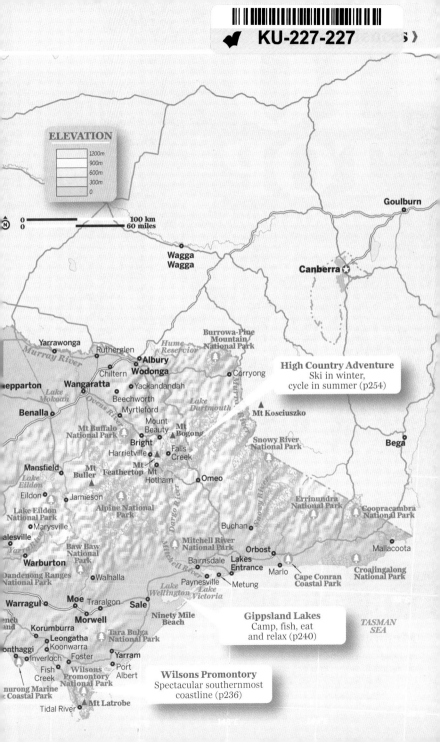

ELEVATION

1200m
900m
600m
300m
0

0   100 km
0   60 miles

Goulburn

Wagga Wagga

Canberra

Murray River

Yarrawonga

Hume Reservoir

Burrowa-Pine Mountain National Park

Rutherglen

Albury
Wodonga

Chiltern

epparton

Wangaratta

Yackandandah

Corryong

High Country Adventure
Ski in winter,
cycle in summer (p254)

Lake Mokoan

Beechworth

Myrtleford

Ovens River

Lake Dartmouth

Mt Kosciuszko

Benalla

Mount Beauty

Mt Buffalo National Park

Mt Bogong

Bright

Harrietville

Snowy River National Park

Bega

Falls Creek

Mansfield

Mt Buller

Mt Feathertop

Mt Hotham

Lake Eildon

Eildon

Jamieson

Omeo

Dargo River

Alpine National Park

Buchan

Snowy River

Errinundra National Park

Coopracambra National Park

alesville

Marysville

Yarra

Mitchell River National Park

Orbost

Mallacoota

Baw Baw National Park

Bairnsdale

Lakes Entrance

Marlo

Cape Conran Coastal Park

Croajingalong National Park

Warburton

Mitchell River

Paynesville

Metung

Dandenong Ranges National Park

Walhalla

Lake Wellington

Lake Victoria

Warragul

Moe

Traralgon

Sale

Ninety Mile Beach

Gippsland Lakes
Camp, fish, eat
and relax (p240)

TASMAN SEA

Morwell

ench and

Korumburra

Leongatha

Koonwarra

Tara Bulga National Park

onthaggi

Inverloch

Foster

Yarram

Port Albert

Wilsons Promontory
Spectacular southernmost
coastline (p236)

Fish Creek

Wilsons Promontory National Park

nurong Marine Coastal Park

Mt Latrobe

Tidal River

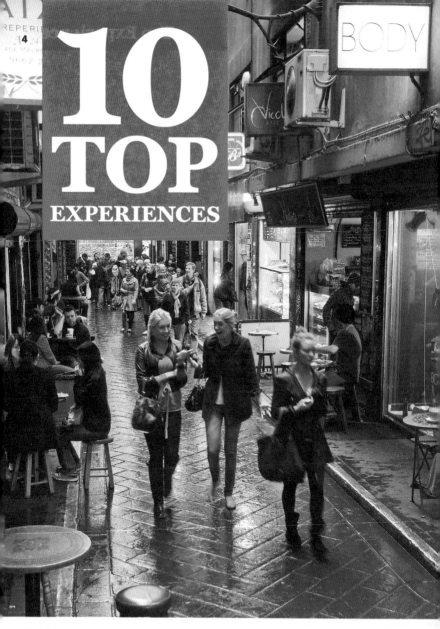

10 TOP EXPERIENCES

Melbourne

1 Head down the many bluestone-laden laneways in Melbourne (p52) to find hidden, yet outstanding, restaurants and bright, bold street art that encapsulates the alternative vibe Melburnians carry so well. Take your place on a milk crate in Degraves St and let a local barista change the way you think about coffee, then window-shop for quirky craft and clothes. Watch evening's arrival by the Yarra River then, almost blindly, head up some stairs or down the very end of a graffiti-covered lane to find a smooth drinking establishment serving up quality Victorian wine and beer. Centre Place, Melbourne

Great Ocean Road

2 The Twelve Apostles (p174) are one of Victoria's most vivid sights. Take it slow while driving along roads that curl beside spectacular beaches then whip slightly inland through rainforests. Spend a few days making this iconic trip and you won't be disappointed; surf at Bells Beach, stop to see kangaroos in Anglesea, searching for the glow-worms that brighten up Lorne's narrow forest roads, then go koala-spotting at Cape Otway. Further along is maritime treasure Port Fairy and Cape Bridgewater. For the ultimate in slow travel, walk the Great Ocean Walk (p171) . *London Bridge, Great Ocean Road*

GRANT DIXON/LONELY PLANET IMAGES ©

Grampians

3 Rising up from otherwise pancake-flat countryside, the landscape of the Grampians (p205) is as timeless as it is tempting. The granite outcrops here are simply made for rock climbing, abseiling and bushwalking. Not that adventurous? You can drive to waterfalls, stunning lookouts and bush camps carpeted in wildflowers, sample local wines and learn stories of how the traditional Indigenous owners lived in a place they call Gariwerd. Families or romantic couples will find just as much to do here as adventurers. *Cave of Hands, Grampians National Park*

Cultural & Sporting Melbourne

4 If it's footy season in Melbourne (p337), you'll know about it. But it's not just winter that sees absolute sporting dedication from Melburnians: come spring it's the racing, summer it's cricket and tennis – and everyone's invited to join in the talk and watch the action. The arts scene is widely blogged and reviewed: explore Melbourne's free art galleries and wear your best black clothes to one of the many literary, theatrical, comedic and musical events that Melburnians pack their diaries with (p24). Cricket match at the Melbourne Cricket Ground

Wilsons Promontory

5 For sheer natural beauty, Wilsons Promontory (p236) has it all. Extending out into Bass Strait, this national park is isolated but accessible, boasting sublime beaches and some of the best wilderness hiking in the state. There's a well-maintained network of trails and bush-camping areas – you just need to grab a map, strap on a pack and disappear into the wilds. The overnight walk across the Prom from Tidal River to Sealers Cove and back is a great way to get started, but serious hikers should tackle the three-day Great Prom Walk, staying a night in the gloriously isolated lighthouse keepers' cottages. Whale Rock, Tidal River

Mildura

6 The riverside towns on the Murray (p279) can take you back to the days of paddle steamers, then fast-forward you to a world of houseboats, water sports and wineries. For the very best of the Murray, Mildura (p282) is an isolated oasis town with a glorious climate, a relaxed attitude, art deco architecture and some of regional Victoria's best gourmet dining. Spend the morning cruising to a winery lunch on a restored paddle steamer, the afternoon swimming, kayaking or golfing, and the evening choosing from the restaurants on the Grand Hotel's 'Feast Street' – get a table at Stefano's if you can! *Emmylou Paddlesteamer on Murray River*

Country Charm

7 There's a lot to like about Victoria's country towns: a strong sense of community spirit, an unhurried pace, and that country air – and many towns are only a short drive from the city (p133). Head up the Calder Hwy to the historic goldfield towns of Kyneton, Castlemaine and Maldon, where grand 19th-century buildings, galleries and markets will keep you occupied for days. Day-trip to Daylesford and Hepburn Springs for a relaxing spa treatment and cafe scene. In the northeast, the gorgeous towns of Beechworth, Yackandandah and Bright are a year-round delight. *Autumn Festival, Bright*

Phillip Island & the Penguin Parade

8 Who can resist the nightly parade of cute little penguins waddling out of the ocean and into their sandy burrows? Not the three million-plus tourists who visit Phillip Island (p225) annually, that's for sure. Luckily there's plenty more to this little island in Western Port Bay: fabulous surf beaches, a MotoGP circuit that will satisfy revheads even when there's no racing on, wildlife parks and loads of things to keep kids busy. For something different, jump on the ferry for the short trip to French Island (p223) where there are no sealed roads and no mains power. Little penguins

Gippsland Lakes

9 Water, water, everywhere. Aside from the famous Ninety Mile Beach, East Gippsland's lakes district (p247) is a glistening patchwork of waterways and inlets where boating and fishing are a way of life. Experience the coastal charm of villages like Paynesville, Metung and gorgeous Mallacoota, cruise the lakes to wineries and waterside pubs, and gorge on the state's freshest seafood. Throw in some of Victoria's wildest coastal parks and you've got a trip to remember. Pier at Mallacoota Inlet

High Country Adventure

10 The mountains and valleys of the High Country (p254) are Victoria's year-round adventure playground. In the 'white season', some of the best skiing, snowboarding and après-ski in the country can be found on the slopes of Mt Hotham, Mt Buller and Falls Creek. In the 'green season', you can make like the Man from Snowy River riding horses on the high plains, or dive into high-adrenalin pursuits like mountain biking and paragliding. If all that gets too much, hit the wine and cheese trail in northeastern Victoria's gourmet region. Hiking, Mt Hotham

Melbourne & Victoria Getaways

Wine, Food & Song »
City Breaks »
State of Play »
Gold Rush »

Lake Tyers Beach, Lakes Entrance (p244)

Wine, Food & Song

Victoria is bursting with wineries, breweries, gourmet food and fresh farm produce, and when music's added to the mix, a festival feeling takes over. Melbourne basks in a culinary glow; the CBD is full of choices but it's the suburbs that hold the most gourmet surprises.

Regional Flavours

1 Fine food comes in some unusual packages around Victoria: top restaurants are hidden in olive groves (Loam; p154), farms (Sunnybrae; p169) and below breathtaking, climbable outcrops (Royal Mail Hotel; p211).

Music Festivals

2 Making the pilgrimage to a music festival is part of the calendar for many Melburnians; Apollo Bay (p171), Meredith (p26), Port Fairy (p181) and Queenscliff (p152) sing out to the sea, while Wangaratta (p304) sees an inland jazz-loving crowd.

Alfresco Life in Holiday Spots

3 Spend summer days outside cafes drinking coffee and catching up on the news with the holiday crowd. Expect fresh air, alfresco dining and plenty of opportunities for people-watching in Sorrento (p219), Daylesford (p144), Lorne (p166) and Queenscliff (p150).

Musical Wineries

4 Wineries don't just make and sell wine in Victoria, they frequently hold music festivals among the vines. Some also host weekend events designed for maximum fun, like the annual Rutherglen Winery Walkabout (p296).

Farm Produce

5 Pick your own berries at Red Hill (p223) on the Mornington Peninsula – or grab a basket and go farm-gate-hopping, trying (and buying) everything from cheese and berries to wine and olives. Jump on a bike and follow the foodie trail in Milawa (p263) in the High Country.

Clockwise from top left
1. Victoria's gourmet cuisine (p321) **2.** Winery, Red Hill (p224) **3** Meredith Music Festival (p26)

City Breaks

From seaside adventures to getting down and groovy with locals in the city's northern suburbs, there's plenty to do that barely involves leaving the city limits.

Seaside Escape

1 Tram it to St Kilda (p77), check in at one of its boutique hotels (p93), then head out for a waterside dinner at the Stokehouse (upstairs; p102). Watch a movie on the roof of the St Kilda Sea Baths (p79) and perhaps throw in a swim in its saltwater pool for good measure.

Get Arty

2 Book into one of the Art Series hotels (p92 and p94, then spend a day in Melbourne checking out both NGV Australia (p53) and NGV International (p66) and the galleries and street art along Flinders Lane. Picnic at Heide (p72) and dine at Mirka's at Tolarno (p102) in St Kilda.

Market Meandering

3 The Queen Victoria Market (p62) doesn't just sell fresh food, it also hosts summer evenings of entertainment and hawker food, offers cooking classes and runs foodie tours. The deli has all the ingredients for a delicious picnic spread – buy up then catch the free tourist bus to the Yarra River or Carlton Gardens to feast.

Northern Fun

4 Stay in Fitzroy (p70) and feel the vibe of Brunswick St and its ultracool neighbour, Gertrude St. Drink or dine at Cutler & Co (p99), partake in a coffee or two at De Clieu (p109), and, on the weekend, browse the Rose Street Artists' Market (p125). The Northcote Social Club (p116) makes live music a short tram ride away, or stay local at the Workers Club (p118).

CBD Delights

5 Book a skyscraper hotel room (p86), then get as low as you can in a downstairs restaurant (p95) or bar (p106), off a graffiti-covered lane. Kayak the Yarra (p80), or if there's sporting action, be guided by the bright lights to the MCG (p68) or Docklands Stadium (p68).

Clockwise from top left
1. Brunswick St's cafe culture (p109) 2. Ian Potter Centre: NGV Australia (p53) 3. Laneway art (p336)

State of Play

The diversity of Victoria's landscape and weather means it's never dull for adventure-seekers. Year-round there's surfing and bushwalking, while winter brings snow and skiing, and summer, when the snow clears, exposes walking and cycling tracks with spectacular views.

Melbourne is not immune to a bit of outdoor action; there's a long river to kayak or canoe along and blustery winds off St Kilda to windsurf and kitesurf in. Head just a short distance out of the city and there are iconic surfing beaches, accessible walking tracks and great camping sites in national parks to rest and recuperate at. Some of Victoria's lakes and rivers have ideal canoeing conditions, and recent rains mean that Victorian lakes that were completely empty are now havens of water-sport activity again. The Murray region is a hive of water-based activity, with windsurfers taking to Yarrawonga's waters and waterskiers enjoying carving up the river in Echuca.

There are some terrific locations for rock climbing and abseiling in Victoria, and the good-looking Grampians and Mt Arapiles top the list. Cyclists get stunning alpine vistas in the High Country (once the skiers and snowboarders have packed up for the year) as well as mad-cap runs through forest paths along the Great Ocean Road. There are organised cycling adventures around Melbourne and the state, which range from one day (and 250km) to nine days. The not-so-serious enjoy much shorter rail trails (besides or along former railway lines) and 'cycle to produce trails' that incorporate food and wine but still require a substantial bit of cycling.

Clockwise from top left

1. Sealers Cove Walk (p239), Wilsons Promontory
2. Fairhaven (p165) 3. Rock climbing, Mt Arapiles (p211)
4. Murray to Mountains Rail Trail (p267)

Gold Rush

Gold made Victoria what it is today; buildings built from the proceeds line Melbourne's streets, and the gold-rush towns of Bendigo and Ballarat still thrive on the history. There are plenty of ways to pay homage to the towns where this boom originated – go history-mad or just rejoice in what these towns have become.

Ballarat's Buildings

1 Forget what century it is and stroll down Lydiard St, past historic buildings that still have an aura of sophistication about them. Stay and play, there's plenty to do (p187).

Hear Bendigo's Story

2 Ride the talking tram around the once gold-filled town of Bendigo (p194). Pass antique stores and grand buildings, then hop off and go underground at Central Deborah Goldmine.

Golden Entertainment

3 Get panning for your own little chunk of gold at Ballarat's historic village of Sovereign Hill (p190). Nighttime sees it glowing under the lights and flames of the reenactment of the Eureka Rebellion.

Chinese History

4 Catch up with the Chinese past and present of Bendigo (p194); check out the city's Joss House and watch Sun Loong, the longest five-clawed dragon in the world, being 'awakened' (very noisily) in the annual Easter Festival.

Small Town Charm

5 Take time out in the smaller former gold towns of Maryborough (p204), Maldon (p203), Castlemaine (p200) and Daylesford (p144), where antique hunting and weekend relaxation has replaced digging for gold.

Right
1. Easter Festival (p196), Bendigo 2. Central Deborah Goldmine (p194), Bendigo

Welcome to Melbourne & Victoria

Keeping up with Melbourne's calendar of cultural and sporting events can be simply exhausting. Thankfully, Melbourne is surrounded by vibrant regions that inspire winding down, or, if you can't get enough, ramping up the adventure.

Outdoors

Victorians spend much of their time living life outdoors. Open spaces, from outback-like deserts to yellow-sanded bayside beaches, attract activity-seekers, weekend wanderers and jovial holidaymakers. Even city folk in the midst of a working week err to the outside, watching movies under the stars and stretching out in parks to lap up the sunshine. Victoria's towns have character and plenty of culture: outdoor food and wine festivals are almost a weekly event; farmers markets liven up school ovals; and family-friendly music festivals take place in front of stunning natural backdrops. Established walking and cycling routes help people ditch the car and get closer to nature, and where there are waves for surfing, or fields for skiing, or rivers for kayaking, there's almost always somewhere to rent the gear and someone to lead you in the right direction.

Indoors

During a bustling gold-rush era in the late 1800s, streets in Melbourne and many of Victoria's small towns were stamped with architectural wonders. These days many of those grand buildings are luxury hotels or hostels, or theatres bursting with talent, or converted – on the inside – to colourful state-of-the-art galleries. Some of Victoria's best old industrial mills and factories live to see another century as smart, yet rough-around-the-edges, restaurants, bars and cafes, filled with folk sipping lattes on designer chairs and dining on delicious, locally sourced food.

Culture

Explore the cultural make-up of Victoria by popping into an Indigenous cultural centre and learning about Victoria as it was pre-settlement or, in Melbourne, go on an Indigenous tour along the Yarra or search for trees just outside the CBD that show remnants of Indigenous culture. Catch a tram to Footscray or Richmond and meander along a bustling market-like street before heading to a restaurant for fabulous African or Vietnamese cuisine. Hide out in Chinatown's laneways. Hang out in arty Fitzroy. The cultural identity of Victoria is evident and explained in many of the state's museums and art galleries, and, in Melbourne itself, on its walls.

Journeys

Packing your bags, jumping into the car and heading out of the city is a national pastime. Well-signposted touring routes, helpful information centres and thousands of different types of places to lay your hat make it almost easier done than said. To the coast? To the mountains? To the small country towns? You can almost be guaranteed a friendly welcome, a good coffee (somewhere), and a decent meal to go along with the stunning vistas. The only obstacle is time; make the most of it.

need to know

Currency
» Australian dollars ($)

Language
» English

When to Go

Warm to hot summers, mild winters
Dry climate

Mildura
GO Jul-Oct

Mt Hotham
GO Jun-Sep

Ballarat
GO Mar-Jun

Cape Otway
GO Jan-Apr

HIGH SEASON
(DEC–FEB)

» Beaches are packed with local holidaymakers soaking up the sun and enjoying school holidays.

» Easter and June/July school holidays are also busy; the latter especially in the ski resorts.

SHOULDER
(FEB–MAR)

» Quieter time with many more accommodation vacancies.

» Late summer's weather can be particularly hot.

LOW SEASON
(APR–AUG)

» Milder weather; often decent rainfall during second low season of September to November.

Setting Your Budget

Budget less than
$100

» Dorm beds: $15–30

» Cheap meals: $10–15; check out fresh food markets

» Free art galleries and live music

» A walking tour

Midrange
$100–200

» Hotel room: $80–100

» Breakfast at a good cafe

» Tapas and a couple of cocktails

» A live gig

Top End
$200+

» Hotel room: $150–300

» The top restaurant in town

» Tickets to an event

Money

» ATMs can be found in most towns, and credit cards are widely accepted.

Visas

» Visas are required for international travellers; check www.immi.gov. au for information.

Mobile Phones

» Local SIM cards are available and cheap. CDMA band phones don't work in Australia; other phones can be set to roaming before leaving.

Driving/ Transport

» Drive on the left; steering wheel is on the right side of the car. Trains and buses cover some regions but services are often daily or less.

Websites

» **Lonely Planet** (www. lonelyplanet.com/ melbourne) Destination information, hotel bookings, traveller forum and more

» **Visit Victoria** (www. visitvictoria.com) Official state tourism site

» **Parks Victoria** (www.parkweb.vic.gov. au) Profiles Victoria's national parks

» **Three Thousand** (www.threethousand. com.au) Local fashion, entertainment and food

» **The Age** (www. theage.com.au) Local news and reviews

» **Bureau of Meteorology** (www. bom.gov.au/weather/ vic) Guidance for the weather

Exchange Rates

Canada	C$1	A$1
Europe	€1	A$1.37
Japan	¥100	A$1.21
New Zealand	NZ$1	A$0.77
UK	£1	A$1.59
US	US$1	A$1

For current exchange rates see www.xe.com

Important Numbers

Callers to Australia need to drop the first '0' in a mobile phone number and the '0' of Victoria's 03 area code.

Country code	61
International access code	00
Police, fire & ambulance	000
Parks Victoria	13 19 63

Arriving in Melbourne

» **Tullamarine Airport**
Bus – SkyBus runs express services every 10 to 30 minutes to/ from Southern Cross Station (see p130)
Taxis – $40; around 25 minutes to the city

» **Avalon Airport**
Bus – Avalon Airport Transfers meets every flight and takes passengers to Melbourne (see p131)
Taxis – $80; around one hour to the city, or 20 minutes to Geelong ($50)

Travelling Without a Car

Melbourne's public transport system has great coverage, but the same can't be said for public transport around the rest of the state. Buses are infrequent and trains only head to certain destinations. To get around this, think about hiring a bike at your destination or bringing your own bike on the train. Some towns are good at encouraging this, including Woodend, and it's also feasible on the Mornington Peninsula and in towns like Echuca.

Private bus tours cover many of Victoria's main sights, though time is often limited so consider arranging to stay over near the sight then returning the next day. Long, long walks are gaining popularity and shuttle-bus services are starting up to connect walkers with accommodation and public transport.

if you like...

Great Food

Farmers markets, slow food, organic – if it's fresh and healthy, Victoria's got it firmly placed in the foodie lexicon. Browse through markets, watch country chefs pick your dinner from their garden, and dine on the results. In the city, too, chefs pride themselves on knowing everything about their ingredients, all the way (which is often not very far) from field to table.

Queen Victoria Market Stock up from this vast market's organic fruit and veg section and fabulous indoor deli, or take a bit more time and join a cooking class or foodie tour (p62)

Royal Mail Hotel Recover from a hike or climb in the Grampians with an outstanding meal at this pub, aka Victoria's 'Restaurant of the Year' in 2011 (p211)

Loam Using plenty of native ingredients is just part of the success story here; diners are encouraged to learn about the food they're going to eat, making it wonderfully interactive (and award-winning) dining (p154)

Harvest Picnic At both Hanging Rock (last Sunday in February; p24) and Werribee (p26; last Sunday in November), these picnics are a celebration of local produce and life outdoors

Wineries

From monolithic warehouses to stunning architect-designed wineries and tiny family-run sheds with equally tiny vintages, wineries are plentiful in Victoria (at last count there were 850). Victoria's been producing wine since the 1830s and today's favourite varieties include Chardonnay, Pinot Noir, Riesling and Sauvignon Blanc.

Mornington Peninsula One or even two days won't be enough to see half the wineries in this former apple- and cherry-growing area; don't miss fort-like Port Phillip Estate and take time to try the area's Pinot Noir (p224)

Yarra Valley It's here at the birthplace of Victoria's wine industry that you'll find cavernous Giant Steps & Innocent Bystander – a fun, warehouse-like pizza-serving winery (p140)

Rutherglen Located by the Murray River, this charming area is known for its Muscat and Tokay; further up the Murray at Echuca and Mildura you'll find small supplies of Italian varietals (p296)

Microbreweries

Microbreweries grow almost as fast as blackberries in Victoria; many towns boast at least one, and the range of beers on tap is often matched with equally enticing meals and snacks. The beer from these breweries is making an appearance in some of Melbourne's bars, so if you can't get to the brewery itself, keep an eye out for the following brews among the local pub's line-up.

Jamieson Brewery This family-friendly brewery has a courtesy bus to help those staying locally get the most out of their brews (p259)

Red Hill Brewery Tucked away in the wine zone of Red Hill is this small, family-friendly brewery offering robust food and free tastings (p223)

Mountain Goat Brewery This large industrial building in urban Richmond is filled with brewing equipment and opens its bar just two evenings a week (Wednesday and Friday) for the dedicated; be there! (p109)

Mildura Brewery Almost worth visiting for its location alone, in what was an art deco theatre (p287)

>> Local beers at the art deco Mildura Brewery (p287)

Fashion

Despite being seemingly in love solely with the colour black, Melbourne does play host to a plethora of designers who keep colour cool and style varying from the draping to the dramatic. That's not to say vintage fabrics don't make an appearance; in Melbourne it can seem that anything goes.

Fitzroy Make your way down Brunswick, Smith and Gertrude Sts to find vintage clothes, ultramodern ware and cute crafty classics (p121)

Chapel St This long street cuts through the heart of South Yarra, Prahran and Windsor and as it does, it works its way through the fashion field. Start with upmarket chain stores, move onto flash independent designers and finish with the best one-offs from local designers and worn-before retro-ware (p126)

Shirt & Skirt Markets This is where emerging local designers strut their stuff on the third Sunday of every month (in a former convent, no less). Accessory searchers will also be happy here (p124)

Shopping

Melbourne's love of the quirky and crafty fills its laneways and market spaces and even reaches outside city boundaries, with suburbs and most small country towns boasting a range of enticing goods in teensy boutiques or laid out in lavish market spreads.

Antiques Regional Victoria is the ideal place to find antiques; look out for roadside megamarkets but don't forget the small curios shops. Daylesford (p149), Ballarat (p193) and small towns in the Yarra Valley (p137) are particularly loaded with trash and treasure gems

Makers Markets From shirts and skirts to stunning images of the city, Melbourne's weekend markets are the ideal place to pick up a treasure. Try the Arts Centre Makers' Market (p67) or the almost beachside Esplanade Market in St Kilda (p129)

Gifts Quirky and smart gift-stores abound in Melbourne's laneways and suburbs, though there's a particular hive of activity near or on Fitzroy's Gertrude St – try Little Salon, SpaceCraft, Meet Me at Mike's and Third Drawer Down (p121)

Markets

Markets liven up towns and cities each weekend, and some regional towns are so decidedly dedicated to antiques that their market-like shops are open daily.

Rose Street Artists' Market This market sees clever and crafty artists gathering each weekend to sell their wares and talk shop (p125)

Camberwell Sunday Market This is where Melburnians purge their belongings, and bargain- or even fashion-hunters can have a field day (p126)

St Andrews Market Each Saturday this park becomes a place of casual commerce; stock up on food as well as the usual jams and preserves

Queen Vic Market From tacky souvenirs to delightful deli produce, the Queen Vic Market is where many locals fill their trolleys for the week ahead

Mill Markets Over the last few years, former factories and mills around regional Victoria have morphed into a chain of retro goods markets. Don't expect fusty furniture here; the focus is firmly on the 1970s. Try Ballarat (p194), Daylesford (p149) or Geelong (p160)

ANDREW BAIN/LONELY PLANET IMAGES ©

>> Great Ocean Walk (p171)

Live Music

Pubs around the state play host to a range of musical talents, but wide open spaces – including wineries, clearings in rainforests and spots by the beach – also get musical, particularly in summer.

The Tote Since thousands of Melburnians came out in force to try to save the Tote from closure in 2010, its name as a beacon for live music (though its rough sounds won't appeal to everybody; p116) has been cemented into folklore

Northcote Social Club Dress down (or just make it look like you did), cruise on in and take your possie for some of the best live independent music in Melbourne (p116)

Seaside Festivals If you're lucky enough to get tickets to the Port Fairy Folk Festival (think one year in advance; p181) or the Apollo Bay (p171) or Queenscliff Music (p152) festivals, book your accommodation and look forward to plenty of local music, sea breezes and happy festival vibes

Musical vineyards Rochford Wines is just one of a bunch of wineries that hosts live music throughout the year (p140)

Arcades & Laneways

It may have started with straight-out graffiti, but many of Melbourne's laneways are also flush with ever-changing paste-ups, stencil art and curious 3D creations (like glass hands sticking out of walls). And the arcades have been a part of Melbourne's shopping society for generations.

ACDC Lane The rockers are still rocking and this lane's U-shape features what are believed to be some Banksy originals. Rocking live-music venue Cherry Bar (p116) adds to the grunge

Hosier Lane Brides and grooms pose for their wedding photos on this bluestone laneway, with graffiti-covered walls (and bins) and swanky Spanish tapas restaurants (p96) as their background

Block Arcade Once the place to 'do the block', this shopping arcade still retains delightful mosaic-covered floors and specialty shops (p56)

Centre Place Beware this location at lunch-hour, but if you manage to nab a seat (or milk crate), grab a latte and watch Melbourne's frantic pace from this prime location

Museums & Galleries

Covering everything from religion to cult movies, Victoria's museums and galleries are frequently free and almost always enthralling. Regional Victoria doesn't miss out: art galleries in major towns may be smaller than their city sisters, but they still hold beautiful pieces of statewide importance.

Australian Centre for the Moving Image (ACMI) A museum of film where you can watch any film from its archives on the spot (or with a bit of notice; p114)

Flinders Lane How many galleries can you fit in one lane? If you can get through all the contemporary galleries here, then you deserve a good lie down (or a coffee boost; p53)

Art Gallery of Ballarat This may be the oldest and largest gallery in regional Australia, but that doesn't mean it shies away from modern art; expect anything from photographic exhibitions of rock gods to collections by internet-bound artists (p190)

If you like... blues music, book yourself a seat on the Blues Train in Queenscliff, drinking local wines and listening to live blues (p152)

If you like... hot springs, head to the natural Peninsula Hot Springs for a session under the stars (p218)

PLAN YOUR TRIP IF YOU LIKE

Country Towns

Victoria's country towns differ dramatically; some revel in their olde worlde nature, others in their blustering beauty, while some celebrate their bushranger or gold-rush heritage with unavoidable passion.

Goldfields Travel up the Calder Hwy to see the 19th-century buildings, art galleries and antique markets that make up Kyneton (p199), Castlemaine (p200) and Maldon (p203)

Northeast The gorgeous towns of Beechworth (known for its gold-rush history and heritage building; p264), Yackandandah (p266) and Bright (where river-swimming is a summer pastime and skiing takes over in Winter; p268) are a year-round delight

Daylesford Despite decades of catering to indulgent travellers in search of its natural mineral springs and spring baths, the tiny town of Daylesford still puts on a glowing smile and extends its hand to visitors in the name of wellbeing – spa treatments in the natural mineral waters in nearby Hepburn Springs are popular (p144)

Walking

The walking ethos starts in Melbourne, with its range of 'city discovery' walking tours. Head out a little further to find rail trails – popular, shortish walks following old railway lines – or go for one of the more substantial walks that Victoria has to offer.

Great Ocean Walk 104km of mostly oceanside walking from Apollo Bay to the Twelve Apostles; this walk can be taken in shorter circuit walks, too (p163)

Great South West Walk This mammoth 250km walk begins and ends in Portland, taking walkers to Nelson River at the border with South Australia (p163)

Australian Alps Walking Track Starts in Walhalla and leads all the way to national capital Canberra in the ACT, covering 650km of mostly alpine terrain (p255)

Wilsons Promontory With 11 'outstations' (camping spots) accessible only by foot, the Prom is ideal for a walking adventure. Shorter walks to Mt Oberon and Lilly Pilly Gully still offer great views and diverse landscapes (p236)

Outdoor Action

Victoria's adventure activities take place with backgrounds of spectacular scenery; expect anything from thrashing oceans to alpine vistas and rocky outcrops.

Snowboarding Mt Buller is a hit with Melbourne daytrippers, and Mt Hotham (the powder capital of Australia) is better for the advanced snowboarder. Close by, Falls Creek is a helicopter ride away. (p254)

Mountain biking In summer, get peddling along the well-developed trails down Mt Buller, Mt Hotham and Falls Creek (p254)

Horse riding Hit the High Country trail on horseback around Mansfield (p259) and the Rubicon Valley near Eildon (p258); trot along the beach at Gunnamatta (p222) or Fairhaven (p165); or take a leisurely ride in the Daylesford region (p144)

Rock climbing Climb the granite outcrops with expert operators around the Grampians (p205), or join the real enthusiasts at Mt Arapiles (p211), Victoria's premier rock-climbing destination

month by month

Top Events

1. **Midsumma Festival,** January
2. **Melbourne International Comedy Festival,** April
3. **Melbourne Writers' Festival,** August
4. **AFL Grand Final,** September
5. **Melbourne Cup,** November

January

It can get asphalt-melting hot, with the only respite to be found in the cool water of beaches or in the High Country. Beach towns are packed with local holidaymakers and their families.

Australian Open

The world's top tennis players and huge merry-making crowds descend on Melbourne Park for Australia's Grand Slam championship. Grab a ground pass or book ahead to see a top seed from the arena seats. www.australianopen.com

Midsumma Festival

Melbourne's gay and lesbian arts festival features over 150 events with a Pride March finale. Expect everything from film screenings to same-sex dance sports and massive riverside dance parties. www.midsumma.org.au

Big Day Out

This national rock-fest comes to town at the end of January. Big names are guaranteed, and if you miss out on the big day, many artists perform 'side shows' at venues around Melbourne. www.bigdayout.com

Chinese New Year

Melbourne has celebrated the Chinese lunar new year since Little Bourke St became Chinatown in the 1860s. The time to touch the dragon happens sometime towards the end of either January or early February. www.chinatownmelbourne.com.au

February

Heat waves are likely, but since school holidays have ended, accommodation is plentiful by the beach. City folk are still in summer mode, filling the long evenings and weekends outside.

St Kilda Festival

This week-long festival ends in a suburb-wide street party on the final Sunday (Festival Sunday). Massive crowds come for both the live music and atmosphere. www.stkildafestival.com.au

Melbourne Food & Wine Festival

Market tours, wine tastings, cooking classes and presentations by celeb chefs take place at venues across the state. Wineries and restaurants across Victoria hold events profiling local produce. www.melbournefoodandwine.com.au

Harvest Picnic at Hanging Rock

Paranormal phenomena don't get a look-in at this enormous group picnic, held at the base of the famous filmic rock. Stalls sell a wide variety of food and wine and there's live entertainment. www.harvestpicnic.com.au

March

Possibly the most festival-packed month of the year, March has fine weather but everyone notices the turning leaves.

Moomba

Moomba's action is focused around the Yarra River, where waterskiing and the wacky Birdman Rally (where competitors launch themselves into the drink in homemade fly-ing machines) take place. www.melbourne.vic.gov.au/moomba

Port Fairy Folk Festival

Historic Port Fairy is charming at any time of year, but fills to the gills with music fans every Labour Day long weekend. Join them for an impressive line-up of roots acts from around the world. www.portfairyfolkfestival.com

Australian Formula One Grand Prix

Normally tranquil Albert Park Lake becomes a fast racetrack and the buzz, both on the streets and in your ears, takes over Melbourne for four fully sick days of revhead action. www.grandprix.com.au

Stawell Gift

The central-west town of Stawell has held a race meet on Easter Mon-day since 1878. The main event is the prestigious 120m dash. It's the richest foot race in the country, at-tracting up to 20,000 visi-tors. www.stawellgift.com

Awakening of the Dragon

Join Bendigo's Chinese com-munity in celebrations with lion dancing, a costume parade and the awakening of Sun Loong with over 100,000 crackers. www.goldendragonmuseum.org

April

Mild weather and the promise of a few laughs and blooms give Melbourne an April glow.

Melbourne International Flower & Garden Show

The Royal Exhibition Build-ing and the surrounding Carlton Gardens are taken over by backyard blitzers, DIY-ers and plenty of dotty old ladies. www.melbflowershow.com.au

Melbourne International Comedy Festival

Local and international comedians entertain Mel-bourne with four weeks of mostly stand-up comedy. After the Melbourne laugh-fest, comedians hit the road to spread the love. www.comedyfestival.com.au

Apollo Bay Music Festival

Ocean views, a laid-back atmosphere and a diverse range of acts make this one of the nicest festivals on the calendar. www.apollobaymusicfestival.com

May

It's time to breathe in the last of the summer fragrances before the jacket has to come too. It's still warm in the northwest, but nights are getting chilly.

St Kilda Film Festival

Australia's first short-film festival has a great grab-bag of genres and talent on show. www.stkildafilmfestival.com.au

Next Wave Festival

Biennial festival that en-courages young artists to do their thing. There's a small international con-tingent, and work includes performance, hybrid and new media and visual arts. The next festivals are scheduled for 2012 and 2014. www.nextwave.org.au

June

It's getting darker earlier and people are rugging up and polishing their skis for a trip to snow-covered alpine regions.

Melbourne International Jazz Festival

International jazz cats head to Melbourne and join locals for gigs at venues around town. www.melbournejazz.com

July

Though cold in Melbourne and icy in the alpine regions, coastal towns like Lorne cosy-up for the weekends.

It does snow in Australia

Head into the snow zones of Mt Buller, Mt Hotham and Falls Creek for skiing and snowboarding. Baw Baw suits families (and won't burn a hole in skiers' pockets).

Melbourne International Film Festival

Midwinter movie love-in brings out Melbourne's black-skivvy-wearing cine-philes in droves. It's held over two weeks at various cinemas across the city. www.miff.com.au

August

It's cold, getting dark early and it's truly time to head inside for some art- and literature-inspired enlightenment.

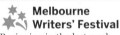 **Melbourne Writers' Festival**

Beginning in the last week of August, the writers' festival features forums and events celebrating reading, writing, books and ideas. www.mwf.com.au

September

The 'last weekend in September' (the AFL grand final) signals the end of rugging up on weekends and the start of sunny days.

⭐ **AFL Grand Final**

It's not easy to get a ticket to the grand final, but it's not hard to get your share of finals fever anywhere in Melbourne. Pubs put on big screens and barbecues (often accompanied by a spot of street kick-to-kick at half-time). www.afl.com.au

⭐ **Melbourne Fringe Festival**

The Fringe showcases experimental theatre, music and visual arts. www.melbournefringe.com.au

⭐ **Royal Melbourne Show**

The country comes to town for this school-holiday fair where carnival rides and junk-filled showbags face off against traditional farming exhibits. www.royalshow.com.au

October

Spring has sprung; the fillies are out as Melbourne glams up for the races.

⭐ **Melbourne International Arts Festival**

Held at various venues around the city, the festival features an always thought-provoking program of Australian and international theatre, opera, dance, visual art and music. www.melbournefestival.com.au

⭐ **Spring Racing Carnival**

Culminating in the prestigious Melbourne Cup in November, these race meets are as much social events as sporting ones. www.springracingcarnival.com.au

⭐ **Wangaratta Festival of Jazz**

Wangaratta hosts over 350 national and international artists each year at Australia's most important jazz festival. The line-up is often stellar; New York greats make regular appearances. www.wangarattajazz.com

⭐ **Australian Motorcycle Grand Prix**

Phillip Island's Grand Prix circuit attracts the world's best motorbike riders for this three-day event. www.motogp.com.au

November

Just when you think it's going to be hot, it's not. Like most of the year, pack for four seasons in one day. The pace in the city heats up as holiday preparations begin.

⭐ **Melbourne Cup**

The Cup, held on the first Tuesday in November, is a horse race that 'stops the nation' (it's a public holiday in Melbourne). www.springracingcarnival.com.au

⭐ **Queenscliff Music Festival**

An out-of-town music festival that's possible in a day trip, but the great range of local acts will make you want to stay for the weekend. www.qmf.net.au

🍴 **Harvest Picnic at Werribee Park**

A friendly annual gathering of wine and food lovers held in Werribee. www.harvestpicnic.com.au

December

It's peak holiday time as school takes a break and offices close down until mid-Jan. Cricket is on the screens and streets.

⭐ **Meredith Music Festival**

Three-day alternative music festival held in a natural amphitheatre out Geelong-way. www.mmf.com.au

⭐ **Boxing Day Test**

Day one of the Boxing Day Test draws out the cricket fans. Crowds are huge and excitable; expect some shenanigans from Bay 13. www.mcg.org.au

⭐ **Falls Festival**

A lively, traffic-jam-inducing, music festival held in rainforest surrounds near Lorne. www.fallsfestival.com.au

Your Weekend Away

Best Weekend Escapes

Bellarine Peninsula Vibrant towns, plenty of foodie options and wonderful sea views to be inspired by.

Yarra Valley So close, with cute villages and more wineries than it's humanly possible to visit in one weekend (but you can try).

Mornington Peninsula Still close, with great food and wine and, naturally, hot springs to end the day in.

Best Winter Weekends

Lorne Redefine the word 'cosy' by stepping inside a gourmet cafe after breezing along the Great Ocean Road.

Marysville & Lake Mountain Everyone seems to be heading here for some snow time, so come on up and join them.

Mildura You'd never know it was winter in this Mediterranean foodie paradise, a one-hour flight away from Melbourne.

Best of the City

St Kilda Get blustered by the bay then settle in for some live music at the Espy.

South Yarra Book into an artist-inspired hotel and let South Yarra and Prahran blow you away with its bars and nightclubs.

Melbourne Start at the Queen Vic Market, squeeze an art gallery into the middle and end the day with an outstanding meal by the Yarra.

Planning Your Trip

When to Go

Heading out of the 'big smoke' is a great idea any time of year, though during school holidays (from December to January, Easter, late June to early July, and also late September to early October) it pays to head away from where the crowds are going, so think High Country in summer, 'stay-cations' over Easter and the beaches in July and October. Though it can still be fun joining the throng over the school holidays, especially if you have children travelling in your entourage.

Best Times

» **Mid-Week** The rates are lower, and, if you stick to Thursday and Friday, the best restaurants and shops in small towns will probably be open.

» **Post Peak** Shoulder periods give you the best of the weather with lower prices and smaller crowds.

Avoid

» **Monday & Tuesday** Restaurants and antique stores often close for a break after a busy weekend.

» **Festival Weekends** Unless you've got a ticket and a bed booked, rocking up during a town mid-festival can be a despairing experience.

Awe-Inspiring Landscapes as Seen from a...Tent

Croajingolong National Park

Disappear into the remote coastal wilderness of this East Gippsland park (p253) and set up camp at Wingan Inlet or Shipwreck Creek.

Grampians

With 11 dedicated camping grounds (some deep in bushland, others easily reached from the Halls Gap–Dunkeld road), the majestic Grampians National Park (p205) is a beautiful spot to set up camp in.

Murray River

Bush camping is free at sites all along the Murray River, where you can walk straight from your tent to your fishing rod. Gunbower Island (p290), between Swan Hill and Echuca, is one of the great riverside camping areas. Wake up to the whistle of paddle steamers.

Wilsons Promontory

Camping meets hiking at the fabulous Wilsons Promontory National Park (p236). Hike from camp to camp in true wilderness, or, if the canvas or weather gets you down, stay in comfort at Tidal River.

Otway Ranges National Park

Blanket Bay (p173) is a romantic's dream spot; if it's full, there are more beachside, koala-laden spots nearby. Check out the local lighthouse in the morning.

Choice Weekend Escapes

Yarra Valley

Winery-hopping, a spell at a brewery, wildlife at Healesville Sanctuary and hiking or driving in Yarra Ranges National Park (p137).

» **Don't forget** To leave room in the car boot for local produce and a case of wine.

Daylesford & Hepburn Springs

Soak in the historic Hepburn Bathhouse & Spa (p144), browse the bookshops and Mill Markets (p149), and wine and dine at some of regional Victoria's best local-produce focused restaurants.

» **Don't forget** To take empty bottles to fill up with the region's natural mineral water.

Mornington Peninsula

Enjoy a long, boozy lunch at one of the great Mornington Peninsula wineries, (carefully) walk the cliff-top paths in the Mornington Peninsula National Park (p222), or play a round of golf at one of the top-notch courses.

» **Don't forget** To take your towel and have a warming soak in the peninsula's (natural) hot springs.

Castlemaine & Maldon

Explore the old mines around historic Maldon (p203), then take the steam train to Castlemaine (p200) to browse the museums and galleries and take in a flick at the classic Theatre Royal.

» **Don't forget** To take some spare change to spend at the local antique shops.

Great Ocean Road

A ride along the coast-clinging Great Ocean Road begins with surf-centric Torquay and takes you past lighthouses, through forests and into the resort town of Lorne. Keep going and you'll be at the Twelve Apostles.

» **Don't forget** To take the surfboard and wetsuit and tackle the waves.

Bellarine Peninsula

Spend the day wandering through the seaside towns of Barwon Heads (p153) and Queenscliff (p150), then take your seat for a music-filled night journey on the Blues Train.

» **Don't forget** To take your camera and keep an eye out for dolphins.

Taking the Family

Phillip Island

Kids will love the Penguin Parade (p225), but they'll also have a ball spotting koalas, fishing for trout, swimming at Cowes Beach, playing at Amaze'n Things (p227) and sampling the goods at the Phillip Island Chocolate Factory (p227). Island-living is always a novelty (even if you actually drive over a bridge to get to it).

Dandenongs

All aboard! Kids (and adults) love winding through the hills on the *Puffing Billy* steam train (p135). In nearby Belgrave, Trees Adventure (p135) is a blast of flying foxes, trees climbs and adventure activities. It's a bargain break for the family, if you make it a day trip out of Melbourne.

Echuca

It's not too expensive to ride the paddle steamers (p292) at this historic Murray River town. There's plenty of family fun in the port area; hire a canoe for paddling on the river or book a few nights on a houseboat. Camp by the Murray River (for free) to get right into the spirit of riverside life.

RESOURCES

There's no lack of information about Victoria's best weekend destinations; start with the following:

» Tourism Victoria (www.visitvictoria.com) Highlights what's on around the state and has an excellent interactive route planner to help you get there.

» Parks Victoria (www.parkweb.vic.gov.au) Up-to-date information on Victoria's parks and camp sites.

» Bureau of Meteorology (www.bom.gov.au) Weather information to help you decide what to pack.

» Wotif.com (www.wotif.com) Lists discounted accommodation in Melbourne and Victoria.

» Lastminute.com.au (www.lastminute.com.au) Lists discounted accommodation in Melbourne and Victoria.

» Mornington Peninsula Tourism (www.visitmorningtonpeninsula.org) For the Mornington Peninsula's highlights and an online accommodation booking service.

» Daylesford Regional Tourism (www.visitdaylesford.com.au) For Daylesford and the surrounding areas and an online section with current vacancies.

» Yarra Valley Regional Tourism (www.visityarravalley.com.au) A comprehensive website with a good search facility to find the right Yarra Valley winery for you.

» Phillip Island Visitor Information Centre (www.visitphillipisland.com) Lists Phillip Island's accommodation and activities and has downloadable brochures.

» Great Alpine Valleys (www.visitalpinevictoria.com.au) Covers the attractions in Bright, Mt Beauty and Myrtleford.

» Bendigo Visitor Information & Interpretive Centre (www.bendigotourism.com) Has an excellent events calendar covering Bendigo.

» Ballarat.com (www.ballarat.com) Outlines Ballarat's accommodation and activities and lists a bunch of special deals.

» EMagine (www.echucamoama.com) News and events from Echuca on the Murray River.

» Discover Murray (www.murrayriver.com.au) Lists specials and packages available along the Murray River and has a good section highlighting kids activities.

» Geelong Otway Tourism (www.visitgeelongbellarine.com) Covers Geelong, the Bellarine, the Surf Coast and the Otways.

» Visit Grampians (www.grampianstourism.com.au) News about the region with links to Visit Victoria's Grampians page.

» The Great Ocean Road (www.greatoceanrd.org.au) Focuses on the accommodation and 'must-do' experiences around the Twelve Apostles.

ACCOMMODATION CHOICES

Victoria's accommodation options are endless. For the independent traveller it's feasible (and quite fun) to take your own van around the state, pulling up at caravan parks or free campsites for the night. Some areas, particularly along the Great Ocean Road, prohibit overnight stays in public areas, so it's wise to check the town's road signage before unpacking the camping equipment and Esky and settling in.

Other options include:

» **Camping Grounds** Some are free, some come complete with local wildlife, but most have heart-stopping views and all of them have their own particular character.

» **Hostels** There's been a trend of 'wiping the slate clean' and starting afresh in Victoria's hostel world, so some, particularly on the Great Ocean Road and in the Grampians, boast architectural merits and very green credentials.

» **Motels** The drive-in style of motel appeared in Victoria in the 1950s and many examples still stand – usually by the side of a main road. Most have had a lick of paint, but it takes a lot to cover up their underlying retro charm.

» **Holiday Parks** Although giant jumping pillows and loading the land with brand new self-contained units is de rigueur, they're great fun and offer good value for families.

» **Hotels** Sitting pretty above the local pub, these rooms are usually basic with shared bathrooms, but there are some renovated standouts. Depending on the crowd downstairs, a night here might not equate to a good night's sleep.

» **Historic Homes** Converted into hotel and B&B accommodation after lives as grand family homes, these offer a unique insight into Victoria's history (and occasionally house the odd ghost).

» **Apartments** For self-contained accommodation, book into an apartment and expect privacy along with the coffee plunger, flat-screen TV and wine glasses.

» **Boutique Accommodation** Varying from Zen-themed tree houses to boomerang-shaped villas and converted trains and churches, these can be an inspiring and refreshing choice.

Ballarat

This former mining town boasts one of the state's best 'living' historic villages: Sovereign Hill (p190). Kids can pan for gold and get dressed up like the locals (err, actors). Add a bit of excitement by staying on the site; accommodation is priced from budget to luxury B&B.

Bendigo

The Central Deborah Goldmine (p194) experience tour will get the whole family 61m below ground, while on the surface, Bendigo's Talking Tram (p194) is a fun way to travel around town and learn about its history. Plenty of motels line the main road, making this an affordable family destination.

Mornington Peninsula

The Mornington Peninsula (p215) is home to three large mazes, calm bay beaches and, in nearby Frankston, a massive sand-sculpturing (aka fancy sandcastles) event that takes over the foreshore from late December to late April.

Torquay

This seaside town (p161) formed the backdrop to many a Melburnian's summer childhood, and though it has expanded (dramatically) in recent years, the pine-tree–clad beaches are still a delightful place to share some fish and chips with the seagulls.

Winter Weekends Away

Mildura

The weather is fine up here, even in July. Ride the paddleboats, play golf, tour wineries and pick up goodies from a bunch of farm gates. Top it off with a meal at Stefano's (p286), one of regional Victoria's best restaurants.

High Country

Winter is a fine time for exploring the wineries and gourmet food producers along the Snow Rd at Milawa and Oxley (p263). Sample cheese, olives, berries and wine, then join the locals by the fire in a country pub.

Mt Buller, Hotham & Falls Creek

Victoria's three adventure mountains are a blast for skiers, snowboarders or just doing the snowshoe shuffle. In the evening relax by the fireside with a glühwein and toasted marshmallow. Buller (p261) is the closest to Melbourne, Hotham (p275) is the most challenging for downhill skiers, and Falls (p272) is the trendiest resort, with ski-in, ski-out accommodation.

Woodend

Just a few kilometres from mysterious Hanging Rock is Woodend (p149), a sweet town easily accessible by train (and car) from Melbourne. You don't need to move far once here: get cosy at one of its restaurants then head into its brewery, which doubles as a hotel (of the sleeping kind). Try a warming paddle of beer with the locals before heading upstairs and staving off winter chills.

Ninety Mile Beach

Don't discount the beach in winter – you might have the place to yourself! Go fishing, boating, beachcombing or camping without the crowds on Victoria's longest stretch of beach (p241). Nearby, Lakes Entrance (p244) has excellent seafood, so stock up (they're happy to pack it in ice) and take it home.

Marysville & Lake Mountain

Pretty Marysville (p142) is a refreshing place for a winter weekend and the gateway to Lake Mountain (p143), Victoria's premier cross-country skiing resort.

Getting into the Theme of Things

Spice up a weekend away with a theme. From wine to antique hunting to pure relaxation, there are probably enough themes for a year's worth of weekends.

Indulgence

Daylesford & Hepburn Springs

Make your way to Daylesford and Hepburn Springs, aka the spa capital of Victoria (p144) . Admire the ducks on a walk around Daylesford's lake, check out the lakeside bookshop, then lunch at the exquisite Lake House. Stock up on handmade chocolates on the main street before heading down to Hepburn Bathhouse & Spa for a long, languorous soak. Both towns have wonderful B&Bs to help complete the experience.

Mornington Peninsula

Get the horses to do the walking while you get to concentrate fully on sampling the great wines of the Mornington Peninsula (see boxed text, p224). Making life easier for nondrivers (and/or wine drinkers) is a priority on the Peninsula, and you can arrange a private shuttle bus that scoots from winery to winery, winery to restaurant and then restaurant to accommodation. Spend the next morning slowly picking strawberries at a farm and complete the indulgence with a well-deserved session at the indoor-outdoor Peninsula Hot Springs (see boxed text, p218).

Wine

Grampians

With a designated driver in tow, take on the Great Grape Rd touring route. It starts in Ballarat (p187) and takes you through the cool-climate wine zones of the Grampians and Pyrenees. Top spots for lingering (and perhaps ending the day) are the villages of Great Western (which may ring bells for sparkling-wine drinkers) and Halls Gap (p208), which has the spectacular Grampians National Park as its backdrop.

Yarra Valley

Start a wine weekend in Coldstream, just 50km away from Melbourne, and don't finish until you've visited every winery in the area (see boxed text, p140). If that's a little ambitious (and, we admit it could be), go slow, taste thoughtfully and dutifully list down which winery makes your favourite Chardonnay, Pinot Noir, Shiraz or Sauvignon Blanc. Healesville is an ideal place to spend the night; there's a lively winery in town, and if, after a day of wine tasting, you'd prefer some hops, there's a brewery, too.

SETTING THE BUDGET

The Budget's Low

But you still want to go... Stick to farmers markets and farm gates for produce and cook up a feast at your accommodation or at a free public BBQ in a picturesque park. The Great Ocean Road and Lakes Entrance are good options; buy fresh seafood, make a salad, and find a beachside BBQ to cook your gourmet meal on. Set aside $30 for an unpowered camping spot, or ramp it up to between $70 and $100 for an on-site van or cabin at a caravan park. Motels can be bargains and also have the effect of taking you back to the family road trips of your childhood, or giving a 1950s edge to the adventure.

Money's No Object

Expect to pay from $150 to $200 a night for a double room at a B&B, or go the full luxury route by finding a self-contained villa (with no shared walls) in a naturally beautiful spot. Dining out in the best restaurant in town will probably set you back around $80 each for drinks, entree, main and, if you can fit it in, dessert.

Food

High Country

Milawa (p263), in the High Country, is just one of the towns where you can 'Peddle to Produce'. It's an idea that has all the right ingredients: borrow a bike with a big basket at the front, pick up a map and let it direct you along (mostly) flat country roads and into the arms (or gates) of farms bursting with produce. Load your basket up with freshly grown or made goodies, and keep on going (the serving suggestion is that you crack your goodies open by the King or Ovens Rivers). The 28km Milawa Gourmet Ride is on flat terrain and is suitable for beginner cyclists and foodies.

Bellarine Peninsula

There are 65 reasons to take foodie dreams to the Bellarine Peninsula (p150); that's how many food-focused operators feature on the Bellarine Taste Trail. Book a night at one of Queenscliff's historic hotels, which tend to have lovely restaurants, and get closely acquainted with the region's wines, mussels, cheeses, boutique beers and blueberries.

Antiques

Ballarat

With more than 20 antique stores in the historic city and its surrounds, Ballarat (p187) is a magnet for the weekend antique hunter. Make sure the car boot has plenty of space and start off in the centre of town before moving your hunt to the towns of Creswick and Newlyn. If you're still not satisfied, then head northeast and keep an eye out for antique stores around the picturesque towns of Daylesford and Trentham.

Mornington Peninsula

Former apple-storage sheds have been given new life as antique stores on the Mornington Peninsula, and antique seekers will be delighted to discover that towns so small they barely appear on a map, actually consist of a milk bar, a service station and shops loaded with secondhand goodies. Tyabb is one such town; its former packing house takes hours to trawl through, and then you discover that there are smaller, yet just as packed, antique centres directly behind it. Bliss.

Victoria Outdoors

Best Walks

Great Ocean Walk Use your feet to get from Apollo Bay to Port Campbell National Park and its Twelve Apostles.
Great South West Walk Head into the wild west and back again on this 250km looping walk from Portland.

Best Fun on the Water

Yarra River Kayak along the river in the middle of Melbourne city.
Murray River Hire a luxury houseboat and meander along the mighty Murray with mates.

Best Bike Trails

High Country Take to the trails of the Alpine region when the snow has dried up.
Apollo Bay Try some downhill madness behind this bay.
Forrest Enjoy 60km of mountain-biking tracks, inland from the Great Ocean Road.

Best Adventure Activities

Snowboarding Take to the snowy slopes for a bit of mid-winter snowboarding.
Rock climbing Climb Mt Arapiles, Victoria's premier rock-climbing destination.
Paragliding Catch the thermals at Mystic Mountain near Bright, or do it the easy way on a powered microlight flight.

Best Surf Breaks

Bells Beach Manages to excite the surfer in anyone.

Outdoor Activities

Victoria's excellent network of national parks and state forests makes it a great playground for outdoor enthusiasts, with countless tracks to follow, mountains to climb, waves to surf and hills to ski.

Boating

» **Port Phillip Bay** (p82) City-based yachties are well catered for by sailing clubs here.

» **Regional Boating Areas** Include the sprawling Gippsland Lakes system, the water-sports playground of Lake Eildon (p258) and the low-key Mallacoota Inlet (p251).

» **Houseboats** Cruising off into the sunset on the Murray River with some good friends is a classic way to spend a holiday in Victoria. There's houseboat hire in Mildura (p286), Swan Hill (p288) and Echuca (p294).

» **Gippsland Lakes** In this sprawling lakes system Metung (p243) has plenty of boat-hire opportunities.

» **High Country** Explore the water-sports playground of Lake Eildon (p258).

» **Wilsons Promontory** The best way to experience low-key Mallacoota Inlet (p251) is by boat.

» **Murray River** Cruising off into the sunset on a houseboat with some good friends is a classic way to spend a holiday in Victoria. There's houseboat hire in Mildura (p286), Swan Hill (p288) and Echuca (p294).

Walking

» **Great Ocean Road** (p163) Has a couple of wonderfully long walks that can be done as an entire leg or in separate sections.

» **High Country** Walking tracks here are exposed as the snow melts away; try Baw Baw National Park (p255), Cathedral Range State Park, Mt Hotham (p275), Mt Beauty (p271) and Mt Buffalo (p268).

» **Wilsons Promontory National Park** (p237) In Gippsland, this national park has stacks of marked trails and lovely camping spots.

» **Grampians National Park** Has more than 150km of well-marked walking tracks (p205) that go past towering waterfalls and sacred Aboriginal rock-art sites.

» **Croajingolong National Park** Near Mallacoota in East Gippsland, this national park (p253) offers rugged inland treks and easier coastal walks.

Canoeing & Kayaking

» **Melbourne's Yarra River** (p80) Popular with paddlers; check out Docklands and Melbourne's CBD from the river, or continue on to enjoy its gentle lower reaches with a bellbird soundtrack.

» **Glenelg River** (p184) On the South Australian border, this is a great place for multiday trips.

The river works its way through deep gorges with stunning riverside wildflowers and birdlife. Best of all, it has special riverside camp sites en route, many of which are only accessible by canoe.

» **Apollo Bay** (p170) A popular spot for short sea-kayaking trips.

How Much

Canoe hire costs from $35 to $75 per day, depending on the operator. Extra expenses may include equipment delivery and pickup.

Cycling

Melbourne has an excellent network of long urban bike trails, and in country areas you'll find thousands of kilometres of diverse cycling terrain, much of it readily accessible by public transport.

» **Melbourne** It's possible to hire a retro bike and take to the streets just like the locals do. If a newer bike appeals, Melbourne's new Bike Share system has just the blue beast for you.

» **Great Ocean Road** One of the world's most spectacular coastal roads has some mighty fine mountain tracks hidden in the hinterlands.

» **High Country** During the 'green' season, there are exhilarating climbs and descents.

RESPONSIBLE BUSHWALKING

» Stay on established trails, avoid cutting corners, and stay on hard ground where possible.

» Before tackling a long or remote walk, tell someone responsible about your plans and contact them when you return, and consider carrying a personal locator beacon (PLB).

» Use designated camping grounds where provided. When bush camping, look for a natural clearing and avoid camping under river red gums, which have a tendency to drop their branches.

» Keep your vehicle on existing tracks or roads.

» Don't feed native animals.

» Take all your rubbish out with you – don't burn or bury it.

» Avoid polluting lakes and streams – don't wash yourself or your dishes in them, and keep soap and detergent at least 50m away from waterways.

» Use toilets where provided – otherwise, bury human waste at least 100m away from waterways (taking a hand trowel is a good idea).

» Boil water for 10 minutes (or purify with a filter or tablets) before drinking it.

» Don't bring dogs or other pets into national parks.

» Use a gas or fuel stove for cooking.

» Don't light fires unless necessary – if you do need a fire, keep it small and use only dead fallen wood in an existing fireplace. Make sure the fire is completely extinguished before moving on. On total fire ban days, don't (under any circumstances) light a fire – and that includes fuel stoves.

HOUSEBOAT HIJINKS

Plan on spending at least $1000 to get yourself and a bunch of friends on a houseboat for a few days. Houseboat life on the Murray (especially in holiday periods) can be raucous and fun, and the houseboats themselves, some with palm trees, kitchen-sized BBQs and spas, match luxury homes in terms of facilities (there can be a whiff of overindulgence).

Events

» **Great Victorian Bike Ride** (www.bv.com.au; adult $800, child under 17yr/6-12yr/under 5yr $600/300/free) A nine-day annual ride attracting 5000 cyclists of all ages and fitness levels. Payment for this fully supported ride includes meals, mechanical support and access to camping grounds. Hosted in different parts of the state each year, cyclists can find themselves pedalling down the scenic Great Ocean Road, powering along from Swan Hill to Melbourne, or tripping from rugged Mt Hotham to coastal Mornington.

» **Around the Bay in a Day** (www.bv.com.au; entry fee $160) This 250km ride is shorter and attracts around 20,000 keen cyclists each year. It covers the length of Port Phillip Bay from Melbourne to Sorrento, across on the ferry to Queenscliff and back to Melbourne (or vice versa, or a variation). Children over 12 years can participate in the shorter legs, and those over 15 can come along for the 210km and 250km rides.

Dangers

» Keep an eye on surrounding cars, of course, but also on the magpies: beware of the occasional dive-bombing attack by these black-and-white birds in spring.

» Wearing an approved bicycle helmet in Victoria is compulsory.

Fishing

Victoria is full of fanatical fisherfolk who rise well before the crack of dawn to head to their favourite fishing hotspot. There are hundreds of places around the state where you can dangle a line or two – whether you want to fly fish for rainbow trout in a mountain stream, lure a yabbie out of a dam, catch a deep-river redfin or hook a yellowtail kingfish from a surf beach.

» **Gippsland Lakes** East of Melbourne, this vast lake system around Bairnsdale, Paynesville, Metung (p243) and Lakes Entrance (p246) has been popular with fisherfolk for decades, with large snapper and bream often on the end of the line.

» **Mallacoota** Right on the NSW border, this is another favourite family fishing spot, with excellent estuary, river and ocean fishing yielding catches of bream, flathead, whiting and mulloway (see p251) .

» **Great Ocean Road** Along here you'll find countless idyllic fishing villages to base yourself, including Apollo Bay and Port Campbell. Warrnambool (p177) is another fave with anglers, offering the chance to hook mullet, bream or garfish in the Merri and Hopkins Rivers, or whiting, Australian salmon and trevally off the wild ocean beaches.

» **Marysville** The place where inland, patient types can learn to cast a fly in search of the elusive trout,

Marine Parks

» Around 5% of Victoria's coastline is protected by marine national parks and smaller marine sanctuaries, and all fishing is banned in these protected areas. For a full list of no-go zones, see the website of **Parks Victoria** (www.parkweb.vic.gov.au).

Licence To Fish

» To fish in Victoria's other marine, estuarine or freshwaters, those between the ages of 18 and 70 need to purchase a Recreational Fishing Licence (RFL), which cost $6 for 48 hours, $12 for 28 days or $25 for a year. They're available online from www.dpi.vic.gov.au (you'll need a credit card and printer to print a copy), from most tackle shops and also Department of Primary Industries (DPI) offices.

Horse Riding

Prices average $40 for a one-hour ride, $80 for a half-day ride and $190 to $220 for a full-day ride.

Mountain

» The sound of thundering hooves, the crackle of undergrowth, the skilful horses and riders weaving through forests and galloping across stunning snow-capped mountains, the swell of the music...

It's impossible to watch *The Man from Snowy River*, the film about 19th-century cattlemen in Victoria's High Country, without getting the itch to saddle up and go trailblazing through this stunning horse-riding terrain. Some of the state's best riding is found in these mountains.

» **Tours** A swag of companies offer visitors the chance to find their inner jackaroo or jillaroo in the High Country, with a choice of one-hour burls to multiday pack trips (some as long as 12 days). See the sections on Mansfield (p260) and Mt Beauty (p271).

Beach

» For those who have dreams of cantering along a lonely windswept beach as the sun sets on the horizon, Victoria's coastline is an enticing alternative. Close to Melbourne, it's possible to ride through bush and beach around Gunnamatta on the Mornington Peninsula (p222), or you can head west to beach locations along the Great Ocean Road, including Aireys Inlet (p165) and Warrnambool (p177).

SKIING & SNOWBOARDING

Skiing in Victoria has come a long way from its modest beginnings in the 1860s when Norwegian gold miners started sliding around Harrietville in their spare time. Today it's a multimillion-dollar industry with three major and six minor ski resorts.

» **Snowfields** Northeast and east of Melbourne, scattered around the high country of the Great Dividing Range. The two largest ski resorts are Mt Buller (p261) and Falls Creek (p272). Mt Hotham

(p275) is smaller, but has equally good skiing, while Mt Baw Baw (p255) and Mt Buffalo (p268) are smaller resorts, popular with families and less-experienced skiers.

» **When to go** The ski season officially commences on the first weekend of June. 'Ski-able' snow usually arrives later in the month, and there's often enough snow until the end of September. Spring skiing can be idyllic, as the weather may be sunnier and warmer, and the crowds smaller. See the **Official Victorian Snow Report** (www.vicsnowreport.com.au) or **Australian Snow Report** (www.ski.com.au) for the latest on snow, weather and road conditions, and check the Park Victoria website (www.parkweb.vic.gov.au) for more info on snow sports in national parks.

» **Daytripping** If you're thinking about a day trip to the snowfields, Mt Buller and Mt Baw Baw are the closest options to Melbourne for downhill skiers, while cross-country skiers can choose between Lake Mountain (p143), Mt Stirling (p261) or Mt St Gwinear (p255). Mt Baw Baw is particularly suited to families.

Note that rates are cheaper if you are hiring for longer periods. For a package deal (which can include meals and/or lessons, lift tickets, ski hire and transport), you can book directly with a lodge, through a travel agent or through an accommodation booking service.

For a listing of on-mountain accommodation, see the relevant Sleeping sections in The High Country chapter. In July and August it is advisable to book your accommodation, especially for weekends. In June or September it's usually possible to find something when you turn up.

COSTS

The following table shows what you'll be up for a day on the slopes mid-week at Mt Baw Baw:

A DAY AT THE SNOW

snow chain rental	$25
car entry	$30
jacket & pants hire	$35
ski, poles & boot hire adult/child	$45/32
toboggan hire	$8
lift pass	$60/40
cross-country pass	$10/5
toboggan pass	$5

Surfing

With its exposure to the relentless Southern Ocean swell, Victoria's rugged coastline provides plenty of quality surf. But the chilly water (even in summer) has even the hardiest surfer reaching for a wetsuit. A full-length 3mm- to 4mm-thick wetsuit is the standard for winter, and booties, helmets and even wetsuit gloves might make that extra-long session a bit easier.

» **Torquay** Local and international surfers gravitate to Torquay (p161) on the Great Ocean Road, home to legendary brands Quicksilver and Rip Curl, as well as the largest surf lifesaving club in the state. Here you'll find mega surf shops at Surf City Plaza, the Surfworld Museum and plenty of experienced waxheads eager to teach you how to ride a wave.

HOW'S THE SWELL?

Surf reports for Lorne, Torquay, the East Coast, 13th-Queenscliff, Phillip Island and the Mornington Peninsula are on **Coastal Watch** (www.coastalwatch.com) while **Swell Net** (www.swellnet.com.au) has reports, 'surfcam' images and forecasts, including 'best days' for the Mornington Peninsula, Phillip Island, Western Port, Barwon Heads, Torquay and Warrnambool.

» **Bells Beach** Near Torquay, Bells Beach (p163) plays host to the Rip Curl Pro every Easter, bringing with it an international entourage of pro surfers, sponsors and spectators. If the waves aren't working, the whole entourage packs up and moves – en masse – to more wave-packed beaches.

» **Mornington Peninsula** Gunnamatta (p222) is among the most popular spots, but it is fairly wild so check with locals before heading in.

» **Bigger Swells** Shipwreck Coast, west of Cape Otway as far as Peterborough, offers possibly the most powerful waves in Victoria. It faces southwest and is open to the sweeping swells of the Southern Ocean. The swell is consistently up to 1m higher than elsewhere, making it the place to go if you're after big waves. However extreme care must be taken, as some breaks are isolated, subject to strong rips and undertows, and are generally only for the experienced surfer. It's probably best to surf with someone who knows the area.

» **And... something for the beginners** For the less experienced, popular places with surf schools include Anglesea (p163) and Lorne (p166), along the Great Ocean Road, or on Phillip Island, (p226) Inverloch (p234) and Lakes Entrance (p244) to the east of Melbourne. The Mornington Peninsula (p222) also has surf schools.

Whether you've got four days or 40, these itineraries provide a starting point for the trip of a lifetime. Want more inspiration? Head online to www.lonelyplanet. com/thorntree to chat with other travellers.

itineraries

Two to Three Days
Melbourne to Melbourne via Sorrento and Queenscliff

》 Head Mornington-way from Melbourne, then cross the Peninsula and have a break in the antique stores at **Tyabb** on the way to **Stony Point**. From here take the ferry to **French Island** for some quiet time, before returning to the mainland and having a stroll along the beach at **Point Leo**. Head inland to check out a couple of **Red Hill wineries**, then turn back to the coast and continue to the **Cape Schanck** lighthouse. Next stop is the Peninsula Hot Springs in **Rye**, then the refined town of **Sorrento**. Keep an eye out for dolphins while you're on the Sorrento-Queenscliff car ferry and take a deep breath as you approach the historic town of **Queenscliff**. Spend a day here, heading out to the foodie spots on the **Bellarine Peninsula** and west to the joined-by-a-bridge towns of **Barwon Heads** and **Ocean Grove**. Get onto the Bellarine Hwy and spend a bit of time admiring Corio Bay from **Geelong**, Victoria's second-biggest city, before returning to Melbourne on the Princes Hwy.

One Week
Murray River

> It's not easy to lose your way on this route: simply find the Murray River (via the Calder Hwy from Melbourne) and stick to it. Start at **Mildura** at the top of the Murray, and head east against the flow. Mildura is a lovely town to get acquainted with; its food and wine are worth the five-hour trip from Melbourne alone. Head to **Swan Hill** and visit its Pioneer Village before tucking into some unexpectedly good Thai and Japanese food. Snap a photo with the Giant Murray Cod by the information centre then set off, stopping at farm gates along the way, for **Echuca**. Here you can hop on a paddle steamer or take some time out admiring the Murray from the towering historic port. You can head back to Melbourne from here (it'll take around 3 hours) or continue on to **Yarrawonga**. Check out Lake Mulwala, and hop on a lunch cruise around this dammed section of the river to get among the sculpture-like remains of long-dead trees. Continue on your way to 'sticky' **Rutherglen**, Victoria's home of fortified wines, before getting on the Hume Fwy back to Melbourne.

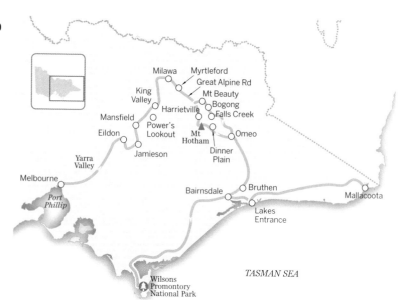

Two Weeks

High Country & Gippsland Touring

》 Victoria's High Country is the best place in the state for car and motorcycle touring, especially outside the winter months, when even the highest roads are clear of snow. Taking the Great Alpine Rd, you can sail right over the mountains and down to the coast at Gippsland. Now that's an adventure.

Start your journey by heading up through the **Yarra Valley**, over the scenic Black Spur and up to **Eildon**, the base for fishing and houseboat holidays on Lake Eildon. From here, take the recently sealed southern road around the lake to **Jamieson**, a quaint little former gold-mining town with a renowned brewery. The road winds north from here to the all-seasons adventure town of **Mansfield**, gateway to Mt Buller and a base for horse riding and mountain biking. The utterly scenic Mansfield-Whitfield Rd winds up and over the ranges before plunging down to the King Valley – don't miss **Power's Lookout** about halfway along. Spend some time in the **King Valley** – an underrated wine region – before hitting the gourmet trail along the Snow Rd between Milawa and Myrtleford. By now you're on the **Great Alpine Rd**. Carry on to Bright, famous for its autumn colours and spring blossoms, before continuing on to **Harrietville** and the winding, hairpin ascent of **Mt Hotham**. Enjoy the expansive Alpine views from the summit before continuing to **Dinner Plain** and through alpine meadows to the historic town of **Omeo**.

An alternative route from Bright is via **Mt Beauty** and **Bogong Village** to **Falls Creek**, then on the recently sealed road linking Falls with the Omeo Hwy. After taking a breather in Omeo, start your descent along the Tambo River though stunning valleys and farmland to **Bruthen**. From here it's an easy drive to **Bairnsdale** or **Lakes Entrance**, where you can recuperate on the beach before deciding whether to continue east to **Mallacoota**, on the remote Wilderness Coast, or turn west and return to Melbourne via the **Gippsland Lakes** and **Wilsons Promontory**.

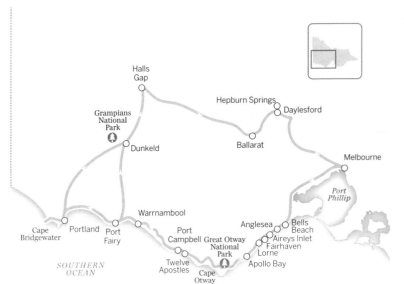

Three Weeks
Great Ocean Road & Grampians

The **Great Ocean Road** is one of the most popular touring routes in the country, and it's no surprise to discover that it is worth the hype. Take two weeks to get the best from this region, then take another week to wind down via the Grampians and Goldfields.

Start in the surfing mecca of Torquay by checking out the waves at **Bells Beach**, then head to family-friendly **Anglesea** to see the kangaroos at its golf course and take a break by its river. **Aireys Inlet** is next; tour the lighthouse before a beach walk at **Fairhaven** and a coffee and overnight stay in the resort town of **Lorne**. The Great Ocean Road is in its element now, but you can break up the sea views with a detour up into the rainforests of the **Otway Ranges**. Back on the Great Ocean Road, head to the fishing village of **Apollo Bay** for a day or two then continue west into the koala and lighthouse zone of **Cape Otway**. It's quite a stretch to Port Campbell National Park and its famed **Twelve Apostles**; take the time to count them and spend a night in **Port Campbell** to get a real feel for the area. Look for whales off the coast of **Warrnambool** then continue west to quaint, and very Irish, **Port Fairy**. If there's time, head to tiny **Cape Bridgewater** to check out the seal population and wind farms, then head inland towards the **Grampians** from **Portland** or Port Fairy.

On the way to the **Grampians** stop for a meal (voted Victoria's best in 2011) in tiny **Dunkeld**. Spend a few days among the granite rock formations at **Halls Gap,** and visit some of the local wineries. Head back Melbourne-way via the gold-rush town of **Ballarat.** Check out its art gallery, antique stores and grand buildings before taking a detour to the goldfield towns of **Daylesford** and **Hepburn Springs**, now more famous for their natural mineral springs. Head through Trentham and Blackwood to the Western Hwy and you'll be back in Melbourne in an hour.

One Day
Dandenongs

> A mere 35km from Melbourne, the Dandenongs' leafy respite is favoured by daytrippers, and you'll find shops, restaurants and sights geared up for visitors. From the Burwood Hwy head east to **Belgrave**; here's where all climb aboard *Puffing Billy* for a steam train journey through the mountains to **Gembrook**. From Belgrave, take the Monbulk Rd through Dandenong Ranges National Park and head to **Sassafras**, which, apart from having a great name, has some good eating options. Head through Olinda to **William Ricketts Sanctuary** and round off the day by taking in the view from nearby **Mt Dandenong** (a view that's even more spectacular at night).

Two Days
Yarra Valley

> This itinerary doesn't take you too far out of Melbourne, but it does show off Melbourne's vineyard-filled backyard. Start in Melbourne and hit the Maroondah Hwy to antique-laden **Coldstream**. Continue along the Maroondah to **Healesville**, a lovely town on the edge of the Yarra Ranges National Park. Eat at the large winery, taste a beer at the brewery and enjoy its small town charm. Head directly west to Yarra Glen, and up to **Dixons Creek**. The area was severely affected by bushfires in 2009 and is still recovering. Be adventurous and head up the Melba Hwy, then take a left west to **Kinglake**. Start the journey back to Melbourne via **St Andrews**, stopping at its market, if you happen to stumble upon the town on a Saturday.

Travel with Children

Melbourne & Victoria for Kids

Melbourne is a great place to travel with kids; they'll love a trip on the free City Circle tram, and museums and art galleries throughout Victoria have dedicated kids areas or, if they don't, often provide activity sheets that you can work on together as you walk on through. Victoria has plenty of parks and gardens to run around in, and some cities and towns, including Melbourne, Geelong and Woodend, have expansive, child-centric playgrounds that adults can get a kick out of too. See also boxed texts on p84 and p73.

Eating Out

Victoria's recent birth-rate boost means families dining out together are common. Cafes not offering 'babycinos' are few and far between, and even staff at Melbourne's best restaurants have been known to make colouring-in sheets and coloured pencils magically appear on their linen-clad dining tables. Still, there is a 'no pusher' camp out there, so perhaps consider leaving strollers at the door rather than pushing through the crowd to your table.

Sleeping

Plenty of Melbourne's midrange hotels offer adjoining rooms (perfect when you need a little space) or are happy to set up another bed for an additional price. Some don't

TRAIN JOURNEYS

The *Puffing Billy*, a steam train chugging along the Belgrave–Gembrook line in the Dandenongs, has long been a family favourite, while the Queenscliff–Drysdale line on the Bellarine Peninsula regularly sees special visits by Thomas the Tank Engine (and friends). Mornington's steam train runs most Sundays, and its special kid-friendly days include a Teddy Bears Day Out and an Easter Bunny and Santa Special.

mind you using the couch if you've brought your own linen. A few regional boutique hotels have a strict 'no children' policy, which is usually made clear at booking stage. When booking rooms through discount websites like www.wotif.com or www.lastminute.com. au, make sure you check the 'maximum occupancy'; often the cheapest rooms are for two adults only.

Entertainment

Music festivals abound in Victoria, and children under 13 often get in free if accompanied by a paying adult. Queenscliff Music Festival has a Kids Klub that features kid-friendly acts. Apollo Bay Music Festival has a Children's Folk Circus and children's events, and the Wangaratta Jazz Festival runs free youth jazz workshops. Community festivals in and around Melbourne usually have activities designed for kids, too.

Children's Highlights
Historic Villages

» Swan Hill's Pioneer Settlement has everything from horse and carriage rides to a sound-and-light show.

» Echuca's historic port is made all the more fun thanks to the frequent long-winded whistles of paddle steamers.

» Warrnambool's Flagstaff Hill is a maritime delight and its sound-and-light show is fun for older kids.

» Ballarat's Sovereign Hill has an exhilarating evening light show and, by day, sports an authentic gold-rush feel.

Wildlife

» Koalas are bountiful in the Cape Otway region of the Great Ocean Road and at Tower Hill near Warrnambool.

» Kangaroos are easy to spot at Anglesea's golf course.

» Penguins are plentiful on Phillip Island, but don't dismiss St Kilda's colony.

» Healesville Sanctuary is a zoo where the kids can catch up with native animals that they may have missed in the wild. Teenagers can be a 'ranger for the day' during school holidays.

» Seals may be smelly (just wait till the kids get a whiff), but they're huge, intriguing and hang around at Cape Bridgewater on the Great Ocean Road and, closer to Melbourne, at Chinaman's Hat, off Sorrento (you'll need to get on a boat tour to see both spots).

» Dolphins are possible to swim with (or watch) if you take charter tours off both Sorrento and Queenscliff (or catch the Sorrento–Queenscliff ferry and keep an eye out).

Rainy-day Activities

» Melbourne's Australian Centre for the Moving Image (ACMI) has age-appropriate video games and movies 'on demand'.

» Melbourne Museum has a fantastic zone for younger kids and great exhibits for older ones.

» The State Library in Melbourne has a terrific Play Pod, and you can also show the kids Ned Kelly's armour here.

» Hop on the free City Circle tram or circle Melbourne on the tourist bus.

» Spend some time in a regional art gallery.

Planning
When to Go

Victoria's beach towns are hot and packed during the school holidays, and while teenagers will appreciate the opportunity to make new friends, babies and toddlers may miss out on the fun and just get hot and sweaty instead. Travelling in low season (out of school-holiday periods) with youngsters has immense appeal: life is calmer, accommodation providers and restaurant staff are happy to see you, and prices are rock-bottom.

Accommodation

Babies

☐ Port-a-cots are often available at an additional cost of $20 to $30 – check first or BYO.

☐ Consider rooms with air-conditioning if travelling during the heights of summer.

Toddlers

☐ Regional properties with dams or ponds require super levels of supervision. Instead, choose properties with fenced-off pools.

☐ YHA hostels have family rooms that sleep three to four, though motels with a double and single bed are usually cheaper.

Kids

☐ This is when 'family rooms' becomes a mantra; even better, hunt down self-contained accommodation with two bedrooms.

Teenagers

☐ Teens need their own space; ensure your accommodation has plenty. The 'family room' mantra is even more important.

☐ In summer, caravan parks are often filled with other families, which is great for teen socialising.

What to Pack

☐ Pretty much everything is available on the road in Victoria, though pharmacies may close early, so pack basic medications.

☐ Basic bedding (sheets and a pillow slip) can be useful if you need to turn the couch into a bed.

Before You Go

☐ Check accommodation is child-friendly.

☐ Book an early meal (6pm is probably the earliest you'll get) in advance for popular restaurants and enquire about children's portions. Even flash restaurants with set five-course menus can often provide a cheaper option for children if asked (nicely).

Regions at a Glance

Melbourne

Activities ✓✓
Food ✓✓✓
Sights ✓

Activities

From being zoomed up 88 floors in mere seconds in the sky-high Eureka Tower, to slowly kayaking down the Yarra River to see the city from the river's point of view, there doesn't need to be a dull moment in Melbourne. Walking tours highlight the stencil-mad city while bike tours take folk out to the nearby 'burbs to show off the fashion precincts. Free art galleries and cheap museums provide joy during rainy spells (and there are plenty), and depending on the season, there's always a sport to become fanatical about, even if it's just for a day.

Food

Dining out is a slight obsession in Melbourne; bloggers snap images of every course and chefs work their hearts out to ensure good reviews. For the mere mortal diner, the pressure equates to restaurants bursting with experimental fervour and dishing up particularly interesting Asian-inspired and Mod Oz dishes. Coffee, cocktails and even beer get the same top-class treatment, so there's no need to settle for less than the best.

Sights

Melbourne's riverside location gives it extra oomph; take a walk from the meeting place of Fed Sq down to Docklands' growing community of city dwellers. Head out on a tram to St Kilda for a fresh bay breeze and an equally breezy community, or stay in town and delight in Melbourne's gold rush–era buildings and arcades.

p52

Around Melbourne

Relaxation ✓✓
Food & Wine ✓✓
Mountains ✓✓

Relaxation

Just a short trip from Melbourne is the delightful town of Daylesford and its spa-town sister, Hepburn Springs. These two towns inspire indulgence and relaxation with their easy-to-access lakes, creeks and natural mineral springs.

Food & Wine

Just an hour from Melbourne are two very different wine and foodie zones: the Yarra Valley, famed for its hills, vineyards and microbreweries; and the Bellarine Peninsula, which adds a sea breeze, splendid sea views and a bit of 'posh' to great locally produced food, wine and beer.

Mountains

Test out the car's brakes with a drive around the forested Dandenong Ranges, and get acquainted with the grand trees and trails of Marysville, which are still in recovery mode after major bushfires in 2009.

p133

Great Ocean Road

Activities ✓
Beaches ✓ ✓ ✓
Sights ✓ ✓ ✓

Activities
There are loads of ways to see this area: mountain bike down rough mountain paths; hop on a horse and ride along beaches; take a scenic helicopter ride around the Twelve Apostles or walk to them along a coastal path that runs the whole way from Apollo Bay.

Beaches
The name Bells Beach rings many bells; it's easily the most famous spread of sand and sea in Victoria. Surfing and paddling beaches dot this coastline, and while it gets pretty rough as you edge west, the whales that calve off Warrnambool's coast don't seem to mind.

Sights
The splendour of the Twelve Apostles is undeniable, and the journey there, along the winding Great Ocean Road, is one of the best road trips in the country. Take time to stop in the small villages and learn about the maritime history of this treacherous stretch of ocean.

p155

Goldfields & Grampians

Activities ✓ ✓ ✓
Food & Wine ✓ ✓
Historic Sights ✓ ✓

Activities
The Grampians is one of Victoria's outstanding natural features, and you don't just get to look: get close and personal while bushwalking, rock climbing or abseiling. Nearby, Mt Arapiles is also a mecca for rock climbers.

Food & Wine
The whole region is dotted with wineries, but spend extra time sussing them out in the Grampians and Pyrenees. Near to the Grampians is one of the state's best – and most spectacularly located – restaurants.

Historic Sights
Within an hour's drive northwest of Melbourne are the central Victorian goldfields. These were some of the richest in the world during the second half of the 19th century, and the grand architecture of Bendigo and Ballarat remains as a sign of those times. Explore the legacy of the mining past in delightful towns such as Castlemaine, Maldon, Kyneton and Maryborough.

p186

Mornington Peninsula & Phillip Island

Activities ✓ ✓
Island Life ✓ ✓
Wine ✓ ✓

Activities
On the Mornington Peninsula, southeast of the city, it's possible to ride a horse from winery to winery, catch some rays on its pretty beaches, then swing over to surf its wild back beaches. Top it off with a relaxing soak in the steamy waters of the peninsula's stunning hot-springs resort.

Island Life
Over in Western Port Bay, French and Phillip Islands are two contrasting islands – one little-visited, the other home to a beguiling colony of little penguins. You can drive to Phillip Island, but you'll be catching a ferry to French.

Wine
The Mornington Peninsula's prosperous wine region takes in Red Hill, Main Ridge and Merricks. It's great for day-trippers but longer-stayers will get to delve into the local Pinot Noir completely.

p214

Gippsland & Wilsons Promontory

National Parks ✓✓✓
Food & Wine ✓
Hiking ✓✓

National Parks
This chapter covers all of eastern Victoria along the coast from Inverloch to Mallacoota, including the Gippsland Lakes and the long sweep of Ninety Mile Beach. Also ripe for exploring are the great national parks of the far east, including the Snowy River National Park and Croajingolong National Park, which sits on the border of New South Wales.

Food & Wine
Lakes Entrance, north of Ninety Mile Beach, is one of the best spots in Victoria for 'straight off the boat' seafood. Match the feast with a local cool-climate wine (there are around 40 wineries in the region).

Hiking
South Gippsland is home to Wilsons Promontory National Park. Otherwise known as 'The Prom', this spot, on the southernmost tip of mainland Australia, is one of the state's most popular places for camping and hiking.

p230

The High Country

Activities ✓✓
Mountains ✓✓
Village Life ✓✓

Activities
This is prime skiing land in winter, and when the snow melts it's a playground for mountain bikers and bushwalkers. Check out the ski resorts of Mt Buller, Mt Hotham and Falls Creek. Fishing for trout is popular in the area's creeks and rivers, especially around Bright.

Mountains
The High Country section covers Victoria's mountain ranges and national parks from Baw Baw to Bogong, the mountain gateway towns in the foothills of northeast Victoria, and the highways that take you all the way over the mountains.

Village Life
The beautiful towns of Beechworth, Bright and Mt Beauty are worth a visit for their shops and character, while wineries feature prominently in the King Valley region.

p254

The Murray

Activities ✓✓
Food & Wine ✓✓
Sights ✓

Activities
This chapter follows Australia's longest river, the Murray, upstream (eastwards) from Mildura to Corryong, via Swan Hill, Echuca, Yarrawonga, Rutherglen and Wodonga. Each of these towns offers a bunch of activities to keep travellers busy, from energetic waterskiing in Echuca to scenic flights over spectacular sections of the Murray in Yarrawonga.

Food & Wine
Yet another winery zone, the Murray's name as the 'fruit bowl' of Victoria also makes it a magnet to seasonal fruit pickers. Farms often sell their produce at the farm gate; keep plenty of room in the car boot.

Sights
Historic villages in Echuca and Swan Hill are worth a peak, and both towns have paddle steamers, which were once the main form of transport but now provide visitors with a unique way of getting to know the waterway.

p279

Look out for these icons:

 Our author's recommendation

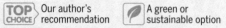 A green or sustainable option

 No payment required

On the Road

Melbourne

POP 4,000,000

Best Places to Eat

» Vue de Monde (p95)

» Cutler & Co (p99)

» Attica (p102)

» HuTong Dumpling Bar (p95)

» Cumulus Inc (p96)

Best Places to Stay

» Punthill Apartments South Yarra (p93)

» Medina Executive Flinders St (p86)

» Melbourne Central YHA (p86)

» Brooklyn Arts Hotel (p91)

» Art Series (The Cullen) (p93)

Why Go?

Melbourne's a vivid city full of colour and contrast. Despite a long-term north–south divide (glitzy, glam St Kilda versus arty, grungy Fitzroy), there's a certain coolness, about its bars, cafes, restaurants and people, that transcends the borders.

The CBD itself sits grid-like on the north side of the river. Here you'll find laneway eateries, street graffiti and fun bars tucked into former industrial buildings. Across the river, Southbank is filled to the brim with glitzy celeb-chef restaurants, and an ever-expanding casino.

Despite the city's attractions, Melbourne's character relies just as much upon its collection of inner-city villages. These slices of Melbourne life have distinct and diverse personalities; don't miss discovering bar-enhanced Northcote, hip Prahran and Windsor or culturally diverse Richmond and Footscray.

It's hard to miss another aspect of Melbourne: sport. In Melbourne, sport knows no boundaries, and Melburnians are intoxicatingly loud-voiced about AFL football (footy), horse racing and cricket.

When to Go
Melbourne

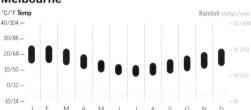

Mid Jan–early Feb Midsumma celebrates queer culture around the city.

Sept–Nov The hats are on and the horses are cantering during spring carnival.

Mar–Sep Rug up and catch a game of footy during the AFL season.

⊙ Sights

CENTRAL MELBOURNE

Melbourne's wide main streets and legion of laneways pop and fizz day and night, seven days a week. The city's little streets have attracted residents and businesses from as far back as the 1850s, a decade in which Melbourne's population quadrupled thanks to the gold rush. CBD living went out of favour but has boomed in the past decade, with some 90,000 claiming CBD abodes as their own. Museums and art galleries are dotted throughout. There are two big ends of town; skyscrapers cluster on the east and west ends of the grid and this is where the city does business. Southern Cross Station sits to the west, with Docklands Stadium and Docklands beyond. Opposite the central Flinders Street Station, Federation Square, known to one and all as Fed Square, squats beside the Yarra, and has become Melbournians' favourite gathering place.

Federation Square LANDMARK
(Fed Sq; Map p58; www.federationsquare.com.au; cnr Flinders & Swanston Sts) Striking Federation Square has become the place to celebrate, protest or party. Occupying a prominent city block, the 'square' is far from square. Its undulating forecourt of Kimberley stone echoes the town squares of Europe.

The surrounding buildings sport a reptilian skin that takes its cue from the endlessly dissecting lines of the city's grid; within are cultural heavyweights such as the Ian Potter Centre and the Australian Centre for the Moving Image (ACMI). It also houses restaurants and bars. At the square's street junction is the subterranean Melbourne **Visitor Centre** (☏9928 0096; ◷9am-6pm; tours per adult $12). Bookings are essential for Fed Sq **tours** that depart from here daily, except Sunday, at 2pm.

Ian Potter Centre: National Gallery of Victoria Australia ART GALLERY
(NGV Australia; Map p58; www.ngv.vic.gov.au; ◷10am-5pm Tue-Sun) This gallery was designed as a showcase of the NGV's extensive collection of Australian paintings, decorative arts, photography, prints, drawings, sculpture, fashion, textiles and jewellery.

The gallery's indigenous collection dominates the ground floor and seeks to challenge ideas of the 'authentic'. There are some particularly fine examples of Papunya painting, such as the epic *Napperby Death Spirit Dreaming* (1980) by Clifford Possum Tjapaltjarri and Tim Leura Tjapaltjarri.

Upstairs there are permanent displays of colonial paintings and drawings by 19th-century Aboriginal artists. There's also the work of the Heidelberg School impressionists and an extensive collection of the work of the modernist 'Angry Penguins', including Sir Sidney Nolan, Arthur Boyd, Joy Hester and Albert Tucker. The permanent collection also has some fabulous examples of the work of local artists such as Jenny Watson, Bill Henson, Howard Arkley, Tony Clark and Gordon Bennett.

There's a great museum shop located here.

MELBOURNE SIGHTS

MELBOURNE IN...

Two Days

Join a walking tour to see Melbourne's street art, then enjoy lunch at **Cumulus Inc**. Chill out at a rooftop bar until it's time to join an evening kayaking tour of the Yarra River. Day two, shop your way to the **Queen Vic market** and find a spot at **Flagstaff Gardens** to eat your quarry. Catch a tram to **St Kilda**, take sunset photos and stroll along the beach. Prop up a bar in lively **Acland St** for the evening.

One Week

Check out **NGV Australia** and **ACMI** before heading **Fitzroy** and **Collingwood** way. Shop along **Gertrude St** and feast at **Cutler & Co**. You're close to **Melbourne Museum**, so spend a couple of hours here then revive with a **Lygon St** coffee. Back in the CBD, dine on dumplings at **HuTong** in **Chinatown**, or at **Flower Drum** across the lane. Spend the next day shopping and people-watching in busy **Prahran**, **Windsor** and **South Yarra**. In winter, catch a footy game at the **MCG** before going low-fi at one of the city's laneway bars. Pop into **Movida Next Door** for some tapas before heading out to the **Northcote Social Club** in Northcote or the **Corner Hotel** in Richmond for live music.

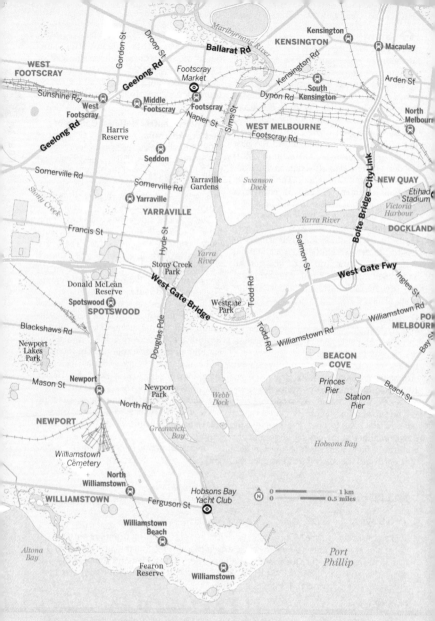

Melbourne Highlights

① Kayak along the CBD section of the **Yarra** (p80)

② Walk to the end of the pier to spot **little penguins** (p79)

③ Invest in some **locally made threads** (p121)

④ Walk down the CBD's **laneways** (p53)

⑤ Taste a Melbourne coffee at **Centre Place** (p106)

⑥ Explore the live music scene in former working-class 'burbs of the inner north, or in sunny **St Kilda** (p115)

See Fitzroy & Around Map (p122)

See Carlton & Around Map (p74)

See Central Melbourne Map (p58)

See East Melbourne & Richmond Map (p69)

See South Yarra, Prahran & Windsor Map (p127)

See St Kilda & Around Map (p112)

Eastern Fwy

FAIRFIELD

To Northcote
Social Club

Victoria
Park

Yarra
Bend
Park

Studley
Park

KEW

Johnston St

FITZROY

Fitzroy

Abbotsford
Convent

Collingwood
Children's
Farm

Studley Park Rd

CARLTON

Elgin St

Grattan St

Collingwood

ABBOTSFORD

Melbourne Museum

Royal Exhibition Building

Queensberry St

Queen
Victoria
Market

Gertrude St Langridge St

North
Richmond

Carlton & United Breweries

Victoria Pde

Victoria St

Barkers Rd

RICHMOND

La Trobe St

Melbourne Central

Parliament

West
Richmond

Church St

Hawthorn

Flagstaff

CBD

Lonsdale St

Bourke St

Treasury
Gardens

Collins St

Southern Cross
(Spencer St)

Wellington Pde

Bridge Rd

Flinders St

Federation
Square

Jolimont

Arts Centre

Alexandra Gardens

Richmond

Burnley St

Burnley

Swan St

BURNLEY

Polly
Woodside

City Rd

East
Richmond

South
Melbourne
Market

Royal
Botanic
Gardens

Morell
Bridge

Herring
Island
Park

Heyington

Kings Way

SOUTH
MELBOURNE

Monash Fwy

Alexandra Ave

Alexandra Ave

Melbourne Sports &
Aquatic Centre

Gunn Island

South
Yarra

Toorak Rd

TOORAK

Albert Rd

Fawkner
Park

SOUTH
YARRA

Williams Rd

Kooyong Rd

Queens Rd

Punt Rd

Commercial Rd

Hawksburn

ALBERT
PARK

Albert
Park
Golf Course

Albert
Park
Lake

Malvern Rd

Chapel St

Victoria
Gardens

Toorak

Beaconsfield Pde

Prahran

High St

Armadale

Beaconsfield Pde

Windsor

WINDSOR

PRAHRAN

ARMADALE

St Kilda
Junction

Dandenong Rd

St Kilda
Rd

ST KILDA

St Kilda
Cemetery

Alma Rd

ST KILDA EAST

Alma Rd

Orrong Rd

Inkerman St

CAULFIELD
NORTH

St Kilda Beach

Carlisle St

Balaclava

Balaclava Rd

BALACLAVA

Buy fresh produce from
the Queen Victoria market and
join the masses eating lunch
at nearby **Flagstaff Gardens**
(p62)

Cycle a vintage bike to
Fitzroy (p131)

Check out the Royal
Exhibition Centre and
neighbouring **Melbourne
Museum** (p73)

Take a wander through
Alexanda Gardens at night and
indulge in some **Art Centre
spire gazing** (p67)

Australian Centre for the Moving Image
MUSEUM

(ACMI; Map p58; www.acmi.net.au; ⊙10am-6pm) Managing to educate, enthral and entertain in equal parts ACMI has enough games and movies on-call for days, or even months of screen time. Screenworld is an exhibition that celebrates the work of mostly Australian cinema and TV, but its exhibitions, games lab and zoetrope will interest anyone, whether they're clued-in about Dexter from *Perfect Match* or not. Upstairs, you'll find the Australian Mediatheque, a venue set aside for the viewing of programs from the National Film and Sound Archive and ACMI. Mini-festivals of cinema classics and the occasional Pixar blockbuster are screened throughout the year, and look out for **Melbourne Cinémathèque** (www. melbournecinematheque.org) screenings. ACMI's programs for young people, both film screenings and workshops, are also very worthwhile.

Birrarung Marr
PARK

(Map p58; btwn Federation Sq & the Yarra River) Featuring grassy knolls, river promenades and a thoughtful planting of indigenous flora, Birrarung Marr is a welcome addition to Melbourne's patchwork of parks and gardens. It's also a scenic route to the Melbourne Cricket Ground (MCG) via the 'talking' William Barak Bridge. Listen out for songs, words and sounds representing Melbourne's cultural diversity as you walk. The promenade runs further along to the Melbourne and Olympic Parks sporting precinct. The sculptural **Federation Bells** (www.federationbells.com.au) perch on the park's upper level and ring out daily (8.30am to 9.30am, noon to 1pm and 5pm to 6pm) with specially commissioned contemporary compositions. An old railway building in the park now hosts creative workshops for two- to 13-year-olds: **ArtPlay** (☑9664 7900; www. artplay.com.au) gets the kids sewing, singing, painting and puppeteering on weekends and during school holidays.

Collins Street
STREET

(Map p58; btwn Spring & Swanston Sts) The top end of Collins St (aka the 'Paris end') is lined with plane trees, grand buildings and luxe boutiques, giving it its moniker.

Straddling Russell St are two of Melbourne's historic churches. **Scots' Church** (www.scotschurch.com; 140 Collins St), the first Presbyterian church in Victoria, was built in the decorative Gothic style (1873). Located opposite here is **St Michael's Uniting Church** (Map p58; www.stmichaels.org.au; 120 Collins St; ⊙10.30am-1.30pm Mon- Sat), designed by Joseph Reed (who also designed the Melbourne Town Hall and the Royal Exhibition Building) in 1866. He chose an unusual Lombardic style, with intricate polychrome brickwork exteriors, open cloisters and sequences of Romanesque arches. The interior is no less striking; it's a theatre-like space with sloping floors and a semicircular gallery. Tours are available during opening hours.

At 188 Collins St, the **Athenaeum** (p115), dating back to 1839, has undergone many a face-lift. The Greek goddess of wisdom, Athena, sits atop the facade, imbuing the theatre with classical gravitas. Across the road, the opulent **Regent Theatre** (p115) was considered one of the most lavish theatres of its kind when it was built in 1929 with the advent of talking movies (talkies). Destroyed by fire and then restored in 1945, the Regent had fallen into disrepair by the 1990s. After a major refurbishment it reopened in late 1996 and is now used for blockbuster stage shows.

Ornate arcades lead off from Collins St. The Block network, comprising Block Pl, Block Arcade and Block Ct, was named after the 19th-century pastime of 'doing the block', which referred to walking the city's fashionable area. The **Block Arcade**, which runs between Collins and Elizabeth Sts, was built in 1891 and features etched-glass ceilings and mosaic floors.

Chinatown
NEIGHBOURHOOD

(Map p58; Little Bourke St) Chinese miners arrived in search of the 'new gold mountain' in the 1850s and settled in this strip of Little Bourke St (between Spring and Swanston Sts), now flanked by traditional red archways. Here you'll find an interesting mix of bars and restaurants, including Flower Drum, one of Melbourne's best (see p95). Come here for *yum cha* (dim sum) or explore its attendant laneways for late-night dumplings or cocktails. Chinatown hosts the city's vibrant Chinese New Year celebrations (see p24).

FREE Parliament House
HISTORIC BUILDING

(Map p58; ☑9651 8911; www.parliament.vic.gov.au; Spring St) The grand steps of Victoria's parliament (c 1856) are often dotted with slow-moving tulle-wearing brides smiling for the camera and placard-holding protesters doing the same. Inside,

FAY JUNE BALL: WIRADJURI WOMAN, SINGER & EDUCATOR, KOORIE HERITAGE TRUST

I run walking tours around Melbourne, showing people the only two indigenous river red gums left in Flagstaff Gardens, and taking them along the Birrarung (Yarra River). It was misnamed the Yarra, which was actually the name of the (now gone) waterfall. Its real name is the Birrarung. People don't realise that Aboriginal language and art is specific to different regions. There are no dots in Victorian art: come to the Koorie Heritage Trust to buy real Victorian art and avoid ripping off Indigenous people.

See
The two scar trees in the MCG car park (**Map p69**) and the Corroboree Tree (**Map p112**) at St Kilda Junction, which the St Kilda community saved.

Listen
Melbourne radio station 3KND (Kool n Deadly) 1503AM.

Eat
Mark Olive runs Black Olive Catering (☑9329 3337; www.blackolive.net.au; 480 Victoria St, North Melbourne), which also sells the native produce range Outback Pride. For a restaurant try Charcoal Lane in Fitzroy (see p99).

Read
When the Wattle Blooms, by Shirley W Wiencke. About William Barak.

Aboriginal Melbourne; the Lost Land of the Kulin People by Gary Presland.

The Melbourne Dreaming; A guide to the Aboriginal Places of Melbourne, by Meyer Eidelson

Did you Know?
Everyone talks about Melbourne's weather, and Melbourne's Wurundjeri had the answer: there are six seasons in Melbourne, not four.

---

the exuberant use of ornamental plasterwork, stencilling and gilt are full of goldrush era pride and optimism. Building began with the two main chambers: the lower house (now the legislative assembly) and the upper house (now the legislative council). The library was added in 1860 and Queen's Hall in 1879. Australia's first federal parliament sat here from 1901, before moving to Canberra in 1927. Though they've never been used, gun slits are visible just below the roof, and a dungeon is now the cleaners' tearoom.

Free half-hour **tours** (⊙9.30am, 10.30am, 11.30am, 1.30pm, 2.30pm & 3.45pm Mon-Fri) are held when parliament is in recess and take you through both houses and the library. Fascinating design features and the symbolism underlying much of the ornamentation are illuminated by the knowledgeable guides. Ask about the mystery of the stolen ceremonial mace that disappeared from the lower house in 1891 – it's rumoured to have ended up in a brothel. Alternatively, see the houses when parliament is sitting.

Melbourne Town Hall   HISTORIC BUILDING
(Map p58; ☑9658 9658; www.melbourne.vic.gov. au; cnr Collins & Swanston Sts) The Melbourne Town Hall has been used as a civic and entertainment venue since 1870. Queen Elizabeth II took tea there in 1954, and the Beatles waved to thousands of screaming fans from the balcony in 1964. In 2001 the town hall's Grand Organ (built in 1929) was given an overhaul; you may want to take the free one-hour **tour** (⊙11am & 1pm Mon-Fri) to find out exactly what having the 'largest grand romantic organ in the southern hemisphere' actually means (book one day in advance). It's a busy venue during the Melbourne International Comedy Festival (see p25).

Council House 2   NOTABLE BUILDING
(CH2; Map p58; www.melbourne.vic.gov.au; 240 Little Collins St) CH2 was completed in 2006 in response to meeting the council's own targets for zero carbon emissions by 2020. Its design is based on 'biomimicry', reflecting the complex ecosystem of the

continued on page 62

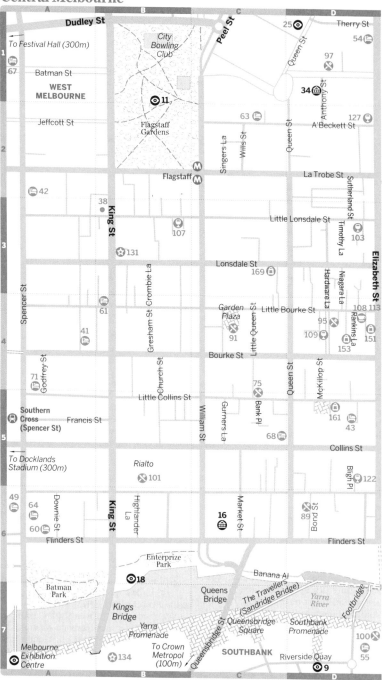

MELBOURNE

Dudley St

City Bowling Club

Peel St

25

Therry St

54

To Festival Hall (300m)

67

Batman St

WEST MELBOURNE

97

Jeffcott St

63

Anthony St

34

A'Beckett St

127

Flagstaff Gardens

Singers La

Wills St

Queen St

La Trobe St

Flagstaff

Sutherland St

42

38

King St

Little Lonsdale St

Timothy La

103

107

131

Lonsdale St

169

Elizabeth St

Spencer St

Gresham St

Crombie La

Garden Plaza

Little Queen St

Little Bourke St

Niagara La

Hardware La

108 113

61

91

95

Rankins La

109

151

41

Bourke St

153

71

Godfrey St

Church St

Little Collins St

William St

Gurners La

Bank Pl

Queen St

McKillop St

75

Southern Cross (Spencer St)

Francis St

161

43

68

Collins St

To Docklands Stadium (300m)

Rialto

101

Bligh Pl

122

49

64

Downie St

Highlander La

Market St

16

Bond St

89

60

Flinders St

Flinders St

Enterprize Park

18

Banana Al

Batman Park

Kings Bridge

Queens Bridge

The Travellers (Sandridge Bridge)

Yarra River

Footbridge

Melbourne Exhibition Centre

Yarra Promenade

134

To Crown Metropol (100m)

Queensbridge St

Queensbridge Square

Southbank Promenade

SOUTHBANK

Riverside Quay

100

55

9

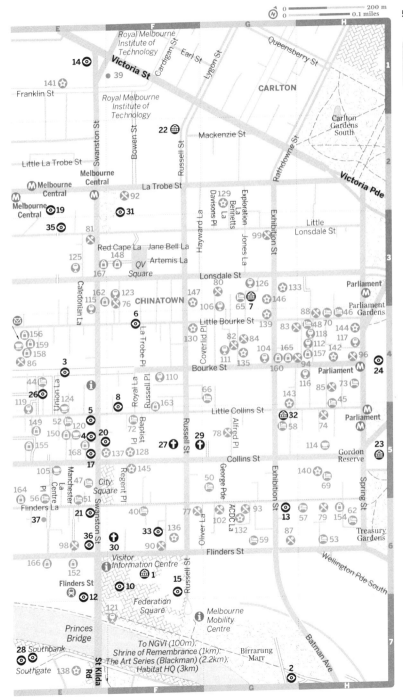

Central Melbourne

continued from page 57

planet. The building uses the sun, water and wind in combination with a slew of sustainable technologies. These include a basement water-mining plant, a facade of richly toned wooden louvres that track the sun (powered by photovoltaic cells), and light and dark air-circulation ducts that either absorb heat or draw in fresh air from the roof. According to post-occupancy studies, productivity of those working in the green building has improved by 10%.

Old Melbourne Gaol
HISTORIC SITE, MUSEUM

(Map p58; ✆8663 7228; www.oldmelbournegaol. com.au; Russell St; adult/child/family $21/11/49; ◷9.30am-5pm) This forbidding monument to 19th-century justice is now a museum. It was built of bluestone in 1841, and was a prison until 1929. The tiny, bleak cells display plaster casts of some of the 130-plus people who were hanged here, a chilling 'by-product' of the era's obsession with phrenology. The dire social conditions that motivated criminals in 19th-century Melbourne are also highlighted.

The last sound that legendary bushranger Ned Kelly (p317) heard was the clang of the trap here in 1880. His death mask, armour and history are on display.

You can also join a **ghost hunt** (www. ghostseekers.com.au; adult $140) or the **Hangman's night tour** (adult/under 15yr $35/30). Evening events are not recommended for children under 12. Book through **Ticketek** (✆13 28 49; http://premier.ticketek.com.au).

Queen Victoria Market
MARKET

(Map p58; www.qvm.com.au; 513 Elizabeth St; ◷6am-2pm Tue & Thu, 6am-5pm Fri, 6am-3pm Sat, 9am-4pm Sun) With over 600 traders, it's the largest open-air market in the southern hemisphere and attracts thousands of shoppers. The market has been on the site for more than 130 years, prior to which it was a burial ground.

This is where Melburnians shop for fresh produce, including organics and Asian specialities. There's a deli, meat and fish hall as well as a fast food and restaurant zone. Saturday mornings are particularly buzzing, with marketgoers having breakfast to the sounds and shows of buskers. Clothing and knick-knack stalls dominate on Sundays; while big on variety, don't come looking for style. If you're in the market for sheepskin moccasins; you'll be in luck.

On Wednesday evenings from mid-November to the end of February the Suzuki Night Market takes over. It's a lively social event featuring hawker-style food stalls, bars and music and dance performances. It also runs a variety of tours and cooking classes.

Royal Arcade
HISTORIC BUILDING

(Map p58; www.royalarcade.com.au; 335 Bourke St Mall) This Parisian-style arcade was built between 1869–1870 and is Melbourne's oldest; the upper walls retain much of the original 19th-century detail. The black-and-white chequered path leads to the mythological figures of giant brothers Gog and Magog, perched with hammers atop the arched exit to Little Collins St. They've been striking the hour here since 1892. The businesses within are a fascinating mix of the classy and the common.

Koorie Heritage Trust
CULTURAL CENTRE

(Map p58; www.koorieheritagetrust.com; 295 King St; entry by gold-coin donation, tours $15; ◷10am-4pm) This cultural centre is devoted to southeastern Aboriginal culture and cares for artefacts and oral history. Its gallery spaces show a variety of contemporary and traditional work, a model scar tree at the centre's heart, as well as a permanent chronological display of Victorian Koorie history.

Behind the scenes, significant objects are carefully preserved; replicas that can be touched by visitors are used in the displays. There's also a shop with books, CDs, crafts and bush-food supplies.

Immigration Museum
MUSEUM

(Map p58; www.museumvictoria.com.au/immigrationmuseum; 400 Flinders St; adult/child $8/free; ◷10am-5pm) The Immigration Museum uses personal and community voices, images and memorabilia to tell the many stories of immigration. Symbolically housed in the old Customs House (1858–70), the restored building alone is worth the visit; its most important space, the **Long Room**, is a magnificent piece of Renaissance revival architecture. It's regularly a venue for celebrating the various cultural groups that make up Melbourne.

Melbourne Aquarium
AQUARIUM

(Map p58; ✆9923 5999; www.melbourneaquarium. com.au; cnr Queenswharf Rd & King St; adult/child/ family $33/19/88; ◷9.30am-6pm Feb-Dec, to 9pm Jan) This aquarium is home to rays, gropers and sharks, all of which cruise around a 2.2-million-litre tank, watched closely by visitors in a see-through tunnel. Penguins

FREE FOR ALL

» Throw a Frisbee, read a book, sprawl on the lawn or smell the flowers at one of Melbourne's parks and gardens. Try the **Royal Botanic Gardens** (p75), **St Kilda Botanic Gardens** (p78) and **Birrarung Marr** (p56).

» Catch a free ride on the **City Circle tram** (see p84). The wine-coloured tram, with recorded commentary, loops along Flinders St, Harbour Esplanade (Docklands), La Trobe and Spring Sts before heading back along Flinders St. It runs every 10 minutes or so between 10am and 6pm (to 9pm Thursday to Saturday during summer), and you can jump on and off at any of the frequent stops.

» Jump on and off the free **Tourist Shuttle** (see p85) at key sights: from the Melbourne Museum to the Shrine of Remembrance.

» Gallery hop: start with some conceptual art at the **Australian Centre for Contemporary Art** (ACCA; p66), Australian art at the **Ian Potter Centre: NGV Australia** (p53) and the permanent collection of the **NGV International** (p66).

» Browse around the **Queen Victoria Market** (p62) and soak up the atmosphere.

» Watch a 'movie on demand' at **ACMI's** Mediatheque (p56).

» Read to your heart's content at the **State Library of Victoria** (p63), play chess in the Chessroom (especially good for a rainy day) or attend one of the fascinating free talks at the nearby **Wheeler Centre** (p63).

» Wander into an AFL game at the **MCG** (p68) at three-quarter time; you'll see the best part of the action and get to sing the winner's theme song at the end.

are the latest addition; see the stunners in icy 'Antarctica'. Three times a day divers are thrown to the sharks; for between $150 to $345 you can join them.

Flinders Street Station HISTORIC BUILDING

(Map p58; cnr Flinders & Swanston Sts) Melbourne's first railway station, Flinders Street, was built in 1854. Two railway workers won the design tender, which might explain why the station contained fabulous facilities for railway workers. Now these, including its ballroom, are, sadly, in disrepair.

Stretching along the Yarra for a block, the station is a city landmark. You'd be hard pressed to find a Melburnian who hasn't uttered 'meet me under the clocks' at one time. On any weekday, well over 100,000 people weave through the station's underpasses, escalators, stairs and platforms. The grand old dame's underground tendrils connect the city's north with its south, with art-filled underpasses (such as Campbell Arcade) linked to Southbank via a pedestrian bridge.

State Library of Victoria LIBRARY

(Map p58; www.slv.vic.gov.au; 328 Swanston St; 10am-9pm Mon-Thu, to 6pm Fri-Sun;) When the library opened in 1856, people entering were required to sign the visitors' book, be over 14 years old and have clean hands. The only requirements today are that you leave your bags in the locker room ($1 to $2 for four hours) and maintain a bit of shush.

When the octagonal **La Trobe Reading Room** was completed in 1913, the reinforced-concrete dome was the largest of its kind in the world. Since 1959 the copper sheeting installed over the skylights had kept the room endearingly fusty. The sheeting was removed during the last round of renovations and natural light now illuminates the ornate plasterwork and the studious Melbourne writers who come here to pen their works. The **Wheeler Centre** (p63) is on the Little Lonsdale St side.

Join a guided tour to see some of the library's vast collection, which includes hundreds of thousands of historical pictures, maps and manuscripts, and almost two million books, newspapers and serials. Interesting permanent and rotating exhibitions feature its rare and unusual treasures, and there's a fabulous Play Pod for children. Bookworm-chic cafe, **Mr Tulk** (cnr La Trobe St & Swanston St; closed Sun) serves lunch, brunch and after-work drinks on Fridays.

Wheeler Centre CULTURAL CENTRE

(Map p58; www.wheelercentre.com; 176 Little Lonsdale St) This new centre, initially funded by Lonely Planet's founders, Maureen and Tony Wheeler, schedules an enthralling range of speakers (usually writers, but also academics and musicians) to talk about all manner of topics. The centre's a celebration of Unesco's acknowledgment of Melbourne as a City of Literature, as well as a way for Melbourne to open up its authors and ideas to everyone. Its free weekly Lunchbox/Soapbox sessions make for a great lunchtime diversion (check online for details).

FREE **Until Never** ART GALLERY
(Map p58; www.untilnever.net; 2nd fl, 3-5 Hosier Lane, enter from Rutledge Lane; ☉11am-5pm Wed-Sat) This gallery space is run by Andrew Mac, one of Melbourne's street art masters, and highlights underground artists. It links in beautifully with the area's street art and ageing city lights project.

FREE **Old Treasury Building** MUSEUM
(Map p58; www.oldtreasurybuilding.org. au; Spring St; ☉10am-4pm, closed Sat) The fine neo-classical architecture of the Old Treasury, built in 1862, is a telling mix of hubris and functionality. The basement vaults were built to house the millions of pounds worth of loot that came from the Victorian goldfields and now feature multimedia displays telling stories from the gold rush. Growing Up in the Old Treasury is a straightforward but charmingly redolent reconstruction of the 1920s caretaker's residence. It beautifully reveals what life in Melbourne was like in the early part of last century.

The adjacent **Treasury Gardens**, to the south of the building, contain the **John F Kennedy Memorial**.

Bourke St Mall STREET
(Map p58; btwn Swanston & Elizabeth Sts) West of Swanston St marks the beginning of the Bourke St Mall. This pedestrian mall unusually includes two tram tracks; don't worry, they'll ding if you get in the way. The mall is thick with the sounds of busking Peruvian bands, shop-front spruikers and the general hubbub from shoppers. The expansive entrances of the mall's main department stores, **Myer** and **David Jones**, consume waves of eager shoppers. In a 60-year tradition, November to early January sees people lining up (sometimes for hours) to get a peek at the animated Christmas puppet show in the Myer windows.

QV NOTABLE BUILDING
(Map p58; www.qv.com.au; cnr Lonsdale & Russell Sts) Taking up a whole city block, this development is on the site of the old Queen Victoria Women's Hospital. It's a medley of commercial and retail spaces designed by

three different architects to give the impression that the block was built up over time. It's both parody and homage to the city itself, with artificial laneways and arcades. It houses supermarkets, department stores, a food court, and eclectic clothing and beaut-smelling body-product stores.

Melbourne Central SHOPPING CENTRE
(Map p58; www.melbournecentral.com.au; La Trobe St) This shopping centre complex (with 300 stores, a cinema complex, bars, eateries and even an underground train station) also houses a lead **shot tower** dating from 1889. The old brick chimney props incongruously beneath a great glass pyramid, a staid structure in a fast-moving retail environment. Ironically, the centre's 2005 redevelopment re-created the alleyways and arcades over which it was built only a decade or so before. For reasons unbeknown to most, small crowds gather on the hour to watch the giant Melbourne Central fob watch and its model cockatoos play Waltzing Matilda.

Chinese Museum MUSEUM
(Map p58; www.chinesemuseum.com.au; 22 Cohen Pl; adult/child $7.50/5.50; ☉10am-5pm) This museum has a temple in the basement and displays of artefacts from the gold-rush era. Its Millennium Dragon bends around the building; in full flight it needs eight people just to hold up its head.

St Patrick's Cathedral CHURCH
(Map p58; www.stpatrickscathedral.org.au; cnr Gisborne St & Cathedral Pl; ☉9am-5pm Mon-Fri, closes at noon on public holidays) Head up McArthur St (the extension of Collins St) to see one of the world's largest and finest examples of Gothic Revival architecture. Designed by William Wardell, St Patrick's was named after the patron saint of Ireland, reflecting the local Catholic community's main origin. Building began in 1863 and continued until the spires were added in 1939. The imposing bluestone exterior and grounds are but a preview of its contents: inside are several tonnes of bells, an organ with 4500 pipes, ornate stained-glass windows and the remains of former archbishops.

St Paul's Cathedral CHURCH
(Map p58; www.stpaulscathedral.org.au; cnr Flinders & Swanston Sts; ☉8am-6pm Sun-Fri, 9am-4pm Sat) Opposite Federation Square stands the Anglican St Paul's Cathedral. Services were celebrated on this site from the city's first days. Built between 1880 and 1891, the present church is the work of distinguished

ecclesiastical architect William Butterfield. It was a case of architecture by proxy, as he did not condescend to visit Melbourne, instead sending drawings from England. It features ornate stained-glass windows (made between 1887 and 1890) and holds excellent music programs.

On the Russell St side of the church is **Mingary** (⊘8am-5pm Mon-Fri, to 1pm Sun), a serene nondenominational 'quiet space' for meditation or contemplation.

Young & Jackson's　　HISTORIC BUILDING, PUB
(Map p58; www.youngandjacksons.com.au; cnr Flinders & Swanston Sts) Across the street from Flinders Street Station is a pub known for more than beer (which it's been serving up since 1861); it's known for its painting of teenager *Chloe*. Painted by Jules Joseph Lefebvre, her yearning gaze, cast over her shoulder and out of the frame, was a hit at the Paris Salon of 1875. The painting caused an outcry in the pursed-lipped provincial Melbourne, however, and was removed from display at the National Gallery of Victoria. Eventually bought by publican and 'art lover' Henry Figsby Young in 1909, *Chloe* found an appreciative audience and permanent home at this pub.

Tasma Terrace　　HISTORIC BUILDING
(2-12 Parliament Pl) The three-storey, grey-stuccoed terraces comprising Tasma Terrace were built in 1879 and designed by Charles Webb, who also designed the famous Windsor Hotel. These are one of Melbourne's finest Victorian terrace rows, with exquisite cast-iron verandas and a restrained ecclesiastical air. They are owned by the **National Trust** (⊘9656 9800; www.nattrust.com.au), an organisation dedicated to preserving historically significant buildings across the state. The National Trust has its offices here. Follow Little Bourke St east to St Andrews Pl, then turn left.

Flagstaff Gardens　　PARK
(Map p58; btwn La Trobe, William, Dudley & King Sts) These small gardens with open lawn are popular with workers taking a lunchtime break.

First known as Burial Hill, this is where most of the city's early settlers ended up. The hill once provided one of the best views out to the bay, so a signalling station was set up here; when a ship was sighted arriving from Britain, a flag was raised on the flagstaff to notify the settlers (it was also significant for the Wurundjeri for the same useful vista). The gardens contain trees that are well over

100 years old including Moreton Bay fig trees, and a variety of eucalypts, including spotted, sugar gums and river red gums.

FREE **Anna Schwartz Gallery**　　ART GALLERY
(Map p58; www.annaschwartzgallery.com; 185 Flinders Lane; ⊘noon-6pm Tue-Fri, 1-5pm Sat) Redoubtable Anna Schwartz keeps some of the city's most respected contemporary artists in her stable, as well as representing midcareer names from around the country. The gallery is your standard white cube – the work is often fiercely conceptual.

FREE **Gallery Gabrielle Pizzi**　　ART GALLERY
(Map p58; www.gabriellepizzi.com.au; 3rd fl, 75-77 Flinders Lane; ⊘10am-5.30pm Tue-Fri, noon-4pm Sat) Gabrielle Pizzi, one of Australia's most respected dealers of indigenous art, ran this Flinders Lane stalwart from the 1980s until her death in 2004. Samantha, her daughter, continues to show contemporary city-based artists such as Julie Gough and Leah King-Smith, as well as traditional artists from the communities of Balgo Hills, Papunya, Utopia, Maningrida, Haasts Bluff and the Tiwi Islands.

FREE **Tolarno Galleries**　　ART GALLERY
(Map p58; www.tolarnogalleries.com; 4th fl, 104 Exhibition St; ⊘10am-5pm Tue-Fri, 1-5pm Sat) Tolarno was an integral player in Melbourne's most famous mid-century marriage between Georges and Mirka Mora. It was once raucously bohemian, but now many years and several sites later, it's a serious, cerebral contemporary space with exhibitions changing monthly.

FREE **West Space**　　GALLERY
(Map p58; www.westspace.org.au; level 1, 15-19 Anthony St; ⊘noon-6pm Wed-Fri, to 5pm Sat) One of Melbourne's oldest nonprofit artist-run galleries, West Space has a varied exhibition program. It features young and emerging artists working in a range of mediums from traditional forms to digital technologies and installation. At the time of research it was in the process of relocating, so check website for new details.

SOUTHBANK & DOCKLANDS

Southbank, once a gritty industrial site, sits directly across the Yarra from Flinders St. Southgate, the first cab off the redevelopment rank, is a shopping mall and behind here you'll find the city's major arts precinct; the NGV International, Arts Centre and arts bodies including the Australian Ballet. Back down by the river, the promenade stretches

As you drive on one of the many roads surrounding Docklands, or catch a train to or from Southern Cross Station, you can't miss *Eagle*. Let's just say this bird has presence. Local sculptor Bruce Armstrong was inspired by the figure of Bunjil, the Wurundjeri creator spirit. The cast aluminium bird contentedly rests on a mammoth jarrah perch, confidently surveying all around with a serene glassy gaze. He's a reminder of the wordless natural world, scaled to provide a gentle parody of the surrounding cityscape's attempted domination. Upon its unveiling, a journalist did have the cheek to call the sculpture 'a bulked-up budgerigar'. Bunjil also makes a looming appearance at the Grand Hyatt and, in the southern suburbs of Melbourne, at Frankston Station.

to the Crown Casino & Entertainment Complex, a self-proclaimed 'world of entertainment', pulling in visitors 24/7. To the city's west lies the Docklands. The once working wharves of Victoria Harbour have given birth to a mini-city of apartment buildings, offices, restaurant plazas, public art and parkland. It's early days, but its manufactured sameness has yet to be overwritten with the organic cadences and colour of neighbourhood life.

National Gallery of Victoria International

ART GALLERY

(NGV International; www.ngv.vic.gov.au; 180 St Kilda Rd; ☺10am-5pm Wed-Mon) Beyond the water wall you'll find international art that runs from the ancient to the contemporary. Key works include a Rembrandt, a Tiepolo and a Bonnard. You might also bump into a Monet and a Modigliani, a Bacon or a Rubens. The gallery also has an excellent decorative arts collection, with pieces from the late Middle Ages to the present day. It's also home to Picasso's *Weeping Woman*, which was the victim of an art heist in 1986.

Its international blockbuster shows are huge, and bring with them long queues. As well as talks and film screenings, the gallery usually has weekly late-night or all-night viewings for these major shows; the mood can be quite festive, with live music and the like.

Completed in 1967, the original NGV building – Roy Grounds' 'cranky icon' – was one of Australia's most controversial but ultimately respected Modernist masterpieces. It was designed with a strict geometry and clear circulation patterns, and made extensive use of wood, glass and blue stone. To deal with 30-odd years of wear and tear and the need for more flexible exhibition spaces, interior remodelling was undertaken from 1996 to 2003, overseen by Mario Bellini. The

new labyrinthine design does away with the stark simplicity of the original but retains key features such as the water wall, Leonard French's stained-glass ceiling in the Great Hall and the austere exterior.

The Australian art collection is on display at the **Ian Potter Centre: NGVA** (p53) at nearby Federation Square.

Eureka Tower & Skydeck 88

LANDMARK

(Map p58; www.eurekaskydeck.com.au; 7 Riverside Quay, Southbank; adult/child/family $18/9/40, the Edge extra $12/8/29; ☺10am-10pm, last entry 9.30pm) Eureka Tower, built in 2006, has 92 storeys. Take a wild elevator ride to almost the top and you'll do 88 floors in less than 40 seconds (check out the photo on the elevator floor if there's time). the 'Edge' – not a member of U2, but a slightly sadistic glass cube – propels you out of the building; you've got no choice but to look down.

FREE Australian Centre for Contemporary Art

ART GALLERY

(ACCA; www.accaonline.org.au; 111 Sturt St; ☺10am-5pm Tue-Fri, 11am-6pm Sat & Sun; 🚊1) ACCA is one of Australia's most exciting and challenging contemporary galleries. Shows include work specially commissioned for the space. The gallery shows a range of local and international artists. The building is, fittingly, sculptural, with a deeply rusted exterior evoking the factories that once stood on the site, and a slick, soaring, ever-adapting interior designed to house often massive installations. From Flinders St Station, walk across Princes Bridge and along St Kilda Rd. Turn right at Grant St then left to Sturt.

Crown Casino & Entertainment Complex

CASINO

(off Map p58; www.crowncasino.com.au; Southbank) The Crown Casino & Entertainment Complex sprawls across two city blocks and includes three luxury hotels linked with **Crown Casino**, which has over 300 tables and 2500 gaming machines open 24/7. It's another world in its no-natural-light interior, where hours can fly by.

Thrown in for good measure are waterfalls, fireballs, a giant cinema complex, a bowling alley, a variety of nightclubs and a 900-seat showroom. The complex is also home to a handful of luxury retailers, chain stores and specialty shops, as well as bars, cafes and a food hall. Restaurants here range from the perfunctory to the sublime, with several major culinary players stretched out along the river (see the boxed text, p98).

Polly Woodside Maritime Museum MUSEUM
(Map p54; www.pollywoodside.com.au; Lorimer St E, Southbank; admission adult/child/family $15/8/42; ⊙9.30am-5pm) A revamped interactive visitors centre opened in early 2011, adding explanations to the story of the iron-hulled merchant ship the *Polly Woodside*, who now resides in what looks like a giant holding pen. A glimpse of her rigging makes for a tiny reminder of what the Yarra would have looked like in the 19th century, dense with ships at anchor.

Southgate SHOPPING
(Map p58; www.southgate-melbourne.com.au; Southbank) Southgate was the first shopping and dining complex built along the south bank of the Yarra, replacing billowing chimneystacks and saw-toothed factories.

You'll find restaurants and cafes with views though quality ranges from some of the city's best to those simply after the tourist dollar. Nearby, check out the **Travellers** along the Sandridge Bridge, a series of sculptures depicting the story of arrival that belongs to many Melburnians.

A number of boat operators are stationed outside Southgate should you want to hail a water taxi to take you to the sporting precinct or cruise over to Williamstown.

Melbourne Recital Centre CULTURAL CENTRE
(☎9699 3333; www.melbournerecital.com.au; 3 Sturt St, Southbank) This award-winning building may look like a framed piece of giant honeycomb, but it's actually the latest addition to the performing arts scene, along with the new Melbourne Theatre Company (p114) building next door, designed by the same architects, Ashton Raggatt McDougall. Its program ranges from local singer-songwriters and quartets to Babar the Elephant; and it's also been a major venue for the Mel-

bourne International Jazz Festival. From Flinders St Station cross the Yarra and turn right at Southbank Blvd.

Victorian Arts Centre CULTURAL CENTRE
(Map p58; www.theartscentre.com.au; 100 St Kilda Rd) The Arts Centre is made up of two separate buildings: the concert hall (**Hamer Hall**, which at the time of writing was undergoing a major redevelopment) and the **theatres building** (under the spire). Both are linked by a series of landscaped walkways.

The **Famous Spiegeltent**, one of the last of the great Belgian mirror tents, occupies the forecourt annually between February and April and is the stage for cabaret, music, comedy and circus. The **George Adams Gallery** and **St Kilda Road Foyer Gallery** are free gallery spaces with changing exhibitions.

There are one-hour **tours** (adult/concession/family $15/10/30) of the complex from 11am on Monday to Saturday. On Sunday you can visit backstage at 12.15pm ($20, 1½ hours). Children under 12 years are not allowed in the backstage area.

The Arts Centre hosts a **makers market** every Sunday from 10am to 4pm. Around 80 artisans sell everything from juggling balls to photographs.

Across the way in the Kings Domain is the **Sidney Myer Music Bowl**, a summer venue with a stage that's been graced by everyone from DJs at huge summer dance parties to Dame Kiri.

The small section of park across St Kilda Rd from the Victorian Arts Centre is the rather endearingly retro **Queen Victoria Gardens**, which contain a memorial statue of the good queen herself, a statue of Edward VII astride his horse, and a huge floral clock.

Docklands NEIGHBOURHOOD
(Map p54; www.docklands.vic.gov.au; ☎70, 86) This waterfront area was the city's main industrial and docking area until the mid-1960s. In the mid '90s, precincts for certain types of activity were developed. Among them are a purpose-built studio complex and residential, retail and entertainment areas. Of most interest to travellers is the first born, **New Quay**, with public art, promenades and a wide variety of cafes and restaurants. **Waterfront City** also has restaurants, bars, a yacht club and, if it rises again, the troublesome observation wheel, which was erected in 2009 then dissembled as structural problems became evident.

Docklands Stadium SPORTS STADIUM
(Etihad Stadium; Map p54; ☑8625 7700; www.
docklands.com; Bourke St, Docklands; ⓡSouthern
Cross; ⓖ70, 75, 86, 96, 109, 112) Upstart Docklands Stadium is never going to live up to
the MCG in terms of atmosphere or classic
design, but it's a well-used, comfortable and
easy-to-access sports arena, seating 52,000
for a range of AFL games, Melbourne Victory soccer matches, the odd Rugby Union
test and the likes of U2. Behind-the-scenes
tours (☑8625 7277; adult/child/concession/
family $14/7/11/37) of the venue are available
Monday to Friday at 11am, 1pm and 3pm,
subject to events.

EAST MELBOURNE & RICHMOND

East Melbourne's sedate wide streets are
lined with grand double-fronted Victorian
terraces, Italianate mansions and art deco
apartment blocks. Locals here commute to
the city on foot, across the Fitzroy Gardens.
During the footy season or when a cricket
match is played, the roar of the crowd shat-
ters the calm; you're in lobbing distance of
the MCG.

Across perpetually clogged Punt Rd/
Hoddle St is the suburb of Richmond, which
stretches all the way to the Yarra. It was
once a raggle-taggle collection of workers
cottages inhabited by generations of labourers, who toiled in the tanneries, clothing-
manufacturing and food-processing industries. It is now rather genteel, although it
retains a fair swag of solid, regular pubs
and is home to a thriving Vietnamese community along the Victoria St strip. Running parallel with Victoria St is clothing
outlet–lined Bridge Rd. Richmond's main
south–north thoroughfare is Church St.
Swan St is a jumble of food outlets, shops
and smart drinking holes. Its proximity to
the MCG sees thousands trekking along
here on match days seeking a postgame ale
and a sympathetic ear as the day's play is
dissected.

Melbourne & Olympic Parks SPORTS STADIUM
(Map p69; www.mopt.com.au; Batman Ave; ⓡJol-
imont, ⓖ48, 70, 75) Stages at these big-event
stadiums morph to accommodate everything from rock gods to cyclists to comedy
galas. Melbourne Park comprises **Hisense
Arena**, the multipurpose venue with a re-
tractable roof, and **Rod Laver Arena**. The
Australian Open Tennis takes over the
whole complex in January. Daily **tours**
(adult/child/family $14/6/28) of the Rod Laver

Arena take you to the dressing rooms, VIP
areas and superboxes. **AAMI Park**, with
its rectangular pitch-shaped stadium designed to hold Melbourne's soccer and rugby
games, held its first match in 2010.

Olympic Park includes **Olympic Stadium**, hosting athletics and home to local
rugby league team, the Melbourne Storm, as
well as the **Westpac Centre**, home to the
Collingwood Football Club.

Melbourne Cricket Ground SPORT STADIUM
(MCG; Map p69; ☑9657 8888; www.mcg.org.au;
Brunton Ave; ⓡJolimont, ⓖ48, 75, 70) It's one of
the world's great sporting venues, and for
many Australians the 'G' is considered hallowed ground.

In 1858 the first game of Aussie Rules
football was played where the MCG and
its car parks now stand, and in 1877 it was
the venue for the first Test cricket match
between Australia and England. The MCG
was also the central stadium for the 1956
Melbourne Olympics and the 2006 Commonwealth Games. It recently underwent
the biggest building works in its 150-year
history, with the William Barak Bridge now
linking it to the CBD, as well as creating a
new members' stand. MCG membership is
a badge of honour for Melburnians of a particular class.

If you want to make a pilgrimage, **tours**
(☑9657 8879; adult/child/family $20/10/50)
take you through the stands, corporate and
coaches' areas, the Long Room and (subject
to availability) the players change rooms
and out onto the ground. Tours run (on non-
match days) between 10am and 3pm. Bookings are not essential but are recommended.

The MCG houses the **National Sports
Museum** (☑9657 8856; www.nsm.org.au; Olympic Stand, Gate 3, MCG; adult/concession/family
$20/10/50, with MCG tour $30/15/60; ◷10am-
5pm), which focuses on Australia's favourite
sports and celebrates historic sporting mo-
ments. There are some choice sports fetish
objects on display: the handwritten notes
used to define the rules of Australian Rules
Football in 1859; Don Bradman's baggy
green cap; olive branches awarded to Edwin
Flack, Australia's first Olympian in 1886;
and our Cathy's infamous Sydney Olympics
swift suit. It also incorporates **Champions**
horse-racing gallery.

Fitzroy Gardens PARK
(Map p69; btwn Wellington Pde, Clarendon, Lansd-
owne & Albert Sts; ⓡParliament, ⓖCity Circle, 48,
75) The city drops away suddenly just east of

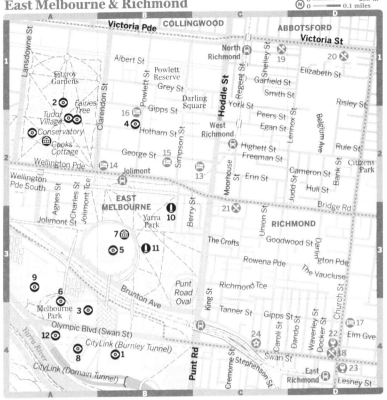

East Melbourne & Richmond

MCG DREAMING

Where did Australian Rules Football come from? There's plenty of evidence to suggest that Aboriginal men and women played a form of football (called Marngrook) prior to white settlement. Did they play it at the MCG site pre-settlement? The MCG has two scar trees from which bark was removed by Aboriginal people to make canoes. These reminders make it clear that Melbourne's footy fans (and perhaps players) were not the first to congregate at the MCG.

Johnston Collection   MUSEUM
(Map p69; ✆9416 2515; www.johnstoncollection. org; East Melbourne; adult/concession $22/18.50; ☐48, 75) The collection of sharp-eyed antique dealer William Johnston is on show in this characteristic East Melbourne mansion. Rooms are decorated in an English country-house style, and also highlight specific interior-decorating fashions from last century – almost as fascinating as the pieces themselves. Visits come with a sense of mystique; for privacy reasons, you need to book a tour and be picked up from the nearby Hilton on the Park (p91) rather than just rocking up to the door. Tours depart three times daily; phone to reserve a place.

FITZROY & AROUND

Fitzroy, Melbourne's first suburb, had a reputation for vice and squalor. Today, despite a long bout of gentrification, it's still where creative people meet up, though now it's more to 'do' lunch and blog about it before checking out the offerings at local 'one-off' boutiques and vintage shops. It's also home to a bunch of art galleries,

Gertrude St, where once grannies feared to tread, is Melbourne's street of the moment. Smith St has some rough edges, though talk is more of its smart restaurants, cafes and boutiques rather than its down-and-out days of old. And as the traditional land of the Wurundjeri people, it's still a social spot for Aboriginals. The streets behind Smith are home to what were the southern hemisphere's largest industrial complexes. These satanic mills are now packed with million-dollar apartments. Down the hill beyond Smith St is the 'Collingwood Flat'. This was once one of the city's most notorious slums. Many houses were cleared in the 1960s to make way for public-housing tower blocks, though many cottages also remain.

To the north is the leafy residential area of North Fitzroy, which centres around the Edinburgh Gardens. Weekends see it full of hipsters having picnics and kids having birthday parties.

Beyond Merri Creek is Northcote, one of Melbourne's fastest gentrifying suburbs, a sprawling neighbourhood of wooden Federation cottages and big backyards. Its sleepy demeanour shifts once the sun goes down, when High St hums to the sound of a thousand Converse hitting the pavement in search of fun.

Spring St, giving way to Melbourne's beautiful backyard, the Fitzroy Gardens. The stately avenues lined with English elms, flowerbeds, expansive lawns, strange fountains and a creek are a short stroll from town.

The design of the path system 'accidentally' resembles a Union Jack. While there's no red, white and blue flowerbeds, the gardens do have a pervasive English nostalgic feel.

Cook's Cottage (www.cookscottage.com.au; adult/child/family $4.50/2/12; ◷9am-5pm) was shipped from Yorkshire in 253 packing cases and reconstructed in 1934 (the cottage actually belonged to the navigator's parents). It's decorated in mid-18th-century style and there is also an exhibition about Captain James Cook's eventful, if controversial, voyages to the Southern Ocean.

Nearby is writer Ola Cohn's equally kooky carved **Fairies Tree**. Efforts to preserve the 300-year-old stump, embellished in 1932 with fairies, pixies, kangaroos, emus and possums, include dissuading true believers from leaving notes to the fairies in the tree's hollows.

Between Cooks' Cottage and the Fairies' Tree is the Fitzroy Gardens **Scarred Tree** (now a stump), which was stripped of a piece of its bark to make a canoe by Aboriginal people.

In the centre of the gardens is a 'model' **Tudor village**. This well-meaning gift was a way of saying thanks for sending food to Britain during WWII.

In the northwestern corner of the gardens is the **People's Path**, a circular path paved with 10,000 individually engraved bricks. The delightful 1930s **Conservatory** (◷9am-5pm) features a range of different floral displays each year.

Collingwood Children's Farm COMMUNITY FARM
(Map p54; www.farm.org.au; 1 St Heliers St, Abbotsford; adult/child/family $8/4/16; ⊙9am-5pm; ⟨R⟩Victoria Park, ⟨◻⟩203) The inner city melts away at this rustic riverside retreat that's not only loved by children. There's a range of frolicking farm animals that children can participate in feeding, as well as rambling gardens and grounds for picnicking on warm days. The farm cafe is open early and can be visited without entering the farm itself. The monthly **farmers market** (www.mfm.com.au; adult/child $2/free; ⊙8am-1pm, 2nd Saturday of the month), held right by the river, is a local highlight, with everything from rabbits to roses to organic milk hoisted into baskets.

Centre for Contemporary Photography
ART GALLERY
(CCP; Map p122; www.ccp.org.au; 404 George St, Fitzroy; admission by donation; ⊙11am-6pm Wed-Fri, noon-5pm weekends; ⟨◻⟩86) This not-for-profit centre has a changing schedule of exhibitions across a couple of galleries. Shows traverse traditional technique and the highly conceptual. There's a particular fascination with work involving video projection, including a nightly after-hours screening in a window. It's a nice space and it also sells a range of Lomo cameras and a small selection of books.

FREE **Gertrude Contemporary Art Spaces** ART GALLERY
(Map p122; www.gertrude.org.au; 200 Gertrude St, Fitzroy; ⊙11am-5.30pm Tue-Fri, 11am-4.30pm Sat; ⟨◻⟩86) This nonprofit gallery and studio

complex has been going strong for nearly 30 years; many of its alumni are now certified famous artists. The monthly openings are refreshingly come-as-you-are, with crowds often spilling onto the street, two-buck wine in hand. The studio open-days, where you get to wander around upstairs and talk to the recipients of the much-sought-after residencies about their work, are worth watching out for.

Abbotsford Convent CULTURAL CENTRE
(Map p54; (⟨☎⟩9415 3600; www.abbotsfordconvent. com.au; 1 St Heliers St, Abbotsford; ⊙7.30am-10pm; ⟨R⟩Victoria Park, ⟨◻⟩203) The convent, which dates back to 1861, is spread over nearly 7 hectares of riverside land. The nuns are long gone – no one is going to ask you if you've been to mass lately – and there's now a rambling collection of creative studios and community offices. The **Convent Bakery** (www.conventbakery.com) supplies impromptu picnic provisions, or Steve at his 1950s-style bar **Handsome Steve's House of Refreshment** (http://houseofrefreshment.com; 1st fl) will mix you up a Campari soda to sip on the balcony while you're overlooking the ecclesiastic architecture and listening to the footy on the radio. There's a **Slow Food Market** (www.mfm.com.au; admission $2; ⊙8am-1pm) every fourth Saturday.

FREE **Alcaston Gallery** ART GALLERY
(Map p122; www.alcastongallery.com.au; 11 Brunswick St, Fitzroy; ⊙10am-6pm Tue-Fri, 11am-5pm Sat; ⟨◻⟩112) Set in an imposing boom-style terrace, the Alcaston's focus is on living indigenous artists. The gallery works directly

END OF THE TRAMLINE TREASURES

Missed your stop? No worries. Here are just a few of the treats that lie at the end – or almost end – of the line:

» **Get to know the Neighbours** Take tram 75 to stop 73 (Springvale Rd), take a right, then a left down Weeden Dve and look out for Pin Oak Court (aka Ramsay St, the oft-filmed court in the long-running Australian soap, *Neighbours*) on your left.

» **Jackson Dodds** (611 Gilbert Rd, West Preston; ⟨◻⟩112) Forgot to get off in North Fitzroy? No matter, eat at this fantabulous cafe while waiting for the tram back.

» **London** (www.thelondon.com.au; 92 Beach St, Port Melbourne; ⟨◻⟩109) Watch the boats depart from this portside pub at the end of the 109 tramline.

» **Pope Joan** (www.popejoan.com.au; 77 Nicholson St, East Brunswick; ⟨◻⟩96) OK, it's not at the end of the line, but industrial-looking Pope Joan has all the right ingredients for an urgent stop – lots of windows, yummy toasted sandwiches and great coffee.

» **Milkwood** (120 Nicholson St, East Brunswick; ⟨◻⟩96) It's uber-tiny, but this end of the tramline treat has heart-shaped cinnamon bread to help share the love. It's packed on weekends and we know why.

If there's one out-of-Melbourne spot that deserves an afternoon dedicated to it, it's **Heide** (www.heide.com.au; 7 Templestowe Rd, Bulleen; ⊙10am-5pm Tue-Sun; ⛟Heidelberg then ⛟903) This, the former home of John and Sunday Reed, is a large public art gallery with wonderful grounds for wandering around and picnicking in. It holds regularly changing exhibitions, many of which include works by the artists that called Heide home, including Sidney Nolan and Albert Tucker. Its grounds are full of sculptures and the two vegetable gardens that Sunday Reed loved so much.

This was a special spot for Melbourne's artists; Sunday was known for feeding and housing them during their rough or creative times. In exchange, she ended up with a shed full of Nolans (almost the entire Ned Kelly series was painted by Sidney Nolan in the dining room of Heide 1 and a thoroughly talented array of house guests.

These days Shannon Bennett's Cafe Vue does the cooking honours (Tuesday to Sunday), and you can eat in, or grab a lunch box ($15) to have by the Yarra. The free tours are a great introduction to Melbourne's early painting scen (see p330).

with indigenous communities and is particularly attentive to cultural sensitivities; it shows a wide range of styles from traditional work to contemporary artists. There's also a space dedicated to works on paper.

FREE **Sutton Gallery** ART GALLERY
(Map p122; www.suttongallery.com.au; 254 Brunswick St, Fitzroy; ⊙11am-5pm Tue-Sat; ⛟112) This gallery is housed in a simple, unassuming warehouse space entered off Greeves St. It's known for championing challenging new work and represents artists such as Nick Mangan, Helga Groves, Gordon Bennett and Lindy Lee.

Carlton & United Breweries BREWERY
(Map p54; (⛟9420 6800; www.carltonbrewhouse. com.au; cnr Nelson & Thompson Sts, Abbotsford; tours adult/child/concession $25/15/20; ⛟109) Just in case Homer Simpson ever makes it to Melbourne, Foster's beer-brewing empire runs 1½-hour **tours** of its Abbotsford operations at 10am, noon and 2pm. You'll encounter enormous 30m-wide vats of beer and a superfast bottling operation, and yes, samples are included in the price. Tours run Monday to Friday; children under 10 and those in open-toed shoes are not admitted. Bookings essential.

Yarra Bend Park PARK
(Map p54; www.parkweb.vic.gov.au; ⛟200/207) Escape the city without leaving town. About 5km northeast of the city centre, the Yarra River flows through bushland, an area cherished by runners, rowers, cyclists, picnickers and strollers.

Yarra Bend Park has huge tracts of densely treed land (not to mention two golf courses and numerous sports grounds) that are great for walking. Cockatoos screech by the banks and grey-headed flying foxes roost in the trees: it's hard to believe you're 10 minutes from office towers and industry. At the end of Boathouse Rd is the 1860s **Studley Park Boathouse** (⛟9853 1972; www.studleyparkboathouse.com.au), which has a kiosk and restaurant, BBQ facilities, flocks of ducks, and boats and canoes for hire (see p80). Kanes suspension footbridge takes you across the river, from where it's about a 20-minute walk to **Dights Falls**, at the meeting of the Yarra River and Merri Creek. You can also walk to the falls along the southern riverbank.

CARLTON & AROUND
Carlton is the traditional home of Melbourne's Italian community and you'll see the *tricolori* unfurled with characteristic passion come soccer finals and the Grand Prix. The heady mix of intellectual activity, espresso and phenomenal food lured bohemians to the area in the 1950s; by the 1970s it was the centre of the city's bourgeoning counterculture scene and has produced some of the city's most legendary theatre, music and literature. Carlton has now well and truly grown up, and despite its public housing and student population, it is a privileged address loaded with liberal and literary residents.

Lygon St reaches out through leafy North Carlton to booming Brunswick. The sprawling University of Melbourne, and its large residential colleges, takes up Carlton's western edge. Here you'll find a vibrant mix of students, long-established families, renovators and newly arrived migrants. The central

Brunswick artery, Sydney Rd, is perpetually clogged with traffic and is packed with Middle Eastern restaurants and grocers. Lygon St, East Brunswick, just keeps getting more fashionable; it has a cluster of restaurants, music venues and bars.

Melbourne Museum
MUSEUM

(Map p74; ☑13 11 02; www.museumvictoria.com.au; 11 Nicholson St, Carlton; adult/child $8/free, exhibitions adult/child $24/16; ☺10am-5pm; ⓇParliament, ⓐCity Circle, 86, 96, ⓠ250, 251, 402) This confident postmodern exhibition space mixes old-style object displays with themed interactive display areas. The museum's reach is almost too broad to be cohesive but provides a grand sweep of Victoria's natural and cultural histories. Walk through the reconstructed laneway lives of the 1800s or become immersed in the legend of champion racehorse and national hero Phar Lap. Bunjilaka, on the ground floor presents indigenous stories and history told through objects and Aboriginal voices. An open-air forest atrium features Victorian plants and animals, and there's some traditional (and nonetheless fascinating) displays of pinned insects. There's a hands-on children's area with weekend activities, as well as an **Imax cinema** (p114) next door.

Royal Exhibition Building
HISTORIC BUILDING

(Map p74; www.museumvicoria.com.au/reb; Nicholson St, Carlton; ⓇParliament, ⓐCity Circle, 86, 96, ⓠ250, 251, 402) Built for the International Exhibition in 1880, and winning Unesco World Heritage status in 2004, this beautiful Victorian edifice symbolises the glory days of the Industrial Revolution, the British Empire and 19th-century Melbourne's economic supremacy. Inside it's equally impressive, with extensive decorative paintwork throughout.

Australia's first parliament was held here in 1901; more than a hundred years later everything from trade fairs to designer sales to dance parties take place. It's also the home of the biennial Melbourne Art Fair. **Tours** (☑13 11 02; adult/child $5/3.50) leave from the **Melbourne Museum** most days at 2pm.

University of Melbourne
UNIVERSITY

(Map p74; www.unimelb.edu.au; Grattan St, Carlton; ⓐ6, 8, 72) The esteemed University of Melbourne was established in 1853 and remains one of Australia's most prestigious universities. Its blend of Victorian Gothic stone buildings, midcentury international-style towers and postmodern showpieces provides a snapshot of changing architectural aspirations. The campus sprawls from Carlton through to the neighbouring suburb of Parkville, and its extensive grounds house the university colleges. Most notable of these is the Walter Burley Griffin–designed **Newman College**.

FREE Ian Potter Museum of Art
ART GALLERY

(Map p74; www.art-museum.unimelb.edu.au; Swanston St, btwn Faraday & Elgin Sts, Parkville; ☺10am-5pm Tue-Fri, noon-5pm Sat & Sun) Part of Melbourne University, the Ian Potter Museum of Art manages the university's extensive art collection, which ranges from antiquities to contemporary Australian work. It's a thoughtfully designed space and always has an exciting exhibition program.

Royal Melbourne Zoo
ZOO

(☑9285 9300; www.zoo.org.au; Elliott Ave, Parkville; adult/child/family $25/13/57; ☺9am-5pm; ⓇRoyal Park, ⓐ55) Melbourne's zoo is one of the city's most popular attractions. Established in 1861, this is the oldest zoo in Australia and the third oldest in the world. Set in spacious, prettily landscaped gardens, the zoo's enclo-

KIDS & SCIENCE

Tired of 'why?' questions from the kids? Then take them to **Spotswood's Scienceworks** (☑9392 4800; www.museumvictoria.com.au/scienceworks; 2 Booker St, Spotswood; Scienceworks adult/child $8/free, Planetarium & Lightning Room additional adult/child $6/4.50; ☺10am-4.30pm; ⓇSpotswood), which wants them to push buttons (not yours, thankfully), lift flaps and pull levers. Scienceworks' range of permanent interactive displays includes the science of sport, household items and the human body. Additional temporary exhibitions are usually scheduled for the school holidays. Scienceworks is *very* popular with school groups; the quietest times are weekday afternoons during school terms and Saturday morning. The museum is a 10-minute signposted walk from Spotswood train station.

The Melbourne Planetarium re-creates the night sky on a 16m-domed ceiling using a hi-tech computer and projection system (and you can guess what the Lightning Room involves). Several shows suitable for children of all ages are also screened.

sures aim to simulate the animals' natural habitats. Walkways pass through the enclosures: you can stroll through the bird aviary, cross a bridge over the lions' park or enter a tropical hothouse full of colourful butterflies. There's also a large collection of native animals in natural bush settings, a platypus aquarium, fur seals, lions and tigers, plenty of reptiles, and an 'Am I in Asia?' elephant enclosure. Allow at least half a day for your visit. In summer, the zoo hosts **Twilight Concerts**, while Roar 'n' Snore (adult/child $195/145, ☉Sep-May) allows you to camp at the zoo and join the keepers on their morning feeding rounds.

Melbourne General Cemetery   CEMETERY
(College Cres, North Carlton; ☉9am-5pm; ☐1, 8) Melbourne has been burying its dead in this cemetery since 1852; it's the final resting place of three Australian prime ministers and the ill-fated explorers Burke and Wills.

Close to a million other people are interred here, mostly along sectarian lines.

Princes Park   PARK
(Princes Park Dr, North Carlton; ☐19) Joggers and walkers pound the 3.2km gravel path around the perimeter of the park, while cricket, rugby league and dog walking fill up the centre. Former home to the Carlton football club (and its current training ground), the ground is known as **MC Labour Park**; the sprawling park has a number of other sporting ovals, a children's playground and barbecues.

Ceres   ENVIRONMENT PARK
(www.ceres.org.au; 8 Lee St, East Brunswick; ☉9am-5pm, market 9am-1pm Wed & Sat; ☐96) Ceres, which was the name of the Roman goddess of agriculture and fertility, also stands for Centre for Education & Research in Environmental Strategies, a 20-something-year-old community environ-

Carlton & Around

ment built on a former rubbish tip. Stroll around the permaculture and bushfood nursery before refuelling with an organic coffee and cake at the pretty (and extremely popular) cafe. There are playgrounds and plenty of natural miniworlds to keep children amused. Or better still, come for the community market where you can buy organic and backyard-produced goodies, and have your tarot read while the kids marvel at the chooks and sheep. Turn right at the last tram stop; it's on your left.

SOUTH YARRA, PRAHRAN & WINDSOR

This neighbourhood has always been synonymous with glitz and glamour; it might be south but it's commonly referred to as the 'right' side of the river. Its elevated aspect and large allotments were always considered prestigious. Access from the CBD to South Yarra was by boat or punt – hence Punt Rd – before Princes Bridge was built in 1850.

Chapel St's South Yarra strip still parades itself as a must-do fashion destination, but

has seen better days; it's been taken over by chain stores, tacky bars and, come sunset, doof-doof cars, but Prahran is still a gutsy and good place, with designer stores, bars and some refreshingly eclectic businesses. Commercial Rd is Melbourne's pumping gay precinct, and has a diverse collection of nightclubs, bars and bookshops. It is also home of the Prahran Market, where the locals shop for fruit, veg and upmarket deli delights. Chapel St continues down to Windsor, a hive of fun cafes and op-shops.

Hawksburn Village, up the Malvern Rd hill, and High St, Armadale make for stylish shopping.

FREE **Royal Botanic Gardens** PARK
(Map p54; www.rbg.vic.gov.au; ⊙7.30am-8.30pm Nov-Mar, to 5.30pm Apr-Oct; ⊕8) One of the finest botanic gardens in the world, the Royal Botanical Gardens are one of Melbourne's most glorious attractions. Sprawling beside the Yarra River, the beautifully designed gardens feature a global selection of plantings as well as specific Australian gardens. Mini-ecosystems, such as a cacti and succulents area, a herb garden and an indigenous rainforest, are set amid vast lawns. Take a book, picnic or Frisbee; most importantly, take your time.

Along with the abundance of plant species, there's a surprising amount of wildlife, including waterfowl, ducks, swans and child-scaring eels in and around the ornamental lake, as well as cockatoos and possums.

The gardens are encircled by the **Tan**, a 4km-long former horse-exercising track, and now used to exercise joggers. During the summer months, the gardens play host to the **Moonlight Cinema** (p114) and theatre performances (see Fridays' 'EG' section of the *Age* newspaper for details).

You can pick up guide-yourself leaflets at the park entrances; these leaflets change with the seasons and tell you what to look out for at the different times of year.

The visitor centre (⊙9am-5pm Mon-Fri, 9.30am-5.30pm Sat & Sun) is at the former centre for stargazers, Observatory Gate, Birdwood Ave. A range of tours departs from here. Choose from a variety of guided walks through assorted horticultural pockets to learn a bit about history, botany and wildlife.

Other features include the Observatory for tours of the night sky and the excellent, nature-based Ian Potter Foundation

Children's Garden (Map p54; www.rbg.vic.gov.
au; Observatory Precinct, Royal Botanic Gardens,
Birdwood Ave, South Yarra; ⊙10am-4pm Wed-
Sun, daily during Victorian school holidays; 🚌8), a
whimsical and child-scaled place that invites
kids and their parents to explore, discover
and imagine. The various mini-environ-
ments are often directed by the seasons and
many plants have been chosen to delight
kids with their intrinsic weirdness or strong
colours. Programs run in the school holidays; see website for details and book ahead.

Next to the visitor centre, the **National
Herbarium**, established in 1853, contains
1.2 million dried botanical specimens used
for identification purposes.

For visitors who can't get enough of
gardens, the Royal Botanical Gardens has
a recently developed **Australian Garden**
(1000 Ballarto Rd) in the outlying suburb of
Cranbourne. Explore 63 hectares of un-
touched heathlands, wetlands and wood-
lands, as well as talk to staff about growing
indigenous plants in a domestic setting. The
award-winning **visitor centre** was designed
by local architect Kerstin Thompson. See
www.rbg.vic.gov.au for its location and opening hours.

Shrine of Remembrance   MONUMENT
(www.shrine.org.au; Birdwood Ave, South Yarra;
⊙10am-5pm; 🚋5, 6, 8, 16, 64, 67, 72) Beside St
Kilda Rd stands the massive Shrine of Remembrance, built as a memorial to Victorians killed in WWI. It was built between 1928
and 1934, much of it with depression-relief
or 'susso' labour. Its bombastic classical
design is partly based on the Mausoleum
of Halicarnassus, one of the seven ancient
wonders of the world. Visible from the other
end of town, planning regulations continue
to restrict any building that would obstruct
the view of the shrine from Swanston St as
far back as Lonsdale St.

Thousands attend the moving Anzac Day
(25 April) dawn service, one of over 120 annual ceremonies hosted at the Shrine. The
Remembrance Day service at 11am on the 11
November commemorates the signing of the
Armistice in 1918 marking the formal end
to WWI. At this precise moment a shaft of
light shines through an opening in the ceiling, passing over the Stone of Remembrance
and illuminating the word 'love'. The forecourt, with its cenotaph and eternal flame,
was built as a memorial to those who died
in WWII, and there are several other specific memorials that surround the shrine.
The complex is under 24-hour police guard;
during opening hours the police are quaintly
required to wear uniforms resembling those
worn by WWI light-horsemen.

Como House   HISTORIC BUILDING
(Map p127; ☎9827 2500; www.comohouse.com.au;
cnr Williams Rd & Lechlade Ave, South Yarra; adult/
child/family $12/6.50/30; ⊙10am-4pm; 🚌8)
This grand colonial residence overlooking
the Yarra was begun in 1840, and underwent renovations up till 1959. The building
has been faithfully restored by the National
Trust and contains some of the Armytage
family's belongings, the last and longest
owners, who lived in the house for 95 years
before passing it on to the National Trust.
The extensive well-tended grounds are faithful to 19th-century landscaping principles
and include a croquet lawn and magnificent flower walks. Contact them for tour
times. The **National Trust** (www.nattrust.com.
au) runs **twilight ghost tours** on the first
Thursday of each month from April to September (tours $35).

**Governor La Trobe's Cottage &
Government House**   HISTORIC BUILDING
(Kings Domain; 🚌48, 75) East of the Shrine of
Remembrance, near the intersection of Birdwood Ave and Dallas Brooks Dr, is **Governor La Trobe's Cottage** (www.nattrust.com.
au), the original government house building
that was sent out in prefabricated form from
the mother country in 1840. Inside, you can
see many of the original furnishings, and the
servants' quarters out the back.

This modest cottage sits in stark contrast
to the Italianate pile of **Government House**
(☎8663 7260; Government House Dr). Built in
1872, it's been the residence of all serving
Victorian governors since, and is a replica
of Queen Victoria's palace on England's Isle
of Wight. As well as being the regal pied-à-
terre, the house and gardens are also used
for an array of state functions and celebrations. Book well in advance to take the Na-

ELVIS IN MELBOURNE

Given that Elvis Presley never actually
performed in Melbourne, it's surprising
to find out that after he died (or did he?)
in 1977, his Melbourne fans erected a
tribute to the King at Melbourne General Cemetery. Look for the large grotto
(and, on his birthday and certain anniversary dates, his fans).

DON'T MISS

WHERE'S WERRIBEE?

Just 30 minutes down the Princes Hwy from the spectacular hump of the Westgate Bridge, among market gardens and new housing estates, is one of Melbourne's most surprising sleeping options. The **Mansion Hotel and Spa** (☑9731 4000; www.lancemore. com.au/mansion; rooms from $220) manages to be both stylish and modern, and has a leisurely country house ambience. Rooms are small – this was a former seminary – but smartly configured and furnished, and there's plenty of space elsewhere to enjoy. Relax among the clever collection of contemporary art in the lounge, library or billiards room. Or do laps of the large indoor pool and collapse in the adjoining spa. A short, bucolic stumble away is **Shadowfax Winery** (www.shadowfax.com.au). Tastings and wood-fired pizzas are available in the stunning Wood Marsh–designed space, or pull up an outside table overlooking the plantings of Shiraz. The **Werribee Mansion** (www.parkweb.vic. gov.au; K Rd, Werribee), a stolid 1870s edifice brimming with colonial arriviste ambition, is also just next door. Werribee Park is the setting for the **Harvest Picnic**, a food, wine and music event held on the last Sunday of November. If the kids are in tow, don't miss the **Werribee Open Range Zoo** (www.zoo.org.au; adult/child $25/13; ☺9am-5pm, last admission 3.30pm), which is also steps away. It's run by the same folk as the Melbourne Zoo, but, with acres and acres of space, allows visitors to jump aboard a bus and go on a 45-minute safari. The meerkats are mesmerising, as usual.

tional Trust **tour** (www.nattrust.com.au; adult/child $10/5), which includes both houses on Monday and Wednesday .

Herring Island   PARK
(Map p127; http://home.vicnet.net.au/~herring) Once an unloved dumping ground for silt, Herring Island is now a prelapsarian garden that seeks to preserve the original trees, shrubs and grasses of the Yarra and provide a home for indigenous animals such as parrots, possums and lizards.

Hidden within is an impressive collection of environmental sculpture, including work by Brit Andy Goldsworthy and locals Julie Collins, Robert Jacks and Robert Bridgewater.

Designated picnic areas, with barbecues, make for a rare retreat just 3km from the city centre. The island is theoretically open to visitors all year round, but can only be reached by boat. A **Parks Victoria punt** (☑13 19 63; per person $2; ☺11.30am-5pm Sat & Sun Dec-Mar) operates from Como Landing on Alexandra Ave in South Yarra.

Prahran Market   MARKET
(Map p127; www.prahranmarket.com.au; 163 Commercial Rd, South Yarra; ☺dawn to 5pm Tue, to 6pm Thu & Fri, dawn-5pm Sat, 10am-3pm Sun; ᵫPrahran, ᵭ72, 78, 79) The Prahran Market has been an institution for over a century and is one of the finest produce markets in the city. It goes without saying that there are numerous stalls stocking fresh seafood, deli items, meats, fruits and vegetables. The market

is also home to the **Essential Ingredient** (☑9827 9047; www.theessentialingredient.com.au) a specialty culinary store. Check its website for details of its cooking school, featuring workshops with Melbourne's most lauded chefs and restaurateurs.

Fawkner Park   PARK
(btwn Toorak & Commercial Rds, South Yarra; ᵭ72) This huge expanse of green is loved and used by the area's sporting folk and lapdogs alike. Walkways lined with elms, oaks and Moreton Bay fig trees provide structure to the otherwise open fields. Barbecues and charming little pavilions are available for public use.

FREE **Uplands Gallery**   ART GALLERY
(Map p127; ☑9510 2374; www.uplandsgallery.com; 247 Chapel St, Prahran; ☺11am-5pm Tue-Fri, noon-4pm Sat; ᵫPrahran, ᵭ78, 79) This gallery shows both emerging and established artists, and while being taken increasingly seriously by collectors, loves to push boundaries. It has over 20 artists in its 'stable'.

ST KILDA & AROUND

Come to St Kilda for its sea breezes, seedy history and a good old bit of people watching. St Kilda was once a playground full of dance halls, a funpark, ice-skating rink, theatres, sea baths and gardens. It got divided up (as many good things do) and now its art deco apartments are worth astronomical real estate prices. There are still mansions dotted around, and its leafy back streets are worth a wander (just remember its reputation as a red light district is not unfounded). There's some great punk history here; the Boys Next Door, fronted by Nick Cave, were based here and played gloriously chaotic gigs at the George Hotel (then known as the Crystal or Seaview Ballroom).

Come dusk, St Kilda's palm trees, bay vistas, briny breezes and pink-stained sunsets are heartbreakingly beautiful. Come the weekend, the volume is turned up, the traffic crawls and the street-party atmosphere sets in. It's still a neighbourhood of extremes, and often exhilarating contrasts: backpacker hostels sit aside fine-dining restaurants, souvlaki bars next to designer shops. Nowhere is this more evident than Fitzroy St, which runs straight from St Kilda Junction to the water's edge. Acland St runs parallel to the Esplanade and from Fitzroy St's Prince Hotel. Its western strip is pleasantly leafy and nostalgically residential. Many long-time locals have turned to Carlisle St's eastern reach, which is traditionally a devout Jewish neighbourhood but is now known for its wine bars and all-day breakfast cafes.

Jewish Museum of Australia
MUSEUM

(☑9534 0083; www.jewishmuseum.com.au; 26 Alma Rd, St Kilda; adult/child/family $10/5/20; ☉10am-4pm Tue-Thu, 11am-5pm Sun; ☐Balaclava) Interactive displays tell the history of Australia's Jewish community from the earliest days of European settlement, while permanent exhibitions celebrate Judaism's rich cycle of festivals and holy days. The museum also has a good curatorial reputation for its contemporary art exhibitions. Follow St Kilda Rd from St Kilda Junction then turn left at Alma Rd.

NOW'S THE TIME

You've got to hand it to Melburnians, they have a certain sentimentality towards neon signs and industrial buildings. Things that set off the average Melburnian's nostalgic ticker include:

» The neon **Nylex Clock** (currently not ticking) atop malt silos near the Yarra River in Richmond.

» The **Skipping Girl** neon sign (renewed and skipping again) near Victoria Gardens in Richmond and.

» The **Uncle Toby's silos** in Sunshine, in Melbourne's industrial west.

Linden Arts Centre & Gallery
ART GALLERY

(Map p112; (☑9534 0099; www.lindenarts.org; 26 Acland St; ☉1-5pm Tue-Fri, 11am-5pm Sat & Sun; ☐16, 96) Housed in a wrought iron–clad 1870s mansion, Linden champions the work of emerging artists. There's a diverting children's sculpture garden and a peaceful front lawn for postshow lolling. The annual postcard show, which coincides with the St Kilda festival in February/March is a highlight.

Luna Park
AMUSEMENT PARK

(Map p112; www.lunapark.com.au; Lower Esplanade; adult/child 1-ride ticket $9.40/7.50, unlimited-ride ticket $42/32; ☉check website for seasonal opening hours; ☐16, 96) It opened in 1912 and still retains the feel of an old-style amusement park with creepy Mr Moon's gaping mouth swallowing you up whole on entering. There's a heritage-listed scenic railway (the oldest operating roller coaster in the world) and a beautifully baroque carousel with hand-painted horses, swans and chariots. There is also the full complement of gut-churning modern rides. For grown-ups, the noise and lack of greenery or shade can pall all too fast.

St Kilda Botanic Gardens
GARDENS

(www.portphillip.vic.gov.au; cnr Blessington & Tennyson Sts, St Kilda; ☉sunrise-sunset; ☐96, 67) Taking pride of place on the southern line of the Barkly, Carlisle and Blessington St triangle, the Botanic Gardens are an unexpected haven from the St Kilda hustle. Wide gravel paths invite a leisurely stroll, and there are plenty of shady spots to sprawl on the open lawns. There are local indigenous plants and a subtropical rainforest conservatory to ponder, as well as the springtime splendour of the Alister Clarke Rose Garden. The duck pond is a favourite with children.

St Kilda Foreshore
BEACH

(Map p112; Jacka Blvd, St Kilda; ☐16, 96) While there are palm-fringed promenades, a parkland strand and a long stretch of sand, still, don't expect Bondi or Noosa. St Kilda's seaside appeal is more Brighton, England than *Baywatch,* despite 20-odd years of glitzy development. And that's the way Melburnians like it: a certain depth of character and an all-weather charm, with wild days on the bay providing for spectacular cloudscapes and terse little waves, as well as the more predictable sparkling blue of summer. It was one of the first Melbourne beaches to ban smoking and glass containers.

Two popular St Kilda restaurants are superbly located in historic foreshore build-

FOOTSCRAY & YARRAVILLE

The city's remaining working docklands divide the western suburbs from the city. Although the distance is not great, the interstitial landscape of containers and their attendant machinery is otherworldly enough to create a strong sense of separateness. The suburbs beyond here have long been proudly working class, though this has changed in the last 15 years, with many young professional families taking advantage of the area's cute cottages, close-to-CBD location and community feel.

The area's 'capital' is the fabulously unfussy Footscray. Almost half of Footscray's population was born overseas, the majority in Vietnam, Africa, China, Italy and Greece. The areas around Barkly St bring those in search of Vietnamese and East African cooking and produce. The **Footscray Market** (Map p54; ☑9687 1205; cnr Hopkins & Leeds Sts; ⊘7am-4pm Tue, Wed & Sat, to 6pm Thu, to 8pm Fri) is testament to the area's diversity.

Heading south from Footscray are the fashionable residential neighbourhoods of Seddon and Yarraville. The latter centres on its train station, with a beautifully well-preserved heritage shopping area around Anderson St; it also boasts some great restaurants, bars and cafes.

For those interested in the west's unique history, head to the **Living Museum** (☑9318 3544; www.livingmuseum.org.au; Van Ness Ave, Maribyrnong; ⊘10am-4pm Mon-Fri, 11am-4pm Sun), set in the grounds of Pipemakers Park, featuring a wetlands area and indigenous gardens. For see boxed text, p99, for eating options.

ings: the stylish **Donovans** (p103), once a bathing pavilion, and the **Stokehouse** (p102), originally an Edwardian teahouse.

The kiosk at the end of St Kilda Pier (an exact replica of the original, which burnt down in 2003, a year short of its centenary) is as much about the journey as the destination. Piers have always made good fodder for music videos (Elton John, Elvis Costello et al) and this one is no different. The clip for Paul Kelly's melancholic '80s hit 'From St Kilda to Kings Cross' was shot here. The breakwater near the pier was built in the '50s as a safe harbour for boats competing in the Olympic Games. It's now home to a colony of little penguins that have, incredibly, chosen the city's most crowded suburb in which to reside. You can also visit and learn about the penguins on an eco **Stand up Paddleboarding** trip (see p82).

During summer, the **Port Phillip Eco Centre** (www.ecocentre.com; 55A Blessington St, St Kilda) also runs a range of tours, including one that starts at a storm-water drain and ends up at the **penguin colony**. Contact **Earthcare St Kilda** (earthcarestkilda@gmail.com) to get involved in penguin research or rakali watch.

On the foreshore south of the pier, the Moorish-style St Kilda Sea Baths (Map p112; ☑9525 4888; www.stkildaseabaths.com.au; 10-18 Jacka Blvd) is a spectacular public folly. The complex contains a health club, shops

and food outlets, but is markedly lacking in atmosphere and visitors, a hard call in this location. There's a heated indoor saltwater pool, but at $13 a dip, it's really only attractive on frosty days.

Elwood Beach   BEACH
(off Map p112; Ormond Esplanade, Elwood) A short drive or concerted foreshore walk will take you to this swimming beach. It tends to be less windswept, though often no less crowded, than St Kilda and is surrounded by leafy Elwood Park and Point Ormond Reserve. There are playgrounds and kiosks.

FREE **Muma**   ART GALLERY
(Monash University Museum of Art; Ground fl, Bldg F, Monash University, Caulfield Campus, Dandenong Rd, Caulfield; ⊘10am-5pm Tue-Fri, noon-5pm Sat; ☐3, ☐Caulfield) Established during the 1960s, Muma's art collection has 1600 art works, and they're a great representation of Australian contemporary art. To house the collection, a new, specially designed gallery opened in 2010, featuring a sculptural commission by artist Callum Morton.

SOUTH MELBOURNE, PORT MELBOURNE & ALBERT PARK

There's something boastful about these suburbs, and it runs along the lines of being close to Melbourne's watery highlights: the beach, expansive Albert Park Lake and the Melbourne Aquatic Centre. These are upmarket suburbs rejoicing in their peaceful environment (though come Grand Prix time, the noise is ramped up big time).

Head to South Melbourne for its market, contemporary homeware shops and top cafes (seems there's a coffee competition going on). At nearby Port Melbourne is Station Pier, the passenger terminal for the ferry service between Melbourne and Tasmania (see p130). Port Melbourne is packed with modern housing and old factories stuffed with new apartments. This end of the bay is Garden City, which is modelled on workers' 'garden suburbs' in Britain. It still faintly hints at what was once a rollicking, working-class port, and many Melburnians don't even know it exists.

South Melbourne Market   MARKET
(Map p54; cnr Coventry & Cecil Sts, South Melbourne; ☺8am-4pm Wed, to 6pm Fri, to 4pm Sat & Sun; ⸬96) The market's labyrinthine interior is packed to overflowing with an eccentric collection of stalls selling everything from carpets to bok choy. It's been on this site since 1864 and is a neighbourhood institution, as are its dim sims. The surrounding streets are conveniently dotted with decent cafes and other interesting speciality shops. There's a cooking school here, too.

Albert Park Lake   LAKE
(Map p54; btwn Queens Rd, Fitzroy St, Aughtie Dr & Albert Rd, Albert Park; ⸬96, 112) Elegant black swans give their inimitable bottoms-up salute as you circumnavigate the 5km perimeter of this man-made lake. Jogging, cycling, walking or clamouring over play equipment is the appropriate human equivalent. Lakeside Dr was used as an international motor-racing circuit in the 1950s, and since 1996 the revamped track has been the venue for

---

DON'T MISS

PORT VIEWS

This is one of Melbourne's most surprising spots: **Station Pier** (Map p54). This pier holds many memories for generations of Victorian immigrants and it's still a working passenger port today (though people are generally arriving from Tasmania rather than distant England). There's a clutch of swish megarestaurants on the pier itself – including Waterfront and 3 Station Pier – serving up bay vistas and variable food to large numbers of visitors.

---

the **Australian Formula One Grand Prix** (p25) each March. Also on the periphery is the **Melbourne Sports & Aquatic Centre**, with an Olympic-size pool and child-munching wave machine.

Station Pier   HISTORIAL SITE.
(Map p54; www.portofmelbourne.com; ☺6am-9pm pedestrians only, closed during some ship visits; ⸬109) Station Pier is Melbourne's main sea passenger terminal, and is where the *Spirit of Tasmania*, cruise ships and navy vessels dock. It has been in operation since 1854, and the first major railway in Australia ran from here to the city. It has great sentimental associations for many migrants who arrived by ship in the 1950s and 60s, and for servicemen who used it during WWII. There has been significant development of the area over the last 10 years and there is now a gaggle of restaurants built on and around the pier, as well as a marina.

🏃 Activities
Canoeing & Kayaking
Kayaking   KAYAKING
(📞0418 106 427; www.kayakmelbourne.com.au; tours $89) Don't miss out on the chance to see Melbourne's Yarra River by kayak. These two-hour tours take you past Melbourne's newest city developments and explain the history of the older ones. Moonlight tours are most evocative and include a dinner of fish and chips. Tours usually depart from Shed 4, North Wharf Rd, Docklands – check website for directions.

Studley Park Boathouse   CANOEING
(📞9853 1828; www.studleyparkboathouse.com.au) Pack a picnic then rent a two-person canoe or kayak from the boathouse for $30 for the first hour.

Cycling
Cycling maps are available from the Visitor Information Centre at Federation Square and Bicycle Victoria (📞8636 8888; www.bv.com.au). The urban series includes the Main Yarra Trail (35km), off which runs the Merri Creek Trail (19km), the Outer Circle Trail (34km) and the Maribyrnong River Trail (22km). There are also paths taking you along Melbourne's beaches.

You'll not be alone on the roads; there's a large club scene, as well as a new breed of 'slow cyclists'.

Wearing a helmet while cycling is compulsory in Melbourne (as it is in the rest of Australia).

WILLIAMSTOWN

Williamstown is a yacht-filled gem just a short boat ride (or drive) from Melbourne's CBD. It has stunning views of Melbourne, and a bunch of touristy shops along its esplanade.

Gem Pier is where passenger ferries dock to drop off and collect those who visit Williamstown by boat. It's a fitting way to arrive, given the area's maritime ambience. **Williamstown Ferries** (☑9517 9444; www.williamstownferries.com.au) plies Hobsons Bay daily, stopping at Southgate and visiting a number of sites along the way, including Scienceworks (p73) and Docklands. **Melbourne River Cruises** (☑9629 7233; www. melbcruises.com.au) also docks at Gem Pier, travelling up the Yarra River to Southgate. Ticket prices vary according to your destination. Pick up a timetable from the very useful visitor centre in Williamstown or at Federation Square, or contact the companies directly; bookings are advised.

Humble Vintage CYCLING
(☑0432 032 450; www.thehumblevintage.com) Get yourself a set of special wheels from this collection of retro racers, city bikes and ladies bikes. Rates start at $30 per day, or $80 per week and include lock, helmet and a terrific map with plenty of ideas of what to do with your non-bike riding hours, too. See also boxed text, p130.

Golf

Some of Melbourne's golf courses are rated among the best in the world. The illustrious Sandbelt refers to 10 courses stretching along the bay; they're built on a sand base, creating perfect conditions year-round. Among them are **Royal Melbourne** (www.royalmelbournegc.com), Australia's best and rated number eight in the world, **Huntingdale** (www.huntingdalegolf .com.au), home of the Australian Masters tournament, and **Kingston Heath** (www .kingstonheath.com.au), ranked number two in Australia and host to high-profile tournaments. Unfortunately, many are private courses: you'll need a letter of introduction from your own club, and often a verifiable handicap, to get a hit.

For public courses, it's best to book ahead. Green fees cost around $25 for 18 holes during the week, and all courses have clubs and buggies for hire. You'll find a summary of the state's courses at www.ausgolf.com.au. Some good public courses close to town include the following.

Albert Park Golf Course GOLF
(☑9510 5588; www.golfvictoria.com.au; Queens Rd, Albert Park; ☉dawn-dusk; ⊠3, 5, 6, 16, 64, 6) This 18-hole championship golf course is set on the fringes of **Albert Park Lake** (Map p54), just 2km from the city. Located alongside the Australian Formula One Grand Prix racing circuit, a separate **driving range** (☑9696 4653; Aughtie Dr; ☉7am-10pm; ⊠96) allows golfers to hit off from 65 two-tier all-weather bays.

Brighton Golf Course GOLF
(☑9592 1388; www.brightongolfclub.com.au; 232 Dendy St, Brighton; ☉dawn-dusk) One of the adored Sandbelt courses for which Melbourne is known, this 18-hole course keeps golfers on their toes with water hazards and deep bunkers. It's about 10km southeast of the CBD.

Yarra Bend Golf Course GOLF
(☑9481 3729; www.parkweb.vic.gov.au; Yarra Bend Rd, Fairfield; ☉dawn-dusk) Yarra Bend is just 4km from the city, and affords views of the Yarra River. It's an 18-hole course that also offers instruction, and a Japanese-speaking staff member is on hand.

Indoor Rock Climbing

Hardrock@Verve ROCK CLIMBING
(Map p58; ☑9631 5300; www.hardrock.com.au; 501 Swanston St; ☉noon-10pm Mon-Fri, 11am-7pm Sat & Sun) Not the bar franchise but an indoor climbing centre with naturalistic surfaces up to 16m-high and city views. There are a few storeys of glass frontage, so the city gets to view you too.

Lawn Bowls

Formerly the domain of senior citizens wearing starched white uniforms, bowling clubs have recently been inundated by younger types: barefoot, with a beer in one hand and a bowl in the other. With a game costing between $10 and $15 (including bowl hire), and cheap beer on tap, bowls makes for a leisurely afternoon with mates.

North Fitzroy Bowls
LAWN BOWLS

(☑9481 3137; www.fvbowls.com.au; 578 Brunswick St, North Fitzroy; ☐112) Officially known as the Fitzroy Victoria Bowling & Sports Club, this centre, north of Alexandra Parade, comes equipped with lights for night bowls, barbecues and a beer garden. The dress code is neat-casual, with slippers or thongs (flip flops) acceptable. Phone to make a booking and for opening times, which vary from day to day.

St Kilda Bowling Club
LAWN BOWLS

(Map p112; ☑9537 0370; 66 Fitzroy St, St Kilda; ☺noon-sunset Tue-Sun; ☐16, 96) The only dress code at this popular bowling club is 'shoes off'. So join the many others who de-shoe to enjoy a beer and a bowl in the great outdoors. This club provides bowls and a bit of friendly instruction for first-timers; Francophiles can opt for *boules*.

Sailing

With about 20 yacht clubs around the shores of Port Phillip, yachting is one of Melbourne's most popular passions. Races and regattas are held on most weekends, and the bay is a memorable sight when it's sprinkled with hundreds of colourful sails. Conditions can change radically and without warning, making sailing on the bay a challenging, and sometimes dangerous, pursuit. Melbourne's two main ocean races are the Melbourne-to-Devonport and Melbourne-to-Hobart events, held annually between Christmas and New Year. The Melbourne to Hobart race goes around Tasmania's wild western coast; the more famous Sydney to Hobart event runs down the eastern coast.

Hobsons Bay Yacht Club
SAILING

(HBYC; Map p54; ☑9397 6393; www.hbyc.asn.au; 268 Nelson Pl, Williamstown) From October to March, Hobsons Bay Yacht Club welcomes volunteer sailors on Wednesday nights (arrive by 5.30pm).

Royal Melbourne Yacht Squadron
SAILING

(RMYC; Map p112; ☑9534 0227; www.rmys.com.au; Pier Rd) Have a go on a yacht on Wednesday nights ($20); arrive by 4pm. Wear nonmarking shoes (white soles) and take along waterproof gear, if you have it.

TENNIS

It's not just as spectators that Melburnians really dig tennis. You'll find enthusiastic clubs and beautifully sited courts scattered throughout the inner city.

Melbourne Park
TENNIS

(Map p69; ☑9914 4133; www.mopt.com.au; Batman Ave) The home of the Australian Open tennis grand slam, Melbourne Park has 23 outdoor and five indoor courts; prices are per hour and vary depending on the time of day and week. Indoor court hire ranges from $36 to $42, and outdoor courts cost between $28 and $36, plus racquet hire.

WINDSURFING, KITE-SURFING & STAND-UP PADDLE BOARDING

Elwood, just south of St Kilda, is a popular sailboarding area and you can have a go at stand up paddle boarding (SUP) up the Yarra River or join a tour out to St Kilda's penguin colony.

RPS – the Board Store
WINDSURFING, PADDLE BOARDING

(☑9525 6475; www.rpstheboardstore.com; 87 Ormond Rd, Elwood) A three-hour introductory course in windsurfing costs $130, while private 1½-hour SUP lessons are $75 ($60 if there are three people). All gear is included; courses are weather-dependent and mainly limited to the summer months. Book at least a week ahead. Follow Marine Pde to Glenhuntly Rd; turn left at Ormond Rd.

Stand Up Paddle Boarding
PADDLE BOARDING

(☑0416 184 994; www.supb.com.au; St Kilda Baths; tours $89-130) Hire out SUP equipment from St Kilda for $25 per hour or join one of their Yarra River or St Kilda Penguin tours.

SWIMMING

In summer, do as most Melburnians do, and hit the sand at one of the city's metropolitan beaches. St Kilda, Middle Park and Port Melbourne are popular patches, with suburban beaches at Brighton and Sandringham. Public pools are also well loved.

Fitzroy Swimming Pool
SWIMMING POOL

(Map p122; ☑9205 5180; Alexandra Pde, Fitzroy; adult/child $4.60/2.10; ☐112) Between laps, locals love catching a few rays up in the bleachers or on the lawn; there are also two toddler pools. The pool's Italian 'Aqua Profonda' sign was painted in 1953 – an initiative of the pool's manager who frequently had to rescue migrant children who couldn't read the English signs. The sign is heritage-listed (misspelled and all – it should be 'Acqua').

Melbourne City Baths
SWIMMING POOL

(Map p58; ☑9663 5888; www.melbournecity baths.com.au; 420 Swanston St, Melbourne; casual swim adult/child/family $5.50/2.60/12, gym $20;

6am-10pm Mon-Thu, 6am-8pm Fri, 8am-6pm Sat & Sun) The City Baths were literally public baths when they first opened in 1860 and were intended to stop people bathing in and drinking the seriously polluted Yarra River. They now boast the CBD's largest pool (it's 30m), plus you get to do your laps in a 1903 heritage-listed building. There is also a public spa, the full complement of gym facilities and squash courts.

Prahran Aquatic Centre SWIMMING POOL
(Map p127; 8290 7140; 41 Essex St, Prahran; adult/child $4.80/2.70; 72, 78, 79) This glam 50m heated outdoor pool is surrounded by a stretch of lawn. The on-site cafe is a must for the locals who can't do without their latte, seminaked or not.

Courses

Book a cooking course at the **South Melbourne Market** (classes $80-120), which has standard classes to masterclass with some of Melbourne's best known chefs; **Queen Victoria Market** (2½hr classes; $90-160) for everything from home brewing to curing; or **Essential Ingredient at the Prahran Market** (9827 9047; classes $110-275) from pizza making to matching food and wine.

The **Centre for Adult Education** (CAE; Map p58; 9652 0611; www.cae.edu.au; 253 Flinders Lane) runs a wide variety of courses from cooking to language to art.

Tours

Aboriginal Heritage Walk WALKING TOUR
(9252 2429; www.rbg.vic.gov.au; Royal Botanic Gardens; adult/child $25/10; 11am Tue & Thu & 1st Sun of the month) The Royal Botanic Gardens are on a traditional camping and meeting place of the original owners, and this tour takes you through their story – from songlines to plant lore, all in 90 fascinating minutes. The tour departs from the visitor centre.

Walkin' Birrarung WALKING TOUR
(8622 2600; www.koorieheritagetrust.com/education; $15) These tours are run mainly for school groups, but you may be able to tag along. They're an exploration of the landscape of the Yarra as well as the dramatic and irrevocable changes to both the people and the place. Its impact on all senses evokes

---

NOW, JUST RELAX...

Melbourne has some luxuriously indulgent day spas that offer the usual range of 'treatments' that go way beyond the basic massage/mani/pedi formula. The trend is definitely to the organic and the spiritual.

Aesop, a Melbourne-based company, runs **Aesop Spa** (Map p127; 9866 5250; www.aesop.net.au; 153 Toorak Rd, South Yarra; treatments from $120; by appointment 10am-4pm Wed-Sat; South Yarra, 8) in South Yarra. If you've been hanging around in the bathrooms of some of Melbourne's finer restaurants, you may be familiar with the citrus tang of its liquid soap. Aesop Spa takes it up a notch, and you can choose from five basic treatments; your lactate surge or detox overhaul will be further customised to your skin while you're wrapped up in a mohair blanket on a cotton futon.

Melbourne's hotels have long been associated with luxury day spas; what better way for some rejuvenation than to spa and sleep in the one locale. The brand new Crown Metropol hotel has residential rooms with staircases leading directly to its spa, **isika** (off Map p58; www.crownmetropol.com.au/isika; 9292 8327; 8 Whiteman St, Southbank; 1hr from $140; 8am-8pm) . Other luxury hotels offering spa treatments are the Prince, with its **Aurora Spa Retreat** (Map p112; www.auroraspatreat.com; 2 Acland St, St Kilda; 1hr from $120; Mon-Fri 8.30am-8pm, Sat 8.30am-6pm, Sun 10am-7pm; 16, 79, 96, 112); **Chuan Spa at the Langham Hotel** (Map p58; 8696 8111; www.chuanspa.com; Langham Hotel, 1 Southgate Ave, Southbank; 1hr from $175; 6am-8.30pm Mon-Fri, 8am-8pm Sat & Sun); and the mother and daughter fave, the **Lyall Spa** (Map p127; 9868 8333; www.thelyall.com; 14 Murphy St, South Yarra; 1hr from $125; 10am-6pm; South Yarra, 8) at the Lyall Hotel.

A cheaper way to feel a million dollars is to visit the **Japanese Bath House** (off Map p122; 9419 0268; www.japanesebathhouse.com; 59 Cromwell St, Collingwood; bath $28, shiatsu from $46; 11am-10pm Tue-Fri, to 8pm weekends, 109). Though urban the setting may be, it's as serene as can be inside this authentic *sentō* (bathhouse). Perfect for some communal skinship (it's nude, segregated bathing, folks), a shiatsu and a postsoak sake in the *tatami* lounge.

MELBOURNE FOR CHILDREN

Melbourne is fairly child-friendly and getting around by tram has become easier thanks to 'super platforms' that allow you to push the stroller straight on. Other trams still require assistance to get on board, and some styles of trams are not stroller-friendly at all.

The best baby-change facilities can usually be found in major department stores, but you can use public facilities at Travellers Aid (at both Flinders St and Southern Cross Stations).

» **Children's Garden** (p75) With tunnels in the rainforest, a kitchen garden and water-play area, this garden is much loved by kids and parents.

» **Collingwood Children's Farm** (p71) Old MacDonald has nothing on this farm, which has an organic, wholesome vibe and a bunch of farm animals (usually) happy to be made a fuss of.

» **ACMI** (p56) Free access to computer games and movies may encourage square eyes, but it's a great spot for a rainy day.

» **Luna Park** (p78) Fairy floss will fuel the hysteria of the Ferris wheel and historic scenic railway.

» **Scienceworks** (p73) Explains the mysteries of the physical world through interactive displays.

» **Royal Melbourne Zoo** (p73) Sleepovers in the historic Elephants' Enclosure are offered. Roar 'n' Snore packages include three meals (BYO sleeping bag and pillow) and take you behind the scenes.

» **ArtPlay** (p56) and **Ian Potter Centre** (NGVA; p53) Have art programs that often take their cues from the current show, if you can't get them interested in that iconic piece of modern art.

» **National Sports Museum** (p68) Just walking in will get your junior champion's heart rate up.

» **Ceres** (p74) Kids are encouraged to participate in their environment, either through playing with the animals or via the interactive education programs on offer.

» **Melbourne Museum** (p73) The Children's Gallery has hands-on exhibits that make kids squeal (especially the creepy-crawly 'Bugs Alive!' exhibit).

memories that lie beneath the modern city. Tours begins at Enterprize Park. Highly recommended.

 Sunset Eco Penguin Tour

PADDLE BOARDING

(Map p77; ☑0416 184 994; www.supb.com.au; $130) See St Kilda's penguin colony while you navigate your paddleboard standing up (a lesson, equipment and wetsuit hire is included).

Balloon Sunrise   HOT-AIR BALLOONING

(☑1800 468 247; www.hotairballooning.com.au; adult/child $345/240) Although perhaps not fully awake (the tour leaves before dawn), you'll certainly feel dreamy floating above the building tops and peering into backyards from a hot-air balloon. This tour includes an hour's air time, plus a champagne breakfast at the Langham Hotel (Map p58), from where tours depart. Balloons go up

every morning (weather permitting) except Christmas and New Year's Day, though you'll need to book a few weeks ahead. Children must be over six years old. They also go up in the Yarra Valley.

FREE **City Circle trams**   TRAM

(www.metlinkmelbourne.com.au) A free service operating from 10am to 6pm daily. This tram travels around the city centre, along Flinders, Spring and Latrobe Sts, and then back along Harbour Esplanade (there are also trams running in the opposite direction). Designed primarily for tourists, and passing many city sights along the way, the trams run every 10 minutes or so. Eight refurbished W-class trams operate on this route. Built in Melbourne between 1936 and 1956, they have all been painted a distinctive deep burgundy and gold. You can even dine on board a tram (www.tramrestaurant. com.au) while taking a scenic night cruise around Melbourne's streets (although this one isn't free).

FREE Melbourne City Tourist Shuttle BUS
(www.thatsmelbourne.com.au) This free shuttle is a 1½ hour round trip, taking passengers to sights including Melbourne Museum, the MCG (when there are no events scheduled) and Docklands. It operates from 9.30am to 4.30pm daily.

Melbourne By Foot WALKING TOUR
(☑1300 311 081; www.melbournebyfoot.com; tours $29) Take a couple of hours out with Dave and experience a mellow, informative walking tour that covers lane art, politics, Melbourne's history and diversity. Highly recommended.

Chocoholic Tours FOOD
(☑9686 4655; www.chocoholictours.com.au; tours from $37) Sure you can check out Melbourne's chocolate shops yourself, but why not join a large bunch of fellow addicts and make a meal of it?

FREE Greeter Service WALKING TOUR
(☑9658 9658; Melbourne Visitor Centre, Federation Sq) Get your bearings on this free two-hour 'orientation tour', which departs Fed Sq daily at 9.30am (bookings required). It's run by the city's volunteer 'greeters'.

Hidden Secrets Tours WALKING TOUR
(☑9663 3358; www.hiddensecretstours.com; tours $70-145) Offers a variety of walking tours covering everything from lanes and arcades, wine, architecture, coffee and cafes, and vintage Melbourne.

Real Melbourne Bike Tours CYCLING
(☑0417 339 203; www.rentabike.net.au; tours incl lunch adult/child $110/79) Offers four-hour cycling tours covering the CBD, parts of the Yarra and Fitzroy. Bike hire is included.

Maribyrnong River Cruises CRUISES
(☑9689 6431; www.blackbirdcruises.com.au; Wingfield St, Footscray; adult/child $20/5; ⏰Tue, Thu, Sat & Sun) The two-hour cruise departs at 1pm and heads up the Maribyrnong River to Avondale Heights, while a one-hour cruise to Docklands departs at 4pm (adult/child $10/5) – you'll see the Lonely Planet head office on the way. Departures are from the end of Wingfield St in Footscray. Buy tickets at the departure point (no phone bookings).

Melbourne River Cruises CRUISES
(☑9681 3284; www.melbcruises.com.au; Berth 5, Lower Promenade, Southgate; adult/child from $23/11) Take a one-hour cruise upstream or downstream, or a 2½-hour return cruise. Regular cruises along the Yarra River depart from a couple of locations – check for details. It also operates a ferry between Southgate and Gem Pier in Williamstown. There are three to nine sailings daily, depending on the season.

Walk to Art WALKING TOUR
(☑8415 0449; www.walktoart.com.au; per person $108) These walking tours take you to galleries, artists' studios and artist-run spaces hidden in Melbourne's buildings and laneways. The tour itinerary, around the CBD and inner neighbourhoods, is always changing, and isn't revealed the day of the walk. The tours operate Wednesday and Saturday, in all weather conditions and last for three hours. Tours include art 'starter pack', and wine and cheese afterwards.

🛏 Sleeping

While you'll have no trouble finding a place to stay that suits your taste and budget, for a city that's big on style Melbourne has surprisingly few truly inspirational boltholes and only a handful of atmospheric, individual small hotels. Still, prices are rarely stratospheric and quality is generally high.

For a standard double room in a top-end hotel, expect to pay upwards of $250, midrange around $150 and for budget doubles from $80 to $100. Prices peak during the Australian Open in January, Grand Prix weekend in March, AFL finals in September and the Spring Racing Carnival in November. Midrange to deluxe hotels publish 'rack rates', but always ask for current specials and for inclusions such as breakfast and parking. All accommodation has a 10% goods and services tax (GST) included in the price.

Apartment-style accommodation is easy to find in Melbourne – there are several local as well as national chains – and suits those who want a smart, functional space to relax in and stow their shopping, but who don't need full hotel accoutrements. There are also plenty of budget hostels, pubs and B&Bs. Many big hostels offer private rooms alongside basic dorms, and Melbourne has an increasing number of 'flashpacker' hostels that provide a raft of comforts while retaining the social hostel vibe.

AIRPORT & AROUND

Melbourne Airport is 25km from the city with no direct public transport links, so odd-

Melbourne's gay and lesbian community is well integrated into the general populace, but clubs and bars are found in two distinct locations: Abbotsford, Collingwood, Prahran and South Yarra. Commercial Rd, which separates Prahran and South Yarra, is home to numerous gay clubs, cafes and businesses. It's more glamorous than the 'northside', which is reputedly more down to earth and a little less pretentious.

Plenty of Melbourne venues get into the spirit during **Midsumma Festival** (www.midsumma.org.au; ☺mid Jan-Feb). It has a diverse program of cultural, community and sporting events, including the popular Midsumma Carnival at Birrarung Marr, St Kilda's Pride March and much more. Australia's largest GLBT film festival, the **Melbourne Queer Film Festival** (www.melbournequeerfilm.com.au) screens 140 films from around the world each March.

MCV (www.mcv.net.au) is a free weekly newspaper, and gay and lesbian community radio station **JOY 94.9FM** (www.joy.org.au) is another important resource for visitors and locals.

Drinking & Nightlife

Xchange Hotel CLUB
(www.xchange.com.au; 119 Commercial Rd, South Yarra; ☺4pm-1am Mon-Thu, 2pm-3am Fri-Sun; ☒Prahran, ☒72) A brand new fitout has added girly 'Pamela's Place' and transformed the 'Boom Boom Room' into an arena-style, multilevel dance floor.

Orlando EVENT
(http://orlandoinbrunswick.wordpress.com; 380 Victoria St, Brunswick; ☺last Fri of month; ☒Brunswick, ☒19) This GLBTIQ indie dance party happens on the last Friday of the month. Victoria St runs west off Sydney Rd.

Laird PUB/CLUB
(www.lairdhotel.com; 149 Gipps St, Collingwood; ☺5pm-late; ☒Collingwood) The Laird's been running its men-only gay hotel for over 30 years now. It's on the Abbotsford side of Gipps St, which runs off Collingwood's Wellington St.

---

hour flights require taxis, a Skybus from the CBD or a sleepover. There are three main airport hotels, ranging from bells, whistles and direct 'air bridge' access at the **Hilton Melbourne Airport** (☎8336 2000; www1.hilton.com; Arrival Drive; r from $255; ❋☞❋) and the smart but slightly further away **Holiday Inn Melbourne Airport** (☎1300 724 944; www.holidayinn.com.au; 10-14 Centre Rd; r from $225; ❋❋), to the **Hotel Formule 1** (☎8336 1811; www.formule1.com.au; 12 Caldwell Drive; r from $109; ❋@☞), which has basic rooms with bunks and is just over 600m away.

CENTRAL MELBOURNE

There are a lot of places across all price ranges that will put you in the heart of the action, whether you've come to town and want to shop, party, catch a match or take in some culture. If you like to take a morning stroll in something resembling nature, choose a hotel towards Spring St for easy access to Fitzroy Gardens, or close to Flinders St for a riverside run. Spencer St has a lot of hotels, historically sited to catch country train passengers; while they're only a few tram stops away from the city centre (and in spitting distance of Docklands Stadium), it's not as atmospheric as staying in Flinders Lane or Little Collins St.

Melbourne Central YHA HOSTEL **$**
(Map p58; ☎9621 2523; www.yha.com.au; 562 Flinders St; dm/d $32/100; @☞) This heritage building has been totally transformed by the YHA gang; expect a lively reception, handsome rooms, and kitchens and common areas on each of the four levels. Entertainment's high on the agenda, and there's a fab restaurant (Bertha Brown) on the ground floor and a grand rooftop area.

Medina Executive Flinders St APARTMENTS **$$**
(Map p58; ☎8663 0000; www.medina.com.au; 88 Flinders St; apt from $165; ❋) These cool monochromatic apartments are extra-large and luxurious. Ask for one at the front for amazing parkland views or get glimpses into Melbourne's lanes from the giant timber-floored studios, all boasting full kitchens.

Sofitel HOTEL **$$$**
(Map p58; ☎9653 0000; www.sofitelmelbourne.com.au; 25 Collins St; r from $270; ❋@☞) Guestrooms at the Sofitel start on the 36th floor,

Glasshouse Hotel
PUB

(www.glass-house.com.au; 51 Gipps St, Collingwood; ☺5pm-late Wed, noon-late Fri & Sun, 4pm-late Sat; 🚋16, 96, 12) Caters for a mostly lesbian crowd with entertainment including live bands, drag kings and DJs. Gipps St runs east off Wellington St.

Peel Hotel
CLUB

(www.thepeel.com.au; cnr Peel & Wellington Sts, Collingwood; ☺9pm-late Thu-Sat; 🚋86) Features a mostly male crowd dancing to house music, retro and commercial dance. It's on Peel St, which runs east off Smith St.

Commercial Hotel
PUB

(238 Whitehall St, Yarraville; ☺Wed-Sat; 🚉Yarraville) A friendly, low-key pub in Melbourne's inner west that presents drag shows on Saturday nights. From the CBD, follow Footscray Rd and turn left down Whitehall.

Greyhound Hotel
LIVE MUSIC, PUB

(www.ghhotel.com.au; cnr Carlisle St & Brighton Rd, St Kilda; 🚋16, 67, 79) The old Greyhound's had a facelift; expect drag-filled evenings from Thursday to Saturday. Follow Carlisle St to the corner of Brighton Rd.

Sleeping

169 Drummond
GUESTHOUSE **$$**

(Map p74; ☎9663 3081; www.169drummond.com.au; 169 Drummond St, Carlton; d $135-145; 🚋1, 8) A privately owned guesthouse in a renovated, 19th-century terrace in the inner north, one block from vibrant Lygon St.

so you're guaranteed views that will make you giddy. The rooms are high international style, opulent rather than minimal, and though the hotel entrance, with its superb IM Pei–designed ceiling, is relentlessly workaday, you'll soon be a world (or at least 36 floors) away. No35 is an excellent restaurant on level, you guessed it, 35.

Nomad's Industry
HOSTEL **$**

(Map p58; ☎9328 4383; www.nomadshostels. com; 198 A'Beckett St; dm $28-36, d $125; @🛜) Flashpacking hits Melbourne's CBD with this smart hostel boasting a mix of dorms (groups can take hold of a four-bed dorm with en suite). There's a rooftop area and plenty of gloss (especially in the girls-only 'Princess Wing').

Pensione Hotel
HOTEL **$**

(Map p58; ☎9621 3333; www.pensione.com.au; 16 Spencer St; r from $100-135; ✺@🛜) With refreshing honesty, the Pensione Hotel names some rooms a 'petit double' but what you don't get in size is more than made up for in spot-on style, room extras and superreasonable rates. It's lovely.

Adelphi Hotel
HOTEL **$$**

(Map p58; ☎8080 8888; www.adelphi.com.au; 187 Flinders Lane; r from $185; ✺@🛜🏊) This discreet Flinders Lane property, designed by Denton Corker Marshall in the early '90s, was one of Australia's first boutique hotels. The cosy rooms with original fittings have stood the test of time and its pool, which juts out over Flinders Lane, has inspired imitators.

Grand Hyatt Melbourne
HOTEL **$$$**

(Map p58; ☎9657 1234; www.melbourne.grand. hyatt.com; 123 Collins St; r from $320; ✺@🛜) This famous Collins St five-star has 546 rooms, many with grand floor-to-ceiling windows, marble baths, designated workspaces and art deco furnishings. Its remodelled foyer is quite over the top, yet you can still find peaceful nooks.

Hotel Lindrum
HOTEL **$$$**

(Map p58; ☎9668 1111; www.hotellindrum.com.au; 26 Flinders St; r from $245; ✺@🛜) This attractive hotel was once the snooker hall of the legendary and literally unbeatable Walter Lindrum. Expect rich tones, subtle lighting and tactile fabrics. Spring for a deluxe room and you'll snare either arch or bay windows and marvellous Melbourne views. Nice as they are, some of the standard rooms feel as if corners have been cut. But it's still easily one of the city's finest boutique hotels. And yes, there's a pool table.

Majorca Apartment 401 APARTMENTS $$$
(Map p58; ☎9428 8104; www.apartment401.com.au; 258 Flinders Lane; apt from $250) This is the ultimate in like-a-local living. The Majorca, a single apartment, is in one of the city's loveliest art deco buildings and watches over a bustling vortex of laneways. It's stylishly furnished, has timber floorboards and the windows are huge. Who needs a concierge when you're right in the centre of things already? There's a two-night minimum.

Hotel Causeway HOTEL $$
(Map p58; ☎9660 8888; www.causeway.com.au; 275 Little Collins St; r incl breakfast from $170; ✳@☎) This art deco gem, with a discreet entrance in the covered arcade Howey Place, will appeal to those who've come to Melbourne to shop and bar-hop. It's intimate in scale, so don't expect the facilities of a big hotel. Rooms are snazzy and feature luxurious linen sheets, robes and slippers.

Robinsons in the City BOUTIQUE HOTEL $$
(Map p58; ☎9329 2552; www.ritc.com.au; 405 Spencer St; r incl breakfast from $185; ✳☎) Robinsons is a gem with six large rooms and warm service. The building is a former bakery, dating from 1850, but it's been given a modern, eclectic look. Bathrooms are not in the rooms; each room has its own in the hall. Service is warm and personal; repeat visits are common.

⌖ Alto Hotel on Bourke HOTEL $$
(Map p58; ☎9606 0585; www.altohotel.com.au; 636 Bourke St; r from 160, apt from $190; ✳@☎) This environment-minded hotel has water-saving showers, energy-efficient light globes, double-glazed windows that open and in-room recycling is promoted. Rooms are also well equipped, light and neutrally decorated. Apartments (but not studios) have full kitchens and multiple LCD TVs, and some have spas. Freebies include organic espresso coffee, apples and access to a massage room.

Crown Metropol HOTEL $$$
(off Map p58; ☎9292 8888; www.crownmetropol.com.au; 8 Whiteman St, Southbank; r from $240; ✳☎) This new Bates Smart–designed addition to the Crown casino empire is lofty and doused in grey, black and white. Huge 'loft' rooms come complete with guest bathrooms and no less than three TVs, but expect semi-open plan bathrooms in other rooms. Room service is provided by Gordon Ramsay's **Maze** restaurant (see boxed text, p98) downstairs. And spa rooms have direct access to **isika** spa (see boxed text, p83).

Grand Hotel Melbourne HOTEL $$$
(Map p58; ☎9611 4567; www.grandhotelmelbourne.com.au; 33 Spencer St; r $235-355; ✳@☎✖) Even the studios are grand in this Italianate building, which housed the Victorian Railways administration back in the day when rail ruled the world. Its self-catering rooms were originally offices, and have high ceilings with mezzanines. All vary in size and layout and are subtly furnished. It fills up rapidly during events at nearby Docklands Stadium.

Sebel Melbourne HOTEL $$$
(Map p58; ☎9211 6600, 1800 500 778; www.mirvachotels.com.au; 394 Collins St; r from $240; ✳@☎) The Sebel is a low-key alternative in the grand Bank of Australasia building, right in the heart of the business district. The clean, minimalist rooms have self-catering facilities and washing machines, and the airy split-level loft suites are spacious. Ask for a room on a higher floor to avoid dim back-alley views.

Park Hyatt HOTEL $$$
(☎9224 1234; www.melbourne.park.hyatt.com; 1 Parliament Sq; r from $355; ✳☎✖) Resembling a Californian shopping mall from the outside, the interior understands luxury to be about wood panelling, shiny surfaces and miles of marble. Rooms are elegantly subdued, and most come complete with supersized baths, clever layouts that maximise your chance of seeing natural light and lovely treetop-level views. There's a lavish indoor pool, plus a great tennis court and whiz-bang business facilities. Perfect if you want to be superclose to the city but also to have some park-fuelled peace and quiet too. To find it, head north along Collins St then Macarthur St and turn right at St Andrews Pl.

Manhattan APARTMENTS $$$
(Map p58; ☎1300 731 299; www.manhattan.punthill.com.au; 57 Flinders Lane; apt from $205; ✳@✖) While not quite avoiding the serviced-apartment furnishing clichés, these loft spaces are set in a former warehouse and have original industrial-age details. Large marble

bathrooms, full granite-bench kitchens, a stylish muted palette and prime laneway location make this a good option. There's also a functional lap pool and gym; ask for a room at the back for an outlook.

Vibe Savoy Hotel
HOTEL **$$**

(Map p58; ☎9622 8888; www.vibehotels.com.au; 630 Little Collins St; r from $169; ❊ @) This lovely heritage building at Collins St's western end has been given a bold makeover, though its grand proportions aren't so in evidence in its somewhat truncated rooms. But they do offer a concoction of traditional hotel comforts, bright colours and contemporary furnishings.

Causeway 353
HOTEL **$$**

(Map p58; ☎9660 8888; www.causeway.com.au; 353 Little Collins St; r incl breakfast from $150; ❊@☎) Who needs a view when you've got a laneway location? Causeway 353's breakfast is in a cafe on a bustling laneway, and you'll be more than relaxed after a night in its simple, stylish rooms which feature long and dark timber bedheads, huge king-sized beds and smart leather furniture.

Greenhouse Backpacker
HOSTEL **$**

(Map p58; ☎9639 6400; www.friendlygroup.com. au; 6/228 Flinders Lane; dm/s/d incl breakfast $32/70/80; ❊@☎) Greenhouse has a fun vibe and is extremely well run – they know what keeps backpackers content. This includes freebies: daily half-hour internet access, pancakes on Sunday, rooftop BBQs, luggage storage and activities. There's also chatty, helpful staff and spic-and-span facilities. There are double-bed bunks for couples in the mixed dorms; solo travellers can opt for single-sex dorms.

Hotel Windsor
HOTEL **$$$**

(Map p58; ☎9633 6000; www.thewindsor.com.au; 103 Spring St; r from $245; ❊@) Showing the strain of being one of Australia's most famous and self-consciously grand hotels, this example of marvellous Melbourne–era opulence was about to undergo a controversial $260 million redevelopment, which would add 300 rooms and 25 stories to the 1883 heritage-listed building.

Mercure
HOTEL **$$**

(Map p58; ☎9205 9999; www.accorhotels.com.au; 13 Spring St; r from $189; ❊@☎) A lively foyer, friendly staff and a perfect 2pm checkout on Sundays add sparkle to the decent rooms. All have a shower over bath and some have sweet park views.

Jasper Hotel
HOTEL **$$**

(Map p58; ☎8327 2777; www.jasperhotel.com.au; 489 Elizabeth St; r from $180; ❊@☎) The old Hotel Y has had a makeover by Jackson Clements Burrows and now sports moody down-lighting, a veritable Pantone swatchbook of colours, louvered bathrooms and some lovely graphic soft furnishings. It's a tad soulless, though. Guests have complimentary use of the sporting facilities at the nearby Melbourne City Baths. All profits go to the YWCA's community and welfare services.

Punt Hill Little Bourke
APARTMENTS **$$**

(Map p58; ☎9631 1111; www.littlebourke.punthill. com.au; 11-17 Cohen Place; apt from $170; ❊☎≋) Neat and modern open-plan apartments have bright colours, balconies and stainless-steel kitchens. Lots of light, an indoor lap pool and a cute Chinatown laneway location lift this little place above the ordinary.

Quest Hero
APARTMENTS **$$**

(Map p58; ☎8664 8500; www.questhero.com.au; 140 Little Collins St; apt from $190; ❊@) These spacious and well-equipped apartments have fabulous urban views. Housed in an architecturally interesting residential building, you're sitting on top of some amazing retailers. Lofts make for good long-term stays and the larger apartments are a great option for families.

Mantra 100 Exhibition
APARTMENTS **$$**

(Map p58; ☎9631 4444; www.mantra.com.au; 100 Exhibition St; apt from $179; @) A great midcity location with streamlined apartment facilities make this a good choice. The big windows and the use of blond wood, white and the odd splash of intense colour are a surprise at this price. Nice location between the bustle of Bourke and the calm of Collins Sts.

City Centre Hotel
HOTEL **$**

(Map p58; ☎9654 5401; www.citycentrebudget hotel.com.au; 22 Little Collins St; s/d/f $70/90/130; @☎) Intimate, independent and inconspicuous, this 38-room budget hotel is a find. It's located at the city's prettier end, down a 'Little' street, up some stairs and inside an unassuming building. All rooms share bathroom facilities but the fresh rooms are light-filled with working windows; there's also free wi-fi and a laundry. On the roof there's a fabulous patch of domesticity – swing seats and banana lounges – amid a sea of midcity slick.

Crossley
HOTEL $$

(Map p58; ☑9639 1639; www.accorhotels.com.au; 51 Little Bourke St; r from $150; ❈@🛜) The hotel's 80-odd rooms are housed in a 1930s building that provides much of its character. Rooms are modern and have updated bathrooms, but are nothing special.

Somerset Gordon Place
APARTMENTS $$

(Map p58; ☑9267 5400; www.somerset.com; 24 Little Bourke St; apt from $145; ❈@🛜🏊) The Somerset's smart, pint-sized apartments are concealed inside a prim heritage building at the top end of town, and ranging from small studios to two-bedroom, some with kitchenettes. A sunny courtyard with an outdoor pool is an unexpected bonus in this midcity location.

City Square Motel
HOTEL $

(Map p58; ☑9654 7011; www.citysquaremotel.com.au; 67 Swanston St; s/d incl breakfast $90/125; ❈) The foyer's not much but the rooms are dirt cheap and the staff charming. Rooms come with double-glazed windows to dull the sound of tram bells, and there's bread, butter and vegemite in the room for breakfast.

Melbourne Connection Travellers Hostel
HOSTEL $

(Map p58; ☑9642 4464; www.melbourneconnection.com; 205 King St; dm $20-35, d $60-80; @) This little 79-bed charmer follows the small-is-better principle. It offers simple, clean and uncluttered budget accommodation with modern facilities, well-organised staff and a basement lounge area.

Atlantis Hotel
HOTEL $$

(Map p58; ☑9600 2900; www.atlantishotel.com.au; 300 Spencer St; r from $140; ❈@🛜🏊) Across from Docklands and Southern Cross Station, this place offers two-bedroom suites perfect for families (and they're only $20 more expensive than the standard room). The low-slung rooms are soothingly neutral, if not super-stylish.

Causeway Inn on the Mall
HOTEL $$

(Map p58; ☑9650 0688; www.causeway.com.au; 327 Bourke St Mall; s/d incl breakfast $119/130; ❈@🛜) Recently refurbished, the Causeway Inn is always busy and often full. Bonuses include helpful staff, free breakfast and daily newspaper, and a location bang in the middle of the city. The hotel entrance is actually in the Causeway.

City Limits
APARTMENTS $$

(Map p58; ☑9662 2544; www.citylimits.com.au; 20 Little Bourke St; r incl breakfast $130; ❈@🛜) If you can ignore the dazzling mix of decor styles (plenty of '80s aesthetics here), the staff are welcoming and you're in an ideal Chinatown location. The rooms have small, but decently stocked kitchenettes.

Victoria Hotel
HOTEL $$

(Map p58; ☑9669 0000; www.victoriahotel.com.au; 215 Little Collins St; s/d $99/120; ❈@🛜🏊) The original Vic opened its doors in 1880 but don't worry: they've updated the plumbing since then. This city institution has around 400 rooms, and all differ slightly. The Bellerive and Heritage rooms are more upmarket, but all have downlights and are comfortable. Facilities include a plunge pool.

Langham Hotel
HOTEL $$$

(Map p58; ☑8696 8888; www.langhamhotels.com; 1 Southgate Ave; r from $310; ❈@🛜) The Langham lobby screams luxury, but its restaurants can feel a little mall-like and the rooms, while perfectly equipped, are past their prime in the style stakes. The **Chuan Spa** (see boxed text, p83) is well regarded.

Urban Central Backpackers
HOSTEL $

(☑1800 631 288, 9639 3700; www.urbancentral.com.au; 334 City Rd, South Melbourne; dm/d/f incl breakfast from $28/115/135; ❈@🛜) This just-south-of-the-river hostel has bright, white dorms with high ceilings and a max of four beds (there are also doubles and family rooms). The bar downstairs has dangerously cheap happy-hour drinks and all dorms have individual lockers with internal charge points to keep your electricals happy.

Crown Promenade
HOTEL $$$

(Map p58; ☑9292 6688; www.crownpromenade.com.au; 8 Whiteman St; r from $245; ❈🛜) This is Crown's 'diffusion line' hotel and linked to the mother ship by an air bridge. It offers large, modern and gently masculine rooms with luxurious bathrooms, big windows and flat screens.

Docklands Apartments Grand Mercure
APARTMENTS $$$

(☑9641 7503; www.docklandsservicedapartments.com.au; 23 Saint Mangos Lane, New Quay, Docklands; apt from $245; 🅿35, 70; ❈@🛜) Spectacular floor-to-ceiling windows make the most of the water and city views. Apartments have balconies, full kitchens with stainless steel appliances and are furnished in a pleasing contemporary style. Free parking is a plus. There's a minimum two-night stay.

Quest Docklands
APARTMENTS $$

(☑9630 1000; www.questdocklands.com.au; 750 Bourke St, Victoria Point, Docklands; apt from $195;

❇☏) Join the new breed of Melburnians on the Docklands frontier. These apartments are serviced daily and all have a fully kitted kitchen. Crisp lines are cushioned with subtle, earthy-toned furniture and fixtures, and most rooms have a balcony. Literally on the doorstep of Docklands Stadium, so perfect for big-game visits.

EAST MELBOURNE & RICHMOND
East Melbourne takes you out of the action and has few attractions of its own apart from the splendid expanses of Fitzroy Gardens, peace and quiet and ready access to the MCG. Richmond's ideal if you also want a local feel only a 20-minute walk or short taxi trip from the city.

Hilton on the Park HOTEL **$$$**
(Map p69; ☏9419 2000; www.hilton.com; 192 Wellington Pde, East Melbourne; r from $295; ⛤Jolimont, ⛟48, 75; ❇@☏⛴) The brown-brick Hilton building, on the verge of the gardens, is a monument to 1970s functionalism. Complete renovations of the rooms have brought in greys, wood-panelled features and simple, stylish artwork. The location is superb for those looking at an MCG-filled weekend.

Villa Donati B&B **$$$**
(Map p69; ☏9428 8104; www.villadonati.com; 377 Church St, Richmond; s/d incl breakfast $195/225; ⛟70; ❇@☏) Donati is an impeccably maintained Italianate villa with touches of Asia. Its four rooms are individually decorated and all have en suites. Villa Donati doesn't give into the heritage cliché that this type of architecture might encourage; instead it's got personality and an endearingly eclectic, haute-bourgeois style.

Knightsbridge Apartments APARTMENTS **$$**
(Map p69; ☏9419 1333; www.knightsbridgeapartments.com.au; 101 George St, East Melbourne; apt from $119; ⛤Jolimont, ⛟48, 75; ❇☏) Rejuvenated studio apartments over three floors each feature a well-equipped kitchen, plus furniture and accessories that suggest a higher price bracket. There's a chirpy welcome and the overall impression is one of 'nothing's too much trouble'. Smaller rooms with 'Hummer' doona covers are not so impressive. If you don't score an apartment with a teensy private courtyard (rooms 7, 8 and 9), opt for the upper floors for a better outlook and light (note there's no lift).

Georgian Court B&B **$$**
(Map p69; ☏9419 6353; www.georgiancourt.com.au; 21 George St, East Melbourne; s/d/f

HELLO POSSUMS

You're certain to spot possums at night in the Fitzroy and Treasury Gardens. Possums are protected and theoretically wild, so shouldn't be fed. They're usually too busy scavenging through all the lunch rubbish discarded by the day's office workers anyway. If you look up, you might also see a flying-fox bat ducking and weaving through the noise and light pollution.

$99/119/159; ⛤West Richmond, ⛟48, 75; ❇☏) This former mansion has a relaxed appeal that's proven popular with families for many years. Rooms are diminutive and slightly overwrought but come with shiny bathrooms (shared or private). The breakfast area is reminiscent of prewar Britain, with period furniture, high ceilings, lead light windows and seemingly bottomless pots of tea.

Magnolia Court HOTEL **$$**
(Map p69; ☏9419 4222; www.magnolia-court.com.au; 101 Powlett St, East Melbourne; r incl breakfast from $110; ⛤Jolimont, ⛟48, 75; ❇@☏) Aim for the high-ceilinged apartments in this former girls' school to feel truly a part of this posh part of town. How posh? Neighbours roared when the heritage building's fence got a fresh coat of paint. Rooms range from standards to a fully self-contained Victorian cottage.

FITZROY & AROUND
Vibrant Fitzroy hums with attractions day and night, and is a walk away from the city. Thankfully some great boutique accommodation options have opened up, but there's still a shortage of places to stay.

TOP CHOICE **Brooklyn Arts Hotel**
BOUTIQUE HOTEL **$$**
(Map p122; ☏9419 9328; www.brooklynartshotel.com; 48-50 George St; r incl breakfast from $95; ⛟86; ☏) There are seven very different rooms in this character-filled and very unique hotel. Owner Maggie has put the call out for artistic people and they've responded by staying, so expect lively conversation around the continental breakfast. Rooms are clean, quirky, colourful and beautifully decorated; one even houses a piano.

Tyrian Apartments APARTMENTS **$$$**
(Map p122; ☏9415 1900; www.tyrian.com.au; 91 Johnston St; r from $200; ⛟112; ❇☏) These

were supposed to be sold off as apartments, but the owners changed their mind, and folks wanting to live the Fitzroy dream for a night or two can thank them that they did. These spacious, self-contained modern apartments have a certain Fitzroy celeb appeal, which you'll feel from the moment you walk down the dimmed hallway to reception. Big couches, flatscreen TVs and balconies add to the appeal.

Home @ The Mansion
HOSTEL $

(Map p122; ☑9663 4212; www.homemansion. au; 80 Victoria Pde; dm $28-34, d $90; ☑96, 109; @☂) This grand-looking heritage building now houses 92 dorm beds and a couple of doubles, all of which are light and bright and have lovely high ceilings. There are two small Playstation and TV-watching areas, a courtyard out the front and a sunny kitchen.

Nunnery
HOSTEL $

(Map p122; ☑9419 8637; www.nunnery.com.au; 116 Nicholson St; dm/s/d incl breakfast $30/75/110; ☑96; @☂) The Nunnery oozes atmosphere, with sweeping staircases and many original features; the walls are dripping with religious works of art and ornate stained-glass windows. You'll be giving thanks for the big comfortable lounges and communal areas. Next door to the main building is the Nunnery Guesthouse, which has larger rooms in a private setting (from $130). It's perennially popular, so try to book ahead.

Royal Gardens Apartments
APARTMENTS $$

(Map p122; ☑9419 9888; www.questroyalgardens. com.au; 8 Royal Lane; apt from $180; ☑86, 96; ✳☂☀) This rather dauntingly monumental complex of apartments is softened by hidden gardens, and has recently been updated with new furniture and full kitchens. Situated in a quiet nook of happening Fitzroy, it's so relaxed you'll feel like a local.

CARLTON & AROUND

Carlton has quite a few midrange places aimed at the university and hospital crowd while North Melbourne has a few budget options.

Downtowner on Lygon
HOTEL $$

(Map p74; ☑9663 5555; www.downtowner.com.au; 66 Lygon St, Carlton; r from $169; ☑1, 8; ✳@☂) The Downtowner is a surprising complex of different sized rooms, including joining rooms perfect for families and couples travelling together. Ask for a light-bathed room if you can. It's perfectly placed between the CBD and Lygon St restaurants.

Rydges on Swanston
HOTEL $$

(Map p74; ☑9347 7811; www.rydges.com; 701 Swanston St, Carlton; r from $178; ☑1, 8; ✳@☂☀) Rydges is a neat little hotel close to the University of Melbourne, with neutral styling and a no-nonsense approach. Even standard rooms sleep three and have good facilities and fresh bathrooms. Park-view rooms have just that, as well as more space and, usually, a better layout. A highlight is the heated rooftop pool, which includes a large area for lazing around, as well as a spa-sauna room.

Vibe Hotel Carlton
HOTEL $$

(☑9380 9222; www.vibehotels.com.au; 441 Royal Pde, Carlton; r from $155; ☑19; @☀) This early 1960s motel was once noted for its glamorous, high-Californian style. Now it's run by small chain Vibe and, apart from overexuberance in the public areas, some period charm does shine through. Rooms have floor-to-ceiling windows, clean lines and there's a signature '60s pool. It's close to parks and the zoo, and the city is a short tram ride away. It's a leap away from Brunswick's lively Sydney Rd.

North Melbourne Serviced Apartments
APARTMENTS $$

(☑9329 3977; www.northmelbourneapartments. com.au; 113 Flemington Rd, North Melbourne; apt from $165; ☑55, 59; ✳@☂) While not particularly stylish, these light-filled, neat and nondescript apartments come in a range of configurations from studio to two-bedroom, and share a communal laundry. Their proximity to Royal Park (they're near the corner of Royal Park and Flemington Rd, which runs off Elizabeth) and the zoo make these apartments a good choice for families.

Arden Motel
MOTEL $

(☑9329 7211; www.lygonst.com/ardenmotel; 15 Arden St, North Melbourne; r incl breakfast from $88; ☑55, 57; ✳) Sometimes you just need a bed. A bastion of budget accommodation, the Arden is emphatically unfashionable and a tad weary in its pink and greys. It's friendly, though, and there's a laundry. From the Queen Vic Market, take a left onto Victoria St and a right down Leveson St – it's on your right.

SOUTH YARRA, PRAHRAN & WINDSOR

South of the river, South Yarra has some tremendous new hotels (including two of the new 'Art Series' hotels), and a number of boutique and upmarket places set in pretty tree-lined residential streets.

Punthill Apartments South Yarra
APARTMENTS **$$**

(Map p127; 1300 731 299; www.punthill.com.au; 7 Yarra St, South Yarra; r from $180; South Yarra;) It's the little things, like a blackboard and chalk in the kitchen for messages, and individually wrapped liquorice allsorts by the bed, which make this a great choice. The bright rooms have laundry facilities and those with balconies come complete with their own (tin) dog on fake grass.

Art Series (The Olsen)
BOUTIQUE HOTEL **$$$**

(Map p127; 9040 1222; www.artserieshotels.com.au/olsen; 637 Chapel St, South Yarra; r from $200; South Yarra, 8;) This new hotel honouring artist John Olsen is where international celebs are staying these days, and we think we know why. The staff are attentive. The modern glam foyer is beaut. The open-plan rooms are delightful. Oh, and the hotel's pool juts out over Chapel Street. You never know who you'll bump into in the lift.

Art Series (The Cullen)
BOUTIQUE HOTEL **$$**

(Map p127; 9098 1555; www.artserieshotels.com.au/cullen; 164 Commercial Rd, Prahran; r from $169; 78,79;) Expect visions of Ned Kelly shooting you from the glam opaque room/bathroom dividers in this new and lively hotel, resplendent in the works of Sydney artist Adam Cullen. Borrow the 'Cullen Car' ($60 per day) or Kronan bike ($5 per hour) and let the whole city know where you're staying.

Lyall
HOTEL **$$$**

(Map p127; 9868 8222; www.thelyall.com; 14 Murphy St, South Yarra; r from $270; South Yarra, 8;) Tucked away in a leafy residential street, the Lyall's spacious rooms are well-appointed, with little luxuries including gourmet cheese in the minibar, laundry facilities, and, in some, televisions in the bathrooms. The **Lyall Spa** (see boxed text, p83) is well regarded and there's a gym, a smart champagne bar and a bistro. The 24-hour room service is a hit.

Hatton
BOUTIQUE HOTEL **$$$**

(9868 4800; www.hatton.com.au; 65 Park St, South Yarra; r incl breakfast from $215; 8;) This Victorian terrace is enjoying a luxurious reincarnation as a boutique hotel. Each room is uniquely styled: waxed floorboards and wooden mantels are matched with stainless steel, while antiques and contemporary local furniture are thrown effortlessly together. It's situated smack bang between Royal Botanic Gardens and Fawkner Park along the tram line.

Royce on St Kilda Road
BOUTIQUE HOTEL **$$$**

(9677 9900; www.roycehotels.com.au; 379 St Kilda Rd, Melbourne; r from $220; 3, 16, 64, 67, 72;) Housed in an ornate 1920s hacienda-style building, close to Kings Domain on St Kilda Rd, the Royce's successful mix of period details and stylish modern fit-out extends from bathroom to bed. Room types do not just differ in size – they also differ in mood from the softly minimal deluxes to the subtly decorative executive suites.

Back Of Chapel
HOSTEL **$**

(Map p127; 9521 5338; www.backofchapel.com; 50 Green St, Windsor; dm $20-28, d $60-80; 78,79;) This clean backpackers in an old Victorian terrace has its own bar (claiming to have the cheapest drinks in Melbourne), and is literally 20 steps away from buzzing Chapel Street. TV is a feature (there are two biggies) and new bathrooms and a bunch of freebies (breakfast, for one) add appeal.

Albany & Bloomfield
HOTEL **$**

(9866 4485; www.thealbany.com.au; cnr Toorak Rd & Millswyn St, South Yarra; r from $70; 8;) This place, made up of the Bloomfield and the Albany, proudly screams fashion and rock 'n' roll. The Bloomfield has thoroughly modern rooms in an 1890s Victorian mansion, while cheap motel-style rooms with original bathrooms are the domain of the Albany. They all fit the rock 'n' roll theme, however would-be rock stars staying at the Albany don't have access to the rooftop pool, and have a very un-rock-star-like 10am checkout.

Hotel Claremont
GUESTHOUSE **$**

(Map p127; 9826 8000, 1300 301 630; www.hotelclaremont.com, South Yarra; 189 Toorak Rd; dm/s/d incl breakfast $34/69/79; South Yarra, 8;) In a large heritage building dating from 1868, the Claremont is good value, with comfortable rooms, high ceilings and shared bathrooms. Don't expect fancy decor: it's simply a clean, welcoming cheapie.

ST KILDA

St Kilda is a budget traveller enclave but there are some stylish options a short walk from the beach, too.

Prince
HOTEL **$$$**

(Map p112; 9536 1111; www.theprince.com.au; 2 Acland St; r incl breakfast from $260; 16, 79, 96, 112;) The Prince has a suitably dramatic lobby and the rooms are an interesting mix of the original pub's proportions, natural materials and a pared-back aesthetic. Larger rooms and suites feature some key pieces of vintage modernist furniture. On-site 'facilities' take in some of the city's most mentioned: the **Aurora day spa** (see boxed text, p83), bars, band rooms (p117) and even a wine shop downstairs. Unless you're in party mode yourself, be prepared for the seepage of nightclub noise, if you're staying the weekend.

Hotel Urban HOTEL $$$
(Map p112; ✆8530 8888; www.urbanstkilda.com. au; 35-37 Fitzroy St; r from $185; ✱16, 79, 96, 112; ✱@☎) Rooms at Hotel Urban use a lot of blonde wood and white to maximise space, and are simple, light and calming. Some rooms have freestanding in-room spas and are Faraway Tree–shaped (ie circular).

Habitat HQ HOSTEL $
(✆9537 3777; www.habitathq.com.au; 333 St Kilda Rd; dm $30-$38, d$139; ✱16, 67, 79; ✱☎) There's not much this clean, new hostel doesn't have. Tick off open plan communal spaces, a beer garden, free breakfast, a travel agent and a pool table for starters. Follow Carlisle St from St Kilda to St Kilda Rd – it's on your left.

Base HOSTEL $
(Map p112; ✆8598 6200; www.basebackpackers. com; 17 Carlisle St; dm from $30, r from $110; ✱16, 79, 96; ✱@☎) Accor spinoff Base has streamlined dorms, each with en suite, or slick doubles. There's a 'sanctuary' floor for female travellers, and a bar and live music nights to keep the good-time vibe happening.

Hotel Tolarno HOTEL $$
(Map p112; ✆9537 0200; www.hoteltolarno.com.au; 42 Fitzroy St; r from $155; ✱16, 79, 96, 112; ✱@☎) Tolarno was once the site of Georges Mora's seminal gallery, Tolarno. The fine-dining restaurant downstairs (p102) now bears the name of his artist wife Mirka, as well as her original paintings. Rooms upstairs are brightly coloured and eclectically furnished, with good beds and crisp white linen. Those at the front of the building might get a bit noisy for some, but have balconies, floorboards and enormous windows.

Home Travellers Motel HOSTEL $
(Map p112; ✆9534 0300; www.hometravellers motel.com.au; 32 Carlisle St; dm $26-32, d$99; ✱16, 79; @☎) Geared to 'young folk' (ie it gets noisy), this hostel in a former motel also has clean and simple doubles with en suites. There's a large kitchen and lounge and an outdoor barbecue.

Ritz HOSTEL $
(Map p112; ✆9525 3501; www.ritzbackpackers.com; 169 Fitzroy St; dm/d incl breakfast $27/70; ✱16, 79; @☎) Above a corner pub renowned for hosting the riotously popular *Neighbours* nights, the Ritz has an excellent location, opposite an inner-city lake and park, and is only a five-minute walk from St Kilda's heart. It can get noisy when live music is cranking downstairs.

Fountain Terrace B&B $$
(Map p112; ✆9593 8123; www.fountainterrace.com. au; 28 Mary St; s/d incl breakfast $150/175; ✱96, 112; @☎) The seven rooms here are lovingly appointed in honour of famous Australians such as Henry Lawson and Melba (the vintage of which will give you a clue to the style and ambience at work here). All are impeccably presented, with brocades, silks and all manner of frills. The Melba Suite is the most lavish, with access to the front verandah.

Hotel Barkly HOTEL $
(Map p112; ✆9525 3354; www.stkildabeach house.com;109 Barkly St; dm/d incl breakfast from $27/130; ✱3, 67; ✱@☎) Hotel Barkly is the party; you're just the guest list. Bright dorms are on the 1st floor; moody, though not luxurious, private rooms, some with balconies and views, are on the 2nd and 3rd floors. Below is a heaving pub, above is a happy house-cranking bar. Noisy? You bet. But if you're up for it, there's definitely fun to be had. Though perhaps not a lot of sleep.

Coffee Palace HOSTEL $
(Map p112; ✆9534 5283; www.coffeepalaceback packers.com.au; 24 Grey St; dm/d incl breakfast from $25/80; ✱16, 79, 96, 112; @) This rambling old-school backpackers has lots of rooms, lots of activities and lots of years behind it. It has a travel desk, communal kitchen, bar, pool tables, lounge and a TV room, plus a rooftop terrace with bay views. Dorms sleep from four to 10, with some for women only. There are also private rooms with shared bathrooms.

AROUND ST KILDA

Art Series (The Blackman) BOUTIQUE HOTEL $$$
(✆9039 1444; www.artserieshotels.com.au/black man; 452 St Kilda Rd, Melbourne; r from $209; ✱3, 5, 6, 8, 16, 64, 67, 72; ☎✱) The most recent of the Art Series hotels to open, it doesn't boast one single original Charles Blackman painting (though loads of prints and Blackman room decals), but it has superb views

(aim for a corner suite for views of Albert Park Lake and the city skyline), luxurious beds and blackout curtains for a sleep-in. Aimed at the corporate market but suits the splurger, too.

Middle Park Hotel
PUB $$
(☏9690 1958; www.middleparkhotel.com.au; 102 Canterbury Rd, Middle Park; r incl breakfast from $180; 🅿112; ❋🏊) With a locked bedside drawer labeled 'x', and an 'x' keyring to match (hello $70 'intimacy' pack), you might be wondering what kind of hotel you've booked yourself into, but relax. A Six Degrees renovation has ensured the rooms feel luxurious and modern – expect iPod docks and rain shower-heads when you reach the top of the wooden staircase. There's a modern pub and restaurant downstairs, and the cooked gourmet breakfast in the dining room is a treat.

✖️ Eating

CENTRAL MELBOURNE
Cafes spring into life at dawn during the week, and there are many places catering to the lunch needs of the city's workers and shoppers. Swanston St, north of Bourke St, is popular with students. Restaurants rarely rely on views and are spread throughout the city, with many hidden down alleys, in arcades or off the 'Little' streets.

TOP CHOICE Vue de Monde
FRENCH, MODERN AUSTRALIAN $$$
(Map p58; ☏9691 3888; www.vuedemonde.com.au; 430 Little Collins St; lunch/dinner menu gourmand from $100/150; ☺lunch & dinner Tue-Fri, dinner Sat) Melbourne's favoured spot for occasion dining is in the throes of relocating to the old 'observation deck' of the Rialto (525 Collins St), so its view will finally match its name. It'll no doubt be the usual fantastic French cuisine thanks to visionary Shannon Bennett. Book ahead. Remaining at the old barrister's chambers will be the same, same, but cheaper Bistro Vue (☏9691 3838) and Cafe Vue (☺7am-4pm Mon-Fri). The cafe rounds off every Friday night with a cocktail night: five dishes matched with five cocktails.

Flower Drum
CHINESE $$$
(Map p58; ☏9662 3655; www.flower-drum.com; 17 Market Lane; mains $35-55; ☺lunch Mon-Sat, dinner daily) The Flower Drum continues to be Melbourne's most celebrated Chinese restaurant. The finest, freshest produce prepared with absolute attention to detail keeps this Chinatown institution booked out for weeks in advance. The sumptuous, but ostensibly simple, Cantonese food is delivered with the slick service you'd expect in such elegant surrounds.

HuTong Dumpling Bar
CHINESE $
(Map p58; www.hutong.com.au; 14-16 Market Lane; mains $12) HuTong's windows face out onto famed Flower Drum, and its reputation for divine dumplings, including *shao-long bao*, means it's just as hard to get a lunchtime seat. Watch the chefs make the delicate dumplings, then hope they don't watch you making a mess of them (there are step-by-step instructions for eating them on the table). There's also a branch in Prahran (Map p95).

Little Press & Cellar
MODERN GREEK $$$
(Map p58; 72 Flinders St; mains $35-49; ☺7am-late Mon-Fri, noon-late weekends) It may not be as large as the Press Club next door, but this 'little press' gives you a taste of George Calombaris' style at a bargain price. Consider its Monday to Friday express lunch menu, which fires off three Greek dishes for $34, but don't miss the 'little snack' of taramosalata with hot chips ($13.50).

Coda
MODERN AUSTRALIAN $$
(Map p58; ☏9650 3155; www.codarestaurant.com.au; basement, 141 Flinders Lane; mains $36-38; ☺lunch & dinner) Coda has a wonderful 'underground' ambience and its dishes are meant to remind you of the wonderful smells of the kitchen of your childhood (hoping that your parents could put together a decent meal). It's a little hit and miss; some taste plates scream 'yes!', such as crispy prawn and tapioca betel leaf, but others don't hit those highs.

Grossi Florentino Grill
ITALIAN $$$
(Map p58; ☏9662 1811; www.grossiflorentino.com; 80 Bourke St; mains $39-55; ☺lunch & dinner Mon-Fri, dinner Sat) The Grossi grid is packed with rich faces taking lunchtime breaks; on offer is authentic regional Italian menu with metropolitan flair and great produce. The **Cellar Bar** next door is intimate and affordable: a great place to have a quick bowl of pasta and a glass of Pinot Grigio. Service is snappy and professional. If you're into grand statements (with mains hitting the $55 mark), upstairs is an opulent fine-dining stalwart.

Gingerboy
ASIAN FUSION $$
(Map p58; ☏9662 4200; www.gingerboy.com.au; 27-29 Crossley St; small dishes $13-16, large dishes $30-36; ☺lunch & dinner Mon-Fri, dinner Sat) Brave the

aggressively trendy surrounds and weekend party scene, as talented Teague Ezard does a fine turn in flash hawker cooking. Flavours pop in dishes such as scallops with green chilli jam or coconut kingfish with peanut and tamarind dressing. There are two dinner sittings, and bookings are required. Ginger-boy upstairs has a long, long cocktail bar.

Comme Kitchen
MODERN AUSTRALIAN **$$**
(Map p58; ☎9631 4000; www.comme.com.au; 7 Alfred Place; small plates $16-23, large plates $28-35; ◎lunch & dinner Mon-Fri, dinner Sat) Comme does great produce-driven European dishes that eschew prissiness in favour of robust flavours. The space is grand but not stuffy. It's unashamedly chic, filled with contemporary statement furniture and black-clad locals lounging on the broad banquettes.

Trunk
ITALIAN, AMERICAN **$$**
(Map p58; ☎9663 7994; www.trunktown.com.au; 275 Exhibition St; mains $28-35; ◎lunch & dinner Mon-Fri, dinner Sat) Trunk turns into a prime CBD watering hole on Friday nights, but don't let Bryan from the marketing department put you off. The building is over a hundred years old and was once a synagogue. Next door, Trunk's diner has a busy yet relaxed vibe. Its organic breakfast waffles are a sweet choice.

Longrain
THAI **$$**
(Map p58; www.longrain.com; 44 Little Bourke St; mains $25-40; ◎lunch Fri, dinner daily) Expect to wait up to two hours (sip a drink and relax, they suggest) before sampling Longrain's fusion-style Thai. The communal tables don't exactly work for a romantic date but they're great for checking out everyone else's meals. Vegetarian options include green curry of tofu and green papaya salad with tamarind and chilli.

Cumulus Inc
MODERN AUSTRALIAN **$$**
(Map p58; www.cumulusinc.com.au; 45 Flinders Lane; mains $21-38; ◎breakfast, lunch & dinner Mon-Sat) One of Melbourne's best for breakfast, lunch and dinner; it gives you that wonderful Andrew McConnell style along with really reasonable prices. The focus is on beautiful produce and simple but artful cooking: from breakfasts of sardines and smoked tomato on toast at the marble bar, to suppers of freshly shucked *clair de lune* oysters tucked away on the leather banquettes.

MoMo
MIDDLE EASTERN, MEDITERRANEAN **$$$**
(Map p58; www.momorestaurant.com.au; 132 Collins St; mains $45-50; ◎dinner Tue-Sat) From the moment you enter the lift and press the MoMo button, you're in for an experience (and no, the lift's not broken!). This underground restaurant features Greg Malouf's famed flavours in an intimate setting. 'Shared plates' is the vibe, but à la carte is possible from Tuesday to Thursday. Nearby, glitzy **Spice Market** (menu also designed by Gref Malouf) is a spectacular spot for a meal or dazzling drink.

Portello Rosso
TAPAS **$$**
(Map p58; www.portellorosso.com.au; 15 Warburton Lane; tapas $15; ◎lunch Tue-Fri, dinner Tue-Sat) Chef Aaron Whitney has travelled to Melbourne via Byron Bay and Majorca so expect excellent (read: real) tapas. There's an olde world cocktail bar upstairs, and the whole space harks back to its industrial past.

Maha
MIDDLE EASTERN **$$**
(Map p58; ☎9629 5900; www.mahabg.com.au; 21 Bond St; small dishes $8-10, large dishes $20-26; ◎lunch & dinner Mon-Fri, dinner Sat) Get your reservation in for a meal at this sexy subterranean space. It pays homage to the richness and complexity of Middle Eastern and eastern Mediterranean cooking, but is done with a light, modern touch. Chef Shane Delia's Maltese heritage gets a look in too – rabbit is only off the menu when it's not in season.

Red Pepper
INDIAN **$**
(Map p58; 18 Bourke St; mains $5-12; ◎9am-3pm) It's mighty rare to get a decent meal for under $10, but it's possible here. The local Indian community knows it's good, and while leather-like seats feign 'upmarket' it's the fresh naan and daal that people come here for. The mango lassis are delicious and you can rock up here any time until 3am.

Dainty Sichuan
CHINESE **$$**
(Map p58; ☎9663 8861; 26 Corrs Lane; mains $12-25; ◎lunch & dinner) This hidden restaurant has a cult following and might just claim you too. If you like it hot, you'd be advised to order from the category 'Tongue burning hot'. Chilli oil, dried chillies, ground chilli seeds, Sichuan peppercorns and well, chillies, join other less than dainty flavourings such as peanuts and vinegar to give you a range of pork, chicken and beef dishes that will rock your world. Bookings advised.

Movida
SPANISH **$$**
(Map p58; ☎9663 3038; www.movida.com.au; 1 Hosier Lane; tapas $4-6, raciones $10-17; ◎lunch & dinner) Movida is nestled in a cobbled laneway emblazoned with one of the world's

densest collections of street art; it doesn't get much more Melbourne than this. Line up along the bar, cluster around little window tables or, if you've booked, take a table in the dining area. Tapas' tired reputation will be dispelled by one look at Frank Camorra's menu. **Movida Next Door**, right next door..., is the perfect place for a pre-show beer and tapas, while related **Movida Aqui** (500 Bourke St) is a huge, open space with milk crate lighting and a fantastic terrace, **Movida Terraza**.

Earl Canteen
CAFE $
(Map p58; www.earlcanteen.com.au; 500 Bourke St; mains $10-16; ⓧlunch Mon-Sat; ☎) This local, free range–driven cafe is a charmer; take away a lime and palm sugar-poached (free range) chicken salad, or go the (free range) pork belly. Prices are reasonable and the ethics are great.

Bar Lourinhã
TAPAS $$
(Map p58; ☑9663 7890; www.barlourinha.com.au; 37 Little Collins St; tapas $9-20; ⓧlunch & dinner Mon-Fri, Sat dinner) Matt McConnell's wonderful northern Spanish–Portuguese specialities have the swagger and honesty of an Iberian shepherd, but with a cluey, metropolitan touch. Start light with the melting, zingy kingfish pancetta and finish with the hearty house-made chorizo or baked *morcilla* (blood sausage). There's an intriguing wine list sourced from the region too. Come Friday night, it's 'fishy Friday'.

Sungs Kitchen
CHINESE $$
(Map p58; 118 Franklin St; mains $15-23; ⓧlunch & dinner) This bright and bustling pan-Chinese restaurant offers a beyond-standard selection of authentic food, including a whole range of duck dishes (tea-smoked is a favourite) and some interesting vegetarian offerings.

Yu-u
JAPANESE $$
(Map p58; ☑9639 7073; 137 Flinders Lane; small dishes $8-15; ⓧlunch & dinner Mon-Fri) The sparsely elegant basement Yu-u does smart Japanese fare, artfully presented and assuredly delivered. Go for the set-lunch menu of bento boxes, soup and noodles. Dinner is a progression of small dishes that can challenge and delight. The sign is the size of a postage stamp and the doorway nondescript, so it's easy to miss.

Papa Goose
MODERN AUSTRALIAN $$$
(Map p58; ☑9663 2800; www.papagoose.com.au; 91-93 Flinders Lane; mains $30-42; ⓧlunch Mon-Fri, dinner Mon-Sat) Featuring locally sourced meats that are cooked lovingly (the sublime salt bush lamb takes 20 hours to cook), this new restaurant does things marvellously. Upstairs is the long marble bar of Loose Goose Bar; try ordering a Gos Sling without laughing.

Rockpool Bar & Grill
STEAKHOUSE, MODERN AUSTRALIAN $$$
(Map p58; ☑8648 1900; www.rockpoolmelbourne.com; Crown Complex, Whiteman St; mains $20-140; ⓧlunch Sun-Fri, dinner daily) The Melbourne outpost of Neil Perry's empire offers his signature seafood raw bar, but it's really all about beef, from grass-fed to full-blood wagyu. This darkly masculine space is simple and stylish, as is the menu. Even a side of humble mac and cheese is done with startlingly fab ingredients. The Waiting Room bar offers the same level of food service with the added bonus of a rather spectacular drinks menu.

Italian Waiters Club
ITALIAN $$
(Map p58; 1st fl, 20 Meyers Pl; mains $15-18; ⓧlunch & dinner) Once inside the Italian Waiters Club, you'll feel as if you have stepped into another era. Opened in 1947, it still bears 1950s drapes, wood panelling and Laminex tables. Once it was only for Italian and Spanish waiters to unwind after work over a game of *scopa* (a card game) and a glass of wine, but now everyone from suits to students are allowed in for hearty plates of red-sauce pasta and the regularly changing roster of specials. Is located down a laneway and up some stairs,

Pellegrini's Espresso Bar
ITALIAN, CAFE $
(Map p58; ☑9662 1885; 66 Bourke St; mains $12-16; ⓧbreakfast, lunch & dinner) The iconic Italian equivalent of a classic '50s diner, Pellegrini's has remained genuinely unchanged for decades. Pick and mix from the variety of pastas and sauces; from the table out the back you can watch it all being thrown together from enormous ever-simmering pots. In summer, finish with a glass of watermelon granita.

Kenzan@GPO
JAPANESE $
(Map p58; 350 Bourke St; mains $10-25; ⓧlunch Mon-Sat, dinner Thu & Fri) The casual kid sister of posh **Kenzan** (56 Flinders Lane) makes the best sushi rolls in Melbourne. Yes, there's spicy tuna, but it also ups the ante with softshell crab, and intriguing sesame-coated inside-outies. All come prewrapped for lasting crunch. There's sashimi, ramen, lunch sets and tea as well.

As well as **Bophi Devi** (p98) and **Rockpool Bar & Grill** (p97) the Crown Casino complex also boasts the following eating options:

» **Nobu** (Map p58; ☎9696 6566; www.noburestaurants.com; mains $18-145; ☺lunch & dinner) The Nobu chain has set up its Melbourne Japanese restaurant in a seductive space (looking to impress?).

» **Maze** (www.gordonramay.com; level 1, Crown Metropol, cnr Whiteman & Clarendon Sts; chef's menu $110; ☺breakfast, lunch & dinner daily) Celeb chef Gordon Ramsay probably won't be heard shouting from the kitchen here (we're pretty sure he's too busy at his other mazes), but this grill and restaurant under the new Crown Metropol hotel (p88) melds French and Australian cuisine in a spacious and bright restaurant.

Sushi Ten JAPANESE $
(Map p58; ☎9639 6296; Port Phillip Arcade, 228 Flinders St; mains $8-15; ☺noon-4pm Mon-Fri) This cheap and cheerful Japanese canteen pulls the lunchtime crowds that know the sushi is fresh. It also does a range of simple but authentic soups and rice dishes.

Camy Shanghai Dumpling Restaurant
CHINESE $
(Map p58; 23-25 Tattersalls Lane; dishes $6.50; ☺lunch & dinner) There's nothing fancy here; pour your own plastic cup of tea from the urn, then try a variety of dumplings with some greens. Put up with the dismal service and you've found one of the last places in town where you can fill up for under $10.

Don Don JAPANESE $
(Map p58; 321 Swanston St; mains $6-8; ☺lunch Mon-Fri) Students, retailers and city kids storm the door come lunch at this uptown Japanese outlet. From the counter, order good quality bento boxes and bowls of curry and noodles (vegetarian options are also available), then keep up the pace and woof it down.

Tutto Bene ITALIAN $$
(Map p58; ☎9696 3334; www.tuttobene.com.au; Midlevel, Southgate; mains $25-55; ☺lunch & dinner) Across the Yarra in Southbank is this Italian restaurant that's especially known for its risotto. They range from a simple Venetian *risi e bisi* (rice and peas) to some fabulously luxe options involving truffles or roast quail or aged balsamic. Don't miss its fine house-made gelato.

Bopha Devi CAMBODIAN $$
(☎9600 1887; www.bophadevi.com; 27 Rakaia Way, Newquay; mains $19-28; ☺lunch & dinner) The modern Cambodian food here is a delightful mix of novel and familiar Southeast Asian flavours and textures. Herb-strewn salads,

noodles and soups manage to be both fresh and filling. Head down Dudley St to find Newquay (off Docklands Drive).

EAST MELBOURNE & RICHMOND
Richmond's main draw is restaurant-packed Victoria St. Most places here offer a similar menu with a long list of Vietnamese and Chinese favourites.

Demitri's Feast GREEK CAFE $
(Map p69; www.demitrisfeast.com.au; 141 Swan St, Richmond; mains $14-16; ☺breakfast & lunch Tue-Sun; ☎70) Warning: don't even attempt to get a seat here on a weekend; aim for a quiet weekday when you'll have time and space to fully immerse yourself in lunches such as calamari salad with ouzo aioli.

Pacific Seafood BBQ House CHINESE $$
(Map p69; ☎9427 8225; 240 Victoria St, Richmond; mains $15-25; ☺lunch & dinner; ☎North Richmond, ☎24, 109) Seafood in tanks and script-only menus on coloured craft paper make for an authentic, fast and fabulous dining experience. Fish is done simply, perhaps steamed with ginger and greens, and washed down with Chinese beer. Book, or be ready to queue.

Richmond Hill Cafe & Larder CAFE $$
(Map p69; www.rhcl.com.au; 48-50 Bridge Rd, Richmond; brunch $12-30; ☺breakfast & lunch; ☎West Richmond, ☎48, 75) Once the domain of well-known cook Stephanie Alexander, it still boasts its lovely cheese room and simple, comforting food such as cheesy toast. There are breakfast cocktails for the brave.

Minh Minh VIETNAMESE, LAOTIAN $$
(Map p69; 94 Victoria St, Richmond; mains $10-18; ☺lunch Wed-Sun, dinner Tue-Sun; ☎North Richmond, ☎109) Minh Minh specialises in fiery Laotian dishes – the herby green and chilli red beef salad is a favourite – but does all the Vietnamese staples too.

Pearl MODERN AUSTRALIAN **$$$**
(Map p127; ☑9421 4599; www.pearlrestaurant.com.
au; 631-633 Church St, Richmond; mains $35-48;
☺lunch & dinner; ⓡSouth Yarra, ⓰69) Owner-
chef Geoff Lindsay proclaims himself 'a
fifth-generation Aussie boy who is seduced
by ginger, chilli and palm sugar, Turkish
delight, chocolate and pomegranate'. We're
seduced too: his exquisitely rendered food
really does epitomise Modern Australian
cooking. The space is slick but comfortable,
though service can be lax.

FITZROY & AROUND
Gertrude St is carrying away the accolades
food-wise, Smith St at the Gertrude end is
also packing some winners, while Bruns-
wick St's long-established reputation is be-
ing buoyed by some thoughtful and fun din-
ing options.

TOP CHOICE **Cutler & Co** MODERN AUSTRALIAN **$$$**
(Map p122; ☑9419 4888; www.cutler
andco.com.au; 55 Gertrude St, Fitzroy; ☺dinner
Tue-Sun, lunch Fri & Sun; ⓰86) Hyped for all
the right reasons, this is Andrew McConnell's latest restaurant and though its decor
might be a little over-the-top, its attentive,
informed staff and joy-inducing meals
(suckling pig is a favourite) have quickly
made this one of Melbourne's best. It's getting bigger as we write; expect an additional
casual dining area soon as it takes up the
shops next door.

St Jude's Cellar MODERN AUSTRALIAN **$$**
(Map p122; www.stjudescellars.com.au; 389-391
Brunswick St, Fitzroy; mains around $22-26; ☺lunch
& dinner Tue-Sun, breakfast Sat & Sun; ⓰112) A
cavernous warehouse space has been given
a clever, cool and humanising fit-out, while
not losing its airy industrial feel. The restau-
rant stretches out from behind the shopfront
cellar, affording respite from the Brunswick
St hustle. Mains include mussels and leek in
Coldstream cider and goat ragout, but try
their innovative desserts, too.

Moroccan Soup Bar
NORTH AFRICAN, VEGETARIAN **$$**
(off Map p122; ☑9482 4240; 183 St Georges Rd,
North Fitzroy; banquet $18; ☺6-10pm Tue-Sun;
⓰112) Prepare to queue before being seated
by stalwart Hana, who will then go through
the menu verbally. Best bet is the banquet,
which, for three courses, is tremendous
value. The sublime chickpea bake has locals
queuing with their own pots and containers
to nab some to take away. It's an alcohol-free

zone, but there's a cute bar next door. Continue along Brunswick St, cross Alexander
Pde; it's on your left past the bowling club.

Cavallero MODERN AUSTRALIAN **$**
(Map p122; www.cavallero.com.au; 300 Smith St,
Collingwood; mains $10-25; ☺breakfast, lunch &
dinner Tue-Sun; ⓰86) A supersmart, subtle fit-
out lets the charm of this grand Victorian
shopfront shine. Served under the gaze of
a deer's head, morning coffee and brioche
make way for fancy toasties and Pinot Gris.
Come teatime, there's shared plates galore,
and, later still, cocktails, cider and music on
the turntable.

Charcoal Lane AUSTRALIAN **$$**
(Map p122; ☑9418 3400; www.charcoallane.
com.au; 136 Gertrude St, Fitzroy; mains $17-35;
☺lunch & dinner Tue-Sat; ⓰86) This training
restaurant for Aboriginal and disadvantaged
young people is one of the best places to try
native flora and fauna; menu items include
wallaby tartare and native-pepper kangaroo.
The sophisticated decor makes a change
from the polished concrete look in nearby
restaurants.

Commoner MODERN BRITISH **$$**
(Map p122; ☑9415 6876; www.thecommoner.com.
au; 122 Johnston St, Fitzroy; mains $13-30; ☺lunch
& dinner Sat & Sun, dinner Wed-Fri; ⓰112) If you
need to be convinced of this off-strip restaurant's serious intent, the wood-fired goat
or pork they offer up come Sunday lunch
should do it. On Sunday nights there's no
menu; you just get fed. The upstairs bar
opens at 6pm, so breeze on up before dinner, and return to imbibe after.

Añada TAPAS **$$**
(Map p122; ☑9415 6101; www.anada.com.au; 197
Gertrude St, Fitzroy; tapas $2-7, raciones $9-30;
☺lunch & dinner Fri-Sun; ⓰86) Dishes in this
lovely little restaurant are alive with hearty
Spanish and Muslim Mediterranean fla-
vours. Go the nine-course banquet (chef's
choice) for $49 or extend yourself with

FILLING UP IN THE WEST

From authentic ethnic cuisine to cafes
with more than just the usual staples;
there's no need to go hungry in the west.
Try **Le Chien** (5 Gamon St, Seddon) cafe
in Seddon, African restaurant **Cafe
Lalibela** (91 Irving St, Footscray) and the
down to earth pho at **Hung Vuong** (128
Hopkins St, Footscray).

something like braised rabbit legs in cocoa and dried peppers with peas. Book ahead.

Boire WINE BAR $$
(Map p122; www.boire.com.au; 92 Smith St, Collingwood; ⊙lunch Fri & Sat, dinner Tue-Sat; 🚊86) It's French for drinking, but new belle in town Boire is also about feeding. The menu changes daily – check the massive blackboard for mostly local and organic bites, including duck breast or organic chicken leg, and finish off with something decadent such as a dark chocolate gateau with rhubarb and homemade chocolate sorbet.

Wabi Sabi Salon JAPANESE $
(Map p122; www.wabisabi.net.au; 94 Smith St, Collingwood; dishes $3-20; ⊙lunch & dinner Mon-Sat; 🚊86) Expect kooky Japanese decor and delish Japanese cuisine, including bento boxes that change daily (you choose meat, fish or veg and the Japanese chefs do the rest). Its garden version **Wabi Sabi Garden** (17 Wellington St, St Kilda; ⊙closed Sun) is worth a visit too.

Old Kingdom CHINESE $$
(Map p122; ☎9417 2438; 197 Smith St, Fitzroy; around $55 per duck; ⊙lunch Tue-Fri, dinner Tue-Sun; 🚊86) The queues here are for three things: duck soup, Peking duck, and duck and bean shoots, OK, make that four: their thin Chinese pancakes. Expect nothing from the decor and make sure you preorder your Peking duck.

Panama Dining Room EUROPEAN $$
(Map p122; www.thepanama.com.au; 3rd fl, 231 Smith St, Fitzroy; mains $18-27; ⊙dinner Tue-Sun; 🚊86) Gawp at the ersatz Manhattan views while choosing between rabbit, pork, mussels and lamb all dutifully sourced from specific growers. The large space also does double duty as a bar, and dinner is usually packed up by 9.30pm.

Marios CAFE $
(Map p122; 303 Brunswick St, Fitzroy; mains $14-25; ⊙breakfast, lunch & dinner; 🚊112) Mooching at Marios is part of the Melbourne 101 curriculum. Breakfasts are big and served all day, the service is swift and the coffee is old-school strong.

Aux Batifolles FRENCH $$
(off Map p122; ☎9481 5015; 400 Nicholson St, North Fitzroy; mains $26-34; ⊙lunch Tue-Sun, dinner daily; 🚊96) This French bistro does the trick for both big occasions or simple weeknight dinners. All the standards are here: duck *confit*, *moules frites* (mussels and French fries) and steak tartare. Desserts too: crème brûlée and

tarte Tatin (upside-down tart) just the way *maman* used to make. Bookings advised.

Babka Bakery Cafe BAKERY, CAFE $
(Map p122; 358 Brunswick St; mains $8-16; ⊙breakfast & lunch Tue-Sun; 🚊112) Russian flavours infuse the lovingly prepared breakfast and lunch dishes, and the heady aroma of cinnamon and freshly baked bread makes even just a coffee worth queuing for. Cakes are notable and can be taken away whole.

Pizza Meine Liebe PIZZA $
(www.pizzarocks.com.au; 231 High St, Northcote; pizza $12-20; ⊙dinner Tue-Sun; 🚊86) While Meine Liebe falls squarely into the 'new pizza' camp, with a wonderful range of simple toppings, it still feels reassuringly old-school, with a central gas oven, simple shopfront space and lots of bustle. Salads and gelato keep the menu suitably simple. Book ahead.

Birdman Eating TAPAS $
(Map p122; www.birdmaneating.com.au; 238 Gertrude St, Fitzroy; mains $8-18; 🚊86) Popular? You bet. Named after the infamous 'Birdman Rally' held during Melbourne's Moomba festival, you'll be glad you don't have to hurl yourself off a bridge to sit pretty on Gertrude St and eat up Welsh rarebit or dip into leek pate. Like the rally, it's a little mad.

Vegie Bar VEGETARIAN $
(Map p122; www.vegiebar.com.au; 380 Brunswick St, Fitzroy; mains $7-15; ⊙lunch & dinner; 🚊112) Delicious thin-crust pizzas, tasty curries and seasonal broths can be eaten right on fab Brunswick St itself, or in its cavernous, shared-table space inside. They do a roaring trade in fresh juices, too.

Brunswick Street Alimentari CAFE $
(Map p122; 251 Brunswick St, Fitzroy; mains $9-14; ⊙breakfast & lunch; 🚊112) Part deli, part fuss-free canteen, Alimentari stocks artisan bread, smallgoods and cheeses. There's a long list of *piadina* (flatbread), wraps and panini, and comforting staples such as meatballs with bread.

Rosamond CAFE $
(Map p122; 191 Smith St, Fitzroy; dishes $5-12; ⊙breakfast & lunch; 🚊86) Located at the rear of this Smith St property, Rosamond's tiny interior is a warm haven for the local freelance creative crew, who like their daily rations simple but well considered. And that they are: free-range eggs only come scrambled, but with first-rate toast and fresh sides, and there's soup, toasties, baguettes, salads and cupcakes.

CARLTON & AROUND

Avoid Carlton's Lygon St spruikers and keep travelling north past Grattan St; some of Melbourne's loveliest cafes and restaurants lie here and beyond. Don't skip North Melbourne, which buzzes on weekends, as does the East Brunswick end of Lygon St.

Rumi   MIDDLE EASTERN $$
(☑9388 8255; 116 Lygon St, East Brunswick; mains $17-22; ☺dinner Tue-Sun; 🚋1, 8) A fabulously well considered place that serves up a mix of traditional Lebanese cooking and contemporary interpretations of old Persian dishes. The *sigara boregi* (cheese and pine-nut pastries) are a local institution, and tasty mains like meatballs are balanced with a large and interesting selection of vegetable dishes (the near-caramelised cauliflower and the broad beans are standouts). It outgrew its old premises and is making the most of the new.

Hellenic Republic   GREEK $$
(☑9381 1222; www.hellenicrepublic.com.au; 434 Lygon St, East Brunswick; mains $21-32; ☺breakfast, lunch & dinner Sat & Sun, lunch Fri-Sun, dinner Mon-Sun; 🚋1, 8) The Iron Bark grill at George Calombaris's northern outpost works overtime grilling up pitta, king prawns, local calamari and snapper, and luscious lamb. Its taramosalata (white cod roe dip) is unbelievably good and there was almost a riot when it ran out for a few months, so keep your fingers crossed.

Embrasse Restaurant   FRENCH $$
(Map p74; ☑9347 3312; www.embrasserestaurant.com.au; 312 Drummond St, Carlton; mains $27-37; ☺dinner Wed-Sun, lunch Thu-Sun) Pressure-cooking chickpeas and daintily serving up emulsions, purees and flowers is Nicolas Poelaert's game, and the crowd is responding enthusiastically. Just off the main Lygon St drag, the space is intimate and formal. Sunday lunch is a four-course ode to France.

Bar Idda   ITALIAN $$
(☑9380 5339; www.baridda.com.au; 132 Lygon St, East Brunswick; mains $18; ☺dinner Tue-Sat; 🚋1, 8) The diner-style table coverings give little clue to the tasty morsels this Sicilian restaurant serves for dinner. Shared plates are the go, and range from pistachio-crumbed lamb loin to vegetarian layered eggplant.

Auction Rooms   CAFE $$
(107 Errol St, North Melbourne; mains $15-25; 🚋57) This insanely busy cafe serves up sweet coffee and inventive mains, though sometimes you may wonder if it's still operating as an auction room (everyone just seems so...polished!) From Queen Vic Market head west along Victoria St, then right at Errol.

Courthouse Hotel   PUB FARE $$
(www.thecourthouse.net.au; 86 Errol St, North Melbourne; mains $30-41; ☺lunch & dinner Mon-Sat; 🚋57) This corner pub has managed to retain the comfort and familiarity of a local while taking food, both in its public bar and its more formal dining spaces, very seriously. The European-style dishes, such as baked bass groper fillet, are both refined and hearty. Lunch deals, including a glass of wine, are great value at $37. From Queen Vic Market head west along Victoria St, then right at Errol.

Libertine   FRENCH $$
(www.libertinedining.com.au; 500 Victoria St, North Melbourne; mains $28-35; ☺lunch Tue-Fri, dinner Tue-Sat; 🚋57) Locals love this small, traditionally decked-out shopfront for its real French country cooking and va-va-voom interiors. The menu includes roasted Daylesford duck and is requisitely strong on other game and cheeses. From Queen Vic Market, head west along Victoria St.

Balzari   MEDITERRANEAN $$
(Map p74; www.balzari.com.au; 130 Lygon St, Carlton; mains $25-38; ☺lunch & dinner; 🚋1, 8, 96) A nice respite right in the heart of the Lygon St mayhem. This place reaches out to embrace Greek cooking as well as Italian and a few other Mediterranean influences. The space is simple but elegant, and dishes – either entrees or soupy mains – are great to share.

Abla's   LEBANESE $$
(Map p74; ☑9347 0006; www.ablas.com.au; 109 Elgin St, Carlton; mains $25; ☺lunch Thu & Fri, dinner Mon-Sat; 🚋1, 8, 96, 🚍205) The kitchen here is steered by Abla Amad, whose authentic,

---

DON'T MISS

BRUNSWICK EATING

Brunswick is Melbourne's Middle Eastern hub, and its busy **A1 Lebanese Bakehouse** (www.a1lebanesebakery.com.au; 643-645 Sydney Rd; ☺7am-9pm) and alcohol-free **Tiba's Restaurant** (www.tibas restaurant.com.au; 504 Sydney Rd; ☺closed Tue) are worth a trip in themselves. Stock up with goodies from **Mediterranean Wholesalers** (☑9380 4777; www.leosim ports.com.au; 482-492 Sydney Rd).

MELBOURNE EATING

Melbourne's ethnic cuisines were once tightly zoned, and although now spread widely over the city, there are still dedicated clusters. Richmond's Victoria St is packed with Vietnamese restaurants and providores; the western suburb of Footscray also draws those looking for the most authentic Vietnamese – as well as great African – food. Lygon St, Carlton, has long been home to simple red-sauce Italian cooking, with a few notable innovators, and the coffee and delis are great. Chinatown is home to one of Australia's most renowned restaurants of any culinary persuasion, Flower Drum (p95). You'll find regional gems such as Dainty Sichuan (p96) as well as Japanese, Malaysian and Korean here too. One street up, Lonsdale St has a handful of Greek tavernas and bars. The northern suburb of Brunswick has a number of wonderful Middle Eastern bakers and grocers, as well as uber trendy cafes.

flavour-packed food has inspired a whole generation of local Lebanese chefs. Bring a bottle of your favourite plonk and settle in for the compulsory banquet on Friday and Saturday night.

Sugardough Panificio & Patisserie
BAKERY **$**
(163 Lygon St, Brunswick; mains $8; ⊘breakfast & lunch Tue-Sun; ⊜1, 8) Sugardough does a roaring trade in homemade pies (try the chicken *makhani*) and homebaked bread and pastries. Mismatched cutlery and cups and saucers make it rather like being at grandmas on family reunion day.

Small Block
CAFE **$**
(130 Lygon St, North Carlton; mains $8-12; ⊘breakfast & lunch; ⊜1, 8) With salvaged service-station signage and concrete floors, plus warm and efficient service, Small Block acts as a community centre with a neighbourly drop-in and stay-awhile vibe. Big, beautiful breakfasts are worth writing home about.

Tiamo
ITALIAN **$$**
(Map p74; ✆9347 5759; www.tiamo.com.au; 303 Lygon St, Carlton; mains $13-20) When you've had enough of pressed, siphoned, slayered, pour over filtered and plunged coffee, head here to one of Lygon St's original Italian cafe-restaurants. There's laughter and the relaxed joie de vivre only a well-established restaurant can have.

ST KILDA & AROUND
Fitzroy St is one of the city's most popular eating strips, and you'll find the good, the very good and the downright ugly along its in-your-face length. Acland St also hums with dining options, as well as its famed cake shops. Carlisle St has more than its fair share of cute cafes and a couple of restaurants that keep the locals happy.

Attica
MODERN AUSTRALIAN **$$$**
(✆9530 0111; www.attica.com.au; 74 Glen Eira Rd, Ripponlea; 8-course tasting menu $144; ⊘dinner Tue-Sat; ⊜Ripponlea) Staking its claim to fame by being the only Melbourne restaurant to make it onto San Pellegrino's Best Restaurant list in 2010, Attica is a suburban restaurant that serves Ben Shewry's creative dishes degustation-style. Expect small portions of texture-oriented delight, such as potatoes cooked in earth, or *sous vide* (water-bathed) bass groper. Many dishes are not complete on delivery; staff perform minor miracles with a sprinkle of this or by pouring on a drop of that. 'Trials' of Shewry's new ideas take place on Tuesday nights ($80 per head). Follow Brighton Rd south to Glen Eira Rd.

Stokehouse
MODERN AUSTRALIAN **$$**
(Map p112; ✆9525 5555; www.stokehouse.com.au; 30 Jacka Blvd; mains upstairs $28-32, downstairs $10-20; ⊘lunch & dinner; ⊜16, 96) Two-faced Stokehouse makes the most of its beachfront position, cleverly catering to families and drop-ins downstairs, and turning on its best upstairs for finer diners. It's a fixture on the Melbourne dining scene and known for its seafood, service and the bay views on offer. Book for upstairs.

Cafe di Stasio
ITALIAN **$$**
(Map p112; ✆9525 3999; www.distasio.com.au; 31a Fitzroy St; mains $27-43; ⊘lunch & dinner; ⊜16, 96, 112) Capricious white-jacketed waiters, a tenebrous Bill Henson photograph and a jazz soundtrack set the mood. The Italian menu has the appropriate drama and grace.

Mirka's at Tolarno
INTERNATIONAL, ITALIAN **$$**
(Map p112; ✆9525 3088; www.mirkatolarno.com; Tolarno Hotel, 42 Fitzroy St; mains $32-36; ⊘breakfast, lunch & dinner; ⊜16, 96, 112) The dark dining room has a history (it's been delighting

diners since the early '60s) and Guy Grossi's carefully tweaked, knowingly retro food – truffle poached eggs, steak tartare, *duck à l'orange* – adds to the sense of occasion. But you don't get gravitas with your Chateaubriand. Beloved painter Mirka Mora's murals grace the wall, uplifting all.

Donovans MEDITERRANEAN $$$

(Map p112; ☎9534 8221; www.donovanshouse.com.au; 40 Jacka Blvd; mains $35-46; ☻lunch & dinner; 🖪16, 96) Donovans has a big reputation and a marquee location to match. Overlooking the beach, the interior conjures up a comforting Long Island bolthole. The food is far from fussy; rather it's solid on flavour and technique, and broad enough to please all comers. Book well ahead.

Cicciolina MEDITERRANEAN $$

(Map p112; www.cicciolinastkilda.com.au; 130 Acland St; mains $19-40; ☻lunch & dinner; 🖪16, 96) This warm room of dark wood, subdued lighting and pencil-sketches is a St Kilda institution. The inspired Mod-Mediterranean menu is smart and generous, and the service warm. They don't take bookings; eat early or while away your wait in the moody little back bar. Check out the owner's new restaurant, Ilona Staller (282 Carlisle St, Balaclava) nearby.

Claypots SEAFOOD $$

(Map p112; 213 Barkly St; mains $25-35; ☻lunch & dinner; 🖪96) A local favourite, Claypots serves up seafood in its namesake dish. Get in early to both get a seat and ensure the good stuff is still available, as hot items go fast.

Lentil as Anything VEGETARIAN $

(Map p112; www.lentilasanything.com; 41 Blessington St; prices at customers' discretion; ☻lunch & dinner; 🖪16, 96) Choosing from the always-organic, no-meat menu is easy. Deciding what to pay can be hard. This unique not-for-profit operation provides training and educational opportunities for marginalised people, as well as tasty, if not particularly notable, vegetarian food. Whatever you do end up paying for your meal goes to a range of services that help new migrants, refugees, people with disabilities and the long-term unemployed. There's also a branch in the Abbotsford Convent (1 St Heliers St, Abbotsford) and on Barkly St, Footscray.

Mr Wolf PIZZA $$

(Map p112; ☎9534 0255; www.mrwolf.com.au; 9-15 Inkerman St; pizza $18-24; ☻lunch Tue-Fri & Sun, dinner Tue-Sun; 🖪16) Local celeb chef Karen Martini's casual, but stylish, space is out of

the action but always packed to the gills. The pizzas here are renowned (crisp and with top-quality ingredients) but there's also a great menu of antipasti and pastas that display her flair for matching ingredients. It's kid-friendly, but for those who have no little ones in tow, the next-door bar is open late.

Lau's Family Kitchen CHINESE $$

(Map p112; ☎8598 9880; www.lauskitchen.com.au; 4 Acland St; mains $16-25; ☻dinner daily, lunch Sun-Fri; 🖪16, 96) The owner's family comes with absolutely flawless pedigree (father Gilbert Lau, is the former owner of famed Flower Drum) and the restaurant is in a lovely leafy location. The mainly Cantonese menu is simple, and dishes are beautifully done if not particularly exciting, with a few surprises thrown in for more adventurous diners. Make a reservation for one of the two dinner sittings.

I Carusi II PIZZA $$

(Map p112; 231 Barkly St; pizza $14-18; ☻dinner; 🖪16, 96) Beautifully located beyond the Acland St chaos in this nostalgic corner shop, I Carusi II was opened (though it's no longer owned) by one of the people who started the real pizza revolution in Melbourne. I Carusi pizzas have a particularly tasty dough and follow the less-is-more tenet, with top-quality mozza, pecorino and small range of other toppings. Bookings advised.

Batch CAFE $

(www.batchespresso.com; 320 Carlisle St, Balaclava; mains $12-16; ☻breakfast & lunch daily, dinner Fri; 🖪Balaclava) Its walls are decorated with bric-a-brac donated by locals who love the food on offer (the scotch-fillet sandwiches are winners) and great coffee. Good luck getting a seat during the weekend-only all-day brunches. Carlisle St runs east off St Kilda Rd.

Banff PIZZA $

(Map p112; www.banffstkilda.com.au; 145 Fitzroy St; mains $9; 🖪16) It's not just the daily happy hour that keeps Banff's Fitzroy St–fronting chairs occupied, it's also the $9 pizzas ($5 for lunch).

Pelican TAPAS $$

(Map p112; cnr Fitzroy & Park Sts; mains $7-20; ☻breakfast, lunch & dinner; 🖪16, 96, 112) This modern space evokes beach shacks of days gone by, and makes for a lovely spot to watch the Fitzroy St circus in full swing. Tapas here is not aiming for Iberian authenticity, just good-tasting accompaniments to the extensive drinks menu.

Take home the recipes of some of Melbourne's most loved and respected chefs.

» *MoVida; Spanish Culinary Adventures* (Frank Camorra & Richard Cornish) The recipe for Frank Camorra's divinely light flaky empanada pastry is worth the sticker-price alone. The bright pages provide a wealth of tapas recipes as well as capturing the verve of this evergreen laneway bar (p96). Their latest book, *MoVida Rustica: Spanish Traditions & Recipes,* explores Spanish food further.

» *The Press Club* (George Calombaris) Beautifully photographed and laid out, George Calombaris' inspired take on Greek cooking at the Press Club (p95), jumps from the pages of this lovely book. His recipes cover all aspects of the cuisine, and the book includes a chapter on ouzo.

» *Saraban* (Greg & Lucy Malouf) The force behind Melbourne's happening modern Middle Eastern scene, Greg Malouf co-wrote this exquisite book focussing on the exciting flavours, techniques and culinary traditions of his Lebanese heritage, with his ex, Lucy. It's a follow on from their book *Arabesque*. See MoMo review on p96.

» *My French Vue: Bistro Cooking at Home* (Shannon Bennett) The author's degustation dining belongs strictly to the don't-try-this-at-home camp of cooking, but this book concentrates on bistro staples. The recipes have his signature creative twist (p95) but are explained thoughtfully and with a nod to solid traditions.

» *Lotus Asian Flavours* (Teage Ezard) Learn all the tricks to conjure up great hawker dishes, curries and fragrant salads. Ezard has a wonderful take on Southeast Asian flavours, which is on show at his casual restaurant Gingerboy (p95), and in this book he shows a knack for demystifying techniques for a non-Asian audience.

» *The Cook's Companion* (Stephanie Alexander) Although she no longer graces the city's stoves on a regular basis, Alexander's work continues via her writing, community programs and lasting influence on a whole generation of chefs. This is one of Australia's most well-thumbed cookbooks.

» *Sunday's Kitchen: Food & Living at Heide* (Lesley Harding & Kendrah Morgan) The recipes and memories from Sunday Reed's kitchen and gardens at Heide, which have fed some of Australia's finest artists (see boxed text, p72).

» *Cooking from Memory: A Journey Through Jewish Food* (Hayley Smorgon, Gaye Weeden & Natalie King) Not exactly a chef's book, but a collection of culinary journeys collected from 21 cooks. It's filled with recipes and stories that reflect the breadth and complexity of Australia's Jewish community, and shows the lasting influence they have had on Melbourne's culinary landscape.

Galleon Cafe CAFE **$**
(Map p112; 9 Carlisle St; ⊖breakfast & lunch; ⊠16,79) Friendly folk, a decent amount of elbow room and low-key music make this a cheery place to down a coffee and muffin in busy St Kilda.

Cacao BAKERY, CAFE **$**
(Map p112; www.cacao.com.au; 52 Fitzroy St; light meals $4.50-11; ⊖7am-7pm; ⊠16, 96, 112) Set among the trees, Cacao creates award-winning chocolates and is mad for macaroons.

SOUTH YARRA, PRAHRAN & WINDSOR
It's perpetual peak hour at Chapel St's many cafes. You'll also find a few excellent dining options in Prahran, including on Greville St as well as the Prahran Market (see p77). The Windsor strip keeps things cheap and cheerful.

Jacques Reymond MODERN AUSTRALIAN **$$$**
(Map p127; ☑9525 2178; www.jacquesreymond.com.au; 78 Williams Rd, Prahran; 3 courses from $98; ⊖lunch Thu-Fri, dinner Tue-Sat; ⊠6) Housed in a Victorian terrace of ample proportions, Reymond was a local pioneer of degustation dining. Degustation plates are now entrée-size, and there's an innovative vegetarian version. Expect a French- influenced, Asian-accented menu with lovely details including house-churned butter.

Da Noi
ITALIAN **$$**

(Map p127; ☎9866 5975; 95 Toorak Rd, South Yarra; mains $25-32; ☺lunch Tue-Sat, dinner Mon-Sat; ☒South Yarra, ☐8) Da Noi serves up beautiful Sardinian dishes that change daily. The spontaneous kitchen might reinterpret the chef's special three times a night. Just go with it; it's a unique experience and harks back to a different way of dining. Bookings advised.

Mama Ganoush
MIDDLE EASTERN **$$**

(Map p127; www.mamaganoush.com; 56 Chapel St, Windsor; mains $28-38; ☺dinner Mon-Sat; ☒Windsor) This is Middle Eastern food that remains true to its roots while being modern and new. The space is full of delicate arabesque screens; the *kibbes* (meatballs), tagines and puddings are full of thought, passion and flavour. It's run by Greg Malouf, the brother of renowned chef and writer Greg Malouf, and he also knows a thing or two about Levantine flavours.

Dino's Deli
SPANISH **$$**

(Map p127; 34 Chapel St, Windsor; mains $22-32; ☺breakfast, lunch & dinner; ☒Windsor) The wine list's way longer than its food list (evidence of prior drinking line the walls), but it's a great spot to dine on Spanish flavours while being looked down on by Parisian dancing girls. It can get very busy.

Outpost
CAFE **$**

(Map p127; 9 Yarra St, South Yarra; mains $14; ☒South Yarra) With the same owners as St Ali, this mighty busy cafe has a range of different rooms to dine and converse in. Our pick of dining rooms? The one where you get to watch the food (including items such as shaved Italian black truffle) being prepared.

Borsch, Vodka & Tears
POLISH **$$**

(Map p127; www.borschvodkaandtears.com; mains $15-25; 173 Chapel St, Windsor; ☺breakfast, lunch & dinner; ☒Prahran, ☐6) We'd consider this one for the name alone, but it's also the business for spruced-up Polish food and an impressive variety of everyone's favourite white spirit, vodka. *Przekazki* spreads let you sample; the dumplings, herrings and blintzes are top-notch, and the borsch is suitably authentic. There are more vegetarian options on the menu than you'd expect too.

Lucky Coq
PIZZA **$**

(Map p127; www.luckycoq.com.au; 179 Chapel St, Windsor; mains $4; ☐6) Bargain pizzas and plenty of late-night DJ action make this a good start to a Chapel St eve. Reports of suit-wearers being denied entry may excite some.

Hooked
FISH & CHIPS **$**

(Map p127; www.hooked.net.au; 172 Chapel St, Windsor; mains $9-15; ☺lunch & dinner; ☒Prahran, ☐72) Great fish and chippery with decor that will make you change your mind on the takeaway and eat in at the communal table. Old-school chips are made on site and fish is either done traditionally or with light Asian accents. Also in **Fitzroy** (Map p122; 384 Brunswick St).

Thai Food to Go
THAI **$**

(Map p127; 141 Chapel St, Windsor; mains $10-21; ☺lunch & dinner; ☒Windsor) The happy hipster nonchalance of the staff and decor, plus a nicely buzzing local crew of diners, make up for fairly standard, though fresh and tasty, Thai food. The menu is flexible and the salads are a steal. Plus they deliver.

SOUTH MELBOURNE, PORT MELBOURNE & ALBERT PARK

These neighbourhoods are perfect for casual footpath dining on a sunny weekend and offer some solidly epicurean options too. While the superscaled restaurants along the bay have stunning views, some also have fairly nondescript food.

Tempura Hajime
JAPANESE **$$$**

(☎9696 0051; 60 Park St, South Melbourne; set meals $73; ☐112) A completely unmarked door, tiny and almost impossible to get a booking? Check. Cult status is assured, and in this case, warranted. Hajime takes you on an edible journey with a set menu of beautifully pondered on and prepared small dishes made with seasonal produce. Park St runs off St Kilda Rd.

Albert Park Hotel Oyster Bar & Grill
SEAFOOD **$$**

(www.thealbertpark.com.au; cnr Montague St & Dundas Pl, Albert Park; mains $15-30; ☐1, 96) With a focus on oysters and seafood as well as bar food, this new incarnation of the Albert Park Hotel (thanks again to Six Degrees) is filling seats with its promise of market-priced fish and wood-barbecued 'big fish' served in five different Mediterranean styles. Its bar is a relaxing place for a brew on a weekend. Head into Albert Park by following Bridport Rd off St Kilda Rd.

Misuzu's
JAPANESE **$$**

(3-7 Victoria Ave, Albert Park; mains $18-30; ☺lunch & dinner; ☐1) Misuzu's menu includes whopping noodle, rice and curry dishes, tempuras and takeaway options from the neatly displayed sushi bar. Sit outside under lantern-hung trees, or inside surrounded by murals and dark wood. Head into Albert Park by following Bridport Rd off St Kilda Rd.

St Ali CAFE **$**
(www.stali.com.au; 12-18 Yarra Pl, South Melbourne; mains $8-45; ⊘breakfast & lunch daily, dinner Wed-Sat; 🚃112) This hideaway warehouse space is a lovely jumble of communal tables, nooks and balconies to accommodate any mood. The food is simple, fresh modern Middle Eastern. Coffee is carefully sourced, roasted and bagged on site, and guaranteed to be good. Dinner comes under categories of two legs and four legs. Just off Clarendon St, between Coventry and York Sts.

Mart 130 CAFE **$**
(☎9690 8831; 107 Canterbury Rd, Middle Park; dishes $6-10; ⊘breakfast & lunch; 🚃96) Where the light-rail trams now run was once a fully fledged railway line with a string of Federation-style stations. Mart 130 has painted the walls and floors a smart black and white, and serves up corn-cakes, granola and eggs with decks overlooking the park. Weekend waits can be long.

🍸 Drinking

Melbourne's bars are legendary, and from laneway hideaways to brassy corner establishments, it's easy to quickly locate a 'local' that will please the senses and drinking palate. The same goes for coffee. Out of the CBD, shopping strips are embedded with shopfront drinking holes: try Fitzroy, Collingwood, Northcote, Prahran and St Kilda. Many inner-city pubs have pushed out the barflies, pulled up the beer-stained carpet, polished the concrete and brought in talented chefs and mixologists, but don't dismiss the character-filled oldies that still exist.

Wine bars are well established in Melbourne, and dedicated cocktail bars are increasingly popular. 'Pop up' bars emerge then disappear from city streets; keep an eye on Three Thousand (www.threethousand.com. au) for the latest.

Bar reviews can be also found on the website of the Age (www.theage.com.au) newspaper.

See also p111 for clubs and p115 for live music venues.

CENTRAL MELBOURNE
The skill of squeezing into a bar/crowded rooftop is often needed, especially during 'Friday night drinks' when office workers let their hair down. To avoid the crunch, some charge between $10 to $15 at the door on Friday and Saturday nights.

Carlton Hotel BAR
(Map p58; www.thecarlton.com.au; 193 Bourke St; ⊘4pm-late) Over-the-top Melbourne rococo gets another workout here and never fails to raise a smile. Check the rooftop **Palmz**, if you're looking for some Miami-flavoured vice or just a great view.

Croft Institute BAR
(Map p58; www.thecroftinstitute.net; 21-25 Croft Alley; ⊘5pm-late Mon-Fri, 8pm-late Sat) Located in a laneway off a laneway, the lab-themed Croft is a test of drinkers' determination. Prescribe yourself a beaker of house-distilled vodka in the downstairs laboratory (some come complete with fat plastic syringes). There's a $10 cover charge on Friday and Saturday nights.

Double Happiness BAR
(Map p58; http://doubledouble.com.au; 21 Liverpool St; ⊘5pm-late Mon-Fri, 6pm-late Sat & Sun) This stylish hole-in-the-wall doesn't just do Chinese-themed decor, it also offers Chinese beers. Try a Tsingtao beer or a cardamom- or ginger-flavoured cocktail.

Gin Palace BAR
(Map p58; www.ginpalace.com.au; 190 Little Collins St; ⊘4pm-late) With a drinks list to make your liver quiver, Gin Palace is the perfect place to grab a soft couch or secluded alcove, sip, and take it slow. Martinis here are legendary and it's open superlate most nights.

Aix Cafe Creperie Salon CAFE
(24 Centre Place; ⊘Mon-Sat 6am-5pm) Settle on a seat out front for true laneway graffiti-views – not only does this grungy French-inspired cafe serve up excellent coffee and crepes, it's also in the best spot on Centre Place to get personal with the laneway attitude.

Sensory Lab CAFE
(Map p58; www.sensorylab.com.au; 297 Little Collins St; ⊘7am-6pm Mon-Wed, 7am-9pm Thu-Fri, 8am-7pm Sat, 9am-6pm Sun) Coffee six ways anyone? Bursting out of David Jones' shopping centre is this little cafe serving coffee all the modern ways. Prices depend on method; a latte is standard, but siphon, cold-drip, pour-over coffees range from $4 to $5.50.

Sweatshop BAR
(Map p58; www.sweatshopbar.com.au; 113 Lonsdale St; ⊘Mon-Sat) There's great Cantonese cuisine upstairs at Seamstress, but it's the dingy sweatshop-like cocktail bar downstairs that

TO BEER, TO NOT TO BEER

Let your beer dreams come true (and we're not talking Victoria Bitter) at Melbourne's top beer bars. All have 'awesome beer from knowledgeable staff' according to James Smith of craftypint.com, which keeps beer drinkers informed about the city's brewers and bars.

» **Local Taphouse** (off Map p112; www.thelocal.com.au; 184 Carlisle St, St Kilda East)

» **Beer DeLuxe** (Map p58; www.beerdeluxe.com.au; Federation Square, Melbourne)

» **Biero** (Map p58; www.biero.com.au; 525 Little Lonsdale St, Melbourne; ⊙Mon-Sat)

» **Mountain Goat Brewery** (www.goatbeer.com.au; 80 North St, Richmond; ⊙from 5pm Wed & Fri)

has it all sewn up. Test the skills of the mixologist while chewing on some crunchy pig's ears (lightly coated in five spice salt).

Madame Brussels BAR
(Map p58; www.madamebrussels.com; Level 3, 59-63 Bourke St; ⊙noon-1am) Head here if you've had it with Melbourne's 'black is the uniform' and all that dark wood. Although named for a famous 19th-century madam, it feels as though you've fallen into a camp '60s rabbit hole, with much Astroturfery and staff dressed à la the country club. The decor might veer towards the hysterical, but it's just the tonic on a chilly winter's day; they even provide lap rugs for the terrace.

Melbourne Supper Club BAR
(Map p58; 1st fl, 161 Spring St; ⊙8pm-4am Sun & Mon, 5pm-late Mon-Sat) Melbourne's own Betty Ford's (the place you go when there's nowhere left to go), the Supper Club is open very late and is a favoured after-work spot for performers and hospitality types. Leave your coat at the door and cosy into a Chesterfield. Browse the encyclopaedic wine menu and relax; the sommeliers will cater to any liquid desire. The upstairs bar has wonderful views and is open to the elements for the cigar smokers.

Loop BAR
(Map p58; www.looponline.com.au; 23 Meyers Pl; ⊙3pm-late) Loop has a large double screen and scattered projectors; find yourself a dark seat or a spot at the bar and watch the 'Video Jockeys' display their wares. It has something on every night, from beats to heartfelt docos.

New Gold Mountain BAR
(Map p58; www.newgoldmountain.org; Level 1, 21 Liverpool St; ⊙6pm-late) Unsignposted, New Gold Mountain's intense Chinoiserie interi-

or comes as a shock. Two upstairs floors are filled with tiny screen-shielded corners, with decoration so delightfully relentless you feel as if you're trapped in an art-house dream sequence. You may need to phone the number on the door to get in.

Brother Baba Budan CAFE
(Map p58; www.sevenseeds.com.au; 359 Little Bourke St) Cute city outpost of indie roasters St Ali. There's coffee, of course, and only the odd *rugelach* or biscuit to distract you.

Workshop BAR
(Map p58; www.theworkshopbar.com.au; 413 Elizabeth St; ⊙10am-late Mon-Fri, 1pm-late Sat & Sun) This industrial bar offers healthy lunches early and live music or DJs playing late. At any time there's perfect Elizabeth St gazing from the flora-filled outdoor area.

1000 £ Bend BAR
(Map p58; www.thousandpoundbend.com.au; 361 Little Lonsdale St; ☎) Breakfasts and lunches and cruisy folk using the free wi-fi – that's not all at this mega warehouse of entertainment. It's also the venue for art shows, plays and an annual bike fest. As we write it's being crowned with a liquor licence, so expect this to be the place to see.

Liaison CAFE
(Map p58; Monaco House, 22 Ridgway Place) With queues on Tuesdays and Fridays for its exclusive macaroons, Liaison, housed in the former garage of the Monaco Consulate, has a cult (well, macaroon and coffee) following.

Campari House COCKTAIL BAR
(Map p58; www.camparihouse.com.au; 25-23 Hardware Lane) It's worth coming here on a sunny day or balmy evening to sip cocktails on the rooftop. Come rainy days the luxury lounge (open from Thursday to Saturday) is perfectly comforting.

TOP ROOFTOPS FOR IMBIBING

» **Madame Brussels** (p107)

» **Supper Club** (p107)

» **Rooftop Bar** (p114)

» **Palmz at the Carlton Hotel** (p106)

» **Movida Terraza** (p96)

» **Campari House** (p107)

1806   COCKTAIL BAR
(Map p58; www.1806.com.au; 169 Exhibition St)
This cocktail bar doesn't pack up its stirrers
until 3am most mornings (and until 5am on
Friday and Saturday). Not only does it serve
a long, long list of cocktails, it also runs sessions designed to bring the mixologist out in
you ($170).

Riverland   BAR
(Map p58; www.riverlandbar.com; Vaults 1-9, Federation Wharf; ⊙7am-midnight) Perched below
Princess Bridge, this bluestone beauty, keeps
things simple with good wine, beer on tap
and bar snacks that hit the mark: charcuterie, cheese and BBQ. A rare riverside drinking
hole that doesn't give off the scent of corporate investors. Outside tables are a treat when
the weather is kind.

Pushka   CAFE
(Map p58; 20 Pesgrave Pl) Relaxed hipster hideaway, off Howey Pl, with home-away-from-
home charm, excellent coffee and Portuguese
custard tarts. Just keep on going up that alley.

Robot   BAR
(Map p58; www.robotsushi.com; 12 Bligh Pl; ⊙5pm-
late Mon-Fri, 8pm-late Sat) If neo-Tokyo is your
thing or you just have a sudden urge for a
sushi handroll washed down with an Asahi,
check out Robot. It has an all-welcome door
policy, big windows that open to the laneway, a cute mezzanine level and attracts a
laid-back young crowd.

Section 8   BAR
(Map p58; www.section8.com.au; 27-29 Tattersalls
Lane; ⊙8am-late Mon-Fri, noon-late Sat & Sun)
Come to the latest in shipping container
habitats, and sink a Mountain Goat with the
after-work crowd, who make do with packing cases for decor.

Sister Bella   BAR
(Map p58; Sniders Lane; ⊙11am-late Mon-Fri, 4pm-
late weekends) This dilapidated laneway warehouse is totally ramshackle, but that's the
way we like it. It's a casual, darkened spot
for a brew and a cheap meal.

New Guernica   BAR
(Map p58; www.newguernica.com.au; 2nd fl, 322
Little Collins St; ⊙5pm-late Mon-Fri, 9pm-late weekends) Huddle away in a fairy-tale world full
of mushrooms and deer in the deep forest
atmosphere of this upstairs bar. It's a picnic
spot for night owls.

Berlin Bar   BAR
(Map p58; www.berlinbar.com.au; 16 Corrs Lane;
⊙Wed-Sat) And why not, we say, create a bar
that goes from one extreme to another in
just a short walk. Plenty of German beers in
your choice of the grungy East section or the
fancy-dancy West.

Federal Coffee Palace   CAFE
(Map p58; GPO, Elizabeth St) Atmosphere plus,
with tables beneath the colonnades of the
GPO and the fashion retailer fave. Space heaters keep you toasty when the city turns chilly.

Switchboard   CAFE
(Map p58; Manchester Unity Arcade, 220 Collins St)
Beneath the Man-U mosaics, there's nana-
style wallpaper, cupcakes and a coffee machine in a cupboard.

Lounge   BAR
(Map p58; www.lounge.com.au; 1st fl, 243 Swanston
St; ⊙11am-late Mon-Fri, 1pm-late weekends; 🛜)
Lounge has seen a lot of years and a lot of
extremely big nights. It still feels like a share
house from the early '90s, and that's the way
the crowd likes it. Evenings are filled with
the sound of DJs (door charge is usually
$20), or escape to Lounge's big balcony with
some cajun fries.

EAST MELBOURNE & RICHMOND

Richmond's factory-fodder roots are evident
in its plethora of corner pubs. This is where
you'll find the Corner Hotel, one of the city's
best live music venues.

TOP CHOICE **Der Raum**   BAR
(Map p69; www.derraum.com.au; 438
Church St, Richmond; ⊙5pm-late; ☒East Richmond, 🚋70, 79) The name conjures up images
of a dark Fritz Lang flick and there's definitely something noirish about the space and the
extreme devotion to hard liquor (evidence of
which hangs over barflies on octopus straps).
Cocktails are not cheap but are muddled and
mixed with fresh juices, premium spirits and
an award-winning knowledge of the craft.

Mountain Goat Brewery   MICROBREWERY
(www.goatbeer.com.au; cnr North & Clark Sts, Richmond; ⊘from 5pm Wed & Fri) This local microbrewery is set in a massive beer-producing warehouse; enjoy its range of beers while nibbling on pizza. There are free brewery tours on Wednesdays. It's tricky to reach: head down Bridge Rd, turn left at Burnley and right at North.

Public House   BAR
(Map p69; www.publichouse.com.au; 433-435 Church St, Richmond; ⊘noon-late; ⌨East Richmond, ⌫70, 79) Not in any way resembling a public house from any period of history, this great Six Degrees fit-out features their signature blend of found glass and earthy raw and recycled materials. There's imported beer on tap and a short but sweet wine list.

FITZROY & AROUND
Possessing the highest density of pubs of any suburb in Melbourne, Fitzroy has a big drinking scene. Neighbouring Collingwood and Northcote along High St also see a lot of action.

Joe's Shoe Store   BAR
(233 High St, Northcote; ⊘4pm-late Tue-Sun; ⌫86) Someone called Joe will no longer sell you lace-up brogues but this dark, groovy drinking hole will have you well wined and beered. It's always packed with Northcote cool kids who order pizza from **Meine Liebe** (p100) or just stick to drinks. Head north along Hoddle St to reach High St.

Builders Arms Hotel   PUB
(Map p122; 211 Gertrude St, Fitzroy; ⊘4pm-late Mon-Thu, 2pm-late Fri-Sun; ⌫86) A completely re-imagined bad old boozer that's retained its charm despite theatrical new threads. Come for a pot by all means, but there's also decent wine by the glass, and traditional food to satisfy the 'gimme a steak!' night crowd. Picnic-style tables on the footpath outside are perfect for taking in Gertrude St.

De Clieu   CAFE
(Map p122; 187 Gertrude St, Fitzroy; ⌫86) From experienced coffee-folk Seven Seeds, comes De Clieu, a funky little cafe with polished concrete floors and a sense of humour. Fancy a glass of homemade red cordial, a bowl of Coco Pops and a coffee? Get it here. And you can be guaranteed it'll be a perfect coffee.

Napier Hotel   PUB
(Map p122; www.thenapierhotel.com; 210 Napier St; ⊘3-11pm Mon-Thu, 1pm-1am Fri & Sat, 1-11pm Sun; ⌫112, 86) The Napier has stood on this corner for over a century; many pots have been pulled as the face of the neighbourhood changed. The nostalgic should note the memorabilia of the sadly departed Fitzroy footy team still adorning the walls. Worm your way around the central bar to the boisterous back dining room or to the skinny passage that serves as a beer garden. The upstairs art gallery features changing exhibitions by local artists.

Little Creatures Dining Hall   MIRCOBREWERY
(Map p122; www.littlecreatures.com.au; 222 Brunswick St, Fitzroy; ☎; ⌫112) With free wi-fi, free community bikes and a daytime kid-friendly groove, this vast drinking hall is the perfect place to meet up, spend up big on pizzas and enjoy a 'spirit-free' drinks list. They focus on locally made drinks including pear cider, Victorian wines and Australian beer.

Naked for Satan   BAR
(Map p122; www.nakedforsatan.com.au; 285 Brunswick St; ⊘noon until late; ⌫112) Vibrant, loud and reviving an apparent Brunswick St legend (a man nicknamed Satan who would get down and dirty, naked because of the heat, in an illegal vodka distillery under the shop), this place packs a punch both with its popular *pintxos* (Basque tapas; $2) and huge range of cleverly-named beverages. It won 'bar of the year' in the *Age's* 2011 *Cheap Eats Guide*.

Gasometer Hotel   PUB
(Map p122; 484 Smith St, Collingwood; ⌫86) A well-practiced team has come together to turn this former Irish pub into a trusty place for entertainment, food with a vegetarian and Spanish bent, and super cocktails. Head here for Mexican Thursday (food and Latin DJs) and trivia Monday, and keep an ear out for its karaoke nights.

Grace Darling   BAR
(Map p122; www.gracedarlinghotel.com.au; 114 Smith St, Collingwood; ⌫86) Adored by Collingwood football fans as the birthplace of the club, Grace has been given a bit of spit and polish by some well-known Melbourne foodies, and while the chicken parma remains, it is certainly not how you know it (more a terracotta bake of chargrilled chook, ham, slow-roasted tomato and parmesan). They also have tasty live music.

Bar Open   LIVE MUSIC, BAR
(Map p122; www.baropen.com.au; 317 Brunswick St, Fitzroy; ⊘3pm-late; ⌫112) This long-established bar, as the name suggests, is often

open when everything else is closed. The bar attracts a relaxed young local crowd ready to kick on. Bands play in the upstairs loft and are almost always free.

CARLTON & AROUND
There are plenty of pubs to be found throughout Carlton and you'll quickly become aware of the area's large student population in many of them. The northern end of Lygon St has a few standouts.

Seven Seeds
CAFE

(www.sevenseeds.com.au; 114 Berkely St, Carlton) This is the most spacious of the Seven Seeds coffee empire; there's plenty of room to store your bike, sip a splendid coffee beside a growing coffee plant and check out all the other lucky people who've found this rather out-of-the-way warehouse-like cafe (follow Elizabeth St from the CBD, then turn right at Queensberry).

Mr Wilkinson
BAR

(295 Lygon St, East Brunswick; ☺closed Tue; ⌂1,8) The owners decked this place out in recycled timber themselves and now concentrate on keeping things mellow and their customers well watered. It's a great place for a natter to the bar staff.

Atticus Finch
BAR

(www.atticusfinch.com.au; 129 Lygon St, East Brunswick; ☺5pm-late Tue-Sun; ⌂1, 8) There's a judicious wine list at this East Brunswick haunt named for everyone's favourite lawyer from literature. The space is smartly and simply done with a slight brooding quality (though perhaps we're overidentifying with the novel). A nice alternative to the bigger pubs in these parts, it still sports the requisite beer garden. Lygon St extends north from Carlton into East Brunswick.

Rrose Bar
BAR

(www.rrosebar.com.au; 7 Errol St, North Melbourne; ☺2pm-late; ⌂57) This small shopfront bar does both stylish and homey in equal measures (something that's harder to pull off than it looks). It's focused on local beverages and has a whopping great seasonal cocktail list.

Alderman
WINE BAR

(134 Lygon St, East Brunswick; ☺Tue-Fri 5pm-late, Sat & Sun 2pm-late; ⌂1, 8) With decks of cards, an upstairs gallery and a resident dog, this local haunt entertains and waters you well while feeding you bites from restaurant Bar Idda next door.

Town Hall Hotel
PUB

(33 Errol St, North Melbourne; ⌂57) The Town Hall is an unfussy local. Live music is staged free in the front room from Thursday to Saturday, otherwise they'll be spinning some classic vinyl. There's a beer garden and pub meals too. From the Queen Vic Market head west along Victoria St, then right at Errol.

Gerald's Bar
WINE BAR

(386 Rathdowne St, North Carlton; ☺5-11pm Mon-Sat; ⌂1, 8, ⌂253) Wine by the glass is democratically selected at Gerald's and they spin some fine vintage vinyl from behind the curved wooden bar. Gerald himself is out the back preparing to feed you whatever he feels like on the day: goat curry, seared calamari, meatballs, trifle. Gerald's bar was awarded 'bar of the year' in 2010 by *Australian Gourmet Traveller* magazine. Continue down Rathdowne St from Carton into North Carlton.

Jimmy Watson's
WINE BAR

(Map p74; www.jimmywatsons.com.au; 333 Lygon St; ☺10.30am-6pm Mon, 11am-late Tue-Sat; ⌂1, 8) Keep it tidy at Watson's wine bar with something nice by the glass, or go a bottle of dry and dry (vermouth and ginger ale) and settle in for the afternoon and evening. If Roy Grounds' stunning midcentury building had ears, there'd be a few generations of writers, students and academics in trouble.

SOUTH YARRA, PRAHRAN & WINDSOR
South Yarra and Windsor may be within walking distance of each other but are a world away in terms of their bar scenes. Windsor has a number of artfully grungy, loungey locals; South Yarra is all about shouting over the music while clutching a lurid-coloured drink. Not so precious Prahran is somewhere in the middle.

Blue Bar 330
BAR

(Map p127; www.bluebar.com.au; 330 Chapel St, Prahran; ⌂Prahran, ⌂72) A narrow and dimly lit sanctum away from the bustle of Chapel St, Blue Bar's linear architecture and streetsmart clientele contrast with the sprawl of couches within. And Blue Bar blessedly debunks the theory that you have to look like a model to drink in Chapel St.

Windsor Castle
PUB

(Map p127; 89 Albert St, Windsor; ⌂Windsor) Cosy nooks, sunken pits, fireplaces and flocked wallpaper make the Windsor Castle extremely attractive.

Carlisle Wine Bar

(137 Carlisle St, Balaclava; ⊘brunch Sat & Sun, dinner daily; ⓡBalaclava, 🚋3, 16) Locals love this often rowdy, wine-worshiping former butcher's shop. The staff will treat you like a regular and find you a glass of something special, or effortlessly throw together a cocktail amid the weekend rush. The rustic Italian food is good too. Carlisle St runs east off St Kilda Rd.

After the Tears Elsternwick

(www.afterthetears.com; 9B Gordon St, Elsternwick; ⊘11am-11pm; ⓡElsternwick, 🚋67) This offshoot of long-time Prahran hang-out Borsch, Vodka & Tears (p105) is next to the Classic Cinema. It serves an astonishing range of vodkas (at last count at least 100) and has an authentic Polish feel. Follow Brighton Rd to Glen Huntly Rd.

George Lane Bar

(Map p112; www.georgelanebar.com.au; 1 George Lane; ⊘6pm-late Wed-Fri, 7pm-late Sat & Sun; 🚋96, 16) Hidden behind the hulk of the George Hotel, tucked away off Grey St, this little bar is a good rabbit hole to dive into. Its pleasantly ad-hoc decor is a relief from the inch-of-its-life design aesthetic elsewhere. There's beer on tap and DJs (and queues) on the weekends.

George Public Bar

(Map p112; www.georgepublicbar.com.au; Basement, 127 Fitzroy St; 🚋96, 16) Upstairs, downstairs divisions live on, even in egalitarian St Kilda. Behind the crumbling paint and Edwardian arched windows of the George Hotel, there's the Melbourne Wine Room and a large front bar that keeps the after-work crowd happy. In the bowels of the building is the George Public Bar, often referred to as the Snakepit. It's often rough, rowdy and the perfect spot to nurse a pot and play some pool.

Mink

(Map p112; www.minkbar.com.au; 2b Acland St; ⊘6pm-late Thu-Sun; 🚋96, 16, 112) In this dimly lit Trans-Siberian–styled bar there's no shortage of vodka and glam good times. Get there early to nab the much sought-after private 'sleeper' and start working your way through the extensive list.

Pause Bar

(www.pausebar.com.au; 268 Carlisle St, Balaclava; ⊘4pm-1am Mon-Fri, noon-1am Sat & Sun; ⓡBalaclava, 🚋3, 16, 79) Pause draws a mixed local crowd (for its cocktails and mezes) who

like to settle into the dim North African–inspired interior for the night. Carlisle St runs east off St Kilda Rd.

Veludo

(Map p112; www.veludo.com.au; 175 Acland St; 🚋96) It's big, it's brassy and it's got a balcony. Over two levels, Veludo's relatively late closing means that most St Kildaites have ducked in here after everything else has closed. Upstairs has live music most nights.

Vineyard

(Map p112; www.thevineyard.com.au; 71a Acland St; 🚋96, 16) The perfect corner position and a courtyard barbie attracts crowds of backpackers and scantily clad young locals who enjoy themselves so much as they drown out the neighbouring roller coaster.

Padre Coffee

(www.padrecoffee.com.au; shop 33 South Melbourne Market, South Melbourne; ⊘Wed, Fri & Sat; 🚋96) Offers perfect (and popular) caffeine-enhanced respite from mad market shopping.

Barkly Hotel

(Map p112; www.hotelbarkly.com; 109 Barkly St; 🚋16, 67, 79) The street-level public bar is the place to go if you're up for sinking a few pints, wiggling to whatever comes on the jukebox and snogging a stranger before last drinks are called. The rooftop bar feigns a bit of class, but things get messy up there too. The look (Gold Coast penthouse, perhaps?) and the music might be just your thing or set your teeth on edge; either way it's worth braving for the abso-bloody-lutely spectacular sunset view across the rooftops to the Palais Theatre and bay beyond.

St Kilda Bowling Club

(Map p112; www.stkildasportsclub.com.au; 66 Fitzroy St; 🚋96, 16, 112) This fabulously intact old clubhouse is tucked behind a neatly trimmed hedge and a splendid bowling green. The long bar serves drinks at 'club prices' (ie cheap) and you'll be joined by St Kilda's hippest and hottest on Sunday afternoons. Francophiles take note: the pétanque club convenes every Friday afternoon.

☆ Entertainment
Nightclubs

Alumbra

(www.alumbra.com.au; Shed 9, Central Pier, 161 Harbour Esplanade, Docklands; ⊘4pm-late Fri-Sun) Great music and a stunning location will impress – even if the Bali-meets-Morocco follies of the decorator don't. If you're going

York St

Hockey Dr

Village Green Dr

Junction Oval

St Kilda Junction
4

Cowderoy St

Park St

Deakin St

Canterbury Rd

Albert Park

14

Beaconsfield Pde

Loch St

Park La

Mary St

ST KILDA WEST

10

6

Fitzroy St

Princes St

Pier Rd

West Beach Rd

16

12

15

29

28

9

Little Grey St

Dalgety St

Dalgety La

Burnett St

Catani Gardens

26

13

17

35

23

Jackson St

Acland St

Eildon Rd

St Leonards Ave

Neptune St

Grey St

Gurner St

Barkly St

Hobsons Bay

3

5

33

Victoria St

36

Neptune La

Robe St

Alfred Pl

30

Inkerman St

25

Alfred Square

7

41

St Kilda Foreshore

ST KILDA

Clyde St

Fawkner St

Havelock St

Blanche St

Vale St

To Local Taphouse (850m)

11

Jacka Blvd

The Esplanade

Lower Esplanade

21

8

Carlisle St

27

34

2

32

37

O'Donnell Gardens

40

18

Belford St

Foster St

20

Cavell St

Shakespeare Gve

Peanut Farm Reserve

Acland St

31

Smith St

St Kilda Botanic Gardens

19

24

Port Phillip

Marine Pde

Spenser St

38

39

22

Chaucer St

Mitford St

Blessington St

Renfrey Gardens

Barkly St

Wordsworth St

St Kilda Marina

To Elwood Beach (1km)

ELWOOD

to do one megaclub in Melbourne (and like the idea of a glass dance floor), this is going to be your best bet. It's in one of the old sheds jutting out into Docklands' Victoria Harbour.

Brown Alley   CLUB
(Map p58; www.brownalley.com; cnr King & Lonsdale Sts, Melbourne; ⊙11.30am-late Mon-Fri, 6pm-late Sat & Sun) This historical pub hides away a fully fledged nightclub with a 24-hour licence. It's enormous, with distinct rooms that can fit up to 1000 people. Their sound equipment is the business and the rota of DJs includes breakbeat, psy-trance and deep house.

Eve   CLUB
(www.evebar.com.au; 334 City Rd, South Melbourne; ⊙dusk-late Thu-Sat) Florence Broadhurst wallpapers, a black granite bar and Louis chairs set the tone, which gets rapidly lower

as the night progresses. Footballers, glamour girls and the odd lost soul come for cocktails and commercial house. Expect to queue after 9pm. Spencer St becomes Clarendon; it's near the corner of City Rd.

Onesixone   CLUB
(Map p127; www.onesixone.com.au; 161 High St, Prahran; ⊙till late Wed-Sat; ⊠Prahran, ⊠6) Front up to the peephole and if you pass muster, snaffle a couch or a pouf. A wiggle on the small dance floor is obligatory. Morning Glory on Sundays starts at 4am and runs until the rest of the world is truly up and about.

Cinemas

Cinema multiplexes are spread throughout Melbourne city, and there are quite a few treasured independent cinemas in both the CBD and surrounding suburbs. Grab a choctop (ice cream dipped in chocolate) and check out movies at the following.

Astor Theatre
CINEMA

(Map p127; ☑9510 1414; www.astor-theatre.com; cnr Chapel St & Dandenong Rd, Windsor; ☑Windsor; ☑64) See a double feature for the price of one. Screens a mix of recent art-house releases and classics in art deco surrounds.

Australian Centre for the Moving Image
CINEMA

(ACMI; Map p58; ☑9663 2583; www.acmi.net. au; Federation Sq, Melbourne) ACMI's cinemas screen a diverse range of films. It programs regular events and festivals for film genres and audiences, as well as screening one-offs.

Cinema Nova
CINEMA

(Map p74; ☑9347 5331; www.cinemanova.com.au; 380 Lygon St, Carlton; ☑1, 8) Nova has the latest in arthouse, documentary and foreign films, and has cheap Monday screenings: sessions before 4pm cost $6 and after 4pm $8 (except public holidays). Special events include Script Alive – readings of unproduced screenplays.

Classic Cinema
CINEMA

(☑9524 7900; www.classictheatre.com.au; 9 Gordon St, Elsternwick; ☑Elsternwick, ☑67) Arthouse classics screen in what is Melbourne's longest-running cinema (it housed a Yiddish theatre troop in the 1950s). It holds 'spit the dummy' sessions for babies and their carers. Follow Brighton Rd to Glen Huntly Rd, turn left, it's on your left.

Kino Cinemas
CINEMA

(Map p58; ☑9650 2100; www.palacecinemas.com. au; Collins Pl, 45 Collins St, Melbourne) The Kino screens art-house films in its comfy licensed cinemas. Monday is cheap (tickets $7).

Imax
3D CINEMA

(Map p74; ☑9663 5454; www.imaxmelbourne.com. au; Melbourne Museum, Carlton Gardens, Carlton; ☑86, 96) Who'd have predicted that 3D films would be relegated to kid-friendly genres? Animal and adventure films in 3D screen on a grand scale here, with movies specially made for these giant screens.

Palace Como
CINEMA

(Map p127; ☑9827 7533; www.palacecinemas. au; cnr Toorak Rd & Chapel St, South Yarra; ☑South Yarra, ☑8) Arthouse and foreign language favourites are shown across four luxury cinemas with a plush foyer, bar and cafe. Fridays have pre-show live music, cocktails and tapas.

Outdoor cinemas are popular in the summer; check the websites for seasonal opening dates and program details. These include:

Moonlight Cinema
OUTDOOR CINEMA

(www.moonlight.com.au; Gate D, Royal Botanic Gardens Melbourne, Birdwood Ave, South Yarra; ☑8) Outdoes itself with its 'Gold Grass' tickets, which include a glass of wine and a reserved bean bed (yes, a bed, not a bag!).

Rooftop Cinema
OUTDOOR CINEMA

(Map p58; www.rooftopcinema.com.au; Level 6, Curtin House, 252 Swanston St, Melbourne) This rooftop is a bar, loved 'beatbox' kitchen and, in summer, a cinema.

St Kilda Open Air Cinema
OUTDOOR CINEMA

(Map p112; www.stkildaopenair.com.au; St Kilda Sea Baths, 10-18 Jacka Blvd, St Kilda; ☑79, 96) Rents out blankets ($4) if a sea breeze hits.

Theatre

Melbourne's theatre district is not limited to the CBD, with individual companies and theatres spread across town. Tickets start at about $20 for independent productions, and $30 for mainstream theatre. See p334 for more on Melbourne's theatre scene. Try Half Tix Melbourne (Map p58; www.halftixmelbourne. com; Melbourne Town Hall; ☑10am-2pm Mon, 11am-6pm Tue-Fri, 10am-4pm Sat) for cheap tickets to the theatre. You need to front up at the Half Tix office in person on the day with cash.

La Mama
THEATRE

(Map p74; ☑9347 6948; www.lamama.com.au; 205 Faraday St, Carlton; ☑19) La Mama is historically significant in Melbourne's theatre scene. This tiny, intimate forum produces new Australian works and experimental theatre, and has a reputation for developing emerging playwrights. It's fought various battles for its funding and, most recently, its building, which, after a huge fundraising effort, it secured.

Malthouse Theatre
THEATRE

(☑9685 5111; www.malthousetheatre.com.au; 113 Sturt St, South Melbourne; ☑1) The Malthouse Theatre Company often produces the most exciting theatre in Melbourne. Dedicated to promoting Australian works, the Malthouse has been housed in the atmospheric Malthouse Theatre since 1990 (when it was known as the Playbox). From Flinders St Station walk across Princes Bridge and along St Kilda Rd. Turn right at Grant St then left into Sturt.

Melbourne Theatre Company
THEATRE

(MTC; ☑8688 0800; www.mtc.com.au; 140 Southbank Blvd, Southbank) Melbourne's major theatrical company stages around 15 productions each year, ranging from contemporary and modern (including many new Australian works) to Shakespearean and other classics. Performances take place in a brand new award-winning venue in Southbank.

Red Stitch Actors Theatre
THEATRE
(Map p127; ☑9533 8082; www.redstitch.net; rear, 2 Chapel St, Windsor) This independent company of actors stages new international works that are often premieres in Australia. The tiny black-box theatre, opposite the Astor (p114) and down the end of the driveway, is a cosy, intimate space.

Theatreworks
THEATRE
(Map p112; ☑9534 3388; www.theatreworks.org.au; 14 Acland St, St Kilda; ☒64) Theatreworks is a community theatre dedicated to supporting a range of arts practitioners.

Comedy
The **Melbourne International Comedy Festival** (p25) is a huge event, but you don't need to wait until April to have a laugh in Melbourne.

Last Laugh at the Comedy Club
COMEDY
(Map p58; www.thecomedyclub.com.au; Athenaeum Theatre, 188 Collins St, Melbourne) The Last Laugh is open Friday and Saturday year-round, with additional nights in summer. This is professional stand-up, featuring local and international artists. Dinner-show packages are available – bookings recommended.

The club is also a venue for acts during the Comedy Festival.

Comic's Lounge
COMEDY
(www.thecomicslounge.com.au; 26 Errol St, North Melbourne; ☒57) There is stand-up every night of the week here. Admission prices vary, but are usually between $15 and $25. Dinner and show nights are popular and feature Melbourne's best-known comedians (many of whom also host radio shows). Tuesday is kind of an open-mic night, where aspiring comics have their eight minutes of fame (or shame). From Queen Vic Market head west along Victoria St, then right at Errol.

Live Music
Melbourne's live music scene has had a rough run of late; residents moving into new apartment buildings have certainly had their voices heard, and as a result some music venues have been forced to close, or reduce the volume. The Tote in Collingwood was an apparent victim of new liquor-licensing laws that meant even small venues must have a security presence; it closed and Melbourne's music-lovers weren't happy. Between 10,000 to 20,000 people rallied in Melbourne's CBD and, as a result, venues were told they could apply to have some of the more obscure conditions removed. There's a happy ending: the Tote got new owners and the music continues.

CURTAINS UP

Blockbuster musicals have the good fortune of playing in Melbourne's graceful old theatres, including the following:

Athenaeum (Map p58; ☑9650 1500; www.ticketmaster.com.au; 188 Collins St) The old dame dates back to the 1830s and the theatre now hosts Melbourne Opera and the International Comedy Festival. Also a Ticketmaster box office.

Comedy Theatre (Map p58; ☑9299 9800; www.marrinertheatres.com.au; 240 Exhibition St) This midsize 1920s Spanish-style venue is dedicated to comedy, theatre and musicals.

Her Majesty's (Map p58; ☑8643 3300; www.hmt.com.au; 219 Exhibition St) On the outside Her Maj is red-brick Second Empire; on the inside it's 1930s Moderne. It's been the home of musicals and comedy since 1880 and is still going strong.

Princess Theatre (Map p58; ☑9299 9800; www.marrinertheatres.com.au; 163 Spring St) This gilded Second Empire beauty has a long and colourful history. It's reputed to have a resident ghost – that of singer Federici, who died as he descended through the stage trap in 1888 after playing Mephistopheles in the opera *Faust*. These days shows range from *Phantom of the Opera* to *Mary Poppins*.

Regent Theatre (Map p58; ☑9299 9500; www.marrinertheatres.com.au; 191 Collins St) The Regent, a Rococo picture palace from the 1920s, is used less as a venue than the Princess, but when it hosts musicals and live acts, it's a fabulous opportunity to experience its elegant grandeur.

TICKETS

Tickets for concerts and music festivals are usually available from one of the agencies listed:

» **Moshtix** (☑1300 438 849; www.moshtix.com.au)

» **Ticketek** (Map p58; ☑13 28 49; www.ticketek.com; 225 Exhibition St, Melbourne)

» **Ticketmaster** (Map p58; ☑13 61 00; www.ticketmaster.com.au; Athenaeum Theatre, 188 Collins St, Melbourne)

Check daily papers, and weekly street magazines *Beat* and *Inpress* for gig info. Radio station 3RRR (102.7FM) broadcasts a gig guide at 7pm each evening (and has it online at www.rrr.org.au), and

Northcote Social Club
LIVE MUSIC, PUB

(☑9489 3917; www.northcotesocialclub.com; 301 High St, Northcote; ☒86) This is one of Melbourne's best live music venues with a stage that's seen plenty of international folk just one album out from star status. Their home-grown line-up is also notable. If you're just after a drink, the front bar buzzes every night of the week, or there's a large deck out the back for lazy afternoons. A perfect, and well-loved, local.

Corner Hotel
LIVE MUSIC, PUB

(Map p69; ☑9427 9198; www.cornerhotel.com; 57 Swan St, Richmond; ☒closed Mon; ☒Richmond, ☒70) The band room here is one of Melbourne's most popular midsized venues and has seen plenty of loud and live action over the years. If your ears need a break, there's a friendly front bar. The rooftop has city views, but gets superpacked, and often with a different crowd from the music fans below. Its Wednesday night trivia has a cult following.

Evelyn Hotel
LIVE MUSIC, PUB

(Map p122; www.evelynhotel.com; 351 Brunswick St, Fitzroy; ☒112) Playing mostly local acts, the Evelyn also pulls the occasional international performer. The Ev doesn't discriminate by genre: if it's quality, it gets a look-in here. Both one-off gigs and band residencies feature from Tuesday to Sunday (free to $30).

The Tote
LIVE MUSIC, PUB

(Map p122; www.thetotehotel.com; cnr Johnston & Wellington Sts, Fitzroy; ☒4pm-late Thu-Sun; ☒86) The Tote's closure in 2010 brought Melbourne to a stop, literally. People protested on the CBD streets against the liquor licensing laws that were blamed for the closure, and there were howls of displeasure on the radio waves. The punters won; there were changes to Melbourne's liquor licensing laws, and, armed with new 'white knight' owners, The Tote reopened to continue its tradition of live bands playing dirty rock.

Cherry Bar
LIVE MUSIC, BAR

(Map p58; ACDC Lane, off 103 Flinders Lane, Melbourne; ☒5pm-late Tue-Fri, 9pm-late Sat) This rock 'n' roll refuge is still going strong. There's often a queue, but once inside a relaxed, slightly anarchic spirit prevails. Music is rarely live but never electronic.

Billboard
LIVE MUSIC

(Map p58; www.billboardthevenue.com.au; 170 Russell St, Melbourne) A little bit of trance and a lot of live music; this place has been around for over 40 years. These days it's attracting a good quality crop of international and local bands (and it still has its famous disco).

Bennetts Lane
JAZZ BAR

(Map p58; www.bennettslane.com; 25 Bennetts Lane, Melbourne; ☒8.30pm-late) Bennetts Lane has long been the boiler room of Melbourne jazz. It attracts the cream of local and international talent and an audience that knows when it's time to applaud a solo. Beyond the cosy front bar, there's another space reserved for big gigs.

Wesley Anne
LIVE MUSIC, BAR

(www.wesleyanne.com.au; 250 High St, Northcote; ☒4pm-late Mon-Fri, 2pm-late Sat & Sun; ☒86) This atmospheric pub set up shop in a church mission's house of assembly. What else can you expect when the demon drink wins out against the forces of temperance? Booze, yes, but also interesting food, live music, a big beer garden with space heaters and a cruisy crowd who often bring their kids along in daylight hours. Head north along Hoddle St to reach High St.

Ding Dong Lounge
LIVE MUSIC, CLUB

(Map p58; www.dingdonglounge.com.au; 18 Market Lane, Melbourne; ☒7pm-late Wed-Sat) Ding Dong walks the rock-and-roll walk and is a top spot to see smaller touring acts or local bands.

East Brunswick Club
LIVE MUSIC, PUB

(www.eastbrunswickclub.com; 280 Lygon St, East Brunswick; ☒1, 8) This live-music venue has a great line-up of local and international acts. The front bar also has a friendly local scene with 12-buck specials on a Monday night: jugs of beer, burgers, parmas and pasta are all $12 each. They also do meatless and dairy-free versions of all the above too for vegos and vegans. Lygon St extends north from Carlton into East Brunswick.

Butterfly Club
CABARET

(www.thebutterflyclub.com; 204 Bank St, South Melbourne; ☺5pm-late Tue-Sun; ☐96, 112) This eccentric little place remains largely undiscovered; expect acts that aren't really theatre, aren't quite straight comedy and that might just throw in a song. The teeny rooms display an extraordinary collection of kitsch, which adds to the feeling that you're never quite sure what you're in for. Follow Spencer St down Clarendon St, then turn right at Bank.

Esplanade Hotel
LIVE MUSIC, PUB

(Map p112; http://espy.com.au; 11 The Esplanade, St Kilda; ☺noon-late Mon-Fri, 8am-late weekends; ☐96, 16) Rock-pigs rejoice. The Espy remains gloriously shabby and welcoming to all. Bands play most nights and there's a spruced-up kitchen out the back. And for the price of a pot you get front row seats for the pink-stained St Kilda sunset.

Prince Bandroom
LIVE MUSIC

(Map p112; www.princebandroom.com.au; 29 Fitzroy St, St Kilda; ☐96, 16, 112) This venue is an institution with the likes of Tricky, Fat Freddy's Drop and Lee Scratch Perry having graced its stage. Its leafy balcony and raucous downstairs bar are added attractions. Dance acts are a feature, but there's also a good mix of indie, electropop, soul and blues.

Retreat
LIVE MUSIC, PUB

(280 Sydney Rd, Brunswick; ☐Brunswick, ☐19) This pub is so big as to be a tad overwhelming. Find your habitat – garden backyard, grungy band room or intimate front bar – and relax. Sundays are very popular with locals who like to laze on the (fake) grass, and while there's live music or DJs most nights, it's also the domain of rock aerobics on Tuesday. Royal Pde becomes Sydney Rd; follow it past Glenlyon Rd.

HEADLINE ACTS

When the rock gods (or more commonly pop, R&B and hip-hop stars) roll into town and are too big for Melbourne's beloved medium-sized venues, such as the Corner Hotel (p116) or the Prince Bandroom (p117), they are likely to play at one of the following venues:

Docklands Stadium (Etihad Stadium; Map p54; www.etihadstadium.com.au; Kings Domain, Melbourne) Has an excellent reputation for staging music giants such as U2 and AC/DC.

Festival Hall (off Map p58; ☐9329 9699; www.festivalhall.com.au; 300 Dudley St, West Melbourne; ☐24, 30, 34, 70) This old boxing stadium is a fave for live music acts.

Palace Theatre (Map p58; www.palace.com.au; 20-30 Bourke St, Melbourne) Features acts ranging from reggae masters to indie darlings.

Forum Theatre (Map p58; www.forummelbourne.com.au, www.marrinertheatres.com.au; 150-152 Flinders St, Melbourne) One of the city's most atmospheric live music venues, it does double duty as a cinema during the Melbourne Film Festival. The Arabic-inspired exterior houses an equally interesting interior, with the southern sky rendered on the domed ceiling. Tickets are booked through Ticketmaster (☐13 61 00; www.ticketmaster.com.au)

Hamer Hall (Melbourne Concert Hall; Map p58; www.theartscentre.net.au; Victorian Arts Centre, 100 St Kilda Rd, Melbourne) The concert hall is undergoing a two-year long redevelopment and should be back in business in 2012.

Palais Theatre (Map p112; ☐9525 3240; www.palaistheatre.net.au; Lower Esplanade) Standing gracefully next to Luna Park, the Palais is a St Kilda icon. Not only is it a beautiful old space, but it also stages some pretty special performances. Tickets booked through Ticketmaster (☐13 61 00; www.ticketmaster.com.au).

Rod Laver Arena (Map p69; www.mopt.com.au; Batman Ave, Melbourne) A giant, versatile space used for headline concerts (from the Eagles to Chemical Brothers) and the **Australian Open tennis** (p24), with a huge sunroof. Not the most atmospheric of venues, but then it's all about the spectacle. Ditto for the nearby **Hisense Arena**.

Sidney Myer Music Bowl (www.theartscentre.net.au; Kings Domain, Melbourne) This beautiful amphitheatre in the park is used for a variety of outdoor events, from the New Year's Day rave **Summerdayze** to the Melbourne Symphony Orchestra.

Revolver Upstairs LIVE MUSIC, CLUB
(Map p127; www.revolverupstairs.com.au; 229 Chapel St, Prahran; ⏰noon-4am Mon-Thu, 24hr Fri-Sun; 🚊Prahran, 🚋6) Rowdy Revolver can feel like an enormous version of your lounge room, but with 54 hours of nonstop music come the weekend, you're probably glad it's not. Live music, interesting DJs and film screenings keep the mixed crowd wide awake.

Cornish Arms LIVE MUSIC/PUB
(www.cornisharms.com.au; 163a Sydney Rd, Brunswick; ⏰3pm-3am Mon-Sat, 3-11pm Sun; 🚊Jewell, 🚋19) The Cornish Arms is a big, friendly venue hosting performances by local talents, some of them firmly from the '80s, but nonetheless interesting. There's entertainment nightly, be it open mic, jazz or DJs.

Workers Club LIVE MUSIC, PUB
(Map p122; www.theworkersclub.com.au; cnr Brunswick & Gertrude Sts, Fitzroy; ⏰4pm-late Sun-Wed, noon-late Thu-Sat; 🚋112,86) The former Rob Roy has been decked out in all retro, offering up six nights of live music, and the front bar serves up cocktails in jugs and offers cheapish mains of the rib-eye or salmon type.

Miss Libertine LIVE MUSIC, CLUB
(Map p58; www.misslibertine.com.au; 34 Franklin St, Melbourne; ⏰8am-late Mon-Fri, noon-late Sat, 9pm-late Sun) Rambling old pub front-bar that goes off, but the main draw is the diverse line-up of local and touring acts, both live and on the turntables. During the day you may hear the tones of Dolly Parton through the speakers.

Night Cat LIVE MUSIC, PUB
(Map p122; www.thenightcat.com.au; 141 Johnston St, Melbourne; ⏰9pm-late Thu-Sun; 🚋112) The Night Cat is a barn-sized space that saw the birth of the upside-down lampshade aesthetic in the mid-'90s. There are two bars, a stage and a black-and-white checked dance floor that sees lots of action. Music is generally in the Latin, jazz or funk vein.

Pony LIVE MUSIC, CLUB
(Map p58; www.pony.net.au; 68 Little Collins St, Melbourne; ⏰6pm-late Thu, 6pm-7am Fri & Sat) Bands thump away upstairs (from Wednesday to Saturday), above the low ceilings and din of downstairs. You can also saddle up for the long haul, with Pony open downstairs until 7am Friday and Saturday night.

Toff in Town LIVE MUSIC, BAR
(Map p58; ☎9639 8770; www.thetoffintown.com; Level 2, Curtin House, 252 Swanston St, Melbourne; ⏰5pm-late Sun-Thu, noon-late Fri) An atmospheric venue well suited to cabaret but also works for intimate gigs by rock gods, avant-folksters or dance-hall queens. The moody bar next door serves post-set drinks of the French wine and cocktail variety. While upstairs is the view-filled Rooftop Bar.

Dance

Melbourne's classical-dance and ballet scene has companies specialising in both traditional ballet performances and genre-busting modern pieces; see also p335.

Australian Ballet BALLET
(☎1300 369 741, 9669 2700; www.australianballet.com.au; 2 Kavanagh St, Southbank) Based in Melbourne and now more than 40 years old, the Australian Ballet performs traditional and new works at the State Theatre in the Victorian Arts Centre. Visit the website for an extensive history as well as upcoming performances. The Southbank centre also includes a school. You can take an hour-long Australian Ballet Centre Tour that includes a visit to the production and wardrobe departments as well as the studios of both the company and the school. It costs $15/8 per adult/child and bookings are essential.

Chunky Move DANCE
(☎9645 5188; www.chunkymove.com; 111 Sturt St, Southbank) The state's contemporary dance company performs at its sexy venue behind the Australian Centre for Contemporary Art. Chunky Move's pop-inspired pieces are internationally acclaimed. The company also runs a variety of dance (contemporary, ballet, funk, breakdance), yoga and pilates classes; see the website for details. From Flinders St Station walk across Princes Bridge and along St Kilda Rd. Turn right at Grant St then left into Sturt.

Kage Physical Theatre DANCE
(☎9417 6700; www.kagephysicaltheatre.com; Abbotsford Convent, 1 St Heliers St, Abbotsford) This modern dance company works between theatre and dance. This is witty and innovative stuff, well worth a look if you're not after a straight narratives. Check the website for performance details.

Classical Music

The following groups are a few of the city's main players. They perform at various venues across town. Check their websites or the local press for venues and concert dates. Melbourne also has a number of small, independent and often very innovative classical groups. Check the *Age* for listings.

Melbourne Symphony Orchestra

ORCHESTRA

(MSO; www.mso.com.au) Averaging 130 performances a year, the MSO has a loyal following. Its reach is broad: while not afraid to be populist (they've done sell-out performances with Burt Bacharach, Neil Sedaka and the Whitlams), it can also do edgy – such as performing with Kiss. The Metropolis series premieres new Australian composition and challenging works from international contemporary composers. The well-regarded Melbourne Chorale has joined forces with the orchestra and is now known as the Melbourne Symphony Orchestra Chorus. The MSO performs regularly at venues around the city including the Melbourne Town Hall, the Malthouse and St Patrick's Cathedral. It also runs a summer series of free concerts at the Sidney Myer Music Bowl.

Musica Viva

ORCHESTRA

(www.musicaviva.com.au) National group Musica Viva stages morning tea tunes (chamber music) five times a year at the **Melbourne Recital Centre** (see p67).

Opera

Melbourne has nurtured internationally acclaimed opera singers and continues to stage world-class productions. People do dress up for a night at the opera, especially opening and weekend nights of Opera Australia, but no one will blink an eyelid if you don't.

Chamber Made Opera

OPERA

(☎9329 7422; www.chambermadeopera.com; Arts House, Meat Market, 1 Blackwood St, North Melbourne; ⊕55, 59) Founded in 1988, Chamber Made Opera showcases contemporary music and music-based performance art. It's innovative, giving iPad opera and Living Room Opera a go (it could be performed in yours). Some performances are free. It's on the corner of Courtney St, which runs off the CBD's Peel St.

Melbourne Opera

OPERA

(☎9614 4188; www.melbourneopera.com; 401 Collins St, Melbourne) A not-for-profit company that performs a classic repertoire in the stunning Athenaeum. Prices are deliberately kept affordable.

Opera Australia

OPERA

(www.opera-australia.org.au) The national opera company performs with some regularity at Melbourne's Victorian Arts Centre (p67).

Victorian Opera

OPERA

(www.victorianopera.com.au) This relatively new company is dedicated to innovation and to accessibility, with B reserve tickets priced at $65. Those aged under 30 can see four operas for $100. Its program pleasingly doesn't always play it safe. It also tours to regional cities.

🔒 Shopping

Melbourne's reputation as a shopping mecca is, we are pleased to announce, utterly justifiable. It's a city of passionate, dedicated retailers catering to a broad range of tastes, whims and lifestyles. City laneways and suburban shopping streets make for eclectic, often reasonably priced, rental spaces that encourage creativity rather than conformity in shop owners; their often brave vision contributes much to the city's identity and atmosphere. Yes, the chains and big global designers are all well represented, and there are shopping malls aplenty, including Chadstone (www.chadstoneshopping.com.au), one of the largest in the southern hemisphere, but the city and its inner suburbs boast a host of alternatives. In this chapter we've highlighted a few of the unique, the useful, the absolutely fashionable and the downright weird.

See also the Fashion & Shopping chapter, (p327) for more information,

OPENING HOURS

Most shops open between 9am and 10am and close between 5pm and 6pm Monday to Thursday and Saturday. Melbourne's late-night shopping night is Friday, with many shops closing between 7pm and 9pm. Department stores are open late on both Thursday (to 7pm) and Friday (to 9pm). On Sunday, stores open between 11am and noon and close from around 4pm to 5pm. Some book shops will keep later hours most nights of the week. In the following listings, we've quoted opening hours only if they vary greatly from these general times; if you are making a special trip, it's always worth a call to check.

CENTRAL MELBOURNE

Melbourne's CBD lets you experience big-city department-store bustle as well as the thrill of finding intriguing individual shops tucked down alleys and hidden up (or down) flights of stairs. The city's main department stores, **Myer** and **David Jones** (DJs), are both on the Bourke St Mall. DJs has stores on either side, as well as a small homewares and bedding department on Little Bourke. Myer reaches over Little Bourke with a walkway. You'll also find the requisite big chain stores on Bourke St Mall too. There's a new breed of 'mini-malls' that have the convenience of lots of shops under one roof, while still retaining varying amounts of character. These include the GPO (p120), QV (p64), Melbourne Central (p64) and Southgate (p67). Walking, with a quick tram boost if your spoils are weighing you down, is the best mode of transport.

Captains of Industry
CLOTHING

(Map p58; www.captainsofindustry.com.au; Level 1, 2 Somerset Place, Melbourne) Where can you get a haircut, a bespoke suit and a pair of shoes made in the one place? Here. The hard-working folk at spacious and industrial Captains also offer homey breakfasts and lunches.

City Hatters
ACCESSORIES

(Map p58; www.cityhatters.com.au; 211 Flinders St, Melbourne) Beside the main entrance to Flinders St Station, this is the most convenient place to purchase an iconic Akubra hat or something a little more unique.

Tomorrow Never Knows
GIFTS

(Map p58; www.tomorrowneverknows.com.au; Capitol Arcade, 113 Swanston St, Melbourne) From quirky kids T-shirts to Melbourne-map cufflinks and very Melbourne sunnies, you'll spot something here to remind you of, well, here. Also at 415 Brunswick St, Fitzroy (Map p122).

Counter
CRAFT, DESIGN

(Map p58; www.craftvic.org.au; 31 Flinders Lane, Melbourne) The retail arm of Craft Victoria, Counter showcases the handmade. Its range of jewellery, textiles, accessories, glass and ceramics bridges the art–craft divide and makes for some wonderful mementos.

Comeback Kid
CLOTHING

(Map p58; www.comebackkid.com.au; Level 1, 8 Rankins Lane, Melbourne) Boys with big wallets come here for hip designer threads from the likes of Limedrop. Look for the glitter ball sparkling up the lane, and check the shop's bathroom for some Mirka Mora originals.

Wunderkammer
ANTIQUES

(Map p58; www.wunderkammer.com.au; 439 Lonsdale St, Melbourne) Surprises abound in this, the strangest of shops: taxidermy, bugs in jars, antique scientific tools, surgical equipment and carnivorous plants to name a few.

Hill of Content
BOOKSTORE

(Map p58; www.hillofcontentbookshop.com; 6 Bourke St, Melbourne) Melbourne's oldest bookshop has a range of general books and extensive stock of arts, classics and poetry.

Metropolis
BOOKS

(Map p58; www.metropolisbookshop.com.au; Level 3, Curtin House, 252 Swanston St) Lovely bookish eyrie with a focus on art, architecture, fashion and film. It also has some very special kids books and a desert-island CD selection.

Alice Euphemia
CLOTHING, JEWELLERY

(Map p58; www.aliceeuphemia.com; Shop 6, Cathedral Arcade, 37 Swanston St, Melbourne) Art-school cheek abounds in the labels sold here and jewellery similarly sways between the shocking and exquisitely pretty.

Self Preservation
JEWELLERY, ACCESSORIES

(Map p58; www.selfpreservation.com.au; 70 Bourke St) Iron cases hold a range of jewels from local artisans, as well as vintage finds. Not only can you shop for silver and gold, you can sit down for breakfast, lunch or dinner (or simply a glass of wine) while you decide. Multitasking never was nicer.

GPO
SHOPPING CENTRE

(Map p58; www.melbournesgpo.com; cnr Bourke & Elizabeth St, Melbourne; 10am-6pm Mon-Thu & Sat, 10am-8pm Fri, 11am-5pm Sun) This was once simply somewhere you went to buy a stamp, but a postfire restoration and subsequent reinvention has made for an airy, atmospheric place to window shop along its galleries. The top floor houses fashion heavyweights, while the middle and lower floors have a smatter-

CBD SHOPPING ZONES

Little Collins St, from Swanston to Russell Sts is, with a few exceptions, a dedicated menswear strip. Little Bourke St, from Elizabeth to Queen Sts, hosts the city's camping, trekking and adventure-travel retailers. Collins St, north from Queen St, but particularly up the hill from Swanston St, is where you will find the city's complement of luxury brands. All the lanes and little streets boast clusters of interesting shops. Don't miss Crossley St, at the Spring St–end of town, as well as the vertical villages of Curtin House (252 Swanston St) and the Nicholas Building (37 Swanston St).

ing of interesting Melbourne designers as well as some global chains.

Nudie
CLOTHING

(Map p58; www.nudiejeans.com; 190 Little Collins St, Melbourne) Cult Swedish jeans are cut from top-quality denim and keep on keeping on (especially if you follow its rock-and-roll dictate to spare them the washing machine for at least a month). It also does a range of T-shirts and underwear, and staff are helpful. Although it's firmly in a menswear zone, Nudies can be worn by both sexes.

NGV Shop at The Ian Potter Centre
BOOKS, GIFTS

(Map p58; www.ngv.vic.gov.au; Federation Sq) This gallery shop has a wide range of international design magazines, a kids section and the usual gallery standards. Also at **NGV International** (off Map p58).

Bison
HOMEWARES

(Map p58; www.bisonhome.com; Shop 9, Howey Pl, 273-277 Little Collins St, Melbourne) David Tunks creates beautifully tonal and tactile stoneware, that begs everyday use. The shop stocks the full range, including his signature milk bottles, plus some textiles, and wooden kitchen and table implements.

Glitzern
JEWELLERY, ACCESSORIES

(Map p58; www.glitzern.com.au; 1a Crossley St, Melbourne) Moi Rogers' horde of vintage accessories and jewellery fills this former storage-cupboard space. Pieces run from high-'70s camp to exquisite art deco Australiana. Rogers' own bold work also features.

Basement Discs
MUSIC STORE

(Map p58; www.basementdiscs.com.au; 24 Block Pl, Melbourne) Apart from a range of CD titles across all genres, Basement Discs has regular in-store performances by big-name touring and local acts. Descend the long, narrow staircase to the basement for a browse; you never know who you might find playing.

Sticky
BOOKS

(Map p58; ☑9654 8559; Shop 10, Campbell Arcade; www.stickyinstitute.com; ☺noon-6pm Mon-Fri, to 5pm Sat). This is a favourite haunt of those who are sick of mainstream press; find hand-photocopied zines here.

FITZROY & AROUND

Gertrude St has become one of the city's most unique shopping strips. Smith St is decidedly vintage, with small boutique stores taking over the Gertrude St/Smith St junction, though its northern end, beyond

MARKETS 121

» **Rose St Artists' Market** (p125)
» **St Kilda Esplanade Sunday Market** (p129)
» **Shirts & Skirts Markets** (p124)
» **Queen Victoria Market** (p62)

Johnston St, is jam-packed with clearance stores. Both North Fitzroy's St Georges Rd and Northcote's High St have interesting collections of homewares, vintage and young designer shops too.

TOP CHOICE Third Drawer Down
DESIGN

(Map p122; www.thirddrawerdown.com; 93 George St, Fitzroy; ☐86) This seller-of-great-things makes life beautifully unusual by stocking everything from sesame-seed grinders to beer-o'clock beach towels. Crazy items from Kiosk also feature in this 'museum of art souvenirs'.

Crumpler
ACCESSORIES

(Map p122; www.crumpler.com.au; cnr Gertrude & Smith Sts, Fitzroy; ☐86) Crumpler's bike-courier bags started it all. Its durable, practical designs can now be found around the world, and it makes bags for cameras, laptops and iPods as well as its original messenger style. If you're after something more specific, hop next door to the **custom store** where you can have a bespoke bag whipped up in your choice of colours.

Little Salon
CRAFT, CLOTHING

(Map p122; www.littlesalon.com.au; 71 Gertrude St, Fitzroy; ☐86) Part art gallery and part retail outlet, this little store is hipster heaven. Wearable art pieces, including bags woven from seat belts, knitted corsages and button bracelets, share space here with decorative items for your wall or shelf. Also a branch in the CBD (Map p58; 1/353 Little Collins St)

Meet Me at Mike's
CRAFT

(Map p122; www.meetmeatmikes.com; 63 Brunswick St, Fitzroy; ☐112) Mixed assortments of '70s greeting cards are sold alongside quilts, DIY kits and Meet Me at Mike's own craft books. This is also the spot to pick up a vintage bike, if your stay in Melbourne is a long one.

Alphaville
CLOTHING

(Map p122; www.alpha60.com.au; 179 Brunswick St, Fitzroy; ☐112) Alphaville keeps the cool kids of both genders happy with Alpha60's sharp clothes.

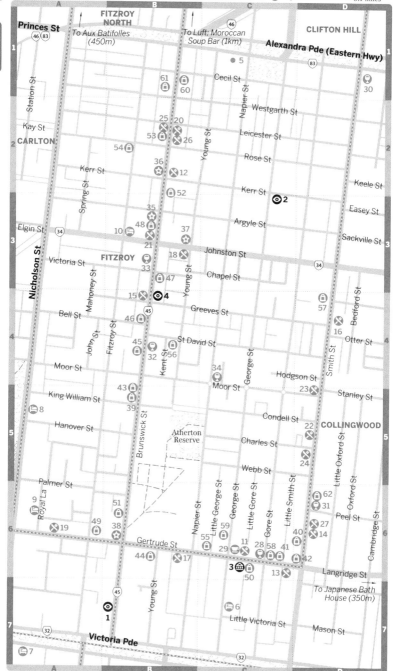

N

0 — 200 m
0 — 0.1 miles

FITZROY NORTH

Princes St
46 83

To Aux Batifolles (450m)

To Luft; Moroccan Soup Bar (1km)

46

CLIFTON HILL

Alexandra Pde (Eastern Hwy)
83

5

Cecil St

30

Station St

61
60

Napier St

Westgarth St

Kay St

Leicester St

CARLTON

25 20
53 26

Young St

Rose St

54

Keele St

Kerr St

36
12

Kerr St
2

Easey St

Spring St

52

Argyle St

Sackville St

Elgin St
34

35
48
10
21

37

Johnston St

34

FITZROY

33
18

Chapel St

Victoria St
Mahoney St

47

Young St

15
4

Bell St

46
45

Greeves St

57

Bedford St

John St

Fitzroy St

45
32

St David St
56

16

Otter St

Moor St

Kent St

34

George St

Hodgson St

King William St

43
39

Moor St

23

Stanley St

8

Condell St

COLLINGWOOD

Hanover St

Atherton Reserve

Charles St

22
24

Webb St

Palmer St

9

Royal La

51

Napier St

Little George St

George St

Little Gore St

Gore St

Little Smith St

Smith St

Brunswick St

Little Oxford St

Oxford St

Cambridge St

62
31

Peel St

49
38
19

Gertrude St

59
55

11
29
28 58 41
50

27
14

40

42

44
17

3
13

Langridge St

To Japanese Bath House (350m)

45

1

Young St

6

Victoria Pde

Little Victoria St

Mason St

32

7

32

Douglas & Hope CLOTHING, CRAFT
(Map p122; www.douglasandhope.com.au; 181 Brunswick St, Fitzroy; ☐112) This quintessentially Melbourne store has Cathy Hope's vintage fabric quilts and other home accessories with a modern sensibility. It's also a good spot to pick up some pieces of Melbourne memorabilia. Also a branch on **Collins St** (Map p58; Block Arcade, 282 Collins St).

Gorman CLOTHING, ACCESSORIES
(Map p122; www.gorman.ws; 285 Brunswick St, Fitzroy; ☐112) Lisa Gorman makes everyday clothes that are far from ordinary: boyish,

but sexy, short shapes are cut from exquisite fabrics, pretty cardies are coupled with relaxed, organic tees. Also in the **city centre** (Map p58; GPO, 250 Bourke St, Melbourne) and **Prahran** (Map p127; 248 Chapel St, Prahran).

Toolz CLOTHING, CRAFTS
(Map p122; www.toolz.com.au; 120 Smith St, Collingwood; ☐86) A unique collection of clothes made in the softest cottons, sourced from Japan and South Korea. Equal parts Marni global sophisticate, Vermont bake-sale ingénue and ascetic Japanese, the artsy, textured aesthetic that emerges is very Smith St.

If there's not an 'owl' and 'deer' appreciation society in Melbourne, then there damn well should be. These little cutsie icons have staged a takeover of Melbourne's independent craft shops and there's no respite from their big eyes in sight. They're on brooches, dangling from ears, on T-shirts and tea towels. Find them in such places as these:

» **Alice Euphemia** (p120; www.aliceeuphemia.com)
» **Counter** (p120; www.craftvic.org.au)
» **Meet Me At Mike's** (p121; www.meetmeatmikes.com)
» **Rose Street Artists' Market** (p125; www.rosestmarket.com.au)
» **Thread Den** (www.threadden.com)

Making your own craft and clothes is a huge trend in Melbourne, and that extends to good old knitting, so don't be surprised if you spot knitters on trams or participating in group knitting in pubs. Craft-wise, Meet Me at Mike's sells two wonderful craft books (*Sew La Tea Do* and *Meet Me at Mike's*) to help you fit in and Thread Den offers classes, use of a sewing lounge, and links to the crafty community.

Shirt & Skirt Markets CLOTHING, CRAFTS
(www.shirtandskirtmarkets.com.au; Abbotsford Convent, 1 St Heliers St, Abbotsford; ☺10am-4pm 3rd Sun of the month; ⍰Victoria Park) Buy limited-run clothes and accessories from emerging designers, for both adults and kids. The Convent makes for leisurely outdoor browsing. Check the website for regular stallholder details. To get here, head east down Johnson St, turn right at Clarke St then left.

Smith Street Bazaar ANTIQUES, CLOTHING
(Map p122; 305 Smith St, Collingwood; ⍰86) A great place to find second-hand Danish delights, electronic games and lamps of all shades and sizes, there's also vintage clothing and shoes. Best of all, it's well organised.

Signet Bureau CLOTHING, SHOES
(Map p122; www.thesignetbureau.com; 165 Gertrude St, Fitzroy; ☺closed Sun; ⍰86) This is a collaboration between cobblers Preston Zly and Munk, and also features designs by Robyn Black and Mm Sohn. Go there for the amazing displays as well as for shoes, clothes and accessories.

ESS CLOTHING
(Map p122; www.ess-laboratory.com; 114 Gertrude St, Fitzroy; ⍰86) Japanese design duo Hoshika Oshimie and her sound artist collaborative partner, Tatsuyoshi Kawabata, have created waves in Melbourne since Hoshinka established Ess Laboratory in 2001. The National Gallery of Victoria has ESS designs in its gallery collection; but don't let that stop you claiming one for yourself.

Books for Cooks BOOKSTORE
(Map p122; www.booksforcooks.com.au; 233-235 Gertrude St, Fitzroy; ⍰86) The breadth of this shop's new and secondhand collection is astounding, ranging from obscure gastronomic histories to Ferran Adrià's recipes in Spanish to the latest celeb chef how-to.

Polyester Books BOOKSTORE
(Map p122; 330 Brunswick St, Fitzroy; ⍰112) Take kinky and subversive and then go several steps beyond. This unapologetic store specialises in literature, magazines and audiovisual materials on topics ranging from satanic cult sex to underground comics, and everything in between. Across the road, **Polyester Records** (Map p122; 387 Brunswick St) sells independent music from around the world. Also has a branch at 288 Flinders Lane, Melbourne.

Simon Johnson FOOD
(Map p122; www.simonjohnson.com; 12-14 Saint David St, Fitzroy; ⍰112) Gourmet retailer Simon Johnson sure knows how to make your tummy rumble (and your credit card quake). This large foodie space is set in a backstreet warehouse that makes browsing a treat. Staff are up for a chat and will make you a complimentary coffee or Mariage Frères tea while you poke around the Welsh salt, Puy lentils and Moroccan pottery. There's also one in **Toorak Village** (471 Toorak Rd).

In The Woods HOMEWARES, DESIGN
(www.inthewoods.com.au; 246 High St, Northcote; ⍰86) A bright blonde-wood interior houses homewares and other witty or well-designed

objects from around the world. Head north along Hoddle St to reach High St.

Luft HOMEWARES, ACCESSORIES
(off Map p122; 212 St Georges Rd, North Fitzroy; ☎112) A neighbourhood favourite for big-name design stars like Eva Solo, iittala and Marimekko; it also knows its lighting. Look for local Marc Pascal's curvy woven shades that can be made to order in a range of colours and shapes.

Spacecraft HOMEWARES, CLOTHING
(Map p122; www.spacecraftaustralia.com; 255 Gertrude St, Fitzroy) An excellent place to find a made-in-Melbourne souvenir that won't end up at the back of the cupboard. Textile artist Stewart Russell's botanical and architectural designs adorn everything from stools to socks to single-bed doonas. Also in East Prahran (Map p127; 572 Malvern Rd).

Rose Street Artists' Market MARKET
(Map p122; www.rosestmarket.com.au; 60 Rose St, Fitzroy; ⊙11am-5pm Sat & Sun; ☎112) One of Melbourne's most popular art-and-craft markets, just a short stroll from Brunswick St. Firmly of the new-gen variety (if you find dolly toilet roll covers, it's because they're the newest thing), here you'll find up to 70 stalls selling jewellery, clothing, furniture, paintings, screen prints and ugly-cute toys. There's also vintage bike-hire from here.

Klein's PERFUME, SKINCARE
(Map p122; 313 Brunswick St, Fitzroy; ☎112) Just what you need in a neighbourhood apothecary: candles, rare scents and unguents from far and wide. Stock ranges from the utterly indulgent (L'Artisan perfumes) to the totally practical (Weleda lip balm). Staff will recommend the perfect gift (and are especially knowledgeable about perfume) and wrap even the most modest purchase with style.

Max Watts Industria VINTAGE, HOMEWARES
(Map p122; 202 Gertrude St, Fitzroy; ☎86) Maps of the world, industrial furniture, wooden letterpress forms, doctor's cabinets, scientific equipment and secondhand designer clothes: it's all here. You can grab something for a few dollars or spend a thousand. This is a favourite locals haunt and a great Ikea antidote.

Retroactive VINTAGE, HOMEWARES
(www.retroactive.net.au; 307 High St, Northcote; ☎86) This modest-looking store yields some fabulous finds. It specialises in Australian modernist furniture and stocks decorative pottery (including German and Italian ceramics). Tram 86 along Smith St will take you right past its door in Northcote.

CARLTON & AROUND

Lygon St in Carlton has a range of practical shops servicing locals and the university population. Fashion here is split between the chains (Country Rd, Witchery, FCUK, Sportsgirl) and elegant shops that would not be out of place in Rome. There's also the fabulous range of delis and food stores you'd expect in a proudly Italian neighbourhood. The seemingly endless strip of Sydney Rd, Brunswick has a host of Middle Eastern grocers as well as shops catering for its rapidly growing hip-kid population.

Readings BOOKSTORE
(Map p74; 309 Lygon St, Carlton; www.readings. com.au; ☎16) A potter around this defiantly prospering indie bookshop can occupy an entire afternoon if you're so inclined. There's a dangerously loaded (and good-value) specials table, switched-on staff and everyone from Lacan to *Charlie & Lola* on the shelves. Its exterior 'housemate wanted' board is legendary.

Eastern Market CLOTHING
(Map p74; www.easternmarket.com.au; 107 Grattan St, Carlton; ☎16) Fashion maven territory with a deconstructed Euro-Tokyo edge. The space is itself an attraction; it's a 19th-century chapel with the owner's inimitable additions.

La Parisienne FOOD
(Map p74; 290 Lygon St, Carlton; ☎16) A French interloper in this most Italian of streets, Parisienne specialises in small goods and take-home dishes that are authentically Gallic. *Boudin blanc* and *noir* (white and dark pork sausage), duck *confit* and its famous pâtés and terrines will not disappoint. It also does a nice range of bread and little pies that are perfect for picnic provisions, and keeps a range of evocatively packaged pantry items.

TOP 5 SHOPS

» **Smith Street Bazaar** (p124)
» **Wunderkammer** (p120)
» **Spacecraft** (p125)
» **Third Drawer Down** (p121)
» **Empire Vintage** (p129)

SOUTH YARRA, PRAHRAN & WINDSOR

Chapel St's South Yarra strip boasts both chains and smaller designer boutiques, but head over to Commercial Rd and into Prahran and Windsor to find a far more eclectic mix. Cute Greville St runs off Chapel, and has a good smattering of shopping opportunities too. Hawksburn village in East Prahran and High St, Armadale, feature stylish boutiques and a wide spread of antique shops.

Chapel Street Bazaar   COLLECTABLES
(Map p127; 217-223 Chapel St, Prahran; ⊠Prahran, ⊠78, 79) Calling this a 'permanent undercover collection of market stalls' won't give you any clue to what's tucked away here. This old arcade is a retro-obsessive riot. It doesn't matter if Italian art glass or Noddy egg cups are your thing, you'll find it here.

Kif & Katast   DESIGN
(Map p127; www.kifandkatast.com.au; 526 Malvern Rd, South Yarra; ⊠Hawksburn, ⊠72) Local designer Katherine Brennan sells notepaper, large screens and fabric featuring images inspired by Melbourne's leafy streetscapes.

Market Imports   HOMEWARES
(www.marketimport.com; 19 Morey St, Armadale; ⊠Armadale) Just off High St, Armadale (near Armadale's train station), Market Imports is a lovely place to source ceramics, textiles, toys and other assorted wares, which, in turn, have been sourced from artisans in Mexico and Italy.

Camberwell Sunday Market

VINTAGE MARKET
(www.sundaymarket.com.au; Station St, Camberwell; admission gold coin donation; ☉7am-12.30pm Sun; ⊠Camberwell, ⊠70, 72, 75) Filled with secondhand and handcrafted goods, this is where Melburnians come to offload their unwanted items and antique hunters come to find them. It's great for finding pre-loved (often rarely worn) items of clothing, restocking a bookcase and finding unusual curios. When traipsing around this car park gets too much, grab a gourmet snag or (less gourmet) doughnut. It's situated behind the corner of Burke and Riversdale Rds.

ak traditions   CRAFT, CLOTHING
(Map p127; www.aktraditions.com; 524 Malvern Rd, Malvern; ⊠72) Ak's stock of exquisitely soulful dolls, toys and quilts are made in Kyrgyzstan using handmade wool felt and yarn-dyed cotton. It also stocks a range of luxurious organic knits for babies, and for the crafty there's inspiring DIY kits and materials. Dinara, its signature doll, can be dressed off the peg, or you can buy knitting patterns to make her clothes yourself.

Collette Dinnigan   CLOTHING
(Map p127; www.collettedinnigan.com.au; 553 Chapel St, South Yarra; ⊠South Yarra, ⊠78, 79) Need a special-occasion frock? New Zealand-born, Australian-claimed and internationally renowned Collette Dinnigan dresses celebrities every other day for premieres and parties. Signature delicate lace gowns and underwear, as well as shimmering satin pieces and the softest cashmere knits are something to celebrate all on their own.

Fool   CLOTHING
(Map p127; 118 Greville St, Prahran; ⊠Prahran, ⊠78, 79) Long-time Greville St resident Rowena Doolan designs practical (though never boring) wearables in compelling rainbow colours. Her winter collections of cable knits and warming wide scarves are particularly strong and well suited to Melbourne's chilly days.

Fat   CLOTHING, ACCESSORIES
(Map p127; www.fat4.com; 272 Chapel St, Prahran; ⊠Prahran, ⊠78, 79) The Fat girls' empire has changed the way Melbourne dresses, catapulting a fresh generation of designers into the city's consciousness, including locals Claude Maus and Dress Up. There are also branches in the city centre (Map p58; GPO, 250 Bourke St, Melbourne) and Fitzroy (Map p122; 209 Brunswick St, Fitzroy).

Scanlan & Theodore   CLOTHING, ACCESSORIES
(Map p127; www.scanlantheodore.com.au; 566 Chapel St, South Yarra; ⊠South Yarra, ⊠78, 79) Scanlan & Theodore helped define the Melbourne look back in the 1980s and are still going strong with superfeminine, beautifully tailored everyday and special-occasion wear. Although now considered a mature, mainstream label, its clothes always manage to make a statement. There are also branches in the city centre (Map p58; 285 Little Collins St, Melbourne), Armadale (1061 High St, Armadale) and a clearance store at Melbourne Central (Map p58).

TL Wood   CLOTHING
(Map p127; www.tlwoodaustralia.com; 216 Chapel St, Prahran; ⊠Prahran, ⊠78, 79) Teresa Liano has styled Melbourne's best dressed behind the scenes for years. Her luscious label gives women what they really want: the loveliest silks and wools, and cuts that both flatter

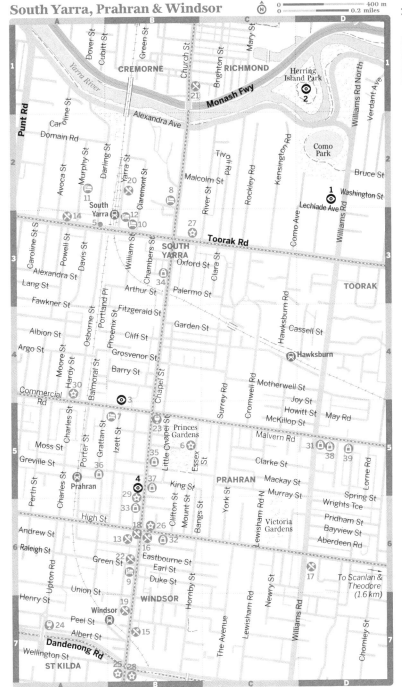

the female form and subtly demand attention. One of her soft knit scarves will keep you warm for years. The shop, which feels more like a very stylish front room, also has a wonderful range of jewellery by local artisans. There's also a branch in the **city centre** (Map p58; QV, 1 Albert Coates Lane, Melbourne).

Angelucci 20th Century   VINTAGE, HOMEWARES
(Map p127; www.angelucci.net.au; 92 High St, Windsor; 🚊6) Specialising in furniture from the 1950s and '60s, Dean Angelucci's store is well known for its treasures. There are smaller pieces such as lighting and ceramics as well as the best-of-the-bunch sofas and sideboards. There's also a branch in **Fitzroy** (Map p122; 113 Smith St, Fitzroy).

ST KILDA & AROUND
As you'd expect from a suburb so dedicated to leisure, St Kilda has a slew of interesting boutiques and a rising number of antique and industrial stores. Things are spread out, and Grey, Blessington and Barkly Sts shouldn't be overlooked.

Chalk N Cheese   CLOTHING
(Map p112; www.chalkncheeseclothing.com.au; 27 Blessington St, St Kilda; 🚊96) Chalk N Cheese offers a limited range of beautifully made kids clothes (for babes and up to six) with a gently nostalgic style and luxurious (though practical) fabrics. The vintage aesthetic carries through to the colours, which are a rich departure from the usual pastels.

Dot & Herbey   CLOTHING, ACCESSORIES
(Map p112; www.dotandherbey.com; 229 Barkly St, St Kilda) Grandma Dot and Grandpa Herb smile down upon this tiny corner boutique from a mural-sized photo, right at home among the vintage floral fabrics and retro style. This is definitely not somewhere to go if you're looking for chain-store same-same; it's also a colourful departure from the Melbourne black dictate.

Monarch Cake Shop   FOOD
(Map p112; 103 Acland St, St Kilda; ⏱7am-10pm; 🚊96) St Kilda's Eastern European cake shops have long drawn crowds that come to peer at the sweetly stocked windows. This is a favourite; its *kugelhopf* (marble cake),

plum cake and poppy-seed cheesecake can't be beaten.

Esplanade Market St Kilda
MARKET
(Map p112; www.esplanademarket.com; Upper Esplanade, St Kilda; ⊘10am-5pm Sun; ⊜96) Fancy shopping with a seaside backdrop? A kilometre of trestle tables joined end-to-end carry individually crafted products from toys to organic soaps to large metal sculptures of fishy creatures. Souvenir alert: long-time stallholder Matt Irwin sells photographic images of Melbourne at its moody best, from postcards to framed prints. The market stretches between Cavell and Fitzroy Sts,

Brotherhood of St Laurence
VINTAGE CLOTHING
(Map p112; 82a Acland St, St Kilda; ⊜96) This op shop is the most retro of welfare organisation Brotherhood of St Laurence's 26-odd op shops. There's a similar branch called Hunter Gatherer in **Fitzroy** (Map p122; 274 Brunswick St, Fitzroy).

SOUTH MELBOURNE & ALBERT PARK
The best spot for designer goodies in South Melbourne is along bustling Coventry St, near the South Melbourne Market.

Nest
HOMEWARES
(291 Coventry St, South Melbourne; ⊜112) This light, bright homewares store stocks Spacecraft screen-printed textiles as well as Aesop skincare. It does its own range of cotton knit 'comfort wear' that's way too nice to hide at home in. Staff are delightful. From South Melbourne Market head along Coventry St.

Empire Vintage
CLOTHING, GIFTS
(63 Cardigan Pl, Albert Park; ⊜1) Lyn Gardener's style is evident in every last piece of stock in this bounteous space. Vintage dresses, aprons, bedspreads, fabrics and jewellery share the shelves with some wonderfully strange industrial paraphernalia. All pieces are sourced from far and wide, or lovingly handcrafted from beautiful materials. Head into Albert Park by following Bridport Rd off St Kilda Rd.

ⓘ Information

Dangers & Annoyances
There are occasional reports of alcohol-fuelled violence in some parts of Melbourne's CBD, in particular King St.

Travelling on public transport without a valid ticket is taken very seriously by ticket inspectors; fines are a hefty $176.

Emergency
For police, ambulance or fire emergencies dial ☑000.

Police There's a centrally located police station at 228 Flinders Lane, Melbourne.

Poisons Information Centre (☑13 11 26)

Centre Against Sexual Assault (CASA; ☑1800 806 292)

Translating & Interpreting Service (☑13 14 50) Available 24 hours.

Internet Access
Wi-fi is available free at central CBD spots such as Federation Square, Crown Casino and the State Library. Hotels charge from $3 to $20 per hour for wi-fi access; it's rarely free and often expensive. If you don't have a laptop or smart phone, there are plenty of internet cafes around Melbourne with terminals (from $2 per hour).

Media
Melbourne's broadsheet the *Age* (www.theage.com.au) covers local, national and international news. The *Herald-Sun* (www.heraldsun.com.au) does the same, only in tabloid form (and with a bit more drama). If you're in town on the last Friday of the month pick up the *Age*'s free *(melbourne) Magazine* for local interest stories and reviews. The *Broadsheet* (www.broadsheet.com.au) is available from cafes.

Music is covered in free street magazines *Beat* (www.beat.com.au) and *Inpress* (www.streetpress.com.au). The latter has an online edition (www.fasterlouder.com.au).

Medical Services
Visitors from Belgium, Finland, Italy, Ireland, Malta, the Netherlands, New Zealand, Sweden and the UK have reciprocal health care agreements with Australia and can access cheaper health services through **Medicare** (☑13 20 11; www.medicareaustralia.gov.au).

Travel Doctor Little Bourke St (TVMC; ☑9935 8100; www.traveldoctor.com.au; Level 2, 393 Little Bourke St, Melbourne); Southgate (☑9690 1433; 3 Southgate Ave, Southbank) Specialises in vaccinations and health advice for overseas trips.

Tambassis Pharmacy (☑9387 8830; cnr Sydney & Brunswick Rds, Brunswick) Open until midnight.

Mulqueeny Midnight Pharmacy (☑9510 3977; cnr High St & Williams Rd, Prahran) Open until midnight.

Royal Melbourne Hospital (www.rmh.org.au; ☑9342 7666; 300 Grattan St, Parkville) Public hospital with an emergency department.

Royal Children's Hospital (www.rch.org.au; ☑9345 5522; cnr Flemington Rd & Gatehouse St, Parkville) Children's hospital.

Money

There are ATMs throughout the CBD and in the surrounding suburbs. Bigger hotels offer a currency exchange service, as do most banks during business hours. There's a bunch of exchange offices on Swanston St.

Post

Melbourne GPO (Map p58; cnr Little Bourke & Elizabeth Sts; ⏰8.30am-5.30pm Mon-Fri, 9am-5pm Sat).

Tourist Information

Melbourne Visitor Centre (MVC; Map p58; ☎9658 9658; Federation Sq, Melbourne; ⏰9am-6pm)

Websites

Lonely Planet's website (www.lonelyplanet.com) has useful links. Other online resources:

Three Thousand (www.threethousand.com.au) A weekly round-up of (groovy) local goings on.

Visit Victoria (www.visitvictoria.com.au) Highlights events in Melbourne and Victoria.

Broadsheet Melbourne (www.broadsheet. com.au) Reviews of drinking and eating places.

That's Melbourne (www.thatsmelbourne.com. au) Downloadable maps, info and podcasts from the City of Melbourne.

🛈 Getting There & Away

Air

Two airports serve Melbourne: Avalon and Tullamarine, though at present only domestic airlines **Tiger** (☎9335 3033; www.tigerairways.com) and **Jetstar** (☎13 15 38; www.jetstar.com) serve Avalon. These two airlines also fly to/from Tullamarine Airport, in addition to the domestic and international flights offered by **Qantas** (☎13 13 13; www.qantas.com) and **Virgin Blue** (☎13 67 89; www.virginblue.com.au).

Two airlines covering Victorian destinations:

» **QantasLink** (☎13 13 13; www.qantas.com.au) Melbourne to Mildura.

» **Regional Express** (☎13 17 13; www. regionalexpress.com.au) Melbourne to Mildura and Portland.

There is a left-luggage facility in Terminal 2 at Tullamarine Airport. It costs $15 to store a backpack or suitcase for 24 hours (International Arrivals; ⏰5.30am-12.30am).

Boat

Spirit of Tasmania (☎1800 634 906; www. spiritoftasmania.com.au) crosses the Bass Strait from Melbourne to Devonport, Tasmania, at least nightly; there are also day sailings during peak season. It takes 11 hours and departs from Station Pier, Port Melbourne (Map p58).

Bus, Car & Motorcycle

Southern Cross Station (Map p58; www.south erncrossstation.net.au) is the main terminal for interstate bus services.

V/Line (www.vline.com.au) Around Victoria.

Firefly (www.fireflyexpress.com.au) To/from Adelaide and Sydney.

Greyhound (www.greyhound.com.au) To/from Australia-wide.

Avalon Airport Transfers (www.sitacoaches. com.au) To/from Avalon Airport $20)

There' s a left luggage facility at Southern Cross Station. It costs $12 to store a backpack or suitcase for 24 hours.

Train

Interstate trains arrive and depart from Southern Cross Station.

🛈 Getting Around

To/From the Airport

TULLAMARINE AIRPORT There are no trains or trams to Tullamarine airport. Taxis charge from $40 for the trip to Melbourne's CBD, or you can catch the **Sky Bus** (☎9335 3066; www. skybus.com.au; adult/child one-way $16/6), a 20-minute express bus service from Southern Cross Station to Tullamarine Airport. The bus departs every 10 to 15 minutes between 4.45am and 1.15am, and every 30 minutes between 1.30am and 4.30am. Sky Bus also offers a free hotel pickup/drop off service to and from Southern Cross Station between 6am and 9.30pm weekdays and 7.30am and 5.30pm weekends.

RENTING RETRO WHEELS

Fancy cruising around Melbourne on an awesome-looking vintage bike? (And we're talking '70s, not penny-farthings). The **Humble Vintage** (www.thehumblevintage.com; ☎0432 032 450) has a special collection of racers, city bikes and ladies bikes for hire for $30 per day, or $80 per week. They come complete with attitude, helmet, lock, light and the Humble Vintage's own custom map and guide. They can be picked up from the CBD, St Kilda and Fitzroy.

Drivers need to be aware that part of the main route into Melbourne from Tullamarine Airport is a toll road run by **CityLink** (☑13 26 29; www. citylink.com.au). You'll need to buy a Tulla Pass ($4.65) or, if you're travelling on toll roads (including CityLink and EastLink) for less than 30 days, a Melbourne Pass ($5.50 start-up fee, plus tolls and a vehicle matching fee). If you have more time and less money, take the exit ramp at Bell St then head up Nicholson St to the CBD.

AVALON AIRPORT **Sita Coaches** (www.sita-coaches.com.au) meets all flights flying into and out of Avalon. It departs from Southern Cross Station around 10 times per day; check website for times. No pre-bookings are required. To/from Avalon Airport $20 one way, 50 minutes.

Bike

Melbourne Bike Share (☑1300 711 590; www. melbournebikeshare.com.au) began in 2010 and has had a slow start, which is mainly blamed on Victoria's compulsory helmet laws. Subsidised safety helmets are now available at 7-Eleven stores around the CBD ($5 with a $3 refund on return). Once armed with a helmet, look out for one of 50 bright blue stations. Memberships are $50 per year, and each first half hour of hire is free (the idea is that they're used for short trips then deposited at another station). Daily ($2.50) and weekly ($8) subscriptions require a credit card and $300 security deposit.

For fun bike hire try **Humble Vintage** (p130).

Car & Motorcycle

CAR HIRE

Avis (☑13 63 33; www.avis.com.au)

Budget (☑1300 362 848; www.budget.com.au)

Europcar (☑1300 131 390; www.europcar. com.au)

Hertz (☑13 30 39; www.hertz.com.au)

Thrifty (☑1300 367 227; www.thrifty.com.au)

Rent a Bomb (☑9696 7555; www.rentabomb. com.au)

CAR SHARING There are currently two car-sharing companies operating in Melbourne: **Go Get** (☑1300 769 389; www.goget.com.au) and **Flexi Car** (☑1300 363 780; www.flexicar. com.au). You rent the cars by the hour or the day and prices includes petrol. Both have join-ing fees (around $30) and Go Get has a fully refundable security deposit of $500 while Flexi Car has an annual insurance fee of $70. The cars are parked in and around the CBD in designated 'car share' car parks. Car sharing costs around $10 per hour depending on the plan you choose.

» **Docklands** 30/48/86
» **St Kilda** 16/67/112 or light rail 96
» **South Melbourne** 1/109/112 or light rail 96
» **South Yarra** 72
» **Prahran** 72 then 78/79 along Chapel St
» **Toorak** 8
» **Richmond** 45/70/75/109
» **Carlton** 1/96
» **North Carlton** 1/96
» **Collingwood** 86
» **Fitzroy** 86/96/112
» **Northcote** 86
» **Parkville/Brunswick** 19
» **North Melbourne** 55/68

PARKING 'Grey Ghosts' (parking inspectors) are particularly vigilant in the CBD; most of the street parking is metered and it's more likely than not that you will be fined (between $60 to $119) if you overstay your metered time. Also keep an eye out for clearway zones. There are plenty of parking garages in the city; rates vary.

Motorcyclists are allowed to park on the footpath.

TOLL ROADS Motorcycles travel free on City-Link; car drivers will need to purchase a pass if they're planning on using one of the two toll roads (CityLink or EastLink, which runs from Ringwood to Frankston).

Public Transport

Flinders Street Station is the main metro train station connecting the city and suburbs. The City Loop runs under the city, linking the four corners of town.

An extensive network of tramlines covers every corner of the city, running north–south and east–west along most major roads. Trams run roughly every 10 minutes Monday to Fri-day, every 15 minutes on Saturday and every 20 minutes on Sunday. Check **Metlink** (www. metlinkmelbourne.com.au) for more informa-tion. Also worth considering is the free City Circle tram (see the boxed text, p63), which loops around town.

Bikes cannot be taken on trams or buses.

TICKETING The myki transport system covers Melbourne's buses, trams and trains and uses a 'touch on, touch off' system. Myki cards ($10 full fare) are available online (www.myki.com.au);

from **Flinders Street Station** (Map p58; cnr Flinders & Swanston Sts, Melbourne); the **Met-Shop** (☑13 16 38) and the **myki discovery centre** (Map p58; Southern Cross Station).

You need to top up your myki card with cash at machines located at most stations (or online, though it can take 24 hours to process). If you're only in town for a few days, short-term tickets can be bought from machines on buses, trains and trams, though fares are slightly more expensive than using a myki. Using myki, Zone 1 ticket fares are $3.02/6.04 for a two-hour/daily, while short-term tickets are $3.80/7

Taxi

Melbourne's taxis are metered and require an estimated prepaid fare when hailed between 10pm and 5am. You may need to pay more or get a refund depending on the final fare. Toll charges are added to fares.

Short Trips from Melbourne

Includes »

Best Places to Eat

Best Places to Stay

Why Go?

Getting out of the city for a day, a weekend or longer is easy – the question is not why, but where to first? Should you hit the surf beaches down south? Spend a day tripping from one winery to the next in the Yarra Valley? Disappear into the tall forest with a pair of walking boots and a keen eye for native wildlife? Or get downright pampered with a massage and mineral spa?

Whatever your taste or emotion, you don't have to go far out from Melbourne's sprawling suburbs to hit the countryside or coast and get a real taste of what Victoria has to offer. And don't think you have to rough it – Daylesford, the Yarra Valley, the Bellarine Peninsula and the Dandenongs have some of the finest boutique accommodation, cafes and restaurants in regional Victoria, with fresh country air to match.

With a short trip you can experience historic towns, mountains, rivers, beaches, bush, vine-covered hills, cycle paths and wildlife. Now go. Enjoy!

When to Go

Dandenong

Feb-May Visit the Yarra Valley when the landscape is at its most colourful; grape harvest starts in February.

Oct-Nov Festivals and spring weather make this a good time to hit the peninsula or Dandenongs

Jun-Sep Cross-country skiing at Lake Mountain or a hot winter soak in Spa Country

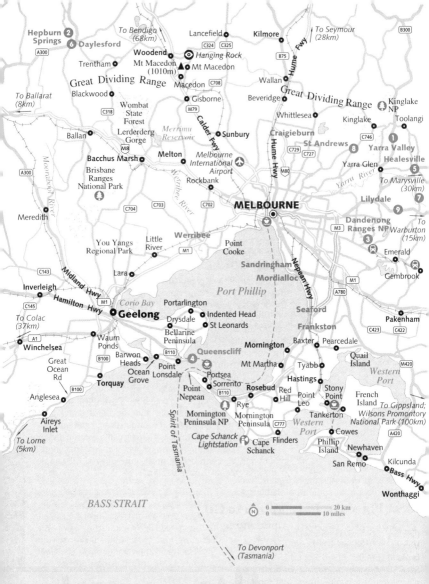

Short Trips from Melbourne Highlights

1 After a dawn balloon ride, sample Australia's finest cool-climate wines in the **Yarra Valley** (p137)

2 Soak in the soothing mineral spa at **Hepburn Springs** (p144)

3 Steam along on Puffing Billy then cruise the hills of the **Dandenongs** (p135)

4 Explore the historic fort or jump aboard the Blues Train at **Queenscliff** (p152)

5 Commune with native wildlife at **Healesville Sanctuary** (p139)

6 Dine in style at the Lake House or Sault in **Daylesford** (p147)

7 Relax in pretty **Marysville** (p142), then hike or ski **Lake Mountain** (p143)

8 Join the alternative crowd at the **St Andrews Community Market** (p142)

9 Cycle the **Lilydale to Warburton Rail Trail** (p141) in the Yarra Valley

THE DANDENONGS

The low ranges of the verdant Dandenongs, just 35km from Melbourne, feel a world away from the city and make a fantastic day trip. On summer weekends, the hills are alive with daytrippers – time your visit for midweek for the best experience. Mt Dandenong, at just 633m, is the tallest peak, but the hills do occasionally get a winter sprinkling of snow. The area was intensively logged and most of the majestic mountain ash had been cleared by the end of the 19th century. European settlers planted deciduous oaks, elms and poplars, and now the landscape is a patchwork of exotic and native flora with a lush understorey of tree ferns. Take care driving on the winding roads – apart from other traffic, you might see a lyrebird wandering across.

The consumption of tea and scones with lashings of jam and cream is de rigueur in the many cafes in the hills, or you can stop for lunch at some quality restaurants in lovely towns such as Olinda, Sassafras and Emerald.

◉ Sights & Activities

Puffing Billy   STEAM TRAIN
(☏9754 6800; www.puffingbilly.com.au; Old Monbulk Rd, Belgrave; Belgrave to Gembrook return adult/child/family $52/26/105) Perennially popular *Puffing Billy* is an iconic restored steam train that toots its way through the hills. There are six departures on holidays, and three or four on other days, so you can hop-on, hop-off and enjoy a picnic or walk. Puffing Billy train station is a short walk from Belgrave train station on Melbourne's suburban network.

Trees Adventure   OUTDOORS
(☏9752 5354; www.treesadventure.com.au; Old Monbulk Rd, Belgrave; 2hr session adult/child/family $16/32/95; ☺11am-5pm Mon-Fri, 9am-5pm Sat & Sun) Nearby to *Puffing Billy* is a blast of tree-climbs, flying foxes and obstacle courses in a stunning patch of old-growth forest boasting sequoia, mountain ash and Japanese oak trees. The safety system for the course ensures you're always attached to a secure line and the beginner sections are suitable for kids as young as five.

Emerald Lake Park   SWIMMING, BOATING
(☏1300 131 683; www.emeraldlakepark.com.au; Emerald Lake Rd, Emerald; admission free, full-day parking $6) Featuring two man-made lakes, Nobelius and Treganowan, this garden has

picnic areas, a water slide and swimming pool, paddle boats and **Emerald Lake Model Railway** (☏5968 3455; adult/child/family $5.50/3.50/14.50; ☺11am-4pm Tue-Sun), the largest HO scale model (1:87) railway in the southern hemisphere.

Dandenong Ranges National Park   WALKING
(☏13 19 63; www.parkweb.vic.gov.au) This national park is made up of the four largest areas of remaining forest in the Dandenongs. The **Ferntree Gully Area** has several short walks, including the popular **1000 Steps** up to One Tree Hill picnic ground (two hours return), part of the **Kokoda Memorial Track**, which commemorates Australian WWII servicemen who served in New Guinea. **Sherbrooke Forest**, just north of Belgrave, has a towering cover of mountain ash trees and several walking trails. **Grants Picnic Area**, at Kallista, attracts flocks of sulphur-crested cockatoos.

National Rhododendron Gardens   GARDENS
(☏9751 1980; www.parkweb.vic.gov.au; Georgian Rd, Olinda; adult/child/family $8.50/3/19.50; ☺10am-5pm) Giant eucalypts tower over shady lawns and brilliant flowerbeds at theses gardens with over 15,000 rhododedrons and 12,000 azaleas.

William Ricketts Sanctuary
                                    SCULPTURE GARDEN
(☏13 19 63; www.parkweb.vic.gov.au; Mt Dandenong Tourist Rd, Mt Dandenong; adult/child/family $7/5/17; ☺10am-4.30pm) This garden features Rickett's sculptures of Aboriginal people, inspired by years spent living among them.

SkyHigh Mt Dandenong   LOOKOUT, MAZE
(☏9751 0443; www.skyhighmtdandenong.com.au; Observatory Rd, Mt Dandenong; vehicle entry $5; ☺9am-10pm Mon-Fri, 8am-10pm Sat & Sun) Drive up to SkyHigh for amazing views over Melbourne and Port Phillip Bay from the highest point in the Dandenongs. The view of the city lights at dusk is even more spectacular. There's a cafe-restaurant, a garden and picnic areas, and a maze (adult/child/family $6/4/16).

🛏 Sleeping

The Dandenongs are an easy day trip from the city but there's plenty of accommodation – most of it luxury cottages and B&Bs aimed squarely at weekenders with deep pockets. Midweek rates are considerably lower. Try the **Dandenong Ranges B&B Booking Service** (☏9751 2347; www.drbnb.com). Camping is not permitted in the national parks.

Observatory Cottages COTTAGES $$$
(📞9751 2436; www.observatorycottages.com.au; 8 Observatory Rd, Mt Dandenong; d $220-280, weekends $560-590; ❄️🤶) Near the peak of Mt Dandenong, the four sumptuous self-contained cottages here are beautifully decorated in heritage style, furnished with antiques and surrounded by lovely grounds with formal hedges. All have a double spa and views.

Glen Harrow Cottages COTTAGES $$
(📞9754 3232; www.glenharrow.com.au; Old Monbulk Rd, Belgrave, d $230-290) The rustic cottages at Glen Harrow are restored former

The Dandenongs

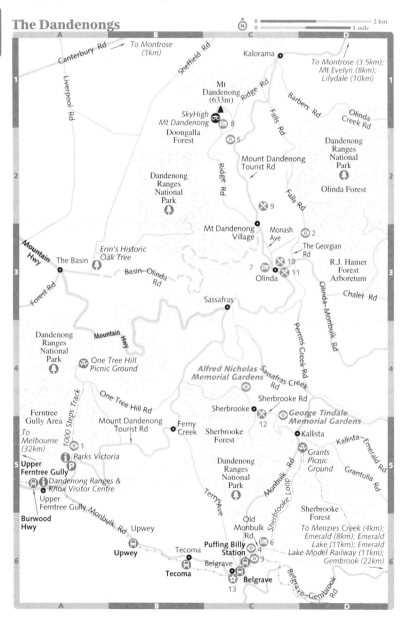

workers' quarters with lots of old-time touches such as cast-iron beds, log fires and antique furnishings, all hidden away in a tangle of gardens and forest. Close to *Puffing Billy* and Trees Adventure.

Loft in the Mill HOTEL **$$**
(☑9751 1700; www.loftinthemill.com.au; 1-3 Harold St, Olinda, d $130-300; ❄@) Right in the centre of Olinda, Loft in the Mill is a welcoming place with nine cosy suites in two bluestone buildings (modelled on an old flour mill and a 19th-century carriage house).

✖ Eating & Entertainment

Cafes and restaurants are scattered around the hills, though Olinda has the greatest concentration of eateries, including the long-running Bavarian buffet experience at the Cuckoo.

Ranges at Olinda MODERN AUSTRALIAN **$$**
(☑9751 2133; www.ranges.com.au; 5 Main St, Olinda; breakfast & lunch $12-26, dinner $18-32; ⊗breakfast & lunch daily, dinner Tue-Sat; ✦) This stylish Mod Oz place has hearty breakfasts, while lunch and dinner might feature thoughtful pasta and risotto dishes, Asian chicken salad and quince-glazed lamb backstrap.

Woods Sherbrooke CAFE, ASIAN FUSION **$$**
(☑9755 2131; www.woodssherbrooke.com.au; 21 Sherbrooke Rd, Sherbrooke; dinner mains $28-34; ⊗11am-11pm, 9am-11pm Sat, 9am-5pm Sun; ✦) Hidden in the hills at Sherbrooke, this is a

The Dandenongs

great casual cafe by day, serious Mod Asian restaurant with Thai and Indian influences by night.

Pig & Whistle Tavern PUB FARE **$$**
(☑9751 2366; www.pigandwhistletavern.com; 1429 Mt Dandenong Tourist Rd, Olinda; mains $17-30; ⊗lunch & dinner) This folksy English-style pub fits well with the vibe of the hills. The dining room is cosy, the meals are generous (duck pie, fish and chips...) and the beer taps dispense ales such as Guinness and Newcastle Brown.

Ivy PIZZA **$$**
(☑9751 2388; www.theivycafe.com.au; 540 Mt Dandenong Tourist Rd, Olinda; mains $20-30; ⊗lunch & dinner Thu-Tue, breakfast Sat & Sun) Cracking, imaginative thin-crust pizzas and a perfect people-watching terrace on Olinda's main strip.

Ruby's Lounge LIVE MUSIC
(☑9754 7445; www.rubyslounge.com.au; 1648 Burwood Hwy, Belgrave; ⊗Tue-Sun from 7pm) For a thumping night out, head to sultry Ruby's – the best live music venue in the Dandenongs. Tuesday and Wednesday nights see local and up-and-coming acts, while things crank up on the weekends with touring bands of all styles, from rock'n'roll to hip hop.

❶ Information

Dandenong Ranges & Knox visitor centre
(☑9758 7522; www.dandenongrangestourism.com.au; 1211 Burwood Hwy, Upper Ferntree Gully; ⊗9am-5pm) Outside the Upper Ferntree Gully train station.

❶ Getting There & Away

Depending on the traffic, it's just under an hour's drive from Melbourne CBD to Olinda, Sassafras or Belgrave. The quickest route is via the Eastern Fwy, exiting on the Burwood Hwy or Boronia Rd. Melbourne's **Metlink** (☑13 16 38; www.metlinkmelbourne.com.au) suburban trains run to Belgrave train station.

YARRA VALLEY

The lush Yarra Valley is Victoria's premier wine region and weekend getaway – partly for its close proximity to Melbourne, but mainly for the 80-plus wineries, superb restaurants, national parks and wildlife. This is the place to rise at dawn in a hot-air balloon over patchwork fields and vineyards, kick back with a Pinot Noir at a winery festival, explore orchards and farms of blueberries

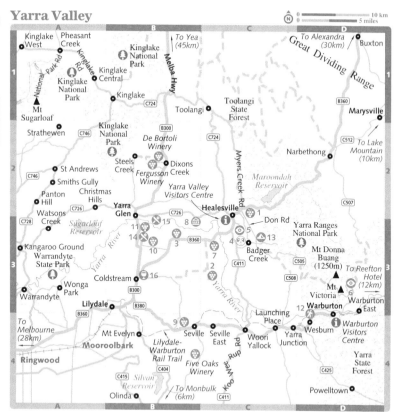

and lavender, or take to the many cycling and walking trails. While the Yarra Valley is a popular day trip from Melbourne, the region boasts some fantastic B&Bs and cottages, and there's much more to do than you can manage in a day.

The namesake Yarra River starts its journey in the upper reaches of Yarra Ranges National Park, passing through Warburton and close to Healesville before winding into Greater Melbourne and emptying into Port Phillip Bay near Williamstown.

The valley covers a huge area from the ruggedly beautiful Yarra Ranges National Park in the east to Kinglake National Park in the west, a huge eucalypt forest on the slopes of the Great Dividing Range. In the centre of the park is Kinglake, a small township devastated by the 2009 bushfires, but rebuilding with a great country pub, a few shops and cafes and an inspiring community spirit. Toolangi, 18km east, was the home

of CJ Dennis, who wrote *The Sentimental Bloke.*

In between is the vine-covered valley itself, with most of the wineries found in the triangle bounded by Healesville, Yarra Glen and Coldstream – the region described in tourism brochures as the 'triangle area'. Further southeast, Warburton is the gateway to the Upper Yarra Valley region, and there's another knot of wineries around Wandin and Seville along the Warburton Hwy (B380).

Healesville & the Lower Yarra Valley

Pretty little Healesville is the main town and base for exploring the triangular area of the Lower Yarra Valley. It's famous for its wildlife sanctuary, and perfectly located for easy access to some of the region's finest wineries – from here it's a scenic drive or cycle circuit to Yarra Glen and Coldstream.

Yarra Valley

Sights & Activities

Healesville Sanctuary   WILDLIFE RESERVE
(5957 2800; www.zoo.org.au; Badger Creek Rd, Healesville; adult/child/family $24.80/12.40/56.80; 9am-5pm) One of the best places in southern Australia to see native fauna, this wildlife park is full of kangaroos, dingoes, lyrebirds, Tasmanian devils, bats, koalas, eagles, snakes and lizards. The Platypus House displays these shy underwater creatures, which are rarely seen in the wild, and the exciting Birds of Prey presentation (noon and 2pm daily) features huge wedge-tailed eagles and owls soaring through the air.

Yarra Valley Railway   HISTORIC RAILWAY
(5962 2490; www.yarravalleyrailway.org.au; Healesville Railway Station; adult/child/family $13/8/34; 10am-4pm Sun & holidays) This historical railway has reopened on restored track with short train rides from Healesville station to Tunnel Hill and back. Future plans including extending the line to Yarra Glen.

Hedgend   MAZE
(5962 3636; www.hedgend.com.au; 163 Albert Rd; adult/child $16/13.50; 10am-4pm Mon, Tue,

Thu & Fri, 10am-5pm Sat & Sun) Just south of town, this place is fun for kids with a bewildering maze, minigolf and giant chess.

TarraWarra Museum of Art   ART GALLERY
(5957 3100; www.twma.com.au; 311 Healesville-Yarra Glen Rd, Healesville; admission $5; 11am-5pm Tue-Sun) In a striking building at TarraWarra Estate, this excellent gallery showcases contemporary Australian art from the 1950s onwards and features regularly changing exhibitions.

Tours

Eco Adventure Tours   WILDLIFE, CULTURAL
(5962 5115; www.ecoadventuretours.com.au; walks from $25) Offers nocturnal wildlife-spotting and cultural walks in the Healesville, Toolangi and Dandenongs area.

Yarra Valley Winery Tours   WINE
(5962 3870; www.yarravalleywinerytours.com.au; tours from $99) Daily tours taking in four or five wineries.

Ballooning
Ballooning over the Yarra Valley is a peaceful way to view the hills and vineyards. One-hour dawn flights with the following operators include a champagne breakfast and cost about $300 (some offer cheaper midweek rates):

Balloon Sunrise (1800 992 105; www.hotairballooning.com.au)

Global Ballooning (9428 5703; www.globalballooning.com.au)

Go Wild Ballooning (9739 0772; www.gowildballooning.com.au)

Sleeping

A number of wineries offer luxury accommodation and there are lots of B&Bs, farm stays and guesthouses in the valley – check out the accommodation booking service at www.visityarravalley.com.au.

Healesville Hotel   HOTEL **$$**
(5962 4002; www.yarravalleyharvest.com.au; 256 Maroondah Hwy/B360, Healesville; d Mon-Thu $100, Fri & Sun $130, Sat incl dinner $315) An iconic Healesville landmark, this restored 1910 hotel offers basic-but-classic upstairs pub rooms with shared bathrooms. The Saturday night accommodation-and-dinner package books out months in advance. Downstairs the formal dining room (mains $29 to $39) is one of the area's culinary show-stoppers.

The Yarra Valley (www.wineyarravalley.com) has more than 80 wineries and 50 cellar doors scattered around its rolling, vine-cloaked hills, and it's recognised as Victoria's oldest wine region – the first vines were planted at Yering Station in 1838. The region produces cool-climate, food-friendly drops such as Chardonnay, Pinot Noir and Pinot Gris but not-half-bad full-bodied reds as well.

Of the many food and wine festivals in the region, our favourite is **Grape Grazing** (www.grapegrazing.com.au) in February, celebrating the beginning of the grape harvest, while Rochford hosts a series of concerts throughout the year. **Shedfest**, in mid-October, is a showcase of the southern wineries near Warburton. Most cellar doors are open from 10am to 5pm daily. Some top Yarra Valley wineries with cellar door sales and tastings include:

» **Boat O'Craigo** (☑8357 0188; 458 Maroondah Hwy, Healesville) Boutique winery with two vineyards producing fruity reds and whites such as Shiraz and Pinot Gris.

» **Coldstream Hills** (☑5964 9410; www.coldstreamhills.com.au; 31 Maddens Lane, Coldstream) The Chardonnay, Pinot Noir and Merlot are the star picks here; good views of the vineyard and valley.

» **Domain Chandon** (☑9738 9200; www.chandon.com.au; 727 Maroondah Hwy, Coldstream) Established by the makers of Moët & Chandon, this slick operation is worth a visit for the free guided tours at 1pm and 3pm, during which you can sample the bubbly.

» **Rochford** (☑5962 2119; www.rochfordwines.com; cnr Maroondah Hwy & Hill Rd, Coldstream) Rochford is a huge complex with restaurant, cafe and regular concerts.

» **TarraWarra Estate** (☑5957 3510; www.tarrawarra.com.au; 311 Healesville-Yarra Glen Rd, Yarra Glen) Convivial bistro and a superb art gallery ($5) come together in a striking building.

» **Wild Cattle Creek Estate** (☑5964 4755; www.wildcattlecreek.com.au; 473 Warburton Hwy, Seville) One of the younger wineries in the Upper Yarra Valley; features good accommodation and the highly regarded Rustic Charm restaurant.

» **Yering Farm Wines** (☑9739 0461; www.yeringfarmwines.com; St Huberts Rd, Yering) A rustic and friendly little cellar door in an old hay shed with lovely views.

» **Yering Station** (☑9730 0100; www.yering.com; 38 Melba Hwy/B300, Yering) A modern complex with a fine restaurant, gourmet providore and bar; it's home to the heady Shiraz-Viognier blend.

Tuck Inn   B&B **$$**
(☑5962 3600; www.tuckinn.com.au; 2 Church St, Healesville; d midweek/weekend from $140/170; ✳) This former Masonic lodge has been refitted in a contemporary style – a beautiful and stylish five-room guesthouse with friendly hosts. Full breakfast included.

Badger Creek Holiday Park   CARAVAN PARK **$**
(☑5962 4328; www.badgercreekholidays.com.au; 419 Don Rd, Badger Creek; powered sites $41, cabin d $100-255; ✳≋) The riverside location here is lovely and the park is well kitted out with an adventure playground, games rooms, a camp kitchen, a pool and tennis courts.

✖ Eating & Drinking

Many of the valley wineries have top-class restaurants and cafes.

Giant Steps & Innocent Bystander
PIZZA, TAPAS **$$**
(☑1800 661 624; www.innocentbystander.com.au; 336 Maroondah Hwy, Healesville; mains $19-42; ◷10am-10pm, weekends from 8am) In town, the industrial-sized Giants Steps & Innocent Bystander is a buzzing restaurant and cellar door – a great place for a lunch of tapas, pizza or cheese platter, a lazy afternoon drink or a spot of in-town wine-tasting.

Bodhi Tree Café   CAFE **$**
(☑5962 4407; 317 Maroondah Hwy, Healesville; mains $9-16; ◷dinner Wed-Fri, lunch & dinner Sat & Sun; ✐) Friendly eco-vibes, salvaged-wood furniture and a pot-belly stove complement the wood-fired pizzas, curries and vegetarian food at this popular hippie hang-out. Live music on Friday and Saturday.

Zonzo

ITALIAN $$

(☎9730 2500; www.zonzo.com.au; 957 Healesville-Yarra Glen Rd, Yarra Glen; pizza $20, share menu $40; ⊙lunch Wed-Sun, dinner Thu-Sat) At the Train Trak Winery, this stylish Italian and traditional pizza restaurant emphasises a family-friendly shared dining experience and fine wines, with super views out over the valley. The thin-crust pizzas just fly off the plate.

Coldstream Brewery

MICROBREWERY, MODERN AUSTRALIAN $$

(☎9739 1794; www.coldstreambrewery.com.au; 694 Maroondah Hwy, Coldstream; mains $23-30; ⊙11am-11pm Wed-Fri, 8am-11pm Sat, 8am-10pm Sun) The unassuming facade of this micro-brewery-restaurant hides a little gem. Apart from brewing some superb beers and cider, the restaurant serves up a brief menu of quality dishes such as smoked trout salad, pizzas or shared plates to accompany your beer tasting.

Healesville Harvest

CAFE $

(☎5962 4002; www.yarravalleyharvest.com.au; 256 Maroondah Hwy, Healesville; snacks $7-15; ⊙breakfast & lunch) Sidling up next to the Healesville Hotel, the Harvest is perfect for fresh Genovese coffee and light meals made with local produce – salads, sandwiches, croissants, breakfast eggs and soups.

🌿 Yarra Valley Dairy

CHEESE, WINE $$

(☎9739 0023; www.yvd.com.au; 70-80 McMeikans Rd, Yering; mains/degustation platters from $18/20; ⊙lunch) This renowned cheesemaker sells cheese, produce and wine from its picturesque farm gate. Eat cheese platters in the dairy's refurbished milking shed, while feasting on the valley views.

❶ Information

Yarra Valley visitor centre (☎5962 2600; www.visityarravalley.com.au; Harker St, Healesville; ⊙9am-5pm) The main info centre for the Lower Yarra Valley.

❶ Getting There & Away

Healesville is 65km north of Melbourne, an easy one-hour drive via the Eastern Fwy and Maroondah Hwy/B360.

Melbourne's **Metlink** (☎13 16 38; www.metlinkmelbourne.com.au) suburban trains run to Lilydale train station. **McKenzie's Bus Lines** (☎5962 5088; www.mckenzies.com.au) runs from Melbourne to Eildon via Lilydale and Healesville.

Warburton & the Upper Yarra Valley

The riverside town of Warburton has a very different feel from its Lower Valley neighbours – most visitors here are more interested in communing with nature than sipping Chardonnay. The youthful **Yarra River** flows right through town and a lovely 6km walking and cycling trail follows both sides of the river.

Warburton has an interesting history, first in gold-mining, then as a timber town. From the early 20th century, much of the industry here was established by the Seventh-day Adventist Church, which operated the Sanitarium Health Food factory (makers of Weet-Bix) here for many years.

Following a disused 1901 railway line, the 38km **Lilydale to Warburton Rail Trail** (☎1300 368 333; www.railtrails.org.au) is a popular cycling route passing through farmland and wine country.

Towering above Warburton is the ruggedly beautiful **Yarra Ranges National Park**. The highest peak, **Mt Donna Buang** (1250m) is snow-topped in winter – there's a lookout tower at the top and toboggans can be rented at the toboggan run (no skiing). A few kilometres before the summit, the **Rainforest Gallery** (☎5966 5996; admission free; Acheron Way), also known as the Mt Donna Buang Skywalk, is a fantastic treetop walk along a 40m observation platform into the rainforest canopy, and a 300m boardwalk through the forest floor.

🛌 Sleeping & Eating

Alpine Retreat Hotel

HOTEL $

(☎5966 2411; www.alpineretreat.com.au; 12 Main St, Warburton; budget d $40, standard $70-95) The sprawling, 33-room, faux-Tudor Alpine Retreat has cheap and cheerful rooms. The cheapest rooms have shared facilities, while the better rooms have an en suite and views of the river. There's good pub food here in art deco surrounds.

Reefton Hotel

PUB $

(☎5966 8555; 1600 Woods Point Rd, McMahons Creek; s/d $50/70, meals $12-26; ⊙lunch & dinner) A bona fide slice of colonial Australiana, the Reefton is a real Aussie bush pub. Eat your homemade pie or Reefton burger out back near the old kiln or in the 'fancier' restaurant. To the side are four cosy little cabins each with separate but private bathroom.

WORTH A DETOUR: ST ANDREWS

Sleepily ensconced in the hills 35km north of Melbourne, this little town is best known for the weekly **St Andrews Community Market** (www.standrewsmarket. com.au; ⊙8am-2pm Sat). Every Saturday morning the scent of eucalypt competes with incense and the birdlife with buskers as an alternative crowd comes to mingle and buy handmade crafts, knitwear and jewellery, fresh produce, herbs and household goods. Enjoy a shiatsu massage, sip chai, have your chakra aligned or just listen to the street musos.

The winding road from St Andrews up to Kinglake is one of the region's great touring routes.

Locals come for live music and jam sessions on weekends. It's 16km east of Warburton at McMahon's Creek.

Good Food Room CAFE $
(☑5966 2464; 3415 Warburton Hwy, Warburton; meals $6-18; ⊙9am-4pm Tue-Fri, 8.30am-5pm Sat & Sun) This slick homestyle cafe does good organic coffee, perfect free-range poached eggs and a range of Boscastle pies.

Polish Jester POLISH $$
(☑5966 9339; 3416 Warburton Hwy/B380, Warburton; mains $10-27; ⊙dinner Thu-Sun, lunch Sat & Sun) A Polish restaurant in a small country town? Try the goulash, soups, dumplings or a Polish platter and wash it down with eastern European beer and vodka.

ⓘ Information

Warburton visitor centre (☑5966 9600; www. warburtoninfocentre.com.au; 3400 Warburton Hwy) The Water Wheel complex was about to close at the time of writing, but the visitor centre should pop up somewhere in town.

Marysville

POP 520

Spread across a valley between Narbethong and Lake Mountain, Marysville was at the epicentre of the tragic 2009 bushfires when most of the town's buildings were destroyed and 34 people lost their lives. While the town and community are steadily and courageously rebuilding, many of the businesses are gone.

Marysville was a private mountain retreat as far back as 1863, and by the 1920s was known as Melbourne's honeymoon capital. Today it's still the main base for the cross-country ski fields at Lake Mountain and is reached via a beautiful drive over the Black Spur from Healesville.

ⓞ Sights & Activities

Spectacular **Steavenson Falls**, about 2km from town, is Victoria's highest waterfall (82m). A short walk from the car park leads to the falls, which are floodlit until midnight.

Bruno's Art & Sculptures Garden
GALLERY, GARDEN
(☑5963 3513; 51 Falls Rd; adult/child $5/free; ⊙garden 10am-5pm daily, gallery 10am-5pm Sat & Sun) This off-beat sculpture garden was badly damaged in the fires but more than 100 of the wonderful terracotta sculptures have been lovingly repaired – a fantasy land of figures representing the world's cultures and characters in an otherworldly rainforest setting.

Crystal Journey of Marysville MUSEUM
(☑5963 4373; 883 Buxton Rd; admission by donation; ⊙10am-5pm Wed-Sun) In the shed at the back is a poignant photographic exhibition depicting the 2009 bushfires and a display of old farm machinery. Is also part souvenir-jewellery shop, part fairy garden.

Marysville Golf Club GOLF
(☑5963 3241; www.marysvillegolfandbowls.com. au; 956 Buxton-Marysville Rd; 18 holes midweek/weekend $20/24) This 18-hole course is in great condition and as scenic as you'll find.

🛏 Sleeping & Eating

Delderfield B&B B&B $$$
(☑5963 4345; www.delderfield.com.au; 1 Darwin St; d $285-340) The two spacious boutique cottages overlooking a gorgeous garden make for a luxurious and romantic retreat, just one street back from Marysville's centre. There are great views through the expansive north-facing courtyard windows, a spa bath and log fires.

Crossways Historic Country Inn MOTEL $$
(☑5963 3290; www.crosswaysmarysville.com.au; 4 Woods Point Rd; d/tw $99/110, 2-bedroom cottages $170) Crossways has been around since the 1920s and, remarkably, survived the bushfires. Family-friendly accommodation includes individual log cabin–style units and the River Cottage, a modern two-bedroom unit.

Marysville Caravan Park
CAMPING GROUND, CABINS **$**
(☑5963 3779; www.marysvillecaravanpark.com.
au; 1130 Buxton Rd; powered site from $33, cab-
ins $85-120) Located in the town centre, the
caravan park has powered sites, a range of
excellent self-contained riverside cabins
and plenty of landscaping improvements
planned.

Fraga's Café
CAFE **$$**
(☑5963 3216; 19 Murchison St; meals $10-26;
☺lunch Thu-Tue, dinner Fri & Sat) Fraga's is a
warm and inviting cafe, serving the town's
best coffee, snacks such as baguettes, pies
and tapas, and creative meals.

ⓘ Information

Marysville visitor centre (☑5963 4567; www.
marysvilletourism.com; Murchison St; ☺9am-
5pm) Should be in a new location across from
the shopping centre.

Lake Mountain

Part of Yarra Ranges National Park, Lake
Mountain (1433m) is the premier cross-
country ski resort in Australia, with 37km
of trails and several toboggan runs. In sum-
mer there are marked hiking and mountain-
biking trails. There's no on-mountain ac-
commodation but Marysville is only 10km
away.

ⓘ Information

During the ski season the daily gate fee is $35
per car on weekends and holidays, and $25
midweek; the trail fee costs from $11.90/5.90
per adult/child. Outside the season there's only
a parking fee of $2.

Lake Mountain Resort (☑5957 7222; www.
lakemountainresort.com.au; Snowy Rd; ☺8am-
4.30pm Mon-Fri Oct-May, 7am-6.30pm daily
Jun-Sep) Has ski hire, a ski school, a cafe and
undercover barbecue areas.

BLACK SATURDAY

Victoria is no stranger to bushfires. In 1939, 71 people died in the Black Friday fires; in 1983 Ash Wednesday claimed 75 lives in Victoria and South Australia. But no one was prepared for the utter devastation of the 2009 bushfires that became known as Black Saturday.

On 7 February, Victoria recorded its hottest temperature on record with Melbourne exceeding 46°C and some parts of the state topping 48°C. Strong winds and tinder-dry undergrowth from years of drought meant extreme fire danger. The first recorded fires began near Kilmore and strong winds from a southerly change fanned flames towards the Yarra Ranges. Within a few devastating hours a ferocious firestorm engulfed the tiny bush towns of Marysville, Kinglake, Strathewen, Flowerdale and Narbethong, while separate fires started at Horsham, Bendigo and an area southeast of Beechworth. The fires virtually razed the towns of Marysville and Kinglake and hit so fast that many residents had no chance of escape. Many fire victims died in their homes or trapped in their cars while trying to escape, some blocked by trees that had fallen across the road.

Fires raged across the state for more than a month, with high temperatures, winds and practically no rainfall making it impossible for fire crews to contain the worst blazes. New fires began at Wilson's Promontory National Park (burning more than 50% of the park area), Dandenong Ranges and the Daylesford area.

The statistics tell a tragic tale: 173 people dead; more than 2000 homes destroyed, and an estimated 7500 people left homeless; and more than 4500 sq km burned out. What followed from the shell-shocked state and nation was a huge outpouring of grief, humanitarian aid and charity. Strangers donated tonnes of clothing, toys, food, caravans and even houses to bushfire survivors, while an appeal set up by the Australian Red Cross raised more than $300 million. A subsequent Royal Commission into the bush-fires made 67 recommendations on bushfire response and safety policies.

Today the blackened forests around Kinglake and Marysville are regenerating as nature intended, and the communities are rebuilding. Tourism is still a big part of the economy here, so visiting the shops, cafes and hotels in the area will continue to boost the recovery.

Daylesford & Hepburn Springs

POP 3600

Set among the scenic hills, lakes and forests of the Central Highlands, Daylesford and Hepburn Springs form the 'spa centre of Victoria', a fabulous year-round destination where you can soak away your troubles and sip wine by the fireside. The health-giving properties of the area's mineral springs were first claimed back in the 1870s, attracting droves of fashionable Melburnians. The well-preserved and restored buildings show the prosperity of these towns, as well as the lasting influence of the many Swiss-Italian miners who came to work the tunnel mines in the surrounding hills.

These days the Daylesford region is one of Victoria's favourite weekend getaways – even if you don't indulge in a spa treatment, there are plenty of great walks, a fabulous foodie scene and an arty, alternative vibe. The local population is an interesting blend of hippies and old-timers, and there's also a thriving gay and lesbian scene here.

◉ Sights & Activities

Daylesford sits above pretty **Lake Daylesford**, a popular fishing and picnicking area; boats and kayaks are available for hire. It's an easy walk or cycle around the lake, passing the Wombat Flat mineral spring. **Jubilee Lake**, about 3km southeast of town, is another pretty picnic spot with canoe hire.

Good local walks include **Sailors Falls**, **Tipperary Springs** and the **Central Springs Reserve**; the visitor centre has maps and walking guides.

Hepburn Bathhouse & Spa   MINERAL SPA
(☎5321 6000; www.hepburnbathhouse.com; Mineral Springs Reserve, Hepburn Springs; ☉9am-6.30pm) Situated within the Hepburn Springs Reserve, this historic bathhouse is an attraction in its own right. Apart from the various spa and hydrotherapy treatments, you can soak in private or public mineral pools. Scattered around the bathhouse are picnic areas, mineral spring pumps (from which you can fill up your own water bottles) and a series of walking trails.

Convent Gallery   GALLERY
(☎5348 3211; www.conventgallery.com.au; cnr Hill & Daly Sts; admission $5; ☉10am-4pm) This beautiful 19th-century convent on Wombat Hill has been brilliantly converted into a craft and art gallery with soaring ceilings, grand archways, winding staircases and magnificent gardens.

Wombat Hill Botanic Gardens   GARDEN
(Central Springs Rd, Daylesford) Oak, pine and cypress trees fill these beautiful gardens, with a picnic area and lookout tower from where you can get fine views of the countryside.

Daylesford Museum   MUSEUM
(☎5348 1453; 100 Vincent St, Daylesford; adult/child $3/1; ☉1.30-4.30pm Sat, Sun & holidays) Next to the visitor centre, the museum houses local historical society memorabilia.

Daylesford Spa Country Railway
    HISTORIC RAILWAY
(☎5348 1759; www.dscr.com.au; Daylesford train station; rides adult/child/family $10/8/25; ☉10am-2.30pm Sun) Popular half-hour rides on an old rail-motor to Musk and back every Sunday – the line to Bullarto was damaged in the 2009 bushfires but repair work is ongoing. It's a leisurely ride, but for extra sparkle go on the first Saturday of the month (at 5.30pm) when the **Silver Streak Champagne Train Journey** (☎0421 780 100; adult $30) indulges you with champagne and finger food served on board.

Chocolate Mill   CHOCOLATE FACTORY
(☎5476 4208; www.chocmill.com.au; 5451 Midland Hwy, Mt Franklin; admission free; ☉10am-4.45pm Tue-Sun, talks at 11am & 2pm) Worth the 10-minute drive out of town, you can watch the Belgian-style chocolates being made by hand (tour at 11.30am) and buy as many as your diet allows.

Boomerang Holiday Ranch   HORSE RIDING
(☎5348 2525; www.boomerangranch.com.au; Ranch Rd, Daylesford; 1hr ride adult/child $35/30) Leisurely trail rides in the state forest.

Hepburn Lagoon Trail Rides   HORSE RIDING
(☎5345 7267; www.hepburnlagoonrides.com.au; 60 Telegraph Rd, Mt Prospect; 2/3hr $80/120, 5hr pub-winery ride $150) Horse riding for all levels, then unwinding by the open fire afterwards.

✸ Festivals & Events

ChillOut Festival   MUSIC, GAY & LESBIAN
(www.chilloutfestival.com.au) Held over the Labour Day weekend in March this gay and lesbian pride festival is Daylesford's

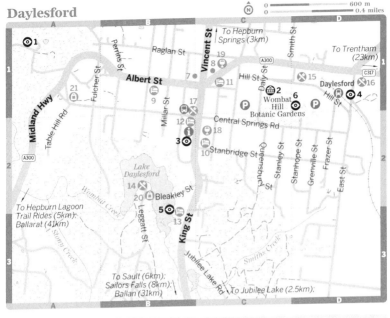

Daylesford

◎ Sights

1 Boomerang Holiday Ranch	A1
2 Convent Gallery	C1
3 Daylesford Museum	B2
4 Daylesford Spa Country Tourist Railway	D1
5 Wombat Flat Mineral Spring	B2
6 Wombat Hill Botanic Gardens	D1

Activities, Courses & Tours

7 Daylesford Day Spa	B1
Endota Spa	(see 17)
8 Massage Healing Centre	C1
Salus	(see 13)

🛏 Sleeping

9 Daylesford Central Motor Inn	B1
10 Daylesford Getaways	C2
11 Daylesford Hotel	C1
Double Nut Chalets	(see 19)
12 Escapes Daylesford	B2
13 Lake House	B3

✴ Eating

14 Boat House Café	B2
15 Cliffy's Emporium	D1
16 Farmers Arms	D1
17 Koukla Café	B1
Lake House	(see 13)

🍷 Drinking

18 Breakfast & Beer	C2
19 Perfect Drop	C1

🛍 Shopping

20 Book Barn	B2
21 Mill Markets	A1

biggest annual event, attracting thousands of people for street parades, music and dance parties.

Swiss Italian Festa   ITALIAN
(www.swissitalianfesta.com) Held in late October, this festival draws on the region's European roots with literary events, music, food, wine and art.

🛏 Sleeping

Even though there are 5000 beds in the region, they fill up fast – most places charge more on weekends and stipulate a two-night stay. Budget accommodation is limited, so book ahead. For cottages and B&Bs there are three online accommodation bookings services with offices in Daylesford:

Daylesford Cottage Directory (☎5348 1255; www.cottagedirectory.com.au; 16 Hepburn Rd), Daylesford Getaways (☎5348 4422; www.dayget.com.au; 123 Vincent St) and Escapes Daylesford (☎5348 1448; www.escapes daylesford.com.au; 94 Vincent St).

DAYLESFORD

Lake House
BOUTIQUE HOTEL $$$
(☎5348 3329; www.lakehouse.com.au; King St; B&B d $500-600, ste $740; ❋🛜) You can't talk about Daylesford without waxing on about the Lake House, a superb family-run property overlooking Lake Daylesford. Set in rambling gardens with bridges and waterfalls, the 33 rooms are split into spacious waterfront rooms with balcony decks, and lodge rooms with private courtyards. They're contemporary chic with free wi-fi and heated floor tiles in the bathrooms. The co-owner can sometimes be found painting in his studio, and his artworks adorn the walls.

Jubilee Lake Holiday Park
CARAVAN PARK $
(☎5348 2186, 1800 686 376; www.jubileelake.com.au; 151 Kale Rd; unpowered/powered sites $33/39, cabins $95-165; ❋🛜) Set in bushland on the edge of pretty Jubilee Lake, this friendly place is the best park in the region. Canoe hire is available and lower rates apply out of the summer high season.

Double Nut Chalets
CHALETS $$$
(☎0418 938 954; www.doublenut.com; 5 Howe St; d incl breakfast $150, weekend $400) The four chalets are spacious and tasteful suites that have gable ceilings and kitchenette, in a lovely garden right in town.

Daylesford Hotel
PUB $
(☎5348 2335; www.daylesfordhotel.com.au; cnr Albert & Howe Sts; d $66) This old pub is the only truly budget accommodation close to the Daylesford town centre. Small, but neat, upstairs rooms have shared facilities and access to the communal balcony overlooking the street.

Daylesford Central Motor Inn
MOTEL $$
(☎5348 2029; www.daylesfordcentralmotorinn.com; 54 Albert St; d/f from $95/130; ❋🛜) An easy stroll from the town centre, this is a standard but comfortable motel.

HEPBURN SPRINGS

Mooltan Guesthouse
GUESTHOUSE $$
(☎5348 3555; www.mooltan.com.au; 129 Main Rd; midweek s/d from $60/85, weekend from $100/130) Behind a well-clipped hedge, this inviting Edwardian country home has large lounge rooms, a billiard table and a tennis court. Bedrooms open onto a broad verandah overlooking the Mineral Springs Reserve. The cheapest rooms have shared facilities.

Shizuka Ryokan
GUESTHOUSE $$$
(☎5348 2030; www.shizuka.com.au; 7 Lakeside Dr; d $250-350) Inspired by traditional places of renewal and rejuvenation in Japan, this traditional minimalist getaway has six rooms

Hepburn Springs 🧭 | 0 — 200 m
0 — 0.05 miles

TAKING TO THE WATERS

The Daylesford and Hepburn Springs region is famous for its rejuvenating mineral spa treatments. Wrap yourself in a fluffy white dressing gown, slip your feet into a hydrotherapy sandals, sit back and relax. You're about to be bubbled and scrubbed, oiled and steamed.

» **Daylesford Day Spa** (☑5348 2331; www.daylesforddayspa.com.au; 25 Albert St, Daylesford) Start with a vitamin-rich mud body mask and steam in a body-care cocoon, before a scalp massage and Vichy shower.

» **Endota Spa** (☑5348 1169; www.endota.com.au; Central Springs Rd, Daylesford) Hot stones and Hawaiian lomi lomi massage.

» **Hepburn Bathhouse & Spa** (☑5321 6000; www.hepburnbathhouse.com; Mineral Springs Reserve, Hepburn Springs) Where it all began in 1896, this renovated resort specialises in hydrotherapy and vanilla milk baths.

» **Massage Healing Centre** (☑5348 1099; www.massagehealingcentre.com.au; 5/11 Howe St, Daylesford) For a modest, down-to-earth alternative to the glitz-and-glam spa resorts listed here, try this place.

» **Mineral Spa at Peppers** (☑5348 6200; www.mineralspa.com.au; Springs Retreat, 124 Main Rd, Hepburn Springs) Have an algae gel wrap, based on an ancient Chinese treatment, then move into the lavender steam room, or take a soft-pack float.

» **Salus** (☑5348 3329; www.lakehouse.com.au; Lake House, King St, Daylesford) The pampering starts as you walk through a small rainforest to your exotic jasmine-flower bath in a cedar-lined tree house overlooking the lake.

» **Shizuka Ryokan** (☑5348 2030; www.shizuka.com.au; 7 Lakeside Dr, Hepburn Springs) Shiatsu massage, geisha facials and spa treatments with natural sea salts and seaweed extracts, ginseng and green tea at this Japanese-style country spa retreat.

with private Japanese gardens, tatami matting and plenty of green tea. Not suitable for children.

Daylesford Wildwood YHA HOSTEL $
(☑5348 4435; www.mooltan.com.au/2008/ww/wildwood.htm; 42 Main Rd; dm/s/d from $27/40/65) You'd hardly know this charming 1920s cottage with a grand lounge room is a youth hostel. The timber deck at the back looks over the garden.

Continental House GUESTHOUSE $
(☑5348 2005; www.hepburnretreatcentre.com.au; 9 Lone Pine Ave; s/d $50/90, cottages $100/130) Also called the Hepburn Retreat Centre, this rambling, timber guesthouse is a little slice of alternative-lifestyle heaven and is as much a yoga retreat as a place to crash. Basic rooms in the house, cottages in the garden, a laid-back vibe, yoga classes and a vegan cooking course. You'll need to BYO linen.

✖ Eating

These two towns combined are walk-in gourmet treats. Every second business on Vincent St in Daylesford is a cafe or food-

store and there's a buzzing atmosphere here on weekends.

DAYLESFORD

Lake House MODERN AUSTRALIAN $$$
(☑5348 3329; www.lakehouse.com.au; King St; mains $36-38; ☺lunch & dinner) The Lake House has long been regarded as Daylesford's top dining experience and it doesn't disappoint with stylish purple high-back furniture, picture windows showing off Lake Daylesford, a superb seasonal menu, an award-winning wine list and impressive service.

Sault MODERN AUSTRALIAN $$$
(☑5348 6555; www.sault.com.au; 2349 Ballan Rd, Sailors Falls; mains $29-40; ☺lunch Fri-Sun, dinner Wed-Sun) Surrounded by lavender and lakes in a grand building about 6km south of Daylesford, stylish Sault is a seriously fine-dining restaurant with a reputation for innovative dishes using local produce. Wednesday is 'locals' night' – a meal and drink is $25.

Cliffy's Emporium DELI, CAFE $$
(☑5348 3279; 28 Raglan St; mains $12-25; ☺breakfast & lunch, dinner Sat; ☑) Behind the vine-covered verandah of this local

institution is an old-world shop crammed with organic vegies, cheese, preserves and the spicy aromas of fruit chutneys and roasting coffee. Occupying a narrow side-section, the busy cafe is perfect for breakfast, pies and baguettes.

Farmers Arms GASTROPUB $$
(✆5348 2091; www.farmersarms.com.au; 1 East St, Daylesford; mains $26-36; ⊘dinner nightly, lunch Sat & Sun) Modern and classical, both in the surroundings and the food, meld tastefully at this classic country gastropub.

Koukla Café PIZZA $$
(✆5348 2363; www.frangosandfrangos.com; 82 Vincent St; mains $15-25; ⊘breakfast, lunch & dinner) Part of Frangos & Frangos, this moody European-style corner cafe is a great place for coffee on the couch, or a sourdough wood-fired pizza for lunch.

Boat House Cafe CAFE $$
(✆5348 1387; 1 Leggatt St; mains $14-24; ⊘breakfast & lunch) On a sunny day the views from the timber deck over Lake Daylesford are reason enough to stop for coffee or a light lunch in this old boatshed.

HEPBURN SPRINGS

Chowder House CAFE $$
(✆5348 2221; 97 Main Rd; mains $6.50-20; ⊘breakfast & lunch Wed-Sun) The creamy seafood chowder here practically walks out the door and it can be hard to snare a seat on the weekends. The chunky soups, including salmon and chicken, are complemented by fresh corn bread, a hearty breakfast menu and cheerful service, even when it's packed to the hilt.

Red Star Café CAFE $$
(✆5348 3329; www.redstar.com.au; 115 Main Rd; mains $10-22; ⊘8am-4pm) The weatherboard shopfront is like someone's home, with loungy couches, bookshelves, great music, a garden out the back and funky local vibe. Great place for a morning coffee or lunch of foccacia, risotto or steak sandwich.

Drinking & Entertainment

Most of the best places to drink around Daylesford and Hepburn Springs are also restaurants serving seriously good food.

Perfect Drop WINE BAR
(✆5348 3373; www.aperfectdrop.com; 5 Howe St, Daylesford; ⊘dinner daily, lunch Sat & Sun) This sweet little wine bar and restaurant really is the place for a perfect drop, with local wines a speciality. It has a relaxed, loungy feel for drinking and chatting, and top-notch food with lots of share plates to sample.

Breakfast & Beer CAFE, BAR
(✆5348 1778; www.breakfastandbeer.com.au; 117 Vincent St, Daylesford) Straight out of a Belgian backstreet, this inspired European-style cafe stocks fine local and imported beer, with a boutique menu strong on local produce including innovative breakfast-brunch fare.

Old Hepburn Hotel PUB
(✆5348 2207; www.oldhepburnhotel.com.au; 236 Main Rd, Hepburn Springs) A great country pub, the Old Hepburn makes for a great night out with live music Friday and Saturday nights and some Sunday afternoons (usually free). The pub food is good and the locals are friendly.

WORTH A DETOUR

Just 10km north of Daylesford, **Mt Franklin** is an extinct volcanic crater that you can drive straight into. Known to the Dja Dja Wurrung traditional owners as Lalgambook, it's a beautiful place with forest-covered walking trails that take you through lush vegetation, a picnic area and a summit lookout. Free short-term camping is permitted in the crater (it's part of the Hepburn Regional Park).

Heading back towards Hepburn Springs, take the turn-off to **Shepherds Flat**, where there are two interesting spots. **Cricket Willow** (✆5476 4277; www.cricketwillow.com.au; 355 Hepburn-Newstead Rd; adult/child/family $3/1.50/9; ⊘10.30am-5.30pm Sat & Sun) was where the Oz cricket bat was developed. Check out the immaculate cricket oval, tour the workshop, willow-tree nursery and museum, or line up against the bowling machine. Further along, **Lavandula** (✆5476 4393; www.lavandula.com.au; 350 Hepburn-Newstead Rd; adult/child $3.50/1; ⊘10.30am-5.30pm Sep–mid-Jul) is a lovely Swiss-Italian farm and stone cottage where you can meet the farm animals, check out the gardens and produce, wander between lavender bushes and enjoy lunch in the Ticinese grotto. There are free tours of the farm and cottage at noon, 2pm and 4pm.

MACEDON RANGES

A short detour off the Calder Fwy, less than an hour's drive north of Melbourne, the Macedon Ranges is a beautiful area of low mountains, native forest and wineries, often enveloped in cloud in winter, but great on a sunny day! It covers the towns of Gisborne, Woodend, Lancefield, Romsey and Kyneton, and the legendary Hanging Rock.

Mt Macedon

The scenic drive up Mt Macedon, a 1010m-high extinct volcano, passes grand mansions and gardens, taking you to picnic areas, walking trails, sweeping lookouts and the huge **memorial cross** near the summit car park. There's a cafe and barbecue area at Cameron's Picnic Area.

Woodend

This pleasant town 13km from Mt Macedon is easily reached by train from Melbourne and makes a popular base for road cyclists and mountain-bikers exploring the Macedon Ranges. It's also the gateway to Hanging Rock.

Woodend Visitor Centre (⏹5427 2033; www.visitmacedonranges.com; High St) has local information.

High St has some great cafes and foodstores. There's retro style at the **Village Larder** (⏹5427 3399; 81 High St; mains $12-19; ⊘breakfast & lunch), where local organic produce is crafted into some interesting dishes. A few doors down, **Maloa House Gourmet Delights** (⏹5427 1608; 97 High St; mains $8-15; ⊘breakfast & lunch Wed-Mon) is another local favourite for breakfast and good coffee.

In the historic Keating's Hotel, **Holgate Brewhouse** (⏹5427 2510; www.holgatebrewhouse.com; 79 High St; mains $26-30; ⊘lunch Tue-Sun, dinner daily) is a cracking brewery pub producing a range of hand-pumped European-style ales and lagers on site. Try a tasting paddle ($10). The kitchen serves hearty Mod Oz bistro food.

Hanging Rock

Made famous by the spooky Joan Lindsay novel (and subsequent film) *Picnic at Hanging Rock*, about the disappearance of a group of 19th-century schoolgirls, **Hanging Rock** (per vehicle $10; ⊘9am-5pm) is an ancient and captivating place. The volcanic rock formations are the sacred site of the traditional owners, the Wurundjeri people, but you're welcome to clamber up the rocks along the 20-minute path to the summit, from where there are views of Mt Macedon and the surrounding countryside. The walk-through Hanging Rock Discovery Centre explains some of the history and geology and there's a good cafe next door.

Spreading out below the rock is a cricket ground and a **racecourse** (www.hangingrockracingclub.com.au), which hosts two excellent picnic race meetings on New Year's Day and Australia Day.

Palais　　　　　　　　　　LIVE MUSIC
(⏹5348 4849; www.thepalais.com.au; 111 Main Rd, Hepburn Springs; ⊘from 6pm Thu-Sun) This Hepburn institution in an atmospheric 1920s theatre is now a restaurant, cafe and cocktail bar with lush lounge chairs and a pool table. There's a regular schedule of gigs featuring well-known touring artists, and open-mic nights on the first Thursday of the month.

 Shopping

Daylesford is jam-packed with shops selling antiques, curios, retro and New Age paraphernalia. Check out the **Daylesford Sun-**day Market (⊘8am-2pm Sun) at the old train station.

Mill Markets　　　　　　　　　MARKET
(⏹5348 4332; www.millmarkets.com.au; 105 Central Springs Rd, Daylesford; ⊘10am-6pm) Large enough to park a Boeing 747, this barn of a market houses a mind-boggling array of antiques and collectables.

Book Barn　　　　　　　　　　BOOKS
(cnr Leggatt & Bleakley Sts, Daylesford; ⊘11am-5.30pm) This tiny bookshop by the lake manages to squeeze in a big range of quality secondhand books, and a great little cafe with a deck overlooking the lake.

ⓘ Information

Daylesford visitor centre (☏5321 6123; www.
visitdaylesford.com; 98 Vincent St, Daylesford;
◷9am-5pm; @) A cheery place, with stacks of
information. It boasts a powerful search engine
which will give you all your accommodation
options, but doesn't handle bookings.

Daylesford library (☏5348 2800; cnr Bridport
& Albert Sts, Daylesford; ◷10am-6pm Mon-Fri,
10am-1pm Sat; @🛜) Free internet access.

ⓘ Getting There & Away

Daily **V/Line** (☏13 61 96) train and coach services connect Melbourne to Daylesford ($10,
two hours): by train to Woodend then bus to
Daylesford. The buses run from Bridport St opposite the fire station.

QUEENSCLIFF & THE BELLARINE PENINSULA

New wineries flank the hillsides of the Bellarine Peninsula, but visitors have been coming
here for its seaside village ambience for centuries. The Bellarine almost forms a connec-
tion with the Mornington Peninsula – there's
only a 3.5km-wide stretch of water between
Point Nepean on the Mornington Peninsula
and the Bellarine's Point Lonsdale. Besides
watching ships being navigated through that
stretch there's gourmet food to try, beaches
to relax on (or dive and snorkel off) and af-
fluent villages to meander through.

Accommodation prices soar from Christmas to the end of January, when even
caravan parks have minimum-stay requirements. Weekends, even in the depths of winter, also see prices rise.

ⓘ Getting There & Away
Bus

McHarry's Buslines (☏5223 2111; www.mcharrys
.com.au) Connects Geelong with most peninsula towns. A two-hour ticket costs $3.20
($3 with myki), taking you to Barwon
Heads (30 minutes), Ocean Grove (45 minutes), Portarlington (45 minutes), Queenscliff (one hour) and Point Lonsdale (55
minutes). Full-day ticket is $6.40 (myki $6).

Car

From Melbourne, the Bellarine Peninsula
is easily accessible via the Princess Fwy
(M1) to Geelong. Rather than taking the
Geelong bypass, head through Geelong to
the Bellarine Hwy (route 91).

Ferry

Queenscliff-Sorrento Car & Passenger Ferries
(☏5258 3244; www.searoad.com.au; one-way
foot passenger adult/child $10/8, 2 adults & car
standard/peak $63/69; ◷hourly 7am-6pm) Runs
between Queenscliff and Sorrento.

Queenscliff
POP 3300

Historic Queenscliff is a lovely spot, popular with daytripping and overnighting Melburnians who come for fine food and wine,
boutique shopping and leisurely walks along
the beach. The views across the Port Phillip
Heads and Bass Strait are glorious, and a
new observation tower by the ferry terminal
shows the town and surrounds off beautifully.

Queenscliff was established for the pilots
who to this day steer all ships through the
treacherous Port Phillip Heads. Known as
'the Rip', this is one of the most dangerous
seaways in the world. In the 1850s Queenscliff was a favoured settlement for diggers
who'd struck it rich on the goldfields, and
wealthy Melburnians and the Western District's squattocracy flocked to the town. Ex-
travagant hotels and guesthouses built then
still operate today, giving Queenscliff a historic charm and grandness.

◉ Sights & Activities

Historic buildings line Gellibrand St. Check
out the old **Ozone Hotel** (now apartments),
Lathamstowe (44 Gellibrand St), **Queenscliff
Hotel** (16 Gellibrand St), and a row of **old pilots'
cottages** (66 & 68 Gellibrand St) dating back to
1853. The main drag, Hesse St, runs parallel to
Gellibrand St. King St takes you to Point Lonsdale, and the ferry terminal is on Larkin Pde.
The visitor centre runs the 45-minute guided
Queenscliff Heritage Walk ($12 incl afternoon
tea) at 2pm each Saturday or by appointment.

FREE **Observation Tower**   LANDMARK
(Wharf Street) Check out the 360-
degree views from this hard-to-miss, and
aptly named, tower.

Fort Queenscliff   HISTORIC SITE
(☏5258 1488; cnr Gellibrand & King Sts; adult/
child/family $10/5/25; ◷tours 1pm & 3pm Sat &
Sun) This fort was built in 1882 to protect
Melbourne from a feared Russian invasion,
although some of the buildings within the
grounds date from the 1860s. The 30-minute
guided tours take in the military museum,
magazine, cells and Black Lighthouse.

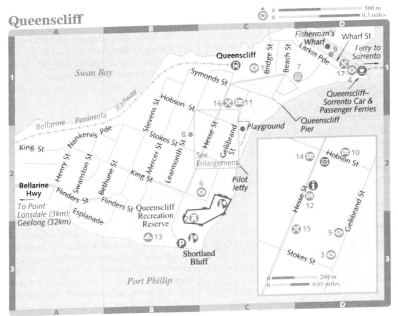

Queenscliff Maritime Museum MUSEUM
(☏5258 3440; 1 Weeroona Pde; adult/child $5/3; ⏱10.30am-4.30pm Mon-Fri, 1.30-4.30pm Sat & Sun) is home of the last lifeboat to serve the Rip, and out back there's a quaint boat shed lined with paintings. They also run 30-minute tours of the working Point Lonsdale Lighthouse.

Bellarine Peninsula Railway STEAM TRAIN
(☏5258 2069; www.bpr.org.au; Queenscliff train station; return adult/child/family $20/12/50; ⏱departs 11.15am, 1.40pm & 2.45pm Sun year-round, Tue & Thu school holidays, daily 26 Dec-9 Jan, Tue-Thu, Sat & Sun mid–late Jan) Run by a group of cheerful volunteer steam-train tragics, and has beautiful trains plying the 1¾-hour return journey to Drysdale. Popular with cyclists, joggers and walkers, the adjacent **Bellarine Rail Trail** runs 34km between the Geelong Showgrounds and Queenscliff.

Sea-All Dolphin Swims
SWIMMING, DOLPHIN-WATCHING
(☏5258 3889; www.dolphinswims.com.au; Larkin Pde; sightseeing adult/child $70/60, 3½hr snorkel $130/115; ⏱8am & 1pm Sep-May) Offers sight-seeing tours and swims with seals and dolphins in Port Phillip Bay.

Queenscliff

Queenscliff Dive Centre
DIVING

(☎5258 1188; www.divequeenscliff.com.au; 37 Learmonth St; per dive with/without gear $125/59) Can get certified divers out to see recently (and deliberately) sunk HMAS *Canberra* ($139/$74) and other wrecks.

★☆ Festivals & Events

Queenscliff Music Festival
MUSIC

(☎5258 4816; www.qmf.net.au; last weekend Nov) Features Australian musos with a folksy, bluesy bent.

Blues Train
MUSIC

(www.thebluestrain.com.au) Get your foot tapping with irregular train trips that feature rootsy music and meals; check the website for dates and artists.

⌁ Sleeping

Vue Grand
HOTEL $$$

(☎5258 1544; www.vuegrand.com.au; 46 Hesse Street; incl breakfast Turret from $400, traditional r $200) The Vue's traditional rooms are nothing on its modern, recently opened, turret suite (boasting 360-degree views) and bayview rooms (with freestanding baths in the lounge), but prices differ by hundreds. If you can't get the room, the turret level deck is a fine spot for a beverage or two on a sunny day.

Queenscliff Hotel
BOUTIQUE HOTEL $$

(☎5258 1066; www.queenscliffhotel.com.au; 16 Gellibrand St; d from $149; ❄@) Classified by the National Trust, this is a superb, authentically old-world luxury hotel. Small Victorian-style rooms have no telephones or TVs, and bathrooms are shared. You can relax in the comfortable guest lounges or dine and drink at the wonderful restaurant and bar.

Athelstane House
BOUTIQUE HOTEL $$

(☎5258 1024; www.athelstane.com.au; 4 Hobson St; r from $160) After changing from a food-focus to an accommodation-focus, Athelstane house has comfortable rooms in a beautifully kept historical building. Its restaurant prices are not bank-breaking.

Queenscliff Inn
HOTEL, HOSTEL $

(☎5258 4600; www.queenscliffinn.com; 59 Hesse St; inn d/f without bathroom incl breakfast $100/200, hostel dm/s/d $30/70/84; ❄🛜) This Edwardian inn has a choice of period-style rooms and four-bed dorms. There's a beautiful common area and a good restaurant on site, as well as a self-catering kitchen.

Queenscliff Tourist Parks
CAMPING GROUND, CABINS $

(☎5258 1765; www.queensclifftouristparks.com. au; 134 Hesse St; unpowered sites $24, cabins $147) This simple, council-run camping ground on Queenscliff's recreation reserve is the closest one to town and right near the beach. Shady sites are scarce.

Queenscliff Dive Centre
HOSTEL $

(☎5258 1188; www.divequeenscliff.com.au; 37 Learmonth St; dm/d incl breakfast $35/140; 🛏) This dive operator has hostel-style accommodation at its Learmonth St office. The terrific shared kitchen and lounge facilities are bright and airy in a central atrium, while the simple rooms are out the back. BYO linen.

✕ Eating

360Q
MODERN AUSTRALIAN $$

(☎5257 4200; www.360q.com.au; 2 Wharf St; mains $19-32; ⊘breakfast Sat & Sun, lunch daily, dinner Fri & Sat) Queenscliff is famous for its seafood, and here's the best location to try it. Sitting pretty at the base of Queenscliff's Observation Tower, 360Q serves up twice-cooked blue-eye fillet and marinated scallops right by the marina.

Café Gusto
CAFE $

(☎5258 3604; 25 Hesse St; breakfast $7-12, lunch $14-16; ⊘breakfast & lunch daily, dinner Fri & Sat) Another favourite Queenscliff eatery, great for breakfast with a spacious garden out the back. Even basics such as sausages become gourmet snags, served in sourdough with onion and homemade tomato relish.

Lix
CAFE $

(Shop 6/4 Wharf St; meals $5; ⊘breakfast & lunch daily) This new water-side cafe serves up simple toasted sandwiches, and more-ish milkshakes and coffee.

Apostle
MODERN AUSTRALIAN $$

(☎5258 3097; www.apostlequeenscliff.com.au; 79 Hesse St; mains $20-32; ⊘breakfast & lunch daily, dinner Fri-Sun) Ensconced in a lofty former church (c 1888), with exquisite stained-glass windows and a terrific sloping floor, Apostle serves up local goodies (like the local mussels in its seafood fettuccine) in a relaxed far-from-churchy environment.

❶ Information

Queenscliff visitor centre (☎5258 4843; www.queenscliffe.vic.gov.au; 55 Hesse St; ⊘9am-5pm; @) Internet access $6 per hour (also available next door at the library).

Point Lonsdale

POP 2500

Point Lonsdale, 5km southwest of Queenscliff, is a laid-back community with cafes and an operational 1902 lighthouse. From the foreshore car park you can walk to the Rip View lookout to watch ships entering the Rip, to Point Lonsdale Pier and to the lighthouse. There's good surf off the rocky beach below the car park.

Below the lighthouse is Buckley's Cave, where William Buckley lived with Aborigines for 32 years after he escaped from the Sorrento convict settlement (see boxed text, p221).

Sleeping & Eating

Point Lonsdale Guest House GUESTHOUSE $$
(☎5258 1142; www.pointlonsdaleguesthouse.com.au; 31 Point Lonsdale Rd; r $110-220; ☒) The huge range of rooms in this former Terminus House (1884) range from basic motel rooms to lavish B&B affairs. Lighthouse views come at a premium. There's a communal kitchen, a tennis court, a games room and barbecue facilities.

Kelp MODERN AUSTRALIAN $$
(67 Point Lonsdale Rd; mains $18-42) Here's a funky, modern cafe-restaurant where locals come for all-day breakfasts, lunchtime pita-bread wraps, and Asian and Mod Oz-inspired evening meals, matched with wine from its long list.

Grow Naturally CAFE $
(59 Point Lonsdale Rd; mains $10-15; ⊘breakfast & lunch) Serving up healthy meals cheaply isn't necessarily easy, but this small cafe succeeds.

Ocean Grove

POP 11,300

Ocean Grove, 3km northeast of Barwon Heads and 12km west of Queenscliff, is the big smoke of the Bellarine Peninsula, where folks come for their supermarket and department-store shopping. There are some good surfing breaks around here, dog-friendly beaches, and some good scuba diving and snorkelling spots beyond the rocky ledges of the bluff.

Sleeping & Eating

Ti-Tree Village CABINS $$
(☎5255 4433; www.ti-treevillage.com.au; 34 Orton St; cottages $170-230; ☒) There's gingerbread

house appeal in this compact, treed resort. Log cabins are cosy and self-contained and some have gardens and spas. The playground and communal barbecue areas make it a popular spot with families grilling their day's catch. On weekends, there's a two-night minimum stay.

Terrace Lofts APARTMENTS $$
(☎5255 4167; www.terracelofts.com.au; 92 The Terrace; d from $175; ❄️🤶) These four luxurious, self-contained, split-level apartments have mezzanine-level bedrooms overlooking open-plan living areas. A short walk to the beach and town, these apartments have wood combustion fires, TVs with DVD and relaxed, modern decor. Kids stay free.

7th Wave MODERN AUSTRALIAN $$
(64b The Terrace; mains $18-33; ⊘lunch & dinner Wed-Sun) Catering to casual cafe diners by day and scrubbed-up dinner guests by night, 7th Wave also features live music. Try the beer-battered local seafood specials.

Barwon Heads

POP 3000

At the mouth of the broad Barwon River, Barwon Heads is a haven of sheltered beaches, tidal river flats and holiday-makers. Barwon Heads was made famous as the setting for *SeaChange,* a popular TV series, and, over a decade on, still trades on the kudos. In a case of life imitating TV, the original bridge linking Barwon Heads with Ocean Grove was recently replaced with two modern bridges.

Feisty Thirteenth Beach, 2km west, is popular with surfers. There are short walks around the headland and the Bluff with panoramic sea vistas, and there are scuba-diving spots under the rocky ledges below.

Sights

Jirrahlinga Koala & Wildlife Sanctuary ZOO
(☎5254 2484; www.jirrahlinga.com.au; Taits Rd; adult/child $15/10). This koala sanctuary also houses roos and reptiles.

Sleeping

Barwon Heads Caravan Park
CAMPING GROUND $
(☎5254 1115; www.barwoncoast.com.au; Ewing Blyth Dr; unpowered/powered sites $24/30, cabin d/f $95/105, beach house f $225) Located right on the Barwon River, this park contains

LOAM

Don't be surprised if you're handed a home-grown beetroot or a sprig of local salt bush to smell – award-winning restaurant Loam (☑5251 1105; 650 Andersons Rd, Drysdale; ☺lunch Thu-Sun, dinner Fri & Sat) is all about stripping food back. Aaron and Astrid Turner's dream restaurant is a stunning success story hidden in the Bellarine hinterland – book months in advance.

Laura's house from *SeaChange* (you can even stay in it). It also has tea tree–shaded sites, tennis courts and playgrounds. Prices almost double between 19 December and 30 Jan.

Seahaven Village APARTMENTS $$
(☑5254 1066; www.seahavenvillage.com.au; 3 Geelong Rd; d $135-295; ✷) Seahaven, opposite Village Park, is a cute cluster of self-contained studios and cottages with electric blankets, open fires, full kitchens and entertainment systems. There's usually a two-night minimum stay.

Private holiday accommodation is managed by agents, including:

Barwon Grove Holiday Rentals (☑5254 3263; www.bgholidayrentals.com.au)

Beds by the Beach (☑5254 2419; www.bedsbythebeach.com.au)

Bellarine Getaways (☑5254 3393; www.bellarinegetaways.com.au)

✕ Eating

Barwon Orange PIZZA $$
(60 Hitchcock Ave; www.barwonorange.com.au; mains $12-27; ☺breakfast, lunch & dinner Thu, Fri & Sat, breakfast & lunch Wed & Sun, closed Mon & Tue winter) Big Bertha – the orange wood-fired oven that cooks up Barwon Orange's crazily topped pizzas – helps the mood along. Innovative menus star and breakfast is served until a civilised 3.30pm.

Starfish Bakery BAKERY $
(78 Hitchcock St; meals $5-9; ☺breakfast & lunch) This relaxed, colourful bakery-cafe makes its own pastries and bread, and serves up good coffee and massive muffins.

At the Heads MODERN AUSTRALIAN $$
(☑5254 1277; www.attheheads.com.au; Jetty Rd; meals $17-50; ☺lunch & dinner daily, breakfast Sat & Sun) Built on stilts over the river, this light, airy cafe-restaurant has huge breakfasts, local fare and the most amazing views. Its bustling family ambience makes it a fun daytime locale. After dark try the seafood bouillabaisse.

Great Ocean Road

Includes »

Best Places to Eat

» Mr Hyde (p159)

» Sunnybrae (p169)

» A La Greque (p166)

» Merrijig Inn (p182)

» Wye General (p169)

Best Places to Stay

» Apollo Bay YHA Eco Beach (p171)

» Annesley House (p183)

» Bellbrae Harvest (p162)

» Woolshed B&B (p162)

» Chapel (p166)

Why Go?

The Great Ocean Road (B100) is one of Australia's most famous road-touring routes. It takes travellers past world-class surfing breaks, through pockets of rainforest, calm sea-side towns and under koala-filled tree canopies. It shows off heathlands, dairy farms and sheer limestone cliffs and gets you up close and personal with the dangerous crashing surf of the Southern Ocean.

Hunt out the isolated beaches and lighthouses in between the towns, and the thick eucalypt forests in the Otway hinterlands to really escape the crowds. Day-tripping tourists from Melbourne rush into and out of the area in less than 12 hours, but in a perfect world you'd ideally spend a couple of weeks here. As we make our way along the Great Ocean Road we pay our respects to the indigenous peoples of this region – from east to west they include the Wathaurung, Gulidjan, Gadubanud, Giraiwurung and the Gunditjmara people.

When to Go?
Cape Otway

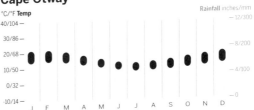

July Check out Lorne mid-winter for bright seascapes and cosy cafes

Easter (March/April) Head to Bells Beach during the Rip Curl Pro to witness spectacular surfing action.

April Chill out with the locals and listen to tunes at the Apollo Bay Music Festival

Highlights

1. Count the upstanding Twelve Apostles near **Port Campbell** (p174)

2. Camp by beaches abutting **Cape Otway lighthouse** (p173)

3. Lap up the resort-style living in **Lorne** (p166)

4. Get tree-top high on the **Otway Fly** (p172)

5. Check out the seals at isolated **Cape Bridgewater** (p184)

6. Stop through Geelong, football-proud and with a wonderful **waterfront** (p157)

7. Keep a lookout for whales off the coast of **Warrnambool's** (p177)

8. Watch the waves at **Bells Beach** (p163)

9. Get a feel for life in a volcano at **Tower Hill Reserve** (p180)

10. Begin exploring the Glenelg River at **Nelson** (p184)

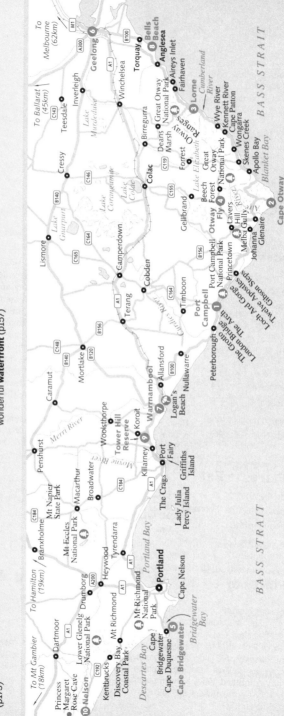

GEELONG

POP 216,000

Geelong is a confident town that's proud of its two icons: Geelong Football team (aka the Cats) and the Ford Motor Company. The Cats have had a fair run in the Australian Football League (AFL) recently, winning the Grand Final in 2007 (for the first time in 44 years) and again in 2009, while Ford, Geelong's other blue-and-white icon, continues to make manufacturing Geelong's largest employer.

The Wathaurung people – the original inhabitants of Geelong – called the area Jillong. Today's Geelong has a new bypass, so travellers can skip the city and head straight to the Great Ocean Road, however there are lots of reasons to make a stop here. Its Corio Bay waterfront has had a makeover, it's a great place for a meal, a wander or a drink in a wine bar. While in Geelong have a squiz at Geelong's wonderful and weird architecture – superb historic buildings and even Bauhaus-style industrial buildings sit next to '70s-era prefab-slab shopping malls. There's a thriving student scene thanks to Deakin University, and you'll find an edgy and bohemian enclave at Geelong's heart.

◉ Sights & Activities

FREE **Geelong Art Gallery**   ART GALLERY
(www.geelonggallery.org.au; Little Malop St; ◷10am-5pm) This gallery houses over 4000 works in one of the city's most impressive buildings. Its Australian collection is strong and includes Frederick McCubbin's 1890 *A Bush Burial*, the gallery's most celebrated painting.

National Wool Museum   MUSEUM
(www.nwm.vic.gov.au; 26 Moorabool St; adult/child/family $7.50/4/20; ◷9.30am-5pm) This museum showcases the history, politics and heritage of wool growing in a lovely 1872 bluestone building. There's a sock-making machine and a massive 1910 Axminster carpet loom that gets chugging on weekends.

Ford Discovery Centre   MUSEUM
(www.forddiscovery.com.au; cnr Gheringhap & Brougham Sts; adult/child/family $8/4/20; ◷10am-5pm Wed-Mon) Get revvy and take a then-and-now look at Ford. See the 'Cars of the Future' display and the Bathurst-winning Falcons, as well as heritage exhibits. You can buy combined Wool Museum and Ford Discovery Centre tickets for $12/6/30 per adult/child/family.

Geelong Waterfront Carousel   CAROUSEL
(Geelong Waterfront; adult/child $4/3.50; ◷10.30am-5pm Mon-Fri, to 8pm Sat, to 6pm Sun) Anyone can ride this ornate hand-carved (and undercover) refurbished 1898 steam-driven carousel (parents ride free with their children).

Freedom Bay Cruises   BOAT CRUISE
(☏0418 522 328; www.freedombaycruises.com.au; Waterfront; cruises adult/child $15/7) Join a 40-minute scenic cruise around Corio Bay.

Geelong Helicopters   SCENIC FLIGHTS
(☏0422 515 151; www.geelonghelicopters.com.au; Waterfront; flights adult/child $45/35) Check out Bells Beach from the air on one of these scenic helicopter flights.

Bay City Seaplanes   SCENIC FLIGHTS
(☏0438 840 205; www.baycityseaplanes.com.au; Waterfront; flights from $35 per person) Swirl around Aireys Inlet Lighthouse on one of these joyrides.

Wander Geelong's revamped waterfront, where you can swim, picnic at a foreshore reserve or just gaze at yachts bobbing on Corio Bay. Walking trails extend from Rippleside Park (Bell Pde), which has a playground, rock pool, jetty, BBQs and picnic tables, right up the hill to Limeburners Point.

Pick up a *Baywalk Bollards* brochure from the information kiosk at Cunningham Pier so you can more formally acquaint yourself with Jan Mitchell's 111 famous painted bollards that give the waterfront its unique character. The newest bollard is a tribute to Mitchell, who died in 2008.

At Eastern Beach, stop for a splash about at the art deco bathing pavilion (admission free), opposite the promenade.

The 1851 Botanic Gardens (Eastern Park; ◷7.30am-7pm) are a peaceful place for a stroll or picnic (or dine in – there's a teahouse onsite). The tiny Old Customs House, in the gardens, is Victoria's oldest timber building, built in Sydney in 1838 and transported here in sections. Eastern Park surrounds the gardens and is Geelong's largest foreshore reserve, with many trees planted as early as 1859. It houses the great and ultra-kid-friendly Geelong Play Space.

✹ Festivals & Events

Audi Victoria Week   SAILING
(☏5229 1418; www.victoriaweek.com.au; ◷Jan) This week-long sailing regatta began in 1854 and these days brings sailing to the public in both Geelong and the Docklands

Geelong

◎ Sights

Activities, Courses & Tours

⌂ Sleeping

✕ Eating

◉ Drinking

✦ Entertainment

▣ Shopping

in Melbourne. Around 450 yachts compete, and there's a heap of shore-based entertainment as well as the opportunity to give sailing a go.

Pako Festa MULTICULTURAL FESTIVAL
(www.pakofesta.com.au; Pakington St, Geelong West; ⊙last Sat in Feb) This celebration of cultural diversity livens up Pakington St annually.

Avalon Airshow AIRCRAFT
(www.airshow.net.au; Avalon Airport; ⊙Mar 2013) This celebration of sky-bound might and power is held every two years and attracts thousands of viewers.

🛏 Sleeping

TOP CHOICE Haymarket BOUTIQUE HOTEL **$$$**
(☑5221 1174; www.haymarkethotel.com. au; 244 Moorabool St; d incl breakfast from $200; ❈🅰) Luxurious rooms in this historic building are furnished with French antiques matching the building's age (1855). The six bedrooms have modern en suites, flatscreen TVs with cable channels, and the ground floor's 'honesty bar' is a refreshing and swanky sight. It's a kid-free zone.

Gatehouse on Ryrie GUESTHOUSE **$**
(☑0417 545 196; www.gatehouseonryrie.com.au; 83 Yarra St; d incl breakfast $75-120; @🅰) This is the best choice for budget travellers; it was built in 1897 and has gorgeous timber floorboards throughout, spacious rooms and a communal kitchen and lounge area. Upstairs rooms have shared bathrooms. Breakfast is held in the glorious front room.

Vailima Waterfront Apartment
APARTMENT **$$$**
(☑0417 300 877; www.vailima.com.au; 26 Eastern Beach Rd; d from $250; ❈) The two-bedroom apartment beside this 1908 Edwardian home is decorated in a maritime theme and has a modern kitchen and laundry, white leather couches and brilliant Corio Bay views from its lounge and sun deck. Not toddler-friendly.

Four Points Sheraton Geelong HOTEL **$$**
(☑5223 1377; www.fourpoints.com/geelong; 10-14 Eastern Beach Rd; r from $160; ❈@🅰≋) The Four Points is on the waterfront, and most rooms have sea views (or glimpses). Rooms are a tad bland, but balconies and sitting areas are lovely additions. Staff are very helpful.

National Hotel Backpackers HOSTEL **$**
(☑5229 1211; www.nationalhotel.com.au; 191 Moorabool St; dm/d $30/70) The 'Nash' (see also p160) is a friendly place and has Geelong's only backpacker accommodation, however the rooms are in desperate need of a basic upgrade and it's only listed here as a last resort.

✕ Eating

TOP CHOICE Go! CAFE **$**
(www.cafego.com.au; 37 Bellarine St; mains from $8; ⊙breakfast & lunch Mon-Sat) Go! is a fun cafe that serves great food (the local mussels are divine) in a riot of colour and amusement. The covered courtyard out the back is huge and welcoming, and staff could not be sweeter. You're not a table number here, you're a stuffed toy (the fluffy toy on your table is how they'll find you).

Mr Hyde CAFE, BAR **$$**
(www.myhyde.com.au; 11 Malop St; mains $15-23; ⊙breakfast, lunch & dinner Tue-Sun) Scoring the top star rating for three years in the *Age's* 'Cheap Eats' guide recently earned Mr Hyde the title 'country Cheap Eats champ', and it's no wonder: the vast, old bank building is filled with booths, secret rooms and stunning bathrooms. Dinner offers meze-style dishes (such as felafel-encrusted lamb cutlets) and a range of Turkish pizzas. Breakfast includes herb omelette and organic granola. Chirpy staff can help you choose from the 90 or so wines it stocks, too.

Le Parisien FRENCH **$$$**
(☑5229 3110; www.leparisien.com.au; 15 Eastern Beach Rd; mains $40-45; ⊙lunch & dinner) You can feast on classic French cuisine *à l'Australienne* (try the kangaroo fillet with bush-tomato chutney) right on the water. All the favourites on the meat-heavy menu are done extremely well.

Jack & Jill MOD AUSTRALIAN **$$**
(☑5229 9935; www.jackandjillrestaurant.com.au; 247 Moorabool St; mains $29-34; ⊙lunch & dinner Mon-Fri, dinner Sat) Choose three or four small dishes from the menu (perhaps parmesan-encrusted scallops, or grilled quail) and they'll all be served to you on one plate. This new spot in Geelong is hitting the spot; book ahead for one of two dinner sittings.

Beach House MOD AUSTRALIAN **$$**
(☑5221 8322; Eastern Beach Reserve; mains $30-42; ⊙dinner Wed-Sat) In a town blessed with fantastic waterfront restaurants, this might be the best. The modern international menu includes ravioli filled with rock flathead and fennel, and market-fresh fish.

Drinking & Entertainment

Beav's Bar
LIVE MUSIC, BAR

(www.beavsbar.com.au; 77 Little Malop St; ⊙4pm-late Wed-Sat) This huge space lined with couches and featuring soft lighting and eclectic decor encourages chilling out. There's live acoustic music each Thursday and Friday night.

CQ
COCKTAIL BAR

(City Quarter; www.thecityquarter.com.au; Cunningham Pier; ⊙noon-late Wed-Sun) Cunningham Pier's redevelopment (partly funded by the Cats' captain Cameron Ling) has brought a restaurant, cafe and boutique bar to this stunning location. Climb the sweeping steps to CQ, and check out its smart fit-out and cocktail and tapas menus. Oh, and the view. You can't miss the view.

National Hotel
LIVE MUSIC, PUB

(The Nash; www.nationalhotel.com.au; 191 Moorabool St) Live bands play regularly at Geelong's rockingest pub, which has a young clientele and upstairs backpacker accommodation (see p159).

Geelong Performing Arts Centre
THEATRE

(GPAC; ⊘5225 1200; www.gpac.org.au; 50 Little Malop St) Geelong's major arts venue uses three theatres and a variety of outdoor venues to show local amateur productions, as well as touring professional dance, musicals and theatre shows.

Skilled Stadium
SPORTS

(Kardinia Park; ⊘5224 9111; www.geelongaustralia.com.au/skilledstadium; Moorabool St; tickets from $23.90) This is the home of the mighty Cats, and on weekends in winter you can join the one-eyed crowd to watch Jimmy Bartel (2007 Brownlow Medal winner), Joel Selwood and Lingie 'run around the park'. Gary Ablett Jnr and his father, legendary Gary Ablett Sr (aka 'God'), once graced this field, as has (in a similar spiritual vein) the Dalai Lama. Tickets can be booked through Ticketmaster (www.ticketmaster.com.au).

Shopping

Head to Pakington St in Geelong West for boutique shops or try these:

Herman Huckleferry
DESIGN

(www.oktoberdee.com.au; studio 7/171-181 Moorabool St) Tucked away in an old-school mall is this tiny treasure. As well as selling her own work, artist Lauren Ferry sells the work of local Geelong designer A Skulk of Foxes.

Mill Markets
COLLECTABLES

(www.themillmarkets.com.au; ⊙10am-6pm); Geelong (20 Brougham St); Newcomb (14 Bellarine Hwy) For collectables, curios and vintage clothes.

Information

Geelong & Great Ocean Road visitor centre (www.greatoceanroad.org; Princes Hwy, Little River; ⊙9am-5pm) Look out for this information container at the service station in Little River, about 20km before Geelong.

National Wool Museum visitor centre (www.visitgreatoceanroad.org.au; 26 Moorabool St; ⊙9am-5pm) Tourist information.

Getting There & Away

Air

For **Jetstar** (⊘13 15 38; www.jetstar.com.au) and **Tiger** (⊘9335 3033; www.tigerairways.com) services to/from Avalon Airport, see p349.

Bus

Avalon Airport Shuttle (⊘5278 8788; www.avalonairportshuttle.com.au) Meets all flights at Avalon Airport and goes to Geelong ($17, 35 minutes) and along the Great Ocean Rd to Lorne ($70, 1¾ hours).

Gull Airport Service (⊘5222 4966; www.gull.com.au; 45 McKillop St) Has 14 services a day between Geelong and Melbourne Airport ($30, 1¼ hours).

McHarry's Buslines (⊘5223 2111; www.mcharrys.com.au) Runs frequent buses from Geelong Station to Torquay and the Bellarine Peninsula ($3.20).

V/Line (⊘13 61 96; www.vline.com.au) Buses run from Geelong Station to Apollo Bay ($13, 2½ hours, two to four daily) via Torquay ($3.20, 25 minutes) and Lorne ($8.50, 1½ hours). On Monday, Wednesday and Friday a bus continues to Port Campbell ($24, four hours) and Warrnambool ($27, six hours). V/Line also runs to Ballarat ($7.50, 1½ hours, three or four daily).

Car

The 25km Geelong Ring Rd runs from Corio to Waurn Ponds, bypassing Geelong entirely. To get to the city, stay on the Princes Hwy (M1). For Geelong's waterfront, take Bell Pde and follow the Esplanade along the bay.

Taxi

Geelong Taxi Network (⊘13 10 08)

Train

V/Line (⊘13 61 96; www.vline.com.au) Runs from Geelong train station (⊘5226 6525; Gordon Ave) to Melbourne's Southern Cross Station ($9, one hour, frequently). Trains also head from Geelong to Warrnambool ($19, 2½ hours, three daily).

CYCLING-MAD FORREST

Mountain-bike riding through Forrest's forest is an adrenaline junkie's dream. Instead of taking the Great Ocean Road to Apollo Bay, then heading inland from Skenes Creek, cycle-mad folk can take the C119 from Geelong to Apollo Bay via Forrest. This sleepy town is tiny but Parks Victoria and the Department of Sustainability & Environment (DSE) have opened more than 50km of **mountain-bike trails** (ranging from beginner to suicidal) nearby. Grab a trail map and a Forrest Mountain Ale from **Forrest Brewing Company** (www.otwaysbrewing.com.au; Apollo Bay Rd, Forrest; ☉Thu-Sun, daily Dec-Jan). Maps can also be downloaded from www.rideforrest.com.au/trails.

The park hosts the **Otway Odyssey Mountain Bike Marathon** (www.rapidascent. com.au) in late February. The 'shorty' route is a long 50km and starts and ends in Forrest, while the longer version (100km) begins in Apollo Bay and ends in Forrest. Forrest is 32km away from Skenes Creek, and you'll be heading through the beautiful Otway hills to get to Apollo Bay. Bike trail 2 heads past Lake Elizabeth, home to platypus. Book a tour through **Otway Eco Tours** (☎5236 6345; www.platypus.net.au; adult/child $85/50) – there's a 95% chance you'll spot one.

Accommodation options include **Forest River Valley B&B** (☎5236 6322; www. forrestrivervalley.com.au; 135 Yaugher Rd; d $250; ❄) outside town, and, in town, **Forrest Accommodation** (☎5236 6381; 59 Grant St; dm/d $40/120) with one massive self-contained apartment sleeping up to 12 (cyclists or a large family) and one lovely B&B-style room, .

TORQUAY

POP 15, 700

In the 1960s and '70s Torquay was just another sleepy seaside town. Back then surfing in Australia was a decidedly counter-cultural pursuit, and its devotees were crusty hippy drop-outs living in clapped-out Kombis, smoking pot and making off with your daughters. Since then surfing has become unabashedly mainstream and a huge transglobal business. Torquay's rise and rise directly parallels the boom of the surfing industry (and especially the surf-apparel industry). The town's proximity to world-famous Bells Beach and status as home of two iconic surf brands – Rip Curl and Quicksilver, both initially wetsuit makers – ensured Torquay's place as the undisputed capital of the Australian surf industry.

Torquay is a good spot if you're after a surf lesson or some serious shopping for surfwear or gear. Otherwise there's not too much to do among the beachside suburban sprawl, where farm paddocks have given way to thousands of new houses.

🞇 Sights & Activities

Surfworld Museum   MUSEUM
(www.surfworld.org.au; adult/child/family $10/6/20; ☉9am-5pm) Embedded at the rear of the **Surf City Plaza** is this homage to Australian surfing, with shifting exhibits, a theatre

and displays of old photos and monster balsa mals (longboards).

Spring Creek Horse Rides   HORSE RIDING
(☎5266 1541; www.springcreekhorserides.com. au; 245 Portheath Rd, Bellbrae; 1hr/2hr $35/60) Guided rides through Spring Creek Valley (the two-hour rides are a little more rugged).

Three companies will help you learn how to **surf**, two-hour lessons cost from $50.
Go Ride A Wave (☎1300 132 441; www. gorideawave.com.au; 1/15 Bell St, Torquay; ☉9am-5pm) Also operates in Anglesea.
Torquay Surfing Academy (☎5261 2022; www.torquaysurf.com.au; 34a Bell St, Torquay; ☉9am-5pm)
Westcoast Surf School (☎5261 2241; www. westcoastsurfschool.com; ☉9am-5pm summer).

Torquay's **beaches** lure everyone from kids in floaties to backpacker surf-school pupils. **Fisherman's Beach**, protected from ocean swells, is the family favourite. Ringed by shady pines and sloping lawns, the **Front Beach** beckons lazy bums, while surf life-savers patrol the frothing **Back Beach** during summer.

There are several good walking trails including the **Foreshore Trail**, which features a giant sundial, and the **Deep Creek Reserve**, which protects Torquay's only remaining native flora.

🛏 Sleeping

TOP CHOICE **Woolshed B&B**　　　　　B&B **$$$**
(☑0408 333 433; www.woolshed.info; 75 Aquarius Ave; apt $250; ✳✸) This restored woolshed is over 100 years old and has been converted into a gorgeous open and airy space with two-bedrooms. It sleeps up to six, and guests can use the pool and tennis court. Chooks ramble around out front, continental breakfast is included, and pets and kids are welcome.

Bellbrae Harvest　　　　APARTMENTS **$$$**
(☑5266 2100; www.bellbraeharvest.com.au; 45 Portreath Rd; d $200; ✳) Far from the madding crowd, here are three separate (and stunning) split-level apartments looking onto a dam. Expect rainwater showers, kitchenettes, huge flatscreen TVs and lots and lots of peace.

Bells Beach Lodge　　　　　HOSTEL **$**
(☑5261 7070; www.bellsbeachlodge.com.au; 51-53 Surfcoast Hwy; dm/d $25/65; @) This grungy budget option is on the highway and has shared facilities and surfboard and bike hire. It's especially popular during events and caters for large groups (so it can be noisy!).

Torquay Foreshore Caravan Park
　　　　CAMPING GROUND, CABINS **$**
(☑5261 2496; www.torquaycaravanpark.com.au; unpowered sites $30-50, cabin d $75-250) Just behind the back beach, this is the largest camping ground on the Surf Coast. It has good facilities and new premium-priced cabins with sea views.

✖ Eating

Moby　　　　　　　　　　CAFE **$**
(41 The Esplanade; mains $9-16; ⊘breakfast & lunch) This old weatherboard on the Esplanade harks back to a time when Torquay was simple, which is not to say its meals are not complicated: fill up on a linguini or honey roasted lamb souvlaki. There's a whopping great playground in the back for kids.

Scorched　　　　MODERN AUSTRALIAN **$$**
(☑5261 6142; www.scorched.com.au; 17 The Esplanade; mains $26-36; ⊘lunch Fri-Sun, dinner Wed-Sun) This might be the swankiest restaurant in Torquay, overlooking the waterfront, with classy understated decor and windows that open right up to let the sea breeze in. Check out the seasonal grazing plate to share.

Imperial Rhino　　　　ASIAN FUSION **$$**
(☑5261 6780; 3 Bell St; mains $15-25; ⊘breakfast, lunch & dinner) Sometimes flat, sometimes sublime, take your chances on this long-established noodle cafe. The relaxed atmosphere is 'mod-Zen', with long wooden tables and loads of natural light – a great place for a late, lazy breakfast.

❶ Information

The two main streets for shopping and eating, Gilbert St and Bell St, run perpendicular to the Esplanade.

Torquay visitor centre (www.greatoceanroad. org; Surf City Plaza, Beach Rd; @) Torquay has a well-resourced tourist office next to the Surfworld Museum.

❶ Getting There & Away

Bus

McHarry's Buslines (☑5223 2111; www.mcharrys. com.au) Runs buses hourly from 9am to 9pm from Geelong to Torquay (with/without myki $3/3.20, 30 minutes), arriving and departing Torquay from the corner of Pearl and Boston Sts (behind the Gilbert St shopping centre).

V/Line (☑13 61 96; www.vline.com.au) Buses run four times daily Monday to Friday (two on weekends) from Geelong to Torquay ($3.20, 25 minutes).

Car

Torquay is 15 minutes south of Geelong on the B100.

WAVE HANDLING

The Great Ocean Road offers fantastic opportunities for surfers with great year-round Southern Ocean swells lashing every beach and point. Wannabes can have lessons in beachside towns including Torquay, Anglesea, Lorne and Warrnambool. The coast offers a mix of breaks for beginners and surf-nazis alike.

» **Bells Beach** (p163) is one of the most famous surfing spots on the planet.

» **Johanna Beach** (p173) has a legendary (read: suicidal) break.

» **Surf City Plaza** (p161) in Torquay is where you can fit yourself out with surf gear, apparel and all possible surfer-guy-chick accoutrements.

TORQUAY TO ANGLESEA

The Great Ocean Road between Torquay and Anglesea heads slightly inland, with a turn-off about 7km from Torquay to Bells Beach. The powerful point break at Bells is part of international surfing folklore (it's here, in name only, that Keanu Reeves and Patrick Swayze have their ultimate showdown in the film *Point Break*). It's notoriously inconsistent, but when the long right-hander is working it's one of the longest rides in the country. Since 1973, Bells has hosted the Rip Curl Pro (www.aspworldtour.com) every Easter. The world championship ASP tour event draws thousands to watch the world's best surfers carve up the big autumn swells – where waves have reached 5m during the contest! The Rip Curl Pro occasionally de-camps to Johanna Beach, two hours west, when fickle Bells isn't working. Contact Surfing Victoria (5261 2907; www.surfing australia.com) for more details.

Nine kilometres southwest of Torquay is the turn-off to spectacular Point Addis, 3km down this road. It's a vast sweep of pristine 'clothing optional' beach that attracts surfers, hang-gliders and swimmers. There's a signposted Koorie Cultural Walk, a 1km circuit trail to the beach through the Ironbark Basin nature reserve.

The Surf Coast Walk (www.surfcoast.vic. gov.au/walkingtracks.htm) follows the coastline from Jan Juc to Moggs Creek south of Aireys Inlet, and can be done in stages – the full route takes 11 hour. It's marked on the *Surf Coast Touring Map*, available from tourist offices.

ANGLESEA

POP 2300

Mix sheer orange cliffs falling into the ocean with hilly, treed 'burbs and a population that booms in summer and you've got Anglesea. Main Beach is the ideal spot to learn to surf, while sheltered Point Roadknight Beach is good for kiddies. The Anglesea heathlands have a huge diversity of flora and fauna and are celebrated each September with a wildflower show.

Sharing fish and chips with seagulls by the Anglesea River is a decade-long family tradition for many, and caravan parks burst at their seams come school holidays. Life hits the fast lane during January when the wide riverbank is taken over by a Sunday market. Downtown Anglesea is just a strip of shops on the Great Ocean Road (look out for the horse statue) but you can get a decent coffee and perhaps tap into some local conversation.

Suck in some sea air and enjoy the wide coastal vistas along Victoria's west coast. Most of the coast's walks take you along beachfronts and over headlands, and can be done in stages or as a complete package. A growing number of B&Bs and transport companies are working together to ensure walkers have a smooth as silk experience (but no one can do much about the blisters).

» **Surf Coast Walk** (p163) is a 30km walk that leaves Torquay and goes to Moggs Creek, past Aireys Inlet.

» **Great Ocean Walk** (p171) starts at Apollo Bay and runs (or walks) all the way to the Twelve Apostles.

» **Great South West Walk** (p184) is a 250km epic that begins and ends in Portland.

Activities

Anglesea Golf Club   GOLF
(www.angleseagolfclub.com.au; Noble St; 9 holes $25) Here's where a resident tagged kangaroo population lives. Watch them graze on the fairways as golfers drive and chip balls around them, particularly at early morning and dusk (but be prepared to be shouted at by golfers if you get in their way).

Eco Logic   NATURE TOURS
(5263 1133; www.ecologic.net.au) Runs kid-oriented nature-based programs during the school holidays, as well as hourly tours of Split Point Lighthouse at Aireys Inlet (until 3pm, or later in summer).

Anglesea Paddleboats   CANOEING
(0408 599 942; www.angleseapaddleandcanoe. com) Hires out canoes and paddleboats by Anglesea River.

Go Ride A Wave   SURFING
(1300 132 441; www.gorideawave.com.au; 143b Great Ocean Rd; 9am-5pm) Hires out kayaks and surfboards and runs two-hour surfing lessons from $75 ($60 if you pay in advance).

⭐ Festivals & Events

Anglesea Music Festival MUSIC
(AMF; www.angleseamusicfest.com) The inaugural AMF took place in November 2010 when a huge bunch of local and regional performers musically enhanced the town for three days. It's an annual event.

🛏 Sleeping

Anglesea Backpackers HOSTEL **$**
(☑5263 2664; www.angleseabackpackers.com; 40 Noble St; dm/d $35/95) This simple backpackers (just two dorm rooms and one double/triple) is clean, bright and welcoming, and in winter the fire glows warmly in the cosy living room.

Rivergums B&B B&B **$$**
(☑5263 3066; www.anglesearivergums.com.au; 10 Bingley Pde; d $100-160; ❄) Tucked by the river with tranquil views, these two spacious, tastefully furnished rooms (a self-contained bungalow and a room attached to the house) are excellent value and the whole set-up is delightfully guest-centric.

Anglesea Overboard COTTAGE **$$**
(☑5289 7424; www.overboardcottages.com.au; 39c O'Donohue Rd; d from $195; ❄) This one-bedroom cottage has ocean views, a spa and a wood fire for those chilly winter nights. Designed for couples, but accepting of babies and dogs (check first), there's also one in Aireys Inlet. Minimum two-night stay.

Anglesea Beachfront Family Caravan Park CAMPING GROUND, CABINS **$$**
(☑5263 1583; www.angleseafcp.com.au; 35 Cameron Rd; powered sites $37, cabin d $100-265; @ 🛜 ❄) This beach- and river-fronting caravan park has a pool, wi-fi, two camp kitchens, a jumping pillow, an indoor spa and a games room. No, you probably won't get that book read.

Surfcoast Holiday Rentals RENTAL HOUSE **$$**
(☑5263 3199; www.surfcoastrentals.com.au; 69 Great Ocean Rd) Has a range of houses starting at $180 per night.

🍴 Eating

TOP CHOICE **Red Till** CAFE **$**
(143A Great Ocean Rd; mains $8-22; ⊙breakfast & lunch Sat-Mon & Thu, daily summer) This cafe, on the outskirts of town towards Aireys Inlet, does coffee and retro decor as good as its Melbourne peers – only the pace of life is different.

River Vu MODERN AUSTRALIAN **$$**
(113 Great Ocean Rd; mains $21-38; ⊙breakfast, lunch & dinner Tue-Sun) It's changed its name a fair few times, but this incarnation offers a simple menu with generous servings. The tables on the front deck make for fine evening alfresco dining.

Angahook Cafe CAFE **$**
(119 Great Ocean Rd; mains $9-15; ⊙breakfast & lunch) This cafe doubles as a gourmet food store and is always busy. You might bump into Estie as she makes her daily delivery of freshly made passionfruit sponge.

Offshore Cafe CAFE **$**
(Shop 16, Anglesea Shopping Centre; mains $6-14; @) This cafe keeps the locals well-caffeinated and fed, and also has internet access (per hour $5).

GREAT OCEAN ROAD DISTANCES & TIMES

DESTINATION	DISTANCE	TIME
Melbourne to Geelong	75km	1hr
Geelong to Torquay	21km	15-20min
Torquay to Anglesea	16km	13min
Anglesea to Aireys Inlet	10km	10min
Aireys Inlet to Lorne	19km	22min
Lorne to Apollo Bay	45km	1hr
Apollo Bay to Port Campbell	88km	1hr 10min
Port Campbell to Warrnambool	66km	1hr
Warrnambool to Port Fairy	28km	20min
Port Fairy to Portland	72km	1hr
Portland to Melbourne	via Great Ocean Rd 440km; direct 362km.	6½hr

HARD YAKKA

The first sections of the Great Ocean Road were constructed by hand (using picks, shovels and crowbars) by returned WWI soldiers. Work began in September 1919 and the road between Anglesea and Apollo Bay was completed in 1932.

ℹ Information

Visitor centre (16/87 Great Ocean Rd; ⊙9am-5pm Sep-May, 10am-4pm Jun-Aug) Located opposite Angahook Cafe, this new information centre sits beside an equally new barbecue area and gives leads on local accommodation and activities.

ℹ Getting There & Away

Car

The new Geelong bypass has reduced the time it takes to drive from Melbourne to Anglesea to around 75 minutes.

AIREYS INLET

Aireys Inlet is midway between Anglesea and Lorne, and is home to glorious stretches of beach, including **Fairhaven** and **Moggs Creek**. Nothing beats a stroll along Fairhaven beach, whether in winter or summer. In Aireys itself, the beaches are backed by tall, volcanic cliffs, with tidal rock pools along the foreshore just below the lighthouse. A Surf Life Saving Club patrols the beach at Fairhaven during summer, while at Moggs Creek, hang-gliders launch themselves from the clifftops and land on the sands below. It's also a popular stretch for horse riding.

The 34m-high **Split Point Lighthouse** and its keepers' cottages were built in 1891. The lighthouse (now fully automated) is still operational and visible 30km out to sea. There's a sweet cafe near its base.

◉ Sights & Activities

Eco Logic   LIGHTHOUSE
(☑5263 1133; www.ecologic.net.au) This Anglesea-based group runs hourly tours of Split Point Lighthouse until 3pm.

Blazing Saddles   HORSE RIDING
(☑5289 7322; www.blazingsaddlestrailrides.com.au; Lot 1 Bimbadeen Dr; 1¼/2¼hr rides $40/65) People come from around the world to hop on a Blazing Saddles horse and head into the bush or along the stunning beach.

Signposted off the main road, on Inlet Crescent, near the lighthouse, is a replica of an 1852 **settler's hut**, which was made from bark, and destroyed by the devastating 1983 Ash Wednesday bushfires.

The lovely 3.5km **Aireys Inlet Cliff Walk** begins at Painkalac Creek, rounds Split Point and makes its way to Sunnymead Beach. The **Surf Coast Walk** continues along the coast here – pick up a copy of *Walks of Lorne & Aireys Inlet* from visitor centres.

🛏 Sleeping

Cimarron B&B   B&B **$$**
(☑5289 7044; www.cimarron.com.au; 105 Gilbert St; d $185; 🞵) This house was built in 1979 from local timbers using only wooden pegs and shiplap joins, and is an idyllic getaway with views over Point Roadknight. Rustic, yet sophisticated, the large lounge area has book-lined walls and a cosy fireplace, while upstairs there are two unique, loft-style doubles with vaulted timber ceilings; otherwise there's a den-like apartment. Out back, it's all state park and wildlife. Gay friendly, but no kids.

Lightkeepers Inn   MOTEL **$$**
(☑5289 6666; www.lightkeepersinn.com.au; 64 Great Ocean Rd; d $110; 🞵🞶) This is the welcome respite for folks who've been enjoying themselves a little too much at the neighbouring restaurant A La Greque. Expect clean motel rooms with extra-thick walls for peace and quiet. Trevor runs the place and has an excellent knowledge of local walks and mountain-biking opportunities.

Pole House   RENTAL HOUSE **$$$**
(☑5220 0200; www.greatoceanroadholidays.com.au; 60 Banool Rd, Fairhaven; overnight midweek from $480) The Pole House, in nearby Fairhaven, is an iconic Great Ocean Road landmark, sitting, as the name suggests, atop a pole, with extraordinary views. It was built in the late '70s and retains its authentic kitsch decor. It was one of the few buildings in the area to survive the 1983 Ash Wednesday bushfires.

Aireys Ocean Inlet at Fairhaven
                              APARTMENTS **$**
(☑5289 7313; www.oceaninlet.com.au; 34 Wybellenna Dr, Fairhaven; d $90) This cute gazebo-style bedsit with sofa bed and floor-to-ceiling windows overlooking native gardens has a teensy cabin next door containing a kitchenette

(with breakfast bar) and bathroom. Well-heeled couples can swing cats in the sleek Coral Cove or Shorehouse apartments for $250 and $275 respectively.

Inlet Caravan Park CABINS $$
(☎5289 6230; www.aicp.com.au; 19-25 Great Ocean Rd; unpowered/powered sites from $33/36, en suite cabin d $105-148; @⊠) This neat little park is more cabin-oriented than a tent city, but it's close to the township's few stores.

✖ Eating

TOP CHOICE **A La Greque** GREEK $$
(☎5289 6922; www.alagreque.com.au; 60 Great Ocean Rd; mains $28-36; ⊗breakfast, lunch & dinner Wed-Sun, daily summer) This modern Greek taverna is outstanding and serves meze including cured kingfish with apple, celery and a lime dressing, and mains such as chargrilled king prawns with fresh oregano. Kosta, the host, ran Kosta's in Lorne for 27 years before decamping to Aireys. The veranda, is an ideal spot to lunch mid-drive, or, better still, make a reservation for dinner.

Truffles Cafe Deli CAFE $$
(☎5289 7402; 34 Great Ocean Rd; mains $15-20; ⊗breakfast & lunch Mon-Sun, dinner Thu-Sun) Truffles does the lot – eat in or takeaway, pizza, pasta, curries, good vegetarian choices, licensed and BYO, coffee, homemade cakes, cheerful efficient service and a happy ambience.

LORNE

POP 1000

Lorne has an incredible natural beauty, something you see vividly as you drive into town from Aireys Inlet. Old, tall gumtrees line its hilly streets and Loutit Bay gleams irresistibly. It's this beauty that has attracted visitors for centuries; Rudyard Kipling's 1891 visit led him to pen the poem 'Flowers': 'Gathered where the Erskine leaps, Down the road to Lorne...'

It gets busy; in summer you'll be competing with day-trippers for restaurant seats and boutique bargains, but, thronged with tourists or not, Lorne is a lovely place to hang out.

◉ Sights & Activities

Qdos Art Gallery ART GALLERY
(☎5289 1989; www.qdosarts.com; 35 Allenvale Rd; ⊗8.30am-6pm Thu-Mon, daily school holidays) Qdos, tucked in the hills behind Lorne, always has something arty in its galleries, and

sculptures dot its lush landscape. Its cafe fare is nothing but delicious and if you really love it, stay the night in one of their luxury zen treehouses ($200 per night, two-night minimum, no kids).

Erskine Falls WATERFALL
Head out of town to see this lovely waterfall. It's an easy walk to the viewing platform or 250 (often slippery) steps down to its base, from which you can explore further or head back on up.

Southern Exposure SURFING, KAYAKING
(☎5261 9170; www.southernexposure.com.au) Offers surfing lessons (one hour $150) and is big on kayaking, and in Torquay, mountain-biking.

Lorne Paddleboat Hire BOATING
(☎0408 895 022; www.lorneswingbridgecafe.com; per 20min $10; ⊗8am-sunset) Churn your way along the Erskine River on a paddleboat.

Kids will love the beachside swimming pool, trampolines and skate park.

There are more than 50km of **walking tracks** through the Otway Ranges around Lorne, but if they sound too long, the Lorne visitors centre has information on the self-guided (and much shorter) **Lorne Historical Walk**, **Tramway Track Walk** (incorporating **Teddy's Lookout**) and the **Shipwreck Plaque Walk**.

✹ Festivals & Events

Falls Festival MUSIC
(www.fallsfestival.com; tickets $350) A three-day knees-up over New Year's on a farm out of town. A top line-up of rock and indie groups; tickets include camping.

Pier to Pub Swim SWIMMING
(www.lornesurfclub.com.au) This popular event in January inspires up to 4500 swimmers to splash their way 1.2km across Loutit Bay to the Lorne Hotel; it's a photo opportunity for local politicians and celebrities.

⌂ Sleeping

There's often a minimum two-night stay on weekends in Lorne, and high-season rates can be nearly double winter prices. For other options, ask at the visitors centre.

Chapel COTTAGE $$$
(☎5289 2622; thechapellorne@bigpond.com; 45 Richardson Blvd; d $200; ❋) Outstanding – this contemporary two-level bungalow, with tasteful Asian furnishings, splashes of co-

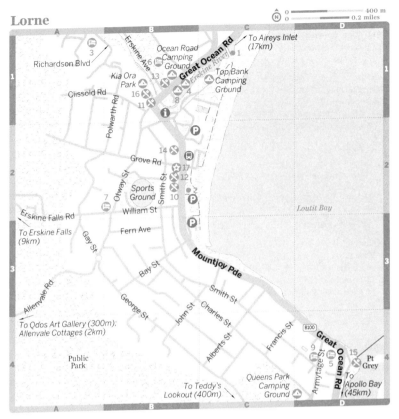

lour and bay windows that open into the forest, has been lifted from the pages of a glossy magazine. It's secluded and romantic, with double shower and complimentary robes.

La Perouse
B&B $$$

(☎0418 534 422; www.laperouselorne.com.au; 26A William St; 2-night minimum d $200; ☎) It's all French at this lovely B&B; expect rooms with amazing attention to detail including imported French toiletries in the bathrooms. It's just up a rise from the town centre.

Allenvale Cottages
COTTAGES $$

(☎5289 1450; www.allenvale.com.au; 150 Allenvale Rd; d from $175) We keep coming back here – four self-contained early-1900s timber cottages that each sleep four (or more) and have been luxuriously restored. They're 2km northwest of Lorne, arrayed among shady trees and green lawns, complete with bridge and babbling brook. There are walking and cycling trails and it's ideal for families.

Ocean Lodge Motel
MOTEL $$

(☎5289 1330; www.oceanlodgelorne.com.au; 6 Armytage St; d $110) Wake up to the sounds of the sea at this simple motel that's been around for eons. Each room has sea views and a kitchenette, while outside there's a tennis court, bird-attracting gardens and a barbecue.

Great Ocean Road Cottages & Backpackers YHA
HOSTEL $

(☎5289 1070; www.yha.com.au; 10 Erskine Ave; tents $25, dm $20-30, d $55-75, cottages $170) Tucked away in the bush among the cockatoos, koalas and other wildlife, this two-storey timber lodge has spacious dorms, bargain tents with beds already set up, and great-value doubles. Unisex bathrooms take some getting used to. The more expensive A-frame cottages sleep up to six people, and come with kitchens and en suite bathrooms.

Lorne

Activities, Courses & Tours

1 Lorne Paddleboat Hire C1
2 Trampolines, Swimming Pool & Skate Park B2

Sleeping

3 Chapel A1
Erskine River Backpackers .... (see 11)
4 Erskine River Park Camping Ground B1
5 Grand Pacific Hotel D4
6 Great Ocean Road Cottages & Backpackers YHA B1
7 La Perouse B2
8 Lorne Camping Grounds Booking Office B1
9 Ocean Lodge Motel D4

Eating

10 Arab B2
11 Ba Ba Lu Bar B1
12 Bottle of Milk B2
13 Foodworks Supermarket B1
14 Kafe Kaos B2
15 Lorne Fisheries D4
16 Pizza Pizza B1

Entertainment

17 Lorne Theatre B2

Lorne Camping Grounds Booking Office CAMPING GROUND $
(☎1300 736 533; www.lornecaravanpark.com.au; 2 Great Ocean Rd; powered sites $30-50, cabin d from $60) Book here for Lorne's five caravan parks. Of these **Erskine River Caravan Park**, where the booking office is located, is the prettiest. It's on the left-hand side as you enter Lorne, just before the bridge. Book well ahead for peak-season stays. The other camping grounds are the Kia-Ora, Ocean Road, Top Bank and Queens Park.

Grand Pacific Hotel PUB $$
(☎5289 1609; www.grandpacific.com.au; 268 Mountjoy Pde; d from $175;) This iconic Lorne landmark, harking back to 1875, has been restored with a sleek modern decor that retains some classic period features. The best rooms have balconies and stunning sea views, though plainer rooms are still luxurious. It's a popular weekend wedding venue.

Erskine River Backpackers HOSTEL $
(☎5289 1496; 6 Mountjoy Pde; dm/d $25/70; summer) Beautiful verandahs line this classic old building locted by the river at the north end of town. It's a relaxed place with four-bunk dorms and great communal spaces.

Eating

Lorne is the Great Ocean Road's gourmet capital, and Mountjoy Pde is bumper-to-bumper with great cafes and restaurants. Most are open day and night during summer, but have shorter winter hours.

Ba Ba Lu Bar SPANISH $$$
(www.babalubar.com.au; 6a Mountjoy Pde; mains $32-42; breakfast, lunch & dinner) It's all a bit Spanish at Ba Ba Lu Bar, what with its wintery paella nights and Chilean singers popping in for a gig in summer. The menu includes inspired tapas and plenty of meat-based mains, and the bar kicks on into the wee hours.

Kafe Kaos CAFE $
(www.kafekaos.com.au; 52 Mountjoy Pde; lunch $8-15; breakfast & lunch) Bright and perky, Kafe Kaos typifies Lorne's relaxed foodie philosophy – barefoot patrons in boardies or bikinis tucking into first-class paninis, bruschettas, burgers and chips. With great veggie options, all-day breakfasts, and coffee, cocktails, beer and wine to wash the sand out of your hair.

Pizza Pizza PIZZA $
(2b Mountjoy Pde; pizzas $12-16; 4-9pm) This tiny shopfront is only big enough for the kitchen – diners takeaway or eat on the footpath tables – but it's a huge hit, offering pizzas such as Punkrock (napoli, mozzarella, roast pumpkin, goat's cheese and fresh rocket).

Bottle of Milk FAST FOOD $
(52 Mountjoy Pde; burgers from $8.50; breakfast, lunch & dinner) Sit back on one of the old school chairs at this cool version of a diner, and tuck into a classic burger stacked with fresh ingredients. The coffee machine gets a good workout, too.

Arab CAFE $$
(94 Mountjoy Pde; mains $20-24; breakfast, lunch & dinner; @) Arab started as a beatnik coffee lounge in 1956, and single-handedly transformed Lorne from a daggy family holiday destination into a place for groovers and shakers. It's been trading ever since, and is *the* spot for coffee and all-day breakfasts. Motorcyclists converge on this place like seagulls flock to a hot chip.

SUNNYBRAE

Sometimes, in what appears to be the middle of nowhere, you'll find a hidden country restaurant. You'll drive up the driveway and see the chef picking the best from the vegetable garden. You won't be able to get a car park (and will need to dodge the farm dog in the search) and then you'll only be allowed in if you've made a booking. **Sunnybrae** (☑5236 2276; www.georgebiron.com; cnr Cape Otway & Lorne Rds, Birregurra; set menu $70; ☺lunch Sat & Sun) is packed on the weekends (that's the only time it's open) but if you manage to reserve a seat in its cottage-like restaurant you'll be handed an A3 sheet with the day's menu written on it. It might include delightful (and very seasonal) morsels such as sugar-cured ocean trout or duck confit with spiced morello cherries. Dessert is your choice from seven dishes including Hungarian poppyseed pancakes. Inspired? Hungry? Book into a Monday cooking class ($110).

There's a well-provisioned **Foodworks Supermarket** (1-3 Great Ocean Rd) at the northern end of town, and for the state's freshest fish and seafood supplies head to **Lorne Fisheries** (Lorne Pier; ☺10am-6pm).

☆ Entertainment

Many of Lorne's restaurants add music to their menus and open until late over summer. Lorne's two pubs offer live bands on weekends.

Lorne Theatre   CINEMA
(☑5289 1272; www.greatoceanroadcinemas.com.au; 78 Mountjoy Pde; adult/child $13/10) This grand old theatre shows new-release films daily during the peak season.

ℹ Information

Lorne visitor centre (☑1300 891 152; www.visitsurfcoast.com.au; 15 Mountjoy Pde; ☺9am-5pm) Stacks of information, helpful staff and an accommodation booking service.

ℹ Getting Around

Lorne Taxi Service (☑0409 892 304)

Cumberland River

Just 7km southwest of Lorne is **Cumberland River**. There's nothing here – no shops or houses – other than the wonderful **Cumberland River Holiday Park** (☑5289 1790; www.cumberlandriver.com.au; Great Ocean Rd; unpowered sites $37, en suite cabins from $105). This splendidly located bushy camping ground is next to a lovely river and high craggy cliffs that rise on the far side. The ocean beach offers surfing and swimming, and there are many walks upriver and over the hills. We've been coming here since we were kids.

Wye River

POP 140

The Great Ocean Road snakes spectacularly around the cliff-side from Cumberland River before reaching this little town with big ideas. Nestled discretely in the pretty (steep) hillsides are some modest holiday houses and a few grander steel-and-glass pole-frame structures built on the 'challenging' housing sites.

🛏 Sleeping & Eating

Wye River Foreshore Camping Reserve   CAMPING GROUND $
(☑5289 0412; sites $30; ☺Dec-Apr) This camping ground offers powered beachside sites during summer.

Wye Beach Hotel   MOTEL $$
(☑5289 0240; www.wyebeachhotel.com.au; 19 Great Ocean Rd; mains $18-30; ☺lunch & dinner; @) People come here for pub food on a verandah with some of the most stunning views of the coast. The hotel also has comfortable motel-style double rooms ($130 to $200) with great views.

Wye General   CAFE $$
TOP CHOICE (www.thewyegeneral.com; 35 Great Ocean Rd; dinner $15-26; ☺breakfast & lunch daily, dinner Fri & Sat winter, dinner daily summer) This cafe has marched into town and there's nothing general about it. From homemade sourdough to perfect coffee, this smart indoor-outdoor joint has polished concrete floors, timber features and a sophisticated retro ambience that will impress.

Holiday Great Ocean Road   RENTAL HOUSES $$
(☑5237 1098; www.holidaygor.com.au) This company manages at least 17 private holiday houses in Wye River. Expect to pay from

$150 per night for a studio and $190 for a two-bedroom cottage, and up to $650 for a mid-week night in its top property 'Horizons'.

Kennett River

Located 5km along from Wye River is **Kennett River**, which has some truly great **koala-spotting** in the town itself, and you'll also spot the furry creatures above the Great Ocean Road towards Apollo Bay (be careful when looking and driving, and watch for mesmerised drivers). In town, just behind the caravan park, walk 200m up Grey River Rd and you'll see bundles of sleepy koalas clinging to the branches. *Ooh aah!* There are also **glow-worms** that shine at night up the same stretch of Grey River Rd (take a torch).

🛏 Sleeping

Kennett River Holiday Park CAMPING, CABINS **$**
(📞1300 664 417, 5289 0272; www.kennettriver.com; unpowered/powered sites $29/35, cabin d from $105; @🛜) This friendly bush holiday park has free wi-fi internet, free BBQs and plans are afoot for a camp kitchen.

Cape Patton to Skenes Creek

Be camera-ready for the roadside **Cape Patton lookout**, about 4km beyond Kennett River. From here to Skenes Creek, the land rolls and folds dramatically in camel-hump hills. **Wongarra**, 8km south of Cape Patton, has an appealing moody, windswept quality.

APOLLO BAY

POP 1800

Apollo Bay is synonymous with music festivals, the Otways and a lovely beach, and it's one of the least claustrophobic hamlets along the Great Ocean Rd. It is getting larger; check the town's real estate offices to see the latest 'new release' housing blocks, and it's impossible to guess how this development will affect the fishing town. Locals – fisherfolk, artists, musicians and sea-changers – may lament the loss of the old pre-yuppie days, but on the flip side, their house values have doubled while you've been reading this.

Majestic rolling hills provide a postcard backdrop to the town, while broad, white-sand beaches dominate the foreground.

It's also an ideal base for exploring magical Cape Otway and Otway National Park. Online, check out www.visitapollobay.com and www.visitotways.com.

⊙ Sights & Activities

Community Market MARKET
(www.apollobay.com/market_place; ⊙8.30am-4.30pm Sat) This market is held along the main strip and is the perfect spot for picking up local apples, locally made souvenirs and just-what-you've-always-wanted table lamps made from tree stumps.

Mark's Walking Tours WALKING
(📞0417 983 985; www.greatoceanwalk.asn.au/markstours; 2-3hr tours adult/child $50/15) Take a walk around the area with local Mark Brack, son of the Cape Otway Lighthouse keeper. He knows this stretch of coast, its history and its ghosts better than anyone around. His daily tours include shipwreck tours, historical tours, glow-worm tours and Great Ocean Walk tours. Minimum two people.

Old Cable Station Museum MUSEUM
(6250 Great Ocean Rd; admission $3; ⊙2-5pm Sat & Sun) Here's a huge collection of photographs and local artefacts relating to the 1859 laying of submarine telegraph cable from Cape Otway to Tasmania. It's a tad old-school, but pleasant all the same.

Apollo Bay Sea Kayaking KAYAKING
(📞0405 495 909; www.apollobaysurfkayak.com.au; 2hr tours $65) Head out to an Australian fur seal colony on a two-seated kayak. Tours (with full instructions for beginners) depart from Marengo beach (to the south of the town centre) and are suitable for children over 12.

Otway Expeditions MOUNTAIN-BIKING
(📞5237 6341; http://otwayexpeditions.tripod.com; argo rides from $45) Take a dual suspension bike through the Otways (minimum six people), or go nuts in an amphibious all-terrain 8x8 argo buggy. Running from November to April is 'iRide': you BYO bike, get carted up the mountain and choose from 17 different tracks to zoom down on. The pros can do 70km, but there are gentler ones, too (and never the twain shall meet).

Apollo Bay Aviation SCENIC FLIGHTS
(📞0407 306 065; www.apollobayaviation.com.au; local flights per person $50) Tour locally or count how many of the Twelve Apostles are left on one of their Twelve Apostles 'Flightseeing' tours. Minimum two people.

DON'T MISS

WALKING THE GREAT OCEAN ROAD

The superb multiday **Great Ocean Walk** (www.greatoceanwalk.com.au) starts at Apollo Bay and runs all the way to the Twelve Apostles. It's possible to start at one point and arrange a pick up at another (public transport options are few and far between). You can do shorter walks or the whole 104km trek over six days. Designated (free) campsites are spread along the Great Ocean Walk catering for walkers only. **Walk 91** (☑5237 1189; www.walk91.com.au; 5-day budget packages per person from $784) arranges transport, and equipment hire, and can take your backpack to your destination so you don't have to. **GOR Shuttle** (☑5237 9278, 0428 379 278) is a recommended shuttle service for luggage and walkers; they'll pick you up when your walking's done (for around $50 a transfer).

Apollo Bay Fishing & Adventure Tours FISHING (☑5237 7888, www.apollobayfishing.com.au; 4hr trips adult/child $90/80) Takes folk out for fishing and scenic cruises.

Signposted **Marriners Lookout** is 1.5km from town back towards Cape Patton – from the car park the lookout is a rewarding 20-minute return walk.

⚜ Festivals & Events

Apollo Bay Music Festival MUSIC (☑5237 6761; www.apollobaymusicfestival.com; weekend pass adult/youth/child under 13yr $162/90/free) Held over a weekend in early April this three-day festival features classical, folk, blues, jazz, rock and some edgy contemporary sounds too. It's an outstanding event, but accommodation can be scarce and expensive – book well ahead.

🛏 Sleeping

TOP CHOICE **YHA Eco Beach** HOSTEL $ (☑5237 7899; 5 Pascoe St; dm $32-38, d $88-95, f $109-145; ❄ @) Even if you're not on a budget this $3 million, architect-designed hostel is an outstanding place to stay. Its eco-credentials are too many to list here, but it's a wonderful piece of architecture with great lounge areas, kitchens, TV rooms, an internet lounge and rooftop terraces. The location, just a block behind the beach in the guts of town, is the icing on the cake.

Nelson's Perch B&B B&B $$ (☑5237 7176; www.nelsonsperch.com; 54 Nelson St; d $160; ❄ @ 🔊) Nelson's looks fresher than some of the town's weary B&Bs. There are three rooms, each with courtyard, and free wi-fi internet throughout.

Surfside Backpackers HOSTEL $ (☑5237 7263; www.surfsidebackpacker.com; cnr Great Ocean Rd & Gambier St; dm $23-30, d $60)

The rooms are a little cramped, but the lounge is blessed with large windows looking out onto the ocean, making this homey place worthwhile.

Angela's Guest House B&B $$ (☑5237 7085; www.angelasguesthouse.com.au; 7 Campbell Ct; d/f from $100/95) This large family home has spotless doubles and family rooms with bright, cheerful decor. They've added a purpose-built version next door, too. Some share a bathroom, most have balconies and they're all excellent value.

Apollo Bay Holiday Park CARAVAN PARK $ (☑5237 7111; www.apollobayholidaypark.com.au; 27 Cawood St; unpowered sites $25, cabin d from $85) This place looks prefab suburban, complete with speed humps, car parks and kit homes. It's at the northern end of town.

🍴 Eating

There's good eating at the two pubs on the main drag, and the **Apollo Bay Fishermen's Co-operative** (Breakwater Rd; ⊙10am-4pm) sells fresh fish and seafood. The **Foodworks Supermarket** (4 Hardy St) is situated just behind the post office.

Chris's at Beacon Point Restaurant GREEK $$$ (☑5237 6411; 280 Skenes Creek Rd; mains $30-44; ⊙breakfast, lunch & dinner) This is a hilltop fine-dining sanctuary with breathtaking views over Bass Strait and Apollo Bay. It's a beautifully designed restaurant with stone feature walls, sandstone floors and vaulted ceilings, under which deliciously fresh seafood is served. You can also stay in its wonderful villas, too (from $265 per night).

Vista SEAFOOD $$ (www.thevistaseafoodrestaurant.com; 155 Great Ocean Rd, mains $25-35; ⊙dinner) This is fab, upmarket dining on the main drag. Spend hours cracking a locally caught crab, supported in your endeavours by local wine.

La Bimba   MODERN AUSTRALIAN $$$
(125 Great Ocean Rd; mains $25-45; ☺breakfast, lunch & dinner Wed-Mon) This upstairs Mod Oz restaurant is outstanding – definitely worth the splurge. It's a warm, relaxed smart-casual place with views, great service and a good wine list. Try the local goodies: Portarlington mussels and blue swimmer crab.

Café Nautigals   CAFE $
(1/57-59 Great Ocean Rd; mains $14-16; ☺breakfast, lunch daily, dinner in summer; ☺) A baby stack of pancakes and a coffee will use up a tenner, which is not bad in anyone's books. It's a laid-back place.

Chill@theBay   TAPAS $
(14 Pascoe St; mains $10-16; ☺breakfast, lunch & dinner) In summer, staff at this modern tapas bar start working the coffee machine early and don't stop until cocktail and tapas time is over. Breakfasts are decent, but it's the wine list and fireplace that have most winter appeal.

Sandy Feet Cafe   CAFE $
(139 Great Ocean Rd; mains $6-12; ☺breakfast & lunch) Tofu, tempeh, wholefoods and good karma.

☆ Entertainment

Lots of Apollo Bay's restaurants have evening bar services, and **Apollo Bay Hotel** (95 Great Ocean Rd) and **Top Pub** (Great Ocean Hotel; 29 Great Ocean Rd) have live bands some weekends.

Apollo Bay Cinema   CINEMA
(☑5289 1272; www.greatoceanroadcinemas.com.au; cnr Great Ocean Rd & Nelson St; adult/child $13/10) Operates from the local hall.

ℹ Information

Great Ocean Rd visitor centre (☑5237 6529; 100 Great Ocean Rd; ☺9am-5pm) In the same building, there's an impressive 'eco-centre' with displays on Aboriginal history, rainforests, shipwrecks and the building of the Great Ocean Road.

Parks Victoria (☑5237 2500; www.parkweb.vic.gov.au; cnr Oak Ave & Montrose St; ☺8am-4.30pm Mon-Fri)

Around Apollo Bay

Head 6km southwest of Apollo Bay along the Great Ocean Rd to the signposted **Shelley Beach** turn-off. It's an unsealed road. There are toilets and wood BBQs in the reserve, a track down to the beach and the 4km **Elliot River Walk**.

The narrow **Barham River Road Scenic Drive** from Apollo Bay runs a delightful 12km past tumbling grassy hills, sheep and stands of colossal eucalypts. Before returning, walk the **Marriners Falls Walk**, which follows the babbling Barham River, and pull into the aptly named **Paradise Valley** picnic area. Seventeen kilometres past Apollo Bay is **Maits Rest Rainforest Boardwalk**, an easy 20-minute rainforest-gully walk.

DETOUR: APOLLO BAY–LAVERS HILL–BEECH FOREST

A great day-drive is from Apollo Bay to Beech Forest via Lavers Hill and Melba Gully State Park. It becomes a loop if you take **Aire Valley Road** (which becomes Binns Track) from Beech Forest back to Apollo Bay, but be warned: this narrow, logging-truck route is not advised for conventional vehicles. It is badly corrugated, mushy clay, arduous driving and certainly no short cut! In winter, it's out of bounds to everyone.

Lavers Hill is 48km from Apollo Bay. This often mist-shrouded hilltop was once a thriving timber town but today it's a favourite feed-stop with two excellent cafes. International folk love the **Fauna Australia Wildlife Retreat** (☑5237 3234; www.faunaaustralia.com.au; 5040 Colac-Lavers Hill Rd, Lavers Hill; d $150) where almost-tame native animals (bred on the property) snoop about at night. You can't pop in for a peek unless you're staying there.

Seven kilometres southwest of Lavers Hill is tiny **Melba Gully State Park**. The marked **Madsen's Track** rainforest nature walk goes under a canopy of blackwoods and myrtle beeches and the fat, 300-year-old 'Big Tree', a messmate eucalypt. After dark, **glow-worms** glimmer in the park. You won't escape the well-signposted **Otway Fly** (see boxed text, p172), 5km from Beech Forest.

Triplet Falls, further along the same road as the Fly (Phillips Track), is also worth the hike. The 900m walk passes an historic timber site. The **Beauchamp** and **Hopetoun Falls** are just past Beech Forest, down the Aire Valley Rd.

CAPE OTWAY

Cape Otway is the second most southerly point of mainland Australia (after Wilsons Promontory) and one of the wettest parts of the state. This coastline is particularly beautiful, rugged and dangerous. More than 200 ships came to grief between Cape Otway and Port Fairy between the 1830s and 1930s, which led to the 'Shipwreck Coast' moniker.

The turn-off for Lighthouse Rd, which leads 12km down to the lighthouse, is 21km from Apollo Bay.

👁 Sights & Activities

Cape Otway Lightstation   LIGHTHOUSE
(✆5237 9240; www.lightstation.com; adult/child/family $17/8/42; ⏰9am-5pm) Cape Otway lighthouse is the oldest surviving lighthouse on mainland Australia and was built in 1848 by more than 40 stonemasons without mortar or cement. The **Telegraph Station** has fascinating displays on the 250km undersea telegraph cable link with Tasmania laid in 1859. A mammoth logistical exercise, the first cable failed after six months.

🛌 Sleeping

TOP
CHOICE **Blanket Bay**   CAMPING GROUND $
(Parks Victoria; ✆13 19 63; www.parkweb. vic.gov.au; sites $20) Blanket Bay is one of those 'secret' camp grounds that Melbournians love to lay claim to discovering. It's serene (depending on your neighbours) and the nearby beach is beautiful. It's not really a secret; in fact it's so popular from Christmas to late January that sites must be won by ballot (held in October). Other sites nearby include **Parker Hill**, **Point Franklin** and **Crayfish Beach**. Contact Parks Victoria for bookings.

Cape Otway Lightstation   B&B $$$
(Cape Otway Lighthouse; www.lightstation.com; d from $200) There is a range of options at this windswept spot; you can book out the whole Head Lightkeeper's House (sleeping 16), or the smaller Manager's House (sleeping two).

🍃 **Great Ocean Ecolodge**   B&B $$$
(✆5237 9297; www.capeotwaycentre.com; 635 Lighthouse Rd; s/d from $160/320) Prebook a room at this ecolodge and check out the native animals, as the attached Cape Otway Centre for Conservation Ecology also serves as an animal hospital for a menagerie of local fauna. The luxurious en suite rooms in the post-and-beam, solar-powered, mud-brick homestead have bush-view decks, and the centre offers walking tours and eco activities.

FURRY GREY MARSUPIALS

This is a terrific spot for koala sightings. Where are they? Look for the cars parked in the middle of the road and look up; they're what's holding up the traffic.

Bimbi Park   CAMPING GROUND $$
(✆5237 9246; www.bimbipark.com.au; Manna Gum Dr; unpowered sites low/high season $20/30, powered sites $30/35, cabin d $60-180) Down a dirt road 3km from the lighthouse is this horse-riding ranch with bush sites, fancy (and not-so-fancy) cabins and horse rides ($45 per hour).

CAPE OTWAY TO PORT CAMPBELL NATIONAL PARK

After Cape Otway, the Great Ocean Road levels out and enters the fertile Horden Vale flats, returning briefly to the coast at tiny Glenaire. Then the road returns inland and begins the climb up to Lavers Hill. On overcast or rainy days the hills here can be seriously fog-bound, and the twists and turns can be challenging when you can't see the end of your car bonnet.

Six kilometres north of Glenaire, a 5km detour goes down Red Johanna Rd winding through rolling hills and grazing cows to the wild thrashing surf of Johanna Beach (forget swimming). The world-famous Rip Curl Pro surfing competition relocates here when Bells Beach isn't working.

About 16km from the former timber town of Lavers Hill is the turn-off to Moonlight Head, a lumpy 5km unsealed road that forks near the coast: to the left is the cemetery and a walking track along the clifftops; to the right is a car park with a track to Wreck Beach and the anchors of the *Marie Gabrielle,* which sank off here in 1869, and the *Fiji,* wrecked in a storm in 1891.

🛌 Sleeping

FREE **Camping Ground**   CAMPING
(✆Parks Victoria 13 19 63; www.parkweb. vic.gov.au) This Johanna campground is on a protected grassy area between the dunes and the rolling hills. Book ahead, but there are no fees due or permits required. There's an ablutions facility, but fires are banned and you'll need to bring in your own drinking water.

Boomerangs APARTMENTS $$$
(☎5237 4213; www.theboomerangs.com; cnr Great Ocean Rd & Red Johanna Rd; d from $230) These boomerang-shaped cabins have vaulted ceilings, jarrah floorboards, leadlighting, spas and commanding views of the Johanna Valley. The onsite owners are lovely.

PORT CAMPBELL NATIONAL PARK

The road levels out after leaving the Otways and enters narrow, flat scrubby escarpment lands that fall away to sheer, 70m cliffs along the coast between Princetown and Peterborough – a distinct change of scene. This is Port Campbell National Park, home to the Twelve Apostles, and the most famous and most photographed stretch of the Great Ocean Road. For eons, waves and tides have crashed against the soft limestone rock, eroding, undercutting and carving out a fascinating series of rock stacks, gorges, arches and blowholes.

The Gibson Steps, hacked by hand into the cliffs in the 19th century by local landowner Hugh Gibson (and more recently replaced by concrete steps), lead down to feral Gibson Beach, an essential stop. This beach, and others along this stretch of coast, are not suitable for swimming because of strong currents and undertows – you can walk along the beach, but be careful not to be stranded by high tides or nasty waves. This is the only place along this stretch of coast where you can access the open beach, and it's possible to walk around the first headland to the west if the tide is low.

The lonely Twelve Apostles are rocky stacks that have been abandoned to the ocean by retreating headland. Today, only seven apostles can be seen from the viewing platforms (see boxed text, p176). The understated roadside lookout (Great Ocean Rd; ☺9am-5pm) at the Twelve Apostles, 6km past Princetown, has public toilets and a cafe. There's pedestrian access to the viewing platforms from the car park via a tunnel beneath the Great Ocean Road. Timber boardwalks run around the clifftops. Helicopters zoom around the Twelve Apostles, giving passengers an amazing view of the rocks. Just behind the car park at the lookout, 12 Apostles Helicopters (☎5598 6161; www.12apostleshelicopters.com.au; 10-min tour from $95) offers a 10-minute tour covering the Twelve Apostles, Loch Ard Gorge, Sential Rock and Port Campbell.

Nearby Loch Ard Gorge is where the Shipwreck Coast's most famous and haunting tale unfolded when two young survivors of the wrecked iron clipper *Loch Ard* made it to shore (see boxed text, p177).

PORT CAMPBELL

POP 400

This small, windswept town is poised on a dramatic, natural bay, eroded from the surrounding limestone cliffs, and almost perfectly rectangular in shape. It was named after Scottish Captain Alexander Campbell, a whaler who took refuge here on trading voyages between Tasmania and Port Fairy. It's a friendly spot with some great bargain accommodation options, and makes an ideal spot for debriefing after the Twelve Apostles. The tiny bay has a lovely sandy beach, the only safe place for swimming along this tempestuous coast.

LIGHT & DARK

In the era of sailing ships, Victoria's beautiful and rugged southwest coastline was one of the most treacherous on Earth. Between the 1830s and 1930s, more than 200 ships were torn asunder along the so-called **Shipwreck Coast** between Cape Otway and Port Fairy. From the early 1850s to late 1880s, Victoria's gold rush and subsequent economic boom brought countless ships of prospectors and hopefuls from Europe, North America and China. After spending months at sea, many vessels (and lives) were lost on the final 'home straight'. The lighthouses along this coast – at **Aireys Inlet** (p165), **Cape Otway** (p173) and **Port Fairy** (p183) – are still operating. The Cape Otway Lighthouse was also involved in the first telegraph cable laid between Tasmania and the Australian mainland in 1859. The spectacular coast around **Port Campbell** (p174) is where the *Loch Ard* famously sank, and the town is littered with material salvaged from this and many other shipwrecks. At **Wreck Beach** (p173) you can see the anchors of the *Marie Gabrielle* which sank in 1869, and the *Fiji*, driven aground in 1891.

OTWAY FLY

Twenty kilometres inland from Lavers Hill on the Colac Rd (C155) is the **Otway Fly** (☑5235 9200; www.otwayfly.com; Phillips Track; adult/child/family $22/9.50/55; ⊙9am-4.30pm, zipline tour adult/child $115/83), 5km from Beech Forest. It's an elevated steel walkway in the forest canopy with a wavy lookout tower. Kids will enjoy the 'prehistoric path' loaded with dinosaurs, and everyone can test their bravery on the zipline tour – where you fly from cloud station to cloud station.

⊙ Sights & Activities

There is stunning **diving** in the kelp forests, canyons and tunnels of the **Arches Marine Sanctuary** and also to the *Loch Ard* wreck. There are shore dives from **Wild Dog Cove** and **Crofts Bay**.

A 4.7km **Discovery Walk**, with signage, gives an introduction to the area's natural and historical features. It's just out of town on the way to Warrnambool.

Port Campbell Touring Company

WALKING, FISHING

(☑5598 6424; www.portcampbelltouring.com.au;half-day tours $65) Runs Apostle Coast tours, a Loch Ard evening walk and fishing trips to Crofts Bay.

Port Campbell Boat Charters   TOURS

(☑5598 6411) Runs diving, scenic and fishing tours.

⊨ Sleeping

Port Campbell Guesthouse   GUESTHOUSE $

(☑0407 696 559; www.portcampbellguesthouse.com.au; 54 Lord St; guesthouse/flashpackers r per person $35/38) It's great to find a home away from home, and this property close to town has a cosy house with four bedrooms out back and a separate motel-style 'flashpackers' section up front. Great for families.

Port Campbell Hostel   HOSTEL $

(☑5598 6305; www.portcampbellhostel.com.au; 18 Tregea St; dm/d $25/70; ✱⊛) This brand new, purpose-built double-storey backpackers has rooms with western views, a huge shared kitchen and an even bigger lounge and bar area. It's big on recycling and the toilets are ecofriendly, too. Hang out in the lounge and read the day's papers or get involved with a *Mills & Boon*.

Port Campbell Holiday Park

CAMPING GROUND, CABINS $

(☑5598 6492; www.pchp.com.au; Morris St; unpowered/powered sites $28/31, cabins $105; ⊛) Neat, small and a two-minute walk to the beach and town.

Port Bayou   B&B $$

(☑5598 6009; www.portbayou.portcampbell.nu; 52 Lord St; d B&B $130, cottage $155; ✱) Choose from the cosy in-house B&B or a rustic self-contained cottage fitted with exposed ceiling beams and corrugated-tin walls (we'd go for the cottage).

Daysy Hill Country Cottages   COTTAGES $$

(☑5598 6226; www.daysyhillcottages.com.au; 2585 Cobden-Port Campbell Rd; d from $145; ✱) These hillside cedar-and-sandstone cottages are a few minutes from town and are decorated in a modern colonial style. The newer cabins have the best views and two have spas.

✕ Eating

Room Six   MODERN AUSTRALIAN $$

(28 Lord St; mains $15-30; ⊙breakfast, lunch & dinner Fri-Wed) Come here for delightful dinners (featuring all the good seafood of the area) or a simple snack during the day. Although only new, its ambience suggests a lovely maturity.

12 Rocks Cafe Bar   CAFE $

(19 Lord St; mains $8-15; ⊙breakfast, lunch & dinner) Watch flotsam wash up on the beach from this busy place, which has the best beachfront views. Try a local Otways beer with a pasta or seafood main, or just duck in for a coffee.

ℹ Information

Port Campbell visitor centre (☑1300 137 255; www.visit12apostles.com.au; 26 Morris St; ⊙9am-5pm) Stacks of regional and accommodation information and interesting shipwreck displays – the anchor from the *Loch Ard* is out the front, salvaged in 1978.

ℹ Getting There & Away

Bus

V/Line buses leave Geelong on Monday, Wednesday and Friday and travel through Port Campbell ($24, four hours) and onto Warrnambool ($27, six hours).

Organised Tours

The following tours depart from Melbourne and often cover the Great Ocean Rd in a day:

Go West Tours (☑1300 736 551; www.gowest. com.au)

Ride Tours (☑1800 605 120; www.ridetours. com.au)

Autopia Tours (☑9391 0261; www.autopia tours.com.au)

Goin South (☑1800 009 858; www.goinsouth. com.au)

Otway Discovery (☑9654 5432; www.otway discovery.com.au)

Adventure Tours (☑1800 068 886; www. adventuretours.com.au)

PORT CAMPBELL TO WARRNAMBOOL

The Great Ocean Road continues west of Port Campbell passing more rock stacks. The next one is the **Arch**, offshore from Point Hesse.

Nearby is **London Bridge**...fallen down! Now sometimes called London Arch, it was once a double-arched rock platform linked to the mainland. Visitors could walk out across a narrow natural bridge to the huge rock formation. In January 1990, the bridge collapsed leaving two terrified tourists marooned on the world's newest island – they were eventually rescued by helicopter. Nearby is the **Grotto**.

The **Bay of Islands** is 8km west of tiny **Peterborough**, where a short walk from the car park takes you to magnificent lookout points.

You can't help but notice the acres and acres of farming land here, and if you're driving, keep an eye out for milk trucks pulling slowly into and out of farms. Slightly tacky **Cheese World** (www.cheeseworld.com.au; Great Ocean Rd, Allansford; ◷9.30am-5pm Mon-Fri, 9am-4pm Sat, 9am-3pm Sun) is opposite the area's main dairy factory, and has a museum, restaurant, cheese cellar and tasty (and cheap) milkshakes. It's 12km before Warrnambool

Timboon, about 16km inland from Peterborough, has a couple of foodie treasures. First up, pop into **L'Artisan Cheese** (cnr Ford & Fells Rd; ◷10.30am-4pm daily Oct-Apr, Wed-Sun May-Sep) and enjoy free tastings of its wonderful cheeses. They're reasonably priced so grab a couple of your favourites for the journey ahead, or get a cheese platter at the on-site cafe. Next stop is the **Timboon Railway Shed Distillery** (www. timboondistillery.com; Bailey St; meals $15-19; ◷10am-5pm, dinner Fri). If you can handle more cheese, this bright former railway goods shed has $20 platters, or try dishes such as Timboon honey and balsamic marinated chicken breast with risoni. There are wood-fired pizzas on Friday nights and, it being a small, recently set up distillery, whisky to try (and buy).

The Great Ocean Road ends near here, where it meets the Princess Hwy (A1), which continues through the traditional lands of the Gunditjmara people into South Australia.

HOW MANY APOSTLES?

The Twelve Apostles are not 12 in number, and, from all records, never have been. From the viewing platform you can clearly count seven Apostles, but maybe some obscure others? We consulted widely with Parks Victoria officers, tourist office staff and even the cleaner at the lookout, but it's still not clear. Locals tend to say 'It depends where you look from', which really is true.

The Apostles are called 'stacks' in geologic lingo, and the rock formations were originally called the 'Sow and Piglets'. Someone in the '60s (nobody can recall who) thought they might attract some tourists with a more venerable name, so they were renamed 'the Apostles'. Since apostles tend to come by the dozen, the number 12 was added sometime later. The two stacks on the eastern (Otway) side of the viewing platform are not technically Apostles – they're Gog and Magog (picking up on the religious nomeclature yet?).

So there aren't 12 stacks; in a boat or helicopter you might count 11. The soft limestone cliffs are dynamic and changeable, constantly eroded by the unceasing waves – one 70m-high stack collapsed into the sea in July 2005 and the Island Archway lost its archway in June 2009. If you look carefully at how the waves lick around the pointy part of the cliff base, you can see a new Apostle being born. The labour lasts many thousands of years.

The Victorian coastline between Cape Otway and Port Fairy was a notoriously treacherous stretch of water in the days of sailing ships, due to hidden reefs and frequent heavy fog. More than 80 vessels came to grief on this 120km stretch in just 40 years.

The most famous wreck was that of the iron-hulled clipper *Loch Ard,* which foundered off Mutton Bird Island at 4am on the final night of its long voyage from England in 1878. Of 37 crew and 19 passengers on board, only two survived. Eva Carmichael, a nonswimmer, clung to wreckage and was washed into a gorge, where apprentice officer Tom Pearce rescued her. Tom heroically climbed the sheer cliff and raised the alarm but no other survivors were found. Eva and Tom were both 19 years old, leading to speculation in the press about a romance, but nothing actually happened – they never saw each other again and Eva soon returned to Ireland (this time, perhaps not surprisingly, via steamship).

WARRNAMBOOL

POP 28,100

Warrnambool was originally a whaling and sealing station – now it's booming as a major regional commercial and whale-watching centre. Its historic buildings, waterways and tree-lined streets are attractive, and there's a large population of students who attend the Warrnambool campus of Deakin University. The major housing and commercial development around the fringes of the city looks much like city suburbs anywhere in Australia, but the regions around the waterfront have largely retained their considerable historic charm.

◉ Sights & Activities

Southern right whales come to mate and nurse their bubs in the waters off Logan's Beach from July to September, breaching and fluking off **Logan's Beach Whale Watching Platform**. It's a major tourist drawcard, but sightings are not guaranteed.

Flagstaff Hill Maritime Village
REPLICA HISTORIC SITE
(☑1800 556 111; www.flagstaffhill.com; Merri St; adult/child/family $16/7/39; ⊙9am-5pm). This major tourist attraction is modelled on an early Australian coastal port. See the cannon and fortifications, built in 1887 to withstand the perceived threat of Russian invasion, and **Shipwrecked** (adult/child/family $26/14/67), an engaging evening sound-and-laser show of the *Loch Ard*'s plunge. Grab a meal at Pippies by the Bay (p179) while you're here.

FREE **Warrnambool Art Gallery** ART GALLERY
(www.warrnambool.vic.gov.au; 165 Timor St; ⊙10am-5pm Mon-Fri, noon-5pm Sat & Sun)

Head here to see the gallery's permanent Australian collection, which includes works by such notable painters as Tom Roberts, James Gleeson and Arthur Boyd.

Dirty Angel MONUMENT
(Liebig St) Standing erect at the bay-end of Liebig St is Warrnambool's war memorial, built in 1925. Take a trip around the roundabout and, from a certain angle, you'll see where it gets its nickname. You can also try a local dark ale named after it.

Rundell's Mahogany Trail Rides
HORSE RIDING
(☑0408 589 546; www.rundellshorseriding.com.au; Millers Lane, Dennington; 2hr beach rides $65) Get to know some of Warrnambool's quiet beach spots by horseback.

Absolute Outdoors SURFING, KAYAKING
(☑5521 7646; www.absoluteoutdoors.com.au; surfing from $40) Runs surfing, kayaking and rock-climbing adventures.

Southern Coast Charters WHALE-WATCHING
(☑5598 3112; www.southerncoastcharters.com.au) Go fishing or whale-watching on one of these charters.

Warrnambool has excellent beaches such as sheltered **Lady Bay**, the main swimming beach, which has fortifications at the breakwater at its western end. **Logan's Beach** has the best surf, and there are breaks at Levy's Beach and Second Bay.

Walking trails in and around Warrnambool include the 3km **Heritage Trail**. The short **Thunder Point** stroll shows off the best coastal scenery in the area; it's also the starting point for the 22km coastal **Mahogany Walking Trail**.

Festivals & Events

Fun4Kids Festival KIDS
(☎5562 4044; www.fun4kids.com.au; various locations) The first week of the winter school holidays (usually in June/July) sees thousands of two- to 12-year-olds (and their parents) head to Warrnambool for this totally kid-oriented festival.

Sleeping

Hotel Warrnambool PUB $$
(☎5562 2377; www.hotelwarrnambool.com.au; cnr Koroit & Kepler Sts; d with/without en suite $140/110; ❋@) Recent renovations in this historic 1894 pub have done wonders with the rooms, which have plasma TVs and access to a kitchenette and lounge. Some have bathrooms and balconies. Downstairs is one of the friendliest pub-eateries in town.

Atwood Motor Inn MOTEL $$
(☎5562 7144; www.atwoodmotorinn.com.au; 8 Spence St; d from $105; ❋☎) Expect spacious

motel-style rooms with flatscreen TVs and bathrooms big enough to wash a (small) whale in. The standard doubles are the smallest, but are still comfortable.

Ban Kor House RENTAL HOUSE $$
(☎0417 156 659; www.bankorhouse.com.au; cnr Banyan & Koroit Sts; d from $180; ❋) This is a nice refit of an old sandstone cottage, retaining many original features. The rooms have been decorated with an eclectic mix of period features and modern styles. The owners also run the place next door, which is similar but with an African theme.

Bayside Lodge MOTEL $$
(☎5562 7323; www.baysidelodge.com.au; 30 Pertobe Rd; q $100-170; ❋☎) These large self-contained two-bedroom apartments are great value for a group or family. Stuck in a '70s time warp, but literally spittin' distance from the beach.

Warrnambool

Warrnambool Beach Backpackers

HOSTEL **$**

(☏5562 4874; www.beachbackpackers.com.au; 17 Stanley St; dm/d $28/80; ﹡@) Close to the sea, this former museum has a huge living area with a bar, internet access, a kitchen and free pick-up service. Its rooms, however, could do with a freshen up. It's a good place to seek casual employment.

Surfside Holiday Park CAMPING GROUND **$$**

(☏5559 4700; www.surfsidepark.com.au; Pertobe Rd; unpowered/powered sites $27/35, cabins from $104) Surfside is one of several Warrnambool caravan parks, and offers good self-contained cabins as well as tent and caravan sites. It's perfectly situated between the town and the beach.

✕ Eating & Drinking

TOP CHOICE **Donnelly's Restaurant**

MODERN AUSTRALIAN **$$**

(78 Liebig St; mains $24-31; ⊙lunch & dinner Tue-Sun, daily in summer) This smart restaurant makes a big deal of its steaks and seafood, and it's no wonder: both are as local as you can get and very satisfying.

Wyton CAFE **$**

(www.wytonevents.com; 91 Kepler St; mains $12; ⊙breakfast & lunch Mon-Fri, breakfast Sat) Come here for sophisticated breakfasts, excellent coffee and healthy lunches (including spicy carrot and risoni pasta), which you can takeaway.

Bojangles PIZZA **$$**

(61 Liebig St; mains $15-31; ⊙breakfast, lunch & dinner) Bojangles is an upmarket pizza restaurant that does great pastas and pizzas. It has an excellent wine list and friendly service.

Pippies by the Bay MODERN AUSTRALIAN **$$**

(Flagstaff Hill Maritime Village, Merri St; mains $28-32; ⊙lunch & dinner daily, breakfast Sat & Sun) A fine restaurant situated in the Flagstaff Hill visitor centre; make an evening of it with a meal and show, or otherwise you can just pop in for a weekend breakfast and admire the view.

Hotel Warrnambool PUB FARE **$$**

(cnr Koroit & Kepler Sts; mains $26-29; ⊙lunch & dinner) This is a cheerful, earthy and cavernous place with exposed mud bricks and railway sleepers, slouchy lounges, a beer garden and live music on the weekends. The bar menu has cheaper mains, including the chef's stir fry, curry of the day and wood-fired pizzas.

Fishtales Cafe MULTICUISINE **$$**

(☏5561 2957; 63 Liebig St; mains $15-25; ⊙breakfast, lunch & dinner) Fishtales is upbeat, friendly and intent on making its eatery the UN of food. It covers India, the Mediterranean, China (and more) and lists its food under 'sea', 'garden' and 'paddock'. Get takeaway or otherwise sit in its cheery courtyard.

Whaler's Inn PUB FARE **$$**

(www.whalersinn.com.au; cnr Liebig & Timor Sts; mains $17-30; ⊙lunch & dinner) It's a family-friendly set-up here and meals are tasty and generous. Prices include an all-you-can-eat salad bar. Fill up for evening karaoke or perhaps the weekend disco.

☆ Entertainment

Loft LIVE MUSIC

(58 Liebig St; ⊙5.30pm-1am Wed, Fri & Sat, daily Dec-Feb) Where the folksy-folk come to play when in Warrnambool.

Warrnambool Entertainment Centre

THEATRE

(☏5564 7885; www.entertainmentcentre.com.au; cnr Liebig & Timor Sts) This is a major venue for live theatre, ballet and music.

Warrnambool Cinema CINEMA
(☎5562 2709; www.villagecinemas.com.au; 54 Kepler St; adult/child/student $14.50/10.50/12.50) Shows mainstream movies. All tickets for sessions starting before 11am are $9.

ℹ️ Information

Warrnambool Library (25 Liebig St; ☻9.30am-5pm Mon-Tue, to 6pm Wed-Fri, 10am-noon Sat; @) Free internet access.

Warrnambool visitor centre (www.visit warrnambool.com.au; Merri St; ☻9am-5pm; @) Signposted off the Princes Hwy (A1) in the Flagstaff Hill complex, it produces a bike map and several walking maps. There's also internet access here ($10 per hour) and bicycle hire ($30 per day).

ℹ️ Getting There & Away

Bus

Three buses a week (Monday, Wednesday and Friday) travel from Geelong along the Great Ocean Road to Warrnambool ($27, six hours).

V/Line (☎13 61 96; www.vline.com.au) has 10 buses a day to Port Fairy ($3.40, 30 minutes) and three continue on to Portland ($9.20, 1½ hours). One bus each weekday goes to Hamilton ($4.60, 1½ hours) and Ballarat ($13.70, three hours), and one on Monday, Wednesday and Friday to Apollo Bay ($15.80, 3½ hours).

Christians Bus Co (☎5562 9432) runs services on Tuesday, Friday and Saturday to Port Fairy ($3.30, departing 8am), continuing to Hamilton ($10.40, two hours), Dunkeld ($13.70, 2½ hours), Halls Gap ($20.40, 3¼ hours) and Ararat ($24, four hours).

Car

Warrnambool is a 45 minute drive west of Port Campbell on the B100.

Train

V/Line (☎13 61 96; www.vline.com.au; Merri St) Trains run to Melbourne ($26, 3¼ hours, three or four daily).

TOWER HILL RESERVE

Tower Hill, 15km west of Warrnambool, is a vast caldera born in a volcanic eruption 35,000 years ago. Aboriginal artefacts unearthed in the volcanic ash show that indigenous people lived in the area at the time. The Worn Gundidj Aboriginal Cooperative operates the **Tower Hill Natural History Centre** (www.worngundidj.org.au; ☻9am-5pm Mon-Fri, 10am-4pm Sat, Sun & public holidays) and Parks Victoria manages the park, which, as a state game reserve, is also open to duck hunters during open season (but not between 9am and 5pm). It's one of the few places where you'll spot wild emus, kangaroos and koalas hanging out together.

There are excellent day walks, including the steep 30-minute **Peak Climb** with spectacular 360-degree views. There's a fascinating painting by Eugene von Guérard of Tower Hill painted in 1855 in the Warrnambool Art Gallery (p181), see the copy at the visitors centre. After a century of deforestation and environmental degradation, this incredibly detailed painting was used to identify species used in a replanting program begun in 1961 when Tower Hill became a state game reserve. Since then over 300,000 trees have been replanted.

PORT FAIRY

POP 2600

This seaside township at the mouth of the Moyne River was settled in 1835, and the first arrivals were whalers and sealers. Port Fairy still has a large fishing fleet and a relaxed, salty feel, with its old bluestone and sandstone buildings, whitewashed cottages, colourful fishing boats and tree-lined streets. The tiny town centre is along and around Sackville St, and the many historic

THE MAHOGANY SHIP

The *Mahogany Ship* is said to be a Portuguese vessel that ran aground off Warrnambool in the 1500s – there have been alleged sightings of the elusive wreck sitting high in the dunes dating back to 1846. Portuguese naval charts from the 16th century, known as the Dieppe Maps, are said to depict parts of Australia's southern coastline, including Armstrong Bay 6km west of Warrnambool, and this has further fuelled the *Mahogany Ship* legend. Alternative theories claim that the *Mahogany Ship* was an even earlier Chinese junk. For 150 years people have been trying to find the remains of the *Mahogany Ship* – some say it's buried deep in the dunes or was swallowed by the sea. There's no direct evidence that the ship ever existed, but every decade or so it all rises to the surface again at the locally held Mahogany Ship Symposium.

ROBIN BOYD

The UFO-like building housing the Tower Hill Natural History Centre was designed by renowned Australian architect Robin Boyd (1919–71) in 1962. While his post-war buildings dot Victoria's landscape, they're usually in the hands of private owners – this one is an exception. Feel the coolness created by using thick walls, and check out the interesting beam-supported ceiling, volcano-like roof and extra-large eaves.

buildings remain authentic to Port Fairy's bygone era. The town is very much a luxury tourist destination and is home to art galleries, antique shops and boutiques.

Port Fairy has a rich and sometimes gloomy heritage that enraptures local history buffs.

◉ Sight & Activities

Port Fairy History Centre   MUSEUM
(www.historicalsociety.port-fairy.com; 30 Gipps St; admission adult/child $3/50c; ⊙2-5pm Wed, Sat & Sun) Housed in the old bluestone courthouse (complete with dusty mannequins acting out a courtroom scene), this museum has shipping relics, old photos and costumes, and a prisoner's cell.

Mulloka Cruises   BOAT CRUISE
(⊋0408 514 382; cruises adult/child $10/free) Runs half-hour cruises of the port, bay and Griffiths Island.

Port Fairy Surf School   CYCLING, SURFING
(⊋5568 2800; www.daktarisport.com.au; 33 Bank St) Hire bikes or learn to surf.

Walks
The visitors centre has brochures and maps that show the popular **Shipwreck Walk** and **History Walk** signposted around town. Also available from the visitors centre is **Art Walk**, a guide to the many local **art galleries**. On **Battery Hill** there's a lookout point, and cannons and fortifications positioned here in the 1860s. Down below there's a lovely one-hour walk around **Griffiths Island** where the Moyne River empties into the sea. The island is connected to the mainland by a footbridge, and is home to a protected **mutton bird colony** (they descend on the town each October and stay until April) and a modest **lighthouse**.

⁂ Festivals & Events

Port Fairy Folk Festival   MUSIC
(www.portfairyfolkfestival.com; tickets $195) Australia's premier folk-music festival is held on the Labour Day long weekend in March. Accommodation for the festival, and the festival itself, is usually booked a year in advance.

🛏 Sleeping

Much of Port Fairy's holiday accommodation is managed by agents, including **Port Fairy Accommodation Centre** (⊋5568 3150; www.portfairyaccom.com.au; 2/54 Sackville St) and **Port Fairy Holiday Rentals** (⊋5568 1066; www.lockettrealestate.com.au; 62 Sackville St). The visitor centre offers a free booking service.

Pelican Waters   BOUTIQUE HOTEL $$
(⊋5568 1002; www.pelicanwatersportfairy.com.au; 34 Regent St; cabins/carriages from $100) Why stay in a hotel when you can sleep in a train? This beautifully presented property has cabins as well as two two-bedroom converted Melbourne train carriages. Great fun.

Port Fairy YHA   HOSTEL $
(⊋5568 2468; www.portfairyhostel.com.au; 8 Cox St; dm $26-30, d/f/apt from $75/115/200; @🖥🛜) In the rambling 1844 home of merchant William Rutledge, this friendly, well-run hostel has a large kitchen, a pool table, free cable TV and peaceful gardens. There's a huge self-contained two-bedroom apartment that has its own lounge and can sleep six, though we bar-rack for the sweet cottage rooms at the back.

Daisies by the Sea B&B   B&B $$
(⊋5568 2355; www.port-fairy.com/daisiesbythesea; 222 Griffiths St; d from $160) Nod off to the sound of the crashing waves just 50m from your door in these two cosy beachfront suites, 1.5km from town. Daisies is a modest, snug and appealing getaway for couples.

Gardens Caravan Park   CAMPING GROUND $$
(⊋5568 1060; www.portfairycaravanparks.com; 111 Griffiths St; unpowered/powered sites $33/38, cabins from $130) One of several local caravan parks, this place is next to the botanical gardens, 200m from the beach and a short walk to the town centre.

Merrijig Inn   PUB $$
(⊋5568 2324; www.merrijiginn.com; cnr Campbell & Gipps Sts; d incl breakfast from $140) Known more for its food than its rooms, Victoria's oldest inn has tiny attic doubles that are about as authentic as you can get. The queen suites are roomier.

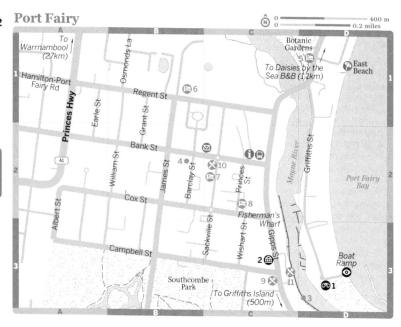

🍴 Eating

TOP CHOICE **Merrijig Inn** MEDITERRANEAN **$$$**
(📞5568 2324; www.merrijiginn.com; cnr Campbell & Gipps Sts; 5 courses $90) Stop here. No, really. Get in here and enjoy some of the best tastes in town. It's superb dining and the menu changes according to what's seasonal. You might get duck breast, baby beetroot, pickled rose, rhubarb and chard one day, and yabbies with asparagus, almonds and nasturtium the next. Delectable food with great service.

Rebecca's Cafe CAFE **$**
(70-72 Sackville St; mains $9-16; ☺breakfast & lunch) Excellent for breakfast and light lunches, Rebecca's has interesting items on the menu including rich wild-rice porridge topped with rhubarb as well as the usual cakes, muffins, slices, scones and biscuits. Lunch runs until 4pm.

Wisharts at the Wharf FISH & CHIPS **$$**
(📞5568 1884; 29 Gipps St; mains $17-23; ☺lunch & dinner) Wharfside dining doesn't come prettier than this. Plump, fresh fish and chips are always assured here. Adventurous presentation and flavours in very relaxed surrounds.

The Hub CAFE **$**
(cnr Bank & Sackville Sts; mains $14; ☺breakfast, lunch & dinner; 🛜) On weekends this corner cafe is packed with people enjoying spicy gourmet breakfasts featuring locally made chorizo sausage, and good old bacon and eggs. The menu steps up a notch for mostly seafood dinners.

ℹ️ Information

Port Fairy Community House (📞5568 2681; Railway Pl; ☺10am-3pm Mon-Fri; @) Internet access costs $4 per hour.

Port Fairy visitor centre (📞5568 2682; www.visitportfairy-moyneshire.com.au; Bank St; ☺9am-5pm) Can recharge your mobile phone battery while providing spot-on tourist information.

ℹ️ Getting There & Away

Bus
V/Line (📞13 61 96; www.vline.com.au) Buses run three times daily on weekdays (twice on Saturday and once on Sunday) to Portland ($6.50, one hour) and Warrnambool ($3.50, 35 minutes).

Viclink (📞13 61 38; www.viclink.com.au) Services connect Port Fairy with Hamilton ($10, 1¼ hours, three weekly), continuing to Halls Gap ($23.50, 2½ hours) and Ararat ($30, 3¼ hours).

Car
Port Fairy is 20 minutes west of Warrnambool on the A1.

Port Fairy

PORTLAND

POP 9800

There's a charm to largish Portland; it has historic houses, a bunch of ghost stories and is a short distance from a lovely lighthouse. It's also the start and end of the Great South West Walk (see p184)

This was Victoria's first European settlement, and became a whaling and sealing base in the early 1800s. The Henty family came here from Van Diemen's Land in 1834 and were the first permanent settlers. Blessed Mary MacKillop, Australia's first saint, arrived here from Melbourne in 1862 and founded Australia's first religious order. Portland is the only deep-water port between Melbourne and Adelaide, and is also home to the massive Portland Aluminium Smelter. The huge industrial wharf is an eyesore on an otherwise attractive colonial-era township.

◎ Sights & Activities

Portland Cable Tram   HISTORIC SITE
(www.portlandcabletrams.com.au; rides adult/child/family $15/12/35; ☺10am-4pm) This restored 1886 cable tram does five trips a day plying an 8km circular route linking the vintage-car museum, botanic gardens, Maritime Discovery Centre and WWII memorial water tower. You can hop on and off as you please.

Powerhouse Motor & Car Museum
                                    MUSEUM
(www.portlandnow.net.au/powerhouse; cnr Glenelg & Percy Sts; adult/child/family $5/1/10) This car-enthusiasts' dream has 30 vintage Australian and American vehicles and motorbikes dating from 1920.

🛏 Sleeping

TOP CHOICE **Annesley House**   BOUTIQUE HOTEL **$$**
(☎0429 852 235; www.annesleyhouse.com.au; 60 Julia St; d from $135) This recently restored former doctor's mansion (c 1878) has six very different self-contained rooms, some featuring clawfoot baths and lovely views. All feature a unique sense of style. Highly recommended.

Clifftop Accommodation   GUESTHOUSE **$$**
(☎5523 1126; www.portlandaccommodation.com.au; 13 Clifton Ct; d from $140; ❇) The panoramic ocean views from the balconies here are incredible. These three self-contained rooms are huge, with big brass beds, telescopes and a modern maritime feel.

Victoria House   GUESTHOUSE **$$**
(☎5521 7577; www.babs.com.au/vic house; 5 Tyers St; s/d incl breakfast from $130/145) This two-storey Georgian bluestone dwelling right in the town centre was built in 1853 and is classified by the National Trust. Its nine heritage-style rooms are showing their age a tad, but the place is buoyed by a comfy lounge with an open fire and some resident ghosts (apparently).

Claremont Holiday Village   CABINS **$**
(☎5523 7567; www.holidayvillage.com.au; 37 Percy St; unpowered sites from $26/35, cabins from $70; @) This central caravan park has decent facilities including a large camp kitchen. The cheaper cabins have shared bathrooms.

✕ Eating

Deegan Seafoods   FISH & CHIPS **$**
(106 Percy St; mains $10; ☺lunch & dinner) Famously, this fish and chip shop serves up the freshest fish in Victoria.

JD's Cafe   FAST FOOD **$**
(70 Percy St; mains $3; ☺breakfast & lunch Mon-Sat) The homemade sausage rolls here are absolutely delicious; nab the recipe if you can!

❶ Information

Parks Victoria (☎5522 3454; www.parkweb.vic.gov.au; 8-12 Julia St; ☺8am-4.30pm Mon-Fri)

Portland visitors centre (☎5523 2671; www. greatoceanroad.org; Lee Breakwater Rd; ☺9am-5pm) In the impressive-looking Maritime Discovery Centre.

① Getting There & Away

Bus

V/Line (☎13 61 96; www.vline.com.au) buses connect Portland with Port Fairy three times daily and once on Sunday ($6.50, 55 minutes) and Warrnambool ($9.50, 1½ hours). Buses depart from Henty St.

Car

Portland is 45 minutes west of Port Fairy on the A1.

PORTLAND TO SOUTH AUSTRALIA

From Portland you can go north to Heywood and rejoin the Princes Hwy to South Australia, or head northwest along the slower, beautiful coastal route known as the Portland-Nelson Rd. This road runs inland from the coast, but along the way there are turn-offs leading to beaches and national parks.

Cape Bridgewater

Cape Bridgewater is an essential 21km detour off the Portland–Nelson Rd. The stunning 4km arc of **Bridgewater Bay** is perhaps one of Australia's finest stretches of white-sand surf beach, backed by pristine dunes. The road continues on to **Cape Duquesne** where walking tracks lead to a **Blowhole** and the **Petrified Forest** on the clifftop. A longer two-hour return walk takes you to a **seal colony** where you can see dozens of fur seals sunning themselves on the rocks.

There's plenty of accommodation available at Cape Bridgewater (enquire at Port-

land visitors centre, p183), but standouts include friendly **Sea View Lodge B&B** (☎5526 7276; www.hotkey.net.au/~seaviewlodge; Bridgewater Rd; d from $140), **Abalone Beach House** (☎0408 808 346; www.abalonehouse.com.au; Bridgewater Rd; house sleeping 4 from $240) and **Cape Bridgewater Bay House** (☎9439 2966; www.capebridgewater.com.au; Bridgewater Rd; up to 4 people $170, extra person $15), an outstanding original bluestone house, refurbished with recycled timber and designer flare, which can sleep eight. **Cape Bridgewater Holiday Camp** (☎5526 7247; www.capebridgewatercoast alcamp.com.au; Blowhole Rd; unpowered sites $15, dm $30, houses $150) has been thoroughly renovated and has lovely dorms, modern self-contained homes and a huge camp kitchen. It also runs incredibly exhilarating **Seals by Sea tours** (adult/child $30/20).

Nelson

POP 230

Tiny Nelson is the last vestige of civilisation before the South Australian border – just a general store, a pub and a handful of accommodation places. It's a popular holiday and fishing spot at the mouth of the **Glenelg River**, which flows through **Lower Glenelg National Park**. Note that Nelson uses South Australia's ☎08 telephone area code. Why? We dunno!

⊙ Sights & Activities

Nelson Boat & Canoe Hire   BOATING
(☎08-8738 4048; www.nelsonboatandcanoehire. com.au) This outfit can rig you up for serious river-camping expeditions – canoe hire costs from $60 a day. It also has paddleboats for hire ($20 per 30 minutes).

Glenelg River Cruises (☎08-8738 4191; cruises adult/child $30/10) departs Nelson daily (except Thursday and Monday) at 1pm for a

GREAT SOUTH WEST WALK

This 250km signposted loop begins and ends at Portland's information centre, and takes in some of the southwest's most stunning natural scenery: from the remote, blustery coast, through the river system of the Lower Glenelg National Park and back through the hinterland to Portland. Brilliantly conceived to connect some of the region's best camping grounds, comfortable accommodation and dining options can also be included. The whole loop would take at least 10 days, but it can be done in sections, and parts can be done as day walks. Maps are available from the Portland visitors centre (p183) and the Parks Victoria and visitor centre in Nelson (p185). All information, FAQs and registration details are available online at www.greatsouthwestwalk.com.

CAPE NELSON LIGHTHOUSE

Cape Nelson Lighthouse (which, be warned, is not on the road to the town of Nelson) is a wonderful spot for a flash bite to eat and some stunning views. **Isabella's Cafe** (☺10am-4pm; antipasta platters $20) takes pride of place at its blustering base and offers excellent deli-style food within its thick bluestone walls. **Lighthouse tours** (adult/child $15/10; ☺10am & 2pm) get you high up, while those wanting to stay a while can book into a self-contained **assistant lighthouse keeper's cottage** (www.capenelsonlighthouse. com.au; d from $180).

leisurely 3½-hour cruise to the **Princess Margaret Rose Cave** (☑08-8738 4171; www. princessmargaretrosecave.com; admission adult/ child/family $14/9/32), but tickets for the cave tour cost extra. If you travel to the cave on your own, it's about 17km from Nelson, towards the border.

🛏 Sleeping

Nelson Hotel   PUB **$**
(☑08-8738 4011; www.nelsonhotel.com.au; Kellett St; d/apt from $40/135; ☺lunch & dinner) This hotel has a dusty stuffed pelican above the bar and a few vegetarian meals on the fishy menu (mains $17 to $30). The quarters are plain, but adequate, with shared facilities, and the attached apartment/studio is great.

Nelson Cottage   COTTAGE **$**
(☑08-8738 4161; www.nelsoncottage.bigpondhost ing.com; cnr Kellett & Sturt Sts; d from $90) This 1848 cottage has old-fashioned rooms with clean shared amenities.

Wrens on Glenelg   B&B **$$**
(☑08-8738 4198; www.wrensonglenelg.com.au; 5 Acacia St; d incl breakfast $160) This swish, modern B&B is done in designer corrugated iron in a nice bush setting, with a private landing on the Glenelg River.

Kywong Caravan Park   CAMPING GROUND **$**
(☑08-8738 4174; www.kywongcp.com; North Nelson Rd; unpowered/powered sites $22/27, cabin d from $53) This 25-acre park is next to the national park and Glenelg River.

There are nine camp sites between Nelson and Dartmoor along the Glenelg River that are popular with canoeists but are also accessible by road, with rain-fed water tanks, toilets and fireplaces (BYO firewood). Camping permits are issued by Parks Victoria in Nelson. Forest Camp South, right on the river, rich in bird life and easily accessible from the Portland-Nelson Rd, is the nicest of these.

ℹ️ Information

Parks Victoria & Nelson visitor centre (☑08-8738 4051; nelsonvic@hotkey.net.au; ☺9am-5pm; @) Just before the Glenelg River bridge.

Getting There & Away

Nelson is 65km from Portland, and 4km from the South Australian border.

Heywood Bus Lines (☑5523 5811) leave Portland for Nelson ($5.70) on Monday and Friday at 9am (returning Monday and Friday at 2pm).

Goldfields & Grampians

Includes »

Why Go?

History, nature and culture combine spectacularly in Victoria's regional heart. It's hard to believe that more than a third of the world's gold came out of Victoria for a brief time in the mid-19th century – most of it from the small but fabulously rich central Victorian goldfields.

Today, the spoils of all that precious metal can be seen in the grand regional cities of Bendigo and Ballarat and the charming-but-not-so-grand-anymore towns of Castlemaine, Kyneton and Maldon. This is a fantastic region for touring, with a range of contrasting landscapes from pretty countryside and green forests to red earth and granite country to farmland, orchards and wineries.

Further west, there's a different type of history to experience at the Grampians National Park, one of Victoria's great natural wonders. The majestic ranges here contain some 80% of Victoria's Aboriginal rock art sites, while for travellers, the Grampians are an adventurer's paradise, standing majestically over the idyllic Wartook Valley and Halls Gaps and Dunkeld.

Best Places to Eat

» Royal Mail Hotel (p211)
» GPO (p198)
» Craig's Royal Hotel (p192)
» Dhaba at the Mill (p200)
» Good Table (p202)

Best Places to Stay

» Shamrock Hotel (p197)
» Theatre Royal Backstage (p202)
» Aspect Villas (p209)
» Little Desert Nature Lodge (p212)
» Steinfeld's (p192)

When to Go
Ballarat

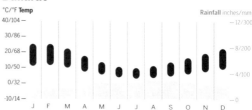

Sep–Nov When the wildflowers bloom in Grampians National Park

Easter Enter the dragon at the Bendigo Easter Festival

Mar–May Autumn colours, hiking and wine touring without the crowds

BALLARAT

POP 78,300

Ballarat was built on gold and it's easy to see the proceeds of those days in the grand Victorian-era architecture around the city centre. The single biggest attraction here is the recreated gold-mining village at Sovereign Hill, but there's plenty m   ore in this busy provincial town to keep you occupied: a day spent admiring the architecture, wandering through the superb art gallery or hanging around Lake Wendouree and the botanical gardens is a day well spent. Rug up if you visit in the winter months – Ballarat is renowned for being startlingly chilly.

History
The area around here was known to the local Koories as 'Ballaarat', meaning 'resting place'. When gold was discovered in August 1851 – sparking the central Victorian gold rush – thousands of diggers flooded in, forming a shanty town of tents and huts. Ballarat's alluvial goldfields were the tip of the golden iceberg, and when deep shaft mines were sunk they struck incredibly rich quartz reefs. In 1854 the Eureka Rebellion pitted miners against the government and put Ballarat at the forefront of miners' rights.

◉ Sights & Activities

Take the time to walk along **Lydiard St**, one of Australia's finest streetscapes for Victorian-era architecture. Impressive buildings include Her Majesty's Theatre (1875), Craig's Royal Hotel (1853), George Hotel (1854) and the art gallery (1884). The main drag, impressive Sturt St, had to be three chains wide (60m) to allow for the turning circle of bullock wagons. The Gold Monument (cnr Sturt & Albert Sts) features a replica of the Welcome Nugget.

The former **Eureka Centre**, telling the story of Ballarat's history and the Eureka Rebellion, was undergoing multimillion-dollar redevelopment at the time of research and is expected to reopen in 2012 as the slightly more verbose Eureka Centre for Australian Democracy (5333 1854; www.eureka ballarat.com; cnr Eureka & Rodier Sts).

THE EUREKA REBELLION

Life on the goldfields was a great leveller, erasing social distinctions as doctors, merchants, ex-convicts and labourers toiled side by side in the mud. But as the easily won gold began to run out, the diggers recognised the inequalities between themselves and the privileged few who held land and the government.

The limited size of claims and the inconvenience of licence hunts coupled with police brutality and taxation without political representation, fired the unrest that led to the Eureka Rebellion.

In September 1854 Governor Hotham ordered the hated licence hunts, to be carried out twice weekly. In the following October a miner was murdered near a Ballarat hotel after an argument with the owner, James Bentley. Bentley was found not guilty by a magistrate (and business associate), and a group of miners rioted and burned his hotel. Bentley was retried and found guilty, but the rioting miners were also jailed, which fuelled their distrust of authority.

Creating the Ballarat Reform League, the diggers called for the abolition of licence fees, a miner's right to vote and increased opportunities to purchase land.

On 29 November 1854 about 800 miners, led by Irishman Peter Lalor, burnt their licences at a mass meeting and built a stockade at Eureka, where they prepared to fight for their rights.

On 3 December the government ordered troopers to attack the stockade. There were only 150 diggers within the barricades at the time and the fight lasted only 20 minutes, leaving 30 miners and five troopers dead.

The short-lived rebellion was ultimately successful. The miners won the sympathy of Victorians and the government chose to acquit the leaders of the charge of high treason.

The licence fee was abolished. A miner's right, costing £1 a year, gave the right to search for gold and to fence in, cultivate and build a dwelling on a moderate-sized piece of land – and to vote. The rebel leader Peter Lalor became a member of parliament some years later.

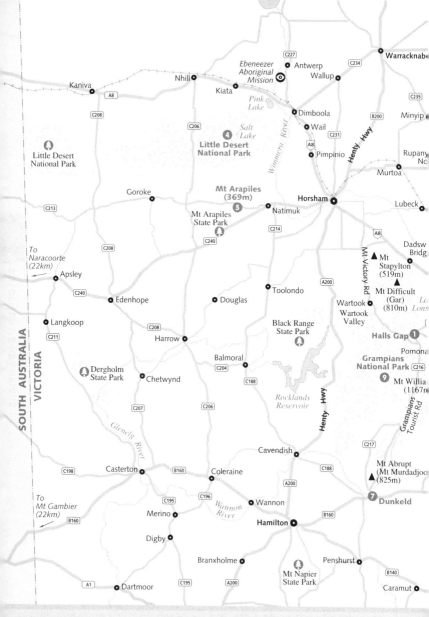

Goldfields & Grampians Highlights

1 Discover the traditional stories of Gariwerd at **Brambuk Cultural Centre** (p208) in Halls Gap

2 Descend deep into a gold mine then ride the talking tram in **Bendigo** (p194)

3 Ride the restored **steam train** (p203) from Maldon to Castlemaine

4 Camp under the stars in **Little Desert National Park** (p212)

5 Scale the granite heights at **Mt Arapiles** (p211), Victoria's best rock-climbing destination

6 Experience the closest thing to a real gold-rush town at Ballarat's **Sovereign Hill** (p190)

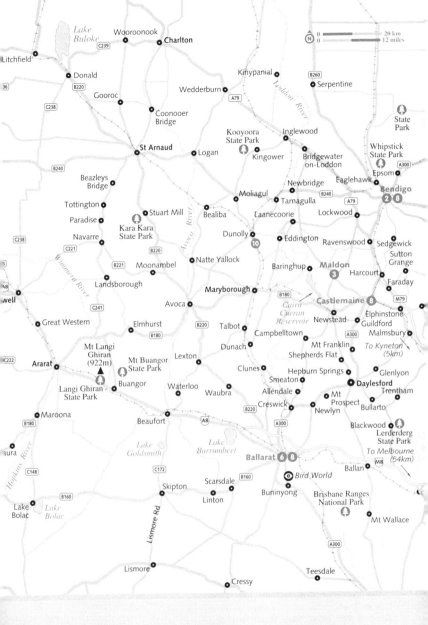

7 Climb Mt Sturgeon then wine and dine in style at the Royal Mail Hotel in **Dunkeld** (p210)

8 Admire the artworks at fabulous regional **galleries** in Bendigo (p196), Ballarat (p190) and Castlemaine (p200)

9 Set up camp and walk to waterfalls and stunning lookouts at **Grampians National Park** (p205)

10 Search for nuggets along the historic **Golden Triangle** (see boxed text, p199) between Maryborough, Maldon and Bendigo

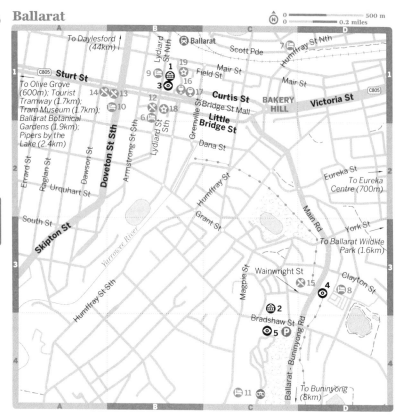

Sovereign Hill HISTORIC SITE, MUSEUM
(☑5337 1100; www.sovereignhill.com.au; Bradshaw
St; adult/child/family $41/19/104; ☉10am-5pm)
You'll need to set aside at least half a day
to visit this fascinating re-creation of an
1860s gold-mining township. The site was
mined in the gold-rush era and much of the
equipment is original, as is the mine shaft.
Kids love panning for gold in the stream,
watching the hourly gold pour and exploring the old-style lolly shop. The main street
is a living history museum with people performing their chores dressed in costumes
of the time. Several places offer food, from
pies at the Hope Bakery to a three-course
lunch at the United States Hotel. Sovereign
Hill opens again at night for the impressive sound-and-light show **Blood on the
Southern Cross** (☑5337 1199; adult/child/
family $50/27/134, combined with Sovereign
Hill $91/46/238), a dramatic simulation of
the Eureka Stockade battle. There are two

shows nightly but times vary so check in advance; bookings are essential.

Your ticket gets you into the nearby **Gold
Museum** (☑5331 1944; Magpie St; adult/child
$9.80/5.20; ☉9.30am-5.20pm), which sits on a
mullock heap from an old mine. There are
imaginative displays and samples from all
the old mining areas, as well as gold nuggets,
coins and a display on the Eureka Rebellion.

FREE **Art Gallery of Ballarat** ART GALLERY
(☑5320 5858; www.balgal.com; 40 Lydiard
St N; ☉9am-5pm) The oldest provincial gallery in Australia, this 1890 architectural
gem houses a wonderful collection of early
colonial paintings, works from noted Australian artists (including Tom Roberts, Sir
Sidney Nolan, Russell Drysdale and Fred
Williams) and contemporary works. Pride
of place goes to the preserved remnants of
the original Eureka flag. Free iPod tours are
available and there are free guided tours at
2pm Wednesday to Sunday.

Ballarat

Lake Wendouree & Around

Lake Wendouree, a large artificial lake created for the 1956 Olympics rowing events, is a natural focal point for the town, especially now that it's full of water again after drying up during the drought. Old timber boatsheds spread along the shore, and a popular walking and cycling track encircles the lake.

On the western side of the lake, Ballarat's beautiful and serene **Botanical Gardens** (Wendouree Pde; admission free; ☉sunrise-sunset) were first planted in 1858. Stroll through the 40 hectares of immaculately maintained rose gardens, wide lawns and the colourful conservatory. Visit the cottage of poet Adam Lindsay Gordon or walk along Prime Ministers' Avenue, a collection of bronze busts of all of Australia's prime ministers. There's a visitor centre in the glass Robert Clark Conservatory.

A **Tourist Tramway** (☎5334 1580; www .btm.org.au; rides adult/child $3/1.50; ☉noon-5pm Sat & Sun) operates on a short section of tramline around the lake, departing from the Tram Museum. Horse-drawn trams

started running in the city in 1887, but were later replaced by electric trams, until 1971.

Ballarat Wildlife Park ZOO
(☎5333 5933; www.wildlifepark.com.au; cnr York & Fussell Sts; adult/child/family $24/15/70; ☉9am-5.30pm, tour at 11am) Ballarat's tranquil wildlife park is strong on native fauna, from the sweet little King Island wallabies to Tasmanian devils, emus, quokkas, snakes, eagles and crocs. There's a daily guided tour, and weekend programs include a koala show, a wombat show, a snake show and crocodile-feeding.

Ballarat Bird World AVIARY
(☎5341 3843; www.ballaratbirdworld.com.au; 408 Eddy Ave, Mt Helen; adult/child/family $10/6/30; ☉10am-5pm) If you prefer feathered wildlife, go to where 40 different types of birds hang out in peaceful gardens with ponds and waterfalls. Located 10km south of Ballarat.

Kirrit Barreet CULTURAL CENTRE
(☎5332 2755; www.aboriginalballarat.com.au; 407 Main Rd; tours $5; ☉9am-5pm Mon-Fri) This excellent cultural centre has a museum and keeping place with displays about the local Wathaurung people, Koori history, art and cultural tours. Distinguished indigenous artists conduct workshops here.

Other Attractions

If Sovereign Hill doesn't wear the kids out, take them to **Gold Rush Mini Golf** (☎5334 8150; www.goldrushgolf.com.au; Western Hwy, Warrenheip; 1/2 rounds adult $12/16, child $7/11, family $32/48; ☉10am-7pm, to 8pm Fri & Sat), with two themed 18-hole courses – naturally the main theme is gold-mining.

Hopeful prospectors can pick up miners' rights and rent metal detectors at the **Gold Shop** (☎5333 4242; www.thegoldshop.com.au; 8a Lydiard St N) in the historic Mining Exchange.

☞ Tours

Eerie Tours HISTORY
(☎1300 856 668; www.eerietours.com.au; tours $25) Relive the ghoulish parts of Ballarat's past with a night-time ghost tour or cemetery tour.

✸ Festivals & Events

Organs of the Ballarat Goldfields MUSIC
(www.ballarat.com/organs) A week of recitals and musical celebrations, held outdoors or in grand cathedrals and churches, in mid-January.

Arts in the Park
MUSIC

(www.ballarat.vic.gov.au) Free music on the foreshore of Lake Wendouree every Sunday from early January to late February.

Begonia Festival
FLOWERS

(www.ballaratbegoniafestival.com) This 100-year-old festival, held over the Labour Day weekend in early March, includes sensational floral displays, a street parade, fireworks, art shows and music.

Ballarat Antique Fair
ANTIQUES

(www.ballaratantiquefair.com.au) Three days in mid-March, with exhibitors and antiques, buyers and sellers from all over Australia.

Royal South Street Eisteddfod
MUSIC

(www.royalsouthstreet.com.au) If you lived in Victoria and learnt music as a child, you were probably dragged off to Australia's oldest eisteddfod; held September or October.

🛏 Sleeping

Ballarat's grand old pubs, B&Bs and cottages all offer gracious accommodation, and there are many motels and holiday resorts.

Sovereign Hill Lodge
HOTEL, HOSTEL $$

(☑5337 1159; www.sovereignhill.com.au; Magpie St) Lots of visitors come to Ballarat to see Sovereign Hill, so it makes sense to stay here, and there's a wide range of accommodation. Within the 1850s village itself, Steinfeld's (s/d $140/160) is the top pick – six elegant heritage rooms and a common lounge overlooking the old township. For $645 a double (Saturday only) you can have the full treatment – period costume, personal township tour, afternoon tea and 'Taste of the Empire' dinner.

The Lodge B&B (d $175, with spa $190) features stylish heritage rooms around a cosy guest lounge with fireplace and bar. There are also motel rooms (s/d/f $125/145/200).

For budget travellers there's the cute four-room YHA Cottage (dm/s/tw $305/49/68). There's also dormitory-style bunkhouse accommodation for groups or families.

George Hotel
HOTEL $$

(☑5333 4866; www.georgehotelballarat.com.au; 27 Lydiard St N; d/f from $120/195; ❉🛜) This grand old pub has seen bags of history since it was first built in 1852. It's right in the thick of things and the recently refurbished rooms are tasteful and comfortable with a good bar and restaurant. If you're thinking of staying here on a weekend, though, remember that the nightclub below is open till 5am.

Ansonia on Lydiard
B&B $$

(☑5332 4678; www.theansoniaonlydiard.com.au; 32 Lydiard St S; d $165-275; ❉🛜) One of Lydiard Sts great hotels, the Ansonia exudes calm with its minimalist design, polished floors and light-filled atrium. Stylish rooms have large-screen TVs and range from studio apartments for two to family suites.

Oscar's
BOUTIQUE HOTEL $$

(☑5331 1451; www.oscarshotel.com.au; 18 Doveton St; d $150-200, spa r $225; ❉🛜) The 13 rooms of this attractive art deco hotel have been tastefully refurbished to include double showers and spas (watch a flat-screen TV from your spa).

Ballarat Goldfields Holiday Park
CARAVAN PARK $

(☑5332 7888; www.ballaratgoldfields.com.au; 108 Clayton St; powered sites $35, cabins $87-170; ❉🛜) Close to Sovereign Hill, with a good holiday atmosphere. The cabins are like miners' cottages, and some have three bedrooms.

Ballarat Backpackers Hostel
HOSTEL $

(☑0427 440 661; www.ballarat.com/eastern station.htm; 81 Humffray St N; s/d/f $40/65/90) In the old Eastern Station Hotel (1862), this refurbished guesthouse is also a decent corner pub with occasional live music. Rooms are fresh and good value.

🍴 Eating

Ballarat offers plenty of dining options around Sturt and Lydiard Sts and there's a nice cafe strip on the Sturt St '400 Block' between Dawson and Doveton Sts. For cheap eats, Bakery Hill, east of the Bridge St Mall, is a global and fast-food area.

Craig's Royal Hotel
CAFE, FRENCH $$

(☑5331 1377; www.craigsroyal.com.au; 10 Lydiard St; mains $26-35; ◷breakfast, lunch & dinner) Even if you can't afford to stay here, you can experience some royal treatment with a cocktail in historic Craig's Bar, or a coffee in Craig's Café & Larder. For fine dining, the Gallery Bistro is a sumptuous atrium dining room serving French-inspired cuisine.

Boatshed Restaurant
MODERN AUSTRALIAN $$

(☑5333 5533; www.boatshed-restaurant.com; Lake Wendouree foreshore; mains $18-32; ◷breakfast, lunch & dinner) At this restaurant perched on stilts over the lake, you can sit on the enclosed deck or stay inside with the open fire and leather armchairs. Good for coffee and cake all day, and a stylish place for a Mod Oz lunch, or a dinner of seafood or steak.

VICTORIA'S GOLD RUSH

When gold was discovered in New South Wales in May 1851, a reward was offered to anyone who could find gold within 300km of Melbourne. By June, a significant discovery was made at Clunes, 32km north of Ballarat, and prospectors headed to central Victoria.

Over the next few months, fresh gold finds were made almost weekly around Victoria. Then in September 1851 the greatest gold discovery ever known was made at Moliagul, followed by others at Ballarat, Bendigo, Mt Alexander and many more.

By the end of 1851 hopeful miners were coming from England, Ireland, Europe, China and the failing goldfields of California across the Pacific.

While the gold rush had its tragic side (including epidemics that swept through the camps), plus its share of rogues (including bushrangers who attacked the gold shipments), it ushered in a fantastic era of growth and prosperity for Victoria. Within 12 years, the population had increased from 77,000 to 540,000. Mining companies invested heavily in the region, the development of roads and railways accelerated, and huge shanty towns were replaced by Victoria's modern provincial cities, most notably Ballarat, Bendigo and Castlemaine, which reached the height of their splendour in the 1880s.

Olive Grove   DELI, CAFE **$**
(☎5331 4455; 1303 Sturt St; dishes $7-12; ☺breakfast & lunch; ☝) The Olive Grove is buzzing with locals lingering over coffee, gourmet baguettes or bagels, or browsing the deli delights of cakes, cold meats and cheeses.

Restauranté Da Uday   INDIAN, ITALIAN **$$**
(☎5331 6655; 7 Wainwright St; mains $14-28; ☺dinner daily, lunch Tue-Sat; ☝) This pretty converted cottage near Sovereign Hill has a lovely atmosphere and the intoxicating aromas of authentic Indian, Thai and (oddly enough) Italian. It's curry meets pizza, with plenty of vegetarian choices and takeaway available.

Pipers by the Lake   CAFE **$$**
(☎5334 1811; Lake Wendouree; mains $18-26; ☺breakfast & lunch) The 1890 Lakeside Lodge was designed by WH Piper and today it's a lovely light-filled cafe with huge windows looking out over the lake and an al fresco courtyard. The $15 lunch-with-a-drink deal is good value.

L'Espresso   ITALIAN **$$**
(☎5333 1789; 417 Sturt St; mains $11-18.50; ☺7am-6pm, to 11pm Fri & Sat) A mainstay on Ballarat's cafe scene, this trendy Italian-style place doubles as a record shop – choose from the whopping jazz, blues and world music CD selection while you wait for your espresso or Tuscan bean soup.

Europa Café   CAFE **$$**
(☎5338 7672; www.europacafe.com.au; 411 Sturt St; mains $12-27; ☺breakfast & lunch daily, dinner Thu-Sun; ☝) With a global range of food including curries, pastas and vegetarian, it's family friendly and there's sharp service.

 Drinking & Entertainment

With its large student population, Ballarat has a lively nightlife. There are some fine old pubs around town but most of the entertainment is centred on Lydiard St and the nearby Camp St precinct.

Irish Murphy's   PUB
(☎5331 4091; 36 Sturt St; ☺to 3am Wed-Sun) The Guinness flows freely at this atmospheric Irish pub. It's a welcoming place and the live music draws people of all ages.

Haida   BAR, LIVE MUSIC
(☎5331 5346; 2 Camp St; ☺5pm-late Wed-Sun) Haida is a loungy two-level bar where you can relax with a cocktail by the open fire or chill out to DJs and live music downstairs.

Karova Lounge   NIGHTCLUB
(☎5332 9122; www.karovalounge.com; cnr Field & Camp Sts; ☺9pm-late Wed-Sat) Ballarat's best original live music venue showcases local and touring bands in a grungy, industrial style.

Her Majesty's Theatre   THEATRE
(☎5333 5888; www.hermaj.com; 17 Lydiard St S) Ballarat's main venue for the performing arts since 1875, 'Her Maj' is in a wonderful Victorian-era building and features theatre, live music, comedy and local productions. Check the website for a calendar of shows.

 Shopping

Ballarat's shopping strip is Sturt St and the streets running off it. At the Ballarat Showgrounds there's a fine Sunday **Trash & Trivia market** (Creswick Rd; ☺8am-1pm Sun).

Mill Markets INDOOR MARKET
(☎5334 7877; www.millmarkets.com.au; 9367 Western Hwy) A little sister of the popular Mill Market at Daylesford, this huge collection of antiques, retro furnishings and knick-knacks is in the old woolsheds.

ℹ️ Information

Ballarat visitor centre (☎1800 446 633, 5320 5741; www.visitballarat.com.au; 43 Lydiard St; ◷9am-5pm) The visitor centre has moved to this temporary location while the Eureka Centre is redeveloped.

ℹ️ Getting There & Away

Greyhound Australia (☎13 14 99; www .greyhound.com.au) buses between Adelaide and Melbourne stop in Ballarat if you ask the driver (departs Adelaide 8.15pm, $72, 8¾ hours). **Airport Shuttle Bus** (☎5333 4181; www.airportshuttlebus.com.au) goes direct from Melbourne Airport to Ballarat train station (adult/child $30/16, 1½ hours, nine daily, seven on weekends).

V/Line (☎13 61 96; www.vline.com.au) has frequent direct trains between Melbourne (Southern Cross station) and Ballarat ($10.40, 1½ hours, 18 daily) and at least three services via Geelong.

BENDIGO

POP 76,000

You don't have to look far to find evidence of Bendigo's heritage – in the magnificent Shamrock Hotel, the Central Deborah Gold-mine and the Chinese dragons that awaken for the Easter Festival.

Modern-day Bendigo is a prosperous, up-beat and thoroughly enjoyable regional city with one of the best regional art galleries in Australia, family attractions and some great wineries in the surrounding district.

History

The fantastically rich Bendigo Diggings cov-ered more than 360 sq km after gold was discovered in nearby Ravenswood in 1851, and later Bendigo Creek. It is said the maids at the Shamrock Hotel mopped the floor ev-ery night to collect the gold dust brought in on the drinkers' boots. The arrival of thousands of Chinese miners in 1854 had a lasting effect on the town, despite the racial tensions that surfaced.

In the 1860s the scene changed again as independent miners were outclassed by the powerful mining companies, with their heavy machinery. The companies poured money into the town and some 35 quartz reefs were found. The ground underneath Bendigo is still honeycombed with mine shafts, and Bendigo Mining successfully re-sumed operations at the Kangaroo Flat mine in 2008.

⊙ Sights

The city's impressive buildings are first seen in Pall Mall as a splendid trio: the **Sham-rock Hotel**, **Law Courts** and former **Post Office**, which is now the visitor centre. Take a look inside all three – the interiors are just as elaborate as the exteriors.

View St is a historic streetscape with some fine buildings, including the **Capital**, which houses the Bendigo Art Gallery, and **Dudley House**, classified by the National Trust.

If you plan on seeing the main sights, the **Bendigo Experience Pass** (adult/child/family $45/24.50/110, valid 3 months) is good value. Ask at the visitor centre.

Central Deborah Goldmine MINE
(☎5443 8322; www.central-deborah.com; 76 Violet St; adult/child/family $26.50/13.50/65; ◷9.30am-5pm) For a very deep experience, descend into this 500m-deep mine with a geologist. The mine has been worked on 17 levels, and about 1000kg of gold has been removed. Af-ter donning hard hats and lights, you're tak-en down the shaft to inspect the operations, complete with drilling demonstrations. There are five tours on weekdays and six on weekends and they last about 75 minutes. Other tours include the 2½ hour Under-ground Adventure ($75/45/190), or, for the claustrophobes, a surface tour ($14/7/35).

Bendigo Talking Tram HISTORIC TRAM
(☎5442 2821; www.bendigotramways.com; adult/child/family $15/9/43, valid 2 days; ◷9.30am-3.30pm) For an interesting tour of the city, hop aboard one of the restored vintage 'talking' trams. The hop-on hop-off trip runs from the Central Deborah Goldmine to the **Tramways Museum** (1 Tramways Rd; admission free with tram ticket; ◷10am-5pm) ev-ery half-hour making half a dozen stops, in-cluding at the Golden Dragon Museum and Lake Weeroona.

 Golden Dragon Museum & Gardens
MUSEUM, GARDEN
(☎5441 5044; www.goldendragonmuseum .org; 1-11 Bridge St; adult/child/family $10/5/25; ◷9.30am-5pm) Bendigo's obvious Chinese

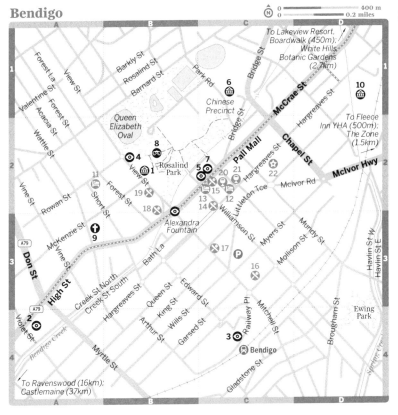

Bendigo

◎ Sights

1 Bendigo Art Gallery	B2
Bendigo Talking Tram	(see 2)
Capital Theatre	(see 1)
2 Central Deborah Goldmine	A4
3 Discovery Science & Technology Centre	C4
4 Dudley House	B2
5 Former Post Office	C2
6 Golden Dragon Museum & Gardens	C1
7 Law Courts	C2
8 Lookout Tower	B2
9 Sacred Heart Cathedral	A3
Shamrock Hotel	(see 13)
10 Tramways Museum	D1

🛏 Sleeping

11 Flynn's Place	A2

12 Old Crown Hotel	C2
13 Shamrock Hotel	C2

🍴 Eating

Barzurk	(see 15)
14 Gillies'	C2
15 GPO	C2
16 Piyawat Thai	C3
17 Toi Shan	C3
18 Whirrakee Restaurant & Wine Bar	B2
19 Wine Bank	B2

🍷 Drinking

20 Dispensary Enoteca	C2
21 Pugg Mahones	C2

🎭 Entertainment

Capital Theatre	(see 1)
22 Pub & Corner Pocket	C2

heritage sets it apart from other goldfields towns, and this fantastic museum and garden is the place to experience it. Walk through a huge wooden door into an awesome chamber filled with dragons including the Imperial Dragons Old Loong (the oldest in the world) and Sun Loong (the longest in the world at over 100m). Old Loong arrived in 1892 to feature in the Easter procession. Sun Loong took over in 1970 when Old Loong retired, and it comes out each year to lead the Easter parade. The museum also displays amazing Chinese heritage items and costumes. Outside, the Yin Yuan (Garden of Joy) classical Chinese gardens are a tranquil little haven with bridges, water features and ornamental shrubs. The tearoom serves simple, Chinese-style dishes. The area outside the museum was redeveloped as the Dai Gum San Chinese precinct, complete with a large lotus flower, and opened in 2010.

Chinese Joss House TEMPLE

(☑5443 8255; Finn St, North Bendigo; adult/child/family $5.50/3.50/11; ⊙11am-4pm Wed, Sat & Sun) Painted red, the traditional colour for strength, this is a practising joss house (a temple where idols are worshipped) and the only one remaining in central Victoria. Exhibits include figures representing the Chinese solar cycle, commemorative tablets to the deceased, paintings and Chinese lanterns.

Bendigo Art Gallery ART GALLERY

(☑5434 6088; www.bendigoartgallery.com.au; 42 View St; admission by donation; ⊙10am-5pm, tours 2pm) One of Victoria's finest regional galleries, the permanent collection here includes outstanding colonial and contemporary Australian art, such as work by Charles Blackman, Fred Williams, Rupert Bunny and Lloyd Rees; the annual temporary exhibitions are cutting edge. The Gallery Café overlooks Rosalind Park and is a good spot for coffee or a light lunch.

FREE Sacred Heart Cathedral CHURCH

(www.sandhurst.catholic.org.au/cathedral; cnr Wattle & High Sts) You can't miss the soaring steeple of this magnificent cathedral. Construction began in the 19th century and was completed in 2001 with the installation of bells from Italy in the belfry. Inside, beneath the high vaulted ceiling, there's a magnificently carved bishop's chair, some beautiful stained-glass windows, and wooden angels jutting out of the ceiling arches.

Lake Weeroona LAKE

(cnr Nolan & Napier Sts) Bendigo's little lake is a favourite spot for boating, kayaking or just walking around the path that encircles it. There are barbecue and picnic areas, toilets, a children's adventure playground on the eastern side and the Boardwalk Restaurant at the southern end.

Parks & Gardens GARDENS

Right in the city centre, Rosalind Park is a lovely green space, with lawns, big old trees, fernery and the fabulous Cascades Fountain, which was excavated after being buried for 120 years. Climb to the top of the lookout tower for sensational 360-degree views, or if you love roses, wander through the Conservatory Gardens.

The White Hills Botanic Gardens, 2km north of town, features many exotic and rare plant species, a small fauna park, aviary, and barbecue facilities.

FREE Bendigo Pottery POTTERY

(☑5448 4404; www.bendigopottery.com.au; 146 Midland Hwy, Epsom; ⊙9am-5pm) Australia's oldest pottery works, the Bendigo Pottery was founded in 1857 and is classified by the National Trust. The historic kilns are still used; watch potters at work, admire the gorgeous ceramic pieces or throw a pot yourself (half-/full day $12/18). The attached museum (adult/child $8/4) tells the story of pottery through the ages.

🏃 Activities & Tours

O'Keefe Rail Trail HIKING, CYCLING

This hike-or-bike trail, along a disused railway line, starts near the corner of Midland Hwy and Baden Stand and meanders for 19km to Axedale.

Balloon Flights of Bendigo

HOT-AIR BALLOONING

(☑544 1127; www.balloonflightsvic.com.au; sunrise flight, breakfast & champagne $280) Offers bird's-eye views of the Bendigo environs.

Central Air Adventures ADVENTURE

(☑0488 059 790; www.centralairadventures.com.au; flights from $469) Strap in for a thrilling one-hour mock-combat flight in an ex-Chinese Air Force Nanchang CJ6-A fighter.

🎊 Festivals & Events

Easter Festival RELIGIOUS

(www.bendigoeasterfestival.org.au) Bendigo's major festival, held in March or April, attracts thousands with its carnival atmo-

Bendigo has lots of parks, gardens and activities to keep kids happy.

About 4km north of the town centre is the **Ironbark Complex** (Watson St), with three major activities: **Ironbark Riding Centre** (☑5436 1565; www.bwc.com.au/ironbark; 1/2hr rides $38/65; ☺8.30am-5pm Mon-Sat) offers trail rides, riding lessons, and the Great Australian Pub Ride to Allies Hotel in Myers Flat (with lunch $85); **Bendigo Gold World** (☑5448 4140; www.bendigogold.com.au; half-/full-day tours $290/350; ☺8.30am-5pm Mon-Sat) has fossicking and detecting tours into the bush with metal detectors, and gold panning – with guaranteed gold! – at the Mobile Gold-panning Centre ($12 per hour); and **Bendigo Water World** (☑5448 4140; www.bendigowaterworld.com.au; admission $3, with slides from $8, family day pass $70; ☺4-7pm Mon-Wed, noon-8pm Thu & Fri, 10.30am-8pm Sat, 10.30am-6pm Sun), where the 'Big Bendi' waterslide zaps you into a pool.

Discovery Science & Technology Centre (☑5444 4400; www.discovery.asn.au; 7 Railway Pl; adult/child/family $12/8/35; ☺10am-4pm, to 5pm Wed), in an old railway goods shed, has a wide range of interesting and educational exhibits, including a planetarium, science lab and kaleidoscope.

A complete kids' entertainment complex, the **Zone** (www.thezone.net.au; 1 Gildea Lane; admission from $15; ☺noon-10pm Mon-Fri, 10am-10pm Sat & Sun) has a playground, minigolf, go-karting and paintball.

Confectionery Capers (☑5449 3111, 0429 409 773; www.confectionerycapers.com; 1028 McIvor Hwy, Junortoun; adult/child/family $6/4/16; ☺10am-5pm Mon-Sat, 1-5pm Sun), 8km southeast of town, is an amazing display of whirls, whizzes, word plays and oddball machines: Barbie dolls in a line? A tree in a toilet? You have to go there for it all to make sense...

sphere and colourful and noisy procession of Chinese dragons, led by Sun Loong, the world's longest imperial dragon.

Bendigo Cup　　　　HORSE RACING
(www.racingvictoria.net.au/vcrc/bendigo) Part of the Spring Racing Carnival; held in November.

Swap Meet　　　　VINTAGE CARS
(www.bendigoswap.com.au) For enthusiasts in search of that elusive vintage-car spare part. It's so popular that accommodation is at a premium. Held in November.

🛏 Sleeping

Several accommodation services offer lovely maisonettes, townhouses, suites and apartments in the heart of the city: **Abode Bendigo** (☑0414 425 447; www.abodebendigo.com.au); **Allawah Bendigo** (☑5444 4655; www.allawah bendigo.com) and **Bendigo Holiday Accommodation** (☑5439 3588; www.bendigoholiday accommodation.com).

TOP
CHOICE　**Shamrock Hotel**　　　HOTEL **$$**
(☑5443 0333; www.hotelshamrock.com .au; cnr Pall Mall & Williamson St; d $120-175, ste $225) One of Bendigo's historic icons, the Shamrock is a stunning Victorian building with stained glass, original paintings, fancy columns and a *Gone with the Wind*–style

staircase. The refurbished upstairs rooms range from small standard rooms to most-spacious deluxe and spa suites.

Fleece Inn YHA　　　　HOSTEL **$**
(☑5443 3086; www.thefleeceinn.com.au; 139 Charleston Rd; dm/s/d/f $35/55/77/110; ✻) This 140-year-old former pub has dorm rooms with partitioned-off beds, cosy private rooms (shared facilities), a communal kitchen and a huge back courtyard with a lounge area, a TV and barbecues. Smart rooms are up the grand original timber staircase. Free continental breakfast.

Flynn's Place　　　BOUTIQUE HOTEL **$$**
(☑5444 0001; www.flynnsplace.com.au; 104 Short St; d $165-195; ✻🛜) The two modern self-contained apartments at Flynn's are sleekly fitted out and furnished in a historic building, with queen beds, wide-screen TVs, DVDs, sound systems and free wi-fi. It's conveniently central, around the corner from the art gallery.

Lakeview Resort　　　MOTEL **$$**
(☑5445 5300; www.lakeviewresort.com.au; 286 Napier St; B&B d/f $140/190; ✻🛜🏊) You've got Lake Weeroona across the road, spacious units around the central courtyard, shaded pool, piazza, and Quills, a fine-dining restaurant with an excellent reputation.

Old Crown Hotel
PUB $

(☎5441 6888; 238 Hargreaves St; r per person $45) Location is the key at this ultra-central pub with clean old-style budget rooms and shared facilities. There are two-bed and four-bed rooms.

A-Line Holiday Village
CABINS, CARAVAN PARK $

(☎5447 9568; www.alineholidayvillage.com.au; 5615 Calder Hwy; en suite sites from $25, cabins $70-90, A-line unit d $85-115; ❄❖) About 10km from the city centre on the Melbourne side of town, this park is set in bushland with immaculate, grassy sites and cute A-frame split-level cottages with all mod-cons.

✕ Eating

Bendigo has an excellent range of cafes, pubs (including the Shamrock) and restaurants, most in the convenient block bounded by Pall Mall, Bull St, Hargreaves St and Mitchell St.

GPO
MEDITERRANEAN $$

(☎5443 4343; www.gpobendigo.com.au; Pall Mall; mains $14-45; ☉lunch & dinner) The food and atmosphere here is superb and rated highly by locals. Confit pork belly and roasted kingfish grace the Mediterranean menu, or go for the innovative pizzas and pasta or tapas plates. The bar is a chilled place for a drink from the impressive wine and cocktail list.

Wine Bank
WINE BAR, CAFE $$

(☎5444 4655; www.winebankonview.com; 45 View St; mains $12-18, ☉lunch & dinner) Wine bottles line the walls in this former bank building, which serves as a wine shop and bar specialising in central Victoria–wines, and an atmospheric Italian-style cafe serving tapas and platters.

Gillies'
BAKERY $

(Hargreaves St Mall; pies from $3-5; ☉daily) The pie window on the corner of the mall here is a Bendigo institution, and the pies are as good as you'll find.

Whirrakee Restaurant & Wine Bar
FRENCH $$$

(☎5441 5557; 17 View St; lunch $19-31, dinner $30-59; ☉lunch & dinner Tue-Sun) In another of Bendigo's historic buildings (the 1908 Royal Bank), Whirrakee has a French-influenced menu featuring Wagyu beef and tortellini of blue swimmer crab. Downstairs there's a small wine bar with cosy sofas, and there's live music in the gold-weighing room on Friday night.

Barzurk
CAFE, BAR $$

(☎5442 4032; 66 Pall Mall; mains $8-28; ☉lunch daily, dinner Wed-Sun) A trendy but casual streetside cafe-bar with pressed tin ceilings and a courtyard out the back. Even light meals are filling and the menu includes Thai dishes, pasta, risotto and gourmet pizza.

Piyawat Thai
THAI $

(☎5444 4450; 136 Mollison St; mains $14-18; ☉dinner Tue-Sun; ✍) Tucked away in a cosy house a couple of blocks south of the centre, this authentic Thai restaurant serves fabulously fragrant curries, noodles and Thai stir-fries at affordable prices.

Bendigo ninesevensix
MODERN AUSTRALIAN $$$

(☎5444 4655; www.bendigoninesevensix.com.au; set menu $98; ☉dinner Sat) Every Saturday night a 1952 Melbourne W-class tram becomes a rolling restaurant, with a set menu including four courses and free drinks – a great way to see the city.

Boardwalk
CAFE $$

(☎5443 9855; Nolan St; mains $18-29; ☉breakfast, lunch & dinner) The location on the edge of Lake Weeroona is the big tick here – full-length windows and an al fresco deck offer prime views of waterbirds and rowers. Good for coffee or a lazy lunch.

Toi Shan
CHINESE $

(☎5443 5811; 67 Mitchell St; mains $12-19, buffet $11.50-14.50; ☉lunch & dinner) For cheap and cheerful Chinese, Toi Shan has been around since the gold rush and you can fill up with the lunchtime smorgasbord.

♟ Drinking & Entertainment

Bendigo has a lively nightlife – uni nights are Tuesday and Thursday. Although some clubs are open as late as 5am, all have a 2am lockout. The main nightlife zone is Bull St and along Pall Mall.

Pugg Mahones
PUB

(☎5443 4916; 224 Hargreaves St; ☉10.30am-late Mon-Sat) With Guinness (and many other beers) on tap, Puggs has a thickly welcoming atmosphere, not-unreasonable doormen, a beer garden and live music every Thursday, Friday and Saturday night till 3am.

Dispensary Enoteca
CAFE, BAR

(☎5444 5885; 9 Chancery Lane; ☉daily from 8am) Hidden down tiny Chancery Lane, the Dispensary serves food throughout the day, but it's also a trendy little cocktail bar with a mind-boggling selection of beers, spirits and wines.

Pub & Corner Pocket LIVE MUSIC
(✆5443 4079; 173 Hargreaves St; ☻Tue-Sat) Bendigo's live-rock venue is a grungy club and pool hall showcasing touring acts from all over Australia; there's free pool till 11pm.

Capital Theatre PERFORMING ARTS
(✆5441 5344; www.bendigo.vic.gov.au; 50 View St) In the beautifully restored Capital Theatre, this is the main venue for the performing arts, with hundreds of performances and exhibitions each year.

Star Theatre CINEMA
(✆5446 2025; www.starcinema.org.au; 1 Peg Leg Rd, Eaglehawk; adult/child $13/7; ☻from 1.30pm) Watch a flick with a beer or wine in decadent armchair comfort at this classic cinema. Located 6km northeast of the city centre.

ℹ Information

Bendigo visitor centre (✆1800 813 153, 5444 4445; www.bendigotourism.com; 51 Pall Mall; ☻9am-5pm) In the historic former post office; offers an accommodation booking service and the Post Office Gallery.

ℹ Getting There & Away

Bendigo Airport Service (✆5444 3939; www .bendigoairportservice.com.au) runs direct between Melbourne Airport and Bendigo train station (one way/return adult $39/74, child $15/30, two hours, four daily). Bookings essential.

V/Line (✆13 61 96; www.vline.com.au) has frequent trains between Melbourne (Southern Cross station) and Bendigo ($15.80, two hours, 12 to 18 daily) via Kyneton and Castlemaine.

GOLDFIELDS TOWNS

As splendid as Ballarat and Bendigo are, to really appreciate this part of the world you need to get out and explore the country towns and former gold-mining relics that make up central Victoria. Touring the likes of Castlemaine, Kyneton, Maldon and Maryborough – and the tiny communities in between – will give you a good understanding of the incredible growth and inevitable decline of the gold towns, but you'll also pass through gorgeous countryside and an increasingly flourishing (and trendy) wine and food region. Head north of Melbourne along the Calder Hwy (M79 and A79) to start the journey.

Kyneton
POP 4300

Kyneton, established a year before gold was discovered, was the main coach stop between Melbourne and Bendigo, and the centre for the farmers who were supplying the diggings with fresh produce. Today Piper St is a historic precinct lined with bluestone buildings that have been transformed into cafes, antique shops, museums and restaurants. The old bank building (1855) is now **Kyneton Historical Museum** (✆5422 1228; 67 Piper St; adult/child $3/1; ☻11am-4pm Fri-Sun), housing a display of local history items – the upper floor is furnished in period style.

It's worth a walk to the **Botanic Gardens** (Clowes St), established by Baron Ferdinand von Mueller in the 1860s, beside the Campaspe River.

GOLDEN TRIANGLE TOURING

The so-called central Victorian 'Golden Triangle' has yielded plenty of gold over the years and is still popular with prospectors and fossickers using metal detectors.

The world's largest alluvial nugget, the 72kg Welcome Stranger, was found in Moliagul in 1869, while the 27kg Hand of Faith (the largest nugget found with a metal detector) was found near Kingower in 1980. A good touring route starts in Castlemaine or Maryborough and heads up to the historic town of Maldon. From there take the back road through the farmland and canola fields of the Loddon Valley to Dunolly. It was here that miners John Deason and Richard Oates first brought the Welcome Stranger nugget, where it was cut into pieces because it was too big to fit on the scales! See a replica of the nugget and the anvil it was cut up on at the **Goldfields Historical Museum** (admission $2; Broadway; ☻1.30-4.30pm Sat & Sun). Dunolly's main street is lined with historic buildings and you can hire metal detectors in town for $45 a day. From here it's a pleasant drive to Moliagul, where signs point to the Moliagul Historic Reserve and the **Welcome Stranger Memorial**, erected in 1897 roughly where the nugget was unearthed. Moliagul is also known as the birthplace of the 'Flying Doctor', the Reverend John Flynn. It's a further 15km east to Tarnagulla, another interesting old mining town, and from there it's an easy drive back to Maldon or across to Bendigo.

✿✿ Festivals & Events

Kyneton is renowned for its daffodils. The annual **Kyneton Daffodil & Arts Festival** (www.kynetondaffodilarts.org.au) is held each September, with 10 days of gala evenings, markets, concerts, fairs, art and flower shows.

Budburst (☑1800 244 711; www.budburst .com) is a wine and food festival hosted at wineries throughout the Macedon Ranges region over several days.

✗ Eating & Drinking

Kyneton's eat street is historic Piper St, with a fabulous cafe and restaurant scene.

Ganim's Market Fresh   MARKET
(☑5422 1653; 17-21 Piper St; ⊙10am-5pm Mon-Fri, 9am-4pm Sat, 11am-4pm Sun) This organic produce market stocks local honey, preserves, fruit and vegies, and has a gelateria and juice bar.

Dhaba at the Mill   INDIAN **$**
(☑5422 6225; www.dhabaatthemill.com; 18 Piper St; mains $10-16; ⊙dinner Thu-Sun, lunch Sat & Sun; ☑) Behind the heavy wooden doors at the old bluestone steam mill, you can tuck into authentic, affordable curries – classics such as butter chicken, palak paneer and lamb vindaloo.

Royal George   MODERN AUSTRALIAN **$$**
(☑5422 1390; www.royalgeorge.com.au; 24 Piper St; mains $27-32; ⊙lunch Thu-Sun, dinner Wed-Sat) The historic Royal George Hotel has been transformed into a glamorous one-hat restaurant and makes for a sublime fine-dining experience.

Ladle Foodstore   CAFE, GROCERY **$**
(☑5422 2430; 30 Piper St; ⊙10am-5pm) Great coffee, bright sunny atmosphere and a cosy lounge area at the back. Local cheeses and preserves are a speciality.

❶ Information

Kyneton visitor centre (☑5422 6110, 1800 244 711; www.visitmacedonranges.com; 127 High St; ⊙9am-5pm) On the southeastern entry to town. Ask for the brochures *Town Walks, Self Drive Tour* and *Campaspe River Walk*.

❶ Getting There & Away

Kyneton is just off the Calder Hwy about 90km northwest of Melbourne. Regular V-line trains on the Bendigo line run here from Melbourne ($8.40, 1¼ hours). The train station is 1km south of the town centre.

Castlemaine

POP 7250

At the heart of the central Victorian gold-fields, Castlemaine is a rewarding working-class town where a growing community of artists and tree-changers live amid some inspiring architecture and gardens. Even after the gold rush subsided, Castlemaine has always had a reputation for industry and innovation – this was the birthplace of the Castlemaine XXXX beer-brewing company (now based in Queensland) and Castlemaine Rock, a hard-boiled sweet lovingly produced by the Barnes family since 1853. It's also the 'Street Rod Centre of Australia', where hot rods have been built and shown off since 1962.

After gold was discovered at Specimen Gully in 1851, the Mt Alexander Diggings attracted some 30,000 diggers and Castlemaine became the thriving marketplace for the goldfields. The town's importance waned as the surface gold was exhausted by the 1860s but, fortunately, the centre of town was well established by then and remains relatively intact.

◉ Sights

Castlemaine has a number of interesting historic buildings, including the Roman basilica façade of the old **Castlemaine Market** (1862) on Mostyn St; the **Theatre Royal** (1856) on Lyttleton St; the **post office** (1894); and the original **courthouse building** (1851) on Goldsmith Cres. For a good view over town, head up to the **Burke & Wills Monument** on Wills St (follow Lyttleton St east of the centre). Robert O'Hara Burke was a police superintendent in Castlemaine before his fateful trek.

See p203 for information on the **Victorian Goldfields Railway** that runs from Castlemaine to Maldon.

Castlemaine Art Gallery & Historical Museum   ART GALLERY
(☑5472 2292; www.castlemainegallery.com; 14 Lyttleton St; adult/student/family $4/2/8; ⊙10am-5pm Mon-Fri, noon-5pm Sat & Sun) A superb art deco building houses this gallery, which features colonial and contemporary Australian art, including work by well-known Australian artists such as Frederick McCubbin and Russell Drysdale. The museum, in the basement, provides an insight into local history, with costumes, china and gold mining relics.

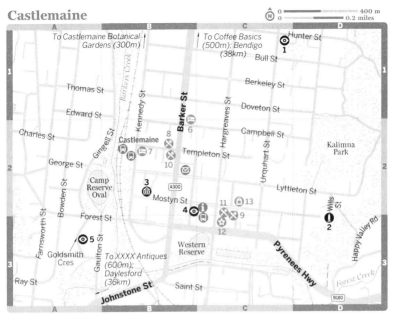

Buda Historic Home & Garden

HISTORIC BUILDING

(☎5472 1032; www.budacastlemaine.org; 42 Hunter St; adult/child/family $9/4/25; ⏰noon-5pm Wed-Sat, 10am-5pm Sun) Home to a Hungarian silversmith and his family for 120 years, Buda has permanent displays of the family's extensive art and craft collections, furnishings and personal belongings. There's an interesting mix of architectural styles: the original Indian-villa influence, and later Edwardian-style extensions dating from 1861.

Castlemaine Botanical Gardens   GARDENS

(cnr Downes Rd & Walker St) These majestic gardens, one of the oldest in Victoria (established 1860), strike a perfect balance between sculpture and wilderness among awe-inspiring National Trust–registered trees and the artificial Lake Joanna.

Castlemaine Rod Shop   MUSEUM

(☎5472 3868, 0428 122 206; Pyrenees Hwy, Chewton; adult/child $5/free) Few people have done more for Castlemaine's reputation as the hot-rod capital than Rod Hadfield, and you can visit his workshop and car display at Chewton, 7km east of Castlemaine. The big green shed contains around 20 custom-built vehicles and drag racers as well as artworks and a trophy display. Call ahead to check it's open.

Castlemaine

✵✵ Festivals & Events

Castlemaine State Festival   ARTS
(www.castlemainefestival.com.au) One of Victoria's leading arts events, featuring theatre, music, art and dance; held in April in odd-numbered years.

Festival of Gardens   GARDEN
(www.festivalofgardens.org) Over 50 locals open their properties to the public; held in November in odd-numbered years.

🛏 Sleeping

Bookings are essential during festival times so make use of the area's free **Accommodation Booking Service** (☏1800 171 888).

Theatre Royal Backstage   BOUTIQUE HOTEL **$$$**
(☏5472 1196; www.theatreroyal.info; 30 Hargreaves St; B&B d $220-240) It's a unique experience staying backstage at this 1854 theatre. The two suites are compact, but beautifully decorated with period furniture and cinema memorabilia, and are literally right behind the velvet curtain – you can clearly hear any performances, though the rate includes admission to all movies screened during your stay. The suites can be rented together for $240 (sleeping four) plus you get the 'Harry Potter' single (under the stairs) free.

Midland Private Hotel   GUESTHOUSE **$$**
(☏5472 1085; www.themidland.com.au; 2 Templeton St; s/d $110/150, en suite d $200, apt d $270) Opposite the train station, this lace-decked 1879 hotel is mostly original so the rooms are old-fashioned but it has plenty of charm, from the art deco entrance to the magnificent guest lounge and attached Maurocco Bar.

Castlemaine Colonial Motel   MOTEL **$$**
(☏5472 4000; www.castlemainemotel.com.au; 252 Barker St; s/d $115/125, spa unit $155, apt $190; ✲🕸) Conveniently central and the best of Castlemaine's motels, the Colonial has modern rooms, some with spa, and high-ceilinged apartments in a beautifully converted school building.

Castlemaine Gardens Holiday Park
   CARAVAN PARK **$**
(☏5472 1125; 1 Doran Ave; unpowered/powered sites $25/30, en suite cabins $85-105) Beautifully situated next to the Botanical Gardens and the public swimming pool.

✗ Eating

Castlemaine's dining scene is constantly evolving and improving, with a good cafe scene at the east end of Mostyn St.

Coffee Basics   CAFE **$**
(☏5470 6270; www.coffeebasics.com.au; 1 Halford St) For great coffee, head north of town to this cafe where they roast and blend their own beans and serve it in their European-influenced cafe.

Good Table   MEDITERRANEAN **$$**
(☏5472 4400; www.thegoodtable.com.au; 233 Barker St; mains $14-25; ⊙lunch & dinner Thu-Sun) There have been numerous incarnations of this lovely corner hotel, but the Good Table does it well with a thoughtful European-influenced menu featuring linguini with yabbies and organic goat pie.

Saffs Cafe   CAFE **$**
(☏5470 6722; 64 Mostyn St; mains $8-24; ⊙lunch daily, dinner Wed-Sat) A local favourite, Saffs is a bright, friendly place with good coffee, cake, brilliant breakfasts, local artwork on the walls and a rear courtyard.

Empyre Hotel   MODERN AUSTRALIAN **$$$**
(☏5472 5166; 68 Mostyn St; lunch $17-25, dinner $34-36; ⊙breakfast & lunch Wed-Sun, dinner Wed-Sat) In a beautifully restored 19th-century hotel, dinner at the Empyre is a sumptuous fine-dining experience. There's more relaxed lunchtime dining in the cafe.

Apple Annie's Bakery & Café   BAKERY, CAFE **$**
(☏5472 5311; 31 Templeton St; mains $6-12; ⊙breakfast & lunch) For fresh baked bread, mouth-watering cakes and pastries, it's hard to beat this country-style cafe and bakery.

☆ Entertainment

Theatre Royal   CINEMA, LIVE MUSIC
(☏5472 1196; www.theatreroyal.info; 30 Hargreaves St; ⊙daily) A continually operating theatre since the 1850s, this is a fabulous entertainment venue – classic cinema (dine while watching a movie), touring live performers, a bar and a cafe. Check the program on the website.

🛍 Shopping

Castlemaine is a good place to go hunting for collectables.

Restorers Barn   VINTAGE
(☏5470 5669; www.restorersbarn.com.au; 129-133 Mostyn St; ⊙10am-5.30pm) An institution in itself, this place is chock-full of interesting bric-a-brac, collectables, tools and old junk.

Book Heaven   BOOKS
(☏5472 4555; 47 Main Rd, Campbells Creek) An awesome secondhand bookshop crammed with 90,000 titles!

XXXX Antiques ANTIQUES
(☎5470 5989; www.xxxxantiques.com.au; 1-5 Elizabeth St; ⏰9.30am-5pm) Houses a museum collection of antiques and collectables, partly in the original XXXX brewery (Bond Store).

ⓘ Information

Castlemaine visitor centre (☎5470 6200; www.maldoncastlemaine.com; Mostyn St; ⏰9am-5pm) In the magnificent old Castlemaine Market, the town's original market building fronted with a classical Roman-basilica facade with a statue of Ceres, the Roman goddess of the harvest, on top.

ⓘ Getting There & Away

V/Line (☎13 61 96) trains run hourly between Melbourne and Castlemaine ($11.60, 1½ hours) and continue on to Bendigo ($3.40).

Around Castlemaine

About 10km northwest of Castlemaine, the **Harcourt** region (bypassed by the new Calder Fwy) is known as Victoria's 'apple centre', but in recent years it has also developed as an excellent mini-wine centre, an extension of the Bendigo wine region – the visitor centre can provide a map and a list of cellar doors. Check out **Bress** (☎5474 2262; www.bress.com.au; 3894 Calder Hwy; ⏰11am-5pm Sat & Sun), a combined winery and cidery; and **Blackjack Wines** (☎5474 2355; www.blackjackwines.net.au; Calder Hwy).

Skydancers (☎5474 2614; Blackjack Rd; adult/child $4/3; ⏰10am-5pm Wed-Sun) is Victoria's only butterfly house where you can flirt with hundreds of butterflies; there are also native gardens and a cafe.

Maldon

POP 1500

Like a pop-up folk museum, the whole of Maldon is a well-preserved relic of the gold-rush era, with many fine buildings constructed from local stone. The population is a scant reminder of the 20,000 who used to work the local goldfields, but this is still a living, working town – packed with tourists on weekends but reverting to its sleepy self during the week.

The town centre consists of High St and Main St, lined with antique stores, cafes, old toy shops, lolly shops, bookshops and the three local pubs – the Maldon, Grand and Kangaroo hotels. Situated behind the visitor centre, the old marketplace is now the **Maldon & District Museum** (☎5474 1633; adult/child $5/1; ⏰1.30-4pm Fri-Wed), with historical photos and a research room. The **Old Post Office** (95 High St), built in 1870, was the childhood home of Henry Handel Richardson. She (yes, she!) writes about it in her autobiography, *Myself When Young* (1948).

Evidence of those heady mining days can be seen around town – you can't miss the 24m-high **Beehive Chimney**, just east of Main St. A short trip south along High St is the remains of the **North British Mine**, where interpretive boards tell the story of what was once one of the world's richest mines. For a hands-on experience, **Carman's Tunnel** (☎5475 2656; carmanstunnel@maldon.vicmail.net; off Parkin's Reef Rd; adult/child $5/2; ⏰tours at 1.30pm, 2.30pm & 3.30pm Sat & Sun, daily during school holidays) is a 570m-long mine tunnel that was excavated in the 1880s, and took two years to dig, yet produced only $300 worth of gold. Now you can descend with a guide for a 45-minute candlelight tour.

Don't miss the 3km drive up to **Mt Tarrengower** for panoramic views from the poppet-head lookout.

If you're in town on a Wednesday or Sunday, ride the beautifully restored steam train along the original line through the Muckleford forest to Castlemaine (and back) with the **Victorian Goldfields Railway** (☎5470 6658, 5475 2966; www.vgr.com.au; adult/child/family return $27/13/60; ⏰departs 10.30am, 1pm & 3pm Wed & Sun). For a little extra, go first class (adult/child/family $40/23/93, Sunday only) in an oak-lined viewing carriage. Magic! The Maldon train station dates from 1884.

Porcupine Township (☎5475 1000; www.porcupinetownship.com.au; cnr Bendigo & Allens Rds; adult/child/family $10/6/30; ⏰10am-5pm) is a quaint theme village recreating the years leading up to the gold rush (1835 to 1853) with a collection of some 40 original slab buildings, including miners' huts, a dance hall and a resident ghost. There are no costumed characters here but kids will enjoy a carriage ride and possibly some panning. There's a cafe for afternoon tea.

⭐ Festivals & Events

Twilight Food & Wine Festival WINE, FOOD
(www.tasteofgold.com) Fine food, lanterns, live music and wine tasting in early January. Arrive by steam train: www.vgr.com.au.

GOLDFIELDS & GRAMPIANS AROUND CASTLEMAINE

Maldon Easter Fair RURAL
(maldoneasterfair.com) Held March or April.

Maldon Folk Festival MUSIC
(www.maldonfolkfestival.com) Maldon's main
event, this four-day festival in early November attracts dozens of performers with
a wide variety of world music at venues
around town and at the main stage at Mt
Tarrengower Reserve.

Sleeping & Eating

There are plenty of self-contained cottages
and charming B&Bs in restored buildings
that are located around town. **Heritage
Cottages of Maldon** (5475 1094; www.
heritagecottages.com.au; 41 High St) manages
numerous properties, and there's also the
**Mt Alexander Accommodation Booking
Service** (1800 171 888, 5470 5866; www.mal
doncastlemaine.com).

Calder House B&B $$
(5475 2912; www.calderhouse.com.au; 44 High
St; d $130-160) If you're in the mood for
grand, you'll step back in time at this formal,
yet very inviting, place.

Penny School Gallery & Café
CAFE, RESTAURANT $$
(5475 1911; www.pennyschoolgallery.com.au; 11
Church St; mains $11-35; 11am-5pm Wed-Sun,
11am-10pm Fri & Sat) Situated in a lovely heritage building tucked away from busy Main
St, this light-filled cafe-restaurant features
changing exhibitions of well-known local
and national artists, including indigenous
art. It's a great spot for coffee but the Mod
Oz menu of pasta, smoked trout and Daylesford venison is hard to beat. There's free
live music on Sunday afternoon and games
of petanque outside. You'll need to book
ahead for dinner.

Bean There Cafe CAFE $
(0419 102 723; 44 Main St; meals $7-15; lunch
Wed-Sun) This tiny licensed cafe is worth a
visit for the yabby pies, made from locally
farmed yabbies.

Information

Maldon visitor centre (5475 2569; www.
maldoncastlemaine.com; 95 High St; 9am-
5pm) Has internet access. Pick up the *Information Guide* and *Historic Town Walk* brochure,
which guides you past some of the most
historic buildings.

Maryborough
POP 7700

Maryborough is part of central Victoria's
'Golden Triangle', where prospectors still turn
up a nugget or two. The town's pride and joy
is the magnificent railway station, and now
that passenger trains are running here again
from Melbourne it's worth a day trip.

The town boasts plenty of impressive
Victorian-era buildings, but **Maryborough
Railway Station** (5461 4683; www.station
antiques.com; 38 Victoria St; admission free;
10am-5pm, to 10pm Thu-Sat, closed Tue) leaves
them all for dead. Built in 1892, the inor-
dinately large station, complete with clock
tower, was described by Mark Twain as 'a
train station with a town attached'. Today it
houses a mammoth antique emporium, a regional wine centre and an excellent cafe. An
antique fair is held here three times a year.

Built in 1894, **Worsley Cottage** (5461
2518; www.vicnet.net.au/~mbhs; 3 Palmerston St;
adult/child $3/free; 10am-noon Tue & Thu, 2-4pm
Sun) is the local historical society museum.
Every room is furnished with pieces from
the times, often donated by local people,
and there's a large photographic collection.
Records held here are used in family history
research.

If you're interested in finding your own
gold nuggets, **Coiltek Gold Centre** (5460
4700; www.coiltek.com.au; 6 Drive-in Ct; 9am-
5pm) offers full-day prospecting courses
(one/two people $120/200) with state-of-
the-art metal detectors. It also sells and
hires out prospecting gear.

Festivals & Events

Highland Gathering SCOTTISH
(www.maryboroughhighlandsociety.com) Have
a fling at Maryborough's Scottish festival,
with races, stalls, tossing the caber and
highland music; held every New Year's
Day since 1857.

Energy Breakthrough Festivals CAR
(www.racvenergybreakthrough.net) Focusing on
alternative energy sources, school groups
bring their inventive vehicles for the
24-hour and 16-hour (for juniors) RACV
Energy Breakthrough Grand Prix; held
late November.

Sleeping & Eating

There's plenty of accommodation in the region. Contact Maryborough visitor centre or

GOLDFIELDS & GRAMPIANS GOLDFIELDS TOWNS

browse its website (www.visitmaryborough .com.au). The historic Bull & Mouth was still undergoing renovations at the time of research but should be open with boutique rooms by the time you read this.

High St is the foodie area, with cafes, restaurants, bakeries, takeaways, pubs and clubs.

Maryborough Caravan Park CARAVAN PARK $
(☑5460 4848; www.maryboroughcaravanpark .com.au; 7-9 Holyrood St; unpowered/powered sites $20/25, bunkhouse dm $25, cabins $60-80; ✳ ☒) Close to the town centre and nicely located beside Lake Victoria, the caravan park is well set up with Maryborough's cheapest accommodation.

Station Cafe CAFE, RESTAURANT $$
(☑5461 4683; 38c Victoria St; mains $16-29; ☺10am-5pm Mon-Wed & Sun, 10am-10pm Thu-Sat) This excellent cafe is in a lovely light-filled room in the grand Maryborough train station. Stop in for a coffee or speciality crepe. The evening menu features pasta and Black Angus steaks; Thursday is roast night.

ℹ Information

Central Goldfields visitor centre (☑1800 356 511, 5460 4511; www.visitmaryborough.com .au; cnr Alma & Nolan Sts; ☺9am-5pm) Loads of helpful maps and friendly staff. There's also a replica of the famous Welcome Stranger gold nugget here, and internet access and a library in the same complex.

ℹ Getting There & Away

The passenger train to Maryborough finally resumed in 2010. Currently there's only one train a day (via Ballarat), departing Melbourne at around 4pm ($23.70, 2½ hours). The return train leaves at 7.25am weekdays, 7am Saturday and 8am Sunday. Maryborough is also connected by bus to Castlemaine and Ballarat.

Rising up from the western Victorian plains and a haven for bushwalkers, rock-climbers and nature-lovers, the Grampians are one of the state's most outstanding natural and cultural features. The rich diversity of wildlife and flora, unique rock formations, Aboriginal rock art, spectacular viewpoints and an extensive network of trails and bush camp sites offer something for everyone. Explorer Major Thomas Mitchell named the ranges the Grampians after the mountains in Scotland. In 1836 he eloquently described them as:

> ...a noble range of mountains, rising in the south to a stupendous height, and presenting as bold and picturesque an outline as a painter ever imagined.

It's really something to be surrounded by these spectacular shapes, whether you're abseiling down in a harness or peering over a cascading waterfall. Over 900 species of native trees, shrubs and wildflowers have been recorded here, with everything from fern gullies to red-gum forests. It's worth visiting at any time of year, but it's at its colourful best in spring when the wildflowers (including 20 species that don't exist anywhere else in the world) are at their peak. After years of very low rainfall (and occasional bushfires), rains came to region in abundance in 2010, followed by damaging floods early in 2011, but fresh water may still be limited at camping areas. Take your own supplies of water to picnic areas and camping grounds.

The four greatest mountain ranges are the **Mt Difficult Range** in the north, **Mt William Range** in the east, **Serra Range** in the southeast and **Victoria Range** in the

ROCK ART

Traditional Aboriginal owners have been occupying Gariwerd for more than 20,000 years and this is the most accessible place in Victoria to see indigenous rock art. Sites include **Bunjil's Shelter**, near Stawell, one of Victoria's most sacred indigenous sites, best seen on a guided tour from the Brambuk Cultural Centre. Other rock art sites in the west of the park are the **Manja Shelter**, reached from the Harrop Track car park; the **Billimina Shelter**, near the Buandik camping ground; and in the north is the **Ngamadjidj Shelter**, reached from the Stapylton camping ground.

These paintings, in protected rock overhangs, are mostly hand prints, animal tracks and stick figures. They indicate the esteem in which these mountains are held by local indigenous communities and should be treated with respect.

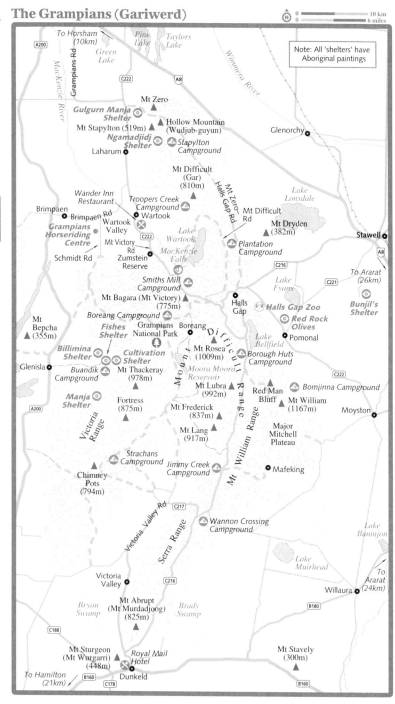

southwest. They spread from Ararat to the Wartook Valley and from Dunkeld up almost to Horsham. **Halls Gap**, the main accommodation base and service town, lies in the Fyans Valley. The smaller **Wonderland Range**, close to Halls Gap, has some of the most splendid and accessible outlooks, scenic drives, picnic grounds and gum-scented walks, such as those that go to the Pinnacles or to Silverband Falls.

There are more than 150km of well-marked **walking tracks**, ranging from half-hour strolls to overnight treks through difficult terrain, all starting from the various car parks, picnic grounds and camping areas. For longer walks, let someone know where you're going (preferably the Parks Victoria rangers).

One of the most popular sights is spectacular **MacKenzie Falls**. From the car park the steep 600m path leads to the base of the falls and a large plunge pool (no swimming). Other popular places include **Boroka Lookout**, with excellent views over Halls Gap and Lake Bellfield, and **Reed Lookout** with the short walk to the **Balconies** and views over Lake Wartook.

Zumstein Reserve in the western Grampians is named after Walter Zumstein, a beekeeper and naturalist who settled in the area in 1910 and developed it into a wildlife reserve. There are picnic facilities, free electric barbecues and short walks. **Mt Stapylton** and **Hollow Mountain** in the north are renowned as abseiling and rock-climbing spots.

👉 Tours

Adventure companies (mostly based in Halls Gap) can organise everything from rock climbing and abseiling to horse riding and 4WD tours.

Absolute Outdoors Australia OUTDOORS
(☑5356 4556; www.absoluteoutdoors.com.au; Shop 4, Stony Ck, Halls Gap) Rock climbing, abseiling, mountain biking, canoeing, and guided nature walks from $55 to $200. Also offers equipment hire.

Brambuk Cultural Centre
INDIGENOUS CULTURE, ROCK ART
(☑5356 4452; www.brambuk.com.au; Grampians Rd/C216; tours adult/child $35/22) Rangers lead a three-hour cultural and rock art tour. Bookings essential.

Grampians Horseriding Centre
HORSE RIDING
(☑5383 9255; www.grampianshorseriding.com .au; 430 Schmidt Rd, Brimpaen, Wartook Valley; 2½hr rides $75; ⏱10am & 2pm) Horse-riding

adventures around a grand property with sweeping views, lakes and wandering bush tracks. Beginners are well looked after.

Grampians Mountain Adventure Company ROCK CLIMBING
(GMAC; ☑5383 9218, 0427 747 047; www. grampiansadventure.com.au; half-day from $75) Specialises in rock-climbing and abseiling adventures and instruction from beginner to advanced.

Grampians Personalised Tours & Adventures OUTDOORS
(☑5356 4654, 0429 954 686; www.grampians tours.com; tours/walks from $59/15) Offers a range of 4WD tours (with off-road options; from $79), rock climbing and abseiling, discovery walks (from half-day to four days) and scenic flights over the ranges ($170/280 for three/five people). Tours include stop-offs at picturesque locations.

Grampians Quad Bike Adventures
QUAD BIKING
(☑5383 9215; www.grampiansquadbikes.com. au; 130 Schmidts Rd, Brimpaen; 2hr/half-day tour $115/180) Tool around the bush on a quad bike (on private property, not in the park). No experience required.

Hangin' Out ROCK CLIMBING
(☑5356 4535, 0407 684 831; www.hanginout .com.au; rock climbing from $65) Rock-climbing specialists who will get you started with a four-hour introductory session ($75) and private guiding from $150. Experienced guide Earl will get you onto the cliff faces with a lively interpretation of the surrounding country as you go. His adventure walk (full day $135) includes rock climbs and abseils – an exhilarating Grampians experience.

Camping

Parks Victoria maintains **sites** (☑5361 4000; sites per vehicle or 6 people $14) throughout the park, with toilets, picnic tables and fireplaces (BYO water). Permits are required; you can register and pay at the office at the Brambuk Cultural Centre. Bush camping is permitted (no camp fires), except in the Wonderland Range area, around Lake Wartook and in parts of the Serra, Mt William and Victoria Ranges.

Pay close attention to fire restrictions – apart from the damage you could do to yourself and the bush, you can be jailed for lighting *any* fire, including a fuel stove, on days of total fire ban.

Information

Parks Victoria (☏13 19 63, 5361 4000; www.parkweb.vic.gov.au; Brambuk the National Park & Cultural Centre, Halls Gap; ⏰9am-5pm) The Brambuk Cultural Centre is the place for park maps and the rangers can advise you about where to go, where to camp and what you might see. They also issue camping permits and fishing permits ($12) required for fishing in local streams.

Halls Gap

POP 7700

Nudging up against the craggy Wonderland Range, Halls Gap is a pretty little town – some might even say sleepy if you visit midweek in winter, but boy does it get busy during holidays! This is the main accommodation base and easiest access for the best of the Grampians. The single street through town has a neat little knot of shops, a supermarket, adventure activity offices, restaurants and cafes. The Halls Gap general store and post office has an ATM and Eftpos.

◉ Sights & Activities

Brambuk Cultural Centre

CULTURAL CENTRE, MUSEUM

(☏5361 4000; www.brambuk.com.au; Grampians Tourist Rd; ⏰9am-5pm) Your first stop should be the superb cultural centre at Brambuk, 2.5km south of Halls Gap. The building itself is a striking design that combines timeless Aboriginal motifs with contemporary design and building materials. Its flowing orange roof represents the open wings of the cockatoo, as well as referencing the peaks of the Grampians. Run by five Koori communities in conjunction with Parks Victoria, the centre offers insights into local culture and history through Koori stories, art, music, dance, weapons, tools and photographs

The **Gariwerd Dreaming Theatre** (adult/child/family $5/3/12) shows hourly films explaining Dreamtime stories of Gariwerd and the creation story of Bunjil. The ceiling here represents the southern right whale (totem of the Gunditjmara people). There's an art room where kids can try their hand at indigenous painting ($3 for a message stone, $7 for a boomerang), and holiday programs are organised. Planted outside are native plants used for food and medicine.

In a separate building – where you first enter the complex – is the Parks Victoria office where rangers can advise on walks and sell camping permits. Also here are interesting educational displays covering the natural features and the history of the Grampians, a souvenir shop and **Brambuk Bush Tucker Café** (meals $11-26; ⏰9am-4pm) with a lovely deck overlooking the gardens.

Grampians Adventure Golf
MINIGOLF

(☏5356 4664; www.grampiansadventuregolf.com.au; 475-481 Grampians Tourist Rd; adult/child/family $12/9/38; ⏰10am-5pm Wed-Sun, daily in school holidays). There's minigolf, and then there's this 18-hole extravaganza squeezed into a bush setting just south of Halls Gap. Great for kids. There's a licensed cafe and the MOCO gallery attached.

Halls Gap Zoo
ZOO

(☏5356 4668; www.hallsgapzoo.com.au; 4061 Pomonal Rd; adult/child/family $18/9/45; ⏰10am-5pm Wed-Mon) Get up close to Australian native animals such as wallabies, grey kangaroos, quolls and wombats, but also exotic critters such as meerkats, spider monkeys, bison and tamarin. This is a top-notch wildlife park with breeding and conservation programs and a natural bush setting. Call ahead to find out about feeding times.

Other Attractions

The road out to Pomonal, 11km southeast of Halls Gap, has a neat little cluster of attractions. Just before the turn-off to the Halls Gap Zoo, you pass **Gap Vineyard** (☏5356 4252; Ararat-Halls Gap Rd; ⏰10am-5pm Wed-Sun), with cellar door sales and tastings.

Next door, **Red Rock Olives** (☏5222 1005; www.redrockolives.com.au; cnr Ararat-Halls Gap & Tunnel Rds; ⏰10am-5pm Sat & Sun) has olive products to sample and buy, or you can just wander around the olive groves.

✦ Festivals & Events

Halls Gap is the focal point for local festivities:

Grampians Jazz Festival
MUSIC

(www.grampiansjazzfestival.com.au) Three days of jazz music around town and a street parade. Held in mid-February.

Grampians Grape Escape
WINE, FOOD

(www.grampiansgrapeescape.com.au) Two-day wine and food extravaganza at various venues and wineries, including live music and kids entertainment. First weekend in May.

Grampians Wildflower Show
FLOWER

(www.grampianswildflowershow.org.au; adult/child $4/0.50) This four-day exhibition in Centenary Hall showcases the wonderful springtime wildflowers of the Grampians. Held in October.

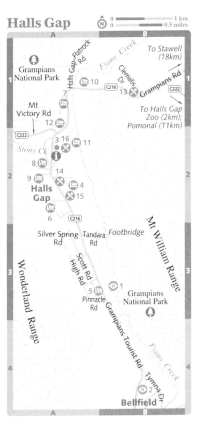

Wonderland ranges through floor to ceiling windows. The villas make the most of local building materials such as Grampians' stone, and sit on a secluded property complete with its own lagoon. With a spa and king-size bed, it's a real couples getaway. There's a minimum two-night stay on weekends.

Halls Gap Film Festival FILM
(www.visithallsgap.com.au/filmfestival) Australian and international films screened at the Classic Cinema in Centenary Hall. Held in November.

🛏 Sleeping

Halls Gap and the surrounding region has a huge range of accommodation – with more than 6000 beds this is regional Victoria's most visited area after the Great Ocean Road. Whether you're camping, backpacking or looking for a motel or log cabin, there's plenty to choose from, but it still gets very busy in holiday periods – book ahead.

Aspect Villas BOUTIQUE VILLA **$$$**
(✆5356 4457; www.aspectvillas.com.au; off Mackey's Peak Rd; d $375; ✱) These two luxury villas are situated close to town but seem a world away when you're reclining on your bed or by the log fire, taking in views of the

D'Altons Resort COTTAGES **$$**
(✆5356 4666; www.daltonsresort.com.au; 48 Glen St; studio/deluxe/family cottages from $100/120/150; ✱✲) These delightful timber cottages, with cosy lounge chairs, cute verandahs and log fires, spread up the hill back from the main road between the gums and kangaroos. It's immaculately kept and the friendly owners are a mine of local information. There's even a tennis court and a saltwater pool.

Mountain Grand Guesthouse
GUESTHOUSE **$$**
(✆5356 4232; www.mountaingrand.com; Grampians Tourist Rd; B&B s/d $146/166; ✱✿) This gracious, old-fashioned timber guesthouse prides itself on being a traditional old-fashioned lodge where you can take a pre-dinner port in one of the lounge areas and mingle with other guests. The rooms are still quaint but with a bright, fresh feel. The Balconies Restaurant here is well regarded.

Pinnacle Holiday Lodge
MOTEL **$$**

(☑5356 4249; www.pinnacleholiday.com.au; 21-45 Heath St; 1-/2-bedroom units $110-160, d with spa $130; ❄❀) Right in the centre of Halls Gap, this gorgeous property behind the Stony Creek shops is a cut above most of Halls Gap's motels. The spacious grounds have a bucolic feel with barbecue areas, an indoor pool and tennis courts. Modern self-contained units, two-bedroom family apartments and a swanky spa suite feature flat-screen TVs and gas log fires.

Grampians YHA Eco-Hostel
HOSTEL **$**

(☑5356 4544; www.yha.com.au; cnr Grampians Tourist Rd & Buckler St; dm/d $34/89) This architecturally designed and ecofriendly hostel utilises solar power and rainwater tanks and makes the most of light and space. It's beautifully equipped with a spacious lounge, a *Master Chef*-quality kitchen and spotless rooms.

Brambuk Backpackers
HOSTEL **$**

(☑53564250;www.brambuk.com.au;Grampians Tourist Rd; B&B dm/d $22/65; @) Across from the cultural centre, this friendly Aboriginal -owned and -run hostel gives you a calming sense of place with a relaxed feel and craggy views out of the lounge windows. All rooms, including dorms, have en suites and the lounge, dining room, kitchen and barbecue deck are all top-notch.

Parkgate Resort
CARAVAN PARK **$**

(☑1800 810 781, 5356 4215; www.parkgateresort .com.au; Grampians Tourist Rd, Halls Gap; powered sites $32-45, cabin/cottage d from $75/110; ❄❀) Just north of the centre, Parkgate is an immaculate, sprawling family holiday park with all the bells and whistles – jumping pillow and playground for kids, tennis courts, a camp kitchen, games and lounge rooms and free barbecues.

Tim's Place
HOSTEL **$**

(☑5356 4288; www.timsplace.com.au; 44 Grampians Rd; dm/s/d $25/55/70, apt $90-150; @) Friendly, spotless backpackers with homely eco-feel; free mountain bikes and herb garden.

Halls Gap Caravan Park
CARAVAN PARK **$**

(☑5356 4251; www.hallsgapcaravanpark.com. au; Grampians Rd; unpowered/powered sites from $25/30, cabins $65-110; ❄) Camping and cabins right in the town centre. Gets crowded at peak times.

✖ Eating

Halls Gap's small knot of eateries are mostly along Grampians Tourist Rd and beside the boardwalk along pretty Stony Creek, where the bakery makes sublime vanilla slices, and the Pink Panther Café does good pizzas. In the Smugglers Hearth souvenir shop you'll find delicious homemade fudge from the Grampians Fudge Factory.

Kookaburra Restaurant
MODERN AUSTRALIAN **$$**

(☑5356 4222; www.kookaburrabarbistro.com.au; 125-127 Grampians Rd; mains $23-34; ⊙dinner Tue-Sat, lunch & dinner Sun) This Halls Gap institution is famed for its sublime crispy-skin duck and Aussie dishes such as barramundi and kangaroo fillet. Since it's only open for dinner, there's a good value 'eat early' deal if you order by 6.30pm. The wine list features mostly Grampians area wines, and there's beer on tap at the convivial bar.

Halls Gap Hotel
PUB **$$**

(☑5356 4566; 2262 Grampians Rd; mains $18-29; ⊙lunch & dinner) For generous no-nonsense bistro food or a family dinner, you can't beat the local pub, about 2km north of town, with views of the Grampians. There are indoor and outdoor play areas for kids, and it's a social place for a beer after a day's bushwalking.

Morningside
CAFE **$**

(☑5356 4222; Grampians Tourist Rd; continental/ cooked breakfast $15/22; ⊙breakfast) The outdoor deck of this cafe at the back of the Colonial Motor Inn is the perfect spot for breakfast with continental buffet or cooked brekky on offer.

ⓘ Information

Halls Gap visitor centre (☑1800 065 599; www.grampianstravel.com.au, www.visithalls gap.com.au; Centenary Hall, 115 Grampians Tourist Rd; ⊙9am-5pm) The staff here are helpful, and can book tours, accommodation and activities.

Dunkeld & the Southern Grampians

The southern access to the Grampians, Dunkeld is a sleepy little town with a very big-name restaurant. The setting is superb, with Mt Abrupt and Mt Sturgeon rising up to the north, while the Grampians Tourist Rd to Halls Gap gives you a glorious passage into the park, the cliffs and sky opening up as you pass between the Serra and Mt William Ranges. Fit hikers can walk to the summit of Mt Abrupt (6.5km, three hours return) and **Mt Sturgeon** (7km, three hours return) for panoramic views of the ranges. Both walks leave from signposted car parks off the Grampians Tourist Rd.

The town was established in the 1860s, but much of it was destroyed by bushfires in 1944. The **Historical Society Museum** (cnr Wills & Templeton Sts, Dunkeld; admission $2; ☺1-5pm Sun), in an old bluestone church, has a local history collection, including Aboriginal artefacts and old photographs.

Dunkeld visitor centre (☎5577 2558; www.sthgrampians.vic.gov.au; Parker St) has useful information.

🛏 Sleeping & Eating

Dunkeld has a couple of cafes in the main street and a number of holiday cottages dotted around the region, but the main attraction is the restaurant at the Royal Mail.

TOP CHOICE **Royal Mail Hotel**

HOTEL, RESTAURANT $$

(☎5577 2241; www.royalmail.com.au; Parker St; d $160-200, apt $290-310) The Royal Mail has been continuously licensed since 1855 but today it's a stylish modern hotel with a fine bar, bistro and one of Victoria's top restaurants (open Tuesday to Sunday). The attached motel-style rooms and apartments, with mountain or garden views, are elegant with all mod-cons, while the cottages across the road make up for the lack of views with their spaciousness. You need to book months ahead to dine in the main restaurant where there's a set menu ($150), but dining in the bistro or at the casual bar is equally enjoyable (mains $16 to $36).

Wartook Valley & the Northern Grampians

Lush Wartook Valley runs along the Grampians' western foothills, giving a completely different perspective of the mountains. Heading to or from Horsham, this is the scenic alternative to the Western Hwy (A8). From Wartook, the sealed Roses Gap Rd and Mount Victoria Rd pass through the park, and there are lots of unsealed roads and tracks passing little creeks, waterfalls and idyllic picnic spots.

You can buy olives and other farm produce at the **Mt Zero Olive Grove** (Mt Zero Rd; ☺10am-4pm). Walk to the top of **Mt Zero** from the nearby picnic area. Further south

off Roses Gap Rd, it's a short walk to the base of **Beehive Falls**.

Wander Inn Restaurant (☎5383 6377; 2637 Northern Grampians Rd; mains $12-25; lunch Tue-Sun, dinner Thu-Sun) has a certain rustic old-world charm in the licensed restaurant and a tranquil tea room and artists' studio attached.

WEST OF THE GRAMPIANS

Horsham

The major town to the northwest of the Grampians and capital of the Wimmera region, Horsham makes a convenient base for exploring the surrounding national parks and Mt Arapiles. The main shopping strip has postal and banking facilities, supermarkets and plenty of other shops and eateries. **Grampians & Horsham visitor centre** (☎1800 633 218, 5382 1832; www.grampians littledesert.com.au; 20 O'Callaghan's Pde; ☺9am-5pm) has information on the surrounding areas.

Horsham Regional Art Gallery (☎5362 2888; www.horshamartgallery.com.au; 80 Wilson St; admission by gold coin donation; ☺10am-5pm Tue-Fri, 1-4.30pm Sat & Sun) houses the Mack Jost Collection of significant Australian artists, including works by Rupert Bunny, Sir Sidney Nolan, John Olsen and Charles Blackman.

Horsham's **Botanic Gardens** (Firebrace St) were established in the 1870s and designed by the curator of Melbourne's Royal Botanic Gardens, William Guilfoyle.

Mt Arapiles State Park

Mt Arapiles, 37km west of Horsham and 12km west of Natimuk, is Australia's premier rock-climbing destination. At 369m it's not a very big mountain but with more than 2000 routes to scale, it attracts salivating climbers from around the world. Popular climbs include the Bard Buttress, Tiger Wall and the Pharos. In the tiny nearby town of Natimuk a community of avid climbers has set up to service the visitors, and the town has also developed into something of a centre for artists – the biennial **Nati Frinj Festival**, held in November in odd years, includes performances and a colourful street parade.

Even if you're not into climbing, there are two short and steep walking tracks from Centenary Park to the summit, or you can drive up along the sealed Lookout Rd.

Arapiles Mountain Shop (☑5387 1529; 67 Main St) sells and hires climbing equipment.

If you want to learn to climb or hire a guide, the **Natimuk Climbing Company** (☑5387 1558; www.climbco.com.au; 117 Main St) and **Arapiles Climbing Guides** (☑5384 0376; www.arapiles.com.au; Natimuk) are two professional outfits offering instruction and group courses.

🛏 Sleeping & Eating

Most climbers head for the popular **Pines Camping Ground** (Centenary Park; camp sites $2) at the base of the mountain.

Duffholme Cabins (☑5387 4246; Natimuk-Goroke Rd; d $44, extra adult $12) comprises a self-contained cottage sleeping seven. Call to make a booking (it's not staffed).

National Hotel (☑5387 1300; 65 Main St; d $65-75) in Natimuk has tidy motel-style units at the back and pub rooms upstairs, plus good counter meals.

Little Desert National Park

Don't expect rolling sand dunes, but this arid park is rich in flora and fauna that thrive in the dry environment. There are over 670 indigenous plant species here, and in spring and early summer the landscape is transformed into a colourful wonderland of wildflowers. The best-known resident is the mallee fowl, an industrious bird that can be seen in an aviary at the Little Desert Lodge.

The park covers a huge 132,000 hectares, and the vegetation varies substantially due to the different soil types, climate and rainfall in each of its three blocks (central, eastern and western). The rainfall often reaches 600mm per year, but summers are dry and very hot.

In the late 1960s the state government announced a controversial plan to clear the area for agriculture. Conservationists and environmentalists protested, and the Little Desert became a major conservation issue. Finally, it was declared a national park and expanded to its present size in 1986.

The Nhill–Harrow road through the park is sealed and the road from Dimboola is gravel, but in the park the tracks are mostly sand and only suitable for 4WD vehicles or walking. Some are closed to 4WDs in the wet season (July to October).

If you want a brief introduction to the park there are several well-signposted walks: south of Dimboola is the **Pomponderoo Hill Nature Walk**, south of Nhill is the **Stringybark Nature Walk** and south of Kiata is the **Sanctuary Nature Walk**. Other longer walks leave from the camping ground south of Kiata, including a 12km trek south to the Salt Lake.

🛏 Sleeping

There are national park camping grounds (sites $13.50) in the eastern block at Horseshoe Bend and Ackle Bend, both on the Wimmera River south of Dimboola; and south of Kiata. They have toilets, picnic tables and fireplaces. Or you can bush camp in the more remote central and western blocks; see the rangers first.

 Little Desert Nature Lodge

CARAVAN PARK, LODGE $

(☑5391 5232; www.littledesertlodge.com.au; unpowered/powered site $17/20, dm $22, B&B s/d from $90/115; ✺) On the northern edge of the desert, 16km south of Nhill, this well-equipped bush retreat is a superb base for exploring the park. With a spacious camping ground, bunkhouse, comfortable en suite motel-style rooms and a restaurant, there's something for everyone. A key attraction here is the tour of the mallee-fowl aviary ($12) where you can see these rare birds in a breeding program, the mallee-fowl sanctuary tour ($110) and the Whimpey's 4WD tours ($65). There's also a night spotlighting walk ($12).

❶ Information

Little Desert Park Office (☑5389 1204; www.parkweb.vic.gov.au; Nursery Rd, Wail) Off the Western Hwy south of Dimboola.

Gateway Towns

DIMBOOLA

On the eastern edge of the Little Desert, beside the Wimmera River (which flooded for the first time in decades early in 2010), Dimboola is a classic country town made famous by Jack Hibberd's play *Dimboola*, and the subsequent 1979 John Duigan film of the same name about a country wedding. The historic Dimboola Hotel was gutted by fire in 2003 and has since lain dormant.

The park entrance is about 4km south of town on a sealed road, but from then on it's gravel. There are numerous easily accessed walks around the flats area along the Wimmera River.

The rare mallee fowl is one of Australia's most fascinating birds. The mature birds are about the size of a small turkey, with wings and backs patterned in black, white and brown, which helps to camouflage them in the mallee scrub. They can fly short distances if necessary. Until the establishment of the Mallee's national parks, the mallee fowl was threatened with extinction.

The life cycle of the mallee fowl is an amazing story of survival and adaptation. The male bird spends up to 11 months preparing the mound for the eggs. First he digs a hole, or opens up an old mound, fills it with leaves, bark and twigs, and covers the lot with sand to create the main egg chamber. When the mound has been saturated by rain so the organic material starts to decompose, he covers it all with more sand – by now it can be up to 1m high and 5m in diameter – and tests the core temperature daily by sticking his beak inside. Once the temperature is stable at 33°C, he lets the female know that she can start laying her eggs.

The female lays between 15 and 20 eggs, which hatch at various stages over spring and summer. The male continues to check the mound temperature daily, and if it varies from 33°C he adjusts it by covering the mound or removing sand.

After hatching, the chicks dig their way up to the surface, can run within a few hours and fly on their first day out. However, the mortality rate is very high. The parents don't recognise or help their own young and, while an average pair of mallee fowl will produce around 90 chicks in their lifetimes, only a few will survive to reproduce.

Beside the Western Hwy about 19km northwest of Dimboola, the **Pink Lake** is a colourful salt lake with a bright pink-purple hue.

Ebeneezer Aboriginal Mission, near Antwerp, 18km north of Dimboola, was established by German missionaries in 1859 and ceased operation in 1904. You can wander around the well-preserved mission buildings and cemetery.

There's tourist information and internet access at **Dim-e-Shop** (☑ 5389 1588; 109 Lloyd St) on the main street.

Dimboola celebrates with a **German Fest** in April, and the **Dimboola Rowing Regatta** in November.

🛏 Sleeping

Riverside Host Farm　　　　CABINS $
(☑ 5389 1550; 150 Riverside Rd; unpowered sites $18, cabins d $77; ❄) This friendly working farm on a bend in the Wimmera River is a lovely place to stay with cosy self-contained cabins, camp sites and a rustic open-sided camp kitchen lounge area with pot-belly stove. Hire canoes, take a boat tour from here into the Little Desert or help out with farm activities.

Dimboola Riverside Caravan Park
CARAVAN PARK $
(☑ 5389 1416; dimboolacaravanpark@bigpond.com; 2 Wimmera St; unpowered/powered sites $20/25, cabins from $50) Set among eucalypts and pine trees beside the Wimmera River.

NHILL

Nhill is the main base for the northern entrance to the park and Kiata campground. It's a big town for this part of the world – the main industries here are wheat farming and producing ducks for Victorian restaurant tables. Nhill is an Aboriginal word meaning 'mist over the water' – check out the artificial **Lake Nhill** and surrounding wetlands to see if there's any water.

Nhill has some grand old pubs, cafes, motels and a caravan park, but your best bet for accommodation is to head down to Little Desert Nature Lodge (p212) near the park entrance.

Hindmarsh visitor centre (☑ 5391 3086; www.hindmarsh.vic.gov.au; Victoria St; ☺ 9am-5pm; @), in Goldsworthy Park in the town centre, has plenty of information on the park and local sights and accommodation.

Mornington Peninsula & Phillip Island

Why Go?

It takes less than an hour to escape the urban sprawl and discover the holiday communities that curl around Port Phillip Bay's eastern half. At the tip of the peninsula, a world of rugged ocean surf beaches, sublime links golf courses and coastal bushwalks opens up. Away from the coast, the peninsula's interior is a wine- and food-lover's paradise, with more than 50 cellar doors and some of Victoria's finest winery restaurants. On the less-developed eastern side of the peninsula, it's a short ferry ride across to wild and isolated French Island and to Phillip Island, sheltering in the waters of Western Port Bay. To reach Phillip Island by car though, you need to drive the long way around. It's certainly worth it: apart from the famous nightly parade of little penguins, Phillip Island is blessed with wonderful surf beaches, accessible wildlife and enough activities to keep you (and the kids) busy for a week.

Best Places to Eat

» Winery restaurants (p224)

» Smokehouse (p220)

» The Rocks (p216)

» Infused (p228)

» Foreshore Bar & Restaurant (p229)

Best Places to Stay

» Carmel of Sorrento (p220)

» Foreshore camping (p218)

» Clifftop (p227)

» Surf & Circuit (p228)

» Royal Hotel (p216)

When to Go

Phillip Island

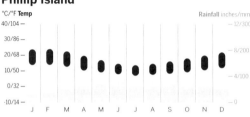

New Year's Eve
Phillip Island goes off with the Pyramid Rock Festival

Nov–Dec The best time to view seals and penguins at Phillip Island

Feb–Mar The perfect time to hit the beaches and wineries, after the holiday crowds have departed

MORNINGTON PENINSULA

The Mornington Peninsula – the boot-shaped area of land between Port Phillip Bay and Western Port Bay – has been Melbourne's summer playground since the 1870s, when paddle steamers ran down to Portsea. Today, much of the interior farming land has been replaced by vineyards and orchards – foodies love the peninsula, where a winery lunch is a real highlight – but it still retains lovely stands of native bushland.

The calm 'front beaches' are on the Port Phillip Bay side, where families holiday at bayside towns from Mornington to Sorrento. The rugged ocean 'back beaches' face Bass Strait and are easily reached from Portsea, Sorrento and Rye; there are stunning walks along this coastal strip, part of the Mornington Peninsula National Park.

The bay heads are so close that it's just a short hop by ferry across from Sorrento to Queenscliff on the Bellarine Peninsula.

❶ Information

Mornington Peninsula visitor centre (☏1800 804 009, 5987 3078; www.visitmornington peninsula.org; 359b Nepean Hwy/B110, Dromana; ◷9am-5pm) The main visitor information centre for the peninsula can book accommodation and tours. There are also visitor centres in Mornington and Sorrento.

❶ Getting There & Away

Moorooduc Hwy (11) and Point Nepean Rd (B110) both feed into the Mornington Peninsula Fwy (11), the main peninsula access. Alternately, exit the Moorooduc Hwy to Mornington and take the coast road around Port Phillip Bay.

Frequent Metlink trains run from Melbourne to Frankston, Hastings and Stony Point.

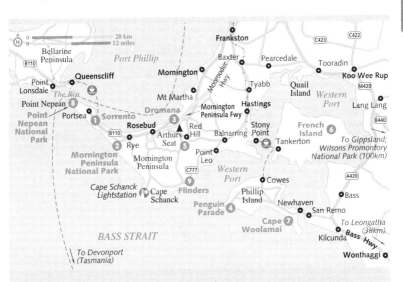

Mornington Peninsula Highlights

❶ Swim with dolphins and soak up the history at **Sorrento** (p219)

❷ Walk the cliff tops and surf the back beaches of **Mornington Peninsula National Park** (p222)

❸ Catch a film at the **Dromana Drive-in** (p218), one of the few left in Australia

❹ Settle in at dusk for the famous **Penguin Parade** (p225) at Phillip Island

❺ Kick off with a long, liquid lunch then an afternoon of wine tasting at the **wineries** (p224) around Red Hill

❻ Take the ferry to **French Island** (p223) and hike or cycle in blissful isolation

❼ Catch a wave at beautiful **Cape Woolamai** (p226)

❽ Cycle out to the peninsula's tip at **Point Nepean National Park** (p221)

❾ Challenge yourself to a round of golf at the **Flinders Golf Club** (p219)

Boat

Inter Island Ferries (☎9585 5730; www.inter islandferries.com.au; return adult/child/bike $21/10/8) runs between Stony Point and Cowes via French Island. See the Phillip Island and French Island sections.

Queenscliff–Sorrento Car & Passenger Ferries (☎5258 3244; www.searoad.com.au; one-way foot passenger adult/child $9/7, 2 adults & car standard/peak $58/64; ☺hourly) sails between Sorrento and Queenscliff, enabling you to cross Port Phillip Bay by car or bicycle.

Bus

Portsea Passenger Service (☎5986 5666; www.grenda.com.au) runs the following bus services:

» 788 from Frankston to Portsea ($5, 1½ hours) via Mornington, Dromana and Sorrento

» 786 from Rye to St Andrews Beach

» 787 from Safety Beach to Sorrento

Peninsula Bus Lines (☎9786 7088; www.grenda.com.au) runs bus 782 from Frankston train station to Flinders ($6, 1½ hours) via Hastings and Balnarring.

Mornington

POP 21,000

Pretty Mornington, with its cute bathing boxes and swimming beaches, is the gateway to the peninsula's holiday coastal strip – just beyond the reaches of Melbourne's urban sprawl. Originally part of the lands of the Boonwurrung people, it was founded as a European township in 1854. The town thrived and by 1890 there were steamers and a daily train service from Melbourne – now sadly defunct.

◉ Sights & Activities

There are several grand old buildings around Main St, including the 1892 **Grand Hotel**. The **Old Court House**, on the corner of Main St and the Esplanade (C783), was built in 1860, and the **Police Lock-Up** behind it was built in 1862. On the opposite corner is the **Old Post Office Museum** (☎5976 3203; cnr Main St & the Esplanade; admission by donation; ☺1.30-4.30pm Sun & public holidays, 11am-3pm Wed in summer) in the 1863 post office building. Nearby is a **monument** to the 15 members of Mornington's football team who lost their lives when their boat, *Process,* sank while returning from a game against Mordialloc in 1892.

For views over the harbour, take a walk along the 1850s **pier** and around the Schnapper Point foreshore boardwalk past the **Matthew Flinders monument** that commemorates his 1802 landing. **Mothers Beach** is the main swimming beach, while at **Fossil Beach**, where limestone was mined in the 1860s, there are remains of a lime-burning kiln. Fossils found here date back 25 million years! At Mills Beach you can see colourful and photogenic **bathing boxes**.

Schnapper Point Boat Hire (☎5975 5479; www.fishingmornington.com; Boatshed 7, Scout Beach) rents out kayaks and small motor boats, and sells fishing tackle and bait.

Away from the beach, the **Mornington Botanical Rose Gardens** (cnr Mornington-Tyabb Rd & Dunns Rd; admission free) is a beautifully landscaped garden with over 4000 flowers. In the Civic Reserve alongside the gardens, **Mornington Peninsula Regional Gallery** (☎5975 4395; www.mprg.mornpen.vic. gov.au; Dunns Rd; adult/child $4/free; ☺10am-5pm Tue-Sun) is an outstanding regional gallery with changing exhibitions and a permanent collection of Australian prints and paintings.

Every Wednesday, the **Mornington Street Market** (Main St; ☺9am-3pm Wed) takes over Main St with stalls and crafts.

On the first three Sundays of each month the popular **Mornington Railway** (☎1300 767 274; www.morningtonrailway.org.au; Mornington train station; return adult/child/family $14/11/38) runs steam locomotives between Mornington and Moorooduc.

🛏 Sleeping & Eating

Main St is lined with cafes and restaurants, particularly at the bay end.

Royal Hotel HOTEL **$$**
(☎5975 9115; www.theroyal.com.au; 770 The Esplanade; d $100-155; ❋) Classified by the National Trust, the Royal is tastefully renovated, offering authentic old-world accommodation in a range of rooms and bay views. The cheapest rooms have shared bathrooms, while the best are the balcony suites with bathrooms and brilliant sea views.

The Rocks SEAFOOD **$$**
(☎5973 5599; www.therocksmornington.com.au; 1 Schnapper Point Dr; mains $18-37; ☺breakfast, lunch & dinner) At the Mornington Yacht Club, this restaurant, with an open-sided deck overlooking the marina, is the perfect place for a drink or light meal. The restaurant is strong on fresh seafood, with oysters done every which way.

Mornington Peninsula

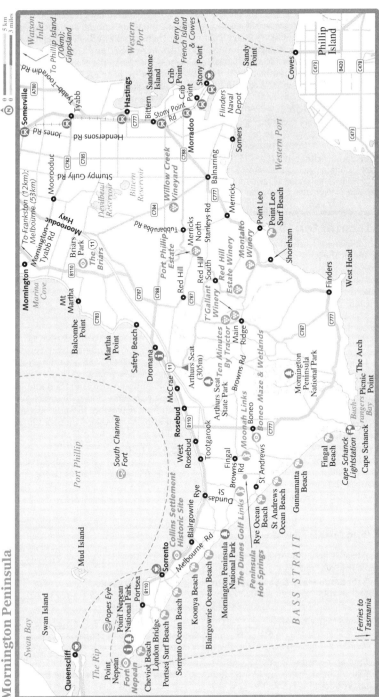

Afghan Marco Polo   MIDDLE EASTERN **$$**
(☑5975 5154; www.afghanmarcopolo.com.au; 9-11 Main St; mains $21-27; ☻dinner) Marco Polo is an atmospheric place with Persian rugs and brass hookahs, and serves traditional Afghan cuisine. Kebabs, kormas, *borani*s and kulfi ice cream – a Central Asian mash up!

❶ Information

Mornington Library (☑5950 1820; Vancouver St; ☻9am-2pm Mon & Sat, to 8pm Tue & Thu, to 6pm Wed & Fri; @🖥) Free internet access.

Mornington visitor centre (☑5975 1644; www.visitmorningtonpeninsula.org; 320 Main St; ☻9am-5pm) Has useful regional information and a Mornington walking-tour map.

Mornington to Blairgowrie

The Esplanade leaves Mornington and heads south for the gorgeous scenic drive towards Sorrento, skirting the rocky Port Phillip Bay foreshore. Inland, the Nepean Hwy (B110) takes a less-scenic route and again becomes the Mornington Peninsula Fwy.

The **Briars** (☑5974 3686; 450 Nepean Hwy, Mt Martha; adult/child $5/4; ☻10am-4pm) is the 1840 homestead of one of the peninsula's first pastoral runs. Sitting on 96 hectares, it includes original farm buildings, parklands and a wildlife reserve. The homestead houses the Dame Mabel Brookes collection of Napoleon relics, which includes locks of the emperor's hair and his death mask.

From **Dromana** take the steep hairpin-bend Arthurs Seat Rd inland up to the lookout at **Arthurs Seat** (called Wonga by the Boonwurrung people), which, at 305m, is the highest point on the Port Phillip Bay coast, with fine views across the bay. The famous chairlift here was closed after a series of accidents but there are plans to revive it, if safety demands can be met. Back at Dromana there's a relic of the 1960s, a time when there were more than 330 drive-in cinemas across Australia. The National Trust–listed **Dromana Drive-In** (☑5987 2492; www.drivein.net.au; 113 Nepean Hwy; adult/child $13/7; ☻Thu-Sun) is one of just a handful that remain.

For a relaxed afternoon of fishing on the bay, **Jillian Fishing Trips** (☑0418 148 426; www.thejillian.com.au; 3/4hr $40/50) has family-friendly morning, afternoon and twilight fishing charters, picking up from Rosebud Pier.

There are lots of spas and massage centres popping up along the peninsula, but none better than **Peninsula Hot Springs** (☑5950 8777; www.peninsulahotsprings.com; Springs La, Rye; bathhouse adult/child Tue-Thu $25/15, Fri-Mon $30/20), a large and luxurious complex that utilises hot, mineral-rich waters pumped from deep underground. There's a huge menu of spa, private bathing and massage treatments available, or you can just relax in the bathhouse. It's about 7km inland from Rye, off Browns Rd.

🛏 Sleeping

There's holiday accommodation all along the coast, and council-managed **foreshore camping** (☑5986 8286; www.mornpen.vic.gov.au; unpowered/powered sites $25/30, peak season $40/45) at Rosebud, Rye and Sorrento. These camping areas are close to the beach and are open from September to April – it's next to impossible to get a site during the Christmas and Easter holidays.

Bayplay Lodge   HOSTEL **$**
(☑5984 0888; www.bayplay.com.au; 46 Canterbury Jetty Rd, Blairgowrie; d/f $45/95; ❀🖥🖨) Tucked away off the Esplanade in Blairgowrie, this rustic house has backpacker-style accom-

THE MAZE TRAIL

When did hedge mazes become so popular? The Mornington Peninsula has a few of these English-garden curiosities to get lost in.

Ashcombe Maze & Lavender Gardens (☑5989 8387; www.ashcombemaze.com.au; 15 Shoreham Rd, Shoreham; adult/child/family $17/10/45; ☻10am-5pm) Brilliant mazes, including a circular rose maze, fields of lavender and blooming gardens.

Boneo Maze & Wetlands (☑5988 6385; www.boneomaze.com.au; 695 Limestone Rd, Fingal; adult/child/family $14/9/39; ☻10am-4pm Mon-Thu, to 5pm Fri-Sun) Several mazes, boardwalks through wetlands and a giant chess set.

Enchanted Maze Garden (☑5981 8449; www.enchantedmaze.com.au; 55 Purves Rd, Arthurs Seat; adult/child/family $17/10/45; ☻10am-6pm) A remarkably well-clipped hedge maze, ornamental garden, sculpture park and lolly shop will make the kids squeal with delight.

TOP FIVE FOR GOLFERS

The Mornington Peninsula has some of Victoria's most picturesque and challenging links golf courses, so if you like slapping the little white ball, try these public access courses, all with ocean views:

The Dunes (☑5985 1334; www.thedunes.com.au; Browns Rd, Rye; 18 holes midweek/weekend $69/52)

Flinders Golf Club (☑5989 0312; www.flindersgolfclub.com.au; Bass St, Flinders; 18 holes midweek/weekend $35/47)

Cape Schanck (☑5950 8000; Boneo Rd/C777, Cape Schanck; 18 holes midweek/weekend $46/42)

Moonah Links (☑5988 2000; www.moonahlinks.com.au; 55 Peter Thomson Dr, Fingal; 18 holes $75-95)

Portsea (☑5984 3521; www.portseagolf.com.au; Relph Ave, Portsea; 18 holes $50)

---

modation, with a big communal lounge and kitchen area, and a pool.

✕ Eating

Two Buoys   TAPAS $
(☑5981 8488; www.twobuoys.com.au; 209 Point Nepean Rd, Dromana; tapas $4-9, mains $11-19; ⏲breakfast, lunch & dinner) This funky Dromana tapas restaurant with a view of the bay is a real shared-dining experience. You can choose from small or medium plates such as twice-cooked pork belly and Dromana mussels, as well as 'flat-bread' pizzas.

Fed-Up Fish Café   SEAFOOD $$
(☑5986 4716; 1571 Point Nepean Rd, Rosebud; mains $15-35; ⏲lunch Wed-Sun, dinner Fri-Sun) It doesn't look like much from the outside, but this fading retro bayside restaurant consistently serves up good, fresh seafood. Try the chowder.

Sorrento

POP 1500

Historic Sorrento is the standout town on the Mornington Peninsula for its beautiful limestone buildings, ocean and bay beaches, and buzzing seaside summer atmosphere. This was the site of Victoria's first official European settlement, established by an expedition of convicts, marines, civil officers and free settlers who arrived from England in 1803.

Sorrento boasts some of the best cafes and restaurants on the peninsula, and the main street is lined with galleries, boutiques, and craft and antique shops – naturally, it gets ridiculously busy in summer. Dolphin swims and cruises are popular, and the trip to Queenscliff on the ferry is a fun outing.

The small **Sorrento visitor centre** (☑5984 5678; 2 St Aubins Way) is on the main street.

◉ Sights & Activities

There are some grand 19th-century buildings constructed from locally quarried limestone around town, including the **Sorrento Hotel** (1871), **Continental Hotel** (1875) and **Koonya Hotel** (1878). They look fabulous in the late-afternoon sun.

The calm bay beach is good for families and you can hire **paddle boards** on the foreshore. At low tide, the **rock pool** at the back beach is a safe spot for adults and children to swim and snorkel, and the surf beach is patrolled in summer. The 10-minute climb up to **Coppins Lookout** offers good views.

Apart from four graves that are believed to hold the remains of 30 original settlers, there's little evidence of Sorrento's original abandoned settlement. The **Collins Settlement Historic Site** (Leggett Way; ⏲1.30-4pm Sat & Sun), midway between Sorrento and Blairgowrie, marks the 1803 settlement site at Sullivan Bay, and a display centre tells its story.

Sorrento Museum (☑5984 0255; 827 Melbourne Rd; adult/child $5/free; ⏲1.30-4.30pm Sat, Sun & public holidays) has interesting displays on the early history of Sorrento and Portsea, and a pioneer garden.

☞ Tours

There are two established operators that run popular dolphin- and seal-swimming cruises from Sorrento Pier.

Moonraker Charters   DOLPHIN
(☑5984 4211; www.moonrakercharters.com.au; adult/child sightseeing $55/44, dolphin & seal swimming $115/105)

Polperro Dolphin Swims
DOLPHIN

(☑5988 8437; www.polperro.com.au; adult/child observers $55/35, all swimmers $125)

Sorrento Tours
BOATING

(☑0418 374 912; www.adventuresails.com.au; adult/child $38/25; ⊙12.30pm & 2.30pm) Sightseeing tours aboard a catamaran. Also sunset sails ($80 per person).

🛏 Sleeping

Carmel of Sorrento
GUESTHOUSE $$

(☑5984 3512; www.carmelofsorrento.com.au; 142 Ocean Beach Rd; d $150-220, self-contained units from $220; ✱) This lovely old limestone house, right in the centre of Sorrento, has been tastefully restored in period style and neatly marries the town's history with contemporary comfort. There are three Edwardian-style suites with bathrooms and continental breakfast, and two modern self-contained units that would suit a small family.

Whitehall Guesthouse & Oceanic Apartments
B&B, APARTMENTS $$

(☑5984 4166; www.oceanicgroup.com.au; 231 Ocean Beach Rd; d $120-255, apt $210-255; ✱☒) This gracious limestone, two-storey guesthouse on the road to the back beach has dreamy views from its timber verandah, though most rooms are small and old-style with shared bathrooms down the hall – the rooms with bathrooms are more spacious. Across the road, Oceanic Apartments ditch the period charm with spruce self-contained split-level apartments.

Hotel Sorrento
HOTEL $$$

(☑5984 8000; www.hotelsorrento.com.au; 5-15 Hotham Rd; motel r $220-280, apt $220-320; ✱@) The legendary Hotel Sorrento is well known as a pub and restaurant but it also has some slick accommodation. The motel-style 'Heritage' and 'Garden' suites are modern and well appointed, but the 'On the Hill' apartments are the ones to go for, with airy living spaces, spacious bathrooms, private balconies, spas and bay views. The hotel has its own spa centre.

Sorrento Beach House YHA
HOSTEL $

(☑5984 4323; www.sorrento-beachhouse.com; 3 Miranda St; dm/d $40/90; @) This purpose-built hostel situated in a quiet but central location maintains a relaxed atmosphere – the back deck and garden is a great place to catch up with other travellers. Staff can also organise horse riding, snorkelling and diving trips.

Also recommended:

Sorrento Foreshore Reserve
CAMPING GROUND

(☑5986 8286; Nepean Hwy; unpowered/powered sites $25/30, high season $40/45) Hilly, bush-clad sites between the bay beach and the main road into Sorrento.

Sorrento Beach Motel
MOTEL

(☑5984 1356; www.sorrentobeachmotel.com.au; 780 Melbourne Rd; d $135-195, with spa $185-225; ✱🛜) The brightly coloured beach-box units at this motel are a cut above most.

🍴 Eating & Drinking

Sorrento's main street, Ocean Beach Rd, has most of the town's cafes and restaurants, with tables and chairs spilling out along the footpaths in summer. The town's three pubs, the historic Hotel Sorrento, Continental Hotel and Koonya Hotel are all good places for a meal or drink, and all have live music in summer.

Smokehouse
PIZZA $$

(☑5984 1246; 182 Ocean Beach Rd; mains $17-32; ⊙dinner Wed-Mon) Gourmet pizzas and pastas are the speciality at this local family favourite. Innovative toppings and the aromas wafting from the wood-fired oven make this restaurant a winner.

The Baths
MODERN AUSTRALIAN $$

(☑5984 1500; www.thebaths.com.au; 3278 Point Nepean Rd; mains $26-32; ⊙lunch & dinner, fish & chippery noon-8pm) The waterfront deck of the former sea baths is the perfect spot for lunch or a romantic sunset dinner overlooking the jetty and the Queenscliff ferry. The menu has some good seafood choices and there's a popular takeaway fish and chippery at the front.

Acquolina Ristorante
ITALIAN $$

(☑5984 0811; 26 Ocean Beach Rd; mains $26-35; ⊙dinner Thu-Mon, closed Jun-Sep) Acquolina set the bar when it opened in Sorrento with its authentic northern-Italian fare. This is hearty, simple food – handmade pasta and ravioli dishes matched with imported Italian wines and homemade tiramisu.

Just Fine Food
CAFE $

(☑5984 4666; 23 Ocean Beach Rd; mains $8-22; ⊙9am-5pm Mon-Fri, to 6pm Sat) Famous for its sublime, fluffy vanilla slices (recipe: top secret), this cafe and deli is a great place for an all-day breakfast or lunch of open sandwiches, foccacia, antipasti and gourmet pies.

In October 1803 William Buckley (1780–1856), a strapping 6ft 7in bricklayer, was transported to Victoria's first settlement (now Sorrento) as a convict for receiving stolen goods.

Buckley and three others escaped in December, though one was shot dead during the escape. The remaining three set off around the bay, thinking they were heading to Sydney, but two turned back and died from lack of food and water.

Buckley wandered for weeks, surviving on shellfish and berries. He was on his last legs when two Wathaurong women found him, and Buckley spent the next 32 years living with the nomadic clan on the Bellarine Peninsula, learning their customs and language.

In 1835 Buckley surrendered to a party from a survey ship. He was almost unable to speak English, and the startled settlers dubbed him the 'Wild White Man'. Buckley was subsequently pardoned and acted as an interpreter and mediator between white settlers and the Wathaurong people. John Morgan's 1852 book *The Life & Adventures of William Buckley* provides an insight into Aboriginal life before white settlement.

The Australian colloquialism 'Buckley's chance' (a very slim or no chance) is said to be based on William Buckley's story, but there's dispute about this. Some claim the expression gained currency in the late 1800s and derived from the name of the Melbourne department store Buckley's & Nunn ('You've got two chances – Buckley's and none').

Stringer's   CAFE, DELI $
(✆5984 2010; 2 Ocean Beach Rd; light meals $4-8; ☺breakfast & lunch) Stringer's is a Sorrento institution, with house-made meals and Mornington wines for sale in the attached grocery shop.

Three Palms   ASIAN FUSION $$
(✆5984 1057; www.threepalms.com.au; 154-164 Ocean Beach Rd; mains $13-25; ☺dinner Wed-Sun, lunch Sat & Sun, daily in summer) Framed by the namesake palms, this relaxed main street bar and restaurant has a rocking side terrace with a 'sarongs and thongs' ambience. The menu features local seafood with Asian influences.

Portsea

POP 650

The last village on the peninsula, wee Portsea is where many of Melbourne's wealthiest families have built seaside mansions. You can walk the Farnsworth Track (1.5km, 30 minutes) out to scenic London Bridge, a natural rock formation, and spot middens of the Boonwurrung people who once called this area home.

Bayplay (✆5984 0888; www.bayplay.com.au; 3755 Point Nepean Rd; ☺8.30am-5.30pm) offers aquatic activities and tours (PADI courses, snorkelling and sea kayaking) and hires equipment (kayaks two/four hours $50/80).

Dive Victoria (✆5984 3155; www.divevictoria.com.au; 3752 Point Nepean Rd; 1/2 dives with

gear $89/163) runs diving and snorkelling trips.

Portsea's pulse is the iconic, sprawling, half-timber **Portsea Hotel** (✆5984 2213; www.portseahotel.com.au; Point Nepean Rd; s/d from $65/110, with bathroom from $125/160), an enormous pub with a great lawn and terrace area looking out over the bay. There's an excellent bistro (mains $20 to $28) and old-style accommodation (most rooms have shared bathrooms) that increases in price based on bay views and season.

Point Nepean National Park

The peninsula's tip is marked by the scenic **Point Nepean National Park** (✆13 19 63; www.parkweb.vic.gov.au; Point Nepean Rd, Portsea), originally a quarantine station and army base. A large section of the park is a former range area and still out of bounds due to unexploded weapons, but there's plenty to see here and long stretches of traffic-free road that make for excellent cycling. There are also plenty of **walking trails** throughout the park and at the tip is **Fort Nepean**, which played an important role in Australian defence from the 1880s to 1945. On the parade ground are two historic **gun barrels** that fired the first Allied shots in WWI and WWII. **Quarantine** is a legendary surf break at the Rip, and is still only accessible by boat.

MORNINGTON PENINSULA & PHILLIP ISLAND PORTSEA

Point Nepean visitor information centre (☎5984 4276; Point Nepean Rd; ⊙9am-6pm Jan, 9am-5pm Feb-Apr & Oct-Dec, 10am-5pm May-Sep) will give you the lowdown on the park and hires bikes for $20 per day. You can walk or cycle to the point (12km return), or take the Point Transporter (adult/child/ family return $9/6/23), a hop-on, hop-off bus service that departs the visitor centre six times daily.

Mornington Peninsula National Park

Stretching from Portsea on the sliver of coastline to Cape Schanck and inland to the Greens Bush area, this national park showcases the peninsula's most beautiful and rugged ocean beaches. Along here are the cliffs, bluffs and crashing surf beaches of **Portsea**, **Sorrento**, **Blairgowrie**, **Rye**, **St Andrews**, **Gunnamatta** and **Cape Schanck**. This is spectacular coastal scenery – well known to the surfers, hikers and fisherfolk who have their secret spots – and it's possible to walk all the way from Portsea to Cape Schanck (26km, eight hours). Swimming and surfing is dangerous at these beaches: the undertow and rips can be severe, and drownings continue to occur. Swim only between the flags at Gunnamatta and Portsea during summer.

If you want to learn to surf, contact **East Coast Surf School** (☎5989 2198, 0417 526 465; www.eastcoastsurfschool.net.au; 226 Balnarring Road, Merricks North; lessons per person $50) or

Mornington Peninsula Surf School (☎0417 338 079; www.greenroomsurf.com.au; 6 Chetwyn Ct, Frankston South; group/private lessons $44/110).

You can ride a horse along wild Gunnamatta Beach with **Gunnamatta Trail Rides** (☎5988 6755; www.gunnamatta.com.au; 150 Sandy Rd, Fingal; rides $45-220) on excursions ranging from half an hour to a full day.

Built in 1859, **Cape Schanck Lightstation** (☎5988 6184, 420 Cape Schanck Rd; museum only adult/child/family $12/8/34, museum & lighthouse $15/12/40, parking $4.50; ⊙10.30am-4pm) is a photogenic working lighthouse with a kiosk, a museum, information centre and regular guided tours. You can stay at **Cape Schanck B&B** (☎5988 6184; www.austpacinns.com.au; 420 Cape Schanck Rd; d from $150) in the limestone Keeper's Cottage.

From the light station, descend the steps of the **boardwalk** that leads to the craggy cape for outstanding views. Longer **walks** include tracks to **Bushrangers Bay**, which can be approached from Cape Schanck or the Bushrangers Bay car park on Boneo Rd (C777) – 5km return. Wild **Fingal Beach** is a 6km return walk,

Flinders

POP 750

Little Flinders, where the thrashing ocean beaches give way to Western Port Bay, has so far been largely spared the development of the bay towns. It's a delightful little community and home to a busy fishing fleet. Surfers have been coming to Flinders for decades,

HAROLD HOLT

On a hot day in December 1967, Harold Holt (1908–67) disappeared in wild surf off Cheviot Beach, while serving as Australia's prime minister. Despite a three-week air and land search – the biggest in Australia's history – his body was never recovered. This, and the fact that it was the height of the Cold War, led to a raft of conspiracy theories.

It was suggested that the CIA had Holt murdered because he wanted to withdraw Australian troops from Vietnam. It was also alleged that various people and companies with vested interest had him bumped off because, with the covert activities of the Atomic Energy Commission (AEC) at Lucas Heights in Sydney, Australia was secretly emerging as a major nuclear energy supplier. Some said that Holt committed suicide because he was depressed and there was a leadership challenge emerging within the Liberal Party. The most colourful theory was that Holt was spying for the Chinese government, and that he climbed aboard a Chinese submarine waiting off Cheviot Beach and died in the mid-1980s, after living out his days with a lover in France.

The lack of a body meant that an inquest was never held, but in 1985 the Victorian Coroners Act was amended so that 'suspected deaths' had to be investigated. The inevitable 2005 coroner's inquest found he died by accidental drowning.

DETOUR: MERRICKS & BALNARRING

On the Western Port Bay side of the peninsula, tiny Merricks is worth a stop for its **Merricks General Store** (☑5989 8088; www.merricksgeneralstore.com.au; 3460 Frankston-Flinders Rd/C777; meals $14-36; ☺9am-5pm). The bistro is renowned for its hearty breakfasts and quality meals using fresh, local produce. The cellar door showcases wines from the Elgee Park, Baillieu Vineyard and Quealy wineries.

Further east, Balnarring has an excellent foreshore camping ground in a bush setting, and the **Balnarring Picnic Races** (☑5986 3755; www.balnarringraces.com; adult/child $10/free), a great country race meeting held at various times throughout the year.

drawn by ocean-side breaks such as Gunnery, Big Left and Cyril's, and golfers know the cliff-top **Flinders Golf Club** course as the most scenic and wind blown in Victoria.

The historic **Flinders Hotel** (☑5989 0201; www.flindershotel.com.au; cnr Cook & Wood Sts; d $150-175; ☀) has been a beacon on this sleepy street corner longer than anyone can remember. Modern motel units are well equipped. The real joy is in the indoor-outdoor **Deck Bar Bistro** (mains $18-36; ☺lunch & dinner) where pub grub goes gastronomic – nothing too fussy, just staple dishes such as steak and parma done really well.

Red Hill Baker (☑5989 0067; 637 Cook St; meals $4-20; ☺9am-6pm) offers fresh-baked bread, pies, pastries and quiches, along with seafood and salad dishes. The crowds show up for live jazz every Sunday from 1pm to 4pm.

Red Hill & Around

POP 480

The undulating hills of the peninsula's interior around Red Hill and Main Ridge are the centre of the region's viticulture and winemaking industries, and a favourite destination for foodies. It's a lovely region of trees and tumbling hills where you can spend a sublime afternoon hopping around the winery cellar doors and restaurants.

The popular **Red Hill Market** (☺8am-1pm) is held the first Saturday of each month.

Red Hill Brewery (☑5989 2959; www.redhillbrewery.com.au; 88 Shoreham Rd; meals $9-24; ☺11am-6pm Thu-Sun) is a great spot to sample some of the 10 handcrafted European-style beers with a plate of mussels or a ploughman's lunch.

If all this booziness is too much, pick your own strawberries at **Sunny Ridge Strawberry Farm** (☑5989 4500; www.sunnyridge.com.au; cnr Shands & Mornington-Flinders Rds;

adult/child $8/4; ☺9am-5pm Nov-Apr, 11am-4pm Sat & Sun May-Oct). Admission includes 500g of strawberries and there's a cafe serving all things strawberry.

FRENCH ISLAND

POP 89

Exposed, windswept and wonderfully isolated, French Island is two-thirds national park and it retains a real sense of tranquillity – you can only get here by passenger ferry, so it's virtually traffic-free, and there's no mains water or electricity! The main attractions are bushwalking and cycling, taking in wetlands, checking out one of Australia's largest **koala colonies** and observing a huge variety of birds.

Pick up the Parks Victoria brochure at the Tankerton Jetty for a list of walks and cycling routes. All roads on the island are unsealed and some are quite sandy.

The island served as a penal settlement for prisoners serving out their final years from 1916 and you can still visit the original prison farm.

The ferry docks at Tankerton; from there it's around 2km to the licensed **French Island General Store** (☑5980 1209; Lot 1, Tankerton Rd, Tankerton; bike hire $25; ☺8am-6pm, from 9am Sun), which also serves as post office, and tourist information and bike-hire centre, and has accommodation ($110 per person). Bikes can also be hired at Tankerton Jetty.

Located 10km from Tankerton to the **Bayview Chicory Kilns** (Bayview Rd; ☺daily), where fourth-generation local Lois will give you a tour of the historic kilns (by donation), show you a few resident koalas and whip up chicory coffee and Devonshire teas in her rustic cafe. Chicory (a coffee substitute) was the island's biggest industry from 1897 to 1963. You can camp here for $8/5 per adult/child.

Most of the peninsula's wineries are in the hills between Red Hill and Merricks, and most have excellent cafes or restaurants attached. Several companies offer winery tours – ask at the visitor centre. Some wineries to consider:

Montalto (☑5989 8412; www.montalto.com.au; 33 Shoreham Rd, Red Hill South; ⊙cellar door 11am-5pm, lunch daily, dinner Fri & Sat) Montalto is one of the Mornington Peninsula's best winery restaurants, and the Pinot noir and Chardonnay here are terrific. There's also the piazza and garden cafe for casual dining, as well as an olive grove and shop.

Port Phillip Estate (☑5989 4444; www.portphillipestate.com.au; 263 Red Hill Rd, Red Hill South; ⊙cellar door 11am-5pm, lunch Wed-Sun, dinner Fri & Sat) Home of Port Phillip Estate and Kooyong wines, this award-winning winery has an excellent, breezy restaurant.

Red Hill Estate (☑5989 2838; www.redhillestate.com.au; 53 Shoreham Rd, Red Hill South; ⊙cellar door 11am-5pm, lunch daily, dinner Fri & Sat) Red Hill Estate's signature Pinot noir and sparkling wines are outstanding, while Max's Restaurant is one of the best on the peninsula.

Ten Minutes By Tractor (☑5989 6080; www.tenminutesbytractor.com.au; 1333 Mornington-Flinders Rd, Main Ridge; ⊙cellar door 11am-5pm, lunch Wed-Sun, dinner Thu-Sat) Another outstanding restaurant and a fine range of Pinot noir, Chardonnay and Pinot gris. The unusual name comes from the three vineyards, which are each 10 minutes apart by tractor.

T'Gallant (☑5989 6565; www.tgallant.com.au; 1385 Mornington-Flinders Rd, Main Ridge; ⊙lunch) This winery pioneered luscious Pinot gris in Australia and produces the country's best. There's fine dining at La Baracca Trattoria and live music on weekends.

Willow Creek Vineyard (☑5989 7448; www.willow-creek.com.au; 166 Balnarring Rd/C784, Merricks North; ⊙lunch daily, dinner Fri & Sat) Renowned for its sparkling wines, Chardonnay and Pinot noir. Chef Bernard McCarthy's Mod Oz Salix Restaurant is a serene place for a light lunch on the deck or an intimate dinner.

☞ Tours

If you want to see the best of the island, especially if your time is limited, a tour is the best way to go. Book ahead and arrange a pick up from Tankerton Jetty.

French Island Biosphere Bus Tours REGION (☑5980 1241, 0412 671 241; www.frenchislandtours. com.au; half-day adult/child $18/10, full day $38/22; ⊙Tue, Thu & Sun, plus Sat in school holidays) Lois from the Chicory Kilns runs these half-day tours with morning or afternoon tea. The full-day tour includes lunch.

French Island Eco Tours ECO TOUR (☑1300 307 054; www.frenchislandecotours. au; half/full day $40/80; ⊙Wed & Sun) Tours around the island explore McLeod Eco Farm, a former prison.

🛏 Sleeping & Eating

Tortoise Head Lodge B&B $ (☑5980 1234; www.tortoisehead.net; 10 Tankerton Rd, Tankerton; budget s/d/f $55/85/110, cabins s/d $80/120) A short stroll from the ferry, this spot has knock out water views and is brilliant value.

🌿**McLeod Eco Farm** GUESTHOUSE $ (☑5980 1224; www.mcleodecofarm.com; McLeod Rd; bunk room d/q $65/110, guesthouse d $98) Formerly the island's prison, this organic farm offers basic bunk rooms in atmospheric old cells with common kitchen facilities and a lounge, but if you're after something more upmarket, the guesthouse rooms (former officers' quarters) are cosy and include breakfast. All have shared bathrooms.

FREE **Fairhaven** CAMPING GROUND $ (☑5986 9100; www.parkweb.vic.gov.au) On the western shore where the wetlands meet the ocean, this camping ground offers a real getaway experience with sites offering little more than a compost toilet. Bookings essential.

ℹ Getting There & Around

Inter Island Ferries (☑9585 5730; www.inter islandferries.com.au; return adult/child/bike $21/10/8) runs a service between Stony Point and Tankerton (10 minutes, at least two daily, four on Tue, Thu, Sat & Sun). You can reach Stony Point directly from Frankston on a Metlink train.

You can hire bikes ($25 per day) from the kiosk at the jetty in summer and from the general store.

PHILLIP ISLAND

POP 7500

Famous for the Penguin Parade and Grand Prix racing circuit, Phillip Island attracts a curious mix of surfers, petrolheads and international tourists making a beeline for those little penguins.

At its heart, Phillip Island is still a farming community, but nature has conspired to turn it into one of Victoria's hottest tourist destinations. Apart from the nightly waddling of the penguins, there's a large seal colony, abundant bird life around the Rhyll wetlands and a koala colony. The rugged south coast has some fabulous surf beaches and the swell of tourists – the holiday population jumps to around 40,000 over summer – means there's a swag of family attractions, plenty of accommodation, and a buzzing cafe and restaurant scene in the island capital, Cowes. Visit in winter, though, and you'll find a very quiet place where the local population of farmers, surfers and hippies go about their business.

'The Island', as it's locally known, is only about 100 sq km, so it's easy and quick to get around by car or bike – it's just a 15-minute drive from Cowes to the Penguin Parade or Grand Prix circuit. It's linked to the mainland by a bridge across the Narrows from San Remo to Newhaven. If you're on foot or bicycle, you can get here by ferry from Stony Point to Cowes.

The Boonwurrung people are the traditional inhabitants of the island, though what they'd have made of coachloads of Penguin Parade tourists and biker gangs making their way over the San Remo bridge is anyone's guess.

⊙ Sights & Activities

PHILLIP ISLAND NATURE PARK

The Phillip Island Nature Park incorporates four of the island's biggest attractions: the Penguin Parade, the Nobbies, Koala Conservation Centre and Churchill Island. A Three Parks Pass (the Nobbies Centre is free) costs $36/18/90 per adult/child/family, or you can buy tickets for each attraction individually.

Penguin Parade   WILDLIFE
(☑5951 2800; www.penguins.org.au; Summerland Beach; adult/child/family $21/11/53; ☉10am-nightfall) The Penguin Parade attracts more than half-a-million visitors annually to see the little penguins (*Eudyptula minor*), the world's smallest, and probably cutest of their kind.

The penguin complex includes concrete amphitheatres that hold up to 3800 spectators who come to see the little fellas just after sunset as they waddle from the sea to their land-based nests. Penguin numbers swell in summer, after breeding, but they're in residence year round. After the parade, hang around the boardwalks for a closer view as the stragglers search for their burrows and mates. Bring warm clothing. There are a variety of specialised **tours** (adult $40-75) where you can be accompanied by rangers to explain the behaviour of penguins, or see the penguins from the vantage of a Skybox (an elevated platform). There's also a cafe and an interpretive centre at the complex.

Koala Conservation Centre   WILDLIFE
(☑5951 2800; www.phillipislandguide.com/koala; Phillip Island Rd; adult/child/family $11/6/27; ☉10am-5pm) From the boardwalks at the Koala Conservation Centre you're certain to see koalas chewing on eucalyptus leaves or dozing away – they sleep about 20 hours a day!

Churchill Island   HISTORIC SITE
(☑5956 7214; off Phillip Island Rd; adult/child/family $11/6/27; ☉10am-4.30pm) Churchill Island, connected to Phillip Island by a bridge near Newhaven, is a working farm where Victoria's first crops were planted. There's a historic homestead and garden here, and pleasant walking tracks looping around the island.

FREE **Seal Rocks & the Nobbies**   NATURE
The Nobbies are a couple of large, craggy, offshore rocks at the island's southwestern tip. Beyond them are Seal Rocks, which are inhabited by Australia's largest fur-seal colony. The **Nobbies Centre** (☑5951 2800; www.penguins.org.au; 1019 Ventnor Rd; tours adult/child $10/5; ☉10am-8pm Dec-Feb, to 5pm Mar-May, 11am-4pm Jun-Aug, to 6pm Sep-Nov) offers great views over the Nobbies and the 6000 distant Australian fur seals that sun themselves here. You can view the seals from boardwalk binoculars or use the centre's underwater cameras ($5). The centre also has some fascinating interactive exhibits, a kids games room and a cafe.

GRAND PRIX CIRCUIT

Even when the motorbikes aren't racing, petrol-heads love the **Grand Prix Motor Racing Circuit** (☑5952 9400; www.phillipislandcircuit.com.au; Back Beach Rd), which was souped up for the Australian Motorcycle Grand Prix in 1989. The **visitor centre** (☉9am-5.30pm) runs **guided circuit tours** (adult/child/family

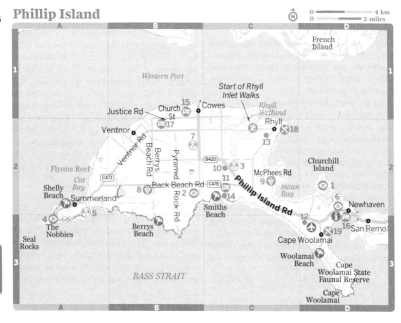

Phillip Island

$19/10/44; ⊙tours 11am & 2pm), or check out the **History of Motorsport Museum** (adult/child/family $14/6/30). The more adventurous can cut laps of the track with a racing driver in hotted-up V8s ($295; bookings essential). Drive yourself in a go-kart around a scale replica of the track with **Champ Karts** (per 10/20/30min $29/53/68).

SWIMMING & SURF BEACHES
Cowes Main Beach is calm and safe for swimming – head over to the long Cowes East Beach for a quieter time. The best surf beaches are along the southern coast. Spectacular **Cape Woolamai** is the most popular surf beach but rips and currents make it suitable for only experienced surfers. Beginners and families head to **Smiths Beach**, which is often teeming with surf-school groups. Both are patrolled in summer. **Berrys Beach** is another beautiful spot and usually quieter than Woolamai or Smiths. Around the Nobbies, **Cat Bay** and **Flynns Reef** will often be calm when the wind is blowing onshore at the Woolamai and Smiths areas.

Island Surfboards (☎5952 3443; www.islandsurfboards.com.au; 225 Smiths Beach & 147 Thompson Ave, Cowes; 2hr lessons $55) offers surfing lessons and hires gear (boards $40 per day).

BIRDS & WILDLIFE

Phillip Island Wildlife Park (☑5952 2038; www.piwildlifepark.com.au; Phillip Island Rd; adult/child/family $15/8/40; ☉10am-5pm), about 2km south of Cowes, has over 100 Australian native wildlife species. Kids love handfeeding the wallabies and kangaroos.

Mutton birds (shearwaters) nest in the Woolamai dunes. They're here from late September to April before returning to Japan and Alaska. There are pelicans (fed at Newhaven at 11.30am), and swans and ibises at **Rhyll Inlet**, where there's a boardwalk around the wetlands.

WINERIES

Phillip Island Winery WINERY
(☑5956 8465; www.phillipislandwines.com.au; Berrys Beach Rd; platters $14-30; ☉11am-5.30pm Thu-Sun, daily in school holidays) Sample excellent estate wines and share platters of cheese, terrine, smoked salmon, trout fillets and pâté.

Purple Hen Winery WINERY
(☑5956 9244; www.purplehenwines.com.au; 96 McPhees Rd, Rhyll; ☉10am-5.30pm Fri-Mon) Try the signature Pinot noir and Chardonnay at the cellar door of this pretty winery off the main tourist route, and with views over Western Port Bay.

OTHER ATTRACTIONS

Amaze'n Things AMUSEMENT PARK
(☑5952 2283; www.amazenthings.com.au; 1805 Phillip Island Rd; adult/child/family $29/20/88; ☉9am-6.30pm) With a maze, crazy illusion rooms, minigolf, a puzzle island and lots of activities, this whacky fun park is great for kids, but gets the adults in too.

Rhyll Trout & Bush Tucker Farm
TROUT FARM
(☑5956 9255; www.rhylltroutandbushtucker.com.au; 36 Rhyll-Newhaven Rd; adult/child/family $9/7/30, rod hire $3; ☉10am-5pm, to 7pm in summer) Another fun day out for kids, here you can fish for trout in a lake or indoor pond or follow the bushtucker trail.

Phillip Island Chocolate Factory FOOD
(Panny's Place; ☑5956 6600; www.phillipisland chocolatefactory.com.au; 930 Phillip Island Rd, Newhaven; factory tours adult/child/family $12/8/36; ☉9am-5pm) Like Willy Wonka's, Panny's place has a few surprises. As well as free samples of handmade Belgian-style chocolate, there's a walk-through tour of the chocolate-making process, including a remarkable gallery of chocolate sculptures, from Michelangelo's

David to an entire model village! Naturally, you can buy chocolate penguins, but most of the chocolate is prepackaged.

Tours

Go West SCENIC TOUR
(☑1300 736 551; www.gowest.com.au; tours $125) One-day tour from Melbourne that includes lunch and iPod commentary in several languages. Includes entry to the Penguin Parade.

Phillip Island Helicopters SCENIC FLIGHT
(☑5956 7316; www.pih.com.au; Phillip Island Tourist Rd, Newhaven; flights per person $70-350) Scenic flights over the island.

Wildlife Coast Cruises WILDLIFE TOUR
(☑1300 763 739, 5952 3501; www.wildlifecoast cruises.com.au; Rotunda Bldg, Cowes Jetty; tours $35-70; ☉Nov-May) Runs a variety of cruises including seal-watching, twilight and cape cruises; also runs a two-hour cruise to French Island (adult/child $30/20) and a full-day cruise to Wilsons Promontory ($190/140).

Festivals & Events

Pyramid Rock Festival MUSIC
(www.thepyramidrockfestival.com) This huge event coincides with New Year's festivities and features some of the best Aussie bands.

Australian Motorcycle Grand Prix
MOTOR RACING
(www.motogp.com.au; ☉Oct) The island's biggest event – three days of bike action in October.

V8 Supercars MOTOR RACING
(www.v8supercar.com.au) Racing events throughout the year.

Sleeping

Most of the accommodation is in and around Cowes, although there are a few places in Rhyll and Newhaven, and B&Bs and caravan parks scattered around the island. During big motor-racing events, Christmas, Easter and school holidays, rates are sky high and you'll need to book way in advance.

Clifftop BOUTIQUE HOTEL $$
(☑5952 1033; www.clifftop.com.au; 1 Marlin St, Smiths Beach; d $145-265; ✷) It's hard to imagine a better location for your island stay than perched above Smiths Beach. Of the seven luxurious suites here, the top four have ocean views and private balconies, while the downstairs rooms open onto gardens – all have fluffy beds and slick contemporary decor.

Surf & Circuit
APARTMENTS $$

(☑5952 1300; www.surfandcircuit.com; 113 Justice Rd, Cowes; apt $135-380; ❄❅) Ideal for families or groups, these eight spacious, modern and comfortable two- and three-bedroom units accommodate up to six and 10 people, respectively. All have kitchens, lounges with plasma TVs, and patios, and some have spas. Outside there are barbecue areas, a tennis court and a playground.

Waves Apartments
APARTMENTS $$

(☑5952 1351; www.thewaves.com.au; 1 The Esplanade, Cowes; d/tr/qd from $180/195/210; ❄) These slick apartments overlook Cowes Main Beach so you can't beat your balcony views if you go for a beachfront unit. The modern, self-contained apartments come with spa, and balcony or patio.

Glen Isla House
BOUTIQUE HOTEL $$$

(☑5952 1882; www.glenisla.com; 230 Church St, Cowes; d incl breakfast $285-425, self-contained cottage $270-330; ❄❅) This brilliant boutique hotel is one of the best addresses on the island. Ensconced in a renovated 1870 homestead and outbuildings, Glen Isla is all about understated, old-world luxury with modern touches such as huge plasma TVs.

Island Spa
COTTAGES $$

(☑5952 6466, 0415 550 201; www.theislandspa. com.au; 183-189 Justice Rd, Cowes; d $150-250) These comfortable, roomy eco-cottages are part of a day spa, so you only have to walk out your front door for some pampering treatment. The self-contained cottages have a private spa as well as a lot of designer touches.

Amaroo Park YHA
HOSTEL $

(☑5952 2548; www.yha.com.au; 97 Church St, Cowes; unpowered sites $30, dm/d/f from $30/95/135; @❅❄) In a shady bush setting, the Amaroo Park YHA is a lovely, old-style guesthouse with a communal kitchen and barbecue areas, a bar, lounge and TV room. There are cabins with bathrooms, and camp sites outside.

Island Accommodation
HOSTEL $

(☑5956 6123; www.theislandaccommodation.com. au; 10-12 Phillip Island Tourist Rd, Newhaven; dm $30-36, d $155; ❄❅) Part of the Islantis Wave complex in Newhaven, this brand-spanking-new backpacker place is perfect for surfers wanting to be close to the action at Woolamai. It's simple but spotless with a rooftop deck and kitchen.

✖ Eating & Drinking

Most of the eateries are in Cowes – the Esplanade and Thompson Ave are crowded with fish-and-chip shops, cafes and takeaways – but there are a few more gems scattered around the island.

COWES

Infused
MODERN AUSTRALIAN $$

(☑5952 2655; www.infused.com.au; 115 Thompson Ave; mains $25-38; ☉lunch & dinner Wed-Mon) Infused's groovy mix of timber, stone and lime-green decor makes it a relaxed place to enjoy a beautifully presented meal , or a late-night cocktail. The eclectic menu is strong on seafood and moves from freshly shucked oysters to Asian curries and Black Angus rib-eye.

Hotel
PUB FARE $$

(☑5952 2060; www.hotelphillipisland.com; 11-13 The Esplanade; mains $10-28; ☉lunch & dinner) So cool that it only goes by its first name (like Cher…), this breezy corner pub is all leather, sleek lines and big windows. The menu is honest and good value with all-day tapas plates, pizza and the standard steak and chicken parma. Has live music on weekends. Its competition, the Isle of Wight, burnt down in 2010.

Madcowes
CAFE $$

(☑5952 2560; 17 The Esplanade; mains $7-17; ☉breakfast & lunch) This stylish cafe-foodstore looks out to the main beach and cooks up some of the heartiest breakfasts and light lunches on the island. Try the ricotta hotcakes or the grazing platter, and browse the selection of wine and produce.

Also recommended:

Café Lugano
CAFE $

(☑5952 5636; 71 Thompson Ave; mains $7-17; ☉breakfast & lunch) Cool hole-in-the-wall joint for good coffee or a healthy lunch of focaccia, rice burger or falafel salad.

Youki's Japanese Takeaway
JAPANESE $

(☑5952 6444; 1/69b Chapel St; sushi rolls $3-12; ☉11am-4pm; ☑) Fresh takeaway sushi rolls, teriyaki and *gyoza* (dumplings).

Panhandle
MEXICAN $$

(☑5952 2741; 145 Thompson Ave; mains $20-26; ☉lunch & dinner) Cheap-and-cheerful, family-friendly Tex-Mex cantina. Tacos, nachos, fajitas and margaritas mixed in with a good atmosphere.

RHYLL

Rhyll has a neat little strip of eateries by the waterfront, including a Greek restaurant and fish and chippery.

Cowes

Foreshore Bar & Restaurant

MODERN AUSTRALIAN **$$**

(☑5956 9520; www.theforeshore.com.au; 11 Beach Rd; mains $21-35; ☺lunch & dinner) The water views and nautical theme from the timber deck of the classy pub-turned-restaurant complement your lunchtime steak sandwich or bowl of mussels. The evening has a relaxed, fine-dining feel with a gastropub menu from bangers and mash to maple pork and Asian duck.

CAPE WOOLAMAI

White Salt   FISH & CHIPS **$**

(☑5956 6336; 7 Vista Pl; fish from $5, meal packs from $20; ☺lunch & dinner Fri-Sun, from 4.30pm Wed & Thu) White Salt serves the best fish and chips on the island – selected fish fillets and hand-cut chips, tempura prawns and marinated barbecue octopus salad with corn, pesto and lemon.

Curry Leaf   INDIAN **$**

(☑5956 6772; 9 Vista Pl; mains $12-18; ☺dinner Wed-Mon, lunch Fri-Sun; ☑) This cheery Indian restaurant and takeaway is popular for its piquant meat, seafood and vegetarian curries, samosas and aromatic biryani dishes.

❶ Information

Phillip Island visitor centres (☑1300 366 422, 5956 7447; www.visitphillipisland.com; ☺9am-5pm, to 6pm in school holidays); Newhaven (895 Phillip Island Tourist Rd); Cowes (cnr Thompson & Church Sts) The main visitor centre for the island is on the main road at Newhaven, and there's a smaller centre at Cowes. Both sell the Three Parks Pass (adult/child/family $36/18/90), and the main centre has a free accommodation- and tour-booking service.

Waterfront Internet Service (☑5952 3312; Shop 1/130 Thompson Ave, Cowes; ☺9am-5pm Mon-Fri, 10am-1pm Sat) Internet access costs $6 per hour.

❶ Getting There & Away

By car, Phillip Island can only be accessed across the bridge from San Remo to Newhaven. From Melbourne take the Monash Fwy (M1) and exit at Pakenham, joining the South Gippsland Hwy at Koo Wee Rup.

Bus

V/Line (☑13 61 96; www.vline.com.au) has train-bus services from Melbourne's Southern Cross Station via Dandenong station or Koo Wee Rup ($11, 2½ hours). There are no direct services.

Ferry

Inter Island Ferries (☑9585 5730; www.interislandferries.com.au; return adult/child/bike $21/10/8) runs between Stony Point on the Mornington Peninsula and Cowes via French Island (45 minutes). There are two sailings Monday and Wednesday, and three on Tuesday, Thursday, Friday, Saturday and Sunday.

❶ Getting Around

Hire bicycles from **Ride On Bikes** (☑5952 2533; www.rideonbikes.com.au; 43 Thompson Ave, Cowes; half-/full day $25/35).

Gippsland & Wilsons Promontory

Best Places to Eat

» Koonwarra Food, Wine & Produce Store (p236)

» Metung Galley (p244)

» Ferryman's Seafood Café (p247)

» Wildfish (p240)

» Café Espas (p243)

Best Places to Stay

» Walhalla Star Hotel (p231)

» Lighthouse Keepers' Cottages (p237)

» Déjà Vu (p246)

» Camping on Ninety Mile Beach (p253)

» Adobe Mudbrick Flats (p252)

Why Go?

The Great Ocean Road may get the crowds, but Gippsland hides all the secrets. Stretching east along the coast from Western Port Bay to Mallacoota and inland to encompass virtually all of eastern Victoria, Gippsland is home to some of the most absorbing, unspoilt and beautiful wilderness areas and beaches in the state.

A trip to Gippsland could mean swimming, fishing, camping and boating along the coast – much of it practically deserted for a good part of the year (yes, it's busy during school holidays!); cycling from town to town on the network of rail trails; or packing the rucksack and hiking boots and heading into the most remote wilderness national parks in the state.

For many, the Gippsland trail starts at the wild and woolly Wilsons Promontory, and heads east through the sublime Lakes District, the Ninety Mile Beach and finally to the Wilderness Coast – some of the most pristine national parks in the country. Out here, the city feels like a lifetime away.

When to Go
Point Hicks

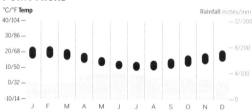

Feb–Mar For toe-tapping jazz festivals at Inverloch and Paynesville.

Oct–Nov Spring is the time for wildflowers and wildlife, as well as bushwalking.

Dec–Jan It gets busy, but there's no better time to hit the oceans and lakes than summer!

WEST GIPPSLAND

The Princes Hwy heads east from Melbourne to the Latrobe Valley, an agricultural area where the increasingly controversial coal-fired power stations supply some 85% of the state's electricity. This industry, along with farming and timber, largely supports the main towns of Moe, Morwell and Traralgon.

North of the valley are the foothills of the Great Dividing Range, where you'll find Baw Baw National Park, the Thomson Dam and the historic gold-mining town of Walhalla.

Walhalla

POP 18

Ensconced high in the green hills and forest of west Gippsland, tiny Walhalla is one of the state's best-preserved and most charming historic towns. In its gold-mining heyday, Walhalla's population was 5000, today it's just 18. There's still plenty to see in here, and the winding forest drive into the town from Rawson or Traralgon is beautiful. Stringers Creek runs through the centre of the township – an idyllic valley encircled by a cluster of sepia-toned historic buildings set into the hillsides. During August the town lights up for the Walhalla Vinter ljusfest (Winter Lights Festival). Remarkably, mains electricity only came to Walhalla a decade ago. Up some steps behind the Star Hotel, a trail leads to the Walhalla Cricket Ground, while the Walhalla Cemetery gives a sombre insight into the history of the area.

◉ Sights & Activities

The best way to see the town is on foot – take the circuit walk (45 minutes) anti-clockwise from the information shelter as you enter town.

Walhalla Historical Museum MUSEUM
(☑5165 6250; www.walhalla.org.au; admission $2; ◷10am-4pm) Located in the old post office in the group of restored shops along the main street, Walhalla Historical Museum also acts as an information centre and books the popular two-hour ghost tours (www.walhallaghosttour.info; adult/child $25/18) on Friday and Saturday nights.

Walhalla Goldfields Railway TRAIN
(☑9513 3969; www.walhallarail.com; return adult/child/family $18/13/40; ◷from Walhalla Station 11am, 1pm & 3pm, from Thomson Station 11.40am, 1.40pm & 3.40pm Wed, Sat, Sun & public holidays) A star attraction is the scenic Walhalla Gold-

fields Railway, which offers a 20-minute ride between Walhalla and Thomson Stations (on the main road, 3.5km before Walhalla). The train snakes along Stringers Creek Gorge, passing lovely, forested gorge country and crossing a number of trestle bridges.

Long Tunnel Extended Gold Mine
GOLD MINE
(☑5165 6259; off Walhalla-Beardmore Rd; tours adult/child/family $20/14/50; ◷tours 1.30pm Mon-Fri, noon, 1.30pm & 3pm Sat & Sun, public & school holidays) Relive the mining past with guided tours exploring Cohens Reef, once one of Australia's top reef-gold producers. Almost 14 tonnes of gold came out of this mine.

☞ Tours

Mountain Top Experience (☑5134 6876; www.mountaintopexperience.com) operates nature-based 4WD tours, including the Walhalla Copper Mine Adventure ($20) and ghost-town tours ($25) on weekends and Wednesdays.

🛏 Sleeping & Eating

You can camp for free at North Gardens, a camp site with toilets and barbecues, at the north end of the village. Walhalla has a handful of cottages and B&Bs, and there are a couple of old-style cafes among the group of shops in the village centre.

Walhalla Star Hotel HOTEL $$
(☑5165 6262; www.starhotel.com.au; Main Rd; d incl breakfast $219, with dinner $319; ✳) The rebuilt historic Star offers stylish boutique accommodation with king-size beds and sophisticated designer decor making good use of local materials such as corrugated-iron water tanks. Guests can dine at the flash Parker's Restaurant (mains from $30; ◷dinner); others need to reserve in advance. Or you can get good breakfasts, coffee and cake at the attached Greyhorse Café (mains from $5; ◷11am-2pm).

Windsor House B&B $$
(☑5165 6237; www.windsorhouse.com.au; off Walhalla Rd; d $160, ste $175-200; ◷Thu-Mon) The five rooms and suites in this beautifully restored two-storey 1878 home are fittingly old fashioned and ghost-free.

Wild Cherry B&B B&B $$
(☑5165 6245; www.wildcherrywalhalla.com.au; Church Hill Rd; d incl breakfast $160) The Wild Cherry is a sweet little B&B perched on the hill above town with comfy motel-style rooms.

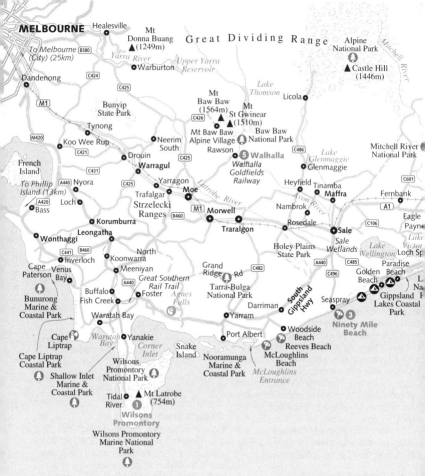

Gippsland & Wilsons Promontory Highlights

1 Hike from Tidal River to Sealers Cove or a remote lighthouse at spectacular **Wilsons Promontory** (p237)

2 Saddle up for the **East Gippsland Rail Trail** (p243), Gippsland's longest cycle path

3 Camp in the dunes and fish from the beach at legendary **Ninety Mile Beach** (p241)

4 Hire a boat and explore the inlet, or visit Gabo Island, from gorgeous little **Mallacoota** (p251)

5 Step back in time at **Walhalla** (p231), an authentic gold-mining village

6 Descend into ancient limestone caves and camp outside at **Buchan** (p248)

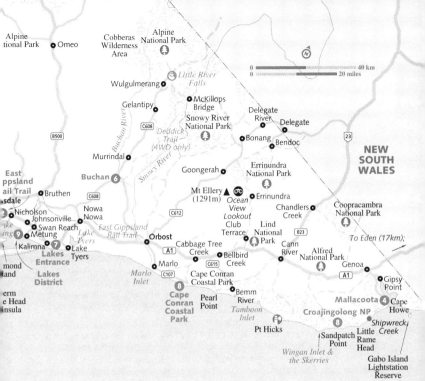

Alpine
tional Park

Omeo

Cobberas
Wilderness
Area

Alpine
National Park

Little River
Falls

Wulgulmerang

Gelantipy

McKillops
Bridge

Snowy River
National Park

Delegate
River

Delegate

Buchan River

C608

Deddick
Trail
(4WD only)

Bonang

Bendoc

B500

Murrindal

East
ppsland
ail Trail
sdale

Buchan

Bruthen

Goongerah

Snowy River

Errinundra
National Park

23

NEW
SOUTH
WALES

Nicholson

C608

Johnsonville

Nowa
Nowa

Mt Ellery
(1291m)

Errinundra

Chandlers
Creek

Coopracambra
National Park

Swan Reach

C612

Ocean
View
Lookout
Club
Terrace

To Eden (17km);

Metung

East Gippsland
Rail Trail

Lake
Tyers

Orbost

Cabbage Tree
Creek

Lind
National
Park

Cann
River

B823

Kalinna

Lake
Tyers

Marlo

A1

C615

Bellbird
Creek

Alfred
National Park

Genoa

Lakes
Entrance

Lakes
District

Marlo
Inlet

C107

Cape Conran
Coastal Park

Cape
Conran
Coastal
Park

Bemm
River

Pearl
Point

Croajingolong NP

A1

Gipsy
Point

Mallacoota

Cape
Howe

Tamboon
Inlet

erm
e Head
nsula

Shipwreck
Creek

Pt Hicks

Sandpatch
Point

Little
Rame
Head

Wingan Inlet &
the Skerries

Gabo Island
Lightstation
Reserve

Bass Strait

0   40 km
0   20 miles

7 Take an afternoon winery
cruise then feast on a seafood
dinner at **Lakes Entrance**
(p245)

8 Find your quiet corner
of the world in humbling
Croajingolong National Park
(p253) and **Cape Conran
Coastal Park** (p251)

9 Cruise the waters of the
Lakes District (p241) from
the tranquil marina villages of
Metung and Paynesville

Rawson Caravan Park
CARAVAN PARK **$**

(☎5165 3439; www.rawsoncaravanpark.com.au; Depot Rd, Rawson; powered sites/dm/cabins $30/45/95) Located About 12km from Walhalla, Rawson Caravan Park has a native bush setting, en suite sites and the popular Stockyard Bar & Bistro, which opens on weekends and features live music and boisterous crowds up from the Latrobe Valley.

Walhalla Lodge Hotel
PUB FARE **$$**

(☎5165 6226; Main St; mains $16-25; ⊘lunch & dinner Wed-Mon) The Wally Pub is a cosy, one-room pub decked out with prints of old Walhalla and serving good-value counter meals – think burgers, pasta, schnitzels and T-bone steaks.

SOUTH GIPPSLAND

South Gippsland has plenty of gems along the coast between Inverloch and Wilsons Promontory – Venus Bay, Cape Liptrap Coastal Park and Waratah Bay are all worth exploring. Inland among the farming communities are some great drives through the Strzelecki Ranges, the Great Southern Rail Trail cycle path and trendy villages such as Koonwarra and Fish Creek.

Inverloch
POP 4140

Fabulous surf, calm inlet beaches and outstanding diving and snorkelling make the coast along the road between Cape Paterson and Inverloch a popular destination. Crowds expand to bursting point during the Christmas school holidays, but somehow the town manages to maintain a down-to-earth vibe. Inverloch also draws the crowds when it hosts the popular Inverloch Jazz Festival (www.inverlochjazzfest. org.au) held on the Labour Day long weekend each March.

If you want to learn to catch a wave, the Offshore Surf School (☎0407 374 743; www. surfingaustralia.com.au; 32 Park St; 2hr lesson $55) offers lessons at the main town surf beach.

🛏 Sleeping & Eating

There's plenty of holiday accommodation around – the visitor centre can help with bookings. Cafes and restaurants are clustered around Williams and A'Beckett Sts.

Inverloch Foreshore Camping Reserve
CAMPING GROUND **$**

(☎5674 1447; www.inverlochholidaypark.com.au; cnr The Esplanade & Ramsay Blvd; unpowered/powered sites from $26/30) Camping is a pleasure at this camp site just back from the inlet beach with shade and privacy.

Lofts
APARTMENTS **$$**

(☎5674 2255; www.theloftapartments.com.au; Scarborough St; apt from $150; ❋) Spread yourself out in these sleek, architect-designed apartments with high ceilings and namesake lofts. They're handily adjacent to the park, beach and shops. Some have water views and most have a spa.

Moilong Express
BOUTIQUE HOTEL **$$**

(☎0439 842 334; 405 Inverloch-Venus Bay Rd; d $120) This quirky former railway train carriage, on a hillside property about 3km from Inverloch, has been converted into very comfortable accommodation with a kitchen, queen-size bed, traditional wood panelling and an old railway station clock.

Tomo
JAPANESE **$$**

(☎5674 3444; www.tomo-modern-jp.com; 23 A'Beckett St; sushi from $4, mains $21-39; ⊘lunch & dinner Tue-Sun, daily Dec-Feb) Modern Japanese cuisine prepared to perfection. Start with tender sushi or sashimi, but don't miss the *gyoza* (dumplings) or tempura tiger prawns.

Red Elk Café
CAFE **$**

(☎5674 3264; 27 A'Beckett St; mains $12-20; ⊘breakfast & lunch) In a weatherboard corner cottage, this new cafe and bar is a buzzing place for coffee and a hearty breakfast.

❶ Information

Inverloch visitor centre (☎1300 762 433; www.visitbasscoast.com; 39 A'Beckett St; ⊘9am-5pm; @) Helpful staff can make accommodation bookings for free.

Bunurong Environment Centre & Shop (☎5674 3738; www.sgcs.org.au; cnr Esplanade & Ramsey Blvd; ⊘10am-4pm Fri-Mon, daily in school holidays) An abundance of books and brochures on environmental and sustainable-living topics. Also here is the Shell Museum ($2) with more than 6000 shells.

❶ Getting There & Away

V/Line (☎13 61 96; www.vline.com.au) trains depart daily from Melbourne's Flinders St and Southern Cross Stations for Dandenong, connecting with buses to Inverloch ($14, 3½ hours). A quicker option (2½ hours) is the V/Line coach with a change at Koo Wee Rup.

Bunurong Marine & Coastal Park

This surprising little marine and coastal park offers some of Australia's best snorkelling and diving, and a stunning, cliff-hugging drive between Inverloch and Cape Paterson. It certainly surprised the archaeological world in the early 1990s when dinosaur remains dating back 120 million years were discovered here. Eagles Nest, Shack Bay, the Caves and Twin Reefs are great for snorkelling. The Oaks is the locals' favourite surf beach. The Caves is where the dinosaur dig action is.

SEAL Diving Services (☎5174 3434; www.sealdivingservices.com.au; 7/27 Princes Hwy, Traralgon) has shore dives at Cape Paterson and boat dives in Bunurong Marine & Coastal Park.

Korumburra

POP 4500

The first sizeable town along the South Gippsland Hwy, Korumburra is scenically situated on the edge of the Strzelecki Ranges.

FREE Coal Creek Village MUSEUM
(☎5655 1811; www.coalcreekvillage.com.au; ⊙10am-4.30pm Thu-Mon, daily during school holidays) Coal Creek Village is an interesting re-creation of a 19th-century mining town, with a museum, activities for kids and a regional visitor centre. V/Line coaches from Melbourne's Southern Cross Station stop outside en route to Leongatha and Yarram.

South Gippsland Railway HISTORIC RAILWAY
(☎5658 1111, 1800 442 211; www.sgr.org.au; adult/child/family return $15/9/48) Volunteers operate heritage diesel trains along scenic tracks from Korumburra to Leongatha and Nyora on Sundays and public holidays (four services).

Koonwarra

POP 750

This tiny township on the South Gippsland Hwy has built itself a reputation around its general store and cafe. There's also an organic fruit-and-vegetable shop and a popular organic Farmers Market (Memorial Park; ⊙8am-1pm 1st Sat of month).

GRAND RIDGE ROAD

The spectacular 132km Grand Ridge Road winds along the top of the Strzelecki Ranges, running from midway between Warragul and Korumburra to midway between Traralgon and Yarram. The (mostly) gravel road provides a fabulous excursion through fertile farmland once covered with forests of giant mountain ash and valleys of giant tree ferns.

The drive makes a great alternative to the Princes Hwy, but if you're going to travel the length of it, allow the best part of a day. Pick the road up (signposted from the highway) south of Warragul. Only 3km along is the excellent Wild Dog Winery (☎5623 1117; www.wilddogwinery.com; Warragul-Korumburra Rd; ⊙10am-5pm), one of Gippsland's first wineries. It produces a great range of cool-climate wines, all grown and bottled on its 30 acres, and has an excellent restaurant with views across the Strzelecki Ranges.

The only community of any size along the Grand Ridge Road is the pretty township of Mirboo North. It's home to Gippsland's only brewery, the award-winning Grand Ridge Brewery & Restaurant (☎9778 6996; www.grand-ridge.com.au; Main St; mains $20-28; ⊙brewery daily, lunch & dinner Wed-Sun), producing a range of chemical- and preservative-free beer. The restaurant food is fresh, prepared from local produce and includes steaks from the local beef producer, tapas plates and roo fillet.

Continuing, you'll pass through the rainforest gully of Tarra-Bulga National Park, one of the last remnants of the magnificent forests that once covered all of south Gippsland. There are some good short walks here, including the Tarra Valley Rainforest Walk to Cyathea Falls (1.5km, 35 minutes return) and the easy Fern Gully Nature Walk (750m, 15 minutes return). Camping is not permitted in the park but you can stay at the nearby Tarra Valley Tourist Park (☎5186 1283; www.tarra-valley.com; 1906 Tarra Valley Rd; unpowered/powered sites $26/36, cabins $115-170), nestled in rainforest, with camping in a pretty riverside setting and cabin accommodation.

For sheer indulgence, stop at the Tarra Valley Rainforest Retreat (☎5186 1313; www.tarravalleyrainforestretreat.com; 1788 Tarra Valley Rd; d $140-160; ❇), elegant Swiss chalet–style accommodation that doubles as a chocolate-making school. Chocolate appreciation courses with the resident chocolate-maker cost $50/55 for guests/nonguests.

☆ Activities

Peaceful Gardens Organic Cooking School COOKING COURSE

(☎5664 2480; Koala Dr; half-/full day from $70/130, children's half-day $30-50) Victoria's first certified-organic cooking school, Peaceful Gardens has the motto 'organic, seasonal, local'. It offers short courses in 'country kitchen' cooking, including making cakes, bread, preserves and traditional pastries and pasta using produce from the owners' local farm. Half-day classes are offered for children.

Koonwarra Day Spa SPA

(☎5664 2332; www.koonwarraspa.com.au; 9 Koala Dr; spa from $30, massage from $50; ⊙9am-5pm Tue-Fri, plus Mon Dec & Jan) Indulge yourself with spas, saunas and body treatments ranging from a 30-minute mineral spa to a six-hour pamper package.

☒ Sleeping & Eating

Lyre Bird Hill Winery & Guest House

B&B $$

(☎5664 3204; www.lyrebirdhill.com.au; 370 Inverloch Rd; guesthouse s/d $125/175, cottage $120; ⊙cellar door 10am-5pm Wed-Mon; ❋) Stay among the vines 4km southwest of Koonwarra. The quaint, old-fashioned B&B has light-filled rooms overlooking the garden, while the self-contained country-style cottage is perfect for a family.

Koonwarra Food, Wine & Produce Store CAFE $$

(☎5664 2285; cnr South Gippsland Hwy & Koala Dr; mains $6-34; ⊙breakfast & lunch daily, dinner Fri; ☒) Simple food with flair is the secret behind this popular cafe, which prides itself on using organic, sustainable suppliers and products. The store stocks local wines and produce, as well as sauces, preserves and pâtés made on site. There's wine and cheese tasting on weekends ($5) and a shady garden area outside.

Fish Creek

POP 700

Travellers in the know have been stopping for a bite to eat at Fish Creek on their way to the coast or the Prom for years, and these days it has developed into a little bohemian artists community with craft shops, galleries, studios, bookshops and some great cafes. The **Great Southern Rail Trail** passes through.

GREAT SOUTHERN RAIL TRAIL

This 49km cycling and walking path (www.railtrails.org.au) follows the old rail line from Leongatha to Foster, passing through the villages of Koonwarra, Meeniyan, Buffalo and Fish Creek – all good places to stop and refuel. The trail meanders through farmland with a few gentle hills, trestle bridges and the occasional views of the coast and Wilsons Prom.

Celia Rosser Gallery (☎5683 2628; www.celiarossergallery.com; Promontory Rd; ⊙10am-4pm Fri-Mon) is a bright art space featuring the works of renowned botanical artist Celia Rosser and various visiting artists. The attached Banksia Café has a sunny deck.

The art deco **Fish Creek Hotel** (☎5683 2416; Old Waratah Rd; mains $16-30; ⊙lunch & dinner), universally known as the Fishy Pub (but also called the Promontory Gate Hotel), is an essential stop for a beer or bistro meal, and there's motel accommodation at the back.

WILSONS PROMONTORY NATIONAL PARK

If you like wilderness bushwalking, stunning coastal scenery and secluded white-sand beaches, you'll absolutely love this place. 'The Prom', as it's affectionately known, is one of the most popular national parks in Australia. Hardly surprising, given its accessibility from Melbourne, network of more than 80km of **walking tracks**, swimming and surf beaches, and abundant wildlife.

Wilsons Promontory was an important area for the Kurnai and Boonwurrung Indigenous peoples, and middens have been found in many places, including Cotters and Darby Beaches, and Oberon Bay. The southernmost part of mainland Australia, the Prom once formed a land bridge that allowed people to walk to Tasmania.

Tidal River, 30km from the park entrance, is the hub, and home to the Parks Victoria office, a general store, cafe and accommodation. The wildlife around Tidal River is incredibly tame: kookaburras and rosellas lurk expectantly (resist the urge to feed them) and wombats nonchalantly waddle out of the undergrowth.

Although there's a staffed **entrance booth** (⊙9am-sunset), where you receive a ticket, entry is free. There's no fuel available in Tidal River.

🏃 Activities

There's an extensive choice of marked **walking trails** here, taking you through forests, marshes, valleys of tree ferns, low granite mountains and along beaches lined with sand dunes. The Parks Victoria office at Tidal River has brochures with details of walks, from 15-minute strolls to overnight and longer hikes. Even nonwalkers can enjoy some of the park's beauty, with car park access off the Tidal River road leading to gorgeous beaches and lookouts. The northern area of the park is much less visited – most walks in this wilderness area are overnight or longer, and mainly for experienced bushwalkers; permits are required.

Swimming is safe from the gorgeous beaches at Norman Bay (Tidal River) and around the headland at Squeaky Beach – the ultra-fine quartz sand here really does squeak beneath your feet!

If you're travelling light, you can hire camping equipment, including tents, stoves, sleeping bags and backpacks, from **Wilsons Prom Hiking Hire** (☑5678 1152; 3670 Prom Rd, Yanakie).

👉 Tours

Bunyip Tours   NATURE
(☑1300 286 947, 9650 9680; www.bunyiptours. com; day tour $120) Proudly carbon-neutral, Bunyip Tours offers a one-day guided tour to the Prom from Melbourne, with the option of staying on another two days to explore by yourself.

First Track Adventures   NATURE
(☑5634 2761; www.firsttrack.com.au) This Yarragon-based company organises customised bushwalking, canoeing and abseiling trips to the Prom for individuals and groups. Prices vary according to group size and activity.

Hiking Plus   HIKING
(☑0418 341 537; www.hikingplus.com; 3-/5-day tours $1100/1800) This tour company organises fully catered and guided hikes to the Prom from nearby Foster, where it has comfortable guesthouse accommodation (including spa) for the start and end of each trip. Packages include a two- to three-day hike, meals, a massage and spa, and you need only carry a light pack.

🛏 Sleeping

Nothing beats a night at the Prom. The main accommodation base is at Tidal River, but there are 11 bush-camping (outstation) areas around the Prom, all with pit or compost toilets, but no other facilities; you need to carry in your own drinking water. Overnight hikers need camping permits (adult/child per night $8/4), which must be booked ahead through Parks Victoria.

TIDAL RIVER

Situated on Norman Bay and a short walk to a stunning beach, Tidal River is incredibly popular. Book accommodation well in advance through **Parks Victoria** (☑1800 350 552, 13 19 63; www.parkweb.vic.gov.au), especially for weekends and holidays.

Camp Sites   CAMPING GROUND $
(unpowered sites per vehicle & 3 people $20-24, powered sites per vehicle & up to 8 people $44-52) Tidal River has 480 camp sites, but only 20 powered sites. For the Christmas school holiday period there's a ballot for sites (apply online by 31 July at www.parkweb.vic.gov.au).

Park Huts   CABINS $
(4-/6-bed huts $65/100) If you're travelling tent-free, these cosy wooden huts are a decent budget option, with bunks and kitchenettes, but no bathrooms.

Lorikeet Units & Cabins   CABINS $$
(d $110-172, additional adult/child $23/15) The spacious and private self-contained cabins sleep up to six people and have large, sliding-glass doors and a deck, and overlook the bush or river. The Lorikeet Units are equally comfortable, sleeping up to four people, but they're closer to the visitor centre and parking area.

Wilderness Retreat   SAFARI TENTS $$$
(d $250, extra person $20) Nestled in bushland at Tidal River, these are the most expensive tents on the Prom! The luxury safari tents, each with their own deck, sleep up to four people and are pretty cool with a bathroom, queen-size beds, heating and a communal tent kitchen.

Lighthouse Keepers' Cottages   COTTAGES $
(8-bed cottages per person $51-83) These isolated, heritage-listed 1850s cottages with thick granite walls are a real getaway, attached to a working lightstation on a pimple of land that juts out into the wild ocean. Kick back after the 19km hike here and watch ships or whales passing by. The cottages have shared facilities, including a fully equipped kitchen.

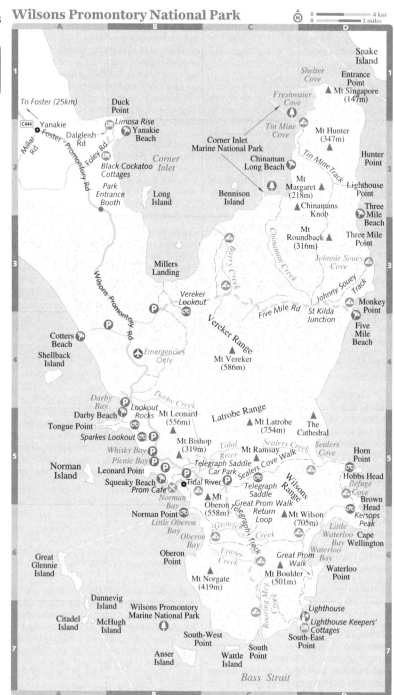

The Prom's delights are best discovered on foot. From November to Easter a free shuttle bus operates between the Tidal River visitors car park and the Telegraph Saddle car park (a nice way to start the Prom Circuit Walk). Here are six of the best:

Great Prom Walk This is the most popular long-distance hike, a moderate 45km circuit across to Sealers Cove from Tidal River, down to Refuge Cove, Waterloo Bay, the lighthouse and the return loop back to Tidal River via Oberon Bay. Allow three days, and coordinate your walks with tide times, as creek crossings can be hazardous. It's possible to visit or stay at the lighthouse by prior arrangement with the parks office.

Sealers Cove Walk The best overnight hike, this two-day walk starts at Telegraph Saddle and heads down Telegraph Track to stay overnight at beautiful Little Waterloo Bay (12km, 4½ hours). The next day walk on the Sealers Cove via Refuge Cove and return to Telegraph Saddle (24km, 7½ hours).

Lilly Pilly Gully Nature Walk An easy 5km (two-hour) walk through heathland and eucalypt forests, with lots of wildlife.

Mt Oberon Summit Starting from the Mt Oberon car park, this moderate-to-hard 7km (2½-hour) walk is an ideal introduction to the Prom with panoramic views from the summit. The free Mt Oberon shuttle bus can take you to the Telegraph Saddle car park and back.

Little Oberon Bay An easy-to-moderate 8km (three-hour) walk over sand dunes covered in coastal tea trees with beautiful views over Little Oberon Bay.

Squeaky Beach Nature Walk Another easy 5km return stroll through coastal tea trees and banksias to a sensational white-sand beach.

YANAKIE & FOSTER
The tiny, dispersed settlement of Yanakie offers the closest accommodation outside the park boundaries – from cabins and camping to luxury cottages. Foster, the nearest main town, has a backpackers and several motels.

Black Cockatoo Cottages　COTTAGES **$$**
(☑5687 1306; www.blackcockatoo.com; 60 Foley Rd, Yanakie; d $160) You can take in glorious views of the national park without leaving your very comfortable bed – or breaking the bank – in these private, stylish, black-timber cottages. There are three modern cottages and a three-bedroom house.

Limosa Rise　COTTAGES **$$$**
(☑5687 1135; www.limosarise.com.au; 40 Dalgleish Rd, Yanakie; d $265-395; ❈) The views are stupendous from these luxury, self-contained cottages near the Prom entrance. The three tastefully appointed cottages (a studio, one-bedroom and two-bedroom) are fitted with full-length glass windows taking complete advantage of sweeping views across Corner Inlet and the Prom's mountains.

Prom Coast Backpackers　HOSTEL **$**
(☑5682 2171; www.yha.com.au; 40 Station Rd, Foster; dm/d/f from $30/70/90; @) The closest backpacker hostel to the park is this friendly YHA in Foster. The cosy renovated cottage sleeps only 10 so it's always intimate.

Warrawee Holiday Apartments
APARTMENTS **$$**
(☑5682 2171; 38 Station Rd, Foster; d $100-130; ❈) Next to Prom Coast Backpackers and under the same management, these comfortable two-bedroom apartments are good value.

 Eating

The General Store in Tidal River stocks grocery items and some camping equipment, but if you're hiking, it's cheaper to stock up in Foster. The **Prom Café** (mains $12-22; ⊙breakfast, lunch & dinner) is open daily for takeaway food and serves breakfast, light lunches and bistro-style meals on weekends and holidays.

ⓘ Information
Parks Victoria (☑1800 350 552, 13 19 63; www.parkweb.vic.gov.au; Tidal River; ⊙8.30am-4.30pm) The helpful visitor centre books all park accommodation, including permits for camping away from Tidal River.

ⓘ Getting There & Away
There's no direct public transport between Melbourne and the Prom, but the **Wilsons Promontory Bus Service** (☑5687 1249; adult/child $8/4), run by Moon's Bus Lines, operates from Foster to Tidal River (via Fish Creek) on Friday at 4.30pm, returning on Sunday at 4.30pm. This service connects with the V/Line bus from Melbourne at Fish Creek.

V/Line (📞13 61 96; www.vline.com.au) buses from Melbourne's Southern Cross Station travel direct to Foster ($17, three hours, four daily).

EAST OF THE PROM

Port Albert

POP 250

This little old fishing village is developing a reputation as a trendy stopover for boating, fishing and sampling the local seafood. The town proudly pronounces itself Gippsland's first established port and the many historic timber buildings in the main street dating from its busy 1850s bear a brass plaque, detailing their age and previous use.

◎ Sights & Activities

The Gippsland Regional Maritime Museum (📞5183 2520; Tarraville Rd; adult/child $5/1; ◎10.30am-4pm daily Sep-May, Sat & Sun Jun-Aug), in the old Bank of Victoria (1861), will give you an insight into the highlights of Port Albert's maritime history, with stories of shipwrecks, the town's whaling and sealing days, and local Aboriginal legends.

You can hire boats and canoes from the Slip Jetty for cruising around the sheltered waters of the Nooramunga Marine & Coastal Park.

🛌 Sleeping & Eating

There's a caravan park at Seabank, about 6km northwest, and a few B&Bs in town.

Port Albert Hotel   MOTEL $
(📞5183 2212; 37 Wharf St; d $80; ◎street counter lunch & dinner daily, restaurant dinner daily, lunch weekends; mains $15-30; 🌐) The old timber pub opposite the wharf lays claim to being Victoria's oldest continually licensed pub (since 1842) and it still draws the crowds with its down-to-earth vibe and quality bistro food. Takeaway fish and chips can be ordered from the street counter (just ring the bell). The motel rooms are clean but faded.

Wildfish   SEAFOOD $$
(📞5183 2007; www.wildfishrestaurant.com.au; 40 Wharf St; lunch $8-17, dinner $26-28; ◎lunch daily, dinner Fri-Sun) With a sublime harbourside location and the freshest local seafood, Wildfish is earning a well-deserved reputation for serving good food. By day it's a cafe serving coffee and sandwiches; by night the

menu turns to thoughtful seafood dishes such as flake-and-scallop pie or tempura garfish fillets.

Port Albert Wharf   FISH & CHIPS $
(📞5183 2002; 40 Wharf St; mains from $6; ◎11am-7.30pm) The fish & chips here are renowned, perfectly presented and as fresh as you'd expect from a town built on fishing.

LAKES DISTRICT

The beautiful Gippsland Lakes form the largest inland waterway system in Australia, with the three main interconnecting lakes – Wellington, King and Victoria – stretching from Sale to beyond Lakes Entrance. The lakes are actually saltwater lagoons, separated from the ocean by the Gippsland Lakes Coastal Park and the narrow coastal strip of sand dunes known as Ninety Mile Beach. You really need a boat to explore the lakes in depth, but it's hard to beat camping and fishing along the beach or hanging out at the pretty seaside communities.

Sale

POP 13, 300

Gateway to the Lakes District, Sale has plenty of accommodation, shops, restaurants and pubs, making it a good town-sized base for exploring Ninety Mile Beach.

The Sale Wetlands Walk (4km, 1½ hours) is a pleasant wander around Lake Gutheridge and its adjoining wetlands and incorporates an Indigenous Art Trail commemorating the importance of the wetlands to the local Kurnai community. Sale Common, a 300-hectare wildlife refuge with bird hides, an observatory, a waterhole, boardwalks and other walking tracks is part of an internationally recognised wetlands system. The best time to visit is early morning or late evening (wear some mosquito repellent), when you'll see lots of bird life.

The Port of Sale is a redeveloped marina area in the town centre with boardwalks, cafes and a canal leading out to the Gippsland Lakes.

FREE Gippsland Art Gallery (📞5142 3372; www.wellington.vic.gov.au/gallery; Civic Centre, 68 Foster St; ◎10am-5pm Mon-Fri, noon-4pm Sat & Sun) exhibits work by locally and nationally renowned artists and hosts touring exhibitions.

🛏 Sleeping & Eating

Minnies B&B **$$**
(☏5144 3344; www.minnies.com.au; 202 Gibsons Rd; s/d $150/160; ❂🐾) It takes some flair to make an outlandish purple-and-green colour scheme look inspired, and indeed it succeeds in the lounge area of this modern B&B. Choose between the funky green room and the more traditional rose room, with its antique-look bedhead complete with rose imprints.

Cambrai Hostel HOSTEL **$**
(☏5147 1600; www.maffra.net.au/hostel; 117 Johnson St, Maffra; dm/d $25/60; ❀) In nearby Maffra, this relaxed hostel is a budget haven and one of the few true backpackers in Gippsland. In a 120-year-old building that was once a doctor's residence, it has a licensed bar, an open fire and a pool table in the cosy lounge, a tiny self-catering kitchen and clean, cheerful rooms. The owners can sometimes arrange work in the region.

Bis Cucina CAFE **$$**
(☏5144 3388; www.biscucina.com.au; 100 Foster St; breakfast & lunch $12-23, dinner $23-36; ⊘breakfast & lunch daily, dinner Fri, Sat & show nights) At the Wellington Entertainment Centre, Bis Cucina offers relaxed and attentive service combined with carefully chosen modern Australian cuisine with Mediterranean influences. This is a good choice for serious foodies, theatre-goers wanting a pre-show meal, or just a coffee or lazy breakfast.

ℹ Information

Wellington visitor information centre
(☏1800 677 520; www.tourismwellington.com.au; 8 Foster St; ⊘9am-5pm; ❀) Internet facilities and a free accommodation-booking service.

ℹ Getting There & Away

V/Line (☏13 61 96; www.vline.com.au) has train and train-bus services between Melbourne and Sale ($21, three hours, six daily) via Traralgon.

Ninety Mile Beach

To paraphrase the immortal words of Crocodile Dundee: that's not a beach...*this* is a beach. Isolated Ninety Mile Beach is a narrow strip of sand backed by dunes, and lagoons and stretching unbroken for more or less 90 miles (150km) from near McLoughlins Beach to the channel at Lakes Entrance – arguably Australia's longest single beach. The area is great for surf fishing, camping and long beach walks, though the crashing surf can be dangerous for swimming, except where patrolled at Seaspray, Woodside Beach and Lakes Entrance.

Between Seaspray and Lakes Entrance, the Gippsland Lakes Coastal Park is a protected area of low-lying coastal shrubs, banksias and tea trees, bursting with native wildflowers in spring. Permits for remote camping can be obtained from Parks Victoria (☏13 19 63; www.parkweb.vic.gov.au).

The main access road to Ninety Mile Beach is the South Gippsland Hwy from Sale or Foster, turning off to Seaspray, Golden Beach and Loch Sport.

SEASPRAY

You'll think you've travelled back to the 1950s at this low-key, low-rise seaside village of prefab houses. It gets busy during the summer holidays but otherwise it's a quiet place with just a few shops, a cafe, holiday accommodation and a near-deserted beach.

Northeast of Seaspray are a string of superb free Parks Victoria camping grounds, just back from the dunes and with beach access. Camp sites include The Honeysuckles, Flamingo Beach, Golden Beach and Paradise Beach. They're hugely popular in summer and during holiday weekends, but at other times you can just drive straight in. Some sites have barbecues and pit toilets, but you need to bring your own water and firewood. Hot showers are available at Golden Beach ($2).

LOCH SPORT & LAKES NATIONAL PARK

⊙ Sights & Activities

The small, bushy holiday town of Loch Sport – where wallabies graze serenely on residents' front lawns – sprawls between the ocean and Lake Victoria. The main road comes to an abrupt halt at Lakes National Park, a narrow strip of coastal bushland surrounded by water. Banksia and eucalypt woodland abound, along with areas of low-lying heathland and some swampy saltmarsh scrub. In spring the park is carpeted with native wildflowers and has one of Australia's best displays of native orchids. A loop road through the park provides good vehicle access, and there are well-marked walking trails. Point Wilson, at the eastern tip of the mainland section of the park, is the best picnic spot and a popular gathering place for kangaroos. Industrial-strength mosquito repellent is a must here.

Sleeping & Eating

90 Mile Beach Holiday Retreat
CARAVAN PARK $

(☑5146 0320; www.90milebeachholidayretreat.com; Track 10, off Golden Beach-Loch Sport Rd; unpowered/powered sites from $26/30, lodge & cottage d from $170) On a huge chunk of land a few kilometres from Loch Sport, this retreat has 2.4km of pristine beach frontage, lots of camp sites and spacious, airy lodges. It's separated from the rest of the world by 6km of dirt track. The whole place is run on solar- and wind-powered generators.

Marina Hotel
PUB FARE $$

(☑5146 0666; Basin Blvd, Loch Sport; mains $16-28; ☺lunch & dinner) Perched by the lake and marina, the local pub has a friendly vibe, superb sunset views and decent seafood dishes on the bistro menu.

Emu Bight Camp Site
CAMPING GROUND $

(unpowered sites per 6 people $15) The only camping area in the park, this place has pit toilets and fireplaces but you must BYO water.

Bairnsdale

POP 11,290

Bairnsdale is East Gippsland's commercial hub and the turn-off north for the Great Alpine Rd (B500) to Omeo or south to Paynesville and Raymond Island. It's a bustling sort of town with a sprinkling of attractions, but most travellers are merely passing through on the way to the coast or the mountains.

Sights & Activities

Krowathunkoolong Keeping Place
(☑5152 1891; 37-53 Dalmahoy St; adult/child/family $6/4/15; ☺9am-5pm Mon-Fri) is a stirring and insightful Koorie cultural exhibition space that explores Kurnai life from the Dreaming until after European settlement. The exhibition traces the Kurnai clan from their Dreaming ancestors, Borun the pelican and his wife Tuk the musk duck, and covers life at Lake Tyers Mission, east of Lakes Entrance, now a trust privately owned by Aboriginal shareholders. The massacres of the Kurnai from 1839 to 1849 are also detailed.

East Gippsland Art Gallery
FREE

(☑5153 1988; www.eastgippslandartgallery.org.au; 2 Nicholson St; ☺10am-4pm Tue-Fri, to 2pm Sat) is a bright, open space that has regular exhibitions, mostly featuring the work of East Gippsland artists. St Mary's Church (Main St) is worth a look inside for the ornate Italian frescoes on the ceiling and walls.

On the edge of town (signposted from the highway at the roundabout as you arrive in Bairnsdale from the west) is the MacLeod Morass Boardwalk, an internationally recognised wetland reserve with walking tracks and bird hides.

Sleeping & Eating

Comfort Inn Riversleigh
HOTEL $$

(☑5152 6966; www.riversleigh.info; 1 Nicholson St; d incl breakfast $135-165; ❄) This Victorian-era boutique hotel offers elegant rooms with heritage furnishings. Breakfast is served in the sunny conservatory, and there's also a formal restaurant here (mains $25 to $38, open for lunch and dinner Monday to Saturday), maximising the use of local ingredients in inventive, modern cuisine.

Mitchell Gardens Holiday Park
CARAVAN PARK $

(☑5152 4654; www.mitchellgardens.com.au; unpowered/powered sites from $23/26, cabins d $56-140; ❄❄) East of the town centre on the

---

EAST GIPPSLAND RAIL TRAIL

The **East Gippsland Rail Trail** (www.eastgippslandrailtrail.com) is a 97km walking/cycling path along the former railway line between Bairnsdale and Orbost, passing through Bruthen and Nowa Nowa and close to a number of other small communities. The trail passes through undulating farmland, temperate rainforest, the Colquhoun Forest and some impressive timber bridges. On a bike the trail can comfortably be done in two days, but allow longer to explore the countryside and perhaps detour on the Gippsland Lakes Discovery Trail to Lakes Entrance. Arty Nowa Nowa is a real biking community, with a new mountain bike park and trails leading off the main rail trail. There are plans to extend the trail from Orbost down to Marlo along the Snowy River.

If you don't have your own bike, **Snowy River Cycling** (☑0428 556 088; www.snowyrivercycling.com.au) offers self-guided tours with a bike (from $30), map and transfers ($25) plus luggage transport. They also run guided cycle adventures.

banks of the Mitchell River, this is a friendly, shady park. The deluxe cabins have a lovely outlook over the Mitchell River.

Grand Terminus Hotel PUB FARE **$$**
(☑5152 4040; www.grandterminus.com.au; 98 McLeod St; s/d $65/75; mains $13-26; ⊙lunch & dinner) This grand old corner pub serves above-average bistro meals with thoughtful pasta and seafood dishes and favourites such as lamb shanks. The upstairs rooms with bathrooms are excellent value.

River Grill MODERN AUSTRALIAN **$$**
(☑5153 1421; 2 Wood St; mains $25-36; ⊙lunch & dinner Mon-Sat) Fine dining with flair comes to Bairnsdale in the form of rustic River Grill, offering contemporary food with a Mediterranean touch.

ℹ Information
Bairnsdale visitor centre (☑1800 637 060, 5152 3444; www.discovereastgippsland.com.au; 240 Main St; ⊙9am-5pm; @) Next to St Mary's Church; free accommodation-booking service.

ℹ Getting There & Away
Bairnsdale is the last stop on the Gippsland rail line. **V/Line** (☑13 61 96; www.vline.com.au) runs trains between Melbourne and Bairnsdale ($25, 3½ hours, three daily). Buses continue on to Lakes Entrance ($6, 40 minutes, three daily) and Orbost ($14, 1¼ hours, one daily).

Paynesville & Raymond Island

◉ Sights & Activities
Paynesville is a relaxed little lake town where life is all about the water, and some residents have their luxury boats moored right outside their house on purpose-built canals. A good reason to detour here is to take the ferry on the five-minute hop across to Raymond Island for some koala spotting. There's a large colony of koalas here, mostly relocated from Phillip Island in the 1950s. The flat-bottom car and passenger ferry operates every half-hour from 7am to 11pm and is free for pedestrians and cyclists.

Several operators hire out boats. **Aquamania** (☑0417 163 365; www.aquamania.com.au) organises boat tours, waterski and wakeboard instruction, and operates a water taxi.

The popular **Paynesville Jazz Festival** (www.paynesvillejazzfestival.com.au) happens on the last weekend in February.

🛏 Sleeping & Eating
Mariners Cove MOTEL **$$**
(☑5156 7444; www.marinerscoveresort.com; d/f $135/165, apt $160-205; ❋) These bright, sunny waterside motel-style units are well located near the Raymond Island ferry. Boat hire is available from $60 for two hours.

Café Espas CAFE **$$**
(☑5156 7275; Raymond Island Foreshore; mains $29-35; ⊙lunch Fri-Sun, dinner Fri & Sat) Over on Raymond Island (turn left off the ferry), Espas has a real island vibe with the owner's artworks on the walls and a well-prepared global menu from Thai seafood salad to paella.

Fisherman's Wharf Pavilion
  CAFE, SEAFOOD **$$**
(☑5156 0366; 70 The Esplanade; lunch $8-24, dinner $24-45; ⊙breakfast & lunch Wed-Sun, dinner Wed-Sat) Perched over the water and with an al fresco deck, this airy cafe is a sublime place for a breakfast of pancakes or a quiche for lunch on a sunny day. By night it's a fine-dining steak-and-seafood restaurant, using fresh, local produce.

Metung
POP 730
Curling around Bancroft Bay, little Metung is one of the prettiest towns in the Lakes District – besotted locals call it the Gippsland Riviera and with its absolute waterfront location and unhurried charm it's hard to argue.

Getting out on the water is easy enough: **Riviera Nautic** (☑5156 2243; www.rivieranautic.com.au; 185 Metung Rd; motor boats per day $140, yachts per 2 days from $1210) hires out boats and yachts for cruising, fishing and sailing on the Gippsland Lakes. At the visitor centre, **Slipway Boat Hire** (☑5156 2969) has small motor boats for hire from $55 per hour to $165 per day, including fuel.

If you'd rather take it easy, take a cruise on board the **Director** (☑5156 2628; www.thedirector.com.au; 2½hr cruise adult/child/family $45/10/105; ⊙departs 3pm Tue, Thu & Sat) to Ninety Mile Beach and back.

At high noon pelicans fly in like dive bombers for fish issued outside the Metung Hotel. Pelicans can tell time – or at least when to get a free feed.

🛏 Sleeping
The only budget accommodation is at the Metung Hotel. The nearest camping ground is up the road at Swan Reach.

McMillans of Metung RESORT $$$
(②5156 2283; www.mcmillansofmetung.com.au; 155 Metung Rd; cottages $145-440, villas $185-415; ✱☎✽) This swish lakeside resort has won stacks of tourism awards for its complex of English country–style cottages set in 3 hectares of manicured gardens, modern villas, private marina and spa centre.

Moorings at Metung APARTMENTS $$$
(②5156 2750; www.themoorings.com.au; 44 Metung Rd; apt $150-390; ✱✽) At the end of the road in Metung village and with water views to either Lake King or Bancroft Bay, this contemporary apartment complex has a range of apartments from spacious studios to two-bedroom, split-level townhouses. Outside the peak season it's good value, with a tennis court, indoor and outdoor pools, spa and marina.

Metung Holiday Villas CABINS $$
(②5156 2306; www.metungholidayvillas.com; cnr Mairburn & Stirling Rds; cabins $110-160; ✱✽) Metung's former caravan park has reinvented itself as a minivillage of semiluxury cabins and one of the best deals in Metung.

✖ Eating

Metung Galley CAFE $$
(②5156 2330; www.themetunggalley.com.au; 50 Metung Rd; lunch $10-22, dinner $21-31; ☉breakfast & lunch daily, dinner Wed-Mon) Felicity and Richard's city hospitality experience shines through in this friendly, innovative cafe, serving up beautifully presented, quality food using local ingredients such as fresh seafood and Gippsland lamb. Recently expanding the cafe into new premises, they've also added a wine bar, and a deli and provedore across the road.

Bancroft Bites CAFE $$
(②5156 2854; www.bancroftbites.com.au; 2/57 Metung Rd; lunch $9-20, dinner $17-32; ☉breakfast, lunch & dinner Thu-Tue) New on the Metung scene, this is another seriously good cafe-by-day, fine-dining-by-night place. Seafood chowder and glazed roast duck grace the contemporary menu.

Metung Hotel PUB FARE $$
(②5156 2206; www.metunghotel.com.au; 1 Kurnai Ave; mains $20-32; ☉lunch & dinner) You can't beat the location overlooking Metung Wharf, and the big windows and outdoor timber decking make the most of the water views. The bistro serves top-notch pub food.

The hotel also has the cheapest rooms in town, with basic doubles for $85 and a bunk room for $30 per person.

❶ Information

Metung visitor centre (②5156 2969; www.metungtourism.com.au; 3/50 Metung Rd; ☉9am-5pm) Accommodation-booking and boat-hire services.

Lakes Entrance

POP 4100

With the shallow Cunninghame Arm waterway separating town from the crashing ocean beaches, Lakes Entrance basks in an undeniably pretty location, but in holiday season it's a packed-out tourist town with a graceless strip of motels, caravan parks, minigolf courses and souvenir shops lining the Esplanade. Still, the bobbing fishing boats, fresh seafood, endless beaches and cruises out to Metung and Wyanga Park Winery should easily win you over. There's plenty here for families and kids, and out of season there's an unhurried pace and accommodation bargains.

The town is named for the channel, artificially created in 1889 to provide ocean access from the lakes system and create a harbour for fishing boats.

◉ Sights & Activities

Lakes Entrance is all about the beach and boating. A long footbridge crosses the Cunninghame Arm inlet from the east of town to the ocean and **Ninety Mile Beach**. From December to Easter, paddle boats, canoes and sailboats can be hired by the footbridge on the ocean side. This is also where the **Eastern Beach Walking Track** (2.3km, 45 minutes) starts, taking you through coastal scrub to the entrance itself.

To explore the lakes, three companies along Marine Pde (on the back-side of the town centre) offer **boat hires** (hire per 1/4/8hr $50/90/150).

On the Princes Hwy on the western side of town is **Kalimna Lookout**, a popular viewing spot with coin-operated binoculars. For an even better view of the ocean and inlet (and a quieter location), take the road directly opposite to **Jemmy's Point Lookout**.

Surfing lessons (gear provided) are run by the **Surf Shack** (②5155 4933; 507 The Esplanade; 2hr lesson $50) at nearby Lake Tyers Beach.

For a bit of indulgence, **Illuka Day Spa** (☎5155 3533; www.illukadayspa.com.au; 1 The Esplanade; ☺9am-5pm Sat-Mon, Wed & Thu, to 8pm Tue, to 7pm Fri), at the Esplanade Resort, has a range of massage therapies, facials and seaweed scrubs from $70.

☞ Tours

Several companies offer cruises on the lakes:

Corque   WINE
(☎5155 1508; www.wyangapark.com.au; lunch/dinner cruise $50/75; ☺lunch daily, dinner Fri & Sat) Among the most enjoyable trips

are the daily lunch and weekend dinner cruises to Wyanga Park Winery. As well as enjoying a relaxing cruise and tasting wine on board, you get to dine at the beautifully located winery. On Thursday the lunch cruise goes via Metung ($55); tours leave from Post Office Jetty.

Lonsdale Cruises   CRUISE
(☎5155 2889; Post Office Jetty; 3hr cruise adult/child/family $45/25/99; ☺1pm) Scenic eco-cruises out to Metung and Lake King on a former Queenscliff–Sorrento passenger ferry.

Lakes Entrance

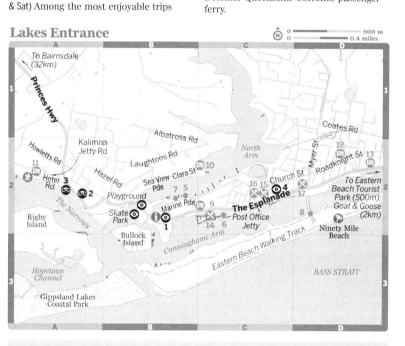

Ⓝ 0 ——————— 800 m
0 ——————— 0.4 miles

Mulloway Fishing Charters FISHING
(☏0427 943 154, 5155 3304; 3hr cruise adult/child $50/25) Fishing cruises departing the jetty opposite 66 Marine Pde. Rods, tackle, bait and morning or afternoon tea provided.

Peels Lake Cruises CRUISE
(☏5155 1246; Post Office Jetty; 4hr Metung lunch cruise adult/child $48/13; ⊘depart 11am) This long-running operator has daily lunch cruises aboard the *Stormbird* to Metung.

 Sea Safari ECO-CRUISE
(☏5155 5027; www.lakes-explorer.com.au; Post Office Jetty; 1/2hr cruise $12/20) These safaris aboard the *Lakes Explorer* have a focus on research and ecology, identifying and counting seabirds, testing water for salinity levels and learning about marine life.

✵ Festivals & Events
The **Seafarers Multicultural Festival** (www.seafarersfestival.com.au), in early December, celebrates the region's culture and fishing industry with a multicultural parade, a Koorie art festival, music and boat races.

🛏 Sleeping
Lakes Entrance has stacks of accommodation, much of it your typical motels, holiday apartments and caravan parks squeezed cheek by jowl along the Esplanade. Prices more than double during holiday periods (book ahead), but there are good discounts out of season.

Déjà Vu B&B $$$
(☏5155 4330; www.dejavu.com.au; 17 Clara St; d $165-300; ✳✉) This imposing, sandstone-coloured, modern home has been built on the slope of a hill to maximise water views, and the lush native garden ensures privacy. Choose from the views of the designer ocean-view apartments, waterfront boathouse or B&B studios.

Goat & Goose B&B $$
(☏5155 3079; www.goatandgoose.com; 16 Gay St; d $160) Bass Strait views are maximised at this wonderfully unusual, multistorey, timber pole–framed house. The friendly owners are long-time locals, and all the gorgeously quaint rooms have spas.

Kalimna Woods COTTAGE $$
(☏5155 1957; www.kalimnawoods.com.au; Kalimna Jetty Rd; d $125-220; ✳) Retreat 2km from the town centre to Kalimna Woods, set in a large rainforest-and-bush garden, complete with friendly resident possums and birds. These self-contained country-style cottages with either spa or wood-burning fireplace are spacious, private and cosy.

Eastern Beach Tourist Park CARAVAN PARK $
(☏5155 1581; www.easternbeach.com.au; 42 Eastern Beach Rd; unpowered/powered sites from $24/29, cabins $110-240; @✉) Most caravan parks in Lakes pack 'em in, but this one has space, grassy sites and a great location away from the hubbub of town in a bush setting back from Eastern Beach. A walking track takes you into town (30 minutes). New facilities are excellent, including a camp kitchen, barbecues and a kids playground.

Lazy Acre Log Cabins CABINS $$
(☏5155 1323; www.lazyacre.com; 35 Roadknight St; d/f $105/125; ✳✉✉) These small, self-contained timber cabins are shaded with old gum trees, and it's a friendly, relaxed place to stay. There are bicycle-hire and babysitting services, and disabled access is available. Rates double in peak holiday periods.

Bellevue on the Lakes HOTEL $$
(☏5155 3055; www.bellevuelakes.com; 201 The Esplanade; d from $159, apt $229; ✳✉✉) Right in the heart of the Esplanade, Bellevue brings a bit of style to the strip with neatly furnished rooms in earthy tones, most with water views. For extra luxury, go for the spacious spa suites or two-bedroom self-contained apartments. The Boathouse Restaurant has a reputation for good seafood.

Riviera Backpackers YHA HOSTEL $
(☏5155 2444; www.yha.com.au; 660-671 The Esplanade; YHA members dm/s/d $23/35/50; @✉) This well-located YHA has clean rooms in old-style brick units, each with two or three bedrooms and a bathroom. There's a big communal kitchen and lounge with pool table and internet access. Bike and fishing-rod hire are available and the owners can sometimes arrange work.

Lakes Beachfront Holiday Retreat
CARAVAN PARK $
(☏5156 5582; www.lakesbeachfront.com.au; 430 Lake Tyers Beach Rd; unpowered/powered sites $30/35, cabin d $110-195, villas $220-350; ✳✉) At pretty Lake Tyers, 11km east of Lakes Entrance, these camp sites are as good as you'll find, surrounded by bush and just a short stroll to the beach.

✕ Eating & Drinking

With the largest fishing fleet in the state, Lakes Entrance is a great place to indulge in fresh seafood. You can sometimes buy shellfish (prawns, bugs) straight from local boats (look for signs) or try Ferryman's. **Omega 3** (Shop 5, Safeway Arcade, Church St) is the shop front for the local Fishermen's Co-op, so the seafood is always fresh.

The best cafe strip is on the Esplanade and around the corner on Myer St, right opposite the Cunninghame Arm footbridge.

Ferryman's Seafood Café   SEAFOOD **$$**
(☎5155 3000; www.ferrymans.com.au; Middle Harbour, The Esplanade; lunch $14-22, dinner $25-42; ⊙brunch, lunch & dinner) It's hard to beat the ambience of dining on the deck of this floating cafe-restaurant, which will fill you to the gills with fish and seafood dishes, including good ol' fish and chips. It's child-friendly and downstairs you can buy fresh seafood, including prawns and crayfish (from 8.30am to 5pm).

Six Sisters & A Pigeon   CAFE **$**
(☎5155 1144; 567 The Esplanade; mains $7-17; ⊙breakfast & lunch Tue-Sun; ⚡) The name alone should guide you to this quirky, licensed cafe on the Esplanade opposite the footbridge. Good coffee, all-day breakfasts – Mexican eggs, French toast or Spanish omelettes – and lunches of focaccias, baguettes and light mains with an Asian-Italian influence.

Miriam's Restaurant   STEAKHOUSE **$$**
(☎5155 3999; cnr The Esplanade & Bulmer St; mains $16-34; ⊙dinner) The upstairs dining room at Miriam's overlooks the Esplanade, and the Gippsland steaks, local seafood dishes and casual cocktail-bar atmosphere are excellent.

Pinocchio Inn   ITALIAN **$**
(☎5155 2565; 569 The Esplanade; pizza & pasta $12-25; ⊙dinner) When you've had enough seafood and only pizza will do, Pinocchio's is a long-running place in the cafe strip. It's also a bar but offers BYO wine for diners – good value.

Waterwheel Beach Tavern   PUB FARE **$$**
(☎5156 5855; www.waterwheeltavern.com; 577 Beach Rd, Lake Tyers; mains $18-32; ⊙lunch & dinner) It's worth the trip out to Lake Tyers, 10 minutes' drive from Lakes Entrance, for a beer at this beachside pub. The setting is superb and the bistro food is classy but unpretentious – Tuesday is steak night, Wednesday parma night.

ℹ Information

Lakes Entrance visitor centre (☎1800 637 060, 5155 1966; www.discovereastgippsland. com.au; cnr Princes Hwy & Marine Pde; ⊙9am-5pm) Free accommodation- and tour-booking services. Also check out www.lakes entrance.com.

The Hub (☎5155 4247; cnr Myer St & The Esplanade; ⊙9.30am-5pm Mon-Fri, 10am-2pm Sat; per hr $5; 🛜) Internet cafe in a quirky, aroma-scented fashion shop.

Lakes Entrance Library (☎5153 9500; 18 Mechanics St; ⊙8.30am-5pm Mon-Fri; @) Free internet access.

ℹ Getting There & Away

V/Line (☎13 61 96; www.vline.com.au) runs a train-bus service from Melbourne to Lakes Entrance via Bairnsdale ($29, 4½ hours, three daily).

EAST GIPPSLAND & THE WILDERNESS COAST

Beyond Lakes Entrance stretches a wilderness area of spectacular coastal national parks and old-growth forest. Much of this region has never been cleared for agriculture and contains some of the most remote and pristine national parks in the state, making logging in these ancient forests a hot issue.

Orbost is the main town and gateway to the Snowy River and Errinundra National Parks, but it's beyond here that things start to get interesting. The magnificent coastal areas of Cape Conran, Croajingolong and Mallacoota are all uncrowded, unspoilt and undeveloped, and even on the highway the winding forest drive to the state's most easterly point is magnificent.

Buchan

POP 330

The sleepy town of Buchan, in the foothills of the Snowy Mountains, is famous for the spectacular and intricate limestone cave system at the **Buchan Caves Reserve**, open to visitors for almost a century. Underground rivers cutting through ancient limestone rock formed the caves and caverns, and they provided shelter for Aboriginal people as far back as 18,000 years ago. **Parks Victoria** (☎5162 1900; www.parks.vic. gov.au; tours adult/child/family $15/9/41; ⊙10am, 11.15am, 1pm, 2.15pm & 3.30pm Oct-Easter, 11am,

1pm & 3pm Easter-Sep) runs guided caves tours daily, alternating between Royal and Fairy Caves. They're both impressive: Royal has more colour, a higher chamber and extinct kangaroo remains; Fairy has more delicate decorations and potential fairy sightings. Tours to both caves cost $22/13/61 per adult/child/family. The rangers also offer hard-hat guided tours to the less-developed Federal Cave during the high season. The reserve itself is a pretty spot with shaded picnic areas, **walking tracks** and grazing kangaroos. Invigoration is guaranteed when taking a dip in the icy **rock pool**.

Sleeping & Eating

Buchan Caves Reserve   CAMPING GROUND $
(5162 1900; www.parks.vic.gov.au; Buchan Caves Reserve; unpowered/powered sites $18/24, cabin d $77, wilderness retreat d $150;) You can stay right by the caves at this serene Parks Victoria camping ground edged by state forest. There are a couple of standard cabins, plus safari-style tents providing a 'luxury' wilderness experience (think comfortable queen-size bed) without having to pitch your own tent.

Buchan Lodge   HOSTEL $
(5155 9421; www.buchanlodge.com.au; 9 Saleyard Rd; dm $20) A short walk from the caves and the town centre, and just by the river, this welcoming pine-log backpackers is great for lounging about and taking in the country views. It boasts a big country-style kitchen, convivial lounge and campfires out the back.

Caves Hotel   PUB FARE $$
(5155 9203; 49 Main St; mains $16-26; lunch & dinner) This century-old timber pub is a good place for a drink and serves decent bistro meals.

Getting There & Away

Buchan is an easy drive 56km north of Lakes Entrance. **Buchan Bus 'n' Freight** (5155 0356) operates a service on Wednesday and Friday from Bairnsdale to Buchan ($17, 1¾ hours, three weekly). It meets the train at Bairnsdale. At other times you'll need your own transport.

Snowy River National Park

Northeast of Buchan, this is one of Victoria's most isolated and spectacular national parks, dominated by deep gorges carved through limestone and sandstone by the Snowy River on its route from the Snowy Mountains in NSW to its mouth at Marlo. The entire park is a smorgasbord of unspoilt, superb bush and mountain scenery. It covers more than 95,000 hectares and includes a huge diversity of vegetation, ranging from alpine woodlands and eucalypt forests to rainforests. Abundant wildlife includes the rare brush-tailed rock wallaby.

On the west side of the park, the views from the well-signposted cliff-top lookouts over **Little River Falls** and **Little River Gorge**, Victoria's deepest gorge, are awesome. From there it's about 20km to **McKillops Bridge**, a huge bridge spanning the Snowy River, making it possible to drive across the park to Errinundra National Park. There are also some sandy river beaches and swimming spots, and several good **short walks** around here. The hilly and difficult **Silver Mine Walking Track** (15km, six hours) starts at the eastern end of the bridge. Walking and canoeing are the most popular activities, but you need to be well prepared for both – conditions can be harsh and subject to sudden change. The classic canoe or raft trip down the Snowy River from McKillops Bridge to a pull-out point near Buchan takes at least four days and offers superb scenery: rugged gorges, raging rapids, tranquil sections and excellent camping spots on broad sandbars.

Sleeping

There is free camping at a number of basic sites around the park, but the main site is **McKillops Bridge**. It's a beautiful spot and has toilets and fireplaces.

Karoonda Park   CABINS $
(5155 0220; www.karoondapark.com; 3558 Gelantipy Rd; dm $30, s/d $50/70, cabins per 6 people $115;) At Gelantipy, 40km north of Buchan on the road to Snowy River National Park, this cattle-and-sheep property has comfortable backpacker and cabin digs. Rates include breakfast; other meals are available. Activities available include abseiling, horse riding, wild caving, white-water rafting, mountain-bike hire and farm activities.

Getting There & Away

The two main access roads to the park are the Buchan-Jindabyne Rd from Buchan, and the Bonang Rd from Orbost. These roads are joined by McKillops Rd (also known as Deddick Valley Rd), which runs across the northern border of the park from Bonang to just south of Wulgulmerang. Various access roads and scenic routes run into and alongside the park from these three main roads. The 43km Deddick Trail, which runs through the middle of the park, is only suitable for 4WDs.

Buchan Bus 'n' Freight (☏5155 0356) operates a bus service from Bairnsdale to Karoonda Park (via Buchan) on Wednesday and Friday ($23, 2¾ hours).

Errinundra National Park

Errinundra National Park contains Victoria's largest cool-temperate rainforest and is one of east Gippsland's most outstanding natural areas. The forests surrounding the park are a constant battleground between loggers and environmentalists.

The national park covers an area of 25,600 hectares and has three granite outcrops that extend into the cloud, resulting in high rainfall, deep, fertile soils and a network of creeks and rivers that flow north, south and east. The park has several climatic zones – some areas of the park are quite dry, while its peaks regularly receive snow. This is a rich habitat for native birds and animals, which include many rare and endangered species such as the potoroo.

◉ Sights & Activities

You can explore the park by a combination of scenic drives, and short- and medium-length walks. Mt Ellery has spectacular views; Errinundra Saddle has a rainforest boardwalk; and from Ocean View Lookout there are stunning views down the Goolengook River

as far as the town of Bemm River. The park also has **mountain plum pines**, some of which are more than 400 years old, are easily accessible from Goonmirk Rocks Rd.

Nestled by the edge of the national park is tiny Goongerah (population 50), where there's a thriving community with two active community environmental organisations.

Goongerah Environment Centre (☏5154 0156; www.geco.org.au) organises ongoing protests and blockades in the forest surrounding the park and has detailed information about park drives and walks on its website.

Environment East Gippsland (☏5154 0145; www.eastgippsland.net.au), the other community group, lobbies extensively on forest issues.

⌂ Sleeping

FREE **Frosty Hollow Camp Site**
CAMPING GROUND $
(☏13 16 93; free camping) This is the only camping area within the national park, on the eastern side. There are also free camping areas on the park's edges – at Ellery Creek in Goongerah and at Delegate River.

Jacarri COTTAGES $
(☏5154 0145; www.eastgippsland.net.au/jacarri; cnr Bonang Hwy & Ellery Creek Track, Goongerah; d/f $80/90) This gorgeous little cottage, made from recycled and plantation timber, is on noted environmentalist and Greens party candidate Jill Redwood's organic farm. It's solar powered, has a slow combustion stove for heating and cooking, and sleeps four.

OFF THE BEATEN TRACK

You can't access most of the Snowy River or Errinundra National Parks with a 2WD, and sections of Croajingolong are only open to a limited numbers of walkers – sometimes the easiest way to see these beautiful wilderness areas is with an organised tour.

An ecotourism award winner, Gippsland High Country Tours (☏5157 5556; www.gippslandhighcountrytours.com.au) is an East Gippsland–based company running easy, moderate and challenging five- to seven-day hikes in Errinundra, Snowy River and Croajingolong National Parks. The Croajingolong trips include three nights' accommodation in the Point Hicks Lighthouse. There's also a five-day bird-watching tour in Snowy River country.

Snowy River Expeditions (☏5155 0220; www.karoondapark.com/sre; Karoonda Park, Gelantipy; tours per day from $85) is an established company, running adventure tours including one-, two- or four-day rafting trips on the Snowy. Half- or full-day abseiling or caving trips are also available. Costs include transport, meals and camping gear.

A mostly volunteer-run organisation based in Orbost, Wilderness Bike Ride (☏0427 859 959; www.wildernessbikeride.com.au) runs a three- or four-day mountain-bike ride as well as other events throughout the year.

ℹ️ Getting There & Around

The main access roads to the park are Bonang Rd from Orbost and Errinundra Rd from Club Terrace. Bonang Rd passes along the western side of the park, while Errinundra Rd passes through the centre. Road conditions are variable and the roads are often closed or impassable during the winter months or after floods (check Parks Victoria in Orbost or Bendoc first) and watch out for logging trucks. Roads within the park are all unsealed, but are 2WD accessible. Expect seasonal closures between June and November, though roads can deteriorate quickly at any time of year after rain.

Orbost

POP 2100

Orbost services the surrounding farming and forest areas. Most travellers fly through as the Princes Hwy passes just south of the town, while the Bonang Rd heads north towards the Snowy River and Errinundra National Parks, and Marlo Rd follows the Snowy River south to Marlo and continues along the coast to Cape Conran Coastal Park.

Orbost visitor information centre (☑5154 2424; cnr Nicholson & Clarke Sts; ◷9am-5pm) is in the historic 1872 Slab Hut.

The impressive **Orbost Exhibition Centre** (☑5154 2634; www.orbostexhibitioncentre.org; Clarke St; adult/child $4/free; ◷10am-4pm Mon-Sat, 1-4pm Sun), next to the visitor centre, showcases stunning works by local timber artists.

Marlo

POP 350

Rather than barrel down the highway from Orbost to Mallacoota, turn off to Marlo, a sleepy beach town at the mouth of the Snowy River just 15km south of Orbost. It's a lovely spot, popular with anglers, and the road continues on to Cape Conran Coastal Park before rejoining the highway.

Aside from the coast, the main attraction here is the **PS Curlip** (☑5154 1699; www.paddlesteamercurlip.com.au; adult/child/family $25/15/60; ◷11.30am & 2.30pm Wed-Sun), a re-creation of an 1890 paddle steamer that once chugged up the Snowy River to Orbost. The vessel was rebuilt as a community project. You can buy tickets at the general store in town.

You can't beat an afternoon beer on the expansive wooden verandah of the **Marlo Hotel** (☑5154 8201; www.marlohotel.com.au; 17 Argyle Pde; d $140, with spa $130-160) with a sublime view of the Snowy River emptying into the sea. The boutique rooms here are above average for a pub – some with spa – and the restaurant serves local seafood such as gummy shark and king prawns (mains $14 to $30).

Cape Conran Coastal Park

This blissfully undeveloped part of the coast is one of Gippsland's most beautiful corners, with long stretches of remote white-sand beaches. The 19km coastal route from Marlo to Cape Conran is particularly pretty, bordered by banksia trees, grass plains, sand dunes and the ocean.

🏃 Activities

Cape Conran is a fabulous spot for **walking**. One favourite is the nature trail that meets up with the East Cape Boardwalk, where signage gives you a glimpse into how Indigenous peoples lived in this area. Following an Indigenous theme, take the West Cape Rd off Cape Conran Rd to **Salmon Rocks**, where there's an Aboriginal **shell midden** dated at more than 10,000 years old.

For some relaxed swimming, canoeing and fishing go to the **Yeerung River**. There's good surfing at **West Cape Beach**. For qualified divers, Lakes Entrance–based **Cross Diving Services** (☑5155 1397, 0407 362 960; www.crossdiving.com.au) offers dives on most weekends (equipment hire available).

If you're staying in the park, keep an eye out for bandicoots and potoroos, whose numbers have increased in recent years following the introduction of the park's fox management program. Check out the **cabbage tree palms**, which can be accessed from a number of points and are a short detour off the road between Cape Conran and the Princes Hwy. This is Victoria's only stand of native palms – a tiny rainforest oasis.

🛏️ Sleeping

Parks Victoria (☑5154 8438; www.conran.net.au) runs the following three excellent accommodation options in Cape Conran Coastal Park:

Banksia Bluff Camping Area

CAMPING GROUND $

(unpowered sites $18-24) This camping ground is right by the foreshore, with generous sites surrounded by banksia woodlands offering shade and privacy. The camping ground has toilets, cold showers and a few fireplaces, but you'll need to bring drinking water. A ballot is held for using sites over the Christmas period.

Cape Conran Cabins
CABINS

(4 people $96-145) These self-contained cabins, which can sleep up to eight people, are surrounded by bush and are just 200m from the beach. Built from local timbers, the cabins are like oversized cubby houses with lofty mezzanines for sleeping. BYO linen.

Cape Conran Wilderness Retreat
SAFARI TENTS

(d $150) Nestled in the bush by the sand dunes are these stylish safari tents. All the simplicity of camping, but with comfortable beds and a deck outside your fly-wire door. Two-night minimum stay.

West Cape Cabins
CABINS $$

(☑5154 8296; www.westcapecabins.com; 1547 Cape Conran Rd; d/f $175/250) Crafted from locally grown or recycled timbers, these self-contained cabins a few kilometres from the park are works of art. The timbers are all labelled with their species, and even the queen-size bed bases are made from tree trunks. The outdoor spa baths add to the joy. The larger cottage sleeps eight. It's a 15-minute walk through coastal bush to an isolated beach.

Mallacoota

POP 980

One of Gippsland's, and indeed Victoria's, little gems, Mallacoota is the state's most easterly town, snuggled on the vast Mallacoota Inlet and surrounded by the tumbling hills and beachside dunes of beautiful Croajingolong National Park. Those prepared to come this far are treated to long, empty, ocean-surf beaches, tidal river mouths and swimming, fishing and boating on the inlet.

On the road in from Genoa you pass turnoffs to Gipsy Point and Karbeethong, beautiful little communities on the inlet offering a few places to stay. At Christmas and Easter Mallacoota is a crowded family holiday spot – it's certainly no secret these days – but most of the year it's pretty quiet and very relaxed.

◉ Sights & Activities

One of the best ways to experience the beauty of Mallacoota is by boat. The calm estuarine waters of Mallacoota Inlet have more than 300km of shoreline. There are many public jetties where you can tie your boat up and come ashore for picnic tables and toilets, or to take a dip. Mallacoota Hire Boats (☑0438 447 558; Main Wharf, cnr Allan & Buckland Drs; motor boats per 2/4/6hr $60/100/140) is centrally located and hires out canoes and boats. No licence required; cash only.

On Gabo Island, 14km offshore from Mallacoota, the windswept 154-hectare Gabo Island Lightstation Reserve is home to seabirds and one of the world's largest colonies of little penguins – far outnumbering those at Phillip Island. Whales, dolphins and fur seals are regularly sighted offshore. The island has an operating lighthouse, built in 1862 and the tallest in the southern hemisphere, and you can stay in the old keepers' cottages here. Mallacoota Air Services (☑0408 580 806; return per 3 adults or 2 adults & 2 children $300) offers fast access to the island on demand, or you can get there by boat with Wilderness Coast Ocean Charters (p252).

There are plenty of great short walks around the town, inlet and in the bush. It's an easy 4km walk or cycle around the inlet to Karbeethong. From there the Bucklands Jetty to Captain Creek Jetty Walk (one-way 5km, 1½ hours) follows the shoreline of the inlet past the Narrows. The Mallacoota Town Walk (7km, five hours) loops round Bastion Point, and combines five different walks. Walking notes with maps are available from the visitor centre.

For good surf, head to Bastion Point or Tip Beach. There's swimmable surf and some sheltered waters at Betka Beach, which is patrolled during Christmas school holidays. There are also good swimming spots along the beaches of the foreshore reserve, at Bastion Point and Quarry Beach.

⌖ Tours

MV Loch-Ard (☑5158 0764; Main Wharf; adult/child 2hr cruise $28/10, 3hr cruise $38/12) Runs several inlet cruises including wildlife spotting and a twilight cruise.

Porkie Bess (☑5158 0109, 0408 408 094; Karbeethong Jetty; 2hr cruise $25, fishing trip $50) A 1940s wooden boat offering fishing trips and cruises around the lakes of Mallacoota Inlet, and ferry services for hikers ($20 per person, minimum four people).

Wilderness Coast Ocean Charters (☑5158 0701, 0417 398 068; wildcoast@dragnet.com.au) Runs day trips to Gabo Island ($60, minimum eight people; $60 each way if you stay overnight) and may run trips down the coast to view the seal colony off Wingan Inlet if there's enough demand.

📖 Sleeping

There are quite a few options here, but during Easter and Christmas school holidays you'll need to book well ahead and expect prices to be significantly higher.

Adobe Mudbrick Flats GUESTHOUSE $
(☑5158 0329; www.adobeholidayflats.com.au; 17 Karbeethong Ave; d $75, q $90-140) A labour of love by Margaret and Peter Kurz, these unique mudbrick flats in Karbeethong are something special. With an emphasis on recycling and eco-friendliness, the flats have solar hot water and guests are encouraged to compost their kitchen scraps. Birds, lizards and possums can be hand-fed outside your door. The array of whimsical apartments are comfortable, well equipped and cheap. A real find.

Mallacoota Foreshore Holiday Park
CAMPING GROUND $
(☑5158 0300; www.mallacootaholidaypark.com. au; cnr Allan Dr & Maurice Ave; unpowered/powered sites $12/18, peak season from $27/32; 🛜) Curling around the waterfront, the grassy sites here morph into one of Victoria's most sociable and scenic caravan parks with sublime views of the inlet and its resident population of black swans and pelicans. No cabins, but the best of Mallacoota's many parks for campers.

Karbeethong Lodge GUESTHOUSE $$
(☑5158 0411; www.karbeethonglodge.com.au; 16 Schnapper Point Dr; d $75-220) It's hard not to be overcome by a sense of serenity as you rest on the broad verandahs of this early 1900s timber guesthouse, with uninterrupted views over Mallacoota Inlet. The large guest lounge and dining room have an open fire and period furnishings, and there's a mammoth kitchen if you want to prepare meals. The pastel-toned bedrooms are small but neat and tastefully decorated.

Mallacoota Wilderness Houseboats
HOUSEBOAT $$
(☑0409 924 016; www.mallacootawildernesshouse boats.com.au; Karbeethong Jetty; 4 nights midweek from $750, 1 week $1200-1600) These six-berth houseboats are not as luxurious as the ones you'll find on the Murray, but they are the perfect way to explore Mallacoota's waterways, and they are economical for a group or family.

Gabo Island Lighthouse COTTAGES $$
(☑Parks Victoria 13 19 63, 5161 9500; www.park web.vic.gov.au; up to 8 people $148-190) For a truly wild experience head out to stay at this remote lighthouse. Accommodation is available in the three-bedroom Assistant Lighthouse Keeper's residence. Watch for migrating whales in autumn and late spring. Pods of dolphins and seals basking on the rocks are also regular sightings. There's a two-night minimum stay, and a ballot for use during the Christmas and Easter holidays.

Mallacoota Hotel Motel MOTEL $$
(☑5158 0455; www.mallacootahotel.com.au; 51-55 Maurice Ave; motel s/d from $75/95, self-contained unit d/tw $115/125; ❄🏊) The neat, good-value motel units next to the hotel orbit a lawn area and swimming pool. There are a range of standard rooms, but all have mod cons.

🍴 Eating & Drinking

Most visitors consider the best eating to be the fish you catch yourself; otherwise there are a few good places along Maurice Ave.

Lucy's CAFE $
(☑5158 0666; 64 Maurice Ave; dishes $10-20; ⏲8am-9pm; @) Lucy's is popular for the delicious and great-value homemade rice noodles with chicken, prawn or abalone, as well as dumplings. It's also good for breakfast.

Croajingolong Cafe CAFE $
(☑5158 0098; Shop 3, 14 Allan Dr; mains $5-14; ⏲breakfast & lunch Tue-Sun; 🛜) Overlooking the inlet, this is the place to spread out the newspaper over coffee, baguettes or a pancake breakfast.

Mallacoota Hotel PUB FARE $$
(☑5158 0455; 51-55 Maurice Ave; mains $17-30; ⏲lunch & dinner) The local pub bistro serves hearty meals from its varied menu, with reliable favourites such as chicken parmigiana and Gippsland steak. Bands play regularly in the summer.

ℹ️ Information

Mallacoota visitor centre (☑5158 0800; www.visitmallacoota.com.au; Main Wharf, cnr Allan & Buckland Dr; ⏲10am-4pm) Operated by friendly volunteers.

Mallacoota Newsagency (☑5158 0888; 14 Allan Dr; ⏲8am-5pm Mon-Sat, to noon Sun; @🛜) Internet access $2.50 per 15 minutes.

ℹ️ Getting There & Away

Mallacoota is 23km southeast of Genoa (on the Princes Hwy). From Melbourne, take the train to Bairnsdale, then the V/Line bus to Genoa ($27, 3½ hours, one daily). **Mallacoota–Genoa Bus Service** (☑0408 315 615) meets the V/Line coach on Monday, Thursday and Friday, plus Sunday during school holidays, and runs to Mallacoota ($4, 30 minutes).

Croajingolong National Park

Croajingolong is one of Australia's finest coastal wilderness national parks, recognised by its listing as a World Biosphere Reserve by Unesco (one of 12 in Australia). The park covers 87,500 hectares, stretching for about 100km from the town of Bemm River to the NSW border. Magnificent, unspoilt beaches, inlets, estuaries and forests make it an ideal park for camping, walking, swimming and surfing. The five inlets, Sydenham, Tamboon, Mueller, Wingan and Mallacoota (the largest and most accessible), are popular canoeing and fishing spots.

Two sections of the park have been declared wilderness areas (which means no vehicles, access to a limited number of walkers only and permits required): the Cape Howe Wilderness Area, between Mallacoota Inlet and the NSW border, and the Sandpatch Wilderness Area, between Wingan Inlet and Shipwreck Creek. The Wilderness Coast Walk, only for the well prepared and intrepid, starts at Sydenham Inlet by Bemm River and heads along the coast to Mallacoota (you can start anywhere in between). Thurra River is a good starting point, making the walk an easy-to-medium hike (59km, five days) to Mallacoota.

Croajingolong is a bird-watcher's paradise, with more than 300 recorded species (including glossy black cockatoos and the rare ground parrot), while the inland waterways are home to myriad water birds, such as the delicate azure kingfisher and the magnificent sea eagle. There are also many small mammals here, including possums, bandicoots and gliders, and some huge goannas.

Park vegetation ranges from typical coastal landscapes to thick eucalypt forests, with areas of warm-temperate rainforest. The heathland areas are filled with impressive displays of orchids and wildflowers in the spring.

Point Hicks was the first part of Australia to be spotted by Captain Cook and the *Endeavour* crew in 1770, and was named after Lieutenant Zachary Hicks. There's a lighthouse (☎5158 4268; www.pointhicks.com. au) here and accommodation in the old cottages. You can still see remains of the SS *Saros*, which ran ashore in 1937, on a short walk from the lighthouse.

Access roads of varying quality lead into the park from the Princes Hwy. Apart from Mallacoota Rd, all roads are unsealed and can be very rough in winter, so check road conditions with Parks Victoria before venturing on, especially during or after rain.

🛏 Sleeping

The park's main camping areas are listed below. Given their amazing beauty, these camping grounds are surprisingly quiet, and bookings only need to be made for the Christmas and Easter holiday periods, when sites are issued on a ballot system. Wingan and Shipwreck can be booked through Parks Victoria (☎13 19 63); Thurra and Mueller through Point Hicks Lighthouse.

Wingan Inlet (unpowered sites $17) This serene and secluded site has superb sandy beaches and great walks. The Wingan River Walk (5km, 2½ hours return) through rainforest has great waterholes for swimming.

Shipwreck Creek (unpowered sites $17) Only 15km from Mallacoota, this is a beautiful camping ground set in forest above a sandy beach. It's a small area with just five sites, and there are lots of short walks to do here.

Mueller Inlet (unpowered sites $20) The calm waters here are fantastic for kayaking and swimming, and the camp sites are only a few metres from the water. It has eight sites, three of them walk in, but it's the only camping ground without fireplaces. There's no vegetation providing privacy, but outside Christmas and Easter holidays it's usually quiet.

Thurra River (unpowered sites $20) This is the largest of the park's camping grounds, with 46 well-designed sites stretched along the foreshore from the river towards the lighthouse. Most of the sites are separated by bush, and there are communal fireplaces and pit toilets.

Point Hicks Lighthouse COTTAGES $$ (☎5158 4268, 5156 0432; www.pointhicks.com.au; bungalow $100-120, cottage $330) This remote lighthouse has two comfortable, heritage-listed cottages and one double bungalow which originally housed the Assistant Lighthouse Keepers. The cottages sleep six people and have sensational ocean views and wood-burning fireplaces.

ℹ Information

Parks Victoria (☎13 19 63, Cann River 5158 6351, Mallacoota 5161 9500; www.parkweb.vic.gov.au) Contact offices in Cann River or Mallacoota for information on road conditions, overnight hiking, camping permits and track notes.

The High Country

Best Places to Eat

» Mansfield Regional Produce Store (p261)

» Provenance (p266)

» King River Café (p263)

» Butter Factory (p268)

» Simone's Restaurant (p271)

Best Places to Stay

» Freeman on Ford (p266)

» Odd Frog (p270)

» Dreamers (p273)

» Houseboat on Lake Eildon (p258)

» Camping, Mt Buffalo (p268)

Why Go?

If you're looking for adventure, you've found the right place. The Great Dividing Range – Australia's eastern mountain spine – curls around eastern Victoria from the Snowy Mountains to the Grampians, peaking in the spectacular High Country. These are Victoria's Alps – a mountain playground attracting skiers and snowboarders in winter and bushwalkers and mountain bikers in summer. Although not particularly high – the highest point is Mt Bogong at 1986m – the mountain air is clear and invigorating, winter snowfalls usually reliable and the scenery spectacular.

There are plenty of year-round activities on offer here, but it's the ski resorts that really pull the crowds. Mt Buller, Mt Hotham and Falls Creek in particular all have good infrastructure. Away from the mountain tops, the High Country offers plenty of summer activities from horse riding, canoeing, abseiling and mountain-bike riding to the more restful pastimes of touring the wineries and gourmet regions of Milawa, the King Valley and Beechworth.

When to Go
Point Hicks

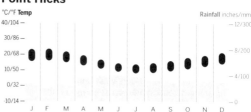

Winter Hit the snowy mountain slopes; July/August is peak season

Apr–May Best time for glorious Autumn colours around Bright and Omeo

Dec–Feb The green season for mountain-biking, horse riding and wine touring

BAW BAW NATIONAL PARK

Baw Baw National Park, an offshoot of the Great Dividing Range, is the southernmost part of Victoria's High Country and is technically in West Gippsland. The Baw Baw Plateau and the forested valleys of the Thomson and Aberfeldy Rivers, are a wonderful places for bushwalking, with marked tracks through subalpine vegetation, ranging from open eucalypt stands to wet gullies and tall forests on the plateau. The 3km **Mushroom Rocks Walk** from Mt Erica car park leads to huge granite tors (blocks of granite broken off from the massif). The highest points are **Mt St Phillack** (1566m) and **Mt Baw Baw** (1564m). The higher sections of the park are snow-covered in winter, when everyone heads for Baw Baw Village ski resort and the **Mt St Gwinear** cross-country skiing area.

There is a camping area in the northeastern section of the park, with picnic tables, fireplaces and pit toilets. Dispersed free bush camping is also allowed on the Baw Baw Plateau (fuel stove only). A section of the **Australian Alps Walking Track**, which starts its 655km journey at Walhalla, passes by a few kilometres from Baw Baw Village.

Baw Baw Village

POP 11

Baw Baw is Victoria's smallest (and also cheapest) downhill-skiing resort and a relaxed option for both beginners and families. The downhill-skiing area is set over 35 hectares with a vertical drop of 140m and seven ski lifts. Baw Baw is also a base for cross-country skiing, with plenty of trails, including one that connects to the Mt St Gwinear trails on the southern edge of the plateau. In winter the day car park costs weekday/weekend $30/35 per car; green season is $5 per day. Lifts per adult/child cost from $59/39 per day midweek and $64/44 weekends; cross-country passes cost $9/5 and toboggan passes $5 per person. **Mt Baw Baw Ski Hire** (☑5165 1120; www.bawbawskihire.com.au; Currawong Rd) hires out equipment. For freestyle riders, **Cactus Rail Park** has rails and kick boxes, and there's the **Big Air Bag**, where you can practise your snowboarding stunts with a guaranteed soft landing!

🛏 Sleeping & Eating

Most lodges and eateries are open year-round.

Kelly's Lodge   B&B, CAFE **$$**
(☑5165 1129; www.kellyslodge.com.au; 11 Frosti Ln; r summer/winter from $100/330) This long-running and superfriendly place, with comfortable rooms and a cosy lounge, is in the centre of everything, The ski-in cafe (mains $14 to $30) is a Baw Baw favourite, with legendary pizzas and lamb shanks.

Alpine Hotel   HOTEL **$**
(☑5165 1136; Currawong Rd; dm summer/winter from $25/30, d from $100/130) Superb value, year-round backpacker and motel-style accommodation. In winter the sports bar-cafe and Powder Lounge is *the* place to hang while local bands belt out rock covers.

Village Central   CAFE-RESTAURANT **$$**
(☑5165 1123; Alpine Resort, Currawong Rd; mains $6-25; ☺daily summer, Fri-Sun winter) The cafe-restaurant at Village Central, specialising in local produce, offers good valley views while you enjoy Mod Oz meals.

ℹ Information

In the centre of the village, **Mt Baw Baw Alpine Resort Management** (☑5165 1136; www.mountbawbaw.com.au) offers general tourist information and an **accommodation service** (☑1300 651 136).

ℹ Getting There & Away

The main access road to Baw Baw Village is the windy Baw Baw Tourist Rd via Noojee, reached off the Princes Hwy at Drouin. The alternative back route from the Latrobe Valley is the unsealed, but all-season, South Face Rd from Rawson, north of Moe. Either way, the last 5km up to Baw Baw Village is probably the steepest road in the country – low gear all the way.

LAKE EILDON NATIONAL PARK

Surrounding most of its namesake lake, Lake Eildon National Park is the low-lying southern gateway to the High Country, covering over 270 sq km and providing superb opportunities for walking and camping. From the 1850s, the areas around Lake Eildon were logged and mined for gold, so much of the vegetation is regrowth eucalypt forest.

Originally called Sugarloaf Reserve, Lake Eildon was created as a massive reservoir for irrigation and hydroelectric schemes. It

The High Country Highlights

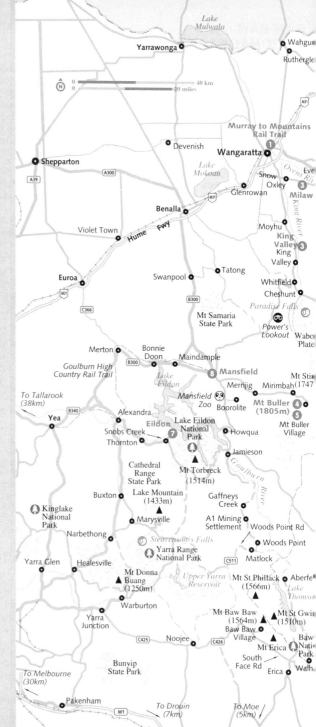

1 Cycle the **Murray to Mountains Rail Trail** (p267), Victoria's longest bike path

2 Visit Ned Kelly's cell in historic **Beechworth** (p265), then sample the brews at Bridge Road Brewers

3 Hit the gourmet trail in **Milawa** (p263) and the **King Valley** (p263), tasting wine, cheese, mustard and olives

4 Mountain-bike the exciting green season trails down **Mt Buller** (p262)

5 Hit the piste at one of the big three ski resorts: **Mt Buller** (p262), **Mt Hotham** (p275) or **Falls Creek** (p273)

6 Enjoy the vibrant colours of the autumn and spring festivals in **Bright** (p270)

7 Holiday on a luxury houseboat or camp by the shores on the beautiful lake at **Eildon** (p258)

8 Make like *The Man from Snowy River* and go horse riding on the high plains around **Mansfield** (p260)

9 Drive along the **Great Alpine Road** (p278) to the isolated goldmining town of **Omeo** (p277)

10 Go caving with glow worms at **Mt Buffalo** (p268)

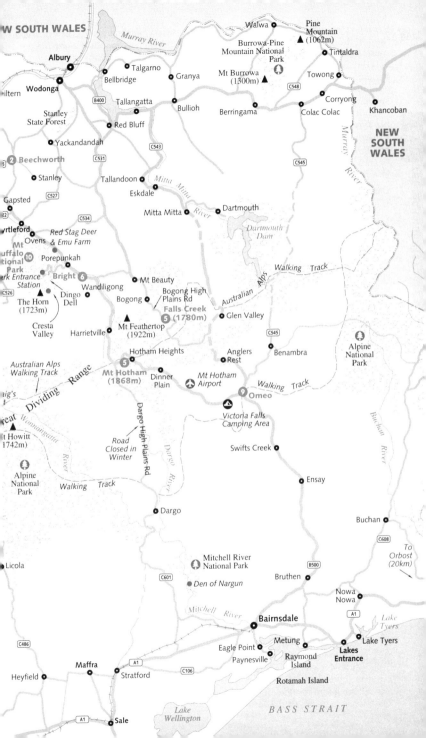

was constructed between 1915 and 1929 and flooded the town of Darlingford and surrounding farm homesteads. Recent rains have brought the lake back to near capacity after years of drought. Behind the dam wall, the 'pondage' (outflow from the dam) spreads below Eildon township.

On the northern arm of the lake is **Bonnie Doon**, a popular weekend base, which reached icon status as the nondescript spot where the Kerrigan family enjoyed 'serenity' in the satirical 1997 Australian film *The Castle*.

Camping

Lake Eildon is a beautiful place for bush camping with several lakeside national park sites. All sites ($18) must be booked online at www.parkweb.vic.gov.au. **Fraser Camping Area**, on Coller Bay 14km northwest of Eildon along Skyline Dr, comprises three separate camp sites, while the **Jerusalem Creek Camping Area** is about 8km southwest of Eildon. If you have your own boat or are prepared to hike in, there are (free) remote camp sites at Taylor's Creek, Mountaineer Creek and Cooper Point.

Houseboats

If the Murray River is too far – or you want more room to manoeuvre – Lake Eildon is the next best place in Victoria to stay on a houseboat. You can hire a luxurious 10- or 12-berth houseboat from one of the following operators (minimum hire per weekend from $1600). Book well ahead for holiday periods:

Eildon Houseboat Hire   HOUSEBOAT
(☑0438 345 366; www.eildonhouseboathire.com.au)

Lake Eildon Marina & Houseboat Hire
                                                   HOUSEBOAT
(☑5774 2107; www.houseboatholidays.com.au)

Eildon

POP 740

The little one-pub town of Eildon, which sits on the edge of the pondage, is a popular recreation- and holiday-base, built in the 1950s to house Eildon Dam project workers.

⊙ Sights & Activities

Lake Eildon and the rivers that feed into it are popular for fishing, but you don't have to be a dedicated angler to have fun here. You can drive up to and across the dam's massive retaining wall to a **lookout point**, with sensational views over the lake, town, and

houseboat building yards. There are quiet walking and cycling trails along the pondage shores that give easy access to the best fishing spots.

Snobs Creek Freshwater Discovery Centre   TROUT FARM
(☑5770 8052; Goulburn Valley Hwy/B349, Snobs Creek; adult/child/family $7/4.50/20; ⊙11am-4pm Fri-Mon, daily during school hols) Kids will love the touch-and-feel tanks and aquariums at this trout farm and hatchery where you can feed the fish and see all sorts of native species in the aquarium.

Eildon Trout Farm   TROUT FARM
(☑5773 2377; www.eildontroutfarm.com.au; 460 Back Eildon Rd, Thornton; entry/fishing $1/2; ⊙9am-5pm) Catching a trout or salmon is guaranteed at this farm located on the back road between Thornton and Eildon.

Goulburn Valley Fly-Fishing Centre
                                                   FLY-FISHING
(☑5773 2513; www.goulburnvlyflyfishing.com.au; 1270 Goulburn Valley Way; fishing introductory/5hr $50/220) If you're looking for specialist tuition and guided fishing trips, either on private waterways or local rivers, this is the place to go.

Rubicon Valley Horse-Riding   HORSE RIDING
(☑5773 2292; www.rubiconhorseriding.com.au; Rubicon Rd, Thornton; rides introductory/2hr/half-day $45/65/90) This company caters for all levels, including children, and runs overnight safaris ($395).

Stockman's Reward   HORSE-RIDING
(☑5774 2322; Goulburn Valley Hwy; rides 1/2hr $35/65) There are horse-riding adventures available for everyone here, with ponies for tiny tots and trail rides in the hills.

Snobs Creek Vineyard   VINEYARD
(☑5774 2017; www.snobscreekvineyard.com.au; 486 Goulburn Valley Hwy, Snobs Creek) For something more leisurely, head to the cellar door at Snobs Creek Vineyard, 5km from Eildon, where you can taste a range of cool-climate Shiraz, Pinot Noir and Chardonnay.

🛏 Sleeping & Eating

There are a few places to stay in Eildon and on the back road to Thornton, but the best accommodation is on board a houseboat (p258) – they build 'em in Eildon. Eating options in town are limited to a few cafes in the small shopping strip and the local pub.

Morning Mist
B&B **$$**

(☑5774 2497; www.morningmist.com.au; 840 Back Eildon Rd; d midweek/weekend $120/175, q $220/320; ☀) On a scenic property overlooking the Goulburn River, this two-bedroom B&B is a wonderful place to relax. The decor has a certain old-fashioned charm but with slick modern touches (even a jukebox) and plenty of privacy.

Golden Trout Hotel Motel
HOTEL **$**

(☑5774 2508; www.goldentrout.com.au; 1 Riverside Dr; d $90) The local pub has standard, slightly tired motel rooms attached, but the location makes up for it – ask for a 'pondage view' room (they're all the same price). The bistro does good pub food ($14 to $28) and is the best bet for an evening meal in town.

Blue Gums Caravan Park
CARAVAN PARK **$**

(☑5774 2576; www.bluegums.com.au; 746 Back Eildon Rd; dm $20, unpowered/powered site $26/29, cabins $100-140; ☀⊛≋) On the banks of the Goulburn River about 5km southwest of Eildon, this is a fabulous family caravan park with two swimming pools, a playground, manicured lawns for camping and slick self-contained cabins.

Eildon Caravan Park
CARAVAN PARK **$**

(☑5774 2105; www.eildoncp.com; Eildon Rd; unpowered/powered site $20/42, cabins $95-180) A rustic little camping ground in a bush setting with pondage frontage.

ℹ Information

Eildon visitors centre (☑5774 2909; www.lakeeildon.com; Main St; ☺10am-2pm winter, to 4pm summer) Friendly staff run this small office opposite the shopping centre.

Jamieson

From Eildon, the sealed and scenic back road skirts the southern edge of the national park to Jamieson, a charming little town where the Goulburn and Jamieson Rivers join Lake Eildon. Jamieson was established as a supply town for goldminers in the 1850s and a number of interesting historical buildings remain.

In the old courthouse is the local **historical museum** (☑5777 0690; adult/child $2.50/1; ☺10am-4pm weekends & holidays).

🍴 Sleeping & Eating

There's good bush camping along the Jamieson and Goulburn Rivers but you must be self-sufficient and camp at least 20m from the water – take the Jamieson-Licola Rd east or the Woods Point Rd to the south. In town, accommodation includes a caravan park and motel.

Twin River Cabins
CABINS **$**

(☑5777 0582; www.twinrivercabins.com.au; 3 Chenery St; s/d $45/75) These rustic little cabins make a great budget retreat close to town. They sleep four to six people and have basic kitchen facilities and shared amenities. The owners rent mountain bikes for $20 a day.

Jamieson Brewery
BREWERY PUB **$$**

(☑5777 0515; www.jamiesonbrewery.com.au; Eildon-Jamieson Rd; mains $16-30; ☺from 11am) An essential stop 3km from town, the Jamieson Brewery produces flavoursome beers on-site, including a raspberry ale and the knockout 'Beast'. Try a tasting plate ($12) and take the free, daily brewery tour at 12.30pm. There's even free tastings of homemade fudge. The bistro serves up good pub food for lunch and dinner daily – enjoy it on the deck overlooking a large garden.

MANSFIELD

POP 2850

Mansfield is the gateway to Victoria's largest snowfields at Mt Buller, but also an exciting all-seasons destination in its own right. There's plenty to do here in *The Man from Snowy River* country, with horse riding and mountain biking popular in summer, and there's a buzzing atmosphere in winter when the snow bunnies hit town.

◉ Sights

The three Mansfield police officers killed at Stringybark Creek by Ned Kelly and his gang in 1878 rest in **Mansfield Cemetery** (cnr Highett St & Stoneleigh Rd).

Mansfield Zoo (☑5777 3576; www.mansfieldzoo.com.au; 1064 Mansfield Woods Point Rd; adult/child/family $15/8/44; ☺10am-5.30pm winter, to 6.30pm summer) is a surprisingly good wildlife park with lots of native fauna and some exotics, such as a pair of lions. If you're older than eight, you can sleep in the paddocks in a swag (adult/child $65/45, including zoo entry for two days) and wake to the dawn wildlife chorus.

🏃 Activities & Tours

Mansfield is an action town. In winter, plenty of places hire chains and ski and snowboarding gear. At other times, this is one of

CRAIG'S HUT

Cattlemen built huts throughout the High Country from the 1850s on, but the most iconic is Craig's Hut, built in 1981 for the film *The Man From Snowy River*. It was converted from a film set into a visitors centre 10 years later, then rebuilt in 2003. In 2006 it was totally burnt down by bushfires, before being rebuilt (again) in 2007. It's on Mt Stirling in the Alpine National Park about 53km east of Mansfield. The last 1.2km is accessible only by walking or 4WD, but it's worth it for the breathtaking views.

the best places in the state for horse riding and mountain biking. Horse riding season in the High Country is generally from late October to May.

Mansfield marks the start or end of the **Goulburn River High Country Rail Trail**, a walking/cycling path that runs from Tallarook to Mansfield via Yea, Alexandra and Bonnie Doon.

All Terrain Cycles   MOUNTAIN BIKING
(☑5775 2724; www.allterraincycles.com.au; 58 High St; bike per day $45-120) Hires out top quality mountain bikes and safety equipment. Also runs guided tours and mountain-biking clinics.

Alpine Helicopter Charter   SCENIC FLIGHTS
(☑0428 376 619; www.alpineheli.com.au; 325 Mt Buller Rd; flights from $150) Themed helicopter flights, such as 'Cattlemen's Huts', 'Ned Kelly Country' and 'Rivers & Waterfalls'. Fly up to Craig's Hut for $315 per person.

High Country Horses   HORSE RIDING
(☑5777 5590; www.highcountryhorses.com.au; Mt Buller Rd, Merrijig; 2hr/half-day rides $80/115, overnight from $500; ☺Oct-May) Based at Merrijig on the way to Mt Buller. High Country Horses offer anything from a short trot to overnight treks to Craig's Hut, Howqua River and Mt Stirling.

McCormack's Mountain Valley Trail Rides
                                      HORSE RIDING
(☑5775 2886; www.mountainvalleytrailrides.com; 43 McCormack's Rd, Merrijig; day ride from $200, overnight from $500; ☺Oct-May) Experienced locals take you into the King Valley and High Country; options include a four-day adventure for $900.

Watson's Mountain Country Trail Rides
                                      HORSE RIDING
(☑5777 3552; www.watsonstrailrides.com.au; Three Chains Rd, Boorolite; 1/2hr $35/60, 1-/2-day rides $200/475) A peaceful property where children can learn with pony rides or short trail rides, or take off on overnight catered rides. One of the highlights is the view from Kate Cameron's Peak, looking down the steep run featured in *The Man From Snowy River*.

✯✯ Festivals & Events

High Country Autumn Festival   AUTUMN
(www.mansfieldmtbuller.com.au) Held over the March Labour Day weekend there are markets, picnics and a rodeo at nearby Merrijig.

Upper Goulburn Wine Region Vintage Celebration   WINE
(www.uppergoulburnwine.org.au) Local wines, musicians and chefs make for three fun days in April.

High Country Festival & Spring Arts   ARTS
(www.highcountryfestival.com.au) A week of arts, bush markets and activities from late October, culminating in the Melbourne Cup day picnic races.

🛏 Sleeping

Mansfield has a good range of accommodation. Prices are slightly higher during ski season.

Mansfield Travellers Lodge   HOSTEL, MOTEL $
(☑5775 1800; www.mansfieldtravellerslodge.com. au; 116 High St; dm/s/d/f $25/90/95/160; ✴) Located lose to the centre of town, this has been a long-time favourite for backpackers and families. The spacious dorms are in a restored heritage building, while the motel section features spotless one- and two-bedroom units. Facilities include a kitchen, games rooms, laundry and drying room.

Highton Manor   B&B $$
(☑5775 2700; www.hightonmanor.com.au; 140 Highton Ln; shared r $65, d incl breakfast stable/manor/tower $120/225/365; ✴) Built in 1896 for Francis Highett, who sang with Dame Nellie Melba, this stately two-storey manor has style and romance but doesn't take itself too seriously. There is group accommodation in the shared room, modern rooms in the converted stables and lavish period rooms in the main house. If you want the royal treatment, choose the tower room.

Banjo's Accommodation
CABINS **$$**

(☑5775 2335; www.banjosmansfield.com.au; cnr Mt Buller Rd & Greenvale Ln; d/q $110/170; ☒) These family-friendly self-contained units on the edge of town can sleep up to five people in the studios and six in the two-bedroom units. They're modern and spacious and the expansive grounds are perfect to let kids run around.

Wappan Station
STATION **$**

(☑5778 7786; www.wappanstation.com.au; Royal Town Rd, Maindample; shearers' quarters adult/child $30/15, cottages d from $150; ☒) Watch farm activities from your deck at this sheep-and-cattle property on the banks of Lake Eildon.

Mansfield Holiday Park
CARAVAN PARK **$**

(☑5775 1383; www.mansfieldholidaypark.com. au; Mt Buller Rd; unpowered/powered sites from $22/25, d cabins $60-100; ☒) On the edge of town, this is a spacious caravan park with a pool, minigolf, camp kitchen and comfortable cabins.

✗ Eating & Drinking

There's some good dining along Main St. Sadly the Mansfield Hotel, an excellent pub-restaurant, was severely damaged by fire in 2010 – the owners plan to rebuild.

On the fourth Saturday of each month, the **Mansfield Farmers Market** (www.man sfieldfarmersmarket.com.au; Highett St; ⊘8.30am-1pm) brings farmers' produce to town at the Mansfield Primary School.

Mansfield Regional Produce Store
CAFE, PROVEDORE **$**

(☑5779 1404; www.theproducestore.com.au; 68 High St; mains $10-18; ⊘breakfast & lunch Tue-Sun, dinner Fri; ☒) The best spot in town for coffee or a light lunch, this rustic store stocks an array of local produce, wine and freshly baked artisan breads. The ever-changing blackboard menu offers full breakfasts, baguettes and salads.

Deck on High
ASIAN FUSION **$$**

(☑5775 1144; www.thedeckonhigh.com.au; 13-15 High St; mains $18-33; ⊘lunch & dinner Wed-Mon, breakfast Sat & Sun) A sophisticated but relaxed bar-restaurant serving up genuinely good Asian-inspired food such as gado gado, pad thai and sushi plates. The upper deck is brilliant for a drink on a summer's afternoon and the downstairs bar, with soft couches and sleek lines, is a cosy place to explore the extensive local wine list in winter.

FORTY one
CAFE **$**

(☑5775 2951; 39-41 High St; mains $8-17; ⊘breakfast & lunch) It's famous for its creamy vanilla slice, but you can enjoy a range of gourmet surprises in the sunny courtyard here.

Delatite Winery Cellar Door & Larder
WINERY **$**

(☑5775 2922; www.delatitewinery.com.au; 26 High St) The family-run Delatite Winery is about 12km from Mansfield and open only by appointment, but you can sample the wines and other local produce at the cellar door in town. Takeaway sushi is available Wednesday to Sunday.

❶ Information

Mansfield & Mt Buller High Country visitors centre (☑1800 039 049; www.mansfieldmt buller.com.au; Maroondah Hwy; ⊘9am-5pm Oct-May, 8am-9pm Jun-Sep) In 'The Station', a modern building next to town's original railway station. Displays include a felt mural of pioneer women and screens featuring local personalities. The centre books general and ski accommodation for the region, and sells lift tickets.

MT BULLER

ELEV 1805M

Victoria's largest and busiest ski resort is also the closest major resort to Melbourne, so it buzzes all winter long. It's also developing into a popular summer destination for mountain bikers and hikers, with a range of cross-country and downhill trails. The extensive lift network includes the Horse Hill chairlift that begins in the day car park and drops you off in the middle of the ski runs. The downhill-skiing area is 180 hectares with a vertical drop of 400m. Cross-country trails link Mt Buller with **Mt Stirling**.

Buller is a well-developed resort with a vibrant village atmosphere in the white season and summer weekends. In winter there's **night skiing** on Wednesday and Saturday, and for nonskiers there's tobogganing, snow-tubing and excellent snowshoeing. **Ducks & Drakes** (www.ducksanddrakes.net; tours $35-45) runs one- to two-hour guided snowshoeing tours, including equipment and hot chocolate, starting at the clock tower.

The only alpine museum in Australia, the **National Alpine Museum of Australia** (NAMA; ☑5777 6077; www.nama.org.au; Level 1, Community Centre, Summit Rd; admission by

Mt Buller has developed into one of the great summer mountain-biking destinations in Victoria, with a network of trails around the summit, and exhilarating downhill tracks. From 26 December to the end of January, the Horse Hill chairlift operates on weekends, lifting you and your bike up to the plateau (all-day lift and trails access $53). If you're not biking you can still ride the chairlift all day (adult/child $16/11).

From 26 December till the Easter weekend a bus shuttle runs every weekend from the **Mirimbah Store** (☑5777 5529; www.mirimbah.com.au; per ride/day $14/30), at the base of the mountain, to the summit car park, from where you can ride all the way back down on a number of trails. The most popular trail is the **River Spur** (60 to 90 minutes), partly following the Delatite River with 13 river crossings. More challenging is the new one-to-1½-hour **Klingsbourne Trail**. The owners of the Mirimbah Store (which, incidentally, is also a fabulous cafe) are experienced riders and a mine of information on the trails.

You can hire quality mountains bikes from **All Terrain Cycles** (☑5775 2724; www.allterraincycles.com.au; 58 High St; $45-120) in Mansfield. During the biking season they also have a hire service at Buller village.

donation; ☉1-4pm winter, by appointment summer), highlights the fascinating history of this area.

Breathtaker on High Spa Retreat (☑1800 088 222; www.breathtaker.com.au; massage per hr from $130) offers the chance to soak and revive with a range of luxurious treatments, a 20m lap pool and a hydrotherapy 'geisha tub', but it's currently open in winter only.

★☆ Festivals & Events

Mt Buller holds an array of event weekends throughout the year. Check the calendar on www.mtbuller.com.au. Summer highlights include the **Buller Beerfest**, in mid-January, and weekend short courses in cooking, art and photography.

🛏 Sleeping

There are over 7000 beds on the mountain, with rates varying throughout the ski season and cheaper rates midweek. A handful of places are open year-round. **Mt Buller Central Reservations** (☑1800 285 537; www.mtbuller.com.au) books accommodation; there's generally a two-night minimum stay on weekends.

Mt Buller Chalet   CHALET $$$
(☑5777 6566; www.mtbullerchalet.com.au; Summit Rd; d incl breakfast summer/winter from $200/350; 🏊) With a central location, the Chalet offers a sweet range of suites, a library with billiard table, well-regarded eateries, an impressive sports centre and a heated pool. The Chalet

also operates nearby **Buller Backpackers** (dm summer/winter $45/55).

Hotel Enzian   CHALET $$
(☑5777 6915; www.hotelenzian.com.au; 69 Chamois Rd; d summer/winter from $140/240) Year-round Enzian has a good range of lodge rooms and apartments (sleeping up to eight) with all the facilities, alpine charm and an in-house restaurant.

Monash University Alpine Lodge   LODGE $
(☑5777 6577; www.sport.monash.edu.au/alpine-lodge.html; 84 Stirling Rd; dm summer/winter from $45/65) Right near the ski-lift ticket office, this grand lodge has four bunks to a room, a pleasant lounge, kitchen, TV room and drying room.

YHA Mt Buller (☑5777 6181; www.yha.com.au; The Ave; dm $79-88) In winter this well-known and cosy little YHA has good facilities and friendly staff.

✕ Eating

You'll find plenty of great dining experiences here in winter, and a few places open year-round. There's a licensed and reasonably well-stocked supermarket in the village centre.

Cattleman's Café   CAFE, BISTRO $
(☑5777 7942; Village Centre; mains $8-18; ☉breakfast & lunch Oct-May, breakfast, lunch & dinner Jun-Sep) At the base of the Blue Bullet chairlift and open year-round, this is the place for breakfast, coffee or a bistro meal of steak, burgers or fish and chips.

Black Cockatoo MODERN AUSTRALIAN **$$**
(☎5777 6566; lunch from $8.50, mains $31-42, 2-/3-course menu $55/65; Summit Rd; ☺breakfast & dinner) At the Mt Buller Chalet, this is year-round fine dining – the best on the mountain. In winter, the Après Bar & Cafe has more casual dining.

Pension Grimus AUSTRIAN **$$**
(☎5777 6396; www.pensiongrimus.com.au; Breathtaker Rd; mains $25-39; ☺dinner daily, lunch Sat & Sun) One of Buller's originals, the Austrian-style food at the Kaptan's Restaurant, impromptu music and a pumping bar that will give you a warm, fuzzy feeling after a day on the slopes.

🍷 Drinking & Entertainment

There's no shortage of entertainment and après-ski fun here in winter, but most places close up for the summer.

Kooroora Hotel PUB, NIGHTCLUB
(☎5777 6050; Village Square; ☺to 3am winter) Rocks hard and late during the ski season. There's live music on Wednesday night and most weekends, and the popular Hoohah Kitchen serves good bistro meals.

Mt Buller Village Cinema CINEMA
(☎5733 7000; Level 4, Community Centre, Summit Rd) This cinema shows latest releases daily during the ski season.

ℹ Information

The **Mt Buller Resort Management Board** (☎5777 6077; www.mtbuller.com.au; Level 5, Community Centre, Summit Rd; ☺8.30am-5pm) also opens an information office in the village square clock tower in winter. Entrance fee to the Horse Hill day car park in winter is $35 per car. Lift tickets cost adult/child $99/54. Combined lift-and-lesson packages start at $145.

ℹ Getting There & Around

Mansfield–Mt Buller Buslines (☎5775 2606, winter 5775 6070; www.mmbl.com.au) runs a winter service from Melbourne on Wednesday, Friday and Sunday (adult/child return $165/125) or from Mansfield (adult/child return $52/36) and charter services in summer.

Ski-season car parking is below the village; a 4WD taxi service transports people to their village accommodation.

Day-trippers park in the Horse Hill day car park and take the quad chairlift into the skiing area, or there's a free day-tripper shuttle-bus service between the day car park and the village. Ski hire and lift tickets are available at the base of the chairlift.

Turning east off the Hume Fwy near Wangaratta and onto the Snow Rd brings you to the King Valley, a prosperous cool-climate wine region and the gourmet capital of the state. The valley extends south along the King River, through the tiny towns of Mohyu, Whitfield and Cheshunt, with a sprinkling of 20 or so wineries noted for Italian varietals and cool-climate wines such as Sangiovese, Barbera, sparkling Prosecco and Pinot Grigio. Check out www.winesoftheking valley.com.au.

Among the best are **Dal Zotto Estate** (☎5729 8321; www.dalzotto.com.au; Main Rd, Whitfield; ☺10am-5pm), which also has an Italian-style trattoria open on weekends; and **Pizzini** (☎5729 8278; www.pizzini.com.au; 175 King Valley Rd, Whitfield; ☺11am-5pm).

There's good **camping** along the King River and a few places to stay around Whitfield.

Milawa Gourmet Region

Back on the Snow Rd, between Wangaratta and Myrtleford, the Milawa/Oxley gourmet region (www.milawagourmet.com) is the place to indulge your tastebuds. As well as wine tasting, you can sample cheese, olives, mustards and marinades, or dine in some of the region's best restaurants

At Oxley, wineries include **John Gehrig Wines** (☎5727 3395; www.johngehrigwines.com. au; Gehrig's Ln; ☺10am-5pm) which has rare varieties like verjuice; and the unmistakeable **Sam Miranda** (☎5727 3888; www.sammiranda. com.au; 1019 Snow Rd; ☺cellar door 10am-5pm, lunch daily) with its architecturally-designed cellar door and wide range of Italian-style wines.

Don't miss a stop at the **King River Cafe** (☎5727 3461; www.kingrivercafe.com.au; 1143 Snow Rd; mains $11-28; ☺lunch Mon & Wed-Sun, dinner Wed-Sun) for scrumptious dishes such as goat's cheese soufflé, and smoked trout, good coffee and local wines.

About 5km further on, the main street of Milawa boasts **Milawa Mustard** (☎5727 3202; www.milawamustard.com.au; Old Emu Inn, The Cross Roads; ☺10am-5pm), which offers tastings of its handmade seeded mustards, herbed vinegars and preserves; the **Olive Shop** (☎5727 3887; www.theoliveshop.com.au; 1605 Snow Rd; ☺10am-5pm Thu-Mon), an olive 'gallery' with oils and tapenades for sampling;

POWER'S LOOKOUT

The back road from Mansfield to Whitfield in the King Valley is a seriously scenic drive – sure beats the Hume Hwy – and about 20km from Whitfield and 3km down a sign-posted gravel road is Power's Lookout, with the greatest view over the King Valley and the Victorian Alps you could hope to see. The lookout was named after Harry Power, a 19th-century bushranger who, some say, teamed up with a young Ned Kelly and taught him a thing or two. Although he committed more than 30 armed crimes, Power was considered something of a gentleman, never killing anyone and occasionally offering not to rob those he thought couldn't afford it. He even apologised as he departed with his loot and horses. Power knew the mountains intimately and may have used this lookout as his hideout, from where he could survey the land for approaching trouble. But in 1870 he was betrayed for a £500 reward, captured here as he slept, and sent to jail for 15 years.

Today, you can survey the valley and ranges just as Power did. There's a lookout at the picnic area, but don't miss the short walk to the rocky No 2 lookout – superb!

and **Walkabout Honey** (☎5727 3468; Snow Rd; ◐10am-5pm), where you can sample a range of honeys.

Next stop is the region's best-known winery, **Brown Brothers Vineyard** (☎5720 5547; www.brownbrothers.com.au; Bobbinawarrah Rd, Milawa; ◐9am-5pm). The winery's first vintage was in 1889, and it has remained in the hands of the same family ever since. As well as the tasting room, there's the superb Epicurean Centre restaurant, a gorgeous garden, kids' play equipment and picnic and barbecue facilities.

About 2km north of Milawa, **Milawa Cheese Company** (☎5727 3589; www.milawacheese.com; Factory Rd; ◐9am-5pm) is our favourite produce store. From humble origins, it now produces a mouth-watering array of cheeses to sample or buy. It excels at soft farmhouse brie (from goat or cow) and pungent washed-rind cheeses. There's a bakery here and the excellent Ageing Frog Bistrot (mains $18-28), where the speciality is a variety of pizzas using Milawa cheese. Also here is the cellar door for **Wood Park Wines** (☎5727 3500; ◐11am-4pm Fri-Wed), so you can complement your cheese tasting with some quality wine tasting, or pop around the back to the **Muse Gallery of Milawa** (☎5727 3599; www.musegallery.com.au; ◐10am-5pm Thu-Mon).

Further northeast on the road to Everton is **EV Olives Groves** (☎5727 0209; www.evolives.com; 203 Everton Rd, Markwood; ◐10am-5pm), offering the fruity taste of the oils, olives and tapenades.

Back in Milawa, the **Milawa Gourmet Hotel** (☎5727 3208; cnr Snow & Factory Rds, Milawa; mains $16-27; ◐lunch & dinner) is a traditional country pub, but it lives up to the region's reputation, serving good bistro food and local produce with gourmet flair.

Just north of Snow Rd on the Ovens River flood plain is the little farming community of Whorouly, home to the **Whorouly Grocer** (☎5727 1220; www.thewhoroulygrocer.com.au; 577 Whorouly Rd; ◐9am-5pm Thu-Mon, to 4pm Sat & Sun), a sweet deli, foodstore and cafe. Nearby is the **Whorouly Hotel** (☎5727 1424; 542 Whorouly Rd; d $50, mains $6-24; ◐lunch & dinner Fri & Sat), a friendly country pub where you can get a hearty bistro meal or stay the night.

Where the Snow Rd meets the Great Alpine Rd (B500), **Gapsted Wines** (☎5751 1383; www.gapstedwines.com.au; Great Alpine Rd; ◐10am-5pm, lunch daily) is another outstanding winery where you can eat from the seasonal lunch menu in beautiful surroundings.

BEECHWORTH

POP 2650

Beechworth's historic honey-coloured granite buildings and wonderful gourmet offerings make this one of northeast Victoria's most enjoyable towns. It's also listed by the National Trust as one of Victoria's two 'notable' towns (the other is Maldon), and you'll soon see why: this living legacy of the gold-rush era will take you back to the days of miners and bushrangers – Ned Kelly was locked up here for the murder of three Mansfield policemen. Most of the town spreads along two intersecting streets – Ford and Camp Sts – where you'll find old-fashioned shops and some of the best foodstores, cafes and restaurants in the region.

⊙ Sights & Activities

HISTORIC PRECINCT

Beechworth's main attraction is the group of well-preserved, honey-tinged buildings that make up the Historic & Cultural Precinct (☎1300 366 321; all sites & 2 guided tours adult/child/family $25/15/50; ⊙9am-5pm). First is the Town Hall, where you'll find the visitors centre and the free *Echoes of History* audio-visual tour. Across the road is the Beechworth Courthouse (adult/child/family $6/4/12; ⊙9am-5pm), where the trials of many key historical figures took place, including Ned Kelly and his mother, whose cells can still be seen. Behind the courthouse is the Old Police Station Museum (admission $2; ⊙10am-2pm Fri-Sun), or you can send a telegram to anywhere in the world from the Telegraph Station on Ford St, the original Morse-code office. Walk through to Loch St to the Burke Museum (adult/child/family $6/4/12; ⊙10am-5pm) – it's named after the hapless explorer Robert O'Hara Burke, who was Beechworth's superintendent of police before he set off on his historic trek north with William Wills.

OTHER ATTRACTIONS

FREE Beechworth Honey Experience (☎5728 1432; www.beechworthhoney. com.au; cnr Ford & Church Sts; ⊙9am-5pm) takes you into the world of honey and bees with a self-guided audio-visual tour, live hive and honey tastings. The shop sells locally made honey, beeswax candles, nougat and soaps.

You'll get all nostalgic over the eye-popping range of old-time sweets and lollies at the Beechworth Sweet Co (www.beechworth sweetco.com.au; 7 Camp St; ⊙daily). So popular it's one-way traffic only!

Old brewery paraphernalia is on display at MB Historic Cellars (☎5728 1304; 29 Last St; admission $1; ⊙10am-4pm), a former brewery that now produces traditional cordials like ginger beer. In the same premises the Carriage Museum, displaying gorgeous old horse-drawn carriages.

The Golden Horseshoes Monument (cnr Sydney Rd & Gorge Scenic Dr) is where, in 1855, a horse was shod with golden shoes and ridden into town by candidate Donald Cameron on the nomination day of Victoria's first parliamentary elections. The Victorian-era PR stunt seemed to work – Cameron was duly elected to parliament.

Down near pretty Lake Sambell you'll find the Chinese Gardens, a tribute to the Chinese gold miners.

☞ Tours

Daily guided walking tours (adult/child/family $7.50/5/15) leave from the visitors centre and feature lots of gossip and interesting details. The Ned Kelly-themed tour starts at 10.15am; the Gold Rush tour at 1.15pm.

Beechworth's most popular after-dark outing is Beechworth Ghost Tours (☎0447 432 816; www.beechworthghosttours. com; adult/child/family $25/15/75; ⊙from dusk), which explore the town's former lunatic asylum by lamplight, with plenty of eerie tales of murder and mayhem. There are four tours on weekends, including a midnight walk.

✪ Festivals & Events

Golden Horseshoes Festival   EASTER
Donald Cameron's ride on a gold-shod horse is re-enacted in a grand parade at this Easter event. Food stalls, Easter-egg hunt, music and fun.

Harvest Celebration   FOOD
(www.harvestcelebration.com.au) Food and wine workshops take to the streets in May.

Beechworth Oktoberfest   BEER
Beer-drinking and oompah in early October, hosted by Bridge Road Brewers.

Celtic Festival   CULTURAL
(www.beechworthcelticfestival.com.au) Art, entertainment, food, music and mayhem in mid-November.

🛏 Sleeping

Beechworth is well-endowed with cottages and heritage B&Bs; check out www.beechworth.com/accommodation.

Freeman on Ford   B&B $$$
(☎5728 2371; www.freemanonford.com.au; 97 Ford St; s/d from $255/275; ❄) In the 1876 Oriental Bank, this sumptuous but homely place offers Victorian luxury in six beautifully renovated rooms, right in the heart of town. The owner, Heidi, will make you feel very special.

Old Priory   GUESTHOUSE $
(☎5728 1024; www.oldpriory.com.au; 8 Priory Lane; dm/s/d $40/55/85, cottages $120) This historic convent is a spooky but charming old place. It's often used by school groups, but it's the best budget choice in Beechworth with lovely gardens and a range of rooms, including beautifully renovated miners' cottages.

La Trobe at Beechworth   APARTMENTS $$
(☎5720 8050; www.latrobeatbeechworth.com. au; Albert Rd; d $105-300, cottages from $175;

) On the hill above town, this was the Beechworth Lunatic Asylum for over 130 years. Today the art deco buildings contain a range of rooms, including cottages and self-contained units. Also here is the Spa at Beechworth wellness retreat.

Lake Sambell Caravan Park CARAVAN PARK **$**
(☑5728 1421; www.caravanparkbeechworth.com. au; Peach Dr; unpowered/powered sites $17/23, cabins $75-125;) This shady park next to beautiful Lake Sambell has great facilities including a camp kitchen, a playground and bike hire. The sunsets reflected in the lake are spectacular.

Eating & Drinking

For a town of its size, Beechworth has some fantastic feasting, from provedores and pantries stocking fresh local produce to serious fine dining restaurants in historic buildings. Most places are close to the intersection of Ford and Camp Sts.

Provenance MODERN AUSTRALIAN **$$**
(☑5728 1786; www.theprovenance.com.au; 86 Ford St; mains $32-40; ⊙dinner Wed-Sun) In an 1856 bank building, Provenance has elegant but contemporary fine dining. Under the guidance of acclaimed local chef, Michael Ryan, the innovative menu features dishes such as Berkshire pork belly, tea-smoked duck breast and some inspiring vegetarian choices. If you can't decide, go for the degustation menu ($85).

Beechworth Bakery BAKERY **$**
(☑5728 1132; 27 Camp St; light meals $3-10; ⊙6am-7pm) Popular with locals and tourists, this is the original in a well-known bakery chain; great for pies, pastries, cakes and sandwiches.

Beechworth Provender CAFE, FOODSTORE **$**
(☑5728 2650; 18 Camp St; ⊙breakfast & lunch) Crammed with delectable local produce (and wines) for filling a gourmet hamper, the Provender is also an excellent cafe.

Bridge Road Brewers BREWERY, PIZZA **$**
(☑5728 2103; www.bridgeroadbrewers.com.au; Ford St; ⊙11am-5pm Mon-Sat, noon-11pm Sun) Hiding behind the imposing Tanswells Commercial Hotel, Beechworth's gem of a microbrewery produces some excellent beers (taste six for $8), and serves freshly baked pretzels and super housemade pizzas ($12 to $21) for lunch Wednesday to Sunday and dinner Sunday night.

Wardens ITALIAN **$**
(☑5728 1377; www.wardens.com.au; 32 Ford St; mains $30-36; ⊙lunch Wed-Sun, dinner Tue-Sat) Modern Italian at its best – think baked Roman gnocchi or roasted swordfish – paired with fine local wines.

Information

Beechworth visitors centre (☑1300 366 321; www.beechworthonline.com.au; 103 Ford St; ⊙9am-5pm) An accommodation and activity booking service located in the Town Hall. Ask about the Golden Ticket, which gives admission to the historic precinct and two guided walking tours (valid for two days).

Getting There & Away

Beechworth is just off the Great Alpine Rd, 36km east of Wangaratta.

V/Line (☑13 61 96; www.vline.com.au) runs a train/bus service between Melbourne and Beechworth with a change at Seymour ($26, four hours, three daily). There are direct buses from Wangaratta ($3.60, 35 minutes, six daily) and Bright ($3.40, 50 minutes, two daily).

YACKANDANDAH

POP 660

An old gold-mining town nestled in beautiful hills and valleys east of Beechworth, 'Yack', as it's universally known, is original enough to be classified by the National Trust. You might even recognise it as the setting for the 2004 film *Strange Bedfellows*, starring Paul Hogan and Michael Caton.

Today many of the historic shops in the main street contain galleries, antiques and curios: **A Bear's Old Wares** (☑02-6027 1114; www.abearsoldwares.com; 12 High St; ⊙9am-5.30pm) is a fascinating shop crammed with Buddhist and Hindu idols, prayer flags, Tibetan jewellery and wall hangings.

Karrs Reef Goldmine (☑0408 975 991; tours adult/child $18.50/16.50; ⊙10am, 1pm & 4pm Fri-Tue) is an old mine dating from 1857. On the 1½-hour guided tours you don a hard hat and descend into the original tunnels to learn a bit about the mine's history. Bookings can be made through the visitors centre.

Other attractions in the region include the **Lavender Patch** (☑02-6027 1603; www.lavenderpatch.com.au; 461 Yackandandah Rd; admission free; ⊙9am-5.30pm) and the studio-gallery at **Kirby's Flat Pottery** (☑02-6027 1416; www.johndermer.com.au; 225 Kirby's Flat Rd; ⊙10.15am-5.30pm Sat & Sun), 4km south of Yackandandah.

The **Murray to Mountains Rail Trail** (www.murraytomountains.com.au) is Victoria's longest bike path and one of the High Country's best walking/cycling trails for families or casual riders – it's sealed and relatively flat for much of the way and passes through spectacular rural scenery of farms, forest and vineyards, with views of the alpine ranges. The 94km trail runs from Wangaratta to Bright via Beechworth, Myrtleford and Porepunkah. A newly completed section heads northwest from Wangaratta to Wahgunyah via Rutherglen, completing the true Murray to Mountains experience.

Break up the journey and explore the area: stop off for a cold beer in a country pub like the Ovens Hotel, sample local produce in the gourmet region, jump off for tastings and lunch at a winery (Pennyweight, Michelton, Boynton's), or spend a day or two in one of the many comfortable local B&Bs.

Aficionados say the 16km between Everton and Beechworth, which detours off the main trail, is the best part of the trail (despite a challenging uphill section), as you're cycling through the bush. Bikes can be hired in Wangaratta and Bright, and towns in between. **Bus-a-Bike** (☑5752 2974) carries up to 11 people and their bikes to wherever, from wherever, along the trail. Ring to arrange your pick-up.

The biggest event of the year is the **Yackandandah Folk Festival** (☑02-6027 1447; http://folkfestival.yackandandah.com), three days of music, parades, workshops and fun in mid- to late-March.

🛏 Sleeping & Eating

Yackandandah Holiday Park   CARAVAN PARK $
(☑02-6027 1380; www.yhp.com.au; Taymac Dr; powered sites $25-35, cabins $85-145) Beside pretty Yackandandah Creek but close to the town, this well-equipped park is a little oasis of greenery and autumn colours.

Star Hotel   PUB $$
(☑02-6027 1493; 30 High St) This 1863 hotel, known locally as the 'top pub', is an old country pub with good bistro meals.

❶ Information

Yackandandah visitors centre (☑02-6027 1988; www.uniqueyackandandah.com.au; 27 High St; ⊙9am-5pm) In the grand, 1878 Athenaeum building. Pick up the free *A Walk in High Street* brochure, which details the history of the shops.

MYRTLEFORD

POP 2700

Along the Great Alpine Hwy near the foothills of Mt Buffalo, Myrtleford is yet another 'Gateway to the Alps', and a worthwhile stop if you're heading to the snowfields or exploring the gourmet region.

The **Murray to Mountains Rail Trail** (p267) follows a path close to the Great Al-

pine Rd from Gapsted (northwest of Myrtleford) southeast to Bright. **Myrtleford Cycle Centre** (☑5752 1511; 59 Clyde St; rental per day $25; ⊙Mon-Sat) rents bikes and helmets.

🛏 Sleeping

Carawah Ridge   B&B $$
(☑5752 2147; www.carawahridge.com.au; 514 Buffalo Creek Rd; d $185; ❄ ⛵) These two secluded apartments, 7km from Myrtleford in the Buffalo Creek Valley, make a delightful getaway. Gorgeous gardens, cosy bedrooms and modern amenities including kitchenette, with a full breakfast delivered to your door.

Motel on Alpine   MOTEL $$
(☑5752 1438; www.motelonalpine.com; 258 Great Alpine Rd; d/f from $140/170; ❄ 🛜 ⛵) Quality motel close to the town centre with a pool and spa, manicured garden and a highly regarded restaurant. Breakfast included.

Myrtleford Caravan Park   CARAVAN PARK $
(☑5752 1598; www.alpineshire.vic.gov.au/myrtlefordcp; Lewis Ave; unpowered/powered sites from $22/28, dm $26, cabins $73-120; ❄) Grassy sites, well-maintained cabins, kids' playground and a 40-bed bunkhouse for groups or backpackers.

🍴 Eating

There's a good range of eateries along the Great Alpine Rd through town, a cafe at the visitors centre and a couple of pubs.

Butter Factory   CAFE, DELI $
(☑5752 2300; www.butterfactory.com.au; 15 Myrtle St; mains $17-25; ⊙breakfast & lunch Thu-Tue, dinner

Fri & Sat; 🖉) This cafe, produce store and restaurant is in an old butter factory, and you can still see butter being churned here or take a short tour on most days. The produce store stocks a wide range of local jams, sauces, honey and pickles, while the cafe is a special place for an organic breakfast or lunch of local trout or innovative tasting plates.

❶ Information

Myrtleford visitors centre (🖉5752 1044; www.visitmyrtleford.com.au, www.visitalpinevictoria.com.au; 38 Myrtle St; @) Information and a booking service for the alpine valley area ski fields. Ask for the *Myrtleford Discovery Trail Guide*, which outlines historical sites around town.

MT BUFFALO NATIONAL PARK

Beautiful **Mt Buffalo** is an easily accessible year-round destination – in winter it's a tiny family-friendly ski resort with gentle runs, and in summer it's a great spot for bushwalking, mountain biking and rock climbing.

It was named in 1824 by the explorers Hume and Hovell on their trek from Sydney to Port Phillip – they thought its bulky shape resembled a buffalo – and declared a national park in 1898. The main access road is out of Porepunkah, between Myrtleford and Bright.

You'll find granite outcrops, alpine lookouts, streams and waterfalls, wildflowers and wildlife here. The **Big Walk**, an 11km, five-hour ascent of the mountain starts from Eurobin Creek Picnic Area, north of Porepunkah, and finishes at the Gorge Day Visitor Area. A road leads to just below the summit of the Horn (1723m), the highest point on the massif. Nearby **Lake Catani** is good for swimming, canoeing and camping. There are 14km of groomed **cross-country ski trails** starting out from the Cresta Valley car park, as well as a **tobogganing area**. In summer Mt Buffalo is a **hang-gliding** paradise, and the near-vertical walls of the Gorge provide some of Australia's most challenging **rock climbing**.

🏃 Activities

Adventure Guides Australia　　ADVENTURE
(🖉0419 280 614, 5728 1804; www.visitmount buffalo.com.au) This established operator offers abseiling (from $55), rock climbing (from $220) and caving with glow worms

through an underground river system (from $99). It also runs a cross-country ski school in winter.

Eagle School of Microlighting　　FLIGHTS
(🖉5750 1174; www.eagleschool.com.au; flights $70-300) Exhilarating tandem flights over the Mt Buffalo region, as well as flying lessons. Flights include an unpowered glide back to base.

🛏 Sleeping

The 100-year-old **Mt Buffalo Chalet**, currently closed and in the hands of Parks Victoria, is still looking for an operator, but could reopen soon.

Remote camping is possible at Rocky Creek, which has pit toilets only. **Lake Catani Campground** (sites $17; ☺Nov-Apr) has a summer campground with toilets and showers. Book through **Parks Victoria** (🖉13 19 63; www.parkweb.vic.gov.au).

BRIGHT

POP 2100

Famous for its glorious autumn colours, Bright is a popular year-round destination in the foothills of the alps and a gateway to Mt Hotham and Falls Creek. Skiers make a beeline through Bright in winter, but it's a lovely base for exploring the Alpine National Park, paragliding, fishing and kayaking on local rivers, bushwalking and exploring the region's wineries. Plentiful accommodation and some sophisticated restaurants and cafes complete the picture.

◉ Sights & Activities

Walking trails around Bright include the 3km loop **Canyon Walk**, 4km **Cherry Walk** and a 6km track to **Wandiligong** that follows Morses Creek.

You could spend an hour or two getting lost among the antiques, retro stuff, junk and collectables at the **Old Tobacco Sheds** (🖉5755 2344; Great Alpine Rd; ☺10am-5pm). There's also a small gold and tobacco museum there.

Wandiligong Maze (🖉5750 1311; www.wan dimaze.com.au; White Star Rd; adult/child/family $10/8/28; ☺10am-5pm Wed-Mon, daily school holidays, closed Aug) is a fun hedge maze, minigolf course and cafe about 8km from Bright.

The **Bright Markets** (☺9am-1pm) are held in Howitt Park on the third Saturday of each month.

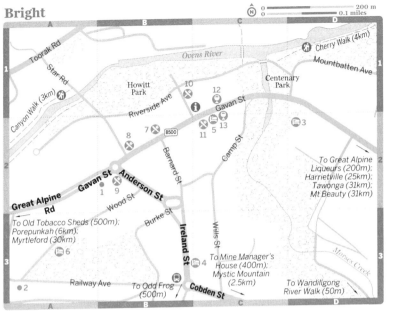

There are plenty of wineries in the region, but for something different you can sample a range of liqueurs, schnapps and brandy distilled on-site at **Great Alpine Liqueurs** (☑5755 1002; www.greatalpineliqueurs.com.au; 36 Churchill Ave; ☺10am-4.30pm Fri-Mon, daily during holidays).

The **Murray to Mountains Rail Trail** (p267) starts (or ends) behind the old train station. Bikes, tandems and baby trailers can be rented from **Cyclepath** (☑5750 1442; www.cyclepath.com.au; 74 Gavan St; per hr from $16, per half-/full day from $22/30).

🖝 Tours

Bright is a base for all sorts of adventure activities, including paragliding – enthusiasts catch the thermals from nearby Mystic Mountain.

Active Flight FLIGHTS
(☑0428 854 455; www.activeflight.com.au) Introductory paragliding course (from $225) or tandem flights (from $130).

Alpine Paragliding PARAGLIDING
(☑0428 352 048; www.alpineparagliding.com; 100 Gavan St; ☺Oct-Jun) Tandem flights from Mystic ($130) and two-day courses $499.

Bright Microflights HANGLIDING
(☑5750 1555; brightmicroflights@swiftdsl.com.au) Takes you on powered hang-glider flights over Porepunkah ($70) or Mt Buffalo ($155).

Elm Lodge Limousine Tours WINERIES
(☑5755 1144; tours from $75) Visit wineries or country pubs in style on a stretch limo tour.

5 Star Adventure Tours   ADVENTURE
(☑5755 5100; www.5staradventure.com.au; 120 Great Alpine Rd) Kayaking, bushwalking, 4WD and snow sports tours.

✯✯ Festivals & Events

Bright Autumn Festival   AUTUMN
(www.brightautumnfestival.org.au) Open gardens, scenic convoy tours and a popular gala day; held April or May.

Bright Spring Festival   SPRING
(www.brightspringfestival.com.au) Celebrate all things Bright and beautiful over the Melbourne Cup weekend in late October/early November.

🛏 Sleeping

There's an abundance of accommodation here, but rooms are scarce during the holiday seasons. There are several good caravan and camping grounds along the Ovens River. If you're stuck, check out **Bright Holiday Accommodation** (www.brightholidays.com.au).

Odd Frog   BOUTIQUE **$$**
(☑5755 2123; www.theoddfrog.com; 3 McFadyens Ln; d $150-195, q $250) Designed and built by the young architect/interior designer owners, these contemporary, ecofriendly studios feature light, breezy spaces and fabulous outdoor decks with a telescope for star gazing. The design features clever use of the hilly site with sculptural steel-frame foundations and flying balconies.

Mine Manager's House   HERITAGE **$$$**
(☑5755 1702; www.brightbedandbreakfast.com.au; 30 Coronation Ave; d $170, B&B $230; 🕱) Dating from 1892 and now sumptuously restored to the finest detail, this traditional B&B offers couples a complete experience. Enjoy warm hospitality, beautiful rooms and a delightful English garden. The claw-foot bath in the self-contained cottage offers an extra treat.

Bright Hikers Backpackers   HOSTEL **$**
(☑5750 1244; www.brighthikers.com.au; 4 Ireland St; dm/s/d/f $25/45/65/130) Right in the centre of town, this clean, well-set-up hostel has a cosy lounge, a great old-style verandah and bike hire ($20 per day).

Elm Lodge Motel   MOTEL **$$**
(☑5755 1144; www.elmlodge.com.au; 2 Wood St; d $100-140, spa cottage $180; 🕱) This slightly quirky set of burgundy and pine units has rooms for all budgets, from a shoebox cheapie to spacious two-bedroom self-contained apartments with polished floor-

boards, and spa rooms. The owners run limousine winery tours (from $75).

Coach House Inn   INN, MOTEL **$$**
(☑5755 1475; www.coachhousebright.com.au; 100 Gavan St; s/d $85/95, motel d/tr/f $110/132/129; ✻🕱) This very central place has simple but supervalue rooms and self-contained motel-style units sleeping from two to six people. In winter there's a ski-hire shop here with discounts for guests, and the popular Lawlers Hut Restaurant next door. High season surcharge is a flat $22 per room.

Bright Caravan Park   CARAVAN PARK **$**
(☑5755 1141; www.brightcaravanpark.com.au; Cherry Ave; unpowered/powered sites from $28/32, cabins $100-180; 🕱) Straddling pretty Morses Creek, this lovely park is five minutes' walk to the shops. The riverside spa cabins are very nice.

Bright Backpackers Outdoor Inn   CAMPING **$**
(☑5755 1154; www.brightbackpackers.com.au; 106 Coronation Dr; unpowered/powered sites from $15/25, d cabins $55; 🕱) This laid-back, friendly park at the foot of Mystic Mountain is popular with paragliders. Cabins are basic but cheap.

🍴 Eating & Drinking

Ireland St, south of the roundabout, has a string of cafes and takeaways and there are more restaurants along Gavan St, the highway through town.

Simone's Restaurant   ITALIAN **$$**
(☑5755 2266; 98 Gavan St; mains $32-35; ⊘dinner Tue-Sat) For 20 years owner–chef Patrizia Simone has been serving outstanding Italian food, with a focus on local ingredients and seasonal produce, in the rustic dining room of this heritage-listed house. This is one of regional Victoria's great restaurants and well worth the splurge. Bookings are essential.

Larder Café & Bar   MODERN AUSTRALIAN **$$**
(☑5755 1537; 2a Anderson St; tapas from $6, mains $18-27; ⊘breakfast, lunch & dinner Fri-Tue) The Larder doesn't look fancy but the philosophy and flavours, using 'native' ingredients like wattleseed, quandong, wild limes and lemon myrtle – perhaps with crocodile tail – are both innovative and something of a taste revelation. Tapas-style plates give you an opportunity to sample the goods.

Beanz of Bright   CAFE **$**
(103 Gavan St; mains $7-16; ⊘breakfast & lunch Tue-Sun) This local favourite is a loungey hole-in-the-wall cafe and bar serving good

coffee and interesting light meals like Thai fish cakes.

Bright Brewery MICROBREWERY
(☑5755 1301; www.brightbrewery.com.au; 121 Gavan St; ☺from noon; ⊕) This small boutique brewery produces a quality range of beers (sample five for $10) and beer-friendly food like pizza, kranskys and nachos. There's a guided tour and tasting on Friday at 3pm ($18), live music on Sunday, or you can learn to be a brewer for a day ($360) – see the website for course dates.

Grape & Grain WINE BAR
([☑5750 1112; www.grapeandgrainbar.com.au; 3/104 Gavan St; ☺Thu-Mon) Swanky bar serving local wines, beers and the good stuff, such as Milawa cheeses and antipasto.

Riverdeck Cafe CAFE $
(☑5755 2199; 119 Gavan St; mains $9-16; ☺breakfast & lunch) Behind the visitor centre, the deck here overlooks the Ovens River and park. Its kid-friendly and a great place for coffee or a pancake breakfast.

Blackbird Café & Food Store CAFE $$
(☑5750 1838; 95 Gavan St; mains $12-21; ☺breakfast & lunch) Newspapers spread across couches and coffee tables, while locals mingle with tourists in this light-filled corner cafe.

❶ Information

Alpine visitor information centre (☑1800 111 885, 5755 0584; www.visitalpinevictoria.com.au, www.brightvictoria.com.au; 119 Gavan St; @) Has a busy accommodation booking service, Parks Victoria information and the attached Riverdeck Cafe. Internet access costs $6 per hour.

❶ Getting There & Away

V/Line (☑13 61 96) runs train/coach services from Melbourne with a change at Seymour ($27, 4½ hours, two daily). Alternatively, take the train to Wangaratta and the bus from there. During the ski season the **Snowball Express** (www.snowball-express.com.au) operates from Bright to Mt Hotham (adult/child return $30/20, 1½ hours).

MT BEAUTY & THE KIEWA VALLEY

POP 1700

Huddled at the foot of Mt Bogong (Victoria's highest mountain) on the Kiewa River, Mt Beauty and its twin villages of Tawonga and Tawonga South are the gateways to Falls

Creek ski resort. It's reached by a steep and winding road from Bright with some lovely alpine views, particularly from Tawonga Gap Lookout. A scenic loop drive is via the **Happy Valley Tourist Road** from Ovens to Mt Beauty.

The **Mt Beauty Music Festival** (www.musicmuster.org.au) brings together folk, blues and country musicians in April.

⊙ Sights & Activities

The 2km **Tree Fern Walk** and the longer **Peppermint Walk** both start from Mountain Creek Picnic and Camping Ground, on Mountain Creek Rd, off the Kiewa Valley Hwy (C531). Located about 1km south of Bogong Village (towards Falls Creek), the 1.5km return **Fainter Falls Walk** takes you to a pretty cascade. For information on longer walks in the area, visit the Alpine Discovery Centre.

There's a fascinating visitor information centre at the **Bogong Power Station** (☑5754 3318; Bogong High Plains Rd; admission free; ☺11am-3pm Wed-Sun), a working hydro-electric plant about 20km from Mt Beauty. The centre explains the history of the hydro scheme and has a water wall and a viewing window into the plant.

Rocky Valley Bikes (☑5754 1118; www.rockyvalley.com.au; Kiewa Valley Hwy; rides beginner/advanced $25/95) hires mountain and cross-country bikes from $20/30 per half-/full-day, and snowsports equipment in the white season.

Annapurna Estate (☑5754 4517; www.annapurnaestate.com.au; 217 Simmonds Creek Rd, Tawonga South; meals $12-30; ☺11am-4pm Fri-Sun), about 3km from Mt Beauty, is a stunning vineyard and restaurant where you can dine on canapés, nori rolls or a kangaroo saddle fillet on the lovely deck looking over the vines.

This is world-renowned trout-fishing territory. **Angling Expeditions** (☑5754 1466; www.anglingvic.com.au; 82 Kiewa Valley Hwy, Tawonga; from $90 per person) specialises in fly-fishing trips to a private creek as well as river expeditions.

Horse riders can experience this beautiful area on horseback with **Bogong Horseback Adventures** (☑5754 4849; www.bogonghorse.com.au; Mountain Creek Rd, Tawonga; 2/3hr/full-day $80/95/190).

⊨ Sleeping

There's camping along the Kiewa River and several motels along the highway.

Dreamers
BOUTIQUE $$$

(☑5754 1222; www.dreamers1.com; Kiewa Valley Hwy; d $200-590) Each of Dreamer's stunning self-contained eco apartments offer something special and architecturally unique. Sunken lounges, open fireplaces, loft bedrooms and balcony spas are just some of the highlights. Great views and a pretty lagoon complete a dreamily romantic five-star experience.

Mount Beauty Holiday Centre
CARAVAN PARK $

(☑5754 4396; www.holidaycentre.com.au; Kiewa Valley Hwy; unpowered/powered sites $26/31, cabins & yurts $80-140; ❄) This family caravan park close to the town centre has river frontage, games and an interesting range of cabins, including hexagonal 'yurts'.

✗ Eating & Drinking

Å Skafferi
SCANDINAVIAN $

(☑5754 4544; www.svarmisk.com.au; 84 Bogong High Plains Rd, Mt Beauty; meals $5-17; ⊙breakfast & lunch) This cool Swedish pantry and foodstore is the latest addition to the Svärmisk apartment complex. Try the grilled Milawa cheese sandwiches for breakfast and the Swedish meatballs or the sampler of herring and *knackebrod* for lunch.

Roi's Diner Restaurant
ITALIAN $$

(☑5754 4495; 177 Kiewa Valley Hwy, Tawonga; mains $26-30; ⊙dinner Thu-Sun) It's hard to believe this unassuming timber shack on the highway 5km from Mt Beauty is an award-winning restaurant, specialising in exceptional modern-Italian cuisine. Great risotto.

Bogong Hotel
PUB $

(☑5754 4449; 169 Kiewa Valley Hwy, Tawonga; mains $16-28; ⊙lunch Sat & Sun, dinner daily) It's hard to beat this country pub for a beer with mountain views from the front verandah. Excellent bistro and the cheaper bar meals and Bogong burgers are a steal.

❶ Information

Mt Beauty visitors centre (☑1800 111 885; www.greatalpinevalleys.com.au; 31 Bogong High Plains Rd) Has an accommodation booking service, a working hydroelectric model and displays on the history and nature of the region.

❶ Getting There & Away

V/Line (☑13 61 96) operates a train/bus/taxi service from Melbourne to Mt Beauty, via Seymour and Bright ($31, 5½hr). In winter **Falls**

Creek Coach Service (☑5754 4024; www.fallscreekcoachservice.com.au) operates direct buses to Mt Beauty from Melbourne on Wednesday, Friday, Saturday and Sunday (one way/return $81/127) and from Albury from Thursday to Sunday ($32/50), both continuing on to Falls Creek ($35/55).

FALLS CREEK

ELEV 1780M

Victoria's glitzy, fashion-conscious resort, Falls Creek combines a picturesque Alpine setting with impressive skiing and infamous après-ski entertainment. **Skiing** is spread over two areas – the **Village Bowl** and **Sun Valley** – with 19 lifts, a vertical drop of 267m and Australia's longest beginner's run at **Wombat's Ramble**. Falls is also the freeride snowboard capital, with four parks. **Night skiing** in the Village Bowl operates several times a week.

Other winter activities include a bungy trampoline ($11), snow bikes ($36), snow-tubing and tobogganing, snowmobile tours (from $120), kiteboarding (from $60) and snowshoe tours ($22). For information, call the **Activities Hotline** (☑1800 204 424).

It's not all snow sports though, and Falls has a great **summer program**, which includes an outdoor cinema on an inflatable screen (free), hiking, mountain biking, horse riding and a rock-climbing wall. The **Summit chairlift** operates during the summer school holidays (per ride/day $12/22). **Mountain biking** is popular here in the green season with downhill trails, three lift-accessed trails, spur fire trails, aqueduct trails, road circuits and bike rental ($50 per day).

The best local **hiking trails** include the walk to **Wallace Hut**, built in 1889, and said to be the oldest cattleman's hut in the High Country, and **Rocky Valley Lake**.

Packers High Country Horse Riding (☑5159 7241; www.horsetreks.com; 1½hr $80, half-/full day $140/200), based at Anglers Rest on the road to Omeo, offers true High Country riding through river valleys and snow-gum forests.

✿ Festivals & Events

Mile High Dragon Boat Festival BOAT
(www.fallscreek.com.au/dragonboats) Gorgeous, glorious dragon boats race on Rocky Valley Lake. Held from 26 to 27 January.

Easter Festival EASTER
(www.fallscreek.com.au/easterfestival) A giant Easter-egg hunt.

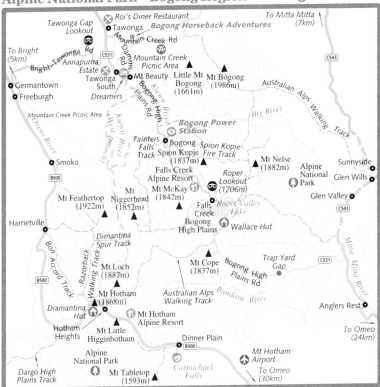

Sleeping

Accommodation at Falls is above the snow-line, so in winter the lodges are truly ski in, ski out. Accommodation can be booked via several agencies, such as **Falls Creek Central Reservations** (☏1800 033 079; www.fallscreek.com.au/centralreservations) or **Falls Creek Reservation Centre** (☏1800 453 525; www.fallscreek.com.au/ResCentre). Most lodges stipulate a minimum two-night stay, particularly on weekends.

Alpha Lodge   LODGE **$**
(☏5758 3488; www.alphaskilodge.com.au; 5 Parallel St; dm summer/winter from $30/109) A spacious, affordable lodge with a sauna, a large lounge with panoramic views, and a communal kitchen.

Viking Alpine Lodge   LODGE **$**
(☏5758 3247; 13 Parallel St; dm/s/d summer $35/65/90, ski season per person $58-137) Viking offers good-value accommodation all year

with excellent communal facilities including lounge, kitchen and great views. Ski in, ski out.

Frueauf Village   APARTMENTS **$$$**
(☏1300 300 709; www.fvfalls.com.au; d summer/winter from $447/554; ☏) These luxurious, architect-designed apartments have everything, including private outdoor hot tubs, plus the funky Milch Cafe Wine Bar.

Eating & Drinking

Quality kiosks, cafes and restaurants abound and there's a supermarket with a bottleshop for self-caterers.

Milch Cafe Wine Bar   WINE BAR **$$**
(☏0408 465 939; 4 Schuss St; mains $12-24) The hip place to see and be seen, this bar-restaurant offers flavoursome Middle Eastern meze and a good wine list. In winter, the bar is packed with skiers conducting post-mortems of their runs.

SLED DOG TOURS

For a real Arctic-style adventure, try a dog-sledding tour, where you're pulled along on a traditional sled behind a team of huskies.

Australian Sleddog Tours (☑0418 230 982; www.sleddogtours.com.au, Dinner Plain; adult/child $115/65) does day tours from Dinner Plain.

Howling Husky Sled Dog Tours (☑0409 517 633; www.howlinghuskysleddogs.com; short rides per double $80, tours per single/double $95/170) offers short rides from their base at Omeo Caravan park, and weekend tours at Mt Baw Baw.

Mo's Restaurant at FeatHertop

MODERN AUSTRALIAN **$$**

(☑5758 3232; 14 Parallel St; mains $18-34; ⊘dinner) This inviting winter-only restaurant at the Feathertop Lodge features leather chesterfield couches, private alcoves and mood lighting.

Huski Produce Store

CAFE **$**

(☑5758 3863; www.huski.com.au; 3 Sitzmark St; ⊘5pm-1.30am) Chic produce store and cafe with great casual dining, coffee and High Country produce.

Man Hotel

PUB

(☑5758 3362; www.fallscreek.com.au/theman hotel; 20 Slalom St; ⊘5pm-1.30am) 'The Man' has been around forever, is open all year and is the heart of Falls' nightlife. In winter it fires up as a club, cocktail bar and live-music venue featuring popular Aussie bands. Good pub dinners and pizzas are available from the **Man Kitchen** ($14-28; ⊘dinner).

ⓘ Information

Ski season daily resort entry is $32 per car. One-day lift tickets per adult/student/child cost $102/69/51. Combined lift-and-lesson packages cost $153/130/104. Lift tickets also cover Mt Hotham. An over-snow taxi service ($34 return) operates between the car parks and the lodges from 7am to midnight daily (to 2am Friday night, to 1am Sat & Sun). Car parking for day visitors is at the base of the village, next to the ski lifts.

Falls Creek Resort Management (☑1800 033 079; www.fallscreek.com.au; 1 Slalom St; ⊘9am-5pm) Has informative pamphlets including *Crosscountry* (about ski trails that are also good for summer walking).

Falls Creek Visitor Information Centre (☑5758 1202; Bogong High Plains Rd; ⊘8am-5pm winter) The helpful visitor centre is near Foodworks supermarket.

ⓘ Getting There & Around

Falls Creek is 375km, and a 4½ hour drive, from Melbourne. During winter **Falls Creek Coach Service** (☑5754 4024; www.fallscreekcoach-service.com.au) operates four times a week between Falls Creek and Melbourne (one way/return $99/161) and also runs services to and from Albury ($57/90) and Mt Beauty ($35/55). There's a reduced service in summer.

If you want to ski Mt Hotham for the day, jump on the **HeliLink** for $125 return (if you have a valid lift ticket).

HARRIETVILLE

POP 280

Harrietville, a pretty little town nestled on the Ovens River below Mt Feathertop, is the last stop before the start of the winding road up to Mt Hotham. During ski season a bus shuttles between the town and Mt Hotham, making it a good spot for slightly cheaper off-mountain accommodation.

Harrietville is the start/finishing point for various **alpine walking tracks**, including the popular Mt Feathertop walk, Razorback Ridge and Dargo High Plains walks. The town is also developing as a mountain-biking centre – you can hire bikes (half-/full day $30/40) from Snowline Hotel, which also runs mountain-bike tours and mountain transfers.

In late November the annual **Bluegrass Festival** (www.bluegrass.org.au) takes over the town.

🛏 Sleeping & Eating

Snowline Hotel

HOTEL, MOTEL **$**

(☑5759 2524; www.snowlinehotel.com.au; Great Alpine Rd; d from $100) The Snowline has been operating for over 100 years, and offers inexpensive off-mountain accommodation in comfortable motel rooms. The **pub bistro** (mains $20-29) has a loyal following, especially for its chicken parma, Harrietville trout and Tasmanian Angus steak.

Shady Brook Cottages

COTTAGES **$$**

(☑5759 2741; www.shadybrook.com.au; Mountain View Walk; 1-/2-bed cottages from $110/150; @❄) A magnificent garden envelopes this lovely, peaceful group of self-contained country-style cottages. Two come with a spa and all have balconies and mod cons.

Bella's
CAFE **$**

(📞5759 2750; 231 Great Alpine Rd; meals $7-17 ⏰breakfast & lunch Thu-Tue) For an all-day breakfast, or lunch of antipasto, damper rolls and pizza with a glass of local wine or hot coffee, this welcoming cafe is Harriet-ville's best.

Big Shed Café
CAFE **$**

(📞5759 2672; Great Alpine Rd, Smoko; meals $6-18; ⏰breakfast & lunch Wed-Mon) You can't miss this giant roadside restaurant in the beauti-fully named hamlet of Smoko, 7km north of Harrietville. The former tobacco shed is now a popular gourmet cafe dishing up focaccias, camembert wedges, and fish and chips.

MT HOTHAM & DINNER PLAIN

ELEV 1868M

Serious hikers, skiers and snowboarders make tracks for Mt Hotham, with some of the best and most challenging downhill runs in the country – the mountain is home to 320 hectares of downhill runs, with a verti-cal drop of 428m and about 80% of the ski trails are intermediate or advanced black di-amond runs. Beginners hit the Big D, which is open for **night skiing** every Wednesday and Saturday in winter. Over at **Dinner Plain**, 10km from Hotham village and linked by a free shuttle, there are excellent **cross-country trails** around the village, including the Hotham-Dinner Plain Ski Trail.

From November to May, Hotham and Din-ner Plain boast some stunning **alpine trails** for hiking and mountain biking. The most popular trail in summer is to **Mt Feathertop** (1922m). This crosses the Razorback Ridge starting at the Diamantina Hut (2.5km from Mt Hotham village). It's 22km return and re-quires sound walking shoes.

Dinner Plain is particularly well set-up for summer activities. Specialising in mountain-bike hire and tours, **Adventures with Alti-tude** (📞5159 6608; www.adventureswithaltitude. com.au; bike hire per hr $15, half-/full day $40/60) provides gear and trail maps. The guided mountain-bike tours start at $80/120 per half-/full day (as well as multiday trips) and they also organise guided bushwalks and horse riding. Also here is a **mountain-bike park** (per day $40; ⏰weekends) with downhill and cross-country trails and jumps.

When the agony ends, head to **Onsen Retreat and Spa** (📞5150 8880; www.onsen. com.au; Big Muster Drive, Dinner Plain; massage/ treatment from $65/135; ⏰daily winter), a divine Japanese-influenced, indoor-outdoor experi-ence where the body gets to feel beautiful. Onsen bathing plus swim, sauna and gym is $45. It's open only during the ski season.

✦ Festivals

Cool Summer Festival
MUSIC

(www.coolsummerfestival.com.au) Three days of music in the middle of nowhere; held in February or March.

Mountain Fresh Festival
FOOD, WINE

(www.mountainfresh.com.au) A week of food and wine with altitude; held in mid-July.

🛏 Sleeping

MT HOTHAM

Leeton Lodge
LODGE **$**

(📞5759 3683; www.leetonlodge.com; Dargo Ct; summer per adult/child $35/20) Classic family ski-club lodge with 30 beds, cooking facili-ties and good views. Open year-round.

General Backpackers
HOSTEL **$**

(📞5759 3523; Great Alpine Rd; dm summer/winter $30/60, apt $150) Behind the General, these brand new fully self-contained apartments have lounge and kitchen and views from the balcony.

MT HOTHAM BOOKING AGENCIES

Ski-season accommodation generally has a minimum two-night stay. Booking agencies:

Mt Hotham Accommodation Service (📞1800 032 061, 5759 3636; www.mthotham accommodation.com.au) Books mountain accommodation during the ski season.

Mt Hotham Central Reservations (📞1800 657 547, 5759 3522; www.skicom.com.au) Books on- and off-mountain accommodation throughout the year.

Dinner Plain Accommodation (📞1800 444 066, 5159 6696; www.accommdinnerplain. com.au; Big Muster Dr).

Dinner Plain Central Reservations (📞1800 670 019, 5159 6451; www.dinnerplain.com; Big Muster Dr)

Arlberg Resort APARTMENTS $$
(☎5759 3618; www.arlberg.com.au; 2 nights low/high season from $410/820; 🛜🏊) The largest resort on the mountain, the Arlberg has a big range of apartments and motel-style rooms, plus restaurants, bars, ski hire and a heated pool. Open during ski season only.

DINNER PLAIN

Currawong Lodge LODGE $$
(☎5159 6452, 1800 635 589; www.currawonglodge.com.au; Big Muster Dr; summer s/d $80/130, ski season 2-night minimum d $210) Currawong Lodge welcomes you with a huge communal lounge-and-kitchen area with a monster open fireplace, TV, DVD and stereo. At this price you can ski with a conscience.

Rundell's Alpine Lodge LODGE $$
(☎5159 6422; www.rundells.com.au; Big Muster Dr; summer d from $198, ski season 2-night minimum $550; 🏊) Originally an Australian Army retreat, this sprawling complex is a well-run hotel with all the comforts – spa, sauna and restaurant/bar – but a definite lack of pretension. The restaurant and cafe (mains $15 to $36) here is open year-round.

🍴 Eating & Drinking

MT HOTHAM

In winter, there are plenty of great eating choices here. In summer a couple of places serve meals and the small supermarket at the General is open.

ALPINE HIGHWAYS

The Victorian High Country has three great 'highways' that will take you up and over the mountains and down to the Gippsland coast. All three link up with Omeo and become the Great Alpine Rd down to Bairnsdale and are a joy for car or motorcycle touring, or for hard-core cyclists!

Great Alpine Road

This much-loved 308km route starts at Wangaratta and follows the Ovens Valley through Myrtleford, Bright and Harrietville before passing over Mt Hotham and Dinner Plain then descending to Omeo and all the way down to Bairnsdale in East Gippsland. It's Australia's highest year-round-accessible sealed road. The section from Omeo southeast to Bruthen is particularly scenic, following the valley of the Tambo River and passing farmland, vineyards and the pretty communities of Swift's Creek and Ensay.

Omeo Highway

Stretching about 155km from the Murray River near Tallangatta to Omeo, the Omeo Hwy (C543) is one of Victoria's most scenic alpine routes. The highway is unsealed in sections (between Mitta Mitta and Glen Willis), and snow often makes it difficult to pass in winter.

   The first section of the road from Tallangatta follows the flatlands of the Mitta Mitta River between wooded mountains. Mitta Mitta is an old gold-mining settlement, and a track leads from the highway to the former Pioneer Mine site, one of the largest hydraulic sluicing operations in Victoria, yielding some 15,000oz (425.25kg) of gold over 16 years.

   At Anglers Rest, beside the Cobungra River, is the **Blue Duck Inn** (☎5159 7220; www.blueduckinn.com.au; Omeo Hwy; mains $18-27; ⊘lunch & dinner Wed-Sun), popular with anglers, motorcyclists, kayakers and bushwalkers for its hearty meals and barbecue area by the river. The two-bedroom self-contained cabins ($130 to $150) here are very cosy.

   Finally, 30km south of Anglers Rest, you reach Omeo and join up with the Great Alpine Rd.

Bogong High Plains Road

In 2009 the Bogong High Plains Rd was finally sealed all the way from Falls Creek to the Omeo Hwy, creating another fabulous all-season tourist route. The journey starts at Mt Beauty and climbs up through Bogong village, where the Bogong Power Station (p271) is worth a visit, to Falls Creek ski resort. From there it skirts Rocky Valley Lake and winds 35km to join the Omeo Hwy about 11km north of Anglers Rest. The result is a superb alpine loop where you can drive from Bright, over Mt Hotham via Omeo to Falls Creek, down to Mt Beauty and back to Bright – a distance of about 250km.

General
PUB $$

(☑5759 3523; Great Alpine Rd; meals $8-30; ☺lunch & dinner; ☻) The ever-reliable 'Gen' is open all year and is a popular watering hole with a menu of pizzas and good bistro meals, as well as internet access.

Zirky's
CAFE $

(☑5759 3518; Great Alpine Rd; meals $10-14; ☺breakfast & lunch Wed-Sun) The Z cafe here at the base of the summit run opens year-round, while Andrew Blake's fine-dining restaurant (open for dinner in winter) is highly regarded.

Good places for an après-ski drink include **Jack Frost**, **Avalanche Bar** and **Swindlers**.

DINNER PLAIN
Dinner Plain Hotel
PUB BISTRO $

(☑5159 6462; mains $9-20; ☺lunch & dinner) The barn-sized local pub is the social hub of Dinner Plain and a friendly place to hang out year-round, with roaring open fires and a bistro serving good pub grub and pizzas.

❶ Information
The ski-season admission fee is $35 per car per day, and $12 for bus passengers (this may be included in your fare). Lift tickets (peak) per adult/student/child cost $102/87/51. Passes are cheaper in September and there are packages that include gear hire and lessons. Lift tickets also cover Falls Creek.

Hotham Central Guest Services (☑5759 4470; Hotham Central) Open during winter.

Mt Hotham Alpine Resort Management Board (☑5759 3550; www.mthotham.com.au) At the village administration centre. Collect a range of brochures with maps for short, eco, heritage and village walks.

Dinner Plain visitor centre (☑1300 734 365; www.visitdinnerplain.com).

❶ Getting There & Around
During the ski season, **Snowball Express** (☑9370 9055, 1800 659 009; www.snowballexpress.com.au) has daily buses from Melbourne to Mt Hotham ($160 return, six hours), via Wangaratta, Myrtleford, Bright and Harrietville.

O'Connell's Bus Lines (☑0428 591 377; www.omeobus.com.au) operates a daily 'Alps Link' service between Omeo and Bright ($9.20) via Mt Hotham and Dinner Plain ($4.40).

A free shuttle runs frequently around the resort from 7am to 3am; a separate shuttle service also operates to Dinner Plain. The free 'zoo cart' takes skiers from their lodges to the lifts between 8am and 6pm.

Mt Hotham Airport services Mt Hotham and Dinner Plain, but it's currently only served in winter by **QantasLink** (www.qantas.com.au) from Sydney, and by charter flights.

Heli-Link (☑5759 4444; return $125, with a lift ticket) takes six minutes to fly to Falls Creek (on clear days) so you can spend a day skiing there.

OMEO

High in the hills, historic Omeo comes as a bit of a surprise after the winding drive up from the coast or down from the mountains. This is the southern access route to Mt Hotham and Falls Creek and the main town on the eastern section of the Great Alpine Rd. The road is sometimes snowbound in winter; always check conditions before heading this way and carry chains. In the gold-rush days of the 1850s, Omeo was the wildest and most remote goldfields in the state. It attracted many Chinese diggers whose legacy you can see today on the **Oriental Claims Walk**. Stay a while to wander the steep main street and breathe in the crisp mountain air.

🛏 Sleeping & Eating
The scenic **Victoria Falls Camping Area**, off the Great Alpine Rd, 18km west of Omeo, has pit toilets and a picnic area. In town, there's a bakery, a couple of cafes and takeaways.

Golden Age Hotel
HOTEL $$

(☑5159 1344; www.goldenageomeo.com.au; Day Ave; budget s/d $50/80, s/d $95/109, d with spa $157) This beautiful art deco corner pub dominates Omeo's main street. Upstairs are simple but elegant pub rooms, some with en suite and spa – the best rooms open onto the balcony. The welcoming **restaurant** (mains $15-25) serves plates piled high with reliable fare of steaks, salads and gourmet pizzas.

Snug as a Bug Motel
MOTEL $$

(☑5159 1311; www.motelomeo.com.au; 188 Great Alpine Rd; d/f from $90/160) There's a range of accommodation here is lovely country-style historic buildings. There are family motel rooms, the main guesthouse, a cute self-contained cottage and the two-room Omeo Backpackers (doubles $65).

Omeo Caravan Park
CARAVAN PARK $

(☑5159 1351; www.omeocaravanpark.com.au; Old Omeo Hwy; unpowered/powered sites $25/28, d cabins from $90) In a pretty valley alongside the Livingstone Creek about 2km from

THE MAN FROM SNOWY RIVER

You've seen the film and probably read Banjo Paterson's famous poem, but out east at Corryong, close to the source of the Murray River, they live the legend. It looked like so much fun in the film that the locals just had to try it – mountain horse-racing where 'the hills are twice as steep and twice as rough'. Yes, it's the **Country Wide Challenge**, Australia's ultimate test of horse-riding prowess! The race is a feature of the **Man From Snowy River Bush Festival** (☏6076 1992; www.manfromsnowyriverbushfestival.com.au; ⊙Mar) – four days of whip-cracking and yarn-spinning fun.

Corryong is a pretty township ringed by mountains – a natural playground for trout fishing, canoeing, cycling and bushwalking. The **Man From Snowy River Museum** (☏6076 1114; www.manfromsnowyrivermuseum.com; 105 Hanson St; adult/child $4/1; ⊙10am-4pm Sep-May) tells the story of Jack Riley, a stockman who lived and worked near Corryong and might have been Paterson's inspiration. It's also a local history museum, featuring a set of snow skis from 1870 and the Jarvis Homestead, a 19th-century slab-timber hut.

Corryong visitors centre (☏6076 2277; www.towong.com; 50 Hanson St; ⊙9am-5pm) has info on the region, including **Jack Riley's Grave** (Corryong Cemetery) which is inscribed with the words, 'In memory of the Man from Snowy River, Jack Riley, buried here 16th July 1914.'

town, this park has spacious, grassy sites. Bike hire is available.

ℹ Information

Omeo visitor information centre (☏03-5159 1679; www.omeoregion.com.au; 152 Day Ave; ⊙10am-3pm)

Omeo Service Station (☏5159 1312; www.omeoskihire.com.au; Main St, Omeo) Ski and chain hire.

ℹ Getting There & Away

Omeo Bus Lines (☏0427 017 732) has one bus on weekdays only between Omeo and Bairnsdale ($17, two hours). **O'Connell's Bus Lines** (☏0428 591 377; www.omeobus.com.au) operates a daily summer 'Alps Link' service between Omeo and Bright ($9.20) via Mt Hotham and Dinner Plain ($4.40). A winter service to Dinner Plain and Mt Hotham operates on Sunday, Wednesday and Friday.

The Murray

Includes »

Best Places to Eat

» Stefano's Restaurant (p286)

» Oscar W's Wharfside (p294)

» Java Spice (p289)

» Pickled Sisters Café (p298)

» Rinaldo's Casa Cucina (p305)

Best Places to Stay

» Houseboat in Mildura (p286) or Echuca (p294)

» Quality Hotel Mildura Grand (p285)

» Camping, Gunbower Island (p290)

» Steam Packet Inn (p293)

» Tuileries, Rutherglen (p297)

Why Go?

State border, irrigation lifeline and recreational magnet for waterskiers, canoeists, campers and golfers, the mighty Murray is Australia's longest and most important inland waterway. It's a stirring place of paddle steamers and houseboat holidays, wineries and orchards, bush camping, balmy weather and red-gum forests.

Most people think of the Murray as a wide, brown, slow-moving strip, but it changes character constantly as it flows from the mountains of the Great Dividing Range in northeastern Victoria to Encounter Bay in South Australia – almost 2400km. Along the way it supplies vital irrigation for orchards, vineyards and farms. Some of Australia's earliest explorers travelled along the river, and long before roads and railways crossed the land, the Murray's paddle steamers carried supplies to and from remote sheep stations.

When to Go
Mildura

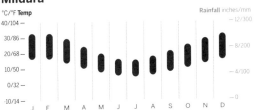

Anytime The Murray region enjoys year-round sunshine, especially Mildura

Sep–Nov Spring-time sees some of the best local festivals, without the heat

Feb–Mar A good time for camping on the river after the holiday crowds have left

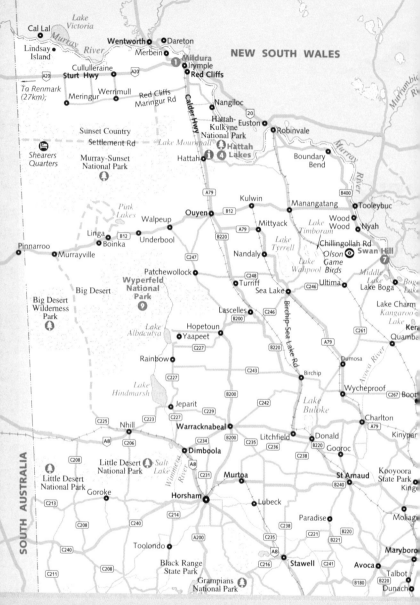

The Murray Highlights

❶ Relax on a houseboat and dine out on 'Feast Street' in sunny **Mildura** (p280)

❷ Ride an original paddle steamer from the **historic Port of Echuca** (p290)

❸ Time your visit to **Rutherglen** (p296) for one of the great winery festivals

❹ Spot the many species of waterbirds at beautiful **Hattah Lakes** (p300)

❺ Set up a bush camp and a fishing rod on the banks of the Murray at **Gunbower National Park** (p289)

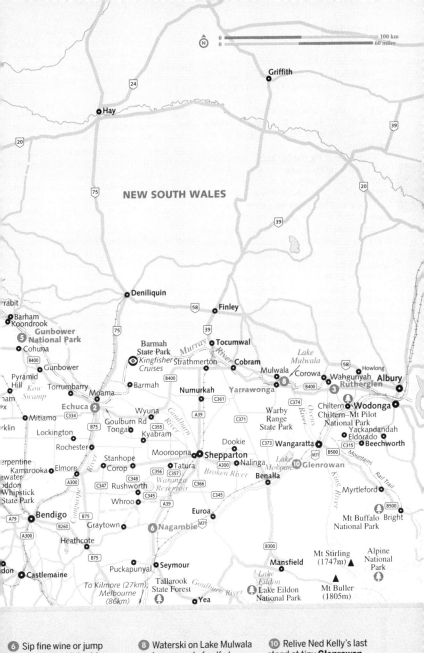

MILDURA

POP 30,000

Sunny, sultry Mildura. After crossing wind-swept deserts and pale-golden wheat fields, it comes as something of a shock to see the miles of fertile vineyards and orchards that thrive is this corner of the state. Mildura (meaning 'red soil') is a true oasis: a modern town with its roots firmly in the grand old pastoralist era.

Considering its remote location, Mildura is a remarkably prosperous and progressive city with fun nightlife, decent shopping, art deco buildings (such as Mildura Brewery, Sandbar and T&G Tower) and some of the best dining in provincial Victoria. Thanks to irrigation, this is one of Australia's richest agricultural areas – it was once a major citrus-growing region and is now the biggest producer of wine in the country. If you're looking for casual work, this is a popular destination for fruit-pickers and agricultural labour.

Of course, the region makes full use of the Murray so it's very easy to get out fishing, swimming, canoeing, waterskiing, house-boating, taking a paddle-steamer cruise or playing riverside golf courses. The weather up here is very much blue sky – you can expect warm, sunny days even in midwinter.

Most places of interest are around the riverside wharf and the main boulevard, Deakin Ave, but Mildura sprawls through the suburbs of Red Cliffs and Irymple, and across the river are the towns of Bunerong and Wentworth.

◉ Sights

Mildura owes much to the Chaffey brothers and their irrigation systems (see boxed text, p284). Pick up a copy of *The Chaffey Trail* from the visitor centre and follow their story. Emerging from the Chaffey vision were the **Mildura Wharf**, now a mooring for paddleboats, the weir and the lock, which is operated at 11am, 12.30pm, 2pm and 3.30pm daily.

Rio Vista & Mildura Arts Centre

HISTORIC BUILDING, GALLERY

(☎5018 8330; www.yourartscentre.com.au; 199 Cureton Ave; admission free; ◷11am-4pm Wed-Mon) Chaffey's grand homestead, the historic Queen Anne–style Rio Vista, has been beautifully preserved and restored, with each room set up as a series of historical displays depicting colonial life in the 19th century, including period furnishings, costumes, photos and a collection of letters and memorabilia.

At the time of writing, the Mildura Arts Centre, in the same complex, was closed for

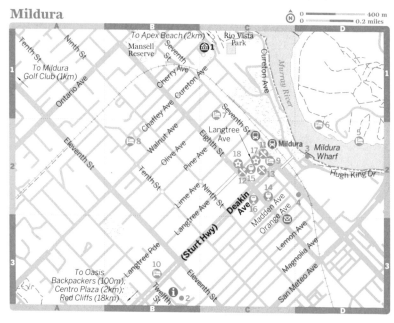

Mildura

extensive redevelopment and due to reopen in late 2011. It combines a modern-art gallery with changing exhibitions and a theatre.

Old Mildura Homestead HISTORIC SITE
(Cureton Ave, Old Mildura House Heritage Park; admission by donation; ⊙9am-6pm) Along the river near Rio Vista, this cottage was the first home of William B Chaffey. The heritage park here contains a few other historic log buildings and has picnic and barbecue facilities.

Old Psyche Bend Pump Station
HISTORIC SITE
(⚹5024 5637; off Cureton Ave, Kings Billabong; adult/family $3/8; ⊙1-4pm Tue & Thu, 10.30am-12.30pm Sun) This station is where Chaffey set up his system to supply irrigation and drainage over 115 years ago. The pumps are electric now and placed a bit further up the river. You can walk around the old centrifugal pumps and Chaffey's triple-expansion steam-engine pump. The station is within Kings Billabong, a pretty nature reserve on the Murray floodplain about 8km southeast of the town centre.

Chateau Mildura WINERY, MUSEUM
(⚹5024 5901; www.chateaumildura.com.au; 191 Belar Ave, Irymple; adult/child $10/free; ⊙10am-4pm) Established in 1888 and still producing table wines, this is a living wine and horticultural museum with wine tasting to help your cultural experience.

Apex Beach BEACH
About 3km northwest of the centre, this is a popular swimming and picnic spot with a

There's almost always a 'twin' town across the Murray River in NSW (technically the river itself is in NSW) but generally the most interesting towns are on the Victorian side – the main exception being Albury-Wodonga (sorry Wodonga!). Before Federation in 1901, all major river crossings had customs houses on each bank, from which the two states levied tariffs on goods carried across their borders. Before poker machines were introduced into Victoria in 1990, many of the twin towns on the NSW side made a fortune from punters travelling across by the busload to play the 'pokies'. Now they're on both sides and gambling has spread like a plague through Victoria!

sandy beach on the Murray. There's a good walking and cycling track from here to the Old Mildura Homestead.

 Activities

Golfers are spoilt for choice in Mildura. **Mildura Golf Club** (⚹5022 8089; www.mildura golfclub.com.au; Twelfth St; 18 holes $25, club hire $22) has a well-maintained and challenging public course in a bush setting beautiful setting. **Riverside Golf Club** (⚹5023 4255; www.visitmildura.com.au/golf; Park St, Nichols Pt; 18 holes $18) is another good course by the river, with a licensed clubhouse.

Mildura

THE CHAFFEY BROTHERS

Mildura partly owes its existence to the Canadian brothers George and William B Chaffey, famous 19th-century engineers who set up an irrigation colony here.

Their promotional scheme was launched in 1887 and attracted more than 3000 settlers to the area. They cleared scrub, dug irrigation channels and built fences, and two massive pumping-station engines were shipped from England.

The early years of the settlement were tough and full of frustrations. There was an economic collapse in the 1890s, rabbit plagues and droughts, and clearing the mallee scrub was a nightmare. George became disillusioned, and in 1896 he returned to North America.

In 1889 William built Rio Vista, a grand riverside homestead, to express his confidence in the new settlement. But his wife, Hattie, died during childbirth before it was finished, and their newborn son died five months later. William later married his deceased wife's niece, also named Hattie, and lived in Mildura until he died in 1926 at the age of 70. Happily, he was there to see the Melbourne–Mildura railway line finally open in 1902, meaning the town's future was assured.

Paddle-steamer Cruises

Paddle-steamer cruises depart from the Mildura Wharf, and most go through a lock: watch the gates opening and the water levels changing. For bookings call ☎5023 2200, or go to www.paddlesteamers.com.au.

PS Melbourne   PADDLE STEAMER

(2hr cruise adult/child $27/12; ⊙cruises 10.50am & 1.50pm) One of the original paddle steamers, and the only one still driven by steam power. Watch the operator stoke the original boiler with wood. On Friday and Saturday this cruise is aboard the PV *Rothbury*.

PV Rothbury   PADDLE STEAMER, WINERY

(winery cruise adult/child $62/30, lunch cruise $29/13) The fastest of the riverboats, it offers a winery cruise from 10.30am on Thursday, with a visit to Trentham Estate Winery and a barbecue lunch at Kings Billabong. On Tuesday there's a lunch cruise to Gol Gol Hotel, where you buy your own meal.

PV Mundoo   PADDLE STEAMER, DINNER

(dinner cruise adult/child $62/30) The newest riverboat has a dinner cruise every Thursday from 7pm. This cruise is sometimes aboard PV *Rothbury*.

☞ Tours

The best tours out of Mildura focus on the region's history, adventure opportunities and cultural heritage. A standout is the extraordinary, ancient natural formations of Mungo National Park (in NSW). Several operators run tours out there, focusing on its culture, 45,000 years of history, and wildlife.

Harry Nanya Tours

NATURE, INDIGENOUS CULTURE

(☎5027 2076; www.harrynanyatours.com.au; tours adult/child $170/110) Indigenous guide Graham Clarke keeps you enchanted with Dreamtime stories and his deep knowledge and understanding of the Mungo region. In summer (November to March), there's a spectacular sunset tour.

Sunraysia Discovery Tours   NATURE

(☎5023 5937; www.sunraysiadiscoverytours.com. au; tours adult/child $140/70) Day tours to Mungo National Park, including lunch and admission fees.

Moontongue Eco-Adventures

KAYAKING

(☎0427 898 317; www.moontongue.com.au; kayak tours $25-50) A sunset kayaking trip is a great way to see the river and its wildlife. Local guide Ian will tell you about the landscape and birdlife as you work those muscles in the magnificent, peaceful surroundings of Gol Gol Creek and the Murray.

Wild Side Outdoors   ADVENTURE

(☎5024 3721, 0428 242852; www.wildside outdoors.com.au) Wild Side is an eco-friendly outfit offering a range of activities including a sunset kayaking tour at Kings Billabong (adult/child $30/10), and a six-hour 4WD tour into the Hattah-Kulkyne National Park (adult/child $80/30). It also has canoe/kayak/mountain-bike hire for $30/20/20 per hour.

Mildura Ballooning   HOT-AIR BALLOONING

(☎5024 6848; www.miiduraballooning.com. au; adult/child $295/195) Enjoy the sunrise from the air with a one-hour dawn balloon flight over the wonderful patchwork of vineyards, orchards and the Murray. Includes champagne breakfast.

Discover Mildura Tours   CITY
(☑5024 7448; www.discovermildura.com.au; tours $125 per person) The four scheduled guided tours (Tuesday to Thursday, and Saturday) here cover wine tasting, a river cruise and farm visits.

🎭 Festivals & Events

Mildura Wentworth Arts Festival   ARTS
(www.artsmildura.com.au/mwaf) Magical concerts by the river, in the sandhills, and all around; held in February/March.

Mildura Country Music Festival   MUSIC
(www.milduracountrymusic.com.au) Ten days of free concerts during the September school holidays.

Mildura Jazz & Wine Festival   MUSIC, WINE
(www.artsmildura.com.au/jazz) Traditional bands, great food, good wine; held in October or November.

Mildura Show   RURAL
(www.mildura.vic.gov.au) One of the largest shows in rural Victoria; held mid-October.

🛏 Sleeping

Mildura is a real holiday destination with dozens of family motels, apartments and caravan parks, and a few big hotels and boutique B&Bs close to the river. For the full experience, consider hiring a houseboat.

TOP CHOICE **Quality Hotel Mildura Grand**
                                        HOTEL $$
(☑5023 0511, 1800 034 228; www.qualityhotelmil duragrand.com.au; Seventh St; B&B standard/grand r $115/175, ste $240-420; ❄🢂🖥) The standard rooms at the Grand aren't the most luxurious in town but staying at this landmark hotel gives you the feeling of being part of something special. It's Mildura's top address, as much for its historical legacy as the modern amenities. Cheaper rooms in the original wing are comfortable but for the full experience, go for one of the stylish suites with private spa. Many rooms open onto a delightful courtyard garden, and there's a gym, pool and spa.

Misty's Manor & Ditto Daddy's
                                    APARTMENT $$
(☑0419 840 451; www.mistysmanormildura.com; 16 Olive Ave; d $155-160; ❄🢂) These two apartments are spectacular in their design and decoration – a beautifully designed but unlikely mix of corrugated iron, stone and recycled timber, with a lilac, mauve and canary-yellow colour scheme in Ditto Daddy's and a tartan theme in Misty's Manor. There are king beds, plasma TVs, modern kitchens, double spa and shower.

Pied-à-terre   B&B $$
(☑5022 9883; www.piedaterre.com.au; 97 Chaffey Ave; d $175, extra adult/child $25/15; ❄🢂) It's French for a home-away-from-home, but we doubt home ever looked this good! Five-bedroom, stylish and luxurious accommodation sleeps up to 10 people with all amenities including free wi-fi, boat and car parking, a barbecue area and holiday vibes.

MILDURA FOR KIDS

Mildura is a great destination for families – aside from swimming or boating on the Murray, there are lots of specialist attractions for kids.

Apex Beach, about 3km northwest of the centre, is a popular swimming spot on the Murray with a sandy beach and picnic areas; watch for currents and snags. For safer swimming head to **Mildura Waves** (☑5023 3747; www.mildurawaves.com.au; cnr Deakin Ave & 12th St; adult/child from $5/2.50; ⊙6am-9pm Mon-Thu, to 7pm Fri, 8am-6pm Sat & Sun), a modern complex with an artificial wave pool and diving boards.

Putt Putt Land of Fun (☑5023 3663; cnr 7th St & Orange Ave; ⊙10am-7.30pm) has minigolf as well as arcade games and dodgem cars. Other play places are **Snakes'N'Ladders** (☑5025 3575; Seventeenth St, Cabarita; admission $8; ⊙9am-4.30pm), with 6 hectares of fun, including a playground and giant slides, and **Woodsies Gem Shop** (☑5024 5797; cnr Morpung & Cureton Ave, Nichols Pt; admission free; ⊙9am-5.30pm), which has a huge garden maze (adult/child $2/1) covered in pretty vines and flowers, a sparkly Aladdin's Cave and a workshop where gems are cut and polished.

Older kids will love the indoor **Mildura Formula K Go Kart Centre** (☑5021 1191; www.formulakartracing.com.au; 55 The Crescent; ⊙10am-late). There's a roller-skating rink in the same building.

Mildura Golf Club Resort
RESORT $$

(☎1300 366 883; www.milduragolfclub.com.au, Twelfth St; d/f from $88/122; ❋❊) Even if golf isn't your thing, this motel-style resort has a lovely setting with tidy rooms looking out over the course and there's a barbecue area, great pools, abundant birdlife, and a bar and bistro. Of course, it helps if you like hitting the little white balls, and there is a range of packages that include room and unlimited golf (from $150).

Sandors Motor Inn
MOTEL $

(☎1800 032 463, 5023 0047; www.sandorsmotor inn.com; 179 Deakin Ave; d $95-125; ❋❊) Mildura has plenty of motels, but Sandors, virtually opposite the visitor centre, is well located with spacious, tidy rooms and an inviting pool set in a tropical garden. Breakfast is included.

Oasis Backpackers
HOSTEL $

(☎5022 8255; www.milduraoasisbackpackers.com. au; 230-232 Deakin Ave; dm/d per week $140/300; ❋@☎❊) Mildura is a big destination for travellers looking for fruit-picking work, so most of the city's half-dozen hostels are set up with them in mind. Oasis is Mildura's best-equipped backpacker hostel with a great pool and patio bar area, ultramodern kitchen and free internet. The owners can organise plenty of seasonal work. Minimum one-week stay.

Apex RiverBeach Holiday Park
CARAVAN PARK $

(☎5023 6879; www.apexriverbeach.com.au; Cureton Ave; unpowered/powered sites $26/29, cabins $82-122; ❋☎) Thanks to a fantastic location on sandy Apex Beach just outside town, this bush park is always popular – prices are 25% higher during school holidays. There are campfires, a bush kitchen, barbecue area, boat ramp, good swimming and a cafe.

Buronga Riverside Caravan Park
CARAVAN PARK $

(☎5023 3040; www.burongacaravanpark.com.au; unpowered/powered sites $24/29, cabins $55-95; ❋) With absolute river frontage, this immaculate, grassy park is across from the wharf in NSW but still the closest park to Mildura's town action.

Houseboats

Staying on a houseboat is bliss. The Mildura region has over a dozen companies that hire houseboats ranging from two- to 12-berth boats and from modest to luxurious. Most have a minimum hire of three days and pric-

es increase dramatically in summer and during school holidays. The following operators are located just across from Mildura Wharf in Buronga:

Acacia Houseboats
HOUSEBOAT $$$

(☎1800 085 500, 5022 1510; www.acaciaboats. com.au; 3 nights $600-1800) Has seven houseboats, ranging from four to 12 berths, with everything supplied except food and drink.

Willandra Houseboats
HOUSEBOAT $$$

(☎5024 7770; www.willandrahouseboats.com. au; 3 nights $700-3600) Willandra has six houseboats sleeping two to 12 people. Offers gourmet and golf packages.

✗ Eating

Mildura's cafe and restaurant precinct runs along Langtree Ave (otherwise known as Feast Street) and around the block dominated by the Grand Hotel. Italian raconteur Stefano de Pieri perhaps single-handedly stamped the town on the foodie map, but others are jumping on board.

TOP CHOICE Stefano's Restaurant
ITALIAN $$$

(☎5023 0511; Grand Hotel, Seventh St; set menu $95; ☺dinner Mon-Sat) Descend into the former underground wine cellar at the Grand Hotel to see Stefano work his magic with the ever-changing five-course Italian dinner. It's an intimate, candlelit experience and very popular – book well in advance.

Restaurant Rendezvous
FRENCH $$

(☎5023 1571; www.rendezvousmildura.com.au; 34 Langtree Ave; mains $28-35; ☺lunch Mon-Fri, dinner Mon-Sat) The warm, casual atmosphere of this long-running place – almost swallowed up by the Grand Hotel – complements the perfectly prepared Mediterranean-style seafood, grills, pastas, crepes and unusual specials.

Stefano's Café Bakery
CAFE, BAKERY $

(☎5021 3627; 27 Deakin Ave; meals $9-22; ☺breakfast & lunch) Fresh bread baked daily, Calabrese eggs, pastries and, of course, good coffee – Stefano's casual daytime cafe and bakery keeps things fresh and simple. It's also a foodstore and wine-cellar door.

New Spanish Bar & Grill
STEAKHOUSE $$$

(☎5021 2377; www.seasonsmildura.com.au; cnr Langtree Ave & Seventh St; mains $28-39; ☺dinner Tue-Sun) In the Grand Hotel, this place keeps it simple with top-quality steaks and barbecue food, including kangaroo and Mallee rump. No tapas, but it is a carnivore's heaven.

Pizza Café at the Grand PIZZA **$**
(☎5022 2223; www.pizzacafe.com.au; 18 Langtree
Ave; pizza & pasta $13-18; ⏰from 11am daily) For
simple, inexpensive, but stylish, family dining – with all the atmosphere of the Grand
Hotel dining strip – Pizza Café is perfect. The
wood-fired pizzas hit the spot but there's a
supporting cast of salads, pastas and chicken
dishes.

 Drinking & Entertainment

Mildura has a compact but lively nightlife
scene, buoyed by an ever-changing crew of
backpackers and itinerant fruit-pickers.

Mildura Brewery BREWERY
(☎5022 2988; www.mildurabrewery.com.au; 20
Langtree Ave; ⏰from 11am) Set in the former
Astor cinema, in the same block as the
Grand Hotel, this is Mildura's trendiest
drinking hole. Shiny stainless-steel vats,
pipes and brewing equipment make a great
backdrop to the stylish lounge, and the beers
brewed here – Honey Wheat and Mallee Bull
among them – are superb. Good food too.
The interior retains many of the sleek art
deco features from the original theatre.

O'Malley's PUB
(☎5021 4236; 56 Deakin Ave) This Irish pub has
Guinness on tap and live music on weekends. Popular for hearty counter meals.

Sandbar BAR
(☎5021 2181; www.thesandbar.com.au; cnr Langtree Ave & Eighth St; ⏰noon-late Tue-Sun) On a
balmy evening locals flock to the fabulous
beer garden at the back of this lounge bar in
a classic art-deco building. Local, national,
original and mainstream bands play in the
front bar nightly from Thursday to Sunday.

Dom's Nightclub CLUB
(☎5021 3822; 28 Langtree Ave, nightclub till 2am Fri
& Sat) The upstairs club at Dom's, in the heart
of Feast Street, attracts the after-pub crowd
on a Saturday night for music and dancing.

Enjoywine WINE BAR
(☎5023 7722; www.enjoywine.com.au; 120 Eighth
St; ⏰7am-late Mon-Sat, 7am-10.30am Sun) You
can taste the local wines here in the lovely
old Hotel Mildura – there are 32 vineyards
represented. Tastings are free (or wines per
glass cost $5 to $7.50).

 Information

Café de la Rue (☎5023 5800; www.cafede
larue.com.au; 51 Deakin Ave; ⏰9am-8pm Mon-
Fri, 10am-6pm Sat & Sun @☎) Coffee, books

and internet access ($1 per half-hour), and you
can also plug your own laptop in or use wi-fi.

Mildura visitor centre (☎1800 039 043, 5018
8380; www.visitmildura.com.au; cnr Deakin Ave
& 12th St; ⏰9am-5.30pm Mon-Fri, to 5pm Sat
& Sun) In the Alfred Deakin Centre. There's a
free accommodation-booking service, interesting displays, local produce, a cafe and very
helpful staff who book tours and activities.

ⓘ Getting There & Away

Air

Regional Express Airlines (Rex; ☎13 17 13;
www.regionalexpress.com.au), **Qantas** (☎13 13
13; www.qantas.com.au) and **Virgin Blue** (☎13
67 89; www.virginblue.com.au) all fly between
Mildura and Melbourne daily. Virgin Blue has
the cheapest fares – as low as $60 one way for
advanced online fares. **Sharp Airlines** (☎1300
556694; www.sharpairlines.com.au) flies direct
between Mildura and Adelaide.

Victoria's busiest regional airport, **Mildura
Airport** (☎5055 0500; www.milduraairport.
com.au) is about 10km west of the town centre
off the Sturt Hwy.

Bus & Train

Long-distance buses operate from a depot at
the train station on Seventh St, but there are
currently no direct passenger trains to or from
Mildura.

V/Line (☎13 61 96) has a train-bus service to/
from Melbourne via Bendigo or Swan Hill ($37,
seven hours, four daily). V/Line's Murraylink
is a daily bus service connecting Mildura with
towns along the Murray: Swan Hill ($22.20, three
hours, three daily), Echuca ($30.40, six hours,
one daily) and Albury-Wodonga ($38, 10 hours,
one daily)

SWAN HILL

POP 9700

Swan Hill is a sleepy river town without
the tourist hype of Mildura and Echuca,
but with undeniable appeal. The riverside
pioneer settlement is one of the best of its
kind in Victoria. Back in 1836, Major Mitchell, explorer and surveyor, was kept awake
all night by swans on the nearby lagoon,
thus giving the town its name. The area was
settled by sheep graziers soon after, and the
original homesteads of the two major properties in the area, Murray Downs and Tyn-
tyndyer, are still looking magnificent. Swan
Hill is a major regional centre surrounded
by fertile irrigated farms that produce
grapes and other fruits, yet it maintains the
easy pace of a country town.

◉ Sights & Activities

Here there are plenty of opportunities for walking, fishing or swimming along the Murray. If you just want a place to picnic, head to **Riverside Park** (Monash Dr), which has barbecue facilities and a playground. From here, the riverside walk explores the banks of the Murray and Marraboor (Little Murray) rivers. If you share Australia's passion for 'big things', check out the **Giant Murray Cod** outside the train station. The **Burke & Wills Tree**, an enormous Moreton Bay fig tree planted to commemorate the explorers as they passed through Swan Hill on their ill-fated journey, is located on Curlewis St.

Pioneer Settlement   OUTDOOR MUSEUM
(☎5036 2410; www.pioneersettlement.com.au; Horseshoe Bend; adult/child/family $24/18/65.50; ⊙9.30am-4pm) Swan Hill's main tourist attraction is a fun re-creation of a riverside port town of the paddle steamer–era. The settlement's displays include the restored PS *Gem,* one of Australia's largest riverboats, a great collection of old carriages and buggies, an old-time photographic parlour, an Aboriginal keeping place, a lolly shop, a school classroom and the fascinating Kaiser Stereoscope. The paddle steamer PS *Pyap* makes short **cruises** (adult/child/ family $18/13/48.50) along the Murray daily at 2.30pm, and at 10.30am weekends and holidays. Other attractions include vintage-car and wagon rides. Every night at dusk the 45-minute **sound-and-light show** (adult/child/family $18/13/48.50) entails a dramatic journey through the settlement in an open-air transporter. A combined package for cruise and show works out to reduce the cost.

Swan Hill Regional Art Gallery   GALLERY
(☎5036 2430; www.swanhill.vic.gov.au/gallery/index.html; Horseshoe Bend; admission by donation; ⊙10am-5pm Tue-Fri, 11am-5pm Sat & Sun) Opposite the Pioneer Settlement, this gallery has a permanent collection of more than 300 works focusing on the works of contemporary and local artists.

Murray Downs Resort   GOLF CLUB
(☎1800 807 574; www.murraydownsresort.com.au; Murray Downs Dr; 9/18 holes $20/35, club hire $22) Itching for a round? One of the Murray's superb public resort golf courses, Murray Downs is 5km east of Swan Hill, in NSW, but is regarded as a Swan Hill club.

★ Festivals & Events

Swan Hill has a racecourse and the three-day **racing carnival** over the Queen's Birthday weekend in June is the main event of the year. It culminates with the Swan Hill Cup on the Sunday. Book accommodation well in advance.

Australian Inland Wine Show   WINE
(www.inlandwine.com; ⊙3rd weekend Oct) Wine festivals are held here every October, including this one. The region's motto: 'Life is too short to drink bad wine.'

⊨ Sleeping

Murray Downs Houseboats   HOUSEBOAT $$
(☎5032 2160, 0428 500 066; www.murraydowns marina.com.au; Murray Downs Marina; 8-/12-berth per 3 nights from $700/1950; ❄) Nothing beats a luxury houseboat for relaxing on the Murray. The 12-berth comes with four bedrooms, two bathrooms and a deck spa. High-season rates are significantly higher ($2650 over the Christmas period). The marina is 2km from town, on the NSW side.

Best's Riverbed B&B   B&B $$
(☎5032 2126; www.bestbnb.com.au; 7 Kidman Reid, Murray Downs; s/d $80/120, spa r $165) On the banks of the Murray, 3km across the border in NSW, this charming B&B has spacious living areas, lounges with open fires and a marvellous view of the river.

Travellers Rest Motor Inn   MOTEL $$
(☎5032 9644; travellersrest.bestwestern.com. au; 110 Curlewis St; s/d/f $110/120/135; ❄❄) Sitting in the shade of the Burke & Wills Tree, rooms here are spacious and comfortable with the usual motel accompaniments. There's a heated spa and outdoor pool.

Pioneer Station Motor Inn   MOTEL $
(☎5032 2017; 421 Campbell St; s/d from $65/75; ❄❄) This good-value budget motel is well kept and close to the town centre and riverside area. The adjacent Carriages Restaurant is a training ground for students from the Swan Hill International College.

Riverside Caravan Park   CARAVAN PARK $
(☎5032 1494; www.swanhillriverside.com.au; Monash Dr; unpowered/powered sites from $29/32, en suite sites from $41, cabins $83-140) On the banks of the Murray, close to the Pioneer Settlement, this park enjoys a fabulous central location. There's a good range of cabins but prices soar by more than 50% in holiday periods.

✖ Eating

The main cafe and dining scene is on Campbell St, or head down to the riverside park for a barbecue or picnic.

Java Spice
THAI **$$**
(☎5033 0511; www.javaspice.com.au; 17 Beveridge St; mains $19-28; ☺lunch Thu-Sun, dinner Tue-Sun; ☑) Dining under open-sided thatched and teak-wood huts in a tropical garden, you'll think you've been transported to Southeast Asia. The authentic cuisine is predominantly Thai, with some Malaysian and Indonesian influences mixed in.

Spoons Riverview Café
CAFE, MODERN AUSTRALIAN **$$**
(☎5032 2601; www.spoonsriverside.com.au; Horseshoe Bend; mains $15-28; ☺breakfast & lunch daily, dinner Thu-Sat) The riverside location alone is enough to lure you to this licensed cafe with its big timber deck overlooking the Marraboor River and Pioneer Settlement. As well as light lunches and innovative dinners, there's a provedore deli selling fresh produce and gourmet hampers.

Yutaka Sawa
JAPANESE **$$**
(☎5032 3515; www.yutakasawa.com.au; 107 Campbell St; mains $14-27; ☺lunch & dinner Wed-Mon, dinner only Sun) A Japanese restaurant in a small country town may sound a bit dodgy but this one has the goods, with expertly prepared sushi and sashimi, and a fine choice of noodle dishes, teriyaka and tempura.

Jilarty Gelato Bar
CAFE, GELATERIA **$**
(☎5033 0042; 233 Campbell St; ☺daily) Gelati on a hot summer's day? Unbeatable. This little cafe specialises in Italian-style gelati with local fruit flavours, along with great coffee and Spanish churros.

❶ Information

Swan Hill Region Information Centre (☎1800 625 373, 5032 3033; www.swanhillonline.com; cnr McCrae & Curlewis Sts) Crammed with helpful maps and brochures on the region.

❶ Getting There & Away

Swan Hill sits on the Murray Valley Hwy 218km from Mildura and 156km from Echuca. **V/Line** (☎13 61 96; www.vline.com.au) runs trains between Melbourne and Swan Hill ($30, four hours, three to four daily), and some train and coach services with a change at Bendigo. There are daily V/line coaches to Mildura ($22.20, three hours) and Echuca ($13.70, two hours).

Around Swan Hill

The Swan Hill region doesn't compare with Mildura in grape production but there are a few wineries you can visit with cellar door sales and tastings, including **Buller Wines** (☎5037 6305; www.buller.com.au; 1374 Murray Valley Hwy, Beverford), the boutique **Dos Rios** (☎5030 3005; www.dosrios.com.au, 3151 Murray Valley Hwy, Nyah) and **Brumby Wines** (☎5030 5366; www.brumbywines.com.au; cnr Murray Valley Hwy & Cannon Lane, Wood Wood).

Historic **Tyntyndyer Homestead** (☎5030 2416; Murray Valley Hwy, Beverford; admission $8.50; ☺open by appointment only), located 16km north of town, has a small museum and many reminders of the hardships of colonial life. Guided group tours require an appointment.

MURRAY COD

The Murray River is great for fishing, from the upper reaches where anglers cast flies in search of trout and salmon, to the slow-moving deepwater sections hiding perch (yellow belly), redfin, bream and the dreaded European carp. The introduced carp has long been a problem in the Murray Darling system, breeding intensively, muddying the waters and generally upsetting the riverine ecology. They are a declared pest, so it's illegal to release them back into the water once caught. And don't bother eating them – they taste like mud.

The big prize, though, is the elusive Murray cod, Australia's largest freshwater fish and native to these waters. The Murray cod is a long-lived fish – the biggest and oldest can weigh upwards of 100kg and there are plenty of tales of the ones that got away. The cod is carnivorous and can be caught using yabbies, grubs, river shrimp, small fish or trolling with a lure. Anything under 60cm must be released back into the water and the bag limit is two. To fish in Victorian waters you need a recreational fishing licence ($12/24.50 per month/year), available from many shops along the Murray or from the **Department of Primary Industries** (new.dpi.vic.gov.au).

Olson Game Birds (☑5030 2648; www. gamebirds.com.au; 2167 Chillingollah Rd; adult/child/family $7/4/18; ☺10am-4pm) is a free-range pheasant and game farm about 32km northwest of Swan Hill where game birds are reared – all destined for restaurant tables. Native birds are on display and peacocks wander around looking gorgeous.

Just 16km southeast of Swan Hill, **Lake Boga** is an interesting little town – especially now that its namesake lake is full of water again. The famous Catalina flying boat *A24-30* is on display at the **Lake Boga Flying Boat Museum** (☑5037 2850; Catalina Park; adult/child/family $6/2.50/12; ☺9.30am-4pm). Flying boats were repaired and tested at Lake Boga during WWII. Inside are lots of displays and photographs.

Further down the highway is a patch-work of lakes, including **Kangaroo Lake** and **Lake Charm**, all popular water-sports destinations. Just before you reach Kerang is the **Middle Lake Ibis Rookery**, where bird-watchers can spy the huge flocks of ibis from a bird hide.

🛏 Sleeping

Burrabliss B&B　　　　　　　　　　B&B **$$**
(☑5037 2527; www.burrabliss.com.au; 169 Lake-side Dr, Lake Boga; d/ste $125/180, villas $300) Overlooking the water at Lake Boga, this luxurious B&B is a fine choice. Go with the friendly owners to see their ultra-fine-wool sheep, go birdwatching in the wetlands, or walk by the lake and enjoy the gardens.

GUNBOWER NATIONAL PARK

One of the great spots for free camping along the Murray River, superb **Gunbower Island** is formed between the Murray River and Gunbower Creek and is said to be the largest inland island in the world. In 2010 Parks Victoria created the 88 sq km Gunbower National Park (previously a state forest) to protect its beautiful river red gum forests. As well as the majestic red gums, which have been extensively logged for timber since the 1870s, the park is home to abundant animals and birdlife. You might see kangaroos, possums, goannas, turtles and snakes, and more than 200 species of birds have been recorded here. A network of 'river tracks' criss-cross the island and lead to more than 100 numbered bush-camping spots by the river

bank (only on the Victorian side). The roads are dirt and a bit rough, but are passable to conventional vehicles when it's dry – after heavy rain though, it's 4WD-only.

The main access points to the island are from Cohuna in the north and tiny Gunbower in the south.

ECHUCA

POP 12,400

Echuca is the paddle-steamer capital of Victoria and a classic Murray River town, bursting with history, nostalgia and, of course, riverboats. The Aboriginal name translates as 'meeting of the waters', as it's here that three great rivers meet – the Goulburn, Campaspe and the Murray. The highlight here is unquestionably the historic port area and the rivers themselves, and while it might feel a bit touristy, the town glows with an upbeat atmosphere and some fabulous restaurants and bars that will bring a smile to the face of riverside campers and travelling gastronomes alike.

History

Echuca was founded in 1853 by ex-convict Harry Hopwood. He settled on the banks of the Murray, converted some rough sheds into an inn and a store, then established punt and ferry crossings over the Murray and Campaspe Rivers. With his monopoly on transport and the gold rush in full swing, he profited handsomely. At the peak of the riverboat era there were more than 100 paddle steamers carting wool, timber and other goods between Echuca and the outback sheep stations.

It was too good to last though: the Melbourne–Echuca railway line opened in 1864, and within a decade the boom years of the riverboat trade had ended.

◉ Sights

HISTORIC PORT OF ECHUCA

Echuca's star attraction is the historic **Port of Echuca** (☑5482 4248; www.portofechuca. org.au; cnr Leslie St & Murray Esp; passport adult/child/family $12.45/8.50/36.25, with paddleboat cruise $29/15/77; ☺9am-5pm, tours at 11.15am). Attractions are spread along the waterfront, and you buy a passport at the entrance that admits you to the three main sections: Echuca Wharf, the Star Hotel and the Bridge Hotel. Everything is original – you're exploring living history as you walk along the pedestrian-only **Murray Esplanade**, which you can wander for free. Complimentary (and very entertaining) **guided tours** set out from the gift shop.

Behind the entrance is **Echuca Wharf**. In the wharf's cargo shed, there's a surprisingly interesting audiovisual presentation and dioramas depicting life on the riverboats.

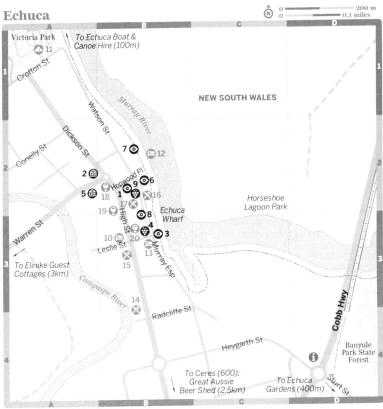

Echuca

Sights

1 Bridge Hotel	B2
2 Echuca Historical Museum	A2
3 Historic Port & Wharf Entrance	B3
4 Murray Esplanade Cellars	B3
5 National Holden Museum	A2
6 Red Gum Works	B2
7 Riverboat Dock	B2
8 Sharp's Magic Movie House & Penny Arcade	B3
9 St Anne's	B2

Sleeping

10 Campaspe Lodge	B3
11 Echuca Caravan Park	A1
12 Murray River Houseboats	B2
Rich River Houseboats	(see 12)
13 Steampacket B&B	B3

Eating

14 Beechworth Bakery	B3
15 Black Pudding Delicatessen	B3
16 Oscar W's Wharfside	B2
17 Star Hotel & Wine Bar	B2

Drinking

18 Echuca Brewing Co	B2
19 Shamrock Hotel	B2
20 Speakeasy	B3

Walk along the various levels of the massive wharf and onto the restored historic **paddle steamers**: PS *Pevensey* (built in 1911) and PS *Adelaide* (1866), the oldest operating paddle steamer in the world. The wharf was built with three tiers because of the changing river levels. There are gauges marking the highest points.

Back on the Esplanade, stop in at the **Star Hotel** (1867) and escape through the underground tunnel, which helped drinkers avoid the police during the years when the pub was a 'sly grog shop'.

On Hopwood Pl at the far end is the **Bridge Hotel**, where your ticket admits you to a historic upstairs gallery. The pub now operates as a restaurant and bistro.

Sharp's Magic Movie House & Penny Arcade (☎5482 2361; Murray Esp; adult/child/family $15/10/45; ☺9am-5pm) has authentic and fully restored penny-arcade machines – you're given a fist-full of pennies. Free fudge tasting is another blast from the past. The movie house shows old films such as Buster Keaton or Laurel and Hardy classics.

Other port-area sights include **Red Gum Works** (Murray Esp; admission free; ☺9am-4pm), a historic sawmill that recreates old timber-milling days. Watch wood-turners and blacksmiths work with traditional equipment, and purchase red-gum products.

There are free tastings of local wines at **Murray Esplanade Cellars** (☎5482 6058; Old Customs House, 2 Leslie St; ☺9.30am-5.30pm) and at **St Anne's** (☎5480 6955; www.stannes winery.com.au; 53 Murray Esplanade; ☺10am-6pm), where the giant port barrels will inspire you to taste the range of ports aged in bourbon and rum barrels.

Other Attractions

Echuca Historical Museum MUSEUM
(☎5480 1325; 1 Dickson St; adult/child $4/1; ☺11am-3pm) This historical museum is located in the old police station, classified by the National Trust. It has a collection of local history items, charts and photos from the riverboat era and early records.

National Holden Museum MUSEUM
(☎5480 2033; www.holdenmuseum.com.au; 7 Warren St; adult/child/family $7/3/16; ☺9am-5pm) Car buffs should check out this museum dedicated to Australia's four-wheeled icon, with more than 40 beautifully restored Holdens, from FJ to Monaro, as well as racing footage and memorabilia.

Great Aussie Beer Shed MUSEUM
(☎5480 6904; www.greataussiebeershed.com.au; 337 Mary Ann Rd; adult/child/family $9.50/3.50/19; ☺9am-5pm Sat, Sun & holidays) This is a wall-to-wall shrine of beer cans in a huge shed. It's the result of 30 years of collecting; one dates back to Federation. Guided tours will take you through the history of beer. Very Aussie.

🏃 Activities

Paddle-steamer Cruises

A paddle steamer cruise here is almost obligatory, and there are at least six operating at one time or another, wood-fired, steam-driven and with interesting commentary. Buy tickets from the port entrance or along the Esplanade. Check out the timetable for lunch and dinner, twilight and sunset cruises.

PS Alexander Arbuthnot RIVER, WINERY
(☎5482 4248; adult/child/family $21/9/54) One-hour cruises four times daily; also winery cruises ($30).

PS Canberra RIVER, WINERY
(☎5482 5244; adult/child/family $22/9.50/57.50) One-hour cruises five times daily; also winery cruises (adult/child $27/12.50).

PS Emmylou RIVER
(☎5480 2237; adult/child/family $29.50/14/77.50) One of the most impressive boats, fully restored and driven by an original engine. Five 1½-hour cruises daily, plus lunch cruises and overnight cruises.

PS Pevensey RIVER, WINERY
(☎5482 4248; adult/child/family $21/9/54) Star of the TV miniseries *All the Rivers Run;* one-hour cruises four times daily and winery cruises ($30).

PS Pride of the Murray RIVER, WINERY
(☎5482 5244) One-hour cruises six times daily, a 2½-hour twilight cruise ($62.50/30) and a winery cruise ($27/12.50)

MV Mary Ann RIVER
(☎5480 2200; www.maryann.com.au; Murray Esp; lunch cruise adult/child $45/10; dinner cruise $75/25) Not a traditional paddle steamer, but this restaurant-boat combines a river cruise with lunch or dinner. Prices include a two-course meal and entertainment. Call ahead for dining times.

Water Sports

Echuca Boat & Canoe Hire BOATING, KAYAKING
(☎5480 6208; www.echucaboatcanoehire.com; Victoria Park Boat Ramp) Hires out tinnies (one/

two hours $40/60), 'barbie boats' (10 people $100/140), kayaks ($16/26) and canoes ($20/30). Multiday self-guided 'campanoeing' trips are also available, where you can arrange to be dropped upstream and canoe back.

River Country Adventours KAYAKING
(📞0428 585 227; www.adventours.com.au; half-/full-/2-day safaris $55/80/155) For organised canoe safaris on the Goulburn River, this Kyabram-based team are the experts in this part of the world, with canoe and camping safaris around the Barmah and Goulburn regions, as well as on the Murray.

Brett Sands Watersports WATERSKIING
(📞5482 1851; www.brettsands.com; Merool Lane, Moama; half/full day $140/220) Several operators offer waterskiing trips and classes, but this outfit will teach you skills behind a boat on skis, wakeboard, kneeboard or barefoot. It also hires out gear.

🖝 Tours
The Echuca region is home to a few wineries and local operators can take you there.

Echuca Limo Tours WINERY
(📞0418 509 493; www.echucalimotours.com.au; 2½/4hr tours $65/105) Visit wineries in style and enjoy cheese platters or lunch.

Echuca Moama Wine Tours WINERY
(📞5480 1839; www.echucamoamawinetours.com. au; tours from $75) Tours include the historic port, a cruise along the Murray and local wineries.

Murray River Fishing Tours FISHING
(📞0418 576 526; www.murrayriverfishingtours. com.au; half/full day $80/160) Fish for Murray cod and yellow belly with the local experts. Children pay half price.

★☆ Festivals & Events
Check the online event calendar (www.echuca moama.com).

Club Marine Southern 80 WATERSKIING
(www.southern80.com.au) The world's largest waterskiing race; held in February.

Riverboats Jazz Food & Wine Festival
MUSIC, WINE
(www.riverboatsjazzfoodandwine.com.au) Music, food and wine by the Murray; held in late February.

Steam, Horse & Vintage Rally HISTORY
(www.echucasteamrally.com.au) On the Queen's Birthday weekend in June; classic and historic vehicles and steam engines powered by all imaginable methods.

Echuca-Moama Winter Blues Festival
MUSIC
(www.winterblues.com.au) Blues and folk musos play in the streets and at venues around town at this weekend music festival in late July.

🛏 Sleeping
Echuca has plenty of accommodation, from quaint B&Bs and backpacker hostels to caravan parks, huge brick motels and old lace-trimmed hotels, much of it conveniently close to the port area.

About 5km east of town, **Christies Beach** is a free camping area on the banks of the Murray. There are pit toilets, but bring water and firewood.

Steam Packet Inn B&B **$$**
(📞5482 3411; www.steampacketinn.com.au; cnr Murray Esplanade & Leslie St; B&B d $149-199; ❄) Staying in the old port area is all part of the Echuca experience and this 19th-century National Trust–classified B&B offers genteel rooms with all the old-fashioned charm, linen and lace, and brass bedstead you could want (but with air-con and flat-screen TVs too). Ask for the large corner rooms for a view of the wharf. The lounge room is cosy and breakfast is served on fine china.

Echuca Gardens HOSTEL, GUESTHOUSE **$**
(📞5480 6522; www.echucagardens.com; 103 Mitchell St; dm/d $30, wagon $80-160, guesthouse from $110) Run by inveterate traveller Kym, this enjoyable place is part YHA hostel and part guesthouse, all set in beautiful gardens with ponds, statues, chooks and fruit trees. The 140-year-old workers cottage has bunk beds, smart bathrooms, a country kitchen and a TV room. The cute 'gypsy wagons' in the garden offer unique accommodation, complete with en suite and kitchenette, and there are two guesthouse rooms in the main house. Something for everyone and a warm atmosphere.

Elinike Guest Cottages COTTAGES **$$**
(📞5480 6311; www.elinike.com.au; 209 Latham Rd; B&B d $185-195) These romantic little self-contained cottages are set in rambling gardens on the Murray River, blending old-world style with modern conveniences such as double spas. The lilac cottage ($195) has a glass-roofed garden room.

Campaspe Lodge MOTEL **$$**
(📞5482 1087; www.echucahotel.com; 567-571 High St; weekday/weekend d $93/125, river-view d $140/160; ❄) Behind the Echuca Hotel, this

group of motel units is great value, with private verandahs and big windows to take in the view of the Campaspe River. There are budget rooms in the pub itself for $40 per person.

Echuca Caravan Park CARAVAN PARK **$**
(☑5482 2157; www.echucacaravanpark.com.au; 51 Crofton St; unpowered/powered sites $31/33, cabin d $95-170; ❋ ⓦ ⛵) Beside the river just a short walk from town, this park is pretty cramped but the facilities are good, with modern timber camp kitchens and shady river red gums.

Houseboats

Echuca is a great place to hire a houseboat. They range from six-berth to luxurious 12-berth craft with spa baths. Four nights midweek in the low season will cost from $660 to $2300 depending on the boat. The following outfits are based at the Riverboat Dock:

Murray River Houseboats HOUSEBOAT **$$$**
(☑5480 2343; www.murrayriverhouseboats.com. au) Five houseboats in the fleet, including the stunning four-bedroom *Indulgence*.

Rich River Houseboats HOUSEBOAT **$$$**
(☑5480 2444; www.richriverhouseboats.com. au) The six beautiful boats here include a budget six-berth and a couple of floating palaces.

✖ Eating

Conveniently, some of the best places to eat in Echuca are around the port area and the top end of High St. Supermarkets, pubs and takeaway can be found in the town centre around Hare St.

TOP CHOICE **Oscar W's Wharfside**
MODERN AUSTRALIAN **$$$**
(☑5482 5133; www.oscarws.com.au; 101 Murray Esp; tapas $9-22, mains $32-37; ❂lunch & dinner) The glorious location in the old port area, with a terrace overlooking the Murray, is unbeatable, but Oscar's really delivers with its food and service. Start with the smaller shared plates or go straight to thoughtful Mod Oz mains of Murray cod and local steak. Big wine list, great atmosphere.

Star Hotel & Wine Bar BAR, BISTRO **$$**
(☑5480 1181; www.starhotelechuca.com.au; 45 Murray Esplanade; mains $10-27; ❂breakfast & lunch daily, dinner Fri & Sat) The historic 'Star Bar' is still one of the liveliest places in town for a meal or drink, especially on weekends when there's live music. Full cooked breakfasts and a reasonably priced lunch of calamari or chicken parma can be enjoyed right beside the port.

Ceres MODERN AUSTRALIAN, ITALIAN **$$$**
(☑5482 5599; www.ceresechuca.com.au; 2 Nish St; tapas $7.50-12.50, mains $13.50-45; ❂lunch & dinner) In a beautifully converted 1881 brick flour mill, Ceres oozes style with its high-back leather chairs, starched tablecloths and occasional couches. It's actually a relaxed place for lunch with all-day coffee and tapas, but there's an atmospheric fine-dining evening restaurant with an innovative menu of Italian-influenced pastas, steaks and roast duckling.

Black Pudding Delicatessen CAFE **$**
(☑5482 2244; 525a High St; meals $10-16; ❂breakfast & lunch) This tiny cafe-deli is a great place for a lazy breakfast or light lunch if you can get a table at the front or the small courtyard at the rear. Good coffee and local produce.

Beechworth Bakery BAKERY **$**
(☑5480 1057; 513 High St; meals $4-12; ❂6am-6pm) In a magnificent old building with wrap-around balcony and deck overlooking the Campaspe River, this cheerful bakery prepares a high standard of breads, pies, cakes and sandwiches.

🍷 Drinking

The Bridge Hotel and Star Bar in the port area are atmospheric places for a drink.

Shamrock Hotel PUB
(☑5482 1036; 583 High St; ❂10am-11pm Mon-Fri, 10am-2am Sat & Sun) Close to the port area, the Shamrock is full of Irish-themed fun and frivolity, with live music, good food and Guinness on tap.

Speakeasy WINE BAR
(☑0408 551 017; 620 High St; ❂from 3pm Thu-Sun, closed Aug) Tucked away behind the port area, Speakeasy is a relaxed bar with a focus on good wines and boutique beers. There's live music at the Sunday sessions from 5pm.

Echuca Brewing Co PUB, BREWERY
(☑5482 4282; www.echucabrewingco.com.au; 609 High St; ❂from 10am Tue-Sun) Although not brewed on site, the four beers on offer here are specially brewed for this label and the bar stocks a big range of microbrewery and boutique beers from around Australia. The kitchen serves fine beer accompaniments – burgers, antipasto and salt-and-pepper squid.

ℹ️ Information

Echuca visitor centre (📞1800 804 446, 5480 7555; www.echucamoama.com; 2 Heygarth St; ⊙9am-5pm) In the old pump station, the visitor centre has helpful staff and an accommodation booking service.

Echuca Library (📞5482 1997; 524-528 High St; ⊙10am-5.30pm Mon, Tue, Thu & Fri, noon-8pm Wed, 10am-1pm Sat, 2-4.30pm Sun) Free internet access.

Tangled Garden Bookshop (📞5480 1333; 495-497 High St; ⊙9am-5.30pm Mon-Sat, 11am-4pm Sun; @🛜) Books, art supplies and internet access ($2 per 15 minutes).

ℹ️ Getting There & Away

V/Line (📞13 61 96; www.vline.com.au) has two direct Melbourne–Echuca trains on weekends and train and bus services (return $20.40, 3½ hours) on weekdays, with changes at Bendigo, Murchison or Shepparton.

AROUND ECHUCA

If you want to entertain the kids for the afternoon, head out to **Billabong Ranch** (📞5483 5122; www.justhorses.com.au; 2831 Tehan Rd; adult/child/family $25/22/75; ⊙9.30am-4pm Mon-Fri, 9am-5pm Sat & Sun) about 10km east of Echuca. There's minigolf, pedal boats, an animal nursery, tenpin bowling, a playground, a cafe, a bar and pony rides, amongst other things – such as off-road buggies ($30 per 15 minutes). It also offers horse riding, including overnight trail rides and winery rides.

Barmah National Park

About 40km northeast of Echuca via the Cobb Hwy in NSW, Barmah is a significant wetlands area of the Murray River floodplain. It's the largest remaining red gum forest in Australia, and the swampy understorey usually floods, creating a wonderful breeding area for many species of fish and birds.

The park entry is about 5km north of the tiny town of Barmah (turn at the pub). From the day-use area, **Kingfisher Cruises** (📞5855 2855; www.kingfishercruises.com.au; adult/child/family $27.50/19/88; ⊙tours at 11am Sun, Mon, Wed, Thu & Sat) takes you out in a flat-bottom boat for an informative two-hour cruise. Your captain points out bird and mammal species along the way. Call ahead for departure times and bookings.

You can camp for free in the park, or at the Barmah Lakes camping area, which has tables, barbecue areas and pit toilets.

YARRAWONGA

POP 5700

Beloved of boaters, waterskiers, golfers and retirees, Yarrawonga supposedly has more sunshine hours than almost anywhere else in Australia. It sits on **Lake Mulwala**, a bulbous body of water created when the Murray River was dammed for irrigation back in 1939. You can cross to the NSW side via the weir or the Mulwala Bridge.

⊙ Sights & Activities

Byramine Homestead   HISTORIC BUILDING
(📞5748 4321; 1436 Murray Valley Hwy; adult/child/family $5/2.50/15; ⊙10am-4pm Sun, Mon, Wed & Thu) When Elizabeth Hume's husband was killed by bushrangers, she moved here and built in 1842 – a safe haven that saw her become the first permanent European settler in the area. The homestead is shaped like a fortress and is set in magnificent grounds, 14km west of town.

Cruises   SIGHTSEEING CRUISE
Two cruise boats, the **Lady Murray** (📞0412 573 460) and the **Paradise Queen** (📞0418 508 616), take you cruising along the lake and the Murray River, pointing out historic spots and birdlife. Both have one-hour barbecue cruises ($24) at noon, scenic cruises ($15) at 2pm, and dinner cruises during summer ($40).

Action Bike & Ski   KAYAKING, CYCLING
(📞5744 3522; www.actionbikeski.com.au; 81 Belmore St; ⊙9am-5.30pm Mon-Fri, to 12.30pm Sat, open some Sun) Hires out kayaks ($45), wakeboard gear ($50) and bikes ($20). To really discover the lake and river, take one of the half-day guided kayak tours ($100).

Yarrawonga & Border Golf Club   GOLF
(📞5744 1911; www.yarragolf.com.au; Gulai Rd, Mulwala; 9/18 holes $26/40) Across the water, in Mulwala, is Australia's largest public golf course, with 45 beautifully manicured holes, resort accommodation and a bar and bistro.

🛏️ Sleeping

Murray Valley Resort   RESORT $$
(📞5744 1844; www.murrayvalleyresort.com.au; Murray Valley Hwy; s/d from $135/160, condos from $270; ✴️♨️) The amazing facilities here

include a gym, indoor and outdoor pools, tennis courts, billiard tables and spas. The condos are stylish self-contained two-bedroom units sleeping up to six people.

Coghill Cottages
COTTAGES $$

(☑5744 2271; www.coghill.com.au; 6 Coghill St; cottages $120-230; ✷▨) These smart, modern self-contained cottages have one, two or three bedrooms and are close to the lake. There's a minimum two-night stay and pets are welcome.

✖ Eating & Drinking

There's a good cafe and pub scene on Belmore St, between the Murray Valley Hwy and the lake.

Nosh Deli
CAFE $

(☑5744 1756; 42 Belmore St; meals $9-18; ☺breakfast & lunch) Top spot for breakfast, coffee, spot-on smoothies or a tasty lunch of enchiladas and frittata. In the evening it becomes a trendy wine bar.

Deck One
PUB $$

(☑5744 3839; www.criterionyarrawonga.com.au; 1 Belmore St; mains $13-25; ☺lunch & dinner) Is this the biggest beer deck in Victoria? It takes up as much real estate as the Criterion Hotel, to which it's attached. Shady umbrellas, good views of the lake and a kids playground. Good pub food is complemented with pizzas and pasta.

ⓘ Information

Yarrawonga visitor centre (☑1800 062 260, 5744 1989; www.yarrawongamulwala.com. au; Irvine Pde; ☺9am-5pm) Right beside the Mulwala Bridge and with a cafe overlooking the lake; book accommodation and tours here.

ⓘ Getting There & Away

V/Line (☑13 61 96; www.vline.com.au) train and coach services run between Melbourne and Yarrawonga ($24, four hours, three daily) with a change at Seymour.

RUTHERGLEN

POP 2000

Rutherglen has plenty of history with some marvellous gold rush–era buildings gracing the town (gold was discovered here in 1860), but today it's red wine that pumps through the region's veins – this is undoubtedly one of northern Victoria's finest wine-growing districts. In town you can dine at some excellent cafes and restaurants, browse antique and bric-a-brac shops, take the self-guided heritage walk, or head out and cycle some of the miles of flat trails.

◉ Sights & Activities

First stop should be the **Rutherglen Wine Experience** (☑1800 622 871; 57 Main St; ☺9am-5pm), with a wine-tasting room where you can sample local fortifieds, book tours and hire bikes ($25/35 per half-/full day).

Four local wineries (Pfeiffer, Cofield, Campbell and Rutherglen Estates) offer free 'Behind the Scenes' **winery tours** on a rotating basis from Monday to Thursday at 2pm. They take you into the world of the winemaking process, but advance bookings through the visitor centre are essential.

The visitor centre provides maps and touring information for **cycling tours** around the region, including the Rutherglen–Wahguynah extension to the **Murray to Mountains Rail Trail**.

The **Common School Museum** (☑02-6033 6300; 57 Main St; admission $2; ☺1-4pm Sun) has an amazing range of weights and measures, local inventions, period pieces and school equipment.

ⓒ Tours

There are lots of ways to get out to the wineries without driving or cycling yourself, including chauffeured limousine tours.

Grapevine Getaways
WINERY

(☑02-6032 8577; www.grapevinegetaways.com. au; 72 Murray St; half/full day tours $35/45) Knowledgeable, personalised tours visiting up to nine wineries aboard the purple bus.

Walkabout Limousines
WINERY

(☑02-6032 9572; www.walkaboutmotel.com.au; Murray Valley Hwy) Winery tours in style.

★ Festivals & Events

There are special events on almost every weekend here, all featuring a wide range of activities, especially focused around eating and drinking. See www.rutherglenvic.com/ events.

Tastes of Rutherglen
WINE, FOOD

Two weekends of total indulgence with food-and-wine packages at dozens of vineyards and restaurants; held in March.

Winery Walkabout Weekend
WINE, MUSIC

Australia's original wine festival – there's music, barrel racing and probably some wine; held in June.

Rutherglen's wineries produce superb fortifieds (port, muscat and tokay) and some potent Durifs and Shirazs – among the biggest, baddest and strongest reds. See the website www.winemakers.com.au for more information. Some of the best:

All Saints (☏02-6035 2222; www.allsaintswine.com.au; All Saints Rd, Wahgunyah; ⊙9am-5.30pm Mon-Sat, 10am-5.30pm Sun) Fairy-tale castle, restaurant and cheese tasting.

Buller Wines (☏1300 794 183; www.buller.com.au; Three Chain Rd; ⊙9am-5pm Mon-Sat, 10am-5pm Sun) Fine Shiraz, plus a bird park.

Morris (☏02-6026 7303; www.morriswines.com; Mia Mia Rd; ⊙9am-5pm Mon-Sat, 10am-5pm Sun)

Pfeiffer (☏02-6033 2805; www.pfeifferwines.com.au; Distillery Rd, Wahgunyah; ⊙9am-5pm Mon-Fri, 10am-5pm Sun)

Rutherglen Estates (☏02-6032 8516; www.rutherglenestates.com.au; Tuileries Complex, Drummond St; ⊙10am-6pm) Closest winery to town.

Stanton & Killeen Wines (☏02-6032 9457; www.stantonandkilleenwines.com.au; Jacks Rd; ⊙9am-5pm Mon-Sat, 10am-5pm Sun)

Vintara (☏0447 327 517; www.vintara.com.au; Fraser Rd; ⊙10am-5pm) Includes Bintara Brewery.

Warrabilla Wines (☏02-6035 7242; www.warrabillawines.com.au; Murray Valley Hwy; ⊙10am-5pm) Small winery but quality reds.

Rutherglen Agriculture & Wine Show

WINE

Don't miss this late-September show: a cowbell is rung at 7am to signal the mad rush.

🛏 Sleeping

Accommodation is tight during major festivals – book ahead. Rates are higher during festivals and on weekends and public holidays.

Tuileries BOUTIQUE HOTEL **$$**

(☏02-6032 9033; www.tuileriesrutherglen.com.au; 13 Drummond St; B&B d $185, with dinner $275; ❄☎) All rooms are individually decorated in bright contemporary tones at this luxurious place next to Jolimont Cellars. There's a guest lounge, a tennis court, a pool and an outstanding restaurant and cafe.

Carlyle House B&B **$$**

(☏02-6032 8444; www.carlylehouse.com.au; 147 High St; B&B $165-195; ❄) The four traditional suits and modern garden apartments are beautifully presented in this lovingly restored home. The Tokay suite boasts a private lounge.

Victoria Hotel PUB **$**

(☏02-6032 8610; www.victoriahotelrutherglen.com.au; 90 Main St; d $50-90, with bathroom $80-120) This beautiful National Trust–classified pub has history, great bistro food and some

very inviting accommodation – the spruced-up front rooms have en suite and views over Main St, with access to the wide, lace-trimmed balcony. At the back is a three-room suite that can be used for families of groups.

Motel Woongarra MOTEL **$**

(☏02-6032 9588; www.motelwoongarra.com.au; cnr Main & Drummond Sts; d/f $90/104; ❄☎) Close to the centre of town, Woongarra has spacious, neat rooms, and little touches, such as the carafe of port on your dresser. Friendly owners run limousine winery tours.

Rutherglen Caravan & Tourist Park

CARAVAN PARK **$**

(☏02-6032 8577; www.rutherglentouristpark.com; 72 Murray St; unpowered/powered sites $18/25, cabin d $51-99) This friendly park with good facilities sits on the banks of Lake King, close to the golf course and swimming pool.

🍴 Eating

Main St is lined with quality cafes, restaurants, pubs and takeaway places – the Vic is the pick of the pubs in town. A number of wineries also have quality restaurants, including All Saints and Vintara.

Beaumont's Café MODERN AUSTRALIAN **$$**

(☏02-6032 7428; www.beaumontscafe.com.au; 84 Main St; mains $18-34; ⊙lunch Fri & Sat, dinner Tue-Sat) Beaumont's offers fine Mod Oz dining in a contemporary dining room and courtyard. Mediterranean and Asian influences produce an interesting menu that features chicken tagine and house-made gnocchi.

Tuileries MODERN AUSTRALIAN $$$
(☑02-6032 9033; 13 Drummond St; lunch $12, dinner $30-34; ☺lunch & dinner) The bright courtyard cafe is a fine place for lunch, and in the evening the fine-dining restaurant produces superb Mediterranean-influenced dishes, with local produce such as Murray cod fillets and Murray Valley pork belly.

Parkers Pies BAKERY $
(☑02-6032 9605; 86-88 Main St; pies $4-6; ☺8am-4.30pm Mon-Sat, 9am-4pm Sun) If you think a pie is a pie, this award-winning local institution might change your mind. Try the gourmet pastries – emu, venison, crocodile or buffalo.

Forks & Corks INTERNATIONAL $$
(☑02-6032 7662; 82 Main St; mains $10-30; ☺lunch daily, dinner Fri & Sat) This is a bright, airy place with artworks on the walls and simple, well-prepared favourites such as fish and chips, curries and pastas. The service is relaxed and cheerful, and the wine list offers some interesting local selections.

❶ Information

Rutherglen Wine Experience (☑1800 622 871; www.rutherglenvic.com; 57 Main St; ☺9am-5pm; ☻) A fun place that combines the visitor centre with a wine-tasting room and a cafe.

❶ Getting There & Away

V/Line (☑13 61 96; www.vline.com.au) has a train and coach service between Melbourne and Rutherglen with a change at Seymour ($26, four hours, eight weekly). During festivals, bus transport to wineries can be organised through the visitor centre.

AROUND RUTHERGLEN

Wahgunyah

POP 800

A short drive northeast of Rutherglen on the Murray River is the idyllic little township of Wahgunyah. At the height of the riverboat era, Wahgunyah was a thriving port town and trade depot. Now, renowned wineries such as All Saints Estate, St Leonards and Pfeiffers surround it, and the historic town of Corowa is just across the bridge in NSW.

In town you can drink or dine at the lovely old **Wahgunyah Empire Hotel** (☑02-6033 1094; 6 Foord Street), where **Fairy's** (mains $14-23; ☺lunch & dinner daily) serves traditional pub fare.

Visit the Cofield winery for tastings and a meal in the excellent **Pickled Sisters Café** (☑02-6033 2377; Distillery Rd, Wahgunyah; mains $19-28; ☺lunch Wed-Mon year-round, dinner Fri & Sat Dec-Feb).

Over in Corowa, in a revamped flour mill, is **Corowa Whisky & Chocolate** (☑0406 059 283; Steele St; ☺9am-4pm), where sampling handmade chocolates and international whiskies should make a change from wine tasting!

Chiltern

POP 1100

Like an old-time movie set, tiny Chiltern is one of Victoria's most historic and charming colonial townships. Its two main streets are lined with 19th-century buildings, antique shops and a couple of pubs – authentic enough that the town has been used as a film set for period films, including the early Walt Disney classic *Ride a Wild Pony*. Originally called Black Dog Creek, it was established in 1851 and prospered when gold was discovered here in 1859.

The **Chiltern visitor centre** (☑5726 1611; www.chiltern.com.au; 30 Main St; ☺10am-4pm) has information about the region and birdwatching in the nearby Chiltern-Mt Pilot National Park. The *Chiltern Touring Guide* walks you around 14 labelled sites. Among the National Trust–classified sites are the **Athenaeum Library & Museum** (☑5726 1467; www.chilternathenaeum.com.au; Conness St; adult/child $2/free; ☺10am-4pm), in the former Town Hall (1866), with a collection of memorabilia, art, photos and equipment from the gold-rush days; **Dow's Pharmacy** (☑5726 1597; Conness St; adult/child $3/1) with lotions and potions from the early days; it's been a chemist since 1859; and **Lake View Homestead** (☑5726 1317; Victoria St), built in 1870 and overlooking Lake Anderson. It was the home of Henry Handel (Ethel Florence) Richardson, who wrote about life here in the book *Ultima Thule* (1929), the third part of her trilogy *The Fortunes of Richard Mahony* (1930).

Star Hotel Museum & Theatre (☑5726 1395; cnr Main & Conness Sts), once used for plays and dances, was the centrepiece of

Chiltern's social and cultural life. Unfortunately the museum here is rarely open these days (call ahead for an appointment). The grapevine in the courtyard is the largest in Australia – you can just see it down the alleyway off Conness St.

There are a couple of classic country pubs in town serving bistro food, and the **Mulberry Tree B&B & Tearooms** (☎5726 1277; www.mulberrytreechiltern.com.au; 28 Conness St; B&B d $135-190), a former bank building with cute B&B rooms (one self-contained) and a garden cafe serving Devonshire teas and light meals.

WODONGA

POP 30,000

The border town of Wodonga is separated from its twin, Albury, by the Murray River. Although a busy little town with a lake formed off Wodonga Creek, most of the attractions and the best of the accommodation are on the NSW side in Albury. The Lincoln Causeway runs from the city centre across Wodonga Creek to the border at the Murray River. The Gateway shopping area, along the Causeway, has art and craft shops where you can watch timber pieces being carved.

There are signed trails for the many walking and bike trails around Gateway Island, along the Murray River and to the beautiful wetlands of **Sumsion Gardens**. This is also the start of the **High Country Rail Trail** (www.highcountryrailtrail.org.au), a cycling and walking path that skirts around the southern end of Lake Hume to Old Tallangatta.

The **Army Museum Bandiana** (☎02-6055 2525; www.defence.gov.au/army/awma_mus; Murray Valley Hwy, Bandiana; adult/child/family $5/2/10; ☺9.30am-5pm) displays a variety of war weaponry, items from missions, and documents. There's also magnificent vintage cars including a Buick and Holden staff cars, Chevrolet and Dodge trucks, carriages and motorbikes.

For 24 years from the end of WWII, **Bonegilla**, 10km east of Wodonga, was Australia's first migrant-reception centre, providing accommodation and training for some 320,000 migrants. At the **Bonegilla Migrant Experience** (☎02-6020 6912; www.bonegilla.org.au; Bonegilla Rd; admission free, tours $5; ☺9.30am-4.30pm) you can visit some of the preserved buildings and see photos and historical memorabilia.

ℹ Information

Gateway visitor information centre (☎1300 796 222; www.alburywodongaaustralia.com.au; Hume Hwy, Gateway Island; ☺9am-5pm) Has 24-hour touch-screen information and an accommodation booking service.

THE WAY NORTH

Heading north to the Murray River from Melbourne opens up some unexpected regions of Victoria – vast desert national parks, sleepy rural towns and the fertile food bowl of the Goulburn Valley to name a few. The main routes north are the Hume Fwy to Wodonga (which continues on to Sydney), the Sunraysia Hwy through the Mallee to Mildura, the Northern Hwy to Echuca and the Goulburn Valley Hwy through Shepparton.

The Mallee

Occupying the relatively vast northwestern corner of Victoria, the Mallee appears as a flat horizon and endless, undulating, twisted mallee scrub and desert. It's dry here, but after years of drought and hardship, welcome rains in 2010 rejuvenated the Wimmera River to the south, in turn filling Lake Hindmarsh, Victoria's largest body of fresh water, and Lake Albacutya. In the north, most of the fresh water is supplied by the Murray. The attractions – other than the sheer solitude – are the semi-arid wilderness areas, such as Wyperfeld National Park, Big Desert Wilderness Park and Murray-Sunset National Park. Collectively these parks cover over 750,000 hectares, and are particularly notable for their abundance of native plants, spring wildflowers and birds. This is 'Sunset Country', the one genuinely empty part of the state. Naturelovers might delight in it, but much of it is inaccessible to all but experienced 4WD enthusiasts. Like most outback areas, visiting here is best avoided in the hot summer months.

The main route through the Mallee is the Sunraysia Hwy, via the towns of Birchip and Ouyen, but if you want to explore the region's national parks, turn off to the historic farming towns of **Jeparit** (birthplace of Sir Robert Menzies and the jumping-off point for Lake Hindmarsh), **Rainbow**, **Yaapeet** and **Hopetoun**.

MALLEE SCRUB

A mallee is a hardy eucalypt with multiple slender trunks. Its roots are twisted, gnarled, dense chunks of wood, famous for their slow-burning qualities and much sought after by woodturners. Mallee gums are canny desert survivors – root systems over 1000 years old are not uncommon – and are part of a diverse and rich biosystem with waterbirds, fish in the huge (but unreliable) lakes, kangaroos and other marsupials, emus, and the many edible plants that thrive in this environment.

When the railway line from Melbourne to Mildura was completed in 1902, much of the region was divided into small blocks for farming. The first Europeans had terrible problems trying to clear the land. They used mullenising (crushing the scrub with heavy red-gum rollers pulled by teams of bullocks, then burning and ploughing the land), but after rain, the tough old mallee roots regenerated and flourished. Farmers also had to deal with rabbit and mouse plagues, sand drifts and long droughts. Today the Mallee is a productive sheep-grazing and grain-growing district, with more exotic crops, such as lentils, also appearing.

WYPERFELD NATIONAL PARK

Wyperfeld is a vast but accessible park of river red gum, mallee scrub, dry lake beds, sand plains and, in the spring, a carpet of native wildflowers. It's a naturalist's paradise, with over 200 species of birds and a network of walking and cycling tracks. A sealed road from the southern park entrance near Yaapeet leads to the visitor centre at Wonga Campground (sites $13.50) with pit toilets, picnic tables and fireplaces. Casuarina Campground (sites free) in the north is reached via a gravel road off the Patchewollock-Baring Rd.

To the west, along the South Australian border, the Big Desert Wilderness Park has no roads, facilities or water. Walking and camping are permitted but only for the experienced and totally self-sufficient.

MURRAY-SUNSET NATIONAL PARK

If you've packed your hat and filled your water bottle, you're ready to enjoy the stunning 6330 sq km of mallee woodland in the Murray-Sunset National Park, reaching from the river red gums of Lindsay Island down to Underbool. Most of the park is remote 4WD-only territory.

The Pink Lakes, near Underbool, get their colour from the millions of microscopic organisms in the lake, that concentrate an orange pigment in their bodies. From Linga, on the Mallee Hwy, there's a signed, unsealed road that was built when salt was harvested from the lakes. Nearby is a basic camping ground, but beyond that you need a 4WD.

It you go for walks along the tracks, leave before dawn and be out of the sun before noon. As the wide sky turns pink at dusk, venture out again to watch the birdlife and the magic of the night sky.

On the western side of the park, the Shearer's Quarters (☑5028 1218; off Settlement Rd; groups $55) has hostel-type accommodation. It's pretty basic (hot and cold water and a fridge are supplied) and is accessible only by 4WD.

ℹ Information

Parks Victoria (☑13 19 63, Underbool 5094 6267, Werrimull 5028 1218; www.parkweb. vic.gov.au) For more information, and to let someone know your whereabouts, contact the rangers in Underbool on the Mallee Hwy, or north at Werrimull.

HATTAH-KULKYNE NATIONAL PARK

The vegetation of the beautiful and diverse Hattah-Kulkyne National Park ranges from dry, sandy mallee-scrub country to the fertile riverside areas closer to the Murray, which are lined with red gum, black box, wattle and bottlebrush.

The Hattah Lakes system fills when the Murray floods, which is great for waterbirds. The many hollow trees here are perfect for nesting, and more than 200 species of birds have been recorded in the area. There are many native animals, mostly nocturnal desert types and wetland species, such as the burrowing frog, which digs itself into the ground and waits until there's enough water to start breeding. Reptiles here include the mountain devil, the inspiration for the Aussie saying, 'flat out like a lizard drinking', because it draws surface water into its mouth by lying flat on the ground.

The main access road is from **Hattah**, 70km south of Mildura on the Calder Hwy. There are two **nature drives**, the Hattah and the Kulkyne, and a network of old camel tracks that are great for **cycling**, although you'll need thorn-proof tubes. Tell the rangers where you're going, and carry plenty of water, a compass and a map.

You can **camp** (unpowered sites $13.50) at Lake Hattah and Lake Mournpoul, but there's limited water and the lake water is undrinkable. Free camping is also possible anywhere along the Murray River frontage.

ℹ Information

Hattah-Kulkyne National Park visitor centre (☑5029 3253; 5km into the park) A cool building with posters, tables and chairs. Ring the ranger to find out if the tracks are passable.

Goulburn Valley

One of Victoria's major inland rivers, the beautiful Goulburn is an important irrigation source that makes intensive agriculture possible. Once a complex of rivers, creeks and billabongs, it has been tamed by dams, levees and channels, although you can still find many pockets of riverine ecology.

The Goulburn Valley is Victoria's 'food bowl', an important centre for fruit, dairy, food processing and some of Australia's oldest and best wineries. To get here, leave the Hume Fwy after Seymour and head north on its little-sister road, the Goulburn Valley Hwy.

NAGAMBIE
POP 1400

On the shores of pretty **Lake Nagambie**, the town of Nagambie was created by the construction of the Goulburn Weir back in 1887. The weir is now popular for water sports such as waterskiing, rowing, canoeing, sailing, fishing and swimming, and the town makes a perfect base for touring local wineries, wetlands, horse studs and the Strathbogie Ranges.

Two of Victoria's best wineries are just south of town: **Mitchelton Wines** (☑5736 2221; www.mitchelton.com.au; Mitchellstown Rd; ☉10am-5pm), with an art gallery and award-winning Shiraz; and **Tahbilk Winery** (☑5794 2555; www.tahbilk.com.au; 254 O'Neils Rd; ☉9am-5pm Mon-Fri, 10am-5pm Sat & Sun). Tahbilk opens onto the **Wetlands & Wildlife Reserve** (admission by gold-coin donation, wetland cruise adult/child $10/free; ☉11am-4pm Mon-Fri, 10am-4.30pm Sat & Sun) with boardwalks and boat tours through a natural area rich in birdlife. Entry is via the excellent **Wetlands Café** (mains $19-28; ☉lunch daily).

Nagambie is also the place to try **skydiving** (see boxed text, p303).

ℹ Information

Nagambie visitor centre (☑1800 444 647, 5794 2647; www.nagambielaketourism.com.au; cnr Goulburn Hwy & Moss Rd; ☉9am-5pm) Staff are passionate about their lake, their town and their region. Enjoy a coffee at the adjacent cafe.

SHEPPARTON
POP 45,000

Laid-back 'Shepp' is the capital of the Goulburn Valley, where the Goulburn and Broken Rivers meet. This is the heart of a rich farming and fruit-growing region – the giant SPC Ardoma cannery is here – so it's popular with travellers looking for fruit-picking work. It's also a decent family destination with lots of activities for kids. Look out for the extraordinarily colourful cows dotted around town – such ironic rural art!

◉ Sights & Activities

Shepparton Art Gallery   GALLERY
(☑5832 9861; www.sheppartonartgallery.com.au; Eastbank Centre, 70 Welsford St; admission free; ☉10am-4pm) Don't miss this regional gallery, where the permanent collection of Australian art includes *Goulburn River near Shepparton* (1862) by Eugene von Guèrard, depicting McGuire's punt crossing the river. A separate gallery houses temporary and touring exhibitions.

Bangerang Cultural Centre
                                          GALLERY, MUSEUM
(☑5831 1020; www.bangerang.org.au; 1 Evergreen Way; admission free; ☉9am-4pm Mon-Fri) This Indigenous gallery, museum and keeping place, is well worth a visit for its unique collection of Koorie art and artefacts, and wonderful dioramas.

Aquamoves   SWIMMING
(☑5832 9400; www.aquamoves.com.au; Tom Collins Dr; adult/child $4.85/3.25; ☉6am-9pm Mon-Thu, 6am-8pm Fri, 8.30am-5pm Sat & Sun) Beside pretty Victoria Park Lake, Aquamoves is an aquatic extravaganza with indoor and outdoor pools, waterslides, a hydrotherapy pool and gym.

Ardmona KidsTown   OUTDOORS
(☑5831 4213; www.kidstown.org.au; Midland Hwy/Mooroopna Causeway; admission by gold coin donation; ☉dawn-dusk) On the road to Mooroopna, this fabulous community adventure park is

great fun for families, with a flying fox, a miniature railway, a giant playground, barbecues, a cafe and more.

🛏 Sleeping & Eating

Shepparton Backpackers HOSTEL $
(☑5831 6556; www.sheppartonbackpackers.com. au; 139 Numurkah Rd; dm/d $25/80; @) Tucked away behind a car wash 3km north of town, this well-equipped hostel is the place to stay if you're looking for agricultural work in the region. There are cheap weekly rates.

Victoria Lake Holiday Park CARAVAN PARK $
(☑5821 5431; www.viclakeholidaypark.com.au; 536 Wyndham St; unpowered/powered sites $24/26, d cabins $77-115) Beside Lake Victoria, this friendly park has plenty of grass and shade, bicycle paths and good facilities.

Cellar 47 ITALIAN $$
(☑5831 1882; 170 High St; mains $15-32; ☺lunch dinner Mon-Sat) With its sleek black-and-glass bar and gourmet wood-fired pizzas, this is a long standard local favourite.

Letizia's Café Bar Restaurant CAFE, BAR $$
(☑5831 8822; 67 Fryers St; mains $12-35; ☺lunch & dinner Tue-Sun) With yum cha, mezes, pasta, bento boxes and Asian-influenced dishes, Letizia's serves up a global selection in a casual, relaxed atmosphere. Great for lunch on the run, or dine in the 100-year-old cellar.

ℹ Information

Shepparton visitor centre (☑1800 808 839, 5831 4400; www.discovershepparton.com.au; Wyndham St; ☺9am-5pm) At the southern end of the Victoria Park Lake.

Up the Hume

The multilane Hume Fwy neatly bypasses every town on its way north from Melbourne to the Victorian border. This used to be a track leading to Sydney, with bullock wagons piled with wheat waiting for those ahead to make the next river crossing. Even 40 years ago, heading north was a jostle of sedans, caravans and trucks on a narrow, potholed road. The highway separates the Goulburn Valley to the west from the foothills of the High Country to the east, and if you have the time to get off the freeway, the minor roads and flat terrain make this the perfect region for either leisurely cycling or to explore the somnolent provincial centres.

SEYMOUR TO BENALLA
Seymour is best known for industry and agriculture, and is central to many activities – contact the **Seymour visitor centre** (☑5799 0233; 47 Emily St; ☺9am-5pm).

Seymour Railway Heritage Centre (☑5799 0515; www.srhc.org.au; Victoria St; admission $2; ☺10am-3pm Tue, Thu, Sat & Sun) has a fantastic collection of heritage Victoria Railway locomotives and carriages and occasional rail tours.

Puckapunyal, 18km west of Seymour, is army country. The **RAAC Tank Museum** (☑5735 7285; www.armytankmuseum.com.au; Hopkins Barracks, Puckapunyal; adult/child/family $7.50/3/15; ☺10am-5pm Tue-Fri, to 4pm last weekend of the month) houses vintage armoured vehicles and tanks (including the Vicker MKII), antitank weapons and historic army displays.

Back on the freeway, turn into **Plunkett Fowles Winery** (☑5796 2150; www.plunkett fowles.com.au; Lambing Gully Rd, Avenel; ☺9am-5pm). The wines made here are full and fresh, and from the excellent **cafe** (meals $8-26) you look across the vineyard to the Strathbogie Ranges.

A little further north, Upton Rd takes you through beautiful countryside to **Avenel Maze** (☑5796 2667; www.avenelmaze.com.au; Upton Rd, Avenel; adult/child/family $9.50/6/27; ☺10am-5pm Thu-Mon, daily during school holidays). There are five bamboozling mazes here, plus the easier rock labyrinth, Kelly Gang connections, minigolf and a licensed cafe.

Benalla has associations with the Ned Kelly legend: Ned made his first court appearance here in 1869 when, aged 14, he was charged with robbery and assault. In 1877 he was again being escorted to the Benalla court when he escaped and hid in a saddle-and-bootmaker's shop on Arundel St. It was here he told police trooper Thomas Lonigan that if ever he shot a man, it would be Lonigan, which he did a year later.

Benalla visitor centre (☑5762 1749; www. benalla.vic.gov.au; Mair St; ☺9am-5pm), by the lake, shares a home with the **Costume & Pioneer Museum** (adult/child $3/2), which has interesting exhibits, a delightful miniature house and a display on local war hero Sir Edward 'Weary' Dunlop.

Benalla Art Gallery (☑5762 3027; www. benallaartgallery.com; Bridge St; ☺10am-5pm) has a collection of Australian art, including paintings from the Heidelberg School, and a cafe that spreads onto a deck overlooking the lake. Outside is the very moving Weary Dunlop Memorial.

COME FLY WITH ME

With calm air-currents, Euroa and Nagambie are the skydiving centres of Victoria, while Benalla, known among enthusiasts worldwide for its thermal activity, is a gliding hotspot. These operators can get you up, up and away:

Go Jump (☑9432 2419; www.skydivingassoc.com.au; Drysdale Rd, Euroa) Start with an introductory scenic flight and tandem jump ($345/385 from 10,000/14,000ft), or take a weekend course ($540) where you end up freefalling with two instructors and pulling your own ripcord.

Skydive Nagambie (☑1800 266 500, 5794 2626; www.skydivenagambie.com; 1232 Kettels Rd, Nagambie) Tandem dives ($365/385 10,000/14,000ft) or a variety of skydiving courses.

Gliding Club of Victoria (☑5762 1058; www.glidingclub.org.au; Samaria Rd Aerodrome; flights from $175) With a base at Benalla airport, go softly, quietly, into a timeless space…

GLENROWAN
POP 350

Ned Kelly's legendary bushranging exploits came to their bloody end here in 1880. The story of Ned and his gang has become an industry in this one-street town – a short detour off the main highway – and you can't drive through Glenrowan without being confronted by the legend and his souvenirs, including a 2m armour-clad statue. The main sites of the capture are signposted, so pick up a walking map and follow the trail.

At the Glenrowan Tourist Centre, **Ned Kelly's Last Stand** (☑5766 2367; 41 Gladstone St; adult/child/family $24/18/64; ☺9.30am-4.30pm, shows every 30min) is an animated theatre where Ned's story is told in a series of rooms by a cast of surprisingly lifelike animatronic characters, and culminates in a smoky shootout and Ned's hanging (it may be too scary for young children). Original props include a handgun owned by Ned, Sgt Kennedy's hitching post and a rare copy of the findings of the Royal Commission into the Kelly manhunt. You can browse the shop and small exhibition of memorabilia for free.

Nearby, underneath Kate's Cottage, a **museum** (☑5766 2448; 35 Gladstone St; adult/child $4.50/1; ☺9am-5.30pm) holds Kelly memorabilia and artefacts gathered from all over the district, and a replica of the Kelly home.

Glenrowan has several country-style cafes and motels, and the local pub.

Buffalo Mountain Wines (☑5766 2180; Gladstone St; ☺daily) is a cellar door with tastings of wines from local vineyards, and stories of the Kelly Gang.

WANGARATTA
POP 15,500

Wangaratta (just plain old 'Wang' to the locals) is a busy commercial centre situated along the Hume Hwy and the turn-off for the ski fields along the Great Alpine Rd, and for the Rutherglen wine region. As such, plenty of people pass through Wang year-round. The name means 'resting place of the cormorants' and the town sits neatly at the junction of the Ovens and King Rivers – the first buildings, in the 1840s, were based around a punt service that operated until 1855. These days, Wangaratta is a modern industrial and textile centre with all the facilities of a provincial town, as well as lots of goldmining and bushranger connections.

◉ Sights & Activities

At the Wangaratta Cemetery, south of town, is the grave of **Dan 'Mad Dog' Morgan**, a notorious bushranger. It contains most of Morgan's remains – after he was fatally shot at nearby Peechelba Station in April 1865, his head was taken to Melbourne for a study of the criminal mind, and his scrotum was supposedly fashioned into a tobacco pouch.

Wangaratta is the start of the **Murray to Mountains Rail Trail**, which runs east via Beechworth to Bright and now links Wangaratta with Rutherglen and Wahgunyah. You can hire bikes from **Bicycle Superstore** (☑5722 2033; www.bicyclesuperstore.com.au; 6-8 Handley St; adult/child per day $29/22), which has a drop-off and pick-up service, baby seats and trailers.

THE KELLY GANG

Bushranger and outlaw he may have been, but Ned Kelly is probably Australia's greatest folk hero. His life and death have been embraced as part of the national culture – from Sidney Nolan's famous paintings to Peter Carey's Booker Prize–winning novel *True History of the Kelly Gang*. Ned himself has become a symbol of the Australian rebel character.

Before he became a cult hero, Edward 'Ned' Kelly was labelled a common horse thief. Born in 1855, Ned was first arrested when he was 14 and spent the next 10 years in and out of jails. In 1878 a warrant was issued for his arrest for stealing horses, so he and his brother Dan went into hiding. Their mother and two friends were arrested, sentenced and imprisoned for aiding and abetting. The Kelly family had long felt persecuted by the authorities, and the jailing of Mrs Kelly was the last straw.

Ned and Dan were joined in their hideout in the Wombat Ranges, near Mansfield, by Steve Hart and Joe Byrne. Four policemen (Kennedy, Lonigan, Scanlon and McIntyre) came looking for them, and, in a shootout at Stringybark Creek, Ned killed Kennedy, Lonigan and Scanlon. McIntyre escaped to Mansfield and raised the alarm.

The government put up a £500 reward for any of the gang members, dead or alive. In December 1878 the gang held up the National Bank at Euroa, and got away with £2000. Then, in February 1879, they took over the police station at Jerilderie, locked the two policemen in the cells, and robbed the Bank of New South Wales wearing the policemen's uniforms. By this time the reward was £2000 a head.

On 27 June 1880, the gang held 60 people captive in a hotel at Glenrowan. A train-load of police and trackers was sent from Melbourne. Ned's plan to destroy the train was foiled when a schoolteacher warned the police. Surrounded, the gang holed up in the hotel and returned fire for hours, wearing heavy armour made from ploughshares. Ned was shot in the legs and captured, and Dan Kelly, Joe Byrne and Steve Hart, along with several of their hostages, were killed.

Ned Kelly was brought to Melbourne, tried, then hanged on 11 November 1880. He met his end bravely; his last words are famously quoted as, 'Such is life.'

His death mask, armour and the gallows on which he died are on display in the Old Melbourne Gaol.

✹ Festivals & Events

Wangaratta Sports Carnival SPORT
An athletics meeting featuring the Wangaratta Gift foot race; held in late January.

Wangaratta Jazz Festival MUSIC
(www.wangarattajazz.com) First held in 1990, this is one of Australia's premier music festivals, featuring traditional, modern and contemporary jazz. It's held on the weekend before the Melbourne Cup in November, with hundreds of musicians and acts, and many awards and workshops. Book accommodation well in advance.

🛏 Sleeping

Wangaratta has a decent range of typical motels, which can be booked online at www.visitwangaratta.com.au.

Hermitage Motor Inn MOTEL $$
(☑5721 7444; www.hermitagemotorinn.com.au; cnr Cusack & Mackay Sts; d/f $115/145; spa r $145; ❄🤶😊) Close to the town centre, the Hermitage is the pick of Wang's motels with spacious rooms, contemporary decor, wi-fi and a pool.

Millers Cottage MOTEL $
(☑5721 5755; www.millerscottage.com.au; 26 Parfitt Rd; s/d from $68/75; ❄😊) The rooms are bog-standard motel, but they're good value and set in a large garden with a pool and playground.

Painters Island Caravan Park

CARAVAN PARK $
(☑5721 3380; www.paintersislandcaravanpark.com.au; Pinkerton Cres; unpowered/powered sites from $26, cabins $60-150; ❄🤶😊) Set on 10 hectares along the banks of the Ovens River, but close to the town centre, this impressive park has a playground, a camp kitchen and a good range of cabins.

🍴 Eating & Drinking

There's a cafe scene along Murphy St and Reid St, and a couple of good restaurants in town.

Rinaldo's Casa Cucina
ITALIAN **$$**

(☎5721 8800; www.rinaldos.com.au; 8-10 Tone Rd; mains $19-27; ⊙lunch & dinner Wed-Sat, lunch Sun) Formerly at the Dal Zotto winery in Whitfield, Rinaldo's has moved its hearty Northern Italian kitchen to this industrial-sized venue in Wang, and is getting plenty of attention. The seasonal menu features fresh pasta dishes and modern Mediterranean versions of steak and seafood. Ask about cooking classes.

Idyl Book Café
CAFE **$**

(☎5722 3545; 64 Faithfull St; ⊙breakfast & lunch Mon-Sat; @) Loads of secondhand books, good coffee and breakfasts with river views.

Vine Hotel
PUB **$$**

(☎5721 2605; Detour Rd; mains $12-24; ⊙lunch & dinner) Ned Kelly and his gang used to hang out here; these days the food is better and you're less likely to get shot. Go underground to the small museum and cellars. The Vine is about 3km north of town, on the road to Eldorado.

Buffalo Brewery
PUB, BREWERY

(☎5726 9215; www.buffalobrewery.com.au; Boorhaman; ⊙daily) At the Boorhaman Hotel, about 15km northwest of Wangaratta, this country pub-brewery produces five award-winning beers, including a wheat beer and a dark ale.

ℹ Information

Wangaratta visitor centre (☎1800 801 065, 5721 5711; www.visitwangaratta.com.au; 100 Murphy St; ⊙9am-5pm; @) In the old library, with displays, internet access, bike hire and videos depicting local rail trails and snippets from the annual Wangaratta Jazz Festival.

Understand
❯ Melbourne & Victoria

Melbourne & Victoria Today

New Brooms

Melbourne's liveability gets a nod year after year, coming in third over at the *Economist,* and number nine on *Monocle's* quality-of-life index. The state hasn't been immune to the global financial crisis but has weathered it better than much of Australia, which in turn has suffered far less than most of the world. Still, if the democratic process can be taken as a gauge of public opinion, Victorians aren't as content as the surveys might suggest.

» Population: 5.53 million

» GSP per capita: $52, 284

» Average house price: $565,000

» Unemployment rate: 5.4%

Julia Gillard's hometown advantage did not translate to votes in the 2010 federal election, and while the Labor Party held onto government by the skin of its teeth, the safe Labor seat of Melbourne was taken by Adam Bandt, the Green's first federal MP.

In the state election that followed a few months later, the Labor party suffered a shock defeat, and the Liberal–National coalition narrowly formed government, with 'hunk from Hawthorn' Ted Baillieu becoming the new premier. Labor cited voter-fatigue after some 11 years in power, but big losses in outer suburban seats suggested infrastructure shortfalls and the high cost of living played a part in their demise.

City Limits

Melbourne now has another title: Australia's most unaffordable city. While conversations in the city centre on the unpopular Windsor Hotel tower redevelopment and whether Docklands will ever see real life beyond its lanyard-land nine-to-fivers and Costco devotees, the state faces considerable urban planning challenges.

The Bracks Labor government's millennial policies to limit sprawl may have been better in theory than practice. Most population growth continued around outer suburban land releases, making for more car-

Top Films

» **The Story of the Kelly Gang** (1906) World's first feature.

» **On the Beach** (1957) Apocalypse Now-ish.

» **Picnic at Hanging Rock** (1975) Elliptical, sensual classic.

» **Dogs in Space** (1986) Chaotic chronicle of the city's punk past.

» **Animal Kingdom** (2010) Menacing, moody crime family thriller.

» **Red Hill** (2010) 'Revisionist' Western-cop thriller genre mash-up, set in breathtaking East Gippsland.

Top Playlist

» 'Carlton (Lygon Street Limbo)', Skyhooks

» 'Shivers', Boys Next Door

» 'Beautiful People', Australian Crawl

» 'Leaps and Bounds', Paul Kelly

» 'Under the Sun', Hunters & Collectors

belief systems
(% of population)

55
Christian

4
Orthodox

3
Buddhism

14
Other

20
No religion

if Victoria were
100 people

70 would be Australian

3 would be European

4 would be English

2 would be New Zealander

4 would be Asian

2 would be Indian

reliant communities that deal daily with soul-destroying commutes and little in the way of local services. The Australian affection for a house on a block of land is hard to discourage by legislation alone; in any case, increased density hasn't equalled affordable inner-city housing.

Baillieu's government has pledged to tackle the housing shortage with what might prove to be contradictory policies of increased land supply and urban renewal, as well as housing more of Victoria's booming population in regional centres such as Geelong (towns like Castlemaine have already seen an influx of savvy buyers). They also slate high-rise development around 'activity centres', sparking concern that the proposed numbers of these – up to 100 – will lead to open-slather development and urban slums. With inner Melbourne already out of reach for low-income home buyers and renters, there's a real threat of 'two Melbournes' emerging.

Cool Capital
As writer and former Next Wave artistic director, Marcus Westbury, says, 'the brain-drain of the young, enthusiastic and talented has worked dramatically in Victoria's favour for quite some time...one of the things that cultural refugees to Victoria cite is Melbourne's impressive smallness: Melbourne does the little things in cultural life exceptionally well'. Long recognised for its street cred and knack for creative, entrepreneurial business, Melbourne just keeps getting cooler. And its cultural players keep getting younger.

Ironically, this scene has become a victim of its own popularity. A wave of alcohol-fuelled violence in the CBD and the rapid gentrification of neighbourhoods that had long been the traditional homes of pubs and live music resulted in what many thought was a far too heavy-handed approach to liquor licensing, aimed at precisely the wrong kind of venue.

» Area of Victoria: 227,415 sq km

» Area of Greater Melbourne: 8806 sq km

» Area of Melbourne CBD: 1.8 sq km

» Highest mountain: Mt Bogong (1986m)

» Victoria's coastline: 1800km

Famous Victorians
» Mary MacKillop
» Dame Nellie Melba
» Barry Humphries
» Nick Cave
» Kylie Minogue
» Julia Gillard
» Julian Assange

Faux Pas
Victorians can be touchy about comparisons with NSW, particularly the Melbourne–Sydney rivalry. This second-city chink in self-esteem is an odd one, as Sydneysiders more often than not express a fondness for the southern capital.

Do & Don't
Don't be afraid of Melbourne's hook turn. When turning right at a designated intersection, pull over to the left, wait for the light to turn red then cross all lanes of traffic to make your turn. This manoeuvre was invented to keep the tram tracks clear.

With the beloved local imperilled, and large crowds of arts and nightlife fans turning out in protest, Victorians wonder if the government will rework the rules, or crackdown harder.

Not Easy Being Green

Sustainability Victoria claims that 86% of Victorians are 'concerned or extremely concerned' about the environmental issues facing the state, a figure that squares with the oh-so green vibe on the streets of inner Melbourne, coastal regions and the tree-changer towns, though not so much with voting patterns.

Melbourne City Council continues to meet and improve on the targets of its *Zero Net Emissions by 2020* policy, and sustainability has become a huge part of many Victorians' everyday lives. Cycling to work and the installation of household grey-water systems are not only popular, but often the core of dinner party conversation. However Victoria's first State of the Environment report, released in 2008, paints a far from optimistic picture. It suggests that the state's growing prosperity masks an alarming decline of natural ecosystems. The biggest issue? Victoria's part in climate change, with the Hazelwood Power Station the most polluting in the country. Despite the end of the drought, water is also of major concern, especially the future of the Murray-Darling Basin. It suggests too that Victoria faces a biodiversity crisis; as Australia's most cleared state, it has the highest number of threatened species.

Victoria is still reeling from its most devastating bushfires, known as Black Saturday. The ensuing 2010 Royal Commission maintained that the 'stay and defend' policy is a sound one, but recommended greater caution in making the decision to do so. The findings continue to be debated in rural communities.

Melbourne's tram network is the largest in the world (topping that of St Petersburg), with around 240km of track, 475 trams and 1813 tram stops. Trams, from the 50-year old W-class to modern level-access models, operate along 27 routes and carry 150-million-plus passengers a year.

Top Non-Fiction

» **Bearbrass** (1995; Robyn Annear)
» **Australian Gothic: A Life of Albert Tucker** (2002; Janine Burke)
» **Yarra: A Diverting History of Melbourne's Murky River** (2005; Kristin Otto)
» **Melbourne Design Guide** (2009)
» **Guide to Melbourne Architecture** (2008; Philip Goad)
» **A Game of Our Own: The Origins of Australian Football** (2010; Geoffrey Blainey)

Local Lingo

» **Like Bourke Street** Very busy
» **The Loop** The five CBD train stations
» **More front than Myer** Cheeky, not at all shy
» **Buckley's** No chance at all (a nod to convict escapee, William Buckley)

History

This is a history that is at once relatively brief and extremely ancient: the state's first people arrived from the north some thousands of decades ago, while European settlement began in the early years of the 19th century and did not flourish until the 1830s. Victoria's early fortunes were tied to sheep and the crops that its rich volcanic soil could produce. It was the discovery of gold, however, that transformed Melbourne from a colonial outpost into one of the world's wealthiest cities. The sudden influx of capital and labour set the stage for Victoria's long-term industrial success. But the state's fondness for a quick buck was to prove its undoing and it was hit particularly hard by the depression of 1889.

Despite the symbolic honour of becoming the new nation's temporary capital in 1901, Melbourne's fortunes didn't really rally until after WWI, and by then its 'first city' status had been long lost to Sydney. When WWI broke out, large numbers of young men from throughout Victoria fought in the trenches of Europe and the Middle East, with enormous losses.

There was a renewed spirit of expansion and construction in Victoria in the 1920s, but this came to a grinding halt with another economic disaster, the Great Depression (in 1931 almost a third of breadwinners were unemployed). When war broke out once again in 1939, Melbourne became the heart of the nation's wartime efforts, and later the centre for US operations in the Pacific. It was boom time again, though no time for celebration.

Postwar immigration was, however, something to be happy about, as Melbourne began its transformation into the multicultural city it is today. Melbourne and Geelong became leading manufacturing centres, and times were good.

During the early 1970s, a bourgeoning counterculture's experiments with radical theatre, drugs and rock and roll rang out through the Melbourne suburb of Carlton. By the later years of that decade, Melbourne's reputation as a prim 'establishment' city was further challenged by

Indigenous Victoria

» Koorie Heritage Trust, Melbourne

» Bunjilaka Aboriginal Cultural Centre, Melbourne Museum

» Brambuk Cultural Centre, Halls Gap

» Harry Nanya Tours, Mildura

» Kirrit Barreet, Ballarat

» Tower Hill Natural History Centre, Warrnambool

TIMELINE	70,000–40,000 BC	1803	1834
	The first humans colonise southeastern Australia. The people of the Kulin Nation live in the catchment of the Yarra River; various other tribes, speaking 38 languages, are spread throughout Victoria.	Victoria's first European settlement is at Sorrento. It is an unmitigated disaster, with no fresh water to be found; the settlers abandon the site after six months and set sail for Van Diemen's Land (Tasmania).	Portland pioneer Edward Henty, his family and a flock of sheep arrive from Van Diemen's Land, marking the first permanent European settlement in the region that will become Victoria.

the emergence of a frantically subversive art, music, film and fashion scene that launched bands like the Birthday Party onto the world stage. During the real-estate boom of the 1980s, a wave of glamorous shops, nightclubs and restaurants made way for Melbourne's emergence as Australia's capital of cool. Changes to the licensing laws in the 1990s saw a huge growth of small bars, cafes and venues – and the birth of the laneway phenomenon.

Indigenous Victoria

Australia's first inhabitants made the journey from Southeast Asia between 70,000 and 40,000 years ago. For the Wurundjeri people who lived in the catchment of the Yarra River, where Melbourne is today, the land and the people were created in the Dreaming by the spirit Bunjil – 'the great one, old head-man, eagle hawk' – who continues to watch over all from Tharangalk-bek, the home of the spirits in the sky.

The Victorian Indigenous peoples lived in some 38 different dialect groups that spoke 10 separate languages: some were matrilineal, others patrilineal. These groups were further divided into clans and sub-clans, each with its own complex system of customs and laws, and each claiming custodianship of a distinct area of land. Despite this, the British considered the continent to be terra nullius – 'a land belonging to no one'.

The Wurundjeri were a tribe of the Woi wurrung, one of five distinct language groups belonging to southern Victoria's Kulin Nation. They often traded and celebrated among the towering red gums, tea trees and ferns of the river's edge with their coastal counterparts the Boonwurrung, as well as other Kulin clans from the north and west.

As the flood-prone rivers and creeks broke their banks in winter, bark shelters were built north in the ranges. Possums were hunted for their meat and skinned to make calf-length cloaks. Possum-skin cloaks were eorn with fur on the inside. The smooth outer hide was rubbed with waterproofing fat and embellished with totemic designs: graphic chevrons and diamonds or representations of emus and kangaroos. During the summer, camps were made along the Yarra and Maribyrnong Rivers and Merri Creek. Food – game, grubs, seafood, native greens and roots – was plentiful. Wurundjeri men and women were compelled to marry out of the tribe, requiring complex forms of diplomacy. Ceremonies and bouts of ritual combat were frequent.

In 1835, when British entrepreneur John Batman arrived from Van Diemen's Land (Tasmania), he travelled through 'beautiful land...rather sandy, but the sand black and rich, covered with kangaroo grass about ten inches high and as green as a field of wheat'. He noted stone dams for catching fish built across creeks, trees that bore the deep scars of bark harvesting and women bearing wooden water containers and woven bags

Estimates suggest that before the Europeans arrived, Victoria's Aboriginal population was between 60,000 and 100,000; by the late 1840s it had dropped to 15,000, and by 1860 scarcely 2000 Aboriginal people survived.

TRAGIC HISTORY

1835	**1837**	**1838**	**1851**
John Batman meets with a group of Aborigines and trades a casket of blankets, mirrors, scissors, handkerchiefs and other assorted curios for around 2400 sq km of land.	The military surveyor Robert Hoddle draws up plans for the city of Melbourne, laying out a geometric grid of broad streets in a rectangular pattern on the northern side of the Yarra River.	The *Melbourne Advertiser*, Melbourne's first newspaper, is 'published', with 10 weekly handwritten editions; in 1839 it rolls off the presses daily as the *Port Phillip Patriot and Melbourne Advertiser*.	Victoria separates from the colony of New South Wales (NSW); gold is discovered in central Victoria and the world's richest gold rush is on.

holding stone tools. However, the Indigenous people's profound spiritual relationship with the land and intimate knowledge of story, ceremony and season would be irrevocably damaged within a few short years.

As European settlement fanned out through Victoria, and the city of Melbourne transformed from pastoral outpost to a heaving, gold-flushed metropolis in scarcely 30 years, the cumulative effects of dispossession, alcohol and increasing acts of organised violence resulted in a shocking decline in Victoria's Indigenous population. From the earliest days, the colonial authorities evicted Aboriginal people from their traditional homes. By the early 1860s the Board for the Protection of Aborigines had begun to gather together surviving Aborigines in reserves run by Christian missionaries at Ebenezer, Framlingham, Lake Condah, Lake Tyers, Ramahyuck and Coranderrk. These reserves developed into self-sufficient farming communities and gave their residents a measure of 'independence' (along with twice-daily prayers and new boots at Christmas), but at the same time inflicted irreversible damage.

European Settlement

The first European settlement in Victoria in 1803 didn't have an auspicious start. With a missed mail ship communiqué and a notoriously supercilious British government calling the shots, Surveyor-General Charles Grimes' recommendations – that the best place to found a southern, French-foiling settlement would be by the banks of the 'Freshwater River' (aka the Yarra) – went unheeded. The alternative, Sorrento, on what is now the Mornington Peninsula, was an unmitigated disaster from the get-go. As Lt David Collins pointed out to his superiors, you can't survive long without drinkable water. The colony moved to Van Diemen's Land, but one extremely tenacious convict escapee, William Buckley, was left behind: he was on the run until John Batman turned up a few decades later.

Australia's European history had begun with intermittent coastal exploration by Dutch seamen some centuries before. In 1770, Captain James Cook formally 'discovered' Australia and in 1788, the first colony was established at Sydney Cove in New South Wales (NSW). After the failed Sorrento colony it was 20-odd years before explorers made their way overland to Port Phillip and another decade before a settlement was founded on the southwest coast at Portland. Around the same time, in the early 1830s, Surveyor-General of NSW, Major Thomas Mitchell, crossed the Murray River (then called the Hume) near Swan Hill and travelled southwest. He was delighted to find the rich volcanic plains of the Western District. His glowing reports of such fertile country included him dubbing the area 'Australia Felix' (fortunate Australia) and encouraged pastoralists to venture into the area with large flocks of sheep and herds of cattle.

ABORIGINAL POPULATION

Around 25,000 people in Victoria have Aboriginal heritage, including about 15,000 in Melbourne and 5000 in the Shepparton region.

1854

Gold miners rebel over unfair licences and conditions, raising the Southern Cross flag at the Eureka Stockade. Brutally suppressed by soldiers and police, their actions enter Australia's nation-building mythology.

1854

Australia's first significant rail line, from Melbourne Terminus on Flinders St, across the Yarra to Station Pier in Port Melbourne, opens.

RICHARD CUMMINS/LONELY PLANET IMAGES ©

» Historical arrival point for immigrants, Station Pier (p80)

Bearbrass One Day, Melbourne the Next

'Modern' Melbourne's story also begins in the 1830s. Australian-born John Batman, an ambitious grazier from Van Diemen's Land, sailed into Port Phillip Bay in mid-1835 with an illegal contract of sale. (Britain's colonial claims of terra nullius relied on the fiction that the original inhabitants did not own the land on which they lived and hence could not sell it.) He sought out some tribal elders and on a tributary of the Yarra – it's been speculated that it was the Merri Creek, in today's Northcote – found some 'fine-looking' men, with whom he exchanged blankets, scissors, mirrors and handkerchiefs for over half a million acres (2400 sq km) of land surrounding Port Phillip.

Despite the fact that the Aborigines from Sydney who were accompanying Batman couldn't speak a word of the local language and vice versa, Batman brokered the deal and signatures were gathered from the 'local chiefs' (all suspiciously called Jika-Jika and with remarkably similar penmanship). He noted a low rocky falls several miles up the Yarra where the Queens Bridge is today. Upstream fresh water made it a perfect place for, as Batman described it, 'a village'. Batman then returned to Van Diemen's Land to ramp up the Port Phillip Association.

It's at this point that the historical narrative becomes as turbid as the Yarra itself. Before Batman could get back to his new settlement of Bearbrass (along with 'Yarra', another cocksure misappropriation of the local dialect), John Pascoe Fawkner, a Launceston publican and childhood veteran of the failed Sorrento colony, got wind of the spectacular opportunity at hand. He promptly sent off a small contingent of settlers aboard the schooner *Enterprize*, who, upon arrival, started building huts and establishing a garden. On Batman's return there were words, and later furious bidding wars over allotments of land. Historians regard the two in various ways, but Fawkner's foremost place in Victoria's story was sealed by the fact he outlived the syphilitic Batman by several decades. Despite the bickering, hubris and greed of the founders, the settlement grew quickly; around a year later, almost 200 brave souls (and some tens of thousands of sheep) had thrown their lot in with the two Johnnies.

New South Wales wasn't happy. Governor Bourke dispatched Captain William Lonsdale south in 1836, quashing any notion of ownership by the Port Phillip Association. This was crown land, by God! Surveyors were sent for and the task of drawing up plans for a city began. Robert Hoddle, Surveyor in Charge, arrived with the governor in March 1837, and was horrified by the lack of order, both that of his unruly staff – they had absconded up river to get drunk or shoot kangaroos one too many times – and the antipodean topography itself. For Hoddle, it was all about straight lines; his grid, demarcated by the Yarra and what was

Various kings, queens and assorted contemporary bigwigs (including Governor Bourke himself) got the nod in the naming of Melbourne's streets.

Chinese migrants founded Melbourne's Chinatown in Little Bourke St in 1851, making it the longest continuous Chinese settlement in any Western country.

1856–60	**1858**	**1880**
Stonemasons building the University of Melbourne strike and the struggle for a shorter working day begins; the subsequent eight hour day campaign transforms Victorian working conditions.	The Melbourne Football Club is formed and Australian Rules football's first recorded match takes place between Scotch College and Melbourne Grammar School.	The International Exhibition is held at the Royal Exhibition Building in Melbourne's Carlton Gardens. Over a million visitors come to see the fruits of the Empire.

» Royal Exhibition Building (

once a 'hillock' where Southern Cross Station now lies, is Melbourne's defining feature. Land sales commenced almost immediately, and so the surveying continued, but with little Romantic notion of exploration or discovery. It was, by all accounts, a real-estate feeding frenzy. The British were well served by their terra nullius concept, as returns on investment were fabulous. The rouseabout 'Bearbrass' was upgraded to the rather more distinguished 'Melbourne', after the serving British prime minister.

During these years, the earliest provincial towns were also established along Victoria's coast, around the original settlement of Portland to the southwest and Port Albert to the southeast. Early inland towns rose up around self-sufficient communities of sheep stations, which at this stage were still the main source of Victoria's fast-increasing fortunes. This, however, was soon to change.

Golden Years

In 1840, a local landowner described the fledgling city of Melbourne as 'a goldfield without the gold'. Indeed, with a steady stream of immigrants and confidence-building prosperity, there had been growing calls for separation from convict-ridden, rowdy New South Wales. By the end of 1850, the newly minted colony of Victoria had got its go-it-alone wish. This quickly seemed like a cruel stroke of fate; gold was discovered near Bathurst in New South Wales in early 1851, sparking a mass exodus. Pastoral riches or not, there was every chance that without a viable labour force (many had already succumbed to the siren call of California) the colony would wither and die.

Melbourne jewellers had for some time been doing a clandestine trade with shepherds who came to town with small gold nuggets secreted in their kerchiefs. Wary of the consequences of a gold rush on civic order, but with few other options, the city's leading men declared that gold must indeed be found. As was the Victorian way, a committee was formed and a reward was offered. Slim pickings were discovered in the Pyrenees and Warrandyte, before a cluey Californian veteran looked north to Clunes. Just over a ridge, in what was to become Ballarat, was the proverbial pot at the end of the rainbow. It wasn't long before miners were hauling 60lb of the magic mineral into Geelong at a time, and the rush was well and truly on.

The news spread around the world and brought hopefuls from Britain, Ireland, China, Germany, Italy, the US and the Caribbean. By August 1852, 15,000 new arrivals were disembarking in Melbourne each month. Crews jumped ship and hotfooted it to the diggings, stranding ships at anchor. Chaos reigned. Everyone needed a place to stay, even if only for a night or two, and when there was no room at the inn, stables were let for exorbitant amounts. Wives and children were often dumped in

Gold Rush Sights

» Sovereign Hill, Ballarat

» Central Deborah Gold Mine, Bendigo

» Central Market, Castlemaine

» Maldon

» Beechworth

By 1840, when the young Queen Victoria took the throne, Melbourne had 10,000 (occasionally upstanding) citizens and was looking decidedly like a city.

1883	**1884**	**1901**	**1923**
Yarra Falls, a rock bridge that spanned the Yarra at Customs House that divided fresh water from salt, and was used as a crossing, was removed by explosives.	HV McKay's invention of the Sunshine stripper harvester in Ballarat makes leaps and bounds in the efficient harvest of cereal crops, and puts Australia on the map as a leading exporter of grain.	Australia's collection of colonies become a nation. The Federation's first parliament is held at the Royal Exhibition Building; parliament will sit in Melbourne for the next 27 years.	Vegemite, a savoury sandwich spread, and Australia's most enduring culinary peccadillo, is invented in Melbourne, using autolysis to break down yeast cells from waste provided by Carlton & United Breweries.

town while husbands continued on to the diggings. Governor La Trobe despaired of his grand civic vision, as shanties and eventually a complete tent village sprung up. Canvas Town, on the south side of the Yarra, housed over 8000 people.

Catherine Spence, a journalist and social reformer, visited Melbourne at the height of the hysteria and primly observed 'this convulsion has unfixed everything. Religion is neglected, education despised...everyone is engrossed with the simple object of making money in a very short time.' The 20 million ounces of gold found between 1851 and 1860 represented a third of the world's total. That said, relatively few diggers struck it lucky. The licensing system favoured large holdings, policing was harsh and scratching out a living proved for many so difficult that dissent became as common as hope had been a few years before.

Over 90% of Australia's $100 million gold haul in the 1850s was found in Victoria.

For some, 1852 was indeed a golden year, but by 1854, simmering tensions exploded in Ballarat.

The Eureka Stockade: Victoria's Rebellion

As the easily won gold began to run out, Victorian diggers despaired of ever striking it rich, and the inequality between themselves and the privileged few who held the land that they worked stoked a fire of dissent.

Men joined together in teams and worked cold, wet, deep shafts. Every miner, whether or not gold was found, had to pay a licence fee of 30 shillings a month. This was collected by policemen who had the power to chain those who couldn't pay to a tree, often leaving them there until their case was heard.

In September 1854, Governor Hotham ordered that the hated licence hunts be carried out twice a week. A month later a miner was murdered near the Ballarat Hotel after an argument with the owner, James Bentley. When Bentley was found not guilty by a magistrate (who happened to be his business associate), miners rioted and burned the hotel down. Though Bentley was retried and found guilty, the rioting miners were also jailed, which enraged the miners.

Kelly Gang Haunts

» Glenrowan

» Warby Range State Park

» Beechworth

» Old Melbourne Gaol

The Ballarat Reform League was born. They called for the abolition of licence fees, democratic reform, including the miners' rights to vote (universal suffrage was yet to exist), and greater opportunity to purchase land.

On 29 November about 800 miners tossed their licences into a bonfire during a mass meeting and then built a stockade at Eureka, led by Irishman Peter Lalor, where they prepared to fight for their rights. A veteran of Italy's independence struggle, Raffaello Carboni, called on the crowd, 'irrespective of nationality, religion and colour', to salute the Southern Cross as the 'refuge of all the oppressed from all the countries on earth'.

On 3 December the government ordered troopers – the mounted colonial police – to attack the stockade. There were only 150 miners within

1925	1930	1953	1956
The first Australian-built Model T Fords roll off an improvised production line in a disused wool store in Geelong.	A plucky young chestnut gelding called Phar Lap wins the Melbourne Cup. His winning streak endears him to the nation; he remains one of the most popular exhibits in the Melbourne Museum.	The first Italian Gaggia espresso machine is imported to Melbourne. Soon Universita Cafe in Lygon St, Pellegrini's in the city and Don Camillo in North Melbourne are serving the city's first cappuccinos.	Melbourne hosts the summer Olympic Games. Despite this mark of sporting bonhomie, the event is marked with political unrest, due to the Suez crisis and the Soviet invasion of Hungary.

Victorian bushranger Ned Kelly (1855–80) became a national legend when he and his gang donned homemade armour in an attempt to deflect the bullets of several dozen members of the constabulary. Kelly's story, set among the hills, valleys and plains of northeastern Victoria, has a Robin Hood–like quality, as well as the whiff of an Irish rebel song.

Kelly's passionate, articulate letters, handed to hostages while he was robbing banks, paint a vivid picture of the harsh injustice of his time, as well as his lyrical intelligence. These, as well as his ability to evade capture for so long, led to public outrage when he was sentenced to death and finally hanged at the Old Melbourne Gaol in 1880.

The enduring popularity of the Kelly legend is evident in the mass of historical and fictional accounts that continue to be written to this day. His life has also inspired a long string of films, from the world's first feature film *The Story of the Kelly Gang* (1906), to two more recent versions, both simply called *Ned Kelly,* the first starring Mick Jagger (1970) and the second, the late Heath Ledger (2003). A series of paintings by Sidney Nolan featuring Kelly in his armour are among Australia's most recognisable artworks.

the makeshift barricades and the fight lasted a short but devastating 20 minutes, leaving 25 miners and four troopers dead.

Though the rebellion was short-lived, the miners won the sympathy and support of many Victorians. The government deemed it wise to acquit the leaders of the charge of high treason. It's interesting to note that only four of the miners were Australian-born: the others hailed from Ireland, Britain, Italy, Corsica, Greece, Germany, Russia, Holland, France, Switzerland, Spain, Portugal, Sweden, the US, Canada and the West Indies.

The licence fee was abolished and replaced by a Miners' Right, which cost one pound a year. This gave miners the right to search for gold; to fence in, cultivate and build a dwelling on a piece of land; and to vote for members of the Legislative Assembly. The rebel miner, Peter Lalor, became a member of parliament some years later. At the Eureka Stockade's 150th anniversary, the then Premier Steve Bracks remarked, 'Eureka was a catalyst for the rapid evolution of democratic government in this country and it remains a national symbol of the right of the people to have a say in how they are governed... This means Eureka is not just a story, it is a responsibility and a calling to ensure we stay true to the Stockade's democratic principles and build on its multicultural heritage – because Eureka was thoroughly multicultural.'

Goldfield brotherhood in 1854, sadly, had its limits. The 40,000 miners who arrived from southern China to try their luck on 'the new gold mountain' were often a target of individual violence and systemic

HISTORY THE EUREKA STOCKADE: VICTORIA'S REBELLION

1964	**1967**	**1970**	**1977**
The Beatles visit Melbourne, staying in the one-time Southern Cross Hotel on Bourke St and creating city-wide 'youthquake' hysteria.	Prime Minister Harold Holt disappears while swimming at Cheviot Beach near Portsea on the Mornington Peninsula; his body is never recovered.	Melbourne's West Gate Bridge collapses during construction, killing 35 workers; the impact and explosion that follows is heard over 20km away.	The Centenary Test, commemorating the first cricket test match between Australia and England, is played at the MCG. Amazingly, Australia triumphs by the same margin as the original, 45 runs.

prejudice. Still, the Chinese community persevered, and it has to this day been a strong and enduring presence in the city of Melbourne and throughout regional Victoria.

Boom & Crash

Gold brought undreamt-of riches and a seemingly endless supply of labour to Victoria. Melbourne became 'Marvellous Melbourne', one of the world's most beautiful Victorian-era cities, known for its elegance, as well as its extravagance. Grand expressions of its confidence include the University of Melbourne, Parliament House, the State Library and the Victorian Mint. Magnificent public parks and gardens were planted both in the city and in towns across the state. By the 1880s, Melbourne had become Australia's financial, industrial and cultural hub. The 'Paris of the Antipodes' claim was invoked; the city was flush with stylish arcades, and grand homes were decorated with ornate iron balconies. The city spread eastwards and northwards over the surrounding flat grasslands and southwards along Port Phillip. A public transport system of cable trams and railways spread into the growing suburbs.

The Welcome Stranger, discovered in 1869 a few centimetres under the ground in the central Victorian town of Moliagul, was, at 72kg, the largest alluvial gold nugget ever found. At the time of its unearthing there were no scales capable of weighing a nugget of its size.

Regional cities, especially those servicing the goldfields, such as Ballarat, Bendigo and Beechworth, also reaped the rewards of sudden prosperity, leaving a legacy of magnificent Victorian architecture throughout the state. 'Selection Acts' enabled many settlers and frustrated miners to take up small farm lots (selections). Although a seemingly reformist, democratic move, these farms were often too small to forge a real living from and life in the bush proved tough. Grinding poverty and the heavy hand of the law led to some settlers turning to bushranging, variously considered a life of crime and or act of subversion against British rule, depending on which side of the economic and religious divide you were on.

In 1880, and again in 1888, Melbourne hosted an International Exhibition, pulling well over a million visitors. The Royal Exhibition Building was constructed for this event; Melbourne's soaring paean to Empire and the industrial revolution is one of the few 19th-century exhibition spaces of its kind still standing.

This flamboyant boast to the world was, however, to be Marvellous Melbourne's swan song. In 1889, after years of unsustainable speculation, the property market collapsed and the decades that followed were marked by severe economic depression.

While the state's Victorian heritage did not fare well during the postwar construction boom (when Melbourne hosted the Olympic Games in 1956, hectares of historic buildings were bulldozed with abandon and this continued apace during the new boom days of the 1980s), significant parts of the city and many goldfield towns still echo with Victorian ambition and aspiration.

1982–84	1983	1988	1992
The Victorian Arts Centre progressively opens at the site now known as Southbank, built to the design of Roy Grounds, after a construction period of some 11 years.	The Ash Wednesday bushfires spread throughout the west, southwest and centre of the state, destroying over 3000 homes and killing 47 Victorians.	The Australian Tennis Open moves from Kooyong to the hard-court venues of Melbourne Park. Attendance jumps by 90%, to well over a quarter of a million spectators.	Southgate shopping centre, built on a former industrial site, opens, connecting the Arts Centre with the city; it marks the beginning of a massive redevelopment of Melbourne's waterfront spaces.

Melbourne's Multicultural Midcentury

In 1901, one of the first things the newly created Australian government did was to pass legislation with the express wish to protect its security and assert its sense of identity as a member of the British Empire. The so-called White Australia policy restricted the entry of non-Europeans, and was followed a couple of years later by the Commonwealth Naturali-

CAPITAL DAYS

Kristin Otto

From *Capital: Melbourne When it was the Capital City of Australia 1901–27*

In 1901 a collection of British colonies – now the states – formed into the Commonwealth of Australia. Melbourne was the political compromise for a temporary capital, while an official site was selected and built upon. Nobody planned on it taking 26 years.

'For the first time in the world's history there will be a nation for a continent and a continent for a nation', said the man who became the first prime minister. In the beginning, he could carry the records of the entire government in his Gladstone bag. Edmund Barton had been one of the founders of the new constitution, writing some of it in the Grand Hotel, now the Hotel Windsor. In the early days, he and Alfred Deakin – the second PM – might boil the billy while sitting up late in an upper room of Parliament House. Barton would occasionally kip there. The third prime minister, Chris Watson, was the first labour leader anywhere to run a country.

Australia was described as 'the social laboratory of the world' and led the way in giving the vote to women, declaring a minimum wage, providing pensions, and having a high standard of living. This nation was born with the 20th century, and in that capital period, the main streams of the modern Melbourne appeared: electricity, film, radio, aeroplanes and cars. The first feature film in the world – *The Story of the Kelly Gang* – was made in and round the city in 1906. Helena Rubinstein began the billion-dollar cosmetics industry in Melbourne when she opened her first salon in the early 1900s.

As a nation, Australia sacrificially blooded itself in WWI, fighting as part of the British Empire. Anzac Day remains an important commemoration of the fact. John Monash, an Australian reserve soldier with a German-Jewish background, became one of the great generals of that war. His domestic engineering expertise can be seen in the Great Domed Reading Room of the State Library of Victoria, and Morell Bridge near the Botanic Gardens. He managed the electrification of the state, and was a director of St Kilda's Luna Park. A university and freeway are both named after him.

The most fascinating artists and writers worked for Keith Murdoch's *Herald* newspaper group (the Flinders St building is now apartments and restaurants). Murdoch later had a son, Rupert. Walter Murdoch (Keith's uncle), wrote in the *Australian Citizen* of 1912, 'The more civilized a nation is, the greater the number of links by which members of that nation are connected.' This was very true of Melbourne, with its rich layers, and some would say, remains true of how Melbourne works today.

JOHN BANAGAN/LONELY PLANET IMAGES ©

1998

Melbourne's Swanston Docks are the main site of Australia's largest industrial dispute in Australia's recent history, as a dispute between the Maritime Union of Australia and Patrick Corporation erupts.

2002

Federation Square opens (a year late to mark the centenary of federation) amid controversy about its final design and cost – $440 million – but to public praise.

» Federation Square (p53)

sation Act, which excluded all non-Europeans from attaining citizenship, and limited both citizen's and non-citizen's ability to bring even immediate family to Australia. This subsequent piece of legislation was particularly devastating to Victoria's Chinese community who maintained strong family and business ties with China.

Victoria's early history of diversity came to an abrupt end. Although the state's loyalties and most of its legal and cultural ties to Britain remained firm, the 1920s did herald change, as small Italian and Greek communities settled in both the city and the state's agricultural heartland, part of a renewed spirit of expansion and construction at the time. They set about establishing food production companies, cafes, restaurants, fish-and-chip shops, delis and grocers; the efforts of these small business pioneers was to prove an inspiration for a new generation of migrants in the 1940s and 50s.

Close to a million non-British immigrants arrived in Australia during the 20 years after WWII; at first Jewish refugees from Eastern and Central Europe, then larger numbers from Italy, Greece, the Netherlands, Yugoslavia, Turkey and Lebanon. With the demise of the blatantly racist White Australia policy in early 1973, many migrants from Southeast Asia also settled in Victoria. These postwar migrants also embraced the opportunity to set up small businesses, adding a vibrancy and character to their new neighbourhoods, such as Carlton, Collingwood, Richmond, Brunswick and Footscray. Melbourne's cultural life was transformed by these communities, and diversity gradually became an accepted, and treasured, way of life.

The former state government encouraged higher-density living and a large amount of student housing was developed in the city centre, seeing many international students become part of the CBD population, with a wave of new businesses servicing them.

The vibrant mix of ethnicities continues to grow, with many recent immigrants from African nations (Victoria has Australia's largest Sudanese population), Eastern Europe and the Middle East. Many immigrants, particularly those from East African countries, have also settled in regional communities.

Less positively, violence against Indian and Pakistani students and claims of unfair working conditions by Indian taxi drivers tarnished the state's reputation for tolerance and harmony as the first decade of the new century came to a close.

During Melbourne's years as the capital, the city's population of just over half a million people was the largest in Australia, and it was second only in size to London in the British Empire.

Tom Roberts' painting *Opening of the First Parliament of the Commonwealth of Australia by HRH The Duke of Cornwall and York, May 9, 1901* includes 250 recognisable portraits of well-known figures present at the Exhibition Building ceremony.

2006

With the failure of late winter and spring rainfalls and the second-driest conditions since 1900, water restrictions are introduced across Victoria.

2006

Melbourne hosts the Commonwealth Games, the largest sporting event ever to be held in the city: in terms of the number of teams, athletes and events it eclipses the 1956 Olympics.

2009

Victoria records its hottest temperatures on record. The Black Saturday bushfires that follow leave 173 people dead, more than 2000 homes destroyed and 4500 sq km burned out.

2011

Victoria is devastated by the worst 'flood events' in its recorded history, with the central and northern parts of the state worst hit, including the towns of Horsham, Shepparton and Swan Hill.

Food & Wine

From Fine Dining to Small Plates

Victoria's food scene is one of almost limitless choice. There is a constant flow of new ideas, new places and new tastes. While Melbourne doesn't have the deeply ingrained traditions and profound self-confidence of, say, Paris or Rome, Bangkok or Tokyo, it has an exuberant culinary culture and a talent for innovation and adaptation.

At the top of the food chain, fine dining thrives. While many Melbourne chefs experiment widely, mixing and matching techniques and ingredients, you'll rarely find chefs doing fusion for fusion's sake. There's too much respect for providence and context. You'll instead find menus that rove across regions and riff on influences. It's rare to find a slavishly followed Anglo-French model (though some, like Jacques Reymond do that, and do it well). There are those that head in a contemporary French direction, such as Shannon Bennett at Vue de Monde and Ben Shewry at Attica, but you're more likely to see a thoughtful pan-Mediterranean menu. Other chefs incorporate both modern Mediterranean and Asian ideas and flavours to greater or lesser degrees; Andrew McConnell at Fitzroy's Cutler & Co and the CBD's Cumulus manages to create a particularly thoughtful but easygoing version of this style, with Pearl upping the Asian flavours.

There's a long tradition of posh Italian dining in the city and it's often exemplary, with chefs such as Guy Grossi at Grossi Florentino. Eastern Mediterranean is also done with five-star flair and a modern sensibility by Greg Malouf at MoMo and George Calombaris' Press Club.

Regional Victoria also has several 'destination' restaurants. Some fit the stereotype of hearty country fare, such as the 'agriturismo'-styled Sardinian cuisine at the Tea Rooms at Yarck, but others, such as the Royal Mail Hotel at Dunkeld, which won the *Age* newspaper's top restaurant award in 2010, surprise with extreme sophistication and creativity.

Given that there's always so much to try, city dwellers love to eat out often rather than saving up restaurants for celebratory big nights out. Melbourne really comes into its own when it comes to a loosened up, grazing style of dining. Small and large plates override the rigid three-course chronology, but an informal menu and more modest price tag doesn't mean quality produce or attention to detail are sacrificed.

A 'no bookings' policy is common at more casual restaurants, meaning that either a drink at the bar or a pre-dinner stroll becomes part of the night out. In a similar manner, bar food is no longer seen as a mere consort to booze, rather it makes for an equal marriage of tastes and experiences. This kind of 'smart casual' eating out is an easy way to join the locals, and also a great way to sample widely without the credit-card king-hit of fine dining. Pub grub is also a big part of Melbourne eating out repertoire, and ranges from a number of ultra-glam restaurants in pub environments to basic counter-meal service with nostalgic dishes such as bangers and mash, steaks, roasts and curries.

The Wine Map of Victoria, by Max Allen, is a great visual guide to the topography, climate, and most widely-planted grape varieties of the state; it also details 900-plus cellar doors, wineries and vineyards.

There's no shortage of really casual food that's cooked with love and is great value for money. Cafes often serve heartier dishes at lunchtime, and casual venues with wine licences are not uncommon. Look for authentic dishes from a smattering of cuisines from across the globe. A steaming bowl of pho (Vietnamese soup), a square of spanakopita (spinach and feta pie), a teriyaki salmon inari (hand roll) or a provolone and prosciutto piadina (Italian flatbread) will probably leave you change from $10, and without doubt about Melbourne's status as a great food city.

Dishing Up Diversity

Take 140 cultures, mix and let simmer for a few decades. While the recipe might not be quite that simple, Victoria's culinary habits are truly multicultural. Many Melburnians have grown up with at least one other culinary heritage besides the rather grim Anglo-Australian fare of the mid-20th century; and they are also inveterate travellers. This makes for a city of adventurous, if often highly critical, palates.

Mod Oz cooking is a loose term that describes a mix of British, European, Asian and Middle Eastern techniques and ingredients, with a seasonal, fresh-produce-driven philosophy similar to Californian cuisine. There's a base of borrowed traditions, yes, but its style and attitude is unique. Its Melbourne manifestation (and the state's culinary offerings in general) tend more towards European and Mediterranean tastes, rather than Sydney's firmly Pacific Rim take on the cuisine. This is both a product of the city's very un-tropical climate – with four distinct seasons and strongly demarked seasonal crops – and also perhaps due to the strong impact Melbourne's Italian, Greek, Eastern European and Middle Eastern communities made on the city from the 1950s on. That's not to say that you won't find wonderful Asian cooking and a host of varied Asian influences – as the city continues to absorb and reinvent these traditions too.

Melbourne has long been a diverse city, but apart from the long-standing influence of the Chinese community via numerous restaurants and importing business, tastes didn't really begin to shift from the Anglo-Celtic basics until the postwar period. As well as importing the goods they couldn't do without, such as olive oil, the city's southern and eastern European migrants set to producing coffee, bread, cheeses and small

THE GHOSTS OF DINNERS PAST

The site of Melbourne was known for its edible delights long before John Batman set eyes on the natural falls of the Yarra. The Wurundjeri thrived because of the area's incredible bounty; the wetlands that spread south of the Yarra were teeming with life, and the Yarra itself brimmed with fish, eels and shellfish. Depending on the season, Indigenous 'Melburnians' would have eaten roast kangaroo, waterfowl, fish and eel, as well as greens, grubs, yam daisies and a sweet cordial concocted from banksia blossoms.

The first Europeans didn't stop to notice the veritable native feast they had stumbled upon, instead they rather quickly went about planting European crops and tending large flocks of sheep. Although many new arrivals were astounded by the ready supply of fresh food, especially the Irish, who were escaping the famine of the 1840s, the early settlers dined mainly on mutton, bread and butter, tea, beer and rum. (Though it's hard to imagine that those familiar with the gentle art of poaching didn't help themselves to ducks and geese.)

A recent archaeological dig in the Little Lonsdale St area of the city revealed bones, seeds and shells that suggested the Melburnians' diet was in fact, by the later part of the 19th century at least, quite diverse. Fine cuts of meat, fresh fruits and vegetables graced the Victorian table. Seafood was also a staple, and judging by the shells found in less salubrious quarters, oysters were far from the luxury they are today.

Vegetarians and vegans (and even raw-food enthusiasts) will have no trouble finding restaurants that cater specifically to them in neighbourhoods such as Fitzroy, Brunswick and St Kilda.

There will also be at least a couple of dishes on most restaurant menus that will please, and few restaurateurs will look askance at special requests. A few fine-dining restaurants (Attica, Jacques Reymond, Ezard) offer vegetarian degustation or tasting menu options, and with advance warning these can usually be made dairy-free.

Most Asian and Indian restaurants will have large meatless menus, but with Chinese, Vietnamese and Thai cooking you'll need to be clear that you don't want the common additives of oyster or fish sauce used. Casual Japanese places also don't have many vegetarian options, though similarly you'll need to ask if they can prepare your dish with dashi, or stock, that hasn't been made with bonito.

goods, which gradually found their way from specialist delis into mainstream supermarkets. These communities also helped shape the agricultural traditions of the state, bringing new crops and production methods to a land that often resembled the parts of the Mediterranean they had left behind. The Vietnamese, Lebanese and Turkish migrants that followed in the 1970s also had a lasting impact on the way Victorians eat. These days, rice-paper rolls, falafel and flat bread wraps are more common on school 'tuckshop' menus than meat pies, and toasted pide bread with avocado is a cafe staple.

Many of the state's culinary leading lights and rising stars are the children or grandchildren of these first generation migrants (or migrants themselves): Guy Grossi, Greg Malouf, Maurice Terzini, Karen Martini, Con Christopoulos, George Calombaris, Rita Macali, Joseph Abboud, Shane Delia, Rosa Mitchell and Pietro Porcu to name just a few.

While Victoria's eating habits have absorbed and incorporated a range of cuisines, creating something new in the process, many of the original inspirations are represented in kitchens across the city, and are constantly joined by those catering to its newest arrivals. Melbourne's ethnic restaurants once clustered in tight community hubs. Although they now flourish all over the city, there are still loosely dedicated zones. Richmond's Victoria Street is packed with Vietnamese restaurants and provedores while the western suburb of Footscray draws those looking for the most authentic Vietnamese, Laotian and Cambodian food (as well as great East African restaurants). Lygon Street, Carlton, has long been home to simple red-sauce Italian cooking – with notable innovators such as DOC – and its coffee and Italian delis are excellent. Chinatown is home to one of Australia's most renowned restaurants of any culinary persuasion, Flower Drum, and there are places doing regional cuisines such as Sichuan- and Beijing-style dumplings up every other laneway. You'll find Japanese, Malaysian and Korean here too. One street up, Lonsdale Street has a handful of Greek taverns and bars. The northern suburb of Brunswick has a number of wonderful Middle Eastern bakers and grocers as well as cafes and restaurants. A large international student population has seen many Indian, Malaysian and Indonesian places spring up in the city, and around the various university campuses, serving inexpensive, fabulously authentic dishes.

Destination Gourmet

» Kyneton
» Milawa
» Beechworth
» Red Hill
» Mildura

Cafes & Coffee Culture

Cafes are an integral part of daily Victorian life. Many city-dwellers are up early so they can catch up with colleagues or just the newspaper over a three-quarter latte and a slice of sourdough before the workday begins, and weekends see cafes across the state fill with those looking for a long leisurely blow-out breakfast. Cafes also fill mid-morning with those out for a morning 'tea' coffee run, or freelancers conducting meetings or working quietly in a corner. This will then be repeated mid-afternoon, with a roaring lunch trade in between.

While socialising is a big part of this ritual, the coffee itself is definitely not an afterthought. Melbourne's coffee wipes the floor with the coffee you'll get in London or Los Angeles, and often tops what you'll find in Italy. Bigger towns throughout the state are also not far behind. In Melbourne, coffee quality is hotly debated; everyone has their preferred bean and blend, and will probably also be on first-name terms with a local barista. Neighbourhood cafes have begun to attract the kind of tribal devotion reserved for AFL teams. Soy coffee is polarising; some purist cafes refuse to offer it, along with skim or 'skinny' milk, while it forms a large part of many others' trade. Within the soy camp, there are two schools: Bonsoy and Vitasoy. Flavoured coffee? Forget about it. Yes, big chains such as Starbucks have sprung up, but an attempt to settle in the cafe heartland of Lygon Street, didn't last long. Who can imagine why you'd need a cookie-cutter multinational to tell you how it's done, when Melbourne's been getting the crème correct for well over 20 years?

The cafe tradition goes back to the early years of last century, with the arrival of Victoria's first wave of Italian and Greek migrants, but really took off post-WWII when large numbers of Italians settled in the inner city and the first Gaggia and La Cimbali espresso machines were imported under licence in 1953. Bourke Street's Pellegrini's is an ever-enchanting survivor of this generation. The brew in their signature Duralex glasses may be unremarkable by today's standards, but the Italian brio, urban bonhomie and original decor are as authentic as it gets. Melbourne *torrefazione* such as Genovese and Grinders also date back to this era, and their bean blends now fuel cafes all over the country. Other local roasters include Atomic, Jasper and Gravity, and Castlemaine's Coffee Basics.

While these original family-run roasters have prospered and become household names, Melbourne is now firmly in the grip of coffee's third wave. Coffee talk now runs to *terroir*. Single origin beans, premium small batch roasts and alternative brewing methods such as the Clover siphon, filter and cold drip have taken coffee appreciation to a new level. Part of a global network that includes Chicago's Intelligentsia and Oslo's Tim Wendelboe, it's the era of extreme coffee excellence.

Third-wave pioneer Mark Dundon's Seven Seeds is part cafe, part retail outlet and part instructional facility, set in a warehouse conversion that wins in the sustainability as well as style stakes. He also runs a city cafe, Brother Baba Budan, and De Clieu in Gertrude Street, Fitzroy. Salvatore Malatesta took over South Melbourne's legendary St Ali from Dundon, and now also runs a stable of cafes, including Sensory Lab, where white-coated staff will analyse customer's palates before recommending a single origin or blend, and Outpost. Other third-wavers include Market Lane at Prahran Market, Monk Bodhi Dharma in East St Kilda and Proud Mary in Collingwood. Many baristas now use beans sourced from Seven Seeds or St Ali.

Cellar Door Dining

» Max's at Red Hill, Mornington Peninsula

» Salix at Willow Creek, Mornington Peninsula

» Yering Station, Yarra Valley

» Port Phillip Estate, Mornington Peninsula

» La Baracca at T'Gallant, Mornington Peninsula

» Merricks General Wine Store, Mornington Peninsula

Eating Local

Over the last decade, the organic and local food movement has gone from strength to strength in Victoria. Shopping at weekly markets and small grocers is a lifestyle choice that's embraced by many and the Slow Food movement has a strong presence state-wide (news and events can be found at www.slowfoodaustralia.com.au/tag/victoria/), as well as a monthly market at the Abbotsford Convent on the fourth Saturday of each month.

Tea and chocolate, although still lurking in coffee's deep shadow, are having something of a renaissance in Melbourne. Many Asian restaurants now offer artisan-produced teas and tisanes, and city hotels like the Windsor and the Langham book out for their traditional fine china and cake stand afternoon teas. The sprightly newcomer is hot chocolate; while you may still come across the drab mix of powdered Cadbury's and frothy milk, the city's bourgeoning artisan chocolate scene means there are a number of chocolatiers serving up ambrosial chocolate made in the Belgian, French or Italian style.

In the city, Queen Victoria Market, and its suburban counterparts in South Melbourne and Prahran, are beloved by locals for their fresh fruit and vegetables, meat and fish, and their groaning deli counters, not to mention a catch up with friends. There is also a weekly rota of inner-city farmers markets (www.mfm.com.au) at Collingwood Children's Farm, Veg Out in St Kilda, and South Melbourne's Gasworks, which bring local artisan producers and fresh, often organic, produce to town. They make for a pleasant Saturday morning coffee spot and food-related stroll.

A huge number of outer suburbs and regional towns also hold community markets, selling local produce (as well as craft and secondhand goods), a comprehensive list can be found at the Australian Farmers Market Association (www.farmersmarkets.org.au). The monthly markets at Red Hill, on the Mornington Peninsula, and St Andrews (www.stan drewsmarket.com.au), around 40 minutes' drive north of Melbourne, are veterans of the scene and incredibly popular. Both are held in atmospheric bush-ringed settings – the bellbird soundtrack is complimentary, no purchase required.

Food tourism is big news right throughout Victoria, with much of the action centred on wine-growing districts such as the Mornington and Bellarine Peninsulas and the Yarra Valley (happy multitasking). The goldfields and spa towns of Kyneton, Daylesford and Castlemaine, and alpine Mansfield, are home to ever-increasing numbers of provedores and cafes offering local produce. The Milawa Gourmet Region, the first to be given the title in Australia is, unsurprisingly, one of the state's richest; the foodie trail here also takes in the surrounding towns of Oxley and Beechworth. Out along the Murray, Mildura is also a destination for its produce and restaurants.

Victorian Vino

Bacchus appears to have smiled upon the state of Victoria. Its small size belies the variety of its climates, which makes for a splendidly diverse wine scene, with around 900 vineyards spread over 21 growing regions. Melbourne itself is surrounded by five of these – the Yarra Valley, Mornington Peninsula, Macedon Ranges, Geelong and Sunbury – all with distinct climates and soils. Wine-region weekends away and grape-grazing festivals are popular with Victorians, and with many of the regions that are also close to favourite beach resorts or ski fields, they also provide a gourmet backdrop to seasonal holidays. Whether it's for confidently working your way through a Melbourne wine list or for creating a cellar door itinerary, understanding what's what only makes the tasting sweeter.

Beginning at Melbourne's suburban fringe, the Yarra Valley is a patchwork of vines, and it's here that you'll find the glamorous big boys of the industry, Chateau Yering and Domaine Chandon. These glistening temples to the grape absorb the tour-bus bustle surprisingly well, with a rota of produce markets and entertainment, as well as striking architecture, making up for the high traffic. The area still has its share of

Famed chef and writer Stephanie Alexander developed a hands-on kitchen garden and cooking curriculum at the inner-city Collingwood College with the aim of instilling a love of fresh produce and the culinary arts in primary school–aged children. While her initial program was inspired by Californian Alice Waters, of Chez Panisse fame, it's found fertile ground in Victoria. Two popular cook books (*Stephanie Alexander's Kitchen Garden Companion* and *Kitchen Garden Cooking with Kids*) and many mini-epicureans later, the program has been rolled out in schools throughout the state. All bodes well for Victoria's continued future as a food destination.

rustic tin sheds where it's just you and the winemaker if that's more your style. Fruity unwooded Pinot Noirs, peachy Chardonnay and crisp sparklings are the darlings here, but there's plenty of experimentation with other grapes too. Wine writer Max Allen recommends the savoury Semillon, Cabernet Merlot and Cabernet Franc blends, and the Merlots from warmer years. Healesville, set in a stunning bush-backed valley, is a good one-stop choice, with a down-to-earth vibe and a downtown cellar door at Giant Steps and Innocent Bystander.

A little further afield in Melbourne's southeast is the rarefied rusticity of the Mornington Peninsula. The hills and valleys of this favourite beach destination hide an embarrassment of riches in terms of small-scale viticulture – there's literally a winemaker around every bend (not to mention symbiotic cellar door, restaurant, gourmet provedore and shop selling French plimsolls). Mornington vignerons are a tenacious, innovative lot, who coax the most out of the volcanic soil and capricious, often chilly, maritime climate to produce beautiful early ripening Pinot Noirs, subtle honeyed Chardonnay and Pinot Gris, as well as fragrant Italian varietals such as Arneis and Pinot Grigio, possibly Australia's best. The vineyards of the Bellarine Peninsula, on the opposite coast, have gained a following of their own, and their delicate maritime-climate aromatic whites are getting a lot of attention.

In Victoria's northeast, wine has been continuously produced since the thirsty days of the gold rush, with Brown Brothers making both fortifieds and table wines right through the 20th century. Northern Italian farmers also made a big contribution to this region's development. They noted similarities in the landscape, and introduced grapes from their home regions that took to the local *terroir*. Today, the gloriously diverse geography, climate and soil, from the flats around Milawa to the high country of Beechworth and the cool, wet King Valley sees a huge variety of wines produced. Rieslings, Sauvignon Blancs and sparklings (including an Italian-styled Prosecco) shine in the King Valley, along with the complex, tightly structured Chardonnay and spicy Shiraz of Beechworth and Milawa's fortifieds, Cabernet Merlots, Sangiovese, Nebbiolos and Pinot Grigios. To the west of here, Rutherglen is also a pioneer and is well known for its fortifieds and unctuous stickies. Big, well, absolutely huge, reds do well here too, but it's the long-cellared Muscats and Tokays (aka liquid Christmas-pud) that keep the faithful coming back.

Other less-visited regions include the Pyrenees, known for its French-influenced sparklings and, somewhat surprisingly, its absolutely Aussie big ripe reds; Macedon, which produces crisp cold-climate sparklings and minerally European-style Chardonnay, Riesling and Sauvignon Blancs; the Goulburn Valley's Ngambie and Shepparton, for Marsanne, Viognier and Rhône Valley reds, some of which are grown from original vines imported from France in the 1850s; and the Grampians for reds, such as Cabernet and Dolcetto, as well as an unforgettable sparkling Shiraz.

Best Victorian Varietals

» Pinot Gris
» Chardonnay
» Viognier
» Arneis
» Savagnin
» Marsanne
» Pinot Noir
» Shiraz
» Gamay
» Durif
» Tokay

Fashion & Shopping

City Style

Fashion plays a huge part in Melbourne's self-image. Whether strictly suited or ultraglam, casual, creative or subversive, Melburnians of both sexes love to look good. They improvise, layer and accessorise, and take every opportunity to express and impress.

Ask any fashionista in Melbourne their favourite time of year and they'll invariably say it's winter – and usually for the fashion opportunities that crisp, cold days deliver. While Melbourne designers do produce swimwear (Gorman, Zoe Elizabeth and We Are Handsome's retro offerings are local favourites), it's during the autumn–winter season of the fashion cycle that the city comes into its own. Temperatures only have to drop a few degrees for boots and jackets emerge, and unpredictable summers see many a cardigan or lightweight scarf thrown in the mix. Transitional pieces are a must.

Melbourne's reputation as a shopping mecca is, we are pleased to announce, utterly justifiable. Passionate retailers roam widely in search of the world's best as well as showcasing abundant local design talent. City laneways and Victorian shopping streets have long provided reasonably priced rental spaces that encourage creativity rather than conformity in shop owners; their vision contributes much to the city's eclectic identity and character. Yes, the chains and big global designers are all well represented, and there are suburban malls aplenty (including the newly glamorous Chadstone, known as Chaddy, the largest in the southern hemisphere and Victoria's oldest; www.chadstoneshopping.com.au), but the city and surrounds offer a host of alternatives. Currently a global darling, the pop-up shop concept (from frock sellers to bakers) has become a Melbourne staple, fitting with the city's indie ethos and lust for the new.

Buoyed by a culture of small shops and an adventurous-minded public, young designers flourish. Rather than adhering to the established studio's hierarchies, many start their own labels straight out of design school, giving the scene an amazing energy and vitality.

Discount factory outlets can be found aplenty in Bridge Rd, Richmond, the lower end of Smith St, Collingwood, or at South Wharf, but savvy Melbourne fashionistas prefer designer-specific sample sales, discovered via word-or-mouth or mailing lists. Missy Confidential (www.missyconfidential.com.au/melbourne.php) has a comprehensive calendar.

Melbourne Black

One constant in Melbourne fashion is colour, or lack of it. You'll not go long without hearing mention of 'Melbourne black', and it's true that inky shades are worn not just during the cold months but right through the hottest days of summer. Perhaps it's because black somehow suits the soft light and often grey days, or maybe it's the subliminal influence of the city's moody bluestone. Some muse that it's the long-lingering fallout of the explosive 1980s postpunk scene or southern European immigration. The fact remains that black clothes sell far better here than in any other city in the country, and it's hard to succeed as a designer if you don't offer up a little darkness in your collection every season. In Melbourne, black is always the new black.

Local Talent

Melbourne's designers are known for their tailoring, luxury fabrics, innovation and blending of global elements, all underscored with a fuss-free Australian sensibility. Those to watch out for include the evergreen Scanlan & Theodore and TL Wood for smart, lyrical elegance; Tony Maticevski and Martin Grant for demi-couture and dark reworkings of the classics; Ess Hoshika, Dhini and Munk for conceptual, deconstructed pieces; Anna Thomas and Vixen for the luxuriously grown-up, either tailored (Thomas) or flowing (Vixen); Gorman, Arabella Ramsay and Obüs for hipster cheek with a delightfully feminine twist; Alpha 60, Schwipe and Claude Maus for clever, urban pieces; Mjölk for precision-cut menswear; and finally, scene stalwarts Bettina Liano for straight-ahead glamour and Alannah Hill for the original girly-girl layers. Millinery is also a local speciality, due to the fondness for racing carnivals, with names such as Richard Nylon, Melissa Jackson and Louise Macdonald being in every stylish Melburnian's contacts list.

Made in Melbourne

» Douglas & Hope
» Aesop
» Spacecraft
» Alice Euphemia
» Fat
» Tomorrow Never Knows

Craft & Markets

Melbourne's penchant for small-scale design goes one further with a bubbling subculture that sells through markets and online. The DIY and craft trend has really taken hold: knitting in pubs, and waiters who harbour business plans for ugly toy empires, have become the stuff of cliché. In this hothouse environment, quality can be overshadowed by enthusiasm, but there are also plenty of artisans who know their stuff.

Craft Victoria is the grand old (if eternally cool) dame of the scene, with a commitment to showing and selling work that, as board member Pene Durston says, demonstrates 'the importance of the "hand" in the

WHERE TO SHOP?

The city has national and international chains spread out over Bourke, Swanston and Collins Sts, as well as the city malls of Melbourne Central, QVB, GPO, Australia on Collins St, Spencer St and South Wharf. Smaller retailers and design workshops inhabit the laneways as well as the vertical villages of Curtin House and the Nicholas Building. Flinders Lane and the arcades and laneways that feed into it are particularly blessed; Manchester Lane has some intriguing pickings. A strip of Little Collins heading north from Swanston is dedicated to sartorially savvy gentlemen, while the length of leafy Collins St is lined with luxury retailers, which tend to cluster ever more tightly as you reach the Spring St end.

Chapel St, South Yarra, has all the chains and classic Australian names, as well as some edgier designers once you hit Prahran. Up the hill, head to Hawksburn Village or High St, Armadale, for bobo-chic, fashion-forward labels, super stylish children's clothes and homewares. You'll find streetwear in Greville St, Prahran, and in Windsor; the latter is also good for vintage shopping.

In the north, Lygon St, Carlton, has some great small shops specialising in European tailoring and local talent. Brunswick St, Fitzroy, has streetwear and vintage shops, and pulses with the energy of young designers, particularly in stores such as the legendary Fat. Gertrude St, Fitzroy, mixes vintage with many of the city's most sought after innovators, as well as some up and coming menswear names, art supply shops and vintage furniture. Quirky fashion and homewares can be found in High St, Northcote, and on St Kilda's Balaclava Rd, in the south. This is just the tip of the well-considered iceberg – don't be surprised to find interesting and unique shops in other neighbourhoods as well.

production of work, and the high level of skill invested by makers in their craft'. Fitzroy's Meet Me At Mike's and Thread Den, in North Melbourne combine a craft, DIY and vintage ethos with classes augmenting their retail offerings. The Nicholas Building (thenicholasbuilding.blogspot. com), at the corner of Swanston St and Flinders Lane, is the city's most concentrated artisan hub, with both small shops (such as Buttonmania and l'uccello) and the much-coveted studios and workshops. Tenants maintain a calendar of open studio days and markets.

To Market, To Market

Melbourne's unpredictable weather hasn't deterred its entrepreneurial spirit, with many markets being held in all-weather venues. The twice-yearly Melbourne Design Market (www.melbournedesignmarket.com. au) is huge, attracting around 10,000 visitors. It showcases 'design-led' stallholders and has a rigorous selection process that keeps quality high. Fitzroy's Rose St Market (www.rosestmarket.com.au) and the Skirts and Shirts Market (www.shirtandskirtmarkets.com.au) at the Abbotsford Convent are as much about the social buzz as the highly individual vendors, while Malvern's Magnolia Square Market (www.magnoliasquare. com.au) is a favourite with the city's yummy-mums as well as serious craft enthusiasts. Monthly markets are also held in pubs (a clever use of drinking downtime in a post-sticky-carpet age). These include the Hello Sailor Vintage Fair at Collingwood's Grace Darling Hotel, held on the last weekend of the month, and the Blackbird Market at Fitzroy's Workers Club, held on the second Saturday.

Vintage style, a persisting global trend, has long flourished in Melbourne, both in the retailing and wearing of vintage pieces and in a general sensibility that pays heed to retro cuts and traditional tailoring. Vintage devotees should head to the city's arcades, and look for shops in Prahran, Fitzroy, Collingwood, Brunswick and Northcote.

The Arts

Visual Arts

Melbourne has always been a city for artists. A dynamic and ever changing network of artist-run spaces, experimental events and exhibitions gives the city an exciting production-house edge, and an excellent public infrastructure of major galleries and museums offers travellers visual culture of serious polish and scale.

Melbourne's first visual culture sprang from the traditions of the Kulin Nation tribes who lived from and belonged to the lands we now associate with the Yarra River, Port Phillip Bay, the Dandenong Ranges, the You Yangs and the country beyond. Both the National Gallery of Victoria Australia and the Melbourne Museum exhibit works of art that predate European settlement, as well as work, like that of William Barak and Tommy McCrae, which captures the first-hand experience of Indigenous life before and after colonisation. The art and artefacts at the Melbourne Museum's Bunjilaka Aboriginal Centre provide a particularly vivid and intimate picture of Victorian Aboriginal culture.

The grand vistas painted by intrepid Europeans visiting the fledgling colony of Melbourne present a very different Australian experience. These vast works offer early views of Australia as a colonial jewel. Bucolic pastures and abundant forests represent a land in the throes of colonisation and environmental upheaval, and offer intriguing catalogues of much that was on the precipice of being lost. Eugène von Guérard's works, such as 'Mount Kosciusko, seen from the Victorian border' (1866; NGV Australia), seen from the Victorian border, capture the wondrous difference of the Australian landscape to the European eye and reward close study with the delight of their lavish attention to detail.

In the late 19th century a generation of Australian-born artists emerged who are fondly remembered for defining a truly Australian vision of the landscape and cities of the day. The artists of the Heidelberg School took the train down the newly laid railway lines to the bush at Melbourne's fringe and camped together, sketching and working rapidly in oils to capture the bright light and dry elegance of the Australian bush. They created a heroic national iconography, ranging from the shearing of sheep to visions of a wide brown land popularly celebrated as offering a chance to all. The most widely reproduced works of the Heidelberg artists, such as Tom Roberts and Arthur Streeton, are majestic in scale and build grand narratives from the contemporary experience of Australians; other smaller works are surprisingly intimate and impressionistically rendered.

Lost (1886; NGV Australia), by Frederick McCubbin, portrays a young girl lost in the bush. The sun shines brightly on the yellowed summer grass, while the repeated vertical staccato of the gum trees divides the

Flinders Lane has the densest concentration of commercial galleries in Australia, with many more dotted throughout the city and inner suburbs. *Art Almanac* has comprehensive listings, with good regional coverage as well.

The Heide Museum of Modern Art is nestled in sprawling grounds by the Yarra, a blissfully bucolic setting but only around 20 minutes' drive north of the city. This area may now be deep suburbia, but was once a fully fledged rural retreat. Here John and Sunday Reed nurtured an artistic community that included Albert Tucker, Sidney Nolan, Arthur Boyd, Joy Hester, John Perceval and Danila Vassilieff.

Heide has an impressive collection of modern and contemporary Australian art housed in three galleries and scattered throughout the tranquil gardens. Each gallery is unique: Heide I is the heritage-listed and beautifully restored Victorian farmhouse that was the Reed's first home; Heide II, a modernist stunner designed by David McGlashan in the 1960s, became their second; while Heide III is a purpose-built exhibition space.

The Reed's kitchen garden is still lovingly tended and the surrounding grounds are landscaped with a combination of European and native trees and dotted with sculpture.

scene, creating a claustrophobic sense through infinite repetition. While portraying an archetypal anxiety, the loss of a child to the land was a particularly poignant concern at the turn of the century. Australians love the landscape, identify with it and take pride in its complexity – its harshness and mysteriousness, its abundance and distinctiveness – and yet it makes us uneasy also; we feel disquiet in the very land that defines us.

Heide, in Melbourne's northern suburbs, was the home of arts patrons John and Sunday Reed, who played a pivotal role in the development of Australian modernism in the early and mid-20th century. Sidney Nolan's epic series celebrating the bushranger Ned Kelly is said to have been painted here, at the Reed's dining-room table. The early Australian modernism forged at Heide was expressively painted and passionately connected to the emotional, social and intellectual worlds of the artists.

Melbourne takes pride in being a city for ideas, a city for contemporary art. Contemporary Victorian artists are strongly concerned with an Australian sense of place, as well as being actively engaged in the more universal concerns of our contemporary, globalised world.

Only a small slice of the mass of work being produced will be evident at any one time, but between the commercial, public and artist-run galleries there is much to discover. The city's strength as a centre for architecture and spatial investigation is reflected in the work of contemporary artists such as Stephen Bram, Callum Morton and Natasha Johns-Messenger.

The practice of the making of art and the reflective ricochet between the real and the represented, are explored by Melbourne artists Ricky Swallow, Nick Mangan, Christian Capurro, Nadine Christensen and Chris Bond.

The impact of technology upon our lives is a subject of much interest to artists such as Stephen Honegger, Anthony Hunt and Patricia Piccinini, artists who are empowered by the digital world as well as being thoughtfully engaged with the ethical dilemmas it generates.

The politics of memory and the borders of empathy are explored by artists such as Susan Norrie, Gordon Bennett, Tom Nicholson and Louisa Bufardeci. Melbourne is also a centre for cross-cultural investigation, with artists such as Kate Beynon, Sangeeta Sandrasegar, Raafat Ishak and Constanze Zikos drawing upon a diversity of cultural perspectives to find their own expressive language.

Geraldine Barlow
Senior Curator and Collection Manager, Monash University Museum of Art

THE ARTS VISUAL ARTS

Regional Gallery Going

» Bendigo Art Gallery

» Art Gallery of Ballarat

» Mornington Peninsula Regional Gallery

» TarraWarra Museum of Art, Yarra Valley

» McClelland Gallery & Sculpture Park, Mornington Peninsula

Literature

Melbourne nourishes the literary types with its tempestuous weather, rich range of cultures and identities, its wine bars and moody architecture. Sometimes it may feel as if words and stories are relegated to the wings, while sport and socialising take centre stage, but scratch the surface and you'll find a city that is home to writers of all descriptions, independent booksellers, a prosperous publishing industry and a thriving culture of reading and discourse on the written word.

This has been recognised by Melbourne's designation as a Unesco City of Literature and the creation of the Wheeler Centre (www.wheelercentre.com), Australia's first Centre for Books, Writing and Ideas. The Centre is located within a newly renovated wing of the State Library of Victoria (www.slv.vic.gov.au) and is home to several literary organisations as well as hosting a very rich program of talks and events, designed to 'get Melburnians thinking'.

Publishing companies Black Inc, Text and Penguin are based here and the city produces a host of magazines, journals and websites that highlight literature and intellectual life. These include the *Australian Book Review, Meanjin,* Black Inc's series of 'best' anthologies and the *Quarterly Essay,* and the short-fiction collection *Sleepers Almanac.*

Has there been a great Victorian novel? Melbourne has certainly provided a variety of memorable backdrops in literary works, from the 19th-century cult crime fiction of *The Mystery of a Hansom Cab* (1886; Fergus Hume) to Christos Tsiolkas' *The Slap* set in the backyards of Brunswick.

Despite a largely urban, multicultural population, it's still up to a novel with a historical, even mythological, bush setting to claim the 'great' title. Peter Carey's *True History of the Kelly Gang,* set in the central Victorian haunts of Australia's most famous bushrangers, took both the Man Booker and Commonwealth Writers' Prize when it was published in 2001.

Bookish Melbourne

» State Library of Victoria
» Wheeler Centre
» Readings
» Hill of Content
» Melbourne Writers Festival

Music

Melbourne's cultural image has involved music since producing two of the most enduringly fascinating talents of the 19th and early 20th centuries. Dame Nellie Melba, opera diva, was an international star who lived

WHITE CUBES

'Melbourne has everything that Milan lacks: a museum and a centre for contemporary art, a studio building with a residency programme for emerging artists, a widely spread network of artist-run spaces, a city-run series of commissions for public art, even a television museum.'
Massimiliano Gioni, curator and director of the Trussardi Foundation Milan

The Melbourne art scene is an energetic and intellectually rigorous one, with a flourishing community of artists, experimental exhibition spaces and events. A good place to tap into this energy is Gertrude Contemporary Art Spaces, for exhibitions by emerging artists and the lowdown on the newest experimental spaces. The Australian Centre for Contemporary Art generates cutting-edge programs of exhibitions as well as developing large-scale projects with Australian and international artists. The Australian Centre for the Moving Image exhibits film and multimedia works by contemporary artists in thematic exhibitions that draw upon a rich diversity of moving-image formats, and the Centre for Contemporary Photography has a strong photo- and film-based program. Melbourne has an active network of university art museums and galleries, among which the Ian Potter Museum at the University of Melbourne and Monash University Museum of Art offer dynamic exhibition programs of work by contemporary artists, as well as reflecting upon the history of Australian art. Regional galleries throughout Victoria also are very strong.

overseas for many years, but retained a sentimental attachment to her home town (hence the name). Percy Grainger, whose innovative compositions and performances prefigured many forms of 20th-century music, was born and brought up in Melbourne. Grainger's eccentric genius extended beyond music to the design of clothing and objects; he was also known for his transgressive sex life.

More recently, Melbourne's live music scene exploded in the mid-60s with a band called the Loved Ones, who broke the imitative mould of American '50s rock and roll. The early 1970s saw groups such as AC/DC, Skyhooks and Daddy Cool capture the experience of ordinary Melbourne life in their lyrics for the first time. By the end of that decade punk had descended; Melbourne's moody weather and grimy backstreets had a natural synergy with the genre. Nick Cave's Boys Next Door and the so-called little bands shrieked their way through gigs at St Kilda's Crystal Ballroom (now the George Hotel), a venue whose dilapidated splendour was straight out of central casting.

Bands and performers that grew out of (and beyond) this scene included the Birthday Party, Sports, the Models, the Johnnys, X, Sacred Cowboys, the Wreckery, Hugo Race, Cosmic Psychos, Hunters & Collectors and Paul Kelly.

Melbourne is still seen as the live-music capital of Australia, and draws musicians here from around the country, despite an increasing dearth of inner-city venues for them to play in. Current darlings include the Drones, Eddie Current Suppression Ring, The Temper Trap and The Basics. For a city so very far away, Melbourne is also blessed with a large number of touring acts each year. Pickings are particularly rich during the summer festival season.

The city also has a healthy club and dance music scene. The mega-clubs of the '80s gave way to a more fluid dance-party culture revolving around techno and other electronic styles. The 'doof' was born; these festivals, often held in bushland settings over several days, peaked in the late '90s, though they still have their devotees. Legendary laneway club Honkytonks took its musical responsibility very seriously and nurtured local DJ talent (and a generation of club kids) through the early years of this decade. Since its demise, other venues have sprung up to fill the gap. Local electronic/synthpop artists who have crossed into the mainstream include Cut/Copy, the Avalanches and DJ Digital Primate.

Australian hip-hop is well represented in Victoria, with locals such as True Live and DJ Peril. Hip-hop has also proven enormously popular with young Aboriginal and Islander musicians (*All You Mob* is an excellent compilation CD of Indigenous artists). Other modern Indigenous musicians, such as Archie Roach, create unique styles by incorporating traditional instruments into modern rock and folk formats.

Jazz also has a dedicated local audience and a large number of respected musicians who are known for improvising, as well as crossing genres into world and experimental electronica. The heart of the scene is the long-running Bennetts Lane, an archetypal up-an-alley jazz club if ever there was one. Its Sunday sessions are legendary, and the venue draws a local crowd that knows its hard bop from its bebop. International and local talent also pull respectable numbers for Melbourne International Jazz Festival and Wangaratta Jazz Festival gigs.

Ninety years after Nellie Melba was made a dame, classical music still has a strong presence in Melbourne. The Melbourne Symphony Orchestra performs works drawn from across the classical spectrum, from the popular to challenging contemporary composition; they are based at the Arts Centre's Hamer Hall (with temporary digs at the Melbourne Town Hall until renovations are complete in 2012). The all-acoustic Melbourne

Beat Magazine (www.beat.com. au) has a weekly all-genre's gig guide, while the 3MBS arts diary (www.3mbs.org. au/arts.html) is an invaluable resource for what's going on in classical music.

Festival Time

» Meredith
» Falls Festival
» Golden Plains
» Port Fairy Folk Festival
» Brunswick Music Festival
» Wangaratta Jazz Festival
» Queenscliff Music Festival
» Apollo Bay Music Festival
» Anglesea Music Festival

Recital Centre (the only venue of its type in Australia) opened in 2009 to rave reviews and hosted around 250 concerts in its first year.

Cinema & Television

Although Sydney might be considered the centre of the Australian film industry, new production facilities at Docklands, a slightly lower cost of getting a film made and generous government subsidies has seen Melbourne wield its movie-making muscle. And Melbourne does looks gorgeous on the big screen. Film-makers tend to eschew the stately and urbane and highlight the city's complexity, from the winsomely suburban to the melancholic and gritty.

Film culture is nurtured in Victoria through local funding projects, tertiary education and exhibition. Funding for features, documentaries, shorts, digital media and game content is provided by Film Victoria (www.film.vic.gov.au), which also provides mentoring schemes. Federation Square has consolidated a big part of Melbourne's screen culture, housing the Australian Centre for the Moving Image and the Special Broadcasting Service (SBS).

The prominence of film in Melbourne is evident in the number of film festivals the city hosts. Apart from the main Melbourne International Film Festival (www.melbournefilmfestival.com.au), there's everything from the Melbourne Underground Film Festival (www.muff.com.au) to shorts at the St Kilda Film Festival (www.stkildafilmfestival.com.au) and the Sydney-import Tropfest (www.tropfest.com.au). Other film-festival genres include foreign-made, seniors, hip-hop, queer and documentary.

Melbourne is a 'must-see' destination for many British travellers primarily because it's home to the TV program *Neighbours*; Pin Oak Ct in Vermont South is the suburban street that has been the show's legendary Ramsay St for 23 years.

There's an enduring affection for police drama and comedy shows on Australian TV, and many of these have emanated from Melbourne. The barely fictionalised Melbourne organised crime series *Underbelly* didn't initially make it to air in the city in which it was set, not because of its tits-and-arse overload, but because a court decided that its plot lines could prejudice concurrent court proceedings. *Rush* and *Offspring* are the latest made-in-Melbourne series to hit the small screen, shot around the streets of Fitzroy, Collingwood and the city's western waterfront. Beloved local comedies include *Kath & Kim,* a hilarious piss-take of nouveau-riche suburban habits and language, and the bitingly satirical *Summer Heights High.* And, of course, there's the never-ending froth of soap opera *Neighbours.*

Theatre

Melbourne's longstanding theatrical heritage is evident in the city's legacy of Victorian-era theatres such as the Princess and Athenaeum. While the blockbusters pack out these grand dames, Melbourne's theatre scene encompasses a wide spectrum of genres.

Melbourne's most high-profile professional theatre company, the Melbourne Theatre Company (MTC; www.mtc.com.au), is also Australia's oldest. It stages up to a dozen performances year-round at the Victorian Arts Centre. Productions are usually firmly focused on satisfying the company's 20,000-strong middle-market subscriber base, though with a new director this may change. Expect works by Australians such as David Williamson, locals Hannie Rayson and Joanna Murray-Smith, and well-known international playwrights.

The Malthouse Theatre (www.malthouse.com.au) is dedicated to the performance of contemporary Australian works and nurturing emerging writers, and is known for relevance, audacity and artistic daring. Marion Potts, the new artistic director, comes to the theatre with a continuing agenda of 'risk, rigour and quest'.

Victoria also has a number of thriving progressive fringe-theatre companies, including Wodonga's HotHouse, Black Lung, Mutation Theatre and Hayloft, which stage residencies in traditional theatre settings and pop up in unusual places.

Humble in size, La Mama, in Carlton has a huge place in the heart of the city's theatre scene. Founded in 1967, it is, as its name might suggest, the mother of independent theatre in Melbourne, and helped forge the careers of David Williamson, Jack Hibberd, Barry Dickens and Graeme Blundell.

Dance

The Australian Ballet (www.australianballet.com.au) is the national ballet company and considered one of the finest in the world. It performs regularly at Melbourne's Victorian Arts Centre, with a program of classical and modern ballets.

Victoria's flagship contemporary dance company, Chunky Move (www. chunkymove.com), is a tidy package of bold, often confronting, choreography, pop culture concepts, technically brilliant dancers, sleek design and smart marketing. The artistic director and choreographer who founded the company in 1995, Gideon Obarzanek, is set to move on in 2012.

Melbourne is also home to another couple of acclaimed contemporary choreographers. Lucy Guerin has a small eponymous company that has attracted high praise from the *New Yorker* magazine's Joan Acocella; she also works with Obarzanek. Shelley Lasica locates her work in non-theatre spaces; collaborating with visual artists and architects, her works blur the lines between dance and performance art.

Architecture & Urban Planning

For a planned city, and a relatively youthful one, Melbourne's streetscapes are richly textured. Long considered one of the world's most lovely Victorian-era cities, Melbourne captures the confident spirit of that age. There's exuberantly embellished Second Empire institutions and hulking former factories that would do Manchester proud. Flinders St Station and the original Queen Victoria Hospital (now part of QVB) herald in the Federation era, when a new Australian identity was being fashioned from the fetching combination of red-brick and ornate wood. Look down Swanston St from Lonsdale and you'll catch a glimpse of a mini-Manhattan. Melbourne's between-the-wars optimism is captured in its string of stunning, if somewhat stunted, art deco skyscrapers like the Manchester Unity Building. Walter Burley Griffin worked in the city at this time too, creating the ornate, organic Newman College in the University of Melbourne and the mesmerising ode to the metropolitan, the Capitol Theatre, now a part-time cinema and university lecture hall.

By mid-century, Modernist architects sought new ways to connect with the local landscape as well as honouring the movement's internationalist roots; the most prominent, Roy Grounds, designed the Arts Centre and the original NGV Australia on St Kilda Rd. Others include Robin Boyd, Kevin Borland and Alistair Knox; their work is mostly residential so it is rarely open to the public. You can, however, visit a beautiful Boyd building anytime: Jimmy Watson's Wine Bar in Carlton. Melbourne also had its own mid-century furniture design stars, Grant and Mary Featherston. Their iconic Contour chair of 1951 is highly prized by collectors, as are their '70s modular sofas.

The 1990s saw a flurry of public building works: Melbourne's architects fell in love with technology and designed with unorthodox shapes, vibrant colours, tactile surfaces and sleek structural features. Denton Corker Marshall's Melbourne Museum, Melbourne Exhibition & Convention Centre, Bolte Bridge, and the CityLink sound tunnel are emblematic of this period. Federation Square, one of the last of these major projects, continues to polarise opinion. Despite the detractors, its cobbled, inscribed

Street Art Sites

» Hosier Lane

» Caledonian Lane

» Centre Way

» Canada Lane, Carlton

Whether you call it street art or graffiti, Melbourne's painted urban landscape is a beacon for visitors from all round the world. 'Caledonian Lane attracts more visiting Brazilians, Londoners and New Yorkers than anywhere else in the city,' says Tai Snaith, a local curator and artist.

It's not just the out-of-towners who are flocking to see the city's street art. Wedding parties seeking street cred record their special day against the gritty backdrop of Hosier Lane. The National Gallery of Australia is considering ways of incorporating stencil art into its collection of Australian prints. Street art is discussed in art and culture journals.

'Street art is a way of artists countering advertising and claiming some of that visual space, which is often subliminally influencing our political ideals,' says Snaith. Does the council's recent acceptance and increasing encouragement mean that the work loses its street credibility and political clout? 'You can see superb sponsored or commissioned work, of course,' says Tai, 'but ultimately work created without pay and often illegally comes from a wilder place.'

piazza has become the city's chosen site for celebration and protest, surely the best compliment a populace can pay an architect. Ashton Raggatt McDougall's Melbourne Recital Centre is a recent architectural prize winner, with an interior that is, according to Melbourne University's Philip Goad, 'like a beautiful violin'.

Melbourne's architectural energy today most often comes not from the monumental but from what goes on in between the new and the old, the towering and the tiny. It's also literally about energy – sustainable practice, in the inner city at least, has become all but de rigueur. Mid-careerists such as Six Degrees, Elenberg Fraser and Kerstin Thompson create witty, inventive and challenging buildings and interiors that see raw or reimagined spaces spring to life.

Sport

The Sporting Life

Cynics snicker that sport is the sum of the Victoria's culture, although they're hard to hear above all that cheering, theme-song singing and applause. Victorians do take the shared spectacle of the playing field very seriously. It's undeniably the state's most dominant expression of common beliefs and behaviour, and brings people from all backgrounds together. It's also a lot of fun; sporting events are followed with such fervour that the crowd is often a spectacle in itself.

Melbourne is the birthplace of Australian Rules football and hosts a disproportionate number of international sporting events, including the Australian Open, Australian Formula One Grand Prix and Melbourne Cup. The city's arenas, tracks, grounds and courts are regarded as the world's best-developed and most well-situated cluster of facilities. Victoria is home to more major events, such as the Rip Curl Pro (aka the Bells Beach Surf Classic), the Australian Motorcycle Grand Prix on Phillip Island, the Stawell Gift and numerous country horse races, including the atmospheric Hanging Rock meet.

Victorians do like to watch their sport, but are also fond of working up a sweat themselves. Personal fitness ranges from a weekly walk in parkland or a swim at the local pool, to boot-camp-style regimes or studio-based pursuits such as Pilates, yoga and indoor rock-climbing. They also love to whack the little white ball, with notable courses in the city's south (Royal Melbourne Golf Club is Australia's best and rated sixth in the world), as well as on the Mornington and Bellarine Peninsulas and the Murray. There's also a huge enthusiasm for tennis; the infectious energy that surrounds the Australian Open in January reveals a deeply tennis-mad city.

The closest ski fields can be reached in under three hours from Melbourne. Although snowfalls have become increasingly erratic over the last few years, when the powder happens, it's just possible for a day trip (after a day off 'with the flu', a goggle tan often gives the snow fiend's game away). Other popular sports include climbing, both indoor and outdoor, and all kinds of watersports. Yachties take to Port Phillip Bay and beyond; the state's bays and waterways also play host to windsurfers, kite-boarders, kayakers, fishing types and divers. Victorian surfers are a privileged if hardy lot, with often-uncrowded access to some of the world's best, if perennially chilly, waves, and the spectacular annual surf pro at Bells Beach.

Australia Rules Football

Underneath the cultured chat and designer threads of your typical Melburnian, you'll find a heart that truly belongs to one thing: the footy. Understanding the basics of Australian Rules Football (AFL, or 'the footy') is definitely a way to get a local engaged in conversation, especially during the winter season. Melbourne is the national centre for the sport, and

The Highlights

» AFL at the MCG
» Boxing Day Cricket Test, MCG
» Bells Beach
» Australian Open
» Formula One Grand Prix
» Stawell Gift

Melbourne's favourite runs include the 4km Tan track around the Royal Botanic Gardens, the 5km path around Albert Park Lake and the sweeping paths of Fitzroy Gardens. The bicycle tracks beside the Yarra River and along the bay also see a lot of well-trained traffic.

the Melbourne-based Australian Football League (AFL; www.afl.com.au) administers the national competition.

During the footy season (March to September), the vast majority of Victorians become obsessed: entering tipping competitions at work, discussing groin injuries and suspensions over the water cooler, and devouring huge chunks of the daily newspapers devoted to mighty victories, devastating losses and the latest bad-boy behaviour (on and off the field). Monday night disciplinary tribunals allocate demerit points for every bit of blood and biffo, and fans follow these proceedings with almost as much attention as the games themselves.

The MCG, affectionately referred to as the 'G', has been the home of football since 1859 and its atmosphere is unforgettable. The AFL now has teams in every mainland state but nine of its 16 clubs are still based in Melbourne, along with regional Geelong. All Melbourne teams play their home games at either the MCG or Etihad Stadium, and those between two local teams ensure a loud, parochial crowd. Barracking has its own lexicon and is often a one-sided 'conversation' with the umpire. One thing is certain: fans always know better. Once disparagingly referred to as 'white maggots' because of their lily-white uniforms, umpires are now decked out in bright orange, so players can spot them in the thick of the game. With the switch, they are now simply called 'maggots'.

After the final siren blows, and the winning club theme song is played (usually several times over), it's off to the pub. Supporters of opposing teams often celebrate and commiserate together. Despite the deep tribal feelings and passionate expression of belonging that AFL engenders, violence is almost unheard of before, during or after games.

The second-tier Victorian Football League (VFL; www.victorianfootballleague.com.au/) fields teams in regional centres Bendigo, Ballarat and Geelong, and in Melbourne suburbs. The old-school atmosphere at these games has begun to attract a new following of footy nostalgics, and those with young families. The Victorian Country Football League (www.vcfl.com.au) has an incredibly dense network of clubs throughout the state, and these games are definitely a way of getting to know the locals.

Cricket

Cricket is Victoria's summer love and it's the game that truly unites the state with the rest of Australia. While it may be the eternal bridesmaid to AFL's limelight-hogging bride, it has a stronghold in Victoria, given the hallowed ground of the MCG and Cricket Australia's base in Melbourne. Seeing a test at the G is a must-do-before-you-die rite of devotion for cricket fans from around the world, and if at all possible, it should be the traditional Boxing Day Test. For many sport-mad Melburnians, it's a bigger deal than Christmas itself. Warm days, cricket's leisurely pace and

In 1963, Melbourne football attendances hit record levels: at least 150,000 diehard fans would be at one of its suburban grounds, or at the MCG, each week. Today the AFL tops English Premiership attendances, with an average of 38,417 footy fans turning out to each of its season games.

AUSTRALIAN TENNIS OPEN

The last two weeks of January is tennis time in Melbourne, when the city hosts the Australian Open (www.australianopen.com) championships. The world's best come to compete at Melbourne Park in the year's first of the big four Grand Slam tournaments. With daily attendance figures breaking world records – well over half a million people come through the turnstiles over the two weeks – a carnival atmosphere prevails. Visitors come from around the world to attend, but it's also a favourite with locals, who make the most of summer holiday leave or amble over to East Melbourne after work. While the entertainment and a few glasses of sparkling in the sunshine are a big part of the draw, there's a hushed respect during matches on centre court. Tensions off the court between ultra-nationalistic fans have erupted in the past, but the most disruptive element is usually the elements themselves. The chance of at least one 40°C scorcher is high.

The roses are in bloom, the city's aflutter, and the nerves of milliners, fashion retailers, dry cleaners, beauty therapists and caterers are beyond frayed. It's Spring Carnival time in Melbourne.

The two-mile (3.2km) Melbourne Cup has been run on the first Tuesday of November, at Flemington Racecourse, since 1861. Watched by 700 million people in over 170 countries, the Cup brings the whole of Australia to a standstill for its three-or-so minutes, and Melburnians have a public holiday. Once-a-year gamblers organise Cup syndicates with friends, and gather to watch the race from pubs, clubs, TAB betting shops and backyard barbecues. Punters, partiers, celebrities and the fashion-conscious (who spend an estimated $54.5 million on clothes and accessories for the event) pack the grandstands, car parks, lawns and marquees of Flemington.

The Cup's heady social whirl gets even headier at Derby Day and Oaks Day, which are considered more glamorous events than the Cup itself, while serious racegoers bet their way through the Cox Plate, the Caulfield Cup, the Dalgety, and the Mackinnon Stakes too.

gangs of supporters who've travelled from far and wide often make for spectator theatrics. A schedule of Tests, one-day internationals, T20 and the Sheffield Shield keep fans happy throughout the rest of the season.

The Rectangle Codes

The original football is most often referred to as soccer in Australia, despite the Football Federation's official assertion of the football tag. Considering all the competition, the game's rise in Melbourne has been spectacular. A new A League national competition was formed in 2005, running from October to May, and with it came a large supporter base and a higher profile for the game. Australia's solid performance in the 2006 FIFA World Cup also contributed to its new-found popularity, as does its status as the 'world game'. The city's original team, Melbourne Victory (www.melbournevictory.com.au), was joined in the competition by Melbourne Heart (www.melbourneheartfc.com.au) in the 2010/11 season. Football's amazingly vocal supporters (including a British-style cheer squad) make for some atmospheric play.

It's yet to be seen what kind of support Rugby Union's first professional foray in the state, the Melbourne Rebels, will receive when they join the national competition in 2011. Union does draw surprisingly large, often sell out, crowds to international matches at Docklands Stadium (it recorded its highest sporting attendance – 56,605 – during a Wallabies tour).

Melbourne Storm (www.melbournestorm.com.au), the first and only Victorian team in the National Rugby League (NRL), enjoyed spectacular success over the last decade, winning the premiership three times, though its moderate supporter numbers continued to be mostly 'expats', drawn from the northern states and across the Tasman. Sadly for Victorian league fans, these titles were stripped for salary cap breaches in 2010.

Melbourne's new purpose-built rectangular stadium, AAMI Park, on the site of Olympic Park Stadium, has a capacity of 30,000, showing the state's continued commitment to embracing 'other' football codes in the future.

Freewheeling

Cycling is more a way of life than a sport. City riders take advantage of the city's extensive 45km network of bike paths and scant hills to commute during the week, or relax on weekends – it's hard to miss the lycra-clad cafe breakfasts of the club scene.

These are the kind of figures that make petrolheads swoon: 300km/h, 950bhp and 19,000rpm. The 5.3km street circuit around normally tranquil Albert Park Lake is known for its smooth fast surface. The buzz, both on the streets and in your ears, takes over Melbourne for four fully sick days in March. Will Australia's own Mark Webber's make it to pole?

Disused railway lines and riverside industrial sites have been gradually turned over to cyclists, with a number of bike paths in greater Melbourne providing excellent touring.

In Melbourne, you will certainly never feel alone on the roads, or in your two-wheeled passion. The city has the Parisian-style Melbourne Bike Share and there are a huge number of shops selling bikes and accessories, as well as volunteer repair workshop at city parks such as Carlton Gardens and Ceres Community Environment Park. If you need to hire a bike, Humble Vintage offers bike hire, and publishes a delightful cycling guide, and Fitzroy's Little Creatures has free bike use for patrons. The fixed-gear and single-speed scene has become an inner-city obsession, along with a cultish appreciation of vintage bikes. Out in the country the state's spectacular landscapes are the perfect backdrop for mountain bikers and road riders alike. The annual Great Victorian Bike Ride is wheeled out to a different region each year.

Bicycle Victoria (www.bv.com.au) and VicRoads (www.vicroads.vic.gov.au) have printable, online maps of the state's cycle paths and other resources..

Survival Guide

Directory A-Z

Accommodation

Accommodation across the state ranges from camping and caravan parks to youth hostels, motels, boutique B&Bs, hotels and resorts. Many tourist offices offer a free accommodation booking service; check out the comprehensive *Accommodation Guide* published by the RACV (www.racv.com.au).

Accommodation prices tend to be seasonal, especially along the coast and the Murray River. Peak time is the Christmas school holidays from mid-December to the end of January, and the Easter holidays, when you'll need to book well in advance and prices skyrocket at popular beach resorts. Winter (June to August) is the cheapest time to travel around most of the state, except at the ski resorts where July and August is peak season. Places at popular getaways such as the Mornington Peninsula and Daylesford often charge more for weekend stays. Accommodation prices in Melbourne are generally steady all year, except for major events such as the Australian Grand Prix and Australian Open tennis tournament.

Camping & Caravanning

Camping holidays are experiencing a resurgence in popularity in Victoria, with some great national park camping grounds and commercial caravan parks to choose from. The only place that camping or caravanning isn't viable is central Melbourne.

At commercial caravan parks, expect to pay around $20/25 for an unpowered/powered site for two people, and from $50 to $120 for a cabin or unit, depending on the size and facilities. These rates will almost certainly double at coastal areas and popular holiday spots during school holidays. **Parks Victoria** (www.parkweb.vic.gov. au) camping grounds range from free to $17, and you can usually have up to six people and one vehicle per site. These should be booked in advance, but often a ranger will come in and collect your money. For the most popular sites, such as Wilsons Prom and Cape Otway, a ballot is held over the Christmas and Easter holiday periods. Free camping is available in many places, including along the Murray and Goulburn Rivers and in the High Country – check with Parks Victoria.

Hostels

Most of Victoria's backpacker hostels are in Melbourne, and the most popular regional centres, such as Hall Gaps, along the Great Ocean Rd, Mildura, Bendigo and Ballarat. There are 16 YHA hostels (www.yha.com.au) in the state, and quite a few more independent backpackers. Expect to pay $25 to $30 for a dorm and from $70 for a double. Some hostels in Melbourne will only admit international travellers – which can be a bit galling and discriminatory for Australians trying to travel in their own country.

B&Bs & Guesthouses

This rapidly growing segment of the accommodation market generally means staying in someone's home or in a purpose-built addition to a home, but increasingly B&Bs are self-contained cottages. It could be a grand historic home, farmhouse, restored miners' cottage or beachside bungalow. In the English tradition, a big cooked breakfast is part of the deal. Rates are usually midrange – from $80 to $180 for a double – but can be much higher if the location and level of luxury is right.

Booking can be made online through Tourism Victoria, or check these sites:

BOOK YOUR STAY ONLINE

For more accommodation reviews by Lonely Planet authors, check out hotels.lonelyplanet.com. You'll find independent reviews, as well as recommendations on the best places to stay. Best of all, you can book online.

Beds & Breakfasts (www.
bedsandbreakfasts.com.au)
Bed & Breakfast (www.
bedandbreakfast.com.au)
Great Places to Stay (www.
greatplacestostay.com.au)

Hotels & Motels

Motels are the most common type of accommodation around the state and popular with travellers looking for central, no frills, familiar accommodation. Motels usually have studios and family apartments from $80 to $200, with TV, en suite, air-conditioning, tea- and coffee-making facilities and usually a pool and barbecue area.

In Melbourne and large provincial centres, hotels are usually aimed at business and luxury travellers, centrally located with business centres and restaurants attached.

In country towns, a hotel refers to the local pub, which may have refurbished rooms upstairs, with shared facilities down the hall. These are often a good budget option, with rooms under $80, where you're sure to rub shoulders with a few locals down in the bar.

Apartments & Holiday Rental Accommodation

Most common along the coast and at ski resorts and popular spots like the Grampians and Murray River, holiday accommodation are generally self-contained with kitchen, one or two bedrooms and parking. Holiday houses along the coast are usually

PRICE RANGES

Price ranges for accommodation in this book are rated with a $ symbol, indicating the price of a standard double room.
$ – under $100
$$ – $100-200
$$$ – over $200

LIGHTHOUSE STAYS

Lighthouse keepers in days of old notoriously endured a lonely, tough existence, but these days you can experience the life in relative comfort. Of Victoria's 20-plus lighthouses, 10 are managed by Parks Victoria, and you can stay in the refurbished keeper's cottages at five of them. Some, like Point Hicks and Gabo Island, are remote, while Cape Otway and Cape Schanck are easily accessible to families:

» Cape Schanck (p222)
» Cape Otway (p173)
» Gabo Island (p252)
» Point Hicks (p253)
» Wilsons Promontory (p237)

just that – an entire house that you can rent for a week or longer and are ideal for families or groups.
Holiday Rentals (www.holidayrentals.com.au)
Holiday Great Ocean Rd (www.holidaygor.com.au)
Holiday Shacks (www.holidayshacks.com.au)
Stayz (www.stayz.com.au)

Houseboat

One of the great ways to stay in Victoria is on a houseboat. They range from basic to luxurious 12-berth craft with deck spa and all mod-cons. The best places to hire:
» Mildura (p286)
» Echuca (p294)
» Eildon (p258)
» Mallacoota (p252)

Business Hours

Opening hours for businesses in this book are listed only if they differ from the following table.

BUSINESS	OPENING HOURS
Bank	9.30am-4pm Mon-Thu, to 5pm Fri
Post Office	9am-5pm Mon-Fri, 9am-noon Sat
Tourist Office	9am-5pm daily

BUSINESS	OPENING HOURS
Shopping Centre	9am-5.30pm, often to 9pm Thu & Fri
Restaurant	lunch noon-3pm, dinner 6-10pm
Cafe	breakfast 8am-11am (later on weekends), all-day lunch
Pub	11am-1am
Bar, Club	4pm-late (between 2am and 5am)

Electricity

240v/50hz

Gay & Lesbian Travellers

Homosexuality is legal and the age of consent is 17. The straight community's attitude towards gays and lesbians is, on the whole, open-minded and accepting.

The gay scene in Victoria is squarely based in Melbourne, where there are exclusive venues and accommodation options. Around the state, places such as Daylesford and Hepburn Springs, Phillip Island, the Mornington Peninsula and Lorne have a strong gay presence and accommodation catering for gays and lesbians. Daylesford's ChillOut Festival (p144) in March is the state's biggest gay and lesbian festival, and there's an annual Gay Pride March in Melbourne.

Health

Few travellers to Victoria will experience anything worse than an upset stomach or a bad hangover, but if you do fall ill the standard of hospitals and health care is high. Tap water is safe to drink. For environmental hazards, see Safe Travel (p346).

Insurance

While the standard of health care in Australia is high and is not overly expensive by international standards, travel insurance should be considered essential for international travellers. Make sure you have appro-priate coverage if you plan on doing any 'dangerous' activities such as skiing, rock climbing, diving or motorcycling.

Vaccinations

Proof of yellow-fever vaccination is required only from travellers entering Australia within six days of having stayed overnight or longer in a yellow fever–infected country. No specific vaccinations are required to travel in Victoria.

Health Care

Australia's Medicare system (www.medicareaustralia. gov.au) covers Australian residents for some health-care costs and emergency care (as well as citizens of New Zealand, Belgium, UK, Netherlands, Sweden, Finland, Italy, Malta and Ireland). Melbourne and the major provincial centres have high quality hospitals.

Internet Access

Melbourne has plenty of internet cafes and wi-fi access is increasingly common, both in public places as well as hotels, cafes and bars. In regional Victoria, most large towns will have an internet cafe, free internet access at the local library, or access at the tourist office. Most caravan parks offer wi-fi these days (sometimes free).

Expect to pay around $2 per hour at an internet cafe in Melbourne, and up to $6 an hour in regional areas.

Legal Matters

Most travellers won't have any contact with the Victorian police or any other part of the legal system. Those that do are likely to experience these while driving. There is a significant police presence on Victoria's roads, and they have the power to stop your car and ask to see your licence (you're required by law to carry it), to check your vehicle for road-worthiness, and also to insist that you take a breath test for alcohol. The blood alcohol limit is 0.05%.

If you are arrested, it's your right to telephone a friend, relative or lawyer before any formal questioning begins. **Legal Aid** (www. legalaid.vic.gov.au) is available only in serious cases and only to the truly needy. However, many solicitors do not charge for an initial consultation.

Money

Currency is the Australian dollar, which is made up of 100 cents. There are 5c, 10c, 20c, 50c, $1 and $2 coins, and $5, $10, $20, $50 and $100 notes.

ATMs

Most bank branches have 24-hour ATMs and will accept debit cards linked to international network systems, such as Cirrus, Maestro, Visa and MasterCard. Most banks charge a fee (around $2) for the privilege of using their ATM if you don't have an account with them. Almost all retail outlets have Eftpos, which allows you to pay for purchases electronically without a fee.

Changing Money

Change foreign currency at most larger banks or foreign-exchange booths in the city and at Melbourne Airport's international terminal. Most

---

SUNBURN & SKIN CANCER

Australia has one of the highest rates of skin cancer in the world, and don't be fooled by Victoria's variable weather and cloudy days. UV exposure here is as dangerous as anywhere in the country. If you're going out in the summer sun, particularly at the beach, use 30-plus water-resistant sunscreen and wear a hat, sunglasses and shirt as much as possible. Do the same for your kids' sensitive skin.

Entering the Region

All visitors to Australia must have a valid passport and visa (New Zealanders receive a 'special category' visa on arrival). Tourist visas are free and valid for three months. The easiest way to obtain a visa is to apply for an Electronic Travel Authority (ETA), which can be done online (www.eta.immi.gov.au) or through your travel agent.

CUSTOMS REGULATIONS

» **What to declare at customs**: cash amounts of more than $A10,000, foodstuffs, goods of animal or vegetable origin, including wooden products and medicines. All drugs and weapons are prohibited. Failure to declare quarantine items can mean an on-the-spot fine or prosecution.

» **Duty-free allowance**: travellers over 18 have a duty-free quota of 2.25L of alcohol, 250 cigarettes and dutiable goods up to the value of $900 (or $450 for those under 18).

» **State restrictions**: There are also restrictions on taking fruit, vegetables, plants or flowers across state borders. There is a particularly strict fruit-fly exclusion zone, which takes in an area along Victoria's northeast border, stretching into NSW and SA. For full details:

Australian Customs (☑1300 363 263; www.customs.gov.au)

Australian Quarantine & Inspection Service (AQIS; www.daffa.gov.au/aqis)

Embassies & Consulates

Most embassies are in Canberra or Sydney, but a number of countries maintain consulates in Melbourne:

Canada (☑9653 9674; Level 27, 101 Collins St, Melbourne)

France (☑9602 5024; Level 7, 60 Queen St, Melbourne)

Germany (☑9864 6888; www.melbourne.diplo.de; 480 Punt Rd, South Yarra)

Ireland (☑9397 8940; Level 1, 295 Queen St, Melbourne)

New Zealand (☑9642 1281; www.nzembassy.com/australia; Level 10, 454 Collins St, Melbourne)

Netherlands (☑9620 2701; Level 3, 50 Market St, Melbourne)

UK (☑9652 1600; 17th fl, 90 Collins St, Melbourne)

USA (☑9526 5900; Level 6, 553 St Kilda Rd, Melbourne)

Practicalities

» Electricity: Power supply is 240V 50Hz.

» Emergency: ☑000

» Newspapers: The **Age** (www.theage.com.au) Melbourne broadsheet covering local, national and international news. **Herald Sun** (www.heraldsun.com.au) Big-selling tabloid strong on sport, especially AFL.

» Radio & TV: The **Australian Broadcasting Commission** (ABC; www.abc.net.au) is the national TV and radio broadcaster; commercial TV networks Seven, Nine, Ten and SBS all have more than one digital channel.

» Weights & Measures: Australia uses the metric system.

Time

Victoria (along with Tasmania, NSW and Queensland) keeps Eastern Standard Time, which is 10 hours ahead of GMT/UTC. That means that when it's noon in Melbourne, it's 9pm the previous day in New York, 2am in London and 11am in Tokyo.

Daylight-saving time, when clocks are put forward an hour, is between the first Sunday in October and the first Sunday in April.

large hotels will also change currency (or travellers cheques) for their guests, but the rate might not be as good as from other outlets.

Credit Cards

The most commonly accepted credit cards are Visa and MasterCard, and to a lesser extent American Express and Diners Club. For lost or stolen card services call the following:

American Express (✆1300 132 639)

Diners Club (✆1300 360 060)

MasterCard (✆1800 120 113)

Visa (✆1800 450 346)

Tipping

Tipping isn't obligatory in Australia, but it's certainly expected in city restaurants and cafes and is appreciated in Melbourne bars. Around 10% is normal at restaurants, with more for notable service. For hotel porters, $2 to $5 should suffice. Tipping is less common in regional or country towns in Victoria.

Post

Australia Post (www. auspost.com.au) divides international destinations into two zones: Asia Pacific and the rest of the world. Airmail letters cost $1.50 and $2.20 respectively. Postage for postcards ($1.30) is the same to any country. It costs 60c to send a standard letter or postcard within Australia. Stamps can be purchased at post offices, newsagents and milk bars.

Public Holidays

Victoria observes the following nine public holidays:

New Year's Day 1 January

Australia Day 26 January

Labour Day First or second Monday in March

Easter Good Friday and Easter Monday in March/April

Anzac Day 25 April

Queen's Birthday Second Monday in June

Melbourne Cup Day First Tuesday in November (Melbourne only)

Christmas Day 25 December

Boxing Day 26 December

Safe Travel

Animal Bites & Stings

Flies & Mosquitoes

For four to six months of the year, you'll have to cope with those two banes of the Australian outdoors: the fly and the mosquito ('mozzie'). Flies aren't too bad in the city but they start getting out of hand in the country, and the further out you go, the more numerous and persistent they seem to be. Widely available repellents such as Aerogard and Rid may also help to deter the little bastards, but don't count on it.

Mozzies are a problem in summer, particularly for campers near water. Try to keep your arms and legs covered as soon as the sun goes down and use insect repellent liberally.

Snakes & Spiders

Bushwalkers should be aware that snakes and spiders, some venomous, are quite common in the Victoria bush, but the risk of getting bitten is very low. Snakes are usually quite timid in nature, and in most instances will move away if disturbed. Wear boots and socks to cover the ankles when walking in summer.

If bitten, a pressure bandage and immobilisation is the best course of action while awaiting medical care. All snake bites can be treated with antivenom. Spiders to watch out for are redback and white-tail spiders.

Ticks & Leeches

The common bush-tick (found in the forest and scrub country all along Australia's east coast) can be dangerous if left lodged in the skin, as the toxin excreted by the tick can cause partial paralysis and, in theory, death. Check your body for lumps every night if you're walking in tick-infested areas. Remove the tick by dousing it with methylated spirits or kerosene and levering it out, but make sure you remove it intact.

Leeches are common, and while they will suck your blood, they are not dangerous and are easily removed by the application of salt or heat.

Bushfires & Blizzards

Bushfires happen every year in Victoria. In hot, dry and windy weather, be extremely careful with any naked flame – cigarette butts thrown out of car windows have started many fires. On a total-fire-ban day it's forbidden even to use a camping stove in the open. Locals will not be amused if they catch you breaking this particular law; they'll happily dob you in, and the penalties are severe.

Bushwalkers should seek local advice before setting out – be careful if a total fire ban is in place, or delay your trip. If you're out in the bush and you see smoke, even a long way away, take it seriously – bushfires move very quickly and change direction with the wind. Go to the nearest open space, downhill if possible. A forested ridge is the most dangerous place to be.

More bushwalkers actually die of cold than in bushfires. Even in summer, temperatures can drop below freezing at night in the mountains and Victorian weather is notoriously changeable. Exposure in even moderately cool temperatures can sometimes result in hypothermia. Always take suitable spare clothing and adequate water and carbohydrates.

Swimming

Popular Victorian beaches are patrolled by surf lifesavers in summer, and patrolled areas are marked off by a pair of red and yellow flags. Always swim between the flags if possible.

Victoria's ocean beaches often have treacherous waves and rips. Even if you're a competent swimmer, you should exercise extreme caution and avoid the water altogether in high surf. If you happen to get caught in a rip when swimming and are being taken out to sea, try not to panic. Raise one arm until you have been spotted, and then swim parallel to the shore – *don't* try to swim bac k against the rip.

A number of people are also paralysed every year in rivers and lakes and from piers by diving into shallow water and hitting a sandbar or submerged log; always check the depth of the water before you leap.

Telephone

The increasingly elusive public payphone is either coin- or card-operated; local calls are unlimited and cost 50c, calls to mobile phones are timed and attract higher charges. Some accept credit cards; many don't work at all.

area code ☑03

country code ☑61

international access code (for dialling out) ☑0011

toll-free ☑1800; ☑1300 are the cost of a local call.

Mobile Phones

All Australian mobile phone numbers have four-digit prefixes beginning with ☑04. Australia's digital network is compatible with GSM 900 and 1800 handsets. Quad-based US phones will also work. Prepaid SIM cards are available from a range of telecommunications providers:

3 Mobile (www.three.com.au)

Dodo (www.dodo.com)

Optus (www.optus.com.au)

Telstra (www.telstra.com)

Virgin (www.virginmobile. com.au)

Vodafone (www.vodafone. com.au)

Phonecards

There's a wide range of local and international phonecards available from most newsagents and post offices for a fixed dollar value (usually $5 to $50). These can be used with any public or private phone by dialling a toll-free access number and then the PIN number on the card.

Tourist Information

Regional centres throughout the state will usually have a visitors centre or tourist information booth in a central location. These are listed throughout this book.

Tourism Victoria (☑13 28 42; www.visitvictoria.com. au) The state tourism body has a thorough website and phone service. Its online travel planner offers maps, travel ideas and a route planner.

Parks Victoria (☑13 19 63; www.parkweb.vic.gov.au) Victoria's national parks, service has a comprehensive website packed with park information; national park camping grounds must be booked through Parks Victoria.

Travellers With Disabilities

Many of the attractions in Melbourne and regional Victoria are accessible for wheelchairs. Trains and newer trams have low steps to accommodate wheelchairs and people with limited mobility. Many car parks in the city have convenient spaces

allocated for disabled drivers. All pedestrian crossings feature sound cues and accessible buttons.

Melbourne Mobility Centre (☑9650 6499, TTY 9650 9316; 1st fl car park, Federation Sq; ☺9am-6pm Mon-Sat, 10am-4pm Sun) Offers TTY phone and web services, equipment hire and general information including a mobility map.

Travellers Aid (www.travellersaid.org.au) City (☑9654 2600; Level 3, 225 Bourke St); Southern Cross Station (☑9670 2072; Lower Concourse); Flinders St Station (☑9610 2030; Main Concourse) These centres are particularly helpful to those with special needs and offer a variety of facilities to travellers, including showers, baby-change facilities, toilets, lounge area, public telephone, lockers, stroller and wheelchair hire, and ironing facilities.

Organisations

City of Melbourne (www. melbourne.vic.gov.au) Online mobility map and information for people with disabilities.

National Information Communication & Awareness Network (Nican; ☑1800 806 769; www.nican. com.au) An Australia-wide directory providing information on access issues, accommodation, sporting and recreational activities, transport and specialist tour operators.

VicDeaf (☑9657 8111; www. vicdeaf.com.au) Auslan interpreter service available.

VicRoads (☑13 11 71; www. vicroads.vic.gov.au) Supplies parking permits for disabled drivers.

Vision Australia (☑1300 847 466; www.visionaustralia. org.au) The Royal Victorian Institute for the Blind has become part of this national organisation.

Women Travellers

Victoria is generally a safe place for women travellers, although the usual sensible precautions apply. It's best to avoid walking alone late at night. And if you're out for a big night on the town, always keep enough money aside for a taxi back to your accommodation. Alcohol-fuelled violence is becoming more common in Melbourne's city centre. The same applies to rural towns, where there are often a lot of unlit, semideserted streets. Lone women should also be wary of staying in basic pub accommodation unless it looks safe and well managed.

Aussie male culture does sometimes manifest in sexist bravado, and sexual harassment isn't uncommon, especially when alcohol is involved.

We do not recommend that women hitchhike alone.

The following organisations offer advice and services for women:

Royal Women's Hospital Health Information Service (☑8345 3045; www.thewomens.org.au)

Royal Women's Hospital Sexual Assault Unit (☑9635 3610; www.thewomens.org.au/SexualAssaultInformation)

Transport

ternational and domestic terminals are within the same complex. There are no direct train or tram services linking it with the city but airport shuttle buses meet flights and taxis descend like flies. See p130 for more information.

GETTING THERE & AWAY

Air

You can fly into Melbourne from most international hubs and from all major cities and tourist destinations in Australia. Not all international flights are direct and you may need to change planes and terminals in Sydney.

Airlines

Qantas (☎13 13 13; www. qantas.com.au) Australia's main carrier with frequent flights to/from Melbourne and regional centres.
Jetstar (☎13 15 38; www. jetstar.com.au) The budget subsidiary of Qantas also has frequent scheduled flights to/from Melbourne and Avalon.
Virgin Blue (☎13 67 89; www.virginblue.com.au) Reliable budget airline flying most domestic routes.
Tiger Airways (☎9335 3033; www.tigerairways. com) Budget flights to/from Melbourne and Avalon to numerous destinations throughout Australia.

Rex (Regional Express: ☎13 17 13; www.rex.com.au) Flights from Melbourne to Adelaide, Sydney and regional centres including Mildura and Albury.
Sharp Airlines (☎1300 556 694; www.sharpairlines. com) Flights from Melbourne Avalon to Portland and Adelaide, and between Adelaide and Mildura.
Skywest Airlines (☎1300 660 088; www.skywest.com.au) Flights from Melbourne to Perth and Kalgoorlie.

Airports

MELBOURNE AIRPORT
Melbourne Airport (☎9297 1600; www.melbourneairport. com.au), often referred to as Tullamarine or Tulla, is around 25km northwest of the city centre. All in-

AVALON AIRPORT
Avalon Airport (☎1800 282 566, 5227 9100; www.avalon airport.com.au) is around 55km southwest of the city centre on the Geelong road. Most Jetstar flights use this airport, as well as some Tiger Airways and Sharp Airlines services. Sita Coaches (☎9689 7999; www. sitacoaches.com.au) operates an airport shuttle, meeting all flights and picking up or dropping off at Southern Cross Station ($20/36 one way/return). Hotel pick-ups can be booked 48 hours prior to departure. The trip takes around 40 minutes.

REGIONAL AIRPORTS
Mildura Airport (www. miluraairport.com.au) has scheduled flights to/from Melbourne and Adelaide. During the ski season, Qantaslink flies from Sydney to Mt Hotham Airport (www. mthotham.com.au).

Land

Bus
Firefly Express (☎1300 730 740; www.fireflyexpress.com. au) Day and overnight buses from Melbourne to Adelaide ($70, 11 hours) and Sydney ($70, 14 hours).

THINGS CHANGE...

The information in this chapter is particularly vulnerable to change. Check directly with the airline or a travel agent to make sure you understand how a fare (and ticket you may buy) works and be aware of the security requirements for international travel. Shop carefully. The details given in this chapter should be regarded as pointers and are not a substitute for your own careful, up-to-date research.

Greyhound Australia (☑1300 473 946; www. greyhound.com.au) Interstate buses between Melbourne's Southern Cross Station and Adelaide ($60, 10 hours), Sydney ($65, 14 hours) and Canberra ($60, nine hours).
Premier Motor Service (☑13 34 10; www.premierms. com.au) Interstate buses between Melbourne and Sydney via Gippsland and the NSW coast ($85, 18 hours), continuing to Brisbane and Cairns.

Train

Countrylink (☑13 22 32; www.countrylink.info) Express trains between Sydney and Melbourne via Albury (from $69, 11 hours, two daily).
Great Southern Rail (☑13 21 47; www.gsr.com.au) Operates the *Overland* between Melbourne and Adelaide (adult/child $90/45, 10 hours, three weekly), departing Melbourne at 8.05am and Adelaide at 7.40am. Cheaper internet fares are available for advance bookings. Take your car on the Motorail from $149.
V/Line (www.vline.com.au) No direct interstate rail services but has train and coach combinations to Adelaide, Sydney, Canberra and Mt Gambier (via the Great Ocean Road).

Sea

Spirit of Tasmania (☑1800 634 906; www.spiritoftasmania. com.au) is a beloved vehicle and passenger ferry sailing nightly to Devonport on Tasmania's northern coast from Station Pier in Port Melbourne, with additional day sailings during summer. The crossing takes around 11 hours. A wide variety of seasonal fares are available, from basic seats to private en suite cabins. Vehicles can be taken across from $79 one-way.

GETTING AROUND

Air

Because of the state's compact size, scheduled internal flights are limited and often ludicrously expensive, with the notable exception of Mildura.

QantasLink (☑13 13 13; www.qantas.com) Flies to Mildura and Mt Hotham.
Regional Express (☑13 17 13; www.rex.com.au) Rex flies to Albury and Mildura.

Bicycle

Without the vast distances of other mainland states, Victoria is perfect for cycling – whether road touring or mountain biking.

Bicycles are carried free on all V/Line regional train services provided you check in 30 minutes before departure. The system of rail trails (disused train lines adapted as bike paths) is growing in country Victoria, and provides scenic, hassle-free cycling. Some routes connect with V/Line train stations. See www.railtrails.com.au for details. V/Line bus services do not carry bicycles.

Bikes can be hired in Melbourne and most towns in regional Victoria, particularly any town where there are well-established cycling paths. Typical hire costs $25 to $45 a day, depending on the quality of the bike.

VICTORIAN RAIL TRAILS

Victoria's rail trails are a great way to see parts of regional Victoria by bike, and more trails are being developed as funding becomes available. Some of the best:

TRAIL	START/FINISH	LENGTH
Murray to Mountains	Wangaratta/Bright	105km
East Gippsland	Bairnsdale/Orbost	94km
Great Southern	Leongatha/Foster	49km
High Country	Bandiana/Old Tallangatta	40km
Lilydale to Warburton	Lilydale/Warburton	40km
Bellarine Peninsula	Geelong/Queenscliff	32.5km
Bass Coast	Anderson/Wonthaggi	16km
Walhalla Goldfields	Erica/Thomson	7km
Goulburn River High Country	Yea/Mansfield	17km
Old Beechy	Colac/Beech Forest	45km
Ballarat–Skipton	Ballarat/Skipton	55km
Port Fairy–Warrnambool	Warrnambool/Port Fairy	37km

CLIMATE CHANGE & TRAVEL

Every form of transport that relies on carbon-based fuel generates CO_2, the main cause of human-induced climate change. Modern travel is dependent on aeroplanes, which might use less fuel per kilometre per person than most cars but travel much greater distances. The altitude at which aircraft emit gases (including CO_2) and particles also contributes to their climate change impact. Many websites offer 'carbon calculators' that allow people to estimate the carbon emissions generated by their journey and, for those who wish to do so, to offset the impact of the greenhouse gases emitted with contributions to portfolios of climate-friendly initiatives throughout the world. Lonely Planet offsets the carbon footprint of all staff and author travel.

Boat

The only scheduled boat transport is the regular daily **Queenscliff-Sorrento Car & Passenger Ferries** (☎5258 3244; www.searoad. com.au) between Queenscliff and Sorrento (p150 and p216); and the **Inter Island Ferries** (☎9585 5730; www .interislandferries.com.au) from Stony Point on the Mornington Peninsula to French Island (p224) and Phillip Island (p225).

Charter boats and cruises can get you around on the water in the Gippsland Lakes and Murray region.

Bus

Victoria's regional bus network **V/Line** (☎13 61 96; www.vline.com.au) offers both a relatively cheap and reliable service, though it can require planning if you intend to do more than straightforward city-to-city trips. The buses basically supplement the train services, so you'll often find yourself on a train and bus combination, changing services en route. For getting between smaller country towns, a bus may well be the only public transport option and it may not even run daily. In some regions, private transport companies run bus services that often connect with V/Line trains and buses.

Airport buses run direct from Melbourne Airport to Bendigo, Ballarat and Geelong, making stops along the way.

Car & Motorcycle

Victoria has some fantastic touring routes for cars and motorcycles, and a lack of public transport in many areas outside the metropolitan area means your own vehicle is often the best way to go.

Driving

Foreign driving licences are valid as long as they are in English or accompanied by a translation. Driving is on the left-hand side of the road. The speed limit in residential areas is 50km/h, rising to 70km/h or 80km/h on some main roads and dropping to 40km/h in specially designated areas such as school zones. On highways the speed limit is generally 100km/h, while on some sections of freeway it's 110km/h.

Wearing seat belts is compulsory, and children up to seven years of age must be belted into an approved safety seat. Motorcyclists must wear crash helmets at all times. The police strictly enforce Victoria's blood-alcohol limit of 0.05% with random breath testing (and drug testing) of drivers.

Toll Roads

Melbourne's **CityLink** (☎13 26 29; www.citylink.com.au) tollway road system has two main routes: the Southern Link, which runs from the southeastern suburb of Malvern to Kings Way on the southern edge of the city centre; and the Western Link, which runs from the Calder Fwy intersection with the Tullamarine Fwy south to the West Gate Fwy.

A CityLink 24-hour pass costs $13.50 and is valid for 24 hours from your first entry through a tollway. A 24-hour Tulla Pass is $4.65 and a weekend pass is $13.15. The easiest way to buy a pass is with a credit card online or by telephoning CityLink.

If you accidentally find yourself on the CityLink toll road (and it's very easy to do), don't panic as there's a three-day grace period. Passes are not required for motorbikes.

EastLink (☎13 54 65; www. eastlink.com.au), which links the Eastern, Monash and Frankston freeways, charges $5.26 for a full-trip pass. To use CityLink and EastLink, you can start a 30-day Melbourne Pass ($5.50 start-up), which will automatically accumulate your tolls and fees.

Automobile Association

Royal Automobile Association of Victoria (RACV; ☎13 19 55; www.racv.com.au) Provides emergency breakdown service, literature, maps and accommodation service. For roadside assistance, RACV has reciprocal agreements with automobile associations in all other states, and many inter-national countries. Basic membership costs $86 (plus $46 joining fee).

Car Hire

The following major car hire companies are represented at the airport, at city locations and in major regional centres:

Avis (☑13 63 33; www.avis.com.au)

Budget (☑1300 362 848; www.budget.com.au)

Europcar (☑1300 13 13 90; www.europcar.com.au)

Hertz (☑13 30 39; www.hertz.com.au)

Thrifty (☑1300 367 227; www.thrifty.com.au)

Campervans

The following companies have offices in Melbourne and a range of van sizes:

Apollo (☑1800 777 779; www.apollocamper.com.au)

Aussie Campervans (☑9395 0771; www.aussiecampervans.com)

Britz Australia (☑8398 8855; www.britz.com.au)

Jucy (☑1800 150 850; www.jucy.com.au)

Travellers Auto Barn (☑9326 3988; www.travellers-autobarn.com.au)

Wicked Campers (☑1800 24 68 69; www.wickedcampers.com.au)

Train

V/Line (☑13 61 96; www.vline.com.au) runs a network of trains around the state, most emanating out of Melbourne's Southern Cross Station. It's a comfortable and efficient way to travel but the rail network is limited to a handful of main lines, so you will often need to rely on train-bus combinations, conveniently also operated by V/Line.

REGIONAL TRAIN LINES	MAIN STATIONS
Geelong	Melbourne, Geelong, Colac, Warrnambool
Bendigo	Melbourne, Kyneton, Bendigo, Swan Hill, Echuca
Ballarat	Melbourne, Ballarat, Ararat, Nhill
Gippsland	Melbourne, Traralgon, Bairnsdale
Seymour	Melbourne, Seymour, Wangaratta, Albury

Tours

If you want to venture further afield but don't feel like trav-elling solo, or are time-poor, there are literally dozens of tours through Victoria to suit all tastes and budgets. Rec-ommended operators:

Adventure Tours Australia (☑1800 068 886; www.adventuretours.com.au) Backpacker-style bus tours between Melbourne and Adelaide, and Melbourne and Sydney, via the coast roads.

Autopia Tours (☑1800 000 507, 9391 0261; www.autopiatours.com.au) Small-group tours to the Grampians, Great Ocean Rd, Yarra Valley and the snowfields.

Bunyip Tours (☑1300 286 947; www.bunyiptours.com) Tours to Great Ocean Road, Phillip Island, Mornington Peninsula and Wilsons Promontory.

Echidna Walkabout (☑9646 8249; www.echidnawalkabout.com.au) Runs na-ture ecotrips (from one- to five-day expeditions) featur-ing bushwalking and koala spotting as far afield as East Gippsland.

Go West (☑1300 736 551; www.gowest.com.au) Day tours to Great Ocean Road and Phillip Island with iPod commentary.

TOP TOURING ROUTES

» **Great Ocean Road** – Torquay to Warrnambool

» **Great Alpine Highway** – Wangaratta to Bairnsdale

» **Eildon-Jamieson Rd** – Eildon to Jamieson

» **Grand Ridge Road** – Warragul to Korumburra

» **Bogong High Plains Rd** – Mt Beauty to Omeo

» **Grampians Tourist Rd** – Halls Gap to Dunkeld, Halls Gap to Wartook

» **Around the Bay** – Melbourne to Melbourne via Sorrento, Queenscliff and Geelong

» **Yarra Ranges** – Healesville to Marysville and Warburton

» **Wilderness Coast** – Orbost to Mallacoota via Marlo and Cann River

» **Goldfields Touring** – Castlemaine, Maldon, Maryborough, Dunolly, Bendigo

TRAIN FARES AT A GLANCE

Sample one-way V/Line fares from Melbourne:

DESTINATION	FARE ($)	DURATION (HR)
Ballarat	10.40	1½
Bendigo	15.80	2
Castlemaine	11.60	1½
Swan Hill	29.90	4¼
Echuca	20.40	3½
Seymour	8.40	1¼
Bairnsdale	26	3½
Echuca	20.40	3½
Warrnambool	26	3½

Groovy Grape (☑1800 661 177; www.groovygrape.com.au) Backpacker-style minibus with tours between Adelaide and Melbourne via the Great Ocean Road.

Steamrail Victoria (☑9397 1953; www.steamrail.com.au) For steam-train devotees, and those who are looking for an unusual day out, this not-for-profit organisation puts old trains back on the tracks for jaunts to various country destinations around the state.

Wild-Life Tours (☑9741 6333; www.wildlifetours.com.au) One- to three-day trips to the Grampians and Phillip Island, and Melbourne to Adelaide via the Great Ocean Road.

behind the scenes

SEND US YOUR FEEDBACK

We love to hear from travellers – your comments keep us on our toes and help make our books better. Our well-travelled team reads every word on what you loved or loathed about this book. Although we cannot reply individually to postal submissions, we always guarantee that your feedback goes straight to the appropriate authors, in time for the next edition. Each person who sends us information is thanked in the next edition – and the most useful submissions are rewarded with a free book.

Visit **lonelyplanet.com/contact** to submit your updates and suggestions or to ask for help. Our award-winning website also features inspirational travel stories, news and discussions.

Note: We may edit, reproduce and incorporate your comments in Lonely Planet products such as guidebooks, websites and digital products, so let us know if you don't want your comments reproduced or your name acknowledged. For a copy of our privacy policy visit lonelyplanet.com/privacy.

OUR READERS

Many thanks to the travellers who used the last edition and wrote to us with helpful hints, useful advice and interesting anecdotes:
Jean-Claude Barthes, William Beeman, Lucy Birchley, Elizabeth Butare, Darryl Cloonan, Marco D'Acunzo, Paul Groenewegen, Mark Lengacher, Aline Riche, Jane Schuppner, Michael Simons, Michael Stuchbery, Helen Walter, David Williams

AUTHOR THANKS

Jayne D'Arcy

Thanks to *M Mag* colleagues Miranda Tay, Dani Valent, James Smith and Penny Modra. Thanks Blakey, Nat, Keshia, Cecilia and the Humes. Thanks Denis from Seaview Lodge: what a welcome sight your B&B's lights were through the fog. Thanks Sharik Billington for your amazing support and our preppie, Miles, for reminding me how great the Great Ocean Road is (those seals!). Thanks Mum, Dad and Kate for Milessitting. Cheers to co-writers Paul Harding and Donna Wheeler, and big thanks to Maryanne Netto.

Paul Harding

Firstly, thanks to my wife Hannah and my beautiful daughter, Layla, who came into the world just before I started working on this book. On the road, many people helped with ideas and advice and the occasional place to stay: Mary and Brian in Castlemaine; Chad and Kylie in Bendigo; Matt and Sim in Yackandandah; Jennifer in Whorouly; Gillian at Mt Buller. Thanks to coordinating author Jayne D'Arcy for such dedication and the debriefing session in Melbourne. Big thanks at Lonely Planet to Maryanne Netto for your help and faith, as well as Liz, David and the rest of the crew.

Donna Wheeler

Thanks to my family, Joe, Rumer and Biba Guario, and *grazie* to *la famiglia* Marolo for entertaining them during writerly lockouts. A kindly Menton hotelier should get a mention, but I didn't catch your name – *merci* in any case. Endless gratitude is due to Melbourne's brave, clever retailers, publicans, chefs, cafe owners, artists and architects: you make my adopted city one of the world's most fascinating. Finally, cheers to my on-the-road colleagues, Jayne D'Arcy and Paul Harding, and Maryanne Netto inhouse.

ACKNOWLEDGMENTS

Climate map data adapted from Peel MC, Finlayson BL & McMahon TA (2007) 'Updated World Map of the Köppen-Geiger Climate Classification', *Hydrology and Earth System Sciences*, 11, 163344.

Cover photograph: The Twelve Apostles at dusk, Mark Sunderland/The Travel Library/Photolibrary.

Many of the images in this guide are available for licensing from Lonely Planet Images: www.lonelyplanetimages.com.

355

This Book

This is the 8th edition of Lonely Planet's Melbourne & Victoria guide. The 1st and 2nd editions were researched and written by Mark Armstrong. Research on the 3rd edition was led by Jon Murray; the 4th by Chris Rowthorn; the 5th by Susie Ashworth; the 6th by Simone Egger; and the 7th edition by Donna Wheeler, assisted by Cath Lanigan, Jocelyn Harewood and Rowan McKinnon. Jayne D'Arcy was the coordinating author on this edition, joined by coauthors Paul Harding and Donna Wheeler; see Our Writers (p368) to find out which destinations they covered. This guidebook was commissioned in Lonely Planet's Melbourne office, and produced by the following:

Commissioning Editor
Maryanne Netto

Coordinating Editor
Trent Holden

Coordinating Cartographer Andras Bogdanovits

Coordinating Layout Designer Paul Iacono

Managing Editor
Liz Heynes

Managing Cartographer
David Connolly

Managing Layout Designer Jane Hart

Assisting Editors Beth Hall, Victoria Harrison, Andi Lien, Joanne Newell, Sophie Splatt, Gabbi Stefanos

Assisting Cartographers Ildiko Bogdanovits, Corey Hutchinson, Peter Shields, Tom Webster

Cover Research
Naomi Parker

Internal Image Research
Rebecca Skinner

Thanks to Helen Christinis, Bruce Evans, Lisa Knights, Anna Metcalfe, Wayne Murphy, Susan Paterson, Celia Wood

BEHIND THE SCENES

NOTES

UCB

index

000 Map pages
000 Photo pages

how to use this book

These symbols will help you find the listings you want:

- ☉ Sights
- 🏃 Activities
- 🤝 Courses
- 👉 Tours
- 🎉 Festivals & Events
- 🛏 Sleeping
- 🍴 Eating
- 🍺 Drinking
- ⭐ Entertainment
- 🛍 Shopping
- ℹ Information/ Transport

Look out for these icons:

TOP CHOICE — Our author's recommendation

FREE — No payment required

🌱 — A green or sustainable option

Our authors have nominated these places as demonstrating a strong commitment to sustainability – for example by supporting local communities and producers, operating in an environmentally friendly way, or supporting conservation projects.

These symbols give you the vital information for each listing:

- 🎵 Telephone Numbers
- ☉ Opening Hours
- P Parking
- ⊖ Nonsmoking
- ❄ Air-Conditioning
- @ Internet Access
- 🛜 Wi-Fi Access
- 🏊 Swimming Pool
- 🥗 Vegetarian Selection
- 📖 English-Language Menu
- 👪 Family-Friendly
- 🐾 Pet-Friendly
- 🚌 Bus
- ⛴ Ferry
- M Metro
- S Subway
- ⊖ London Tube
- 🚋 Tram
- 🚆 Train

Reviews are organised by author preference.

Map Legend

Sights
- ☻ Beach
- ▲ Buddhist
- ⊗ Castle
- ✤ Christian
- ⊕ Hindu
- ☺ Islamic
- ✡ Jewish
- ❶ Monument
- ⊕ Museum/Gallery
- ✪ Ruin
- ✿ Winery/Vineyard
- ☺ Zoo
- ⊙ Other Sight

Activities, Courses & Tours
- ☺ Diving/Snorkelling
- ⊛ Canoeing/Kayaking
- ⊕ Skiing
- ⊙ Surfing
- ⊛ Swimming/Pool
- ☺ Walking
- ⊙ Windsurfing
- • Other Activity/ Course/Tour

Sleeping
- ⊜ Sleeping
- ▲ Camping

Eating
- ☺ Eating

Drinking
- ☺ Drinking
- ☺ Cafe

Entertainment
- ☺ Entertainment

Shopping
- ⊙ Shopping

Information
- ☺ Post Office
- ❶ Tourist Information

Transport
- ✈ Airport
- ⊗ Border Crossing
- 🚌 Bus
- ⊕ Cable Car/ Funicular
- ⊛ Cycling
- ⊕ Ferry
- Ⓜ Metro
- ⊕ Monorail
- P Parking
- S S-Bahn
- ☺ Taxi
- ⊕ Train/Railway
- ⊕ Tram
- ⊙ Tube Station
- Ⓤ U-Bahn
- • Other Transport

Routes
- Tollway
- Freeway
- Primary
- Secondary
- Tertiary
- Lane
- Unsealed Road
- Plaza/Mall
- Steps
-)= = Tunnel
- Pedestrian Overpass
- Walking Tour
- Walking Tour Detour
- Path

Boundaries
- International
- State/Province
- Disputed
- Regional/Suburb
- Marine Park
- Cliff
- Wall

Population
- ◉ Capital (National)
- ◉ Capital (State/Province)
- ● City/Large Town
- • Town/Village

Geographic
- ⌂ Hut/Shelter
- ♟ Lighthouse
- ☺ Lookout
- ▲ Mountain/Volcano
- ☺ Oasis
- ⊕ Park
-)(Pass
- ☺ Picnic Area
- ☺ Waterfall

Hydrography
- River/Creek
- Intermittent River
- Swamp/Mangrove
- Reef
- Canal
- Water
- Dry/Salt/ Intermittent Lake
- Glacier

Areas
- Beach/Desert
- + + + Cemetery (Christian)
- × × × Cemetery (Other)
- Park/Forest
- Sportsground
- Sight (Building)
- Top Sight (Building)

OUR STORY

A beat-up old car, a few dollars in the pocket and a sense of adventure. In 1972 that's all Tony and Maureen Wheeler needed for the trip of a lifetime – across Europe and Asia overland to Australia. It took several months, and at the end – broke but inspired – they sat at their kitchen table writing and stapling together their first travel guide, *Across Asia on the Cheap*. Within a week they'd sold 1500 copies. Lonely Planet was born.

Today, Lonely Planet has offices in Melbourne, London and Oakland, with more than 600 staff and writers. We share Tony's belief that 'a great guidebook should do three things: inform, educate and amuse'.

OUR WRITERS

Jayne D'Arcy

Coordinating author, Melbourne, Short Trips Around Melbourne, Great Ocean Road Growing up in the Victorian seaside suburb of Frankston had its advantages for Jayne; it motivated her to catch the train through all three zones to hang out in Prahran's Greville St, Fitzroy's Brunswick St, St Kilda and the Queen Vic Market. She hit 18 and swapped countries before returning and swapping geographical sides of the bay, making Geelong and Anglesea her home while she studied journalism. After a longish spell working in community radio in East Timor, she finally settled with her family in Melbourne's vibrant north (in Zone 1, just). When she's not riding her French 1970s folding bike around North Fitzroy, booking flights or pretending to renovate, Jayne writes for the *Age* in Melbourne. This is her seventh book for Lonely Planet.

Paul Harding

Short Trips Around Melbourne, Goldfields & Grampians, Mornington & Phillip Island, Gippsland & Wilsons Promontory, The High Country, The Murray Melbourne-born but country-raised, Paul spent childhood summers in the Gippsland Lakes, and later many fishing and camping trips along the Murray River and ski trips to Mt Hotham. He's since seen (and written about) a good part of the world, but still calls this part of Australia home. For this edition, Paul travelled around most of regional Victoria and discovered – yet again – what a beautiful state this is. A freelance writer and photographer, Paul has contributed to more than 30 Lonely Planet guides, including numerous Australian titles.

Donna Wheeler

Melbourne Today, History, Food & Wine, Fashion & Shopping, The Arts, Sport Sydney-born and raised, Donna fell in love with Melbourne as a teenage art student. Various stints in New York, London, rural Ireland and Italy aside, she has spent the better part of two decades trying to get used to Victoria's weather. After careers as an editor, art director, digital producer and content strategist, Donna has embraced the solitude of the writer's life and published widely on contemporary art, design, history and food. She is *ninemsn Travel's* Melbourne Insider and has written guides to Melbourne, Milan and Tunisia for Lonely Planet. She is also an occasional trend forecaster and consultant. Currently based in Turin, Donna misses Melbourne's easy-going but always spot-on style, gingerbread breakfasts at Cumulus Inc, and all her haunts on Smith St, Collingwood.

Published by Lonely Planet Publications Pty Ltd
ABN 36 005 607 983
8th edition – July 2011
ISBN 978 1 74179 588 2
© Lonely Planet 2011   Photographs © as indicated 2011
10 9 8 7 6 5 4 3 2 1
Printed in China